Roxy Wilson

SOLUTIONS TO EXERCISES

CHEMISTRY
THE CENTRAL SCIENCE
Ninth Edition

Brown LeMay Bursten

Prentice Hall

Upper Saddle River, NJ 07458

Project Manager: Kristen Kaiser
Senior Editor: Nicole Folchetti
Editor in Chief: John Challice
Executive Managing Editor: Kathleen Schiaparelli
Assistant Managing Editor: Dinah Thong
Production Editor: Natasha Wolfe
Supplement Cover Management/Design: Paul Gourhan
Manufacturing Buyer: Ilene Kahn
Cover Image Credit: Ken Eward/Biografx

Prentice Hall

Pearson Education, Inc.
Upper Saddle River, NJ 07458

Printed in the United States of America

10 9 8 7 6 5 4 3

ISBN 0-13-009790-X

Pearson Education Ltd., *London*
Pearson Education Australia Pty. Ltd., *Sydney*
Pearson Education Singapore, Pte. Ltd.
Pearson Education North Asia Ltd., *Hong Kong*
Pearson Education Canada, Inc., *Toronto*
Pearson Educacíon de Mexico, S.A. de C.V.
Pearson Education—Japan, *Tokyo*
Pearson Education Malaysia, Pte. Ltd.
Pearson Education, *Upper Saddle River, New Jersey*

Contents

Introduction

Chemistry: The Central Science, 9th edition, contains nearly 2400 end-of-chapter exercises. Considerable attention has been given to these exercises because one of the best ways for students to master chemistry is by solving problems. Grouping the exercises according to subject matter is intended to aid the student in selecting and recognizing particular types of problems. Within each subject matter group, similar problems are arranged in pairs. This provides the student with an opportunity to reinforce a particular kind of problem. There are also a substantial number of general exercises in each chapter to supplement those grouped by topic. Integrative exercises, which require students to integrate concepts from several chapters, are a continuing feature of the 9th edition. Answers to the odd numbered topical exercises plus selected general and integrative exercises, about 1100 in all, are provided in the text. These appendix answers help to make the text a useful self-contained vehicle for learning.

This manual, **Solutions to Black Exercises** in **Chemistry: The Central Science, 9th edition,** was written to enhance the end-of-chapter exercises by providing documented solutions for those problems *not* answered in the appendix of the text. The manual assists the instructor by saving time spent generating solutions for assigned problem sets and aids the student by offering a convenient independent source to check their understanding of the material. Most solutions have been worked in the same detail as the in-chapter sample exercises to help guide students in their studies.

When using this manual, keep in mind that the numerical result of any calculation is influenced by the precision of the numbers used in the calculation. In this manual, for example, atomic masses and physical constants are typically expressed to four significant figures, or at least as precisely as the data given in the problem. If students use slightly different values to solve problems, their answers will differ slightly from those listed in the appendix of the text or this manual. This is a normal and a common occurrence when comparing results from different calculations or experiments.

Rounding methods are another source of differences between calculated values. In this manual, when a solution is given in steps, intermediate results will be rounded to the correct number of significant figures; however, unrounded numbers will be used in subsequent calculations. By following this scheme, calculators need not be cleared to re-enter rounded intermediate results in the middle of a calculation sequence. The final answer will appear with the correct number of significant figures. This may result in a small discrepancy in the last significant digit between student-calculated answers and those given in this manual. Variations due to rounding can occur in any analysis of numerical data.

The first step in checking your solution and resolving differences between your answer and the listed value is to look for similarities and differences in problem-solving methods. Ultimately, resolving the small numerical differences described above is less important than understanding the general method for solving a problem. The goal of this manual is to provide a reference for sound and consistent problem-solving methods in addition to accurate answers to text exercises.

Extraordinary efforts have been made to keep this manual as error-free as possible. All exercises were worked and proof-read by at least three chemists to ensure clarity in methods and accuracy in mathematics. The work and advice of Dr. Mary Ellen Biggin, Augustana College and Dr. Angela Manders Cannon, University of Illinois have been invaluable to this project. However, in a written work as technically challenging as this manual, typos and errors inevitably creep in. Please help us find and eliminate them. We hope that both instructors and students will find this manual accurate, helpful and instructive.

Roxy B. Wilson
University of Illinois
School of Chemical Sciences
601 S. Mathews Ave., Box A-2
Urbana, IL 61801
rbwilson@uiuc.edu

1 Introduction: Matter and Measurement

Classification and Properties of Matter

1.2 (a) homogeneous mixture (b) heterogeneous mixture (particles in liquid)
(c) pure substance (d) heterogeneous mixture

1.4 (a) C (b) K (c) Cl (d) Zn (e) P (f) Ar (g) Ca (h) Ag

1.6 (a) chromium (b) iodine (c) lithium (d) selenium (e) lead
(f) vanadium (g) mercury (h) gallium

1.8 Before modern instrumentation, the classification of a pure substance as an element was determined by whether it could be broken down into component elements. Scientists subjected the substance to all known chemical means of decomposition, and if the results were negative, the substance was an element. Classification by negative results was somewhat ambiguous, since an effective decomposition technique might exist, but not yet have been discovered.

1.10

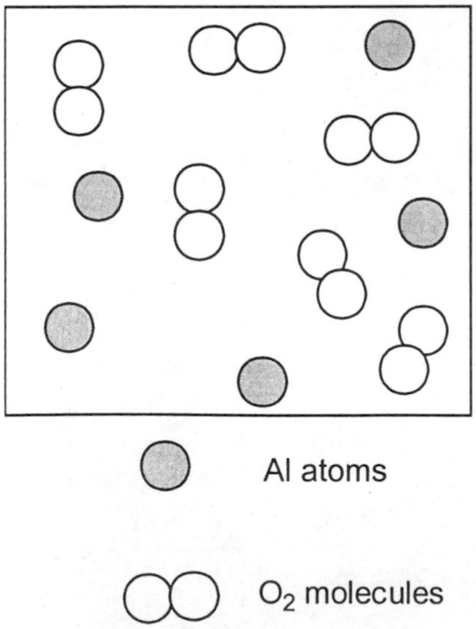

1.12 Physical properties: silver-grey (color); melting point = 420°C; hardness = 2.5 Mohs; density = 7.13 g/cm³ at 25°C. Chemical properties: metal; reacts with sulfuric acid to produce hydrogen gas; reacts slowly with oxygen at elevated temperatures to produce ZnO.

1.14 (a) chemical (b) physical (c) physical (The production of H_2O is a chemical change, but its **condensation** is a physical change.) (d) physical (The production of soot is a chemical change, but its **deposition** is a physical change.)

1.16 (a) Take advantage of the different water solubilities of the two solids. Add water to dissolve the sugar; filter this mixture, collecting the sand on the filter paper and the sugar water in the flask. Evaporate the water from the flask to reproduce solid sugar.

(b) Either the melting-point difference or magnetism difference between iron and sulfur can be used to separate these two elements. Heat the mixture until the sulfur melts, then decant (pour off) the liquid sulfur. Or, use a magnet to attract the iron particles, leaving the solid sulfur behind.

Units and Measurement

1.18 (a) $6.5 \times 10^{-6}\ \text{m} \times \frac{1\ \mu\text{m}}{1 \times 10^{-6}\ \text{m}} = 6.5\ \mu\text{m}$

(b) $6.35 \times 10^{-4}\ \text{L} \times \frac{1\ \text{mL}}{1 \times 10^{-3}\ \text{L}} = 0.635\ \text{mL}\ (635\ \mu\text{L})$

(c) $2.5 \times 10^{-3}\ \text{L} \times \frac{1\ \text{mL}}{1 \times 10^{-3}\ \text{L}} = 2.5\ \text{mL}$

(d) $4.23 \times 10^{-9}\ \text{m}^3 \times \frac{1^3\ \text{mm}^3}{(1 \times 10^{-3})^3\ \text{m}^3} = 4.23\ \text{mm}^3\ (4.23\ \mu\text{L};\ 1\ \text{mm}^3 = 1\ \text{uL})$

$4.23\ \text{mm}^3 \times \frac{(10^{-1})^3\ \text{cm}^3}{1^3\ \text{mm}^3} \times \frac{1\ \text{mL}}{1\ \text{cm}^3} \times \frac{1 \times 10^{-3}\ \text{L}}{1\ \text{mL}} \times \frac{1\ \mu\text{L}}{1 \times 10^{-6}\ \text{L}} = 4.23\ \mu\text{L}$

(e) $12.5 \times 10^{-8}\ \text{kg} \times \frac{1 \times 10^{3}\ \text{g}}{1\ \text{kg}} \times \frac{1\ \text{mg}}{1 \times 10^{-3}\ \text{g}} = 0.125\ \text{mg}\ (125\ \mu\text{g})$

(f) $3.5 \times 10^{-11}\ \text{s} \times \frac{1\ \text{ps}}{1 \times 10^{-12}\ \text{s}} = 35\ \text{ps}\ (0.035\ \text{ns})$

(g) $6.54 \times 10^{9}\ \text{fs} \times \frac{1 \times 10^{-15}\ \text{s}}{1\ \text{fs}} \times \frac{1\ \mu\text{s}}{1 \times 10^{-6}\ \text{s}} = 6.54\ \mu\text{s}$

1.20 (a) $1.48 \times 10^{2}\ \text{kg} \times \frac{1 \times 10^{3}\ \text{g}}{1\ \text{kg}} \times = 1.48 \times 10^{5}\ \text{g}$

(b) $0.0023\ \mu\text{m} \times \frac{1 \times 10^{-6}\ \text{m}}{1\ \mu\text{m}} \times \frac{1\ \text{nm}}{1 \times 10^{-9}\ \text{m}} = 2.3\ \text{nm}$

(c) $7.25 \times 10^{-4}\ \text{s} \times \frac{1\ \text{ms}}{1 \times 10^{-3}\ \text{s}} = 0.725\ \text{ms}$

1.22 (a) volume (b) area (c) volume (d) density (e) time (f) length (g) temperature

1.24 (a) volume = length^3 (cm^3); density = mass/volume (g/cm^3)

volume = $(1.500)^3$ cm^3 = 3.375 cm^3

$$\text{density} = \frac{76.31\ g}{3.375\ cm^3} = 22.61\ g/cm^3\ \text{osmium}$$

(b) $$65.8\ mL \times \frac{1\ cm^3}{1\ mL} \times \frac{4.51\ g}{1\ cm^3} = 296.758 = 297\ g\ \text{titanium}$$

(c) $$0.1500\ L \times \frac{1\ mL}{1 \times 10^{-3}\ L} \times \frac{0.8787\ g}{1\ mL} = 131.8\ g\ \text{benzene}$$

1.26 (a) $$\frac{21.95\ g}{25.0\ mL} = 0.878\ g/mL$$

The tabulated value has 4 significant figures, while the experimental value has 3. The tabulated value rounded to 3 figures is 0.879. The values agree within 1 in the last significant figure of the experimental value; the two results agree. The liquid could be benzene.

(b) $$15.0\ g \times \frac{1\ mL}{0.7781\ g} = 19.3\ mL\ \text{cyclohexane}$$

(c) r = d/2 = 5.0 cm/2 = 2.5 cm

$V = 4/3\ \pi r^3 = 4/3 \times \pi \times (2.5)^3\ cm^3 = 65\ cm^3$

$$65.4498\ cm^3 \times \frac{11.34\ g}{cm^3} = 7.4 \times 10^2\ g$$

(The answer has 2 significant figures because the diameter had only 2 figures.)

Note: This is the first exercise where "intermediate rounding" occurs. In this manual, when a solution is given in steps, the intermediate result will be rounded to the correct number of significant figures. However, the **unrounded** number will be used in subsequent calculations. The final answer will appear with the correct number of significant figures. That is, calculators need not be cleared and new numbers entered in the middle of a calculation sequence. This may result in a small discrepancy in the last significant digit between student-calculated answers and those given in the solution manual. These variations occur in any analysis of numerical data.

For example, in this exercise the volume of the sphere, 65.4498 cm^3 is rounded to 65 cm^3, but 65.4498 is retained in the subsequent calculation of mass, 7.4×10^2 g. In this case, 65 cm^3 × 11.34 g/cm^3 also yields 7.4×10^2 g. In other exercises, the correctly rounded results of the two methods may not be identical.

1.28 Calculate the volume of the rod:

$$2.17\ kg \times \frac{1000\ g}{1\ kg} \times \frac{1\ cm^3}{2.33\ g} = 931.3 = 931\ cm^3$$

$V = \pi r^2 h$; $d = 2r$, $r = d/2$; $V = \pi \left(\frac{d}{2}\right)^2 h$; $d^2 = \frac{4\,V}{\pi\,h}$; $d = \left(\frac{4\,V}{\pi\,h}\right)^{1/2}$

$$d = \left(\frac{4\,(931.3)\,cm^3}{\pi\,(16.8)\,cm}\right)^{1/2} = 8.401 = 8.40\ cm$$

1.30 (a) °C = 5/9 (87°F - 32°) = 31°C

(b) °F = 9/5 (755°C) + 32 = 1391°F

(It could be argued that the result of 9/5 (755) has 3 sig figs, so the final answer should have 3 sig figs, 1390°F.)

(c) °F = 9/5 (- 95°C) + 32 = -139°F (with 2 sig figs, -140°F)

(d) K = 25°C + 273 = 298 K; °F = 9/5 (25°C) + 32 = 77°F

(e) melting point = -248.6°C + 273.15 = 24.6 K
boiling point = -246.1°C + 273.15 = 27.1 K

Uncertainty In Measurement

1.32 Exact: (b), (e) (The number of students is exact on any given day.)

1.34 140°C. The temperature can be read to the nearest 50°C and estimated to the nearest 5-10°C. Since there is uncertainty in the tens digit, the measurement has two significant figures.

1.36 (a) 4 (b) 3 (c) 4 (d) 5 (e) 6

1.38 (a) 1.44×10^5 (b) 9.75×10^{-2} (c) 8.90×10^5
(d) 6.76×10^4 (e) 3.40×10^4 (f) -6.56

1.40 (a) -2.3×10^3 (The intermediate result has 2 significant figures, so only the thousand and hundred places in the answer are significant.)

(b) $[285.3 \times 10^5 - 0.01200 \times 10^5] \times 2.8954 = 8.260 \times 10^7$ (Since subtraction depends on decimal places, both numbers must have the same exponent to determine decimal places/sig figs. The intermediate result has 1 decimal place and 4 sig figs, so the answer has 4 sig figs)

(c) $(0.0045 \times 20{,}000.0)$ + (2813×12) = 3.4×10^4
2 sig figs /0 dec pl   2 sig figs /first 2 digits

(d) 863 × [1255 - (3.45×108)] = 7.62×10^5
3 sig figs /0 dec pl
3 sig figs × 0 dec pl/3 sig figs = 3 sig figs

Dimensional Analysis

1.42 (a) $\frac{1.6093 \text{ km}}{1 \text{ mi}}$; when converting miles to kilometers, miles goes in the denominator so that it cancels the original unit, leaving km in the numerator.

(b) $\frac{453.59 \text{ g}}{16 \text{ oz}} = \frac{28.349 \text{ g}}{1 \text{ oz}}$ (c) $\frac{1 \text{ L}}{1.0567 \text{ qt}}$

1.44 (a) $\frac{2.998 \times 10^8 \text{m}}{\text{s}} \times \frac{1 \text{ km}}{1000 \text{ m}} \times \frac{60 \text{ s}}{1 \text{ min}} \times \frac{60 \text{ min}}{1 \text{ hr}} = 1.079 \times 10^9 \text{ km/hr}$

(b) $1.35 \times 10^9 \text{ km}^3 \times \frac{(1 \times 10^3)^3 \text{ m}^3}{1^3 \text{ km}^3} \times \frac{1^3 \text{ dm}^3}{(1 \times 10^{-1})^3 \text{ m}^3} \times \frac{1 \text{ L}}{1 \text{ dm}^3} = 1.35 \times 10^{21} \text{ L}$

(c) $\frac{232 \text{ mg cholesterol}}{100 \text{ mL blood}} \times \frac{1 \text{ mL}}{1 \times 10^{-3} \text{ L}} \times 5.2 \text{ L} \times \frac{1 \times 10^{-3} \text{ g}}{1 \text{ mg}} = 12 \text{ g cholesterol}$

1.46 (a) $145.7 \text{ ft} \times \frac{1 \text{ yd}}{3 \text{ ft}} \times \frac{1 \text{ m}}{1.094 \text{ yd}} = 44.39 \text{ m}$

(b) $0.570 \text{ qt} \times \frac{1 \text{ L}}{1.057 \text{ qt}} \times \frac{1 \text{ mL}}{1 \times 10^{-3} \text{ L}} = 539 \text{ mL}$

(c) $\frac{3.75 \text{ μm}}{\text{s}} \times \frac{1 \times 10^{-6} \text{ m}}{1 \text{ μm}} \times \frac{1 \text{ km}}{1 \times 10^3 \text{ m}} \times \frac{60 \text{ s}}{1 \text{ min}} \times \frac{60 \text{ min}}{1 \text{ hr}} = 1.35 \times 10^{-5} \text{ km/hr}$

(d) $3.977 \text{ yd}^3 \times \frac{1 \text{ m}^3}{(1.0936)^3 \text{ yd}^3} = 3.0407 = 3.041 \text{ m}^3$

(e) $\frac{\$2.99}{\text{lb}} \times \frac{2.205 \text{ lb}}{1 \text{ kg}} = \$6.59/\text{kg}$

(f) $\frac{9.75 \text{ lb}}{\text{ft}^3} \times \frac{453.59 \text{ g}}{1 \text{ lb}} \times \frac{1 \text{ ft}^3}{12^3 \text{ in}^3} \times \frac{1 \text{ in}^3}{2.54^3 \text{ cm}^3} \times \frac{1 \text{ cm}^3}{1 \text{ mL}} = 0.156 \text{ g/mL}$

1.48 (a) $1486 \text{ mi} \times \frac{1 \text{ km}}{0.62137 \text{ mi}} \times \frac{\text{charge}}{225 \text{ km}} = 10.6 \text{ charges}$

Since charges are integral events, 11 charges are required.

(b) $\frac{14 \text{ m}}{\text{s}} \times \frac{1 \text{ km}}{1 \times 10^3 \text{ m}} \times \frac{1 \text{ mi}}{1.6093 \text{ km}} \times \frac{60 \text{ s}}{1 \text{ min}} \times \frac{60 \text{ min}}{1 \text{ hr}} = 31 \text{ mi/hr}$

(c) $450 \text{ in}^3 \times \frac{(2.54)^3 \text{ cm}^3}{1 \text{ in}^3} \times \frac{1 \text{ mL}}{1 \text{ cm}^3} \times \frac{1 \times 10^{-3} \text{ L}}{1 \text{ mL}} = 7.37 \text{ L}$

(d) $2.4 \times 10^5 \text{ barrels} \times \frac{42 \text{ gal}}{1 \text{ barrel}} \times \frac{4 \text{ qt}}{1 \text{ gal}} \times \frac{1 \text{ L}}{1.057 \text{ qt}} = 3.8 \times 10^7 \text{ L}$

1.50 $9.0 \text{ ft} \times 14.5 \text{ ft} \times 18.8 \text{ ft} = 2453.4 = 2.5 \times 10^3 \text{ ft}^3$

$$2453.4 \text{ ft}^3 \times \frac{(1 \text{ yd})^3}{(3 \text{ ft})^3} \times \frac{(1 \text{ m})^3}{(1.094 \text{ yd})^3} \times \frac{48 \text{ μg CO}}{1 \text{ m}^3} \times \frac{1 \times 10^{-6} \text{ g}}{1 \text{ μg}} = 3.3 \times 10^{-3} \text{ g CO}$$

1.52 (a) $$26.73 \text{ g total} \times \frac{0.90 \text{ g Ag}}{1 \text{ g total}} \times \frac{1 \text{ tr oz}}{31.1 \text{ g Ag}} \times \frac{\$1.18}{1 \text{ tr oz}} = \$0.91$$

(b) $$\$25.00 \times \frac{1 \text{ tr oz}}{\$5.30} \times \frac{31.1 \text{ g}}{1 \text{ tr oz}} \times \frac{1 \text{ g total}}{0.90 \text{ g Ag}} \times \frac{1 \text{ coin}}{26.73 \text{ g}} = 6.1 \text{ coins}$$

Since coins come in integer numbers, 7 coins are required.

1.54 Select a common unit for comparison, in this case the cm.

1 in ≈ 2.5 cm, 1 m = 100 cm

57 cm = 57 cm

14 in ≈ 35 cm

1.1 m = 110 cm

The order of length from shortest to longest is 14-in shoe < 57-cm string < 1.1-m pipe.

Additional Exercises

1.56 A gold coin is probably a **solid solution**. Pure gold (element 79) is too soft and too valuable to be used for coinage, so other metals are added. However, the simple term "gold coin" does not give a specific indication of the other metals in the mixture.

A cup of coffee is a **solution** if there are no suspended solids (coffee grounds). It is a heterogeneous mixture if there are grounds. If cream or sugar are added, the homogeneity of the mixture depends on how thoroughly the components are mixed.

A wood plank is a **heterogeneous mixture** of various cellulose components. The different domains in the mixture are visible as wood grain or knots.

The ambiguity in each of these examples is that the name of the substance does not provide a complete description of the material. We must rely on mental images and these vary from person to person.

1.57 (a) A **hypothesis** is a possible explanation for certain phenomena based on preliminary experimental data. A **theory** may be more general, and has a significant body of experimental evidence to support it; a theory has withstood the test of experimentation.

(b) A scientific **law** is a summary or statement of natural behavior; it tells how matter behaves. A **theory** is an explanation of natural behavior; it attempts to explain why matter behaves the way it does.

1.59 (a) I. (22.52 + 22.48 + 22.54)/3 = 22.51

II. (22.64 + 22.58 + 22.62)/3 = 22.61

Based on the average, set I is more accurate. That is, it is closer to the true value of 22.52%.

(b) Average deviation = $\sum |\text{value} - \text{average}|/3$

I. $|22.52 - 22.51| + |22.48 - 22.51| + |22.54 - 22.51|/3 = 0.02$

II. $|22.64 - 22.61| + |22.58 - 22.61| + |22.62 - 22.61|/3 = 0.02$

The two sets display the same precision, even though set I is more accurate.

1.60 (a) Inappropriate - The circulation of a widely read publication would vary over a year's time, and could simply not be counted to the nearest single subscriber. Probably about four significant figures would be appropriate. (b) Appropriate - It might be possiblé to do better than two significant figures, but an estimate to two significant figures should easily be possible. (c) Rainfall can be measured to within 0.02 in., but it is probably not possible to record an entire year's rainfall to the nearest 0.01 in. Further, the variation from year to year is sufficiently large that it does not make much sense to report the annual average to this number of significant figures. Probably two significant figures would be appropriate. (d) Assuming that the statement is based on survey data from a reasonably large sample, two (6.8%) or three (12.0%) significant figures are appropriate. If the sample contained less than 1000 participants, three significant figures is not appropriate.

1.62 (a) $\frac{\text{m}}{\text{s}^2}$ (b) $\frac{\text{kg}\bullet\text{m}}{\text{s}^2}$ (c) $\frac{\text{kg}\bullet\text{m}}{\text{s}^2} \times \text{m} = \frac{\text{kg}\bullet\text{m}^2}{\text{s}^2}$

(d) $\frac{\text{kg}\bullet\text{m}}{\text{s}^2} \times \frac{1}{\text{m}^2} = \frac{\text{kg}}{\text{m}\bullet\text{s}^2}$ (e) $\frac{\text{kg}\bullet\text{m}^2}{\text{s}^2} \times \frac{1}{\text{s}} = \frac{\text{kg}\bullet\text{m}^2}{\text{s}^3}$

1.63 $$\frac{40 \text{ lb peat}}{14 \times 20 \times 30 \text{ in}^3} \times \frac{1 \text{ in}^3}{(2.54)^3 \text{ cm}^3} \times \frac{453.6 \text{ g}}{1 \text{ lb}} = 0.13 \text{ g/cm}^3 \text{ peat}$$

$$\frac{40 \text{ lb soil}}{1.9 \text{ gal}} \times \frac{1 \text{ gal}}{4 \text{ qt}} \times \frac{1.057 \text{ qt}}{1 \text{ L}} \times \frac{1 \times 10^{-3} \text{ L}}{1 \text{ mL}} \times \frac{1 \text{ mL}}{1 \text{ cm}^3} \times \frac{453.6 \text{ g}}{1 \text{ lb}} = 2.5 \text{ g/cm}^3 \text{ soil}$$

No. The densities tell us that a certain volume of peat moss is "lighter" (weighs less) than the same volume of top soil. Volume must be specified in order to compare mass.

1.65 The most dense liquid, Hg, will sink; the least dense, cyclohexane, will float; H_2O will be in the middle.

1.67 (a) density = (35.66 g – 14.23 g)/4.59 cm³ = 4.67 g/cm³

(b) $34.5 \text{ kg} \times \frac{1000 \text{ g}}{1 \text{ kg}} \times \frac{1 \text{ mL}}{13.6 \text{ g}} \times \frac{1 \text{ L}}{1000 \text{ mL}} = 2.54 \text{ L}$

(c) $V = 4/3 \pi r^3 = 4/3 \pi (28.9 \text{ cm})^3 = 1.0111 \times 10^5 = 1.01 \times 10^5 = 1.01 \times 10^5 \text{ cm}^3$

$1.011 \times 10^5 \text{ cm}^3 \times \frac{3.52 \text{ g}}{\text{cm}^3} = 3.56 \times 10^5 \text{ g}$

The sphere weighs 356 kg or 785 pounds. The student is unlikely to be able to carry the sphere.

1.68 mass of toluene = 58.58 g – 32.65 g = 25.93 g

volume of toluene = $25.93 \text{ g} \times \frac{1 \text{ mL}}{0.864 \text{ g}} = 30.0116 = 30.0 \text{ mL}$

volume of solid = 5.00 mL – 30.0116 mL = 19.9884 = 20.0 mL

density of solid = $\frac{32.65 \text{ g}}{19.9884 \text{ mL}} = 1.63 \text{ g/mL}$

1.70 (a) *Plan.* Calculate the total distance in miles, the total time in hours.

$192 \text{ yd} \times \frac{3 \text{ ft}}{1 \text{ yd}} \times \frac{1 \text{ mi}}{5280 \text{ ft}} = 0.10909 = 0.109 \text{ mi}$

If the distance can be measured to the nearest yard, or 0.0006 mi, there is uncertainty in the fourth and probably third decimal place, so the total distance is reported to 3 decimal places and 5 sig figs.

[total distance = 13 + 0.109 = 13.109 mi]

$44 \text{ min} \times \frac{1 \text{ hr}}{60 \text{ min}} = 0.7333 = 0.73 \text{ hr}$

$18 \text{ sec} \times \frac{1 \text{ min}}{60 \text{ sec}} \times \frac{1 \text{ hr}}{60 \text{ min}} = 0.0050 \text{ hr}$

Time can be measured to the nearest second, or 0.0003 hr, so the total time is reported with 4 decimal places and 5 sig figs.

total time = 1 + 0.7333 + 0.0050 = 1.7383 hr

$$\text{avg. speed} = \frac{13.109\text{ mi}}{1.7383\text{ hr}} = 7.5413\text{ mi/hr}$$

(b) $$\frac{1\text{ hr}}{7.5413\text{ mi}} \times \frac{60\text{ min}}{1\text{ hr}} = 7.9562\text{ min/mi}$$

$$\frac{1\text{ hr}}{7.5413\text{ mi}} \times \frac{60\text{ min}}{1\text{ hr}} \times \frac{60\text{ s}}{1\text{ min}} = 477.37\text{ s/mi}$$

1.72 (a) $$575\text{ ft} \times \frac{12\text{ in}}{1\text{ ft}} \times \frac{2.54\text{ cm}}{1\text{ in}} \times \frac{10\text{ mm}}{1\text{ cm}} \times \frac{1\text{ quarter}}{1.55\text{ mm}} = 1.1307 \times 10^5$$

$$= 1.13 \times 10^5\text{ quarters}$$

(b) $$1.1307 \times 10^5\text{ quarters} \times \frac{5.67\text{ g}}{1\text{ quarter}} = 6.41 \times 10^5\text{ g} \quad (641\text{ kg})$$

(c) $$1.1307 \times 10^5\text{ quarters} \times \frac{1\text{ dollar}}{4\text{ quarters}} = \$28{,}268 = \$2.83 \times 10^4$$

(d) $$\$4.9 \times 10^{12} \times \frac{1\text{ stack}}{\$28{,}268} = 1.7 \times 10^8\text{ stacks}$$ (approximately 170 million stacks)

1.73 (a) $$\frac{\$2480}{\text{acre} \bullet \text{ft}} \times \frac{1\text{ acre}}{4840\text{ yd}^2} \times \frac{3\text{ ft}}{1\text{ yd}} \times \frac{(1.094\text{ yd})^3}{(1\text{ m})^3} \times \frac{(1\text{ m})^3}{(10\text{ dm})^3} \times \frac{(1\text{ dm})^3}{1\text{ L}} =$$

$\$2.013 \times 10^{-3}$/L or 0.2013 ¢ / L (0.201 ¢/L to 3 sig figs)

(b) $$\frac{\$2480}{\text{acre} \bullet \text{ft}} \times \frac{1\text{ acre} \bullet \text{ft}}{2\text{ households} \bullet \text{year}} \times \frac{1\text{ year}}{365\text{ days}} \times 1\text{ household} = \frac{\$3.397}{\text{day}} = \frac{\$3.40}{\text{day}}$$

1.75 $$11.86\text{ g ethanol} \times \frac{1\text{ cm}^3}{0.789\text{ g ethanol}} = 15.0317 = 15.03\text{ cm}^3\text{, volume of cylinder}$$

$$V = \pi r^2 h;\ r = (V/\pi h)^{1/2} = \left[\frac{15.0317\text{ cm}^3}{\pi \times 15.0\text{ cm}}\right]^{1/2} = 0.5648 = 0.565\text{ cm}$$

d = 2r = 1.13 cm

1.77 A solution can be separated into components by physical means, so separation would be attempted. If the liquid is a solution, the solute could be a solid or a liquid; these two kinds of solutions would be separated differently. Therefore, divide the liquid into several samples and do different tests on each. Try evaporating the solvent from one sample. If a solid remains, the liquid is a solution and the solute is a solid. If the result is negative, try distilling a sample to see if two or more liquids with different boiling points are present. If this result is negative, the liquid is probably a pure substance, but negative results are never entirely conclusive. We might not have tried the appropriate separation technique.

1.78 The separation is successful if two distinct spots are seen on the paper. To quantify the characteristics of the separation, calculate a reference value for each spot that is

$$\frac{\text{distance travelled by spot}}{\text{distance travelled by solvent}}$$

If the values for the two spots are fairly different, the separation is successful. (One could measure the distance between the spots, but this would depend on the length of paper used and be different for each experiment. The values suggested above are independent of the length of paper.)

1.80 Study (a) is likely to be both precise and accurate, because the errors are carefully controlled. The secondary weight standard will be resistant to chemical and physical changes, the balance is carefully calibrated, and weighings are likely to be made by the same person. The relatively large number of measurements is likely to minimize the effect of random errors on the average value. The accuracy and precision of study (b) depend on the veracity of the participants' responses which cannot be carefully controlled. It also depends on the definition of "comparable lifestyle". The percentages are not precise, because the broad definition of lifestyle leads to a range of results (scatter). The relatively large number of participants improves the precision and accuracy. In general, controlling errors and maximizing the number of data points in a study improves precision and accuracy.

2 Atoms, Molecules, and Ions

Atomic Theory and Atomic Structure

2.2 (a) 6.500 g compound - 0.384 g hydrogen = 6.116 g sulfur

(b) *Conservation of mass*

(c) According to postulate 3 of the atomic theory, atoms are neither created nor destroyed during a chemical reaction. If 0.384 g of H are recovered from a compound that contains only H and S, the remaining mass must be sulfur.

2.4 (a) 1: $\frac{3.56 \text{ g fluorine}}{4.75 \text{ g iodine}} = 0.749$ g fluorine/1 g iodine

2: $\frac{3.43 \text{ g fluorine}}{7.64 \text{ g iodine}} = 0.449$ g fluorine/1 g iodine

3: $\frac{9.86 \text{ g fluorine}}{9.41 \text{ g iodine}} = 1.05$ g fluorine/1 g iodine

(b) To look for integer relationships among these values, divide each one by the smallest. If the quotients aren't all integers, multiply by a common factor to obtain all integers.

1: 0.749/0.449 = 1.67; 1.67 × 3 = 5

2: 0.449/0.449 = 1.00; 1.00 × 3 = 3

3: 1.05/0.449 = 2.34; 2.34 × 3 = 7

The ratio of g fluorine to g iodine in the three compounds is 5:3:7. These are in the ratio of small whole numbers and, therefore, obey the *law of multiple proportions*. This integer ratio indicates that the combining fluorine "units" (atoms) are indivisible entities.

2.6 (a) The electron itself has a negative charge so it is repelled by the negatively charged plate and attracted to the positively charged plate.

(b) As the charge on the plates is increased, the respective repulsion and attraction of the electron increases (Coloumb's Law) and the amount of bend should increase.

(c) As the mass of the particle increases, a greater force is required to deflect it. If the strength of the magnetic field is constant, the bend should decrease as the mass increases.

(d) Since the unknown particle is deflected in the opposite direction, it is attracted to the (-) plate and repelled by the (+) plate. The unknown particle is positively charged. The magnitude of the deflection is less than that of the electron, so the unknown particle has greater mass than the electron. The unknown is a positively charged particle of greater mass than the electron.

2.8 (a) The droplets contain different charges because there may be 1, 2, 3 or more excess electrons on the droplet.

(b) The electronic charge is likely to be the lowest common factor in all the observed charges.

(c) Assuming this is so, we calculate the apparent electronic charge from each drop as follows:

A: $1.60 \times 10^{-19} / 1 = 1.60 \times 10^{-19}$ C

B: $3.15 \times 10^{-19} / 2 = 1.58 \times 10^{-19}$ C

C: $4.81 \times 10^{-19} / 3 = 1.60 \times 10^{-19}$ C

D: $6.31 \times 10^{-19} / 4 = 1.58 \times 10^{-19}$ C

The reported value is the average of these four values. Since each calculated charge has three significant figures, the average will also have three significant figures.

$(1.60 \times 10^{-19}\ \text{C} + 1.58 \times 10^{-19}\ \text{C} + 1.60 \times 10^{-19}\ \text{C} + 1.58 \times 10^{-19}\ \text{C}) / 4 = 1.59 \times 10^{-19}\ \text{C}$

2.10 In the scattering experiment, most alpha particles, massive positively charged helium nuclei, passed directly through the foil, but a few were deflected at large angles. The diffuse positive charge in the 'plum pudding' model would not have produced a repulsion strong enough to deflect the alpha particles at large angles. In Rutherford's model, the positive charge in the atom is concentrated in the small nucleus. If an alpha particle strikes a gold nucleus directly, it is deflected at a large angle.

Modern View of Atomic Structure; Atomic Weights

2.12 (a) $r = d/2;\ r = \dfrac{2.5 \times 10^{-8}\ \text{cm}}{2} \times \dfrac{1\ \text{Å}}{1\ 10^{-8}\ \text{cm}} = 1.25 = 1.3\ \text{Å}$

$r = \dfrac{2.5 \times 10^{-8}\ \text{cm}}{2} \times \dfrac{1\ \text{m}}{100\ \text{cm}} = 1.25 \times 10^{-10} = 1.3 \times 10^{-10}\ \text{m}$

(b) Aligned Rh atoms have **diameters** touching. $d = 2.5 \times 10^{-8}\ \text{cm} = 2.5 \times 10^{-10}\ \text{m}$

$6.0\ \mu\text{m} \times \dfrac{1 \times 10^{-6}\ \text{m}}{1\ \mu\text{m}} \times \dfrac{1\ \text{Rh atom}}{2.5 \times 10^{-10}\ \text{m}} = 2.4 \times 10^{-4}$ Rh atoms

(c) $V\ 4/3\ \pi r^3 \quad r = 1.25 \times 10^{-10} = 1.3 \times 10^{-30}\ \text{m}$

$V = (4/3)(\pi(1.25 \times 10^{-10})^3\ \text{m}^3 = 8.2 \times 10^{-8}\ \text{m}^3$

2.14 (a) The nucleus has most of the mass **but occupies very little** of the volume of an atom.

(b) True

(c) The number of electrons in an atom is equal to the number of **protons** in the atom.

(d) True

2.16 (a) ^{32}P has 15 p, 17 n (b) ^{51}Cr has 24 p, 27 n (c) ^{60}Co has 27 p, 33 n

(d) ^{99}Tc has 43 p, 56 n (e) ^{131}I has 53 p, 78 n (f) ^{201}Tl has 81 p, 120 n

2.18

Symbol	^{121}Sb	^{88}Sr	^{182}W	^{139}La	^{239}Pu
Protons	51	38	74	57	94
Neutrons	70	50	108	82	145
Electrons	51	38	74	57	94
Mass No.	121	88	182	139	239

2.20 Since the two nuclides are atoms of the same element, by definition they have the same number of protons, 54. They differ in mass number (and mass) because they have different numbers of neutrons. ^{129}Xe has 75 neutrons and ^{130}Xe has 76 neutrons.

2.22 (a) 12 amu

(b) The atomic weight of carbon reported on the front-inside cover of the text is the abundance-weighted average of the atomic masses of the two naturally-occurring isotopes of carbon, ^{12}C and ^{13}C. The mass of a ^{12}C atom is exactly 12 amu, but the atomic weight of 12.011 takes into account the presence of some ^{13}C atoms in every natural sample of the element.

2.24 Average atomic mass (atomic weight) = $\sum$ fractional abundance × mass of isotope

Average atomic mass = 0.6917(62.9296) + 0.3083(64.9278) = 63.5456 = 63.55 amu

2.26 (a) The purpose of the magnet in the mass spectrometer is to change the path of the moving ions. The magnitude of the deflection is inversely related to mass, which is the basis of the discrimination by mass.

(b) The atomic weight of Cl, 35.5, is an average atomic mass. It is the average of the masses of two naturally occurring isotopes, weighted by their abundances. See Solution 2.21(b).

(c) The single peak at mass 31 in the mass spectrum of phosphorus indicates that the sample contains a single isotope of P, and the mass of this isotope is 31 amu.

2.28 (a) Three peaks: $^1H-{}^1H$, $^1H-{}^2H$, $^2H-{}^2H$

(b) $^1H-{}^1H = 2(1.00783) = 2.01566$ amu

$^1H-{}^2H = 1.00783 + 2.01410 = 3.02193$ amu

$^2H-{}^2H = 2(2.01410) = 4.02820$ amu

[The mass ratios are 1 : 1.49923 : 1.99845 or 1 : 1.5 : 2]

(c) $^1H-{}^1H$ is largest, because there is the greatest chance that two atoms of the more abundant isotope will combine.

$^2H-{}^2H$ is the smallest, because there is the least chance that two atoms of the less abundant isotope will combine.

The Periodic Table; Molecules and Ions

2.30 (a) lithium (metal) (b) scandium (metal) (c) germanium (metalloid) (d) ytterbium (metal) (e) manganese (metal) (f) gold (metal) (g) tellurium (metalloid)

2.32 C, carbon, nonmetal; Si, silicon, metalloid; Ge, germanium, metalloid; Sn, tin, metal; Pb, lead, metal

2.34 Compounds with the same empirical but different molecular formulas differ by the integer number of empirical formula units in the respective molecules. Thus, they can have very different molecular structure, size and mass, resulting in very different physical properties.

2.36 A molecular formula contains all atoms in a molecule. An empirical formula shows the simplest ratio of atoms in a molecule or elements in a compound.

(a) molecular: B_2H_6; empirical: BH_3

(b) molecular: $C_6H_{12}O_6$; empirical: CH_2O

2.38 (a) 4 (b) 6 (c) 9

2.40 (a) C_2H_5Br

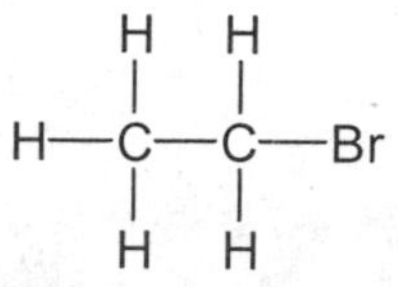

(b) C_2H_7N

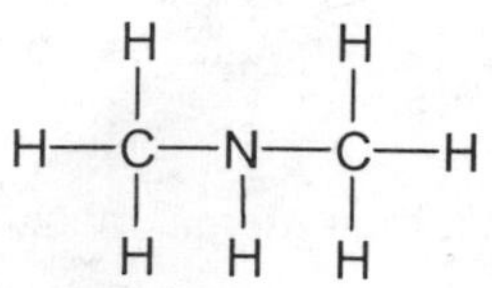

(c) CH_2Cl_2

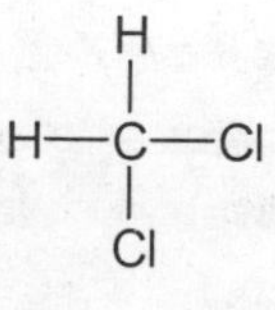

(d) NH_2OH

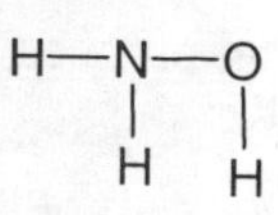

2.42 CH: C_2H_2, C_6H_6

CH_2: C_2H_4, C_3H_6, C_4H_8

NO_2: N_2O_4, NO_2

2.44 (a) Sc^{2+} or Sc^{3+} (b) Sr^{2+} (c) P^{3-} (d) K^{+} (e) F^{-}

2.46 (a) AgI (b) Ag_2S (c) AgF

2.48 (a) $(NH_4)_2SO_4$ (b) Cu_2S (c) LaF_3 (d) $Ca_3(PO_4)_2$ (e) Hg_2CO_3

2.50 Molecular (all elements are nonmetals): (a) PF_5 (c) SCl_2
Ionic (formed from ions, usually contains a metal cation): (b) NaI
(d) $Ca(NO_3)_2$ (e) $FeCl_3$ (f) LaP (g) $CoCO_3$ (h) $(NH_4)_2SO_4$

Naming Inorganic Compounds; Organic Molecules

2.52 (a) selenate (b) selenide (c) hydrogen selenide (biselenide)
(d) hydrogen selenite (biselenite)

2.54 (a) lithium oxide (b) iron(III) carbonate (ferric carbonate)
(c) sodium hypochlorite (d) ammonium sulfite (e) strontium cyanide
(f) chromium(III) hydroxide (chromic hydroxide) (g) cobalt(II) nitrate (cobaltous nitrate)
(h) sodium dihydrogen phosphate (i) potassium permanganate (j) silver dichromate

2.56 (a) $K_2Cr_2O_7$ (b) $Co(NO_3)_2$ (c) $Cr(C_2H_3O_2)_3$ (d) NaH (e) $Ca(HCO_3)_2$
(f) $Ba(BrO_3)_2$ (g) $Cu(ClO_4)_2$

2.58 (a) HBr (b) H_2S (c) HNO_2 (d) carbonic acid (e) chloric acid (f) acetic acid

2.60 (a) dinitrogen monoxide (b) nitrogen monoxide (c) nitrogen dioxide
(d) dinitrogen pentoxide (e) dinitrogen tetroxide

2.62 (a) $NaHCO_3$ (b) $Ca(OCl)_2$ (c) HCN (d) $Mg(OH)_2$ (e) SnF_2
(f) CdS, H_2SO_4, H_2S

2.64 (a) *-ane*
(b) All alkanes are hydrocarbons; they are composed of hydrogen and carbon only.

(c)

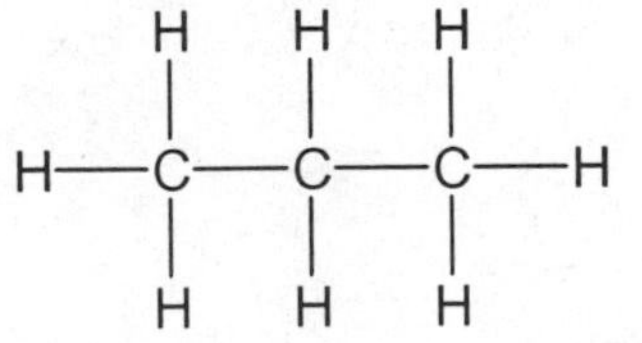

(d) **Hexane** has 6 carbons in its chain.

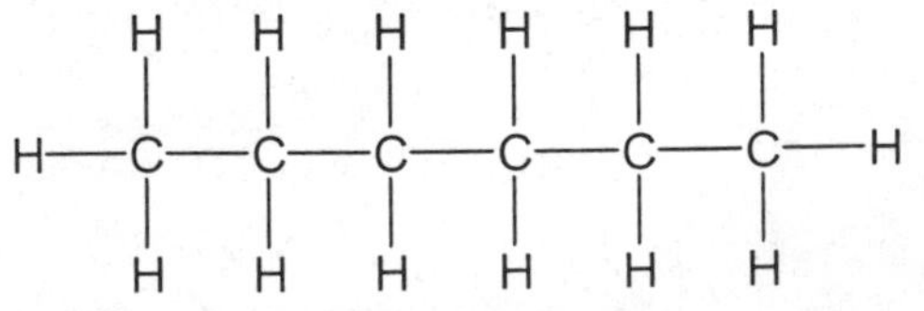

molecular: C_6H_{14}

empirical: C_3H_7

2.66 (a) They all have two carbon atoms in their molecular backbone, or chain.

(b) In 1-propanol one of the H atoms on an outer (terminal) C atom has been replaced by an –OH group.

(c) Ethanoic acid has two carbons in its chain. One of these C atoms is bound to two O atoms in the way that is characteristic of a *carboxylic acid* functional group. Propanoic acid has three C atoms in its chain and one of the outer C atoms is part of the carboxylic acid functional group.

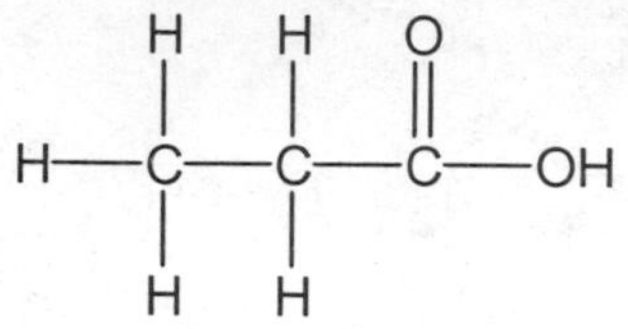

molecular formula: $C_3H_6O_2$ or C_2H_5COOH

Additional Exercises

2.67 (a) Based on data accumulated in the late eighteenth century on how substances react with one another, **Dalton** postulated the atomic theory. Dalton's theory is based on the indivisible atom as the smallest unit of an element that can combine with other elements.

(b) By determining the effects of electric and magnetic fields on cathode rays, **Thomson** measured the mass-to-charge ratio of the electron. He also proposed the "plum pudding" model of the atom in which most of the space in an atom is occupied by a diffuse positive charge in which the tiny negatively charged electrons are imbedded.

(c) By observing the rate of fall of oil drops in and out of an electric field, **Millikan** measured the charge of an electron.

(d) After observing the scattering of alpha particles at large angles when the particles struck gold foil, **Rutherford** postulated the nuclear atom. In Rutherford's atom, most of the mass of the atom is concentrated in a small dense region called the nucleus and the tiny negatively charged electrons are moving through empty space around the nucleus.

2.68 (a) Droplet D would fall most slowly. It carries the most negative charge, so it would be most strongly attracted to the upper (+) plate and most strongly repelled by the lower (-) plate. These electrostatic forces would provide the greatest opposition to gravity.

(b) Calculate the lowest common factor.

A: $3.84 \times 10^{-8} / 2.88 \times 10^{-8} = 1.33$; $1.33 \times 3 = 4$

B. $4.88 \times 10^{-8} / 2.88 \times 10^{-8} = 1.66$; $1.66 \times 3 = 5$

C. $2.88 \times 10^{-8} / 2.88 \times 10^{-8} = 1.00$; $1.00 \times 3 = 3$

D. $8.64 \times 10^{-8} / 2.88 \times 10^{-8} = 3.00$; $3.00 \times 3 = 9$

The total charge on the drops is in the ratio of 4:5:3:9. Divide the total charge on each drop by the appropriate integer and average the four values to get the charge of an electron in warmombs.

A: $3.84 \times 10^{-8} / 4 = 9.60 \times 10^{-9}$ wa

B: $4.80 \times 10^{-8} / 5 = 9.60 \times 10^{-9}$ wa

C: $2.88 \times 10^{-8} / 3 = 9.60 \times 10^{-9}$ wa

D: $8.64 \times 10^{-8} / 9 = 9.60 \times 10^{-9}$ wa

The charge on an electron is 9.60×10^{-9} wa

(c) The number of electrons on each drop are the integers calculated in part (b). A has 4 e^-, B has 5 e^-, C has 3 e^- and D has 9 e^-.

(d) $$\frac{9.60 \times 10^{-9}\ \text{wa}}{1\ e^-} \times \frac{1\ e^-}{1.60 \times 10^{-16}\ \text{C}} = 6.00 \times 10^{7}\ \text{wa/C}$$

2.70 (a) Most of the volume of an atom is empty space in which electrons move. Most alpha particles passed through this space. The path of the massive alpha particle would not be significantly altered by interaction with a "puny" electron.

(b) Most of the mass of an atom is contained in a very small, dense area called the nucleus. The few alpha particles that hit the massive, positively charged gold nuclei were strongly repelled and essentially deflected back in the direction they came from.

(c) The Be nuclei have a much smaller volume and positive charge than the Au nuclei; the charge repulsion between the alpha particles and the Be nuclei will be less, and there will be fewer direct hits because the Be nuclei have an even smaller volume than the Au nuclei. Fewer alpha particles will be scattered in general and fewer will be strongly back scattered.

2.71 (a) 2 protons and 2 neutrons (b) the nuclear strong force

(c) The charge of an α particle is twice the magnitude of the charge of an electron, with the opposite sign. That is, $2\ (+1.6022 \times 10^{-19})\ \text{C} = +3.2044 \times 10^{-19}\ \text{C}$.

(d) $$\frac{3.2044 \times 10^{-19}\ \text{C}}{4.8224 \times 10^{4}\ \text{g/C}} = 6.6448 \times 10^{-24}\ \text{g}$$

$$6.6448 \times 10^{-24}\ \text{g} \times \frac{1\ \text{amu}}{1.66054 \times 10^{-24}\ \text{g}} = 4.0016\ \text{amu}$$

(e) The sum of the particle masses in an α particle is 2(1.0073 amu) and 2(1.0087) amu = 4.0320 amu. The actual particle mass, 4.0016 amu, is less than the sum of the masses of the components. The difference is the nuclear binding energy, the energy released when protons and neutrons combine to form a nucleus. Mass and energy are interchangeable according to the Einstein relationship $E = mc^2$.

2.73 (a) Calculate the mass of a single gold atom, then divide the mass of the cube by the mass of the gold atom.

$$\frac{197.0 \text{ amu}}{\text{gold atom}} \times \frac{1 \text{ g}}{6.022 \times 10^{23} \text{ amu}} = 3.2713 \times 10^{-22} = 3.271 \times 10^{-22} \text{ g/gold atom}$$

$$\frac{19.3 \text{ g}}{\text{cube}} \times \frac{1 \text{ gold atom}}{3.271 \times 10^{-22} \text{ g}} = 5.90 \times 10^{22} \text{ Au atoms in the cube}$$

(b) The shape of atoms is spherical; spheres cannot be arranged into a cube so that there is no empty space. The question is, how much empty space is there? We can calculate the two limiting cases; no empty space and maximum empty space. The true diameter will be somewhere in this range.

No empty space: volume cube/number of atoms = volume of one atom

$V = 4/3\pi r^3$; $r = (3\pi V/4)^{1/3}$; $d = 2r$

$$\text{vol. of cube} = (1.0 \times 1.0 \times 1.0) = \frac{1.0 \text{ cm}^3}{5.90 \times 10^{22} \text{ Au atoms}} = 1.695 \times 10^{-23}$$

$$= 1.7 \times 10^{-23} \text{ cm}^3$$

$r = [\pi (1.695 \times 10^{-23} \text{ cm}^3)/4]^{1/3} = 3.4 \times 10^{-8}$ cm; $d = 2r = 6.8 \times 10^{-8}$ cm

Maximum empty space: assume atoms are arranged in rows in all three directions so they are touching across their diameters. That is, each atom occupies the volume of a cube, with the atomic diameter as the length of the side of the cube. The number of atoms along one edge of the gold cube is then
$(5.90 \times 10^{22})^{1/3} = 3.893 \times 10^7 = 3.89 \times 10^7$ atoms/1.0 cm.

The diameter of a single atom is 1.0 cm/3.89×10^7 atoms = $2.569 \times 10^{-8} = 2.6 \times 10^{-8}$ cm.

The diameter of a gold atom is between 2.6×10^{-8} cm and 6.8×10^{-8} cm (2.6 - 6.8 Å).

(c) Some atomic arrangement must be assumed, since none is specified. The solid state is characterized by an orderly arrangement of particles, so it isn't surprising that atomic arrangement is required to calculate the density of a solid. A more detailed discussion of solid-state structure and density appears in Chapter 11.

2.74 (a) In arrangement A the number of atoms in 1 cm^2 is just the square of the number that fit linearly in 1 cm.

$$1.0 \text{ cm} \times \frac{1 \text{ atom}}{4.95 \text{ Å}} \times \frac{1 \times 10^{10} \text{ Å}}{1 \text{ m}} \times \frac{1 \text{ m}}{100 \text{ cm}} = 2.02 \times 10^7 = 2.0 \times 10^7 \text{ atoms/cm}$$

$1.0 \text{ cm}^2 = (2.02 \times 10^7)^2 = 4.081 \times 10^{14} = 4.1 \times 10^{14}$ atoms/cm^2

(b) In arrangement B, the atoms in the horizontal rows are touching along their diameters, as in arrangement A. The number of Rb atoms in a 1.0 cm row is then 2.0×10^7 Rb atoms. Relative to arrangement A, the vertical rows are offset by 1/2 of an atom. Atoms in a 'column' are no longer touching along their vertical diameter. We must calculate the vertical distance occupied by a row of atoms, which is now less than the diameter of one Rb atom.

Consider the triangle shown below. This is an isosceles triangle (equal side lengths, equal interior angles) with a side-length of 2d and an angle of 60°. Drop a bisector to the uppermost angle so that it bisects the opposite side.

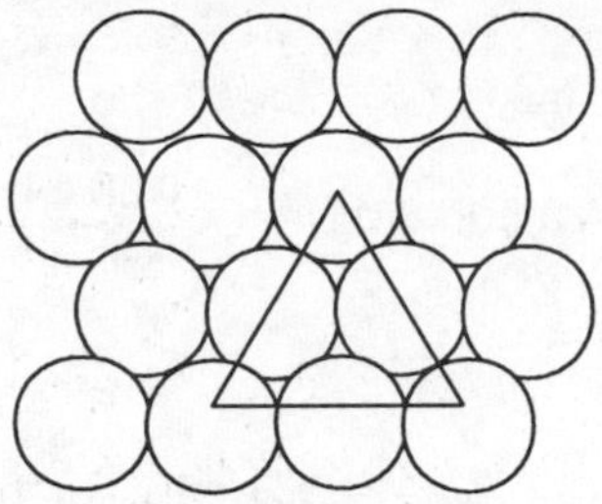

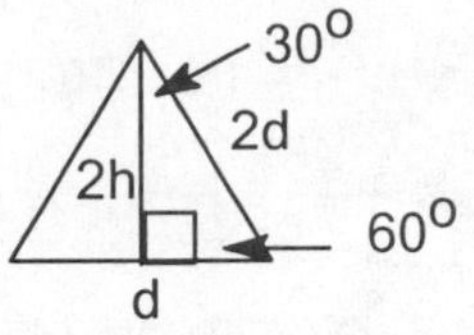

The result is a right triangle with two known side lengths. The length of the unknown side (the angle bisector) is 2h, two times the vertical distance occupied by a row of atoms. Solve for h, the "height" of one row of atoms.

$(2h)^2 + d^2 = (2d)^2$; $4h^2 = 4d^2 - d^2 = 3d^2$; $h^2 = 3d^2/4$

$h = (3d^2/4)^{1/2} = (3(4.95\ \text{Å})^2/4)^{1/2} = 4.2868 = 4.29\ \text{Å}$

The number of rows of atoms in 1 cm is then

$$1.0\ \text{cm} \times \frac{1\ \text{row}}{4.2868\ \text{Å}} \times \frac{1 \times 10^{10}\ \text{Å}}{1\ \text{m}} \times \frac{1\ \text{m}}{100\ \text{cm}} = 2.333 \times 10^7 = 2.3 \times 10^7$$

The number of atoms in a 1.0 cm^2 square area is then

$$\frac{2.020 \times 10^7\ \text{atoms}}{1\ \text{row}} \times 2.333 \times 10^7\ \text{rows} = 4.713 \times 10^{14} = 4.7 \times 10^{14}$$

Note that we have ignored the loss of "1/2" atom at the end of each horizontal row. Out of 2.0×10^7 atoms per row, one atom is not significant.

(c) The ratio of atoms in arrangement B to arrangement A is then 4.713×10^{14} atoms/4.081×10^{14} = 1.555 = 1.2:1. Clearly, arrangement B results in less empty space per unit area or volume. If extended to three dimensions, arrangement B would lead to a greater density for Rb metal.

2.75 (a) diameter of nucleus = 1×10^{-4} Å; diameter of atom = 1 Å

$V = 4/3\ \pi r^3$; $r = d/2$; $r_n = 0.5 \times 10^{-4}$ Å; $r_a = 0.5$ Å

volume of nucleus = $4/3\ \pi\ (0.5 \times 10^{-4})^3\ \text{Å}^3$

volume of atom = $4/3\ \pi\ (0.5)^3\ \text{Å}^3$

$$\text{volume fraction of nucleus} = \frac{\text{volume of nucleus}}{\text{volume of atom}} = \frac{4/3\ \pi\ (0.5 \times 10^{-4})^3\ \text{Å}^3}{4/3\ \pi\ (0.5)^3\ \text{Å}^3} = 1 \times 10^{-12}$$

diameter of atom = 5 Å, $r_a = 2.5$ Å

$$\text{volume fraction of nucleus} = \frac{4/3\ \pi\ (0.5 \times 10^{-4})^3\ \text{Å}^3}{4/3\ \pi\ (2.5)^3\ \text{Å}^3} = 8 \times 10^{-15}$$

Depending on the radius of the atom, the volume fraction of the nucleus is between 1×10^{-12} and 8×10^{-15}; that is, between 1 part in 10^{12} and 8 parts in 10^{15}.

(b) mass of proton = 1.0073 amu

$1.0073 \text{ amu} \times 1.66054 \times 10^{-24} \text{ g/amu} = 1.6727 \times 10^{-24} \text{ g}$

$$\text{diameter} = 1.0 \times 10^{-15} \text{ m, radius} = 0.50 \times 10^{-15} \text{ m} \times \frac{100 \text{ cm}}{1 \text{ m}} = 5.0 \times 10^{-14} \text{ cm}$$

Assuming a proton is a sphere, $V = 4/3\ \pi\ r^3$.

$$\text{density} = \frac{\text{g}}{\text{cm}^3} = \frac{1.6727 \times 10^{-24} \text{ g}}{4/3\ \pi\ (5.0 \times 10^{-14})^3 \text{ cm}^3} = 3.2 \times 10^{15} \text{ g/cm}^3$$

2.77 Weight is the force exerted by the mass of an object under the acceleration due to gravity. The SI unit of weight is the Newton, or kg • m/s^2. Mass is a fundamental quantity with SI units of kg. The weight of an object varies depending on the position of the object relative to Earth, but mass is invariant with position. Atomic 'weights', with units of grams, are the same on the moon as on Earth. Clearly, they are masses rather than weights.

2.79 (a) There are 24 known isotopes of Ni, from ^{51}Ni to ^{74}Ni.

(b) The five most abundant isotopes are

^{58}Ni, 57.935346 amu, 68.077%

^{60}Ni, 59.930788 amu, 26.223%

^{62}Ni, 61.928346 amu, 3.634%

^{61}Ni, 60.931058 amu, 1.140%

^{64}Ni, 63.927968 amu, 0.926%

Data from *Handbook of Chemistry and Physics*, 74th Ed. [Data may differ slightly in other editions.]

2.80 (a) A Br_2 molecule could consist of two atoms of the same isotope or one atom of each of the two different isotopes. This second possibility is twice as likely as the first. Therefore, the second peak (twice as large as peaks 1 and 3) represents a Br_2 molecule containing different isotopes. The mass numbers of the two isotopes are determined from the masses of the two smaller peaks. Since 157.836 ≈ 158, the first peak represents a ^{79}Br–^{79}Br molecule. Peak 3, 161.832 ≈ 162, represents a ^{81}Br–^{81}Br molecule. Peak 2 then contains one atom of each isotope, ^{79}Br–^{81}Br, with an approximate mass of 160 amu.

(b) The mass of the lighter isotope is 157.836 amu/2 atoms, or 78.918 amu/atom. For the heavier one, 161.832 amu/2 atoms = 80.916 amu/atom.

(c) The relative size of the three peaks in the mass spectrum of Br_2 indicates their relative abundance. The average mass of a Br_2 molecule is

0.2569(157.836) + 0.4999(159.834) + 0.2431(161.832) = 159.79 amu

(Each product has four significant figures and two decimal places, so the answer has two decimal places.)

(d) $\dfrac{159.79 \text{ amu}}{\text{avg. } Br_2 \text{ molecule}} \times \dfrac{1\ Br_2 \text{ molecule}}{2 \text{ Br atoms}} = 79.895 \text{ amu}$

(e) Let x = the abundance of ^{79}Br, 1-x = abundance of ^{81}Br. From (b), the masses of the two isotopes are 78.918 amu and 80.916 amu, respectively. From (d), the mass of an average Br atom is 79.895 amu.

$$x(78.918) + (1 - x)(80.916) = 79.895,\ x = 0.5110$$

$$^{79}Br = 51.10\%,\ ^{81}Br = 48.90\%$$

2.82 copper: Cu, 1B (coinage metals, transition metal)
tin: Sn, 4A
zinc: Zn, 2B
phosphorus: P, 5A
lead: Pb, 4A

2.83 (a) an alkali metal: K (b) an alkaline earth metal: Ca (c) a noble gas: Ar
(d) a halogen: Br (e) a metalloid: Ge (f) a nonmetal in 1A: H
(g) a metal that forms a 3+ ion: Al (h) a nonmetal that forms a 2− ion: O
(i) an element that resembles Al: Ga

2.85 (a) chlorine gas: ii (b) propane: v (c) nitrate ion: i
(d) sulfur trioxide: iii (e) methylchloride: iv

2.86

Symbol	$^{102}Ru^{3+}$	$^{80}Se^{2-}$	$^{192}Os^{2+}$	$^{127}I^{-}$	$^{140}Ce^{3+}$
Protons	44	34	76	53	58
Neutrons	58	46	116	74	82
Electrons	41	36	74	54	55
Net Charge	3+	2-	2+	1-	3+

2.88 (a) IO_3^- (b) IO_4^- (c) IO^- (d) HIO (e) HIO_4 or (H_5IO_6)

2.89 (a) perbromate ion (b) selenite ion (c) AsO_4^{3-} (d) $HTeO_4^-$

2.91 (a) potassium nitrate (b) sodium carbonate (c) calcium oxide
(d) hydrochloric acid (e) magnesium sulfate (f) magnesium hydroxide

2.92 (a) CaS, $Ca(HS)_2$ (b) HBr, $HBrO_3$ (c) AlN, $Al(NO_2)_3$ (d) FeO, $Fe_2O_3$2
(e) NH_3, NH_4^+ (f) K_2SO_3, $KHSO_3$ (g) Hg_2Cl_2 , $HgCl_2$ (h) $HClO_3$, $HClO_4$

2.93

	Formula	Name	Density, g/mL	Melting Point, °C	Boiling Point, °C
(a)	PF_3	phosphorus trifluoride	3.907	-151.5	-101.5
(b)	$SiCl_4$	silicon tetrachloride	1.483	-70	57.57
(c)	C_2H_6O (C_2H_5OH)	ethanol	0.7893	-117.3	78.5

2.95 (a) $\frac{0.0774 \text{ g H}}{0.9226 \text{ g C}} = \frac{\text{x g H}}{1.000 \text{ g C}}$; 0.0839 g H/1 g C

(b) xylene: $\frac{0.0949 \text{ g H}}{0.9051 \text{ g C}} = \frac{\text{x g H}}{1.000 \text{ g C}}$; 0.105 g H/1 g C

biphenyl: $\frac{0.0654 \text{ g H}}{0.9346 \text{ g C}} = \frac{\text{x g H}}{1.000 \text{ g C}}$; 0.0700 g H/1 g C

mesitylene: $\frac{0.1006 \text{ g H}}{0.8994 \text{ g C}} = \frac{\text{x g H}}{1.000 \text{ g C}}$; 0.112 g H/1 g C

toluene: $\frac{0.0875 \text{ g H}}{0.9125 \text{ g C}} = \frac{\text{x g H}}{1.000 \text{ g C}}$; 0.0959 g H/1 g C

(c) If 0.0839 g H/1 g C is a 1:1 combining ratio, dividing the g H/1 g C obtained in (b) by 0.083 should indicate the ratio of H:1C in the other compounds.

(d) Empirical formulas follow the combining ratios.

xylene: $\frac{0.105 \text{ g H/1 g C}}{0.0839 \text{ g H/1 g C}}$ = 1.25H : 1C = 5H : 4C; C_4H_5

biphenyl: $\frac{0.0700 \text{ g H/1 g C}}{0.0839 \text{ g H/1 g C}}$ = 0.834H : 1C = 5H : 6C; C_6H_5

mesitylene: $\frac{0.112 \text{ g H/1 g C}}{0.0839 \text{ g H/1 g C}}$ = 1.33H : 1C = 4 H : 3C; C_3H_4

toluene: $\frac{0.0959 \text{ g H/1 g C}}{0.0839 \text{ g H/1 g C}}$ = 1.14H: 1C = 8H : 7C = C_7H_8

2.96 (a) In an alkane, all C atoms have 4 single bonds, so each C in the partial structure needs 2 more bonds. All alkanes are hydrocarbons, so 2 H atoms will bind to each C atom in the ring.

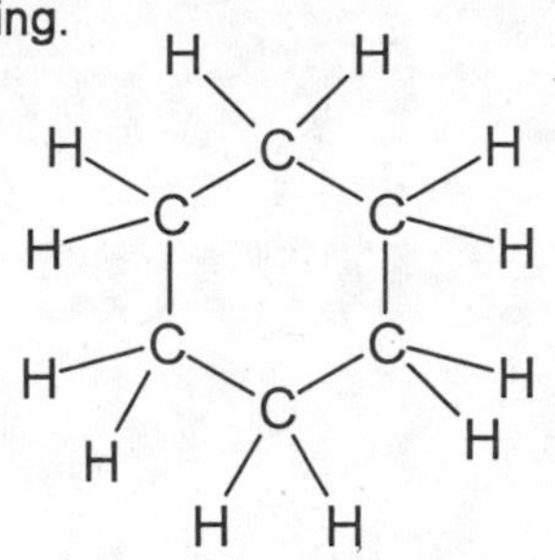

(b) The molecular formula of cyclohexane is C_6H_{12}; the molecular formula of *n*-hexane is C_6H_{14} (see Solution 2.64(d)). Cyclohexane can be thought of as *n*-hexane in which the two outer (terminal) C atoms are joined to each other. In order to form this C-C bond, each outer C atom must lose 1 H atom. The number of C atoms is unchanged and each C atom still has 4 single bonds. The resulting molecular formula is $C_6H_{14-2} = C_6H_{12}$.

(c) On the structure in part (a), replace 1 H atom with an OH group.

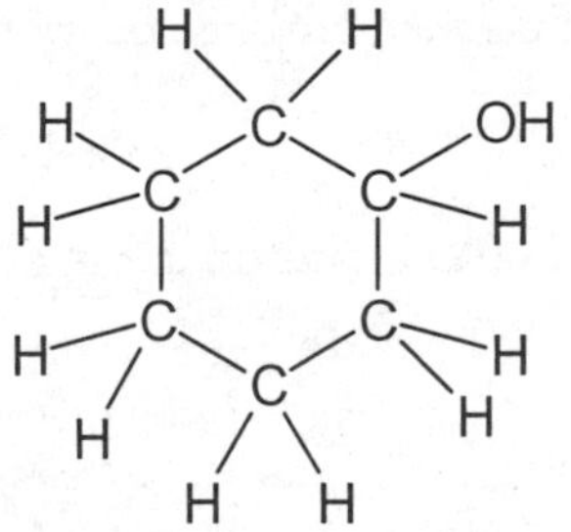

(d) Note that ethene, which contains a C-C double bond, has one fewer H atom per C atom than ethane. The C-C double bond in cyclohexene will have the same effect.

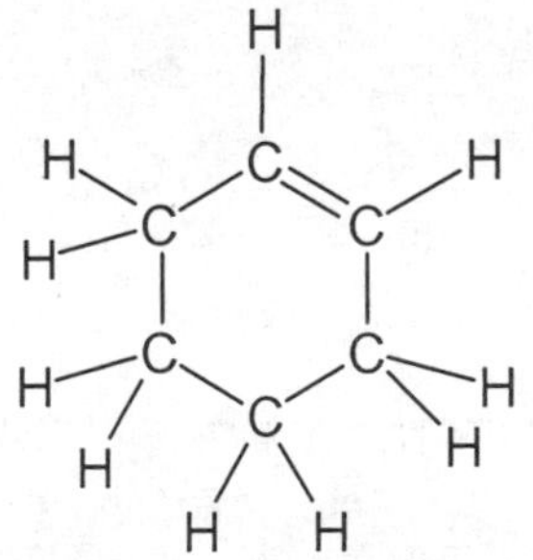

molecular formula: C_6H_{10}

The molecular formula of cyclohex**ene**, C_6H_{10}, is different than the molecular formula of cyclohex**ane**, C_6H_{12}.

2.97 Elements are arranged in the periodic table by increasing atomic number and so that elements with similar chemical and physical properties form a vertical column or group. By its position in the periodic chart, we know whether an element is a metal, nonmetal or metalloid, and the common charge of its ion. Members of a group have the same common ionic charge and combine in similar ways with other elements.

3 Stoichiometry: Calculation with Chemical Formulas and Equations

Balancing Chemical Equations

3.2 (a) H_2O_2 indicates that there are 2 hydrogen atoms and 2 oxygen atoms bound by chemical bonds into a single molecule (of hydrogen peroxide). $2H_2O$ indicates 2 molecules (of water), each of which contains 2 hydrogen atoms and 1 oxygen atom. The composition of the different molecules, H_2O_2 and H_2O, is different and the physical and chemical properties of the two compounds they constitute are very different. The subscript 2 changes molecular composition and thus properties of the compound. The prefix 2 indicates how many molecules (or moles) of the original compound are under consideration.

(b) No. There are more H and O atoms on the reactant side than the product side. The coefficient 6 before $H_2O(l)$ in the products would balance the equation.

3.4

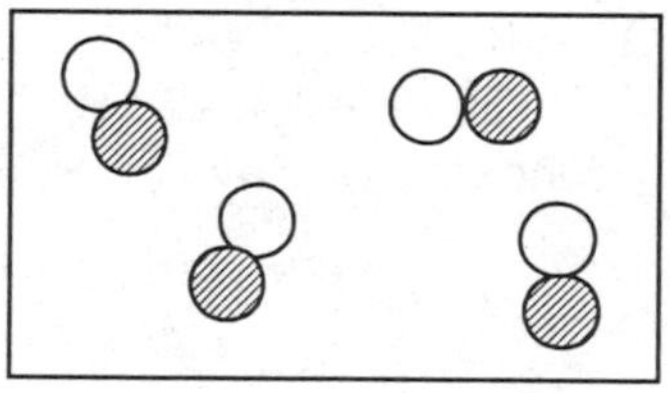

Write the balanced equation for the reaction.

$$2H_2 + CO \rightarrow CH_3OH$$

The combining ratio of H_2: CO is 2:1. If we have 8 H_2 molecules, 4 CO molecules are required for complete reaction. Alternatively, you could examine the atom ratios in the formula of CH_3OH, but the balanced equation is most direct.

3.6 (a) $\mathbf{6}Li(s) + N_2(g) \rightarrow \mathbf{2}Li_3N(s)$

(b) $TiCl_4(l) + \mathbf{2}H_2O(l) \rightarrow TiO_2(s) + \mathbf{4}HCl(aq)$

(c) $\mathbf{2}NH_4NO_3(s) \rightarrow \mathbf{2}N_2(g) + O_2(g) + \mathbf{4}H_2O(g)$

(d) $Ca_3P_2(s) + \mathbf{6}H_2O(l) \rightarrow \mathbf{3}Ca(OH)_2(s) + \mathbf{2}PH_3(g)$

(e) $Al(OH)_3(s) + \mathbf{3}HClO_4(aq) \rightarrow Al(ClO_4)_3(aq) + \mathbf{3}H_2O(l)$

(f) $\mathbf{2}AgNO_3(aq) + Na_2SO_4(aq) \rightarrow Ag_2SO_4(s) + \mathbf{2}NaNO_3(aq)$

(g) $\mathbf{2}N_2H_4(g) + N_2O_9(g) \rightarrow \mathbf{4}H_2O(g) + \mathbf{3}N_2(g)$

3.8 (a) $SO_3(g) + H_2O(l) \rightarrow H_2SO_4(aq)$
(b) $B_2S_3(s) + \mathbf{6}H_2O(l) \rightarrow \mathbf{2}H_3BO_3(aq) + \mathbf{3}H_2S(g)$
(c) $\mathbf{4}PH_3(g) + \mathbf{8}O_2(g) \rightarrow \mathbf{6}H_2O(g) + P_4O_{10}(s)$
(d) $\mathbf{2}Hg(NO_3)_2(s) \xrightarrow{\Delta} \mathbf{2}HgO(s) + \mathbf{4}NO_2(g) + O_2(g)$
(e) $Cu(s) + \mathbf{2}H_2SO_4(aq) \rightarrow CuSO_4(aq) + SO_2(g) + \mathbf{2}H_2O(l)$

Patterns of Chemical Reactivity

3.10 (a) Neutral Ca atom loses $2e^-$ to form Ca^{2+}. Neutral O_2 molecule gains $4e^-$ to form $2O^{2-}$. The formula of the product will be CaO, because the cationic and anionic charges are opposite and equal. $2Ca(s) + O_2(g) \rightarrow 2CaO$
(b) The products are $CO_2(g)$ and $H_2O(l)$. $C_3H_6O(l) + 4O_2(g) \rightarrow 3CO_2(g) + 3H_2O(l)$

3.12 (a) $\mathbf{2}Al(s) + \mathbf{3}Br_2(l) \rightarrow \mathbf{2}AlBr_3(s)$
(b) $SrCO_3(s) \xrightarrow{\Delta} SrO(s) + CO_2(g)$
(c) $C_7H_{16}(l) + \mathbf{11}O_2(g) \rightarrow \mathbf{7}CO_2(g) + \mathbf{8}H_2O(l)$
(d) CH_3OCH_3 is C_2H_6O. $C_2H_6O(l) + \mathbf{3}O_2(g) \rightarrow \mathbf{2}CO_2(g) + \mathbf{3}H_2O(l)$

3.14 (a) $\mathbf{2}C_3H_6(g) + \mathbf{9}O_2(g) \rightarrow \mathbf{6}CO_2(g) + \mathbf{6}H_2O(l)$ combustion
(b) $NH_4NO_3(s) \rightarrow N_2O(g) + \mathbf{2}H_2O(l)$ decomposition
(c) $C_5H_6O(l) + \mathbf{6}O_2(g) \rightarrow \mathbf{5}CO_2(g) + \mathbf{3}H_2O(l)$ combustion
(d) $N_2(g) + \mathbf{3}H_2(g) \rightarrow \mathbf{2}NH_3(g)$ combination
(e) $K_2O(s) + H_2O(l) \rightarrow \mathbf{2}KOH(aq)$ combination

Formula Weights

3.16 Formula weight in amu to 1 decimal place.
(a) N_2O: FW = 2(14.0) + 1(16.0) = 44.0 amu
(b) $HC_7H_5O_2$: 7(12.0) + 6(1.0) + 2(16.0) = 122.0 amu
(c) $Mg(OH)_2$: 1(24.3) + 2(16.0) + 2(1.0) = 58.3 amu
(d) $(NH_2)_2CO$: 2(14.0) + 4(1.0) + 1(12.0) + 1(16.0) = 60.0 amu
(e) $CH_3CO_2C_5H_{11}$: 7(12.0) + 14(1.0) + 2(16.0) = 130.0 amu

3.18 (a) C_2H_2: FW = 2(12.0) + 2(1.0) = 26.0 amu

$$\%\ C = \frac{2(12.0)\ \text{amu}}{26.0\ \text{amu}} \times 100 = 92.3\ \%$$

(b) $(NH_4)_2SO_4$: FW = 2(14.0) + 8(1.0) + 1(32.1) + 4(16.0) = 132.1 amu

$$\%\ H = \frac{8(1.0)\ \text{amu}}{132.1\ \text{amu}} \times 100 = 6.1\%$$

(c) $HC_6H_7O_6$: FW = 6(12.0) + 8(1.0) + 6(16.0) = 176.0 amu

$$\%\ O = \frac{6(16.0)\ \text{amu}}{176.0\ \text{amu}} \times 100 = 54.5\%$$

(d) $PtCl_2(NH_3)_2$: FW = 1(195.1) + 2(35.5) + 2(14.0) + 6(1.0) = 300.1 amu

$$\% \text{ Pt} = \frac{1(195.1)\text{ amu}}{300.1\text{ amu}} \times 100 = 65.01\%$$

(e) $C_{18}H_{24}O_2$: FW = 18(12.0) + 24(1.0) + 2(16.0) = 272.0 amu

$$\% \text{ C} = \frac{18(12.0)\text{ amu}}{272.0\text{ amu}} \times 100 = 79.4\%$$

(f) $C_{18}H_{27}NO_3$: FW = 18(12.0) + 27(1.0) + 1(14.0) + 3(16.0) = 305.0 amu

$$\% \text{ C} = \frac{18(12.0)\text{ amu}}{305.0\text{ amu}} \times 100 = 70.8\%$$

3.20 (a) CO_2: FW = 1(12.0) + 2(16.0) = 44.0 amu

$$\% \text{ C} = \frac{12.0\text{ amu}}{44.0\text{ amu}} \times 100 = 27.3\%$$

(b) CH_3OH: FW = 1(12.0) + 4(1.0) + 1(16.0) = 32.0 amu

$$\% \text{ C} = \frac{12.0\text{ amu}}{32.0\text{ amu}} \times 100 = 37.5\%$$

(c) C_2H_6: FW = 2(12.0) + 6(1.0) = 30.0 amu

$$\% \text{ C} = \frac{2(12.0)\text{ amu}}{30.0\text{ amu}} \times 100 = 80.0\%$$

(d) $CS(NH_2)_2$: FW = 1(12.0) + 1(32.1) + 2(14.0) + 4(1.0) = 76.1 amu

$$\% \text{ C} = \frac{12.0\text{ amu}}{76.1\text{ amu}} \times 100 = 15.8\%$$

The Mole

3.22 (a) exactly 12 g (b) 6.0221421×10^{23}, Avogadro's number

3.24 3.0×10^{23} H_2O_2 molecules contains (4 atoms × 0.5 mol) = 2 mol atoms

32 g O_2 contains (2 atoms × 1 mol) = 2 mol atoms

2.0 mol CH_4 contains (5 atoms × 2 mol) = 10 mol atoms

3.26 250 million = $250 \times 10^6 = 2.50 \times 10^8$ people

$$\frac{6.022 \times 10^{23}\ ¢}{2.50 \times 10^8\text{ people}} \times \frac{\$1}{100\ ¢} = \frac{\$6.022 \times 10^{21}}{2.50 \times 10^8\text{ people}} = \$2.41 \times 10^{13}/\text{person}$$

\$5.5 trillion = $\$5.5 \times 10^{12}$ $$\frac{\$2.41 \times 10^{13}}{\$5.5 \times 10^{12}} = 4.4$$

Each person would receive an amount that is 4.4 times the dollar amount of the national debt.

3.28 (a) molar mass = 1(24.31) + 2(35.45) = 95.21 g

$$2.50 \times 10^{-2} \text{ mol } MgCl_2 \times \frac{95.21 \text{ g}}{1 \text{ mol}} = 2.38 \text{ g } MgCl_2$$

(b) molar mass = 1(14.01) + 4(1.008) + 1(35.45) = 53.49 g/mol

$$76.5 \text{ g } NH_4Cl \times \frac{1 \text{ mol}}{53.49 \text{ g}} = 1.43 \text{ mol } NH_4Cl$$

(c) $$0.0772 \text{ mol } HCHO_3 \times \frac{6.022 \times 10^{23} \text{ molecules}}{1 \text{ mol}} = 4.65 \times 10^{22} \text{ } HCHO_2 \text{ molecules}$$

(d) $$4.88 \times 10^{-3} \text{ mol } Al(NO_3)_3 \times \frac{3 \text{ mol } NO_3^-}{1 \text{ mol } Al(NO_3)_3} \times \frac{6.022 \times 10^{23} \text{ } NO_3^- \text{ ions}}{1 \text{ mol}}$$

$$= 8.82 \times 10^{23} \text{ } NO_3^-$$

3.30 (a) molar mass = 55.847 + 30.974 + 4(16.00) = 150.82 = 150.8 g

$$0.0714 \text{ mol } FePO_4 \times \frac{150.8 \text{ g } FePO_4}{1 \text{ mol}} = 10.77 = 10.8 \text{ g } FePO_4$$

(b) molar mass = 2(14.01) + 8(1.008) + 12.01 + 3(16.00) = 96.09 g

$$4.97 \text{ g } (NH_4)_2CO_3 \times \frac{1 \text{ mol}}{96.09 \text{ g } (NH_4)_2CO_3} \times \frac{2 \text{ mol } NH_4^+}{1 \text{ mol } (NH_4)_2 CO_3} = 0.0103 \text{ mol } NH_4^+$$

(c) molar mass = 9(12.01) + 8(1.008) + 4(16.00) = 180.154 = 180.2 g

$$6.52 \times 10^{21} \text{ molecules} \times \frac{1 \text{ mol}}{6.022 \times 10^{23} \text{ molecules}} \times \frac{180.2 \text{ g } C_9H_8O_4}{1 \text{ mol aspirin}} = 1.95 \text{ g } C_9H_8O_4$$

(d) $$\frac{15.86 \text{ g Valium}}{0.05570 \text{ mol}} = 284.7 \text{ g Valium/mol}$$

3.32 (a) molar mass = 14(12.01) + 18(1.008) + 2(14.01) + 5(16.00) = 294.30 g

(b) $$1.00 \text{ mg aspartame} \times \frac{1 \times 10^{-3} \text{ g}}{1 \text{ mg}} \times \frac{1 \text{ mol}}{294.3 \text{ g}} = 3.398 \times 10^{-6}$$

$$= 3.40 \times 10^{-6} \text{ mol aspartame}$$

(c) $$3.398 \times 10^{-6} \text{ mol aspartame} \times \frac{6.022 \times 10^{23} \text{ molecules}}{1 \text{ mol}} = 2.046 \times 10^{18}$$

$$= 2.05 \times 10^{18} \text{ aspartame molecules}$$

(d) $$2.046 \times 10^{18} \text{ aspartame molecules} \times \frac{18 \text{ H atoms}}{1 \text{ aspartame molecule}} = 3.68 \times 10^{19} \text{ H atoms}$$

3.34 (a) 3.08×10^{21} H atoms $\times \dfrac{19 \text{ C atoms}}{28 \text{ H atoms}} = 2.09 \times 10^{21}$ C atoms

(b) 3.08×10^{21} H atoms $\times \dfrac{1\ C_{19}H_{28}O_2 \text{ molecule}}{28 \text{ H atoms}} = 1.100 \times 10^{20}$

$= 1.10 \times 10^{20}\ C_{19}H_{28}O_2$ molecules

(c) $1.100 \times 10^{20}\ C_{19}H_{28}O_2$ molecules $\times \dfrac{1 \text{ mol}}{6.022 \times 10^{23} \text{ molecules}} = 1.827 \times 10^{-4}$

$= 1.83 \times 10^{-4}$ mol $C_{19}H_{28}O_2$

(d) molar mass = 19(12.01) + 28(1.008) + 2(16.00) = 288.41 = 288.4 g

1.827×10^{-4} mol $C_{19}H_{28}O_2 \times \dfrac{288.4 \text{ g } C_{19}H_{28}O_2}{1 \text{ mol}} = 0.0527$ g $C_{19}H_{28}O_2$

3.36 25×10^{-6} g $C_{21}H_{30}O_2 \times \dfrac{1 \text{ mol } C_{21}H_{30}O_2}{314.5 \text{ g } C_{21}H_{30}O_2} = 7.95 \times 10^{-8} = 8.0 \times 10^{-8}$ mol $C_{21}H_{30}O_2$

7.95×10^{-8} mol $C_{21}H_{30}O_2 \times \dfrac{6.022 \times 10^{23} \text{ molecules}}{1 \text{ mol}} = 4.8 \times 10^{16}\ C_{21}H_{30}O_2$ molecules

Empirical Formulas

3.38 (a) The box contains 4 C atoms and 16 H atoms, so the empirical formula of the hydrocarbon is CH_4.

(b) If the molecular formula of the hydrocarbon is the same as the empirical formula, the reactants' box would contain 4 CH_4 molecules and 8 O_2 molecules. At this stage, you have no basis for knowing whether or not there might be a hydrocarbon molecule other than CH_4 that has this same empirical formula. It turns out, however, that there are none. In general, the molecular formula of a substance does not have to be identical with its empirical formula.

3.40 (a) Calculate the simplest ratio of moles.

0.104 mol K / 0.052 = 2
0.052 mol C / 0.052 = 1
0.156 mol O / 0.052 = 3

The empirical formula is K_2CO_3.

(b) Calculate moles of each element present, then the simplest ratio of moles.

5.28 g Sn $\times \dfrac{1 \text{ mol Sn}}{118.7 \text{ g Sn}}$ = 0.04448 mol Sn; 0.04448 / 0.04448 = 1

3.37 g F $\times \dfrac{1 \text{ mol F}}{19.00 \text{ g FSn}}$ = 0.1774 mol F; 0.1774 / 0.04448 ≈ 4

The integer ratio is 1 Sn : 4 F; the empirical formula is SnF_4.

(c) Assume 100 g sample, calculate moles of each element, find the simplest ratio of moles.

$$87.5\%\ N = 87.5\ g\ N \times \frac{1\ mol\ N}{14.01\ g} = 6.25\ mol\ N; \quad 6.25 / 6.25 = 1$$

$$12.5\%\ H = 12.5\ g\ H \times \frac{1\ mol}{1.008\ g} = 12.4\ mol\ H; \quad 12.4 / 6.25 \approx 2$$

The empirical formula is NH_2.

3.42 See Solution 3.41 for stepwise problem-solving approach.

(a)

$$55.3\ g\ K \times \frac{1\ mol\ K}{39.10\ g\ K} = 1.414\ mol\ K;\ 1.411/0.4714 \approx 3$$

$$14.6\ g\ P \times \frac{1\ mol\ P}{30.97\ g\ P} = 0.4714\ mol\ P;\ 0.4714/0.4714 = 1$$

$$30.1\ g\ O \times \frac{1\ mol\ O}{16.00\ g\ O} = 1.881\ mol\ O;\ 1.881/0.4714 \approx 4$$

The empirical formula is K_3PO_4.

(b)

$$24.5\ g\ Na \times \frac{1\ mol\ Na}{22.99\ g\ Na} = 1.066\ mol\ Na;\ 1.066/0.5304 \approx 2$$

$$14.9\ g\ Si \times \frac{1\ mol\ Si}{28.09\ Si} = 0.5304\ mol\ si;\ 0.5304/0.5304 = 1$$

$$60.6\ g\ F \times \frac{1\ mol\ F}{19.00\ g\ F} = 3.189\ mol\ F;\ 3.189/0.5304 \approx 6$$

The empirical formula is Na_2SiF_6.

(c)

$$62.1\ g\ C \times \frac{1\ mol\ C}{12.01\ g\ C} = 5.17\ mol\ C; \quad 5.17 / 0.864 \approx 6$$

$$5.21\ g\ H \times \frac{1\ mol\ H}{1.008\ g\ H} = 5.17\ mol\ O; \quad 5.17 / 0.864 \approx 6$$

$$12.1\ g\ N \times \frac{1\ mol\ N}{14.01\ g\ N} = 0.864\ mol\ N; \quad 0.864 / 0.864 = 1$$

$$20.7\ g\ O \times \frac{1\ mol\ O}{16.00\ g\ O} = 1.29\ mol\ O; \quad 1.29 / 0.864 \approx 1.5$$

Multiplying by two, the empirical formula is $C_{12}H_{12}N_2O_3$.

3.44 (a) FW 12.01 + 1.008 + 2(16.00) = 45.0. $\frac{\mathcal{M}}{FW} = \frac{90.0}{45.0} = 2$

The molecular formula is $H_2C_2O_4$.

(b) FW = 2(12) + 4(1) + 16 = 44. $\frac{\mathcal{M}}{FW} = \frac{88}{44} = 2$.

The molecular formula is $C_4H_8O_2$.

3.46 Assume 100 g in the following problems.

(a) $75.69 \text{ g C} \times \frac{1 \text{ mol C}}{12.01 \text{ g C}} = 6.30 \text{ mol C}; 6.30/0.969 = 6.5$

$8.80 \text{ g H} \times \frac{1 \text{ mol H}}{1.008 \text{ g H}} = 8.73 \text{ mol H}; 8.73/0.969 = 9.0$

$15.51 \text{ g O} \times \frac{1 \text{ mol O}}{16.00 \text{ g O}} = 0.969 \text{ mol O}; 0.969/0.969 = 1$

Multiply by 2 to obtain the integer ratio 13:18:2. The empirical formula is $C_{13}H_{18}O_2$, FW = 206 g. Since the empirical formula weight and the molar mass are equal (206 g), the empirical and molecular formulas are $C_{13}H_{18}O_2$.

(b) $59.0 \text{ g C} \times \frac{1 \text{ mol C}}{12.01 \text{ g C}} = 4.91 \text{ mol C}; \quad 4.91 / 0.550 \approx 9$

$7.1 \text{ g H} \times \frac{1 \text{ mol H}}{1.008 \text{ g H}} = 7.04 \text{ mol H}; \quad 7.04 / 0.550 \approx 13$

$26.2 \text{ g O} \times \frac{1 \text{ mol O}}{16.00 \text{ g O}} = 1.64 \text{ mol O}; \quad 6.64 / 0.550 \approx 3$

$7.7 \text{ g N} \times \frac{1 \text{ mol N}}{14.01 \text{ g N}} = 0.550 \text{ mol N}; \quad 0.550 / 0.550 = 1$

The empirical formula is $C_9H_{13}O_3N$, FW = 183 amu (or g). Since the molecular weight is approximately 180 amu, the empirical formula and molecular formula are the same, $C_9H_{13}O_3N$.

3.48 (a) *Plan.* Calculate mol C and mol H, then g C and g H; get g O by subtraction. *Solve*:

$6.32 \times 10^{-3} \text{ g } CO_2 \times \frac{1 \text{ mol } CO_2}{44.01 \text{ g } CO_2} \times \frac{1 \text{ mol C}}{1 \text{ mol } CO_2} = 1.436 \times 10^{-4} = 1.44 \times 10^{-4} \text{ mol C}$

$2.58 \times 10^{-3} \text{ g } H_2O \times \frac{1 \text{ mol } H_2O}{18.02 \text{ g } H_2O} \times \frac{2 \text{ mol H}}{1 \text{ mol } H_2O} = 2.863 \times 10^{-4} = 2.86 \times 10^{-4} \text{ mol H}$

$1.436 \times 10^{-4} \text{ mol C} \times \frac{12.01 \text{ g C}}{1 \text{ mol C}} = 1.725 \times 10^{-3} \text{ g C} = 1.73 \text{ mg C}$

$2.863 \times 10^{-4} \text{ mol H} \times \frac{1.008 \text{ g H}}{1 \text{ mol H}} = 2.886 \times 10^{-4} \text{ g H} = 0.289 \text{ mg H}$

mass of O = 2.78 mg sample - (1.725 mg C + 0.289 mg H) = 0.77 mg O

$0.77 \times 10^{-3} \text{ g O} \times \frac{1 \text{ mol O}}{16.00 \text{ g O}} = 4.81 \times 10^{-5} \text{ mol O}$. Divide moles by 4.81×10^{-5}.

C: $\frac{1.44 \times 10^{-4}}{4.81 \times 10^{-5}} \approx 3$; H: $\frac{2.86 \times 10^{-4}}{4.81 \times 10^{-5}} \approx 6$; O: $\frac{4.81 \times 10^{-5}}{4.81 \times 10^{-5}} = 1$

The empirical formula is C_3H_6O.

(b) *Plan*. Calculate mol C and mol H, then g C and g H. In this case, get N by subtraction. *Solve*:

$$14.242 \times 10^{-3} \text{ g } CO_2 \times \frac{1 \text{ mol } CO_2}{44.01 \text{ g } CO_2} \times \frac{1 \text{ mol C}}{1 \text{ mol } CO_2} = 3.2361 \times 10^{-4} = \text{mol C}$$

$$4.083 \times 10^{-3} \text{ g } H_2O \times \frac{1 \text{ mol } H_2O}{18.02 \text{ g } H_2O} \times \frac{2 \text{ mol H}}{1 \text{ mol } H_2O} = 4.5316\ 10^{-4} = 4.532 \times 10^{-4} \text{ mol H}$$

$$3.2361\ 10^{-4} \text{ g mol C} \times \frac{12.01 \text{ g C}}{1 \text{ mol C}} = 3.8866 \times 10^{-3} \text{ g C} = 3.8866 \text{ mg C}$$

$$4.532 \times 10^{-4} \text{ mol H} \times \frac{1.008 \text{ g H}}{1 \text{ mol H}} = 0.45683 \times 10^{-3} \text{ g H} = 0.4568 \text{ mg H}$$

mass of N = 5.250 mg sample – (3.8866 mg C + 0.4568 mg H) = 0.9066 = 0.907 mg N

$$0.9066 \times 10^{-3} \text{ g N} \times \frac{1 \text{ mol N}}{14.01 \text{ g N}} = 6.47 \times 10^{-5} \text{ mol N}.$$ Divide moles by 6.47×10^{-5}.

$$\text{C: } \frac{3.24 \times 10^{-4}}{6.47 \times 10^{-5}} \approx 5; \quad \text{H: } \frac{4.53 \times 10^{-4}}{6.47 \times 10^{-5}} \approx 7; \quad \text{N: } \frac{6.47 \times 10^{-5}}{6.47 \times 10^{-5}} = 1$$

The empirical formula is C_5H_7N, FW = 81. A molar mass of 160 ± 5 indicates a factor of 2 and a molecular formula of $C_{10}H_{14}N_2$.

3.50 The reaction involved is $MgSO_4 \cdot xH_2O(s) \rightarrow MgSO_4(s) + xH_2O(g)$. First, calculate the number of moles of product $MgSO_4$; this is the same as the number of moles of starting hydrate.

$$2.472 \text{ g } MgSO_4 \times \frac{1 \text{ mol } MgSO_4}{120.4 \text{ g } MgSO_4} \times \frac{1 \text{ mol } MgSO_4 \cdot x\,H_2O}{1 \text{ mol } MgSO_4} = 0.02053 \text{ mol } MgSO_4 \cdot x\,H_2O$$

$$\text{Thus, } \frac{5.061 \text{ g } MgSO_4 \cdot x\,H_2O}{0.02053} = 246.5 \text{ g/mol} = \text{FW of } MgSO_4 \cdot x\,H_2O.$$

FW of $MgSO_4 \cdot x\,H_2O$ = FW of $MgSO_4$ + x(FW of H_2O).

246.5 = 120.4 + x(18.02). x = 6.998. The hydrate formula is $MgSO_4 \cdot \underline{7}H_2O$.

Alternatively, we could calculate the number of moles of water represented by weight loss: (5.061 - 2.472) = 2.589 g H_2O lost.

$$2.589 \text{ g } H_2O \times \frac{1 \text{ mol } H_2O}{18.02 \text{ g } H_2O} = 0.1437 \text{ mol } H_2O; \quad \frac{\text{mol } H_2O}{\text{mol } MgSO_4} = \frac{0.1437}{0.02053} = 7.000$$

Again the correct formula is $MgSO_4 \cdot \underline{7}H_2O$.

Calculations Based on Chemical Equations

3.52 The **integer coefficients** immediately preceding each molecular formula in a chemical equation give information about relative numbers of moles of reactants and products involved in a reaction.

3.54 $C_2H_5OH(l) + 3O_2(g) \rightarrow 2CO_2(g) + 3H_2O(g)$

$C_3H_8(g) + 5O_2(g) \rightarrow 3CO_2(g) + 4H_2O(g)$

$CH_3CH_2COCH_3(l) + 11/2\ O_2(g) \rightarrow 4CO_2(g) + 4H_2O(l)$

In a combustion reaction, all H in the fuel is transformed to H_2O in the products. The reactant with most mol H/mol fuel will produce the most H_2O. C_3H_8 and $CH_3CH_2COCH_3$ (C_4H_8O) both have 8 mol H/mol fuel, so 1.5 mol of either fuel will produce the same amount of H_2O.
1.5 mol C_2H_5OH will produce less H_2O.

3.56 $C_6H_{12}O_6(aq) \rightarrow 2C_2H_5OH(aq) + 2CO_2(g)$

(a) $0.400 \text{ mol } C_6H_{12}O_6 \times \dfrac{2 \text{ mol } CO_2}{1 \text{ mol } C_6H_{12}O_6} = 0.800 \text{ mol } CO_2$

(b) $7.50 \text{ g } C_2H_5OH \times \dfrac{1 \text{ mol } C_2H_5OH}{46.07 \text{ g } C_2H_5OH} \times \dfrac{1 \text{ mol } C_6H_{12}O_6}{2 \text{ mol } C_2H_5OH} \times \dfrac{180.2 \text{ g } C_6H_{12}O_6}{1 \text{ mol } C_6H_{12}O_6}$

$= 14.7 \text{ g } C_6H_{12}O_6$

(c) $7.50 \text{ g } C_2H_5OH \times \dfrac{1 \text{ mol } C_2H_5OH}{46.07 \text{ g } C_2H_5OH} \times \dfrac{2 \text{ mol } CO_2}{2 \text{ mol } C_2H_5OH} \times \dfrac{44.01 \text{ g } CO_2}{1 \text{ mol } CO_2} = 7.16 \text{ g } CO_2$

3.58 (a) $CaH_2(s) + 2H_2O(l) \rightarrow Ca(OH)_2(aq) + 2H_2(g)$

(b) $5.00 \text{ g } H_2 \times \dfrac{1 \text{ mol } H_2}{2.016 \text{ g } H_2} \times \dfrac{1 \text{ mol } CaH_2}{2 \text{ mol } H_2} \times \dfrac{42.10 \text{ g } CaH_2}{1 \text{ mol } CaH_2} = 52.2 \text{ g } CaH_2$

3.60 $2C_8H_{18}(l) + 25O_2(g) \rightarrow 16CO_2(g) + 18H_2O(l)$

(a) $0.750 \text{ mol } C_8H_{18} \times \dfrac{25 \text{ mol } O_2}{2 \text{ mol } C_8H_{18}} = 9.375 = 9.38 \text{ mol } O_2$

(b) $5.00 \text{ g } C_8H_{18} \times \dfrac{1 \text{ mol } C_8H_{18}}{114.2 \text{ g } C_8H_{18}} \times \dfrac{25 \text{ mol } O_2}{2 \text{ mol } C_8H_{18}} \times \dfrac{32.00 \text{ g } O_2}{1 \text{ mol } O_2} = 17.5 \text{ g } O_2$

(c) $1.00 \text{ gal } C_8H_{18} \times \dfrac{3.7854 \text{ L}}{1 \text{ gal}} \times \dfrac{1000 \text{ mL}}{1 \text{ L}} \times \dfrac{0.692 \text{ g}}{1 \text{ mL}} = 2619.5 = 2.62 \times 10^3 \text{ g } C_8H_{18}$

$2619.5 \text{ g } C_8H_{18} \times \dfrac{1 \text{ mol } C_8H_{18}}{114.2 \text{ g } C_8H_{18}} \times \dfrac{25 \text{ mol } O_2}{2 \text{ mol } C_8H_{18}} \times \dfrac{32.00 \text{ g } O_2}{1 \text{ mol } O_2} = 9{,}175.1 \text{ g}$

$= 9.18 \times 10^3 \text{ g } O_2$

3.62 (a) *Plan.* Calculate a "mole ratio" between nitroglycerine and total moles of gas produced. (12 + 6 + 1 + 10) = 29 mol gas; 4 mol nitro: 29 total mol gas. *Solve*:

$3.00 \text{ mL nitro} \times \dfrac{1.592 \text{ g}}{\text{mL}} \times \dfrac{1 \text{ mol nitro}}{227.1 \text{ g nitro}} \times \dfrac{29 \text{ mol gas}}{4 \text{ mol nitro}} = 0.15247 = 0.152 \text{ mol gas}$

(b) $0.15247 \text{ mol gas} \times \dfrac{55 \text{ L}}{\text{mol}} = 8.3859 = 8.4 \text{ L}$

(c) $3.00 \text{ mL nitro} \times \frac{1.592 \text{ g}}{\text{mL}} \times \frac{1 \text{ mol nitro}}{227.1 \text{ g nitro}} \times \frac{6 \text{ mol } N_2}{4 \text{ mol nitro}} \times \frac{28.01 \text{ g } N_2}{1 \text{ mol } N_2} = 0.884 \text{ g } N_2$

Limiting Reactants, Theoretical Yields

3.64 (a) *Theoretical yield* is the maximum amount of product possible, as predicted by stoichiometry, assuming that the limiting reactant is converted entirely to product.

Actual yield is the amount of product actually obtained, less than or equal to the theoretical yield. *Percent yield* is the ratio of (actual yield to theoretical yield) × 100.

(b) No reaction is perfect. Not all reactant molecules come together effectively to form products; alternative reaction pathways may produce secondary products and reduce the amount of desired product actually obtained, or it might not be possible to completely isolate the desired product from the reaction mixture. In any case, these factors reduce the actual yield of a reaction.

3.66 $2NO + O_2 \rightarrow 2NO_2$. O_2 = , NO_2 = 

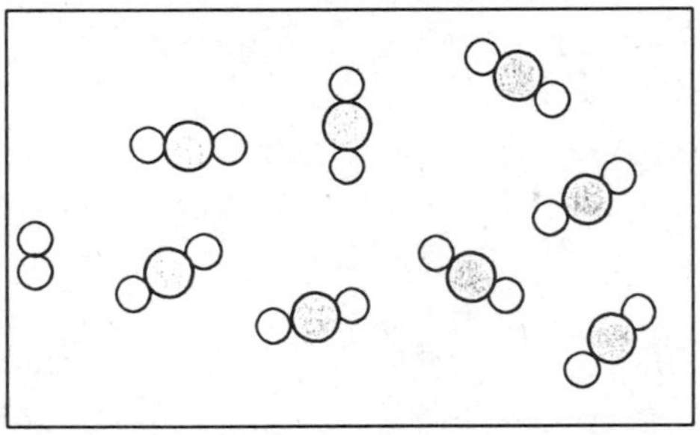

Each NO molecule reacts with 1 O atom (1/2 of an O_2 molecule) to produce 1 NO_2 molecule. Eight NO molecules react with 8 O atoms (4 O_2 molecules) to produce 8 NO_2 molecules. One O_2 molecule doesn't react (is in excess). NO is the limiting reactant.

3.68 (a) $39{,}375 \text{ L beverage} \times \frac{1 \text{ bottle}}{0.355 \text{ L}} = 110{,}915.49 = 1.11 \times 10^5$ portions of beverage

(The uncertainty in 355 mL limits the precision of the number of portions we can reasonably expect to deliver to 3 significant figures.)

115,350 bottles; 122,500 caps; 111,000 bottles can be filled and capped.

(b) 122,500 caps - 111,000 portions = 11,500 caps remain
115,350 empty bottles - 111,000 portions = 4350 bottles remain

(c) The volume of beverage limits production.

3.70 $0.450 \text{ mol Al(OH)}_3 \times \frac{3 \text{ mol } H_2SO_4}{2 \text{ mol Al(OH)}_3} = 0.675 \text{ mol } H_2SO_4$ needed for complete reaction

Only 0.550 mol H_2SO_4 available, so H_2SO_4 limits.

$0.550 \text{ mol } H_2SO_4 \times \frac{1 \text{ mol } Al_2(SO_4)_3}{3 \text{ mol } H_2SO_4} = 0.1833 = 0.183 \text{ mol } Al_2(SO_4)_3$ can form

$0.550 \text{ mol } H_2SO_4 \times \frac{2 \text{ mol Al(OH)}_3}{3 \text{ mol } H_2SO_4} = 0.3666 = 0.367 \text{ mol Al(OH)}_3$ react

0.450 mol $Al(OH)_3$ initial - 0.367 mol react = 0.083 mol $Al(OH)_3$ remain

(This result has 3 **decimal places** because it was obtained by subtraction, and thus only 2 sig. figs.)

3.72 $4NH_3(g) + 5O_2(g) \rightarrow 4NO(g) + 6H_2O(g)$

(a) Follow the approach in Sample Exercise 3.19.

$2.25 \text{ g } NH_3 \times \frac{1 \text{ mol } NH_3}{17.03 \text{ g } NH_3} = 0.1321 = 0.132 \text{ mol } NH_3$

$3.75 \text{ g } O_2 \times \frac{1 \text{ mol } O_2}{32.00 \text{ g } O_2} = 0.1172 = 0.117 \text{ mol } O_2$

$0.1172 \text{ mol } O_2 \times \frac{4 \text{ mol } NH_3}{5 \text{ mol } O_2} = 0.09375 = 0.0938 \text{ mol } NH_3$ required

More than 0.0938 mol NH_3 is available, so O_2 is the limiting reactant.

(b) $0.1172 \text{ mol } O_2 \times \frac{4 \text{ mol NO}}{5 \text{ mol } O_2} \times \frac{30.01 \text{ g NO}}{1 \text{ mol NO}} = 2.81 \text{ g NO}$ produced

(c) 0.1321mol NH_3 - 0.0938 mol NH_3 reacted = 0.0383 = 0.038 mol NH_3 remain

$0.0383 \text{ mol } NH_3 \times \frac{17.03 \text{ g } NH_3}{1 \text{ mol } NH_3} = 0.652 \text{ g } NH_3$ remain

3.74 *Plan.* Write balanced equation; determine limiting reactant; calculate amounts of excess reactant remaining and products, based on limiting reactant.

Solve. $H_2SO_4(aq) + Pb(C_2H_3O_2)_2(aq) \rightarrow PbSO_4(s) + 2HC_2H_3O_2(aq)$

$7.50 \text{ g } H_2SO_4 \times \frac{1 \text{ mol } H_2SO_4}{98.09 \text{ g } H_2SO_4} = 0.07646 = 0.0765 \text{ mol } H_2SO_4$

$7.50 \text{ g } Pb(C_2H_3O_2)_2 \times \frac{1 \text{ mol } Pb(C_2H_3O_2)_2}{325.3 \text{ g } Pb(C_2H_3O_2)_2} = 0.023056 = 0.0231 \text{ mol } Pb(C_2H_3O_2)_2$

1 mol H_2SO_4:1 mol $Pb(C_2H_3O_2)_2$, so $Pb(C_2H_3O_2)_2$ is the limiting reactant.

0 mol $Pb(C_2H_3O_2)_2$, (0.07646 - 0.023056) = 0.0530 mol H_2SO_4, 0.0231 mol $PbSO_4$,

(0.023056 × 2) = 0.0461 mol $HC_2H_3O_2$ are present after reaction

$0.053405 \text{ mol } H_2SO_4 \times 98.09 \text{ g/mol} = 5.2385 = 5.24 \text{ g } H_2SO_4$

$0.023056 \text{ mol } PbSO_4 \times 303.3 \text{ g/mol} = 6.9928 = 6.99 \text{ g } PbSO_4$

$0.046111 \text{ mol } HC_2H_3O_2 \times 60.05 \text{ g/mol} = 2.7690 = 2.77 \text{ g } HC_2H_3O_2$

Check. The initial mass of reactants was 15.00 g; and the final mass of excess reactant and products is 15.00 g; mass is conserved.

3.76 (a) $C_2H_6 + Cl_2 \rightarrow C_2H_5Cl + HCl$

$$125 \text{ g } C_2H_6 \times \frac{1 \text{ mol } C_2H_6}{30.07 \text{ g } C_2H_6} = 4.157 = 4.16 \text{ mol } C_2H_6$$

$$255 \text{ g } Cl_2 \times \frac{1 \text{ mol } Cl_2}{70.91 \text{ g } Cl_2} = 3.596 = 3.60 \text{ mol } Cl_2$$

Since the reactants combine in a 1:1 mole ratio, Cl_2 is the limiting reactant. The theoretical yield is:

$$3.596 \text{ mol } Cl_2 \times \frac{1 \text{ mol } C_2H_5Cl}{1 \text{ mol } Cl_2} \times \frac{64.51 \text{ g } C_2H_5Cl}{1 \text{ mol } C_2H_5Cl} = 231.98 = 232 \text{ g } C_2H_5Cl$$

(b) $$\% \text{ yield} = \frac{206 \text{ g } C_2H_5Cl \text{ actual}}{232 \text{ g } C_2H_5Cl \text{ theoretical}} \times 100 = 88.8\%$$

3.78 $H_2S(g) + 2NaOH(aq) \rightarrow Na_2S(aq) + 2H_2O(l)$

$$2.00 \text{ g } H_2S \times \frac{1 \text{ mol } H_2S}{34.08 \text{ g } H_2S} = 0.05868 = 0.0587 \text{ mol } H_2S$$

$$2.00 \text{ g NaOH} \times \frac{1 \text{ mol NaOH}}{40.00 \text{ g NaOH}} = 0.0500 \text{ mol NaOH}$$

By inspection, twice as many mol NaOH as H_2S are needed for exact reaction, but mol NaOH given is less than mol H_2S, so NaOH limits.

$$0.0500 \text{ mol NaOH} \times \frac{1 \text{ mol } Na_2S}{2 \text{ mol NaOH}} \times \frac{78.05 \text{ g } Na_2S}{1 \text{ mol } Na_2S} = 1.95125 = 1.95 \text{ g } Na_2S \text{ theoretical}$$

$$\frac{92.0\ \%}{100} \times 1.95125 \text{ g } Na_2S \text{ theoretical} = 1.7951 = 1.80 \text{ g } Na_2S \text{ actual}$$

Additional Exercises

3.80 The formulas of the fertilizers are NH_3, NH_4NO_3, $(NH_4)_2SO_4$ and $(NH_2)_2CO$. Qualitatively, the more heavy, non-nitrogen atoms in a molecule, the smaller the mass % of N. By inspection, the mass of NH_3 is dominated by N, so it will have the greatest % N, $(NH_4)_2SO_4$ will have the least. In order of increasing % N: $(NH_4)_2SO_4 < NH_4NO_3 < (NH_2)_2CO < NH_3$.

Check by calculation:

$(NH_4)_2SO_4$: FW = 2(14.0) + 8(1.0) + 1(32.1) + 4(16.0) = 132.1 amu

% N = [2(14.0)/132.1] × 100 = 21.2%

NH_4NO_3: FW = 2(14.0) + 4(1.0) + 3(16.0) = 80.0 amu

% N = [2(14.0)/80.0] × 100 = 35.0 %

$(NH_2)_2CO$: FW = 2(14.0) + 4(1.0) = 1(12.0) + 1(16.0) = 60.0 amu

% N = [2(14.0)/60.0] × 100 = 46.7% N

NH_3: FW = 1(14.0) + 3(1.0) = 17.0

% N = [14.0/17.0] × 100 = 82.4 % N

3.82 (a)

$$\frac{5.342 \times 10^{-21}\text{ g}}{1\text{ molecule penicillin G}} \times \frac{6.0221 \times 10^{23}\text{ molecules}}{1\text{ mol}} = 3217\text{ g/mol penicillin G}$$

(b) 1.00 g hemoglobin (hem) contains 3.40×10^{-3} g Fe.

$$\frac{1.00\text{ g hem}}{3.40 \times 10^{-3}\text{ g Fe}} \times \frac{55.85\text{ g Fe}}{1\text{ mol Fe}} \times \frac{4\text{ mol Fe}}{1\text{ mol hem}} = 6.57 \times 10^{4}\text{ g/mol hemoglobin}$$

3.84 *Plan.* Assume 100 g, calculate mole ratios, empirical formula, then molecular formula from molar mass. *Solve:*

$$68.2\text{ g C} \times \frac{1\text{ mol C}}{12.01\text{ g C}} = 5.68\text{ mol C; } 5.68/0.568 \approx 10$$

$$6.86\text{ g H} \times \frac{1\text{ mol H}}{1.008\text{ g H}} = 6.81\text{ mol H; } 6.81/0.568 \approx 12$$

$$15.9\text{ g N} \times \frac{1\text{ mol N}}{14.01\text{ g N}} = 1.13\text{ mol N; } 1.13/0.568 \approx 2$$

$$9.08\text{ g O} \times \frac{1\text{ mol O}}{16.00\text{ g O}} = 0.568\text{ mol O; } 0.568/0.0568 = 1$$

The empirical formula is $C_{10}H_{12}N_2O$, FW = 176 amu (or g). Since the molar mass is 176, the empirical and molecular formula are the same, $C_{10}H_{12}N_2O$.

3.86 Since all the C in the vanillin must be present in the CO_2 produced, get g C from g CO_2.

$$2.43\text{ g }CO_2 \times \frac{1\text{ mol }CO_2}{44.01\text{ g }CO_2} \times \frac{12.01\text{ g C}}{1\text{ mol C}} = 0.6631 = 0.663\text{ g C}$$

Since all the H in vanillin must be present in the H_2O produced, get g H from g H_2O.

$$0.50\text{ g }H_2O \times \frac{1\text{ mol }H_2O}{18.02\text{ g }H_2O} \times \frac{2\text{ mol H}}{1\text{ mol }H_2O} \times \frac{1.008\text{ g H}}{1\text{ mol H}} = 0.0559 = 0.056\text{ g H}$$

Get g O by subtraction. (Since the analysis was performed by combustion, an unspecified amount of O_2 was a reactant, and thus not all the O in the CO_2 and H_2O produced came from vanillin.) 1.05 g vanillin - 0.663 g C - 0.056 g H = 0.331 g O

$0.6631 \text{ g C} \times \frac{1 \text{ mol C}}{12.01 \text{ g C}} = 0.0552 \text{ mol C}$; $0.0552 / 0.0207 = 2.67$

$0.0559 \text{ g H} \times \frac{1 \text{ mol H}}{1.008 \text{ g H}} = 0.0555 \text{ mol C}$; $0.0555 / 0.0207 = 2.68$

$0.331 \text{ g O} \times \frac{1 \text{ mol O}}{16.00 \text{ g O}} = 0.0207 \text{ mol O}$; $0.0207 / 0.0207 = 1.00$

Multiplying the numbers above by **3** to obtain an integer ratio of moles, the empirical formula of vanillin is $C_8H_8O_3$.

3.88 The mass percentage is determined by the relative number of atoms of the element times the atomic weight, divided by the total formula mass. Thus, the mass percent of bromine in $KBrO_x$ is given by $0.5292 = \frac{79.91}{39.10 + 79.91 + x(16.00)}$. Solving for x, we obtain x = 2.00. Thus, the formula is $KBrO_2$.

3.89 (a) Let AW = the atomic weight of X.

According to the chemical reaction, moles XI_3 reacted = moles XCl_3 produced

$0.5000 \text{ g } XI_3 \times 1 \text{ mol } XI_3 / (AW + 380.71) \text{ g } XI_3$

$= 0.2360 \text{ g } XCl_3 \times \frac{1 \text{ mol } XCl_3}{(AW + 106.36) \text{ g } XCl_3}$

$0.5000 (AW + 106.36) = 0.2360 (AW + 380.71)$

$0.5000 AW + 53.180 = 0.2360 AW + 89.848$

$0.2640 AW = 36.67$; $AW = 138.9$ g

(b) X is lanthanum, La, atomic number 57.

3.91 $2NaCl(aq) + 2H_2O(l) \rightarrow 2NaOH(aq) + H_2(g) + Cl_2(g)$

Calculate mol Cl_2 and relate to mol H_2, mol NaOH.

$1.5 \times 10^6 \text{ kg} \times \frac{1000 \text{ g}}{1 \text{ kg}} \times \frac{1 \text{ mol } Cl_2}{70.91 \text{ g } Cl_2} = 2.115 \times 10^7 = 2.1 \times 10^7 \text{ mol } Cl_2$

$2.115 \times 10^7 \text{ mol } Cl_2 \times \frac{1 \text{ mol } H_2}{1 \text{ mol } Cl_2} \times \frac{2.016 \text{ g } H_2}{1 \text{ mol } H_2} = 4.26 \times 10^7 \text{ g } H_2 = 4.3 \times 10^4 \text{ kg } H_2$

$4.3 \times 10^7 \text{ g} \times \frac{1 \text{ metric ton}}{1 \times 10^6 \text{ g (1 Mg)}} = 43 \text{ metric tons } H_2$

$2.115 \times 10^7 \text{ mol } Cl_2 \times \frac{2 \text{ mol NaOH}}{1 \text{ mol } Cl_2} \times \frac{40.0 \text{ g NaOH}}{1 \text{ mol NaOH}} = 1.69 \times 10^9 = 1.7 \times 10^9 \text{ g NaOH}$

$1.7 \times 10^9 \text{ g NaOH} = 1.7 \times 10^6 \text{ kg NaOH} = 1.7 \times 10^3 \text{ metric tons NaOH}$

3.93 (a) *Plan*. Calculate the total mass of C from g CO and g CO_2. Calculate the mass of H from g H_2O. Calculate mole ratios and the empirical formula. *Solve*:

$$0.467 \text{ g CO} \times \frac{1 \text{ mol CO}}{28.01 \text{ g CO}} \times \frac{1 \text{ mol C}}{1 \text{ mol CO}} \times 12.01 \text{ g C} = 0.200 \text{ g C}$$

$$0.733 \text{ g } CO_2 \times \frac{1 \text{ mol } CO_2}{44.01 \text{ g } CO_2} \times \frac{1 \text{ mol C}}{1 \text{ mol } CO_2} \times 12.01 \text{ g C} = 0.200 \text{ g C}$$

Total mass C is 0.200 g + 0.200 g = 0.400 g C.

$$0.450 \text{ g } H_2O \times \frac{1 \text{ mol } H_2O}{18.02 \text{ g } H_2O} \times \frac{2 \text{ mol H}}{1 \text{ mol } H_2O} \times \frac{1.008 \text{ g H}}{1 \text{ mol H}} = 0.0503 \text{ g H}$$

(Since hydrocarbons contain only the elements C and H, g H can also be obtained by subtraction: 0.450 g sample - 0.400 g C = 0.050 g H.)

$$0.400 \text{ g C} \times \frac{1 \text{ mol C}}{12.01 \text{ g C}} = 0.0333 \text{ mol C}; \quad 0.0333 / 0.0333 = 1.0$$

$$0.0503 \text{ g H} \times \frac{1 \text{ mol H}}{1.008 \text{ g H}} = 0.0499 \text{ mol H}; \quad 0.0499 / 0.0333 = 1.5$$

Multiplying by a factor of 2, the emprical formula is C_2H_3.

(b) Mass is conserved. Total mass products - mass sample = mass O_2 consumed. 0.467 g CO + 0.733 g CO_2 + 0.450 g H_2O - 0.450 g sample = 1.200 g O_2 consumed

(c) For complete combustion, 0.467 g CO must be converted to CO_2.

$2CO(g) + O_2(g) \rightarrow 2CO_2(g)$

$$0.467 \text{ g CO} \times \frac{1 \text{ mol CO}}{28.01 \text{ g C}} \times \frac{1 \text{ mol } O_2}{2 \text{ mol CO}} \times \frac{32.00 \text{ g } O_2}{1 \text{ mol } O_2} = 0.267 \text{ g } O_2$$

The total mass of O_2 required for complete combustion is 1.200 g + 0.267 g = 1.467 g O_2.

3.94 $N_2(g) + 3H_2(g) \rightarrow 2NH_3(g)$

Determine the moles of N_2 and H_2 required to form the 2.0 moles of NH_3 present after the reaction has stopped.

$$2.0 \text{ mol } NH_3 \times \frac{3 \text{ mol } H_2}{2 \text{ mol } NH_3} = 3.0 \text{ mol } H_2 \text{ reacted}$$

$$2.0 \text{ mol } NH_3 \times \frac{1 \text{ mol } N_2}{2 \text{ mol } NH_3} = 1 \text{ mol } N_2 \text{ reacted}$$

mol H_2 initial = 2.0 mol H_2 remain + 3.0 mol H_2 reacted = 5.0 mol H_2

mol N_2 initial = 2.0 mol N_2 remain + 1.0 mol N_2 reacted = 3.0 mol N_2

In tabular form:	$N_2(g)$	+	$3H_2(g)$	→	$2NH_3(g)$
initial	3.0 mol		5.0 mol		0 mol
reaction	-1.0 mol		-3.0 mol		+2.0 mol
final	2.0 mol		2.0 mol		2.0 mol

(Tables like this will be extremely useful for solving chemical equilibrium problems in Chapter 15.)

3.96 (a) $2C_2H_2(g) + 5O_2(g) \rightarrow 4CO_2(g) + 2H_2O(g)$

(b) Following the approach in Sample Exercise 3.19,

$$10.0\text{ g } C_2H_2 \times \frac{1\text{ mol } C_2H_2}{26.04\text{ g } C_2H_2} \times \frac{5\text{ mol } O_2}{2\text{ mol } C_2H_2} \times \frac{32.00\text{ g } O_2}{1\text{ mol } O_2} = 30.7\text{ g } O_2 \text{ required}$$

Only 10.0 g O_2 are available, so O_2 limits.

(c) Since O_2 limits, 0.0 g O_2 remain.

Next, calculate the g C_2H_2 consumed and the amounts of CO_2 and H_2O produced by reaction of 10.0 g O_2.

$$10.0\text{ g } O_2 \times \frac{1\text{ mol } O_2}{32.00\text{ g } O_2} \times \frac{2\text{ mol } C_2H_2}{5\text{ mol } O_2} \times \frac{26.04\text{ g } C_2H_2}{1\text{ mol } C_2H_2} = 3.26\text{ g } C_2H_2 \text{ consumed}$$

10.0 g C_2H_2 initial - 3.26 g consumed = 6.74 = 6.7 g C_2H_2 remain

$$10.0\text{ g } O_2 \times \frac{1\text{ mol } O_2}{32.00\text{ g } O_2} \times \frac{4\text{ mol } CO_2}{5\text{ mol } O_2} \times \frac{44.01\text{ g } CO_2}{1\text{ mol } CO_2} = 11.0\text{ g } CO_2 \text{ produced}$$

$$10.0\text{ g } O_2 \times \frac{1\text{ mol } O_2}{32.00\text{ g } O_2} \times \frac{2\text{ mol } H_2O}{5\text{ mol } O_2} \times \frac{18.02\text{ g } H_2O}{1\text{ mol } H_2O} = 2.25\text{ g } H_2O \text{ produced}$$

3.97 (a) $$1.5 \times 10^2\text{ g } C_9H_8O_4 \times \frac{1\text{ mol } C_9H_8O_4}{180.2\text{ g } C_9H_8O_4} \times \frac{1\text{ mol } C_7H_6O_3}{1\text{ mol } C_9H_8O_4} \times \frac{138.1\text{ g } C_7H_6O_3}{1\text{ mol } C_7H_6O_3}$$

$$= 1.1496 \times 10^2 = 1.1 \times 10^2\text{ kg } C_7H_6O_3$$

(b) If only 80 percent of the acid reacts, then we need 1/0.80 = 1.25 times as much to obtain the same mass of product: $1.25 \times 1.15 \times 10^2$ kg = 1.4×10^2 kg.

(c) Calculate the number of moles of each reactant:

$$1.85 \times 10^5\text{ g } C_7H_6O_3 \times \frac{1\text{ mol } C_7H_6O_3}{138.1\text{ g } C_7H_6O_3} = 1.340 \times 10^3 = 1.34 \times 10^3\text{ mol } C_7H_6O_3$$

$$1.25 \times 10^5\text{ g } C_4H_6O_3 \times \frac{1\text{ mol } C_4H_6O_3}{102.1\text{ g } C_4H_6O_3} = 1.224 \times 10^3 = 1.22 \times 10^3\text{ mol } C_4H_6O_3$$

We see that $C_4H_6O_3$ limits, because equal numbers of moles of the two reactants are consumed in the reaction.

$$1.224 \times 10^3\text{ mol } C_4H_6O_3 \times \frac{1\text{ mol } C_9H_8O_4}{1\text{ mol } C_7H_6O_3} \times \frac{180.2\text{ g } C_9H_8O_4}{1\text{ mol } C_9H_8O_4} = 2.206 \times 10^5$$

$$= 2.21 \times 10^5\text{ g } C_9H_8O_4$$

(d) percent yield = $\frac{1.82 \times 10^5 \text{ g}}{2.206 \times 10^5 \text{ g}} \times 100 = 82.5\%$

Integrative Exercises

3.99 (a) *Plan*: volume of Ag cube $\xrightarrow{\text{density}}$ mass of Ag → mol Ag → Ag atoms

Solve: $(1.000)^3 \text{ cm}^3 \text{ Ag} \times \frac{10.49 \text{ g Ag}}{1 \text{ cm}^3 \text{ Ag}} \times \frac{1 \text{ mol Ag}}{107.87 \text{ g Ag}} \times \frac{6.022 \times 10^{23} \text{ atoms}}{1 \text{ mol}}$

$= 5.8562 \times 10^{22} = 5.856 \times 10^{22}$ Ag atoms

(b) 1.000 cm^3 cube volume, 74% is occupied by Ag atoms

0.7400 cm^3 = volume of 5.856×10^{22} Ag atoms

$\frac{0.7400 \text{ cm}^3}{5.8562 \times 10^{22} \text{ Ag atoms}} = 1.2636 \times 10^{-23} = 1.264 \times 10^{-23} \text{ cm}^3 / \text{Ag atom}$

Since atomic dimensions are usually given in Å, we will show this conversion.

$1.264 \times 10^{-23} \text{ cm}^3 \times \frac{(1 \times 10^{-2})^3 \text{ m}^3}{1 \text{ cm}^3} \times \frac{1 \text{ Å}^3}{(1 \times 10^{-10})^3 \text{ m}^3} = 12.64 \text{ Å}^3 / \text{Ag atom}$

(c) $V = 4/3 \pi r^3$; $r^3 = 3V/4\pi$; $r = (3V/4\pi)^{1/3}$

$r_{Å} = (3 \times 12.636 \text{ Å}^3 / 4\pi)^{1/3} = 1.4449 = 1.445 \text{ Å}$

3.101 *Plan*. We can proceed by writing the ratio of masses of Ag to $AgNO_3$, where y is the atomic mass of nitrogen. *Solve*:

$$\frac{\text{Ag}}{\text{AgNO}_3} = 0.634985 = \frac{107.8682}{107.8682 + 3(15.9994) + y}$$

Solve for y to obtain y = 14.0088. This is to be compared with the currently accepted value of 14.0067.

3.103 (a) *Plan*. Calculate the kg of air in the room and then the mass of HCN required to produce a dose of 300 mg HCN/kg air. *Solve*:

12 ft × 15 ft × 8.0 ft = 1440 = 1.4×10^3 ft^3 of air in the room

$1440 \text{ ft}^3 \text{ air} \times \frac{(12 \text{ in})^3}{1 \text{ ft}^3} \times \frac{(2.54 \text{ cm})^3}{1 \text{ in}^3} \times \frac{0.00118 \text{ g air}}{1 \text{ cm}^3 \text{ air}} \times \frac{1 \text{ kg}}{1000 \text{ g}} = 48.12$

= 48 kg air

$48.12 \text{ kg air} \times \frac{300 \text{ mg HCN}}{1 \text{ kg air}} \times \frac{1 \text{ g}}{1000 \text{ mg}} = 14.43 = 14 \text{ g HCN}$

(b) $2NaCN(s) + H_2SO_4(aq) \rightarrow Na_2SO_4(aq) + 2HCN(g)$

The question can be restated as: What mass of NaCN is required to produce 14 g of HCN according to the above reaction?

$$14.43 \text{ g HCN} \times \frac{1 \text{ mol HCN}}{27.03 \text{ g HCN}} \times \frac{2 \text{ mol NaCN}}{2 \text{ mol HCN}} \times \frac{49.01 \text{ g NaCN}}{1 \text{ mol NaCN}} = 26.2 = 26 \text{ g NaCN}$$

(c) $$12 \text{ ft} \times 15 \text{ ft} \times \frac{1 \text{ yd}^2}{9 \text{ ft}^2} \times \frac{30 \text{ oz}}{1 \text{ yd}^2} \times \frac{1 \text{ lb}}{16 \text{ oz}} \times \frac{454 \text{ g}}{1 \text{ lb}} = 17{,}025$$

$$= 1.7 \times 10^4 \text{ g acrilan in the room}$$

50% of the carpet burns, so the starting amount of CH_2CHCN is
$0.50(17{,}025) = 8{,}513 = 8.5 \times 10^3$ g

$$8{,}513 \text{ g } CH_2CHCN \times \frac{50.9 \text{ g HCN}}{100 \text{ g } CH_2CHCH} = 4333 = 4.3 \times 10^3 \text{ g HCN possible}$$

If the actual yield of combustion is 20%, actual g HCN = 4,333(0.20) = 866.6 = 8.7×10^2 g HCN produced. From part (a), 14 g of HCN is a lethal dose. The fire produces much more than a lethal dose of HCN.

4 Aqueous Reactions and Solution Stoichiometry

Electrolytes

4.2 No. Electrolyte solutions conduct electricity because the dissolved ions carry charge through the solution (from one electrode to the other).

4.4 Although H_2O molecules are electrically neutral, there is an unequal distribution of electrons throughout the molecule. There are more electrons near O and fewer near H, giving the O end of the molecule a partial negative charge and the H end of the molecule a partial positive charge. Ionic compounds are composed of positively and negatively charged ions. The partially positive ends of H_2O molecules are attracted to the negative ions (anions) in the solid, while the partially negative ends are attracted to the positive ions (cations). Thus, both cations and anions in an ionic solid are surrounded and separated (dissolved) by H_2O molecules.

4.6 (a) $MgI_2(aq) \rightarrow Mg^{2+}(aq) + 2I^-(aq)$ (b) $Al(NO_3)_3(aq) \rightarrow Al^{3+}(aq) + 3NO_3^-(aq)$
(c) $HClO_4(aq) \rightarrow H^+(aq) + ClO_4^-(aq)$ (d) $(NH_4)_2SO_4(aq) \rightarrow 2NH_4^+(aq) + SO_4^{2-}(aq)$

4.8 Both AX and BY are weak electrolytes, because some but not all molecules ionize when they dissolve. BY will be the better conductor of electricity because it produces more ions per mole of dissolved solute.

4.10 (a) acetone (nonelectrolyte): $CH_3COCH_3(aq)$ molecules only; hypochlorous acid (weak electrolyte): $HClO(aq)$ molecules, $H^+(aq)$, $ClO^-(aq)$; ammonium chloride (strong electrolyte): $NH_4^+(aq)$, $Cl^-(aq)$

(b) NH_4Cl, 0.2 mol solute particles; HClO, between 0.1 and 0.2 mol particles; CH_3OCH_3, 0.1 mol of solute particles

Precipitation Reactions and Net Ionic Equations

4.12 According to Table 4.1:

(a) $Ni(\mathbf{OH})_2$: insoluble
(b) $Pb\mathbf{SO_4}$: insoluble, Pb^{2+} is an exception to soluble sulfates
(c) $Ba(\mathbf{NO_3})_2$: soluble
(d) $Al\mathbf{PO_4}$: insoluble
(e) $Ag\mathbf{C_2H_3O_2}$: soluble

4 Aqueous Reactions — Solutions to Black Exercises

4.14 In each reaction, the precipitate is in bold type.

(a) $Sn(NO_3)_2(aq) + 2NaOH(aq) \rightarrow$ **$Sn(OH)_2(s)$** $+ 2NaNO_3(aq)$

(b) No precipitate, and therefore, no reaction. There is no chemical change to any of the reactant ions.

(c) $Na_2S(aq) + Cu(C_2H_3O_2)_2(aq) \rightarrow$ **$CuS(s)$** $+ 2NaC_2H_3O_2(aq)$

4.16 Spectator ions are those that do not change during reaction.

(a) $2Cr^{3+}(aq) + 3CO_3^{2-}(aq) \rightarrow Cr_2(CO_3)_3(s)$; spectators: NH_4^+, SO_4^{2-}

(b) $2Ag^+(aq) + SO_4^{2-}(aq) \rightarrow Ag_2SO_4(s)$; spectators: K^+, NO_3^-

(c) $Pb^{2+}(aq) + 2OH^-(aq) \rightarrow Pb(OH)_2(s)$; spectators: K^+, NO_3^-

4.18 Br^- and NO_3^- can be ruled out because the Ba^{2+} salts are soluble. (Actually all NO_3^- salts are soluble.) CO_3^{2-} forms insoluble salts with the three cations given; it must be the anion in question.

4.20

Compound	$Ba(NO_3)_2$ result	NaCl result
$AgNO_3(aq)$	no ppt	AgCl ppt
$CaCl_2(aq)$	no ppt	no ppt
$Al_2(SO_4)_3$	$BaSO_4$ ppt	no ppt

This sequence of tests would definitively identify the contents of the bottle.

Acid-Base Reactions

4.22 (a) NH_3 produces OH^- in aqueous solution by reacting with H_2O (hydrolysis): $NH_3(aq) + H_2O(l) \rightleftharpoons NH_4^+(aq) + OH^-(aq)$. The OH^- causes the solution to be basic.

(b) The term "weak" refers to the tendency of HF to dissociate into H^+ and F^- in aqueous solution, not its reactivity toward other compounds.

(c) H_2SO_4 is a **diprotic** acid; it has two ionizable hydrogens. The first hydrogen completely ionizes to form H^+ and HSO_4^-, but HSO_4^- only **partially** ionizes into H^+ and SO_4^{2-} (HSO_4^- is a weak electrolyte). Thus, an aqueous solution of H_2SO_4 contains a mixture of H^+, HSO_4^- and SO_4^{2-}, with the concentration of HSO_4^- greater than the concentration of SO_4^{2-}.

4.24 Use Table 4.2. (a) strong base (b) weak acid (c) weak acid (d) strong acid

4.26 Since the solution does conduct some electricity, but less than an equimolar NaCl solution (a strong electrolyte) the unknown solute must be a weak electrolyte. The weak electrolytes in the list of choices are NH_3 and H_3PO_3; since the solution is acidic, the unknown must be **H_3PO_3**.

4.28 (a) HBrO: weak (b) HNO_3: strong (c) KOH: strong
(d) CH_3OCH_3: non (e) $CoSO_4$: strong (f) $C_{12}H_{22}O_{11}$: non

4.30 (a) $HC_2H_3O_2(aq) + KOH(aq) \rightarrow KC_2H_3O_2(aq) + H_2O(l)$
$H^+(aq) + OH^-(aq) \rightarrow H_2O(l)$
(b) $Cr(OH)_3(s) + 3HNO_3(aq) \rightarrow Cr(NO_3)_3(aq) + 3H_2O(l)$
$Cr(OH)_3(s) + 3H^+(aq) \rightarrow 3H_2O(l) + Cr^{3+}(aq)$
(c) $Ca(OH)_2(aq) + 2HClO(aq) \rightarrow Ca(ClO)_2(aq) + 2H_2O(l)$
$OH^-(aq) + H^+(aq) \rightarrow H_2O(l)$ The 2 must be cancelled

4.32 (a) $CaCO_3(s) + 2HNO_3(aq) \rightarrow Ca(NO_3)_2(aq) + H_2O(l) + CO_2(g)$
$2H^+(aq) + CaCO_3(s) \rightarrow H_2O(l) + CO_2(g) + Ca^{2+}(aq)$
(b) $FeS(s) + 2HBr(aq) \rightarrow FeBr_2(aq) + H_2S(g)$
$2H^+(aq) + FeS(s) \rightarrow H_2S(g) + Fe^{2+}(aq)$

4.34 $K_2O(aq) + H_2O(l) \rightarrow 2KOH(aq)$, molecular; $O^{2-}(aq) + H_2O(l) \rightarrow 2OH^-(aq)$, net ionic
base: (H^+ ion acceptor) $O^{2-}(aq)$; acid: (H^+ ion donor) $H_2O(aq)$; spectator: K^+

Oxidation-Reduction Reactions

4.36 Oxidation and reduction can only occur together, not separately. When a metal reacts with oxygen, the metal atoms lose electrons and the oxygen atoms gain electrons. Free electrons do not exist under normal conditions. If electrons are lost by one substance they must be gained by another, and vice versa.

4.38 Platinum and gold are called the noble metals because they are especially unreactive and difficult to oxidize. The alkali and alkaline earth metals are called active because they are very easily oxidized and chemically reactive.

4.40 (a) +4 (b) +4 (c) +3 (d) -3 (e) +3 (f) +6

4.42 (a) acid-base reaction
(b) oxidation-reduction reaction; Fe is reduced, C is oxidized
(c) precipitation reaction
(d) oxidation-reduction reaction; Zn is oxidized, N is reduced

not +ve Ni

4.44 (a) $2HCl(aq) + Ni(s) \rightarrow NiCl_2(aq) + H_2(g)$; $Ni(s) + 2H^+(aq) \rightarrow Ni^{2+}(aq) + H_2(g)$

(b) $H_2SO_4(aq) + Fe(s) \rightarrow FeSO_4(aq) + H_2(g)$; $Fe(s) + 2H^+(aq) \rightarrow Fe^{2+}(aq) + H_2(g)$

(c) $2HBr(aq) + Mg(s) \rightarrow MgBr_2(aq) + H_2(g)$; $Mg(s) + 2H^+(aq) \rightarrow Mg^{2+}(aq) + H_2(g)$

(d) $2HC_2H_3O_2(aq) + Zn(s) \rightarrow Zn(C_2H_3O_2)_2(aq) + H_2(g)$;

$Zn(s) + 2HC_2H_3O_2(aq) \rightarrow Zn^{2+}(aq) + 2C_2H_3O_2^-(aq) + H_2(g)$

Acetic acid is weak ∴ it doesn't associate

4.46 (a) $Fe(s) + Cu(NO_3)_2(aq) \rightarrow Fe(NO_3)_2(aq) + Cu(s)$

(b) $Zn(s) + MgSO_4(aq) \rightarrow$ NR

(c) $Sn(s) + 2HBr(aq) \rightarrow SnBr_2(aq) + H_2(g)$

(d) $H_2(g) + NiCl_2(aq) \rightarrow$ NR

(e) $2Al(s) + 3CoSO_4(aq) \rightarrow Al_2(SO_4)_3(aq) + 3Co(s)$

4.48 (a) $Br_2 + 2NaI \rightarrow 2NaBr + I_2$ indicates that Br_2 is more easily reduced than I_2. $Cl_2 + 2NaBr \rightarrow 2NaCl + Br_2$ shows that Cl_2 is more easily reduced than Br_2. The order for ease of reduction is $Cl_2 > Br_2 > I_2$. Conversely, the order for ease of oxidation is $I^- > Br^- > Cl^-$.

(b) Since the halogens are nonmetals, they tend to form anions when they react chemically. Nonmetallic character decreases going down a family and so does the tendency to gain electrons during a chemical reaction. Thus, the ease of reduction of the halogen, X_2, decreases going down the family and the ease of oxidation of the halide, X^-, increases going down the family.

(c) $Cl_2 + 2KI \rightarrow 2KCl + I_2$; $Br_2 + LiCl \rightarrow$ no reaction

Solution Composition; Molarity

4.50 (a) The concentration of the remaining solution is unchanged, assuming the original solution was thoroughly mixed. Molar concentration is a **ratio** of moles solute to liters solution. Although there are fewer moles solute remaining in the flask, there is also less solution volume, so the ratio of moles solute/solution volume remains the same.

(b) The second solution is 5 times as concentrated as the first. An equal volume of the more concentrated solution will contain 5 times as much solute (5 times the number of moles and also 5 times the mass) as the 0.50 *M* solution. Thus, the mass of solute in the 2.50 *M* solution is 5 × 4.5 g = 22.5 g.

Mathematically:

$$\frac{\dfrac{2.50 \text{ mol solute}}{1 \text{ L solution}}}{\dfrac{0.50 \text{ mol solute}}{1 \text{ L solution}}} = \frac{x \text{ grams solute}}{4.5 \text{ g solute}}$$

$$\frac{2.50 \text{ mol solute}}{0.50 \text{ mol solute}} = \frac{x \text{ g solute}}{4.5 \text{ g solute}}; \quad 5.0(4.5 \text{ g solute}) = 23 \text{ g solute}$$

The result has 2 sig figs; 22.5 rounds to 23 g solute

4.52 (a) $M = \frac{\text{mol solute}}{\text{L solution}}; \quad \frac{0.145 \text{ mol } Na_2SO_4}{0.750 \text{ L}} = 0.193 \ M \ Na_2SO_4$

(b) $\text{mol} = M \times \text{L}; \quad \frac{0.0850 \text{ mol } KMnO_4}{1 \text{ L}} \times 0.125 \text{ L} = 1.06 \times 10^{-2} \text{ mol } KMnO_4$

(c) $\text{L} = \frac{\text{mol}}{M}; \quad \frac{0.255 \text{ mol HCl}}{11.6 \text{ mol HCl/L}} = 2.20 \times 10^{-2} \text{ L or } 22.0 \text{ mL}$

4.54 $M = \frac{\text{mol}}{\text{L}}$; $\text{mol} = \frac{\text{g}}{\mathcal{M}}$ ($\mathcal{M}$ is the symbol for molar mass in this manual.)

(a) $\frac{0.850 \text{ mol } K_2Cr_2O_7}{1 \text{ L}} \times 50.0 \text{ mL} \times \frac{1 \text{ L}}{1000 \text{ mL}} \times \frac{294.2 \text{ g } K_2Cr_2O_7}{1 \text{ mol } K_2Cr_2O_7} = 12.5 \text{ g } K_2Cr_2O_7$

(b) $2.50 \text{ g } (NH_4)_2SO_4 \times \frac{1 \text{ mol } (NH_4)_2SO_4}{132.2 \text{ g } (NH_4)_2SO_4} \times \frac{1}{250. \text{ mL}} \times \frac{1000 \text{ mL}}{1 \text{ L}} = 0.0756 \ M \ (NH_4)_2SO_4$

(c) $1.00 \text{ g } CuSO_4 \times \frac{1 \text{ mol } CuSO_4}{159.6 \text{ g } CuSO_4} \times \frac{1 \text{ L}}{0.387 \text{ mol } CuSO_4} \times \frac{1000 \text{ mL}}{1 \text{ L}} = 16.2 \text{ mL solution}$

4.56 (a) 0.10 mol NaCl/250 mL = 0.40 mol NaCl/1000 mL = 0.40 M NaCl

0.15 M KCl < 0.10 M $CaCl_2$ < 0.10 mol NaCl in 250 mL

(b) $NaCl \rightarrow Na^+ + Cl^-$; 0.35 M × 0.040 L = 0.014 mol Cl^-

$CaCl_2 \rightarrow Ca^{2+} + 2Cl^-$; 0.25 M × 0.025 L = 0.00625 mol $CaCl_2$ × 2 = 0.0125 = 0.013 mol Cl^-

The NaCl solution has slightly more moles Cl^-.

4.58 (a) H^+: $\frac{0.100 \ M \times 20.0 \text{ mL} + 0.500 \ M \times 10.0 \text{ mL}}{30.0 \text{ mL}} = 0.233 \ M \ H^+$

Cl^-: concentration Cl^- = concentration H^+ = 0.233 M Cl^-

(b) Na^+: $\frac{2(0.300 \ M \times 15.0 \text{ mL})}{25.0 \text{ mL}} = 0.360 \ M$; K^+: $= \frac{0.200 \ M \times 10.0 \text{ mL}}{25.0 \text{ mL}} = 0.0800 \ M$

SO_4^{2-}: $\frac{0.300 \ M \times 15.0 \text{ mL}}{25.0 \text{ mL}} = 0.180 \ M$; Cl^-: $\frac{0.200 \ M \times 10.0 \text{ mL}}{25.0 \text{ mL}} = 0.0800 \ M$

(c) Na^+: $\frac{3.50 \text{ g NaCl}}{0.050 \text{ L}} \times \frac{1 \text{ mol}}{58.44 \text{ g}} = 1.198\ M$; Ca^{2+}: 0.500 M

Cl^- : 1.198M (from NaCl(s)) + 1.000 M (from $CaCl_2$(aq)) = 2.198 M

4.60 (a) $V_1 = M_2V_2/M_1$; $\frac{0.500\ M\ HNO_3 \times 500 \text{ mL}}{12.0\ M\ HNO_3} = 20.833 = 20.8$ mL conc. HNO_3

(b) $M_2 = M_1V_1/V_2$; $\frac{12.0\ M\ HNO_3 \times 25.0 \text{ mL}}{500 \text{ mL}} = 0.600\ M\ HNO_3$

4.62 (a) The amount of $AgNO_3$ needed is: 0.200 M × 0.1000 L = 0.0200 mol $AgNO_3$

$$0.0200 \text{ mol } AgNO_3 \times \frac{169.88 \text{ g } AgNO_3}{1 \text{ mol } AgNO_3} = 3.3976 = 3.40 \text{ g } AgNO_3$$

Add this amount of solid to a 100 mL volumetric flask, dissolve in a small amount of water, bring the total volume to exactly 100 mL and agitate well.

(b) Dilute the 6.0 M HNO_3 to prepare 250 mL of 1.0 M HNO_3. To determine the volume of 6.0 M HNO_3 needed, calculate the moles HNO_3 present in 250 mL of 1.0 M HNO_3 and then the volume of 6.0 M solution that contains this number of moles.

0.250 L × 1.0 M = 0.250 mol HNO_3 needed;

$$L = \frac{mol}{M};\ L\ 6.0\ M\ HNO_3 = \frac{0.250 \text{ mol needed}}{6.0\ M} = 0.0417 \text{ L} = 42 \text{ mL}$$

Thoroughly clean, rinse and fill a 50 mL buret with the 6.0 M HNO_3, taking precautions appropriate for working with a relatively concentrated acid. Dispense 42 mL of the 6.0 M acid into a 250 mL volumetric flask, add water to the mark and mix thoroughly.

4.64 $50.000 \text{ mL glycerol} \times \frac{1.2656 \text{ g glycerol}}{1 \text{ mL glycerol}} = 63.280 \text{ g glycerol}$

$$63.280 \text{ g } C_3H_8O_3 \times \frac{1 \text{ mol } C_3H_8O_3}{92.094 \text{ g } C_3H_8O_3} = 0.687124 = 0.68712 \text{ mol } C_3H_8O_3$$

$$M = \frac{0.687124 \text{ mol } C_3H_8O_3}{0.25000 \text{ L solution}} = 2.7485\ M\ C_3H_8O_3$$

Solution Stoichiometry; Titrations

4.66 *Plan.* M × L = mol $Fe(NO_3)_2$; balanced equation → mol ratio → mol NaOH → g NaOH

Solve. $\frac{0.500 \text{ mol } Fe(NO_3)_2}{1 \text{ L}} \times 0.02500 \text{ L} = 0.0125 \text{ mol } Fe(NO_3)_2$

$Fe(NO_3)_2(aq) + 2NaOH(aq) \rightarrow Fe(OH)_2(s) + 2NaNO_3(aq)$

$$0.0125 \text{ mol } Fe(NO_3)_2 \times \frac{2 \text{ mol NaOH}}{1 \text{ mol } Fe(NO_3)_2} \times \frac{40.00 \text{ g NaOH}}{1 \text{ mol NaOH}} = 1.0 \text{ g NaOH}$$

4.68 (a) $2HCl(aq) + Ba(OH)_2(aq) \rightarrow BaCl_2(aq) + 2H_2O(l)$

$$\frac{0.101 \text{ mol } Ba(OH)_2}{1 \text{ L } Ba(OH)_2} \times 0.0500 \text{ L } Ba(OH)_2 \times \frac{2 \text{ mol HCl}}{1 \text{ mol } Ba(OH)_2} \times \frac{1 \text{ L HCl}}{0.120 \text{ mol HCl}} = 0.0842 \text{ L or } 84.2 \text{ mL HCl soln}$$

(b) $H_2SO_4(aq) + 2NaOH(aq) \rightarrow Na_2SO_4(aq) + 2H_2O(l)$

$$0.200 \text{ g NaOH} \times \frac{1 \text{ mol NaOH}}{40.00 \text{ g NaOH}} \times \frac{1 \text{ mol } H_2SO_4}{2 \text{ mol NaOH}} \times \frac{1 \text{ L } H_2SO_4}{0.125 \text{ mol } H_2SO_4} = 0.0200 \text{ L or } 20.0 \text{ mL } H_2SO_4 \text{ soln}$$

(c) $BaCl_2(aq) + Na_2SO_4(aq) \rightarrow BaSO_4(s) + 2NaCl(aq)$

$$752 \text{ mg} = 0.752 \text{ g } Na_2SO_4 \times \frac{1 \text{ mol } Na_2SO_4}{142.1 \text{ g } Na_2SO_4} \times \frac{1 \text{ mol } BaCl_2}{1 \text{ mol } Na_2SO_4} \times \frac{1}{0.0558 \text{ L}} = 0.0948 \, M \text{ } BaCl_2$$

(d) $2HCl(aq) + Ca(OH)_2(aq) \rightarrow CaCl_2(aq) + 2H_2O(l)$

$$0.0427 \text{ L HCl} \times \frac{0.208 \text{ mol HCl}}{1 \text{ L HCl}} \times \frac{1 \text{ mol } Ca(OH)_2}{2 \text{ mol HCl}} \times \frac{74.10 \text{ g } Ca(OH)_2}{1 \text{ mol } Ca(OH)_2} = 0.329 \text{ g } Ca(OH)_2$$

4.70 $$\frac{0.102 \text{ mol NaOH}}{1 \text{ L}} \times 0.0355 \text{ L} \times \frac{1 \text{ mol } HC_2H_3O_2}{1 \text{ mol NaOH}} \times \frac{60.05 \text{ g } HC_2H_3O_2}{1 \text{ mol } HC_2H_3O_2}$$

$$= 0.21744 = 0.217 \text{ g } HC_2H_3O_2 \text{ in } 2.50 \text{ mL}$$

$$1.00 \text{ qt vinegar} \times \frac{1 \text{ L}}{1.057 \text{ qt}} \times \frac{1000 \text{ mL}}{1 \text{ L}} \times \frac{0.21744 \text{ g } HC_2H_3O_2}{2.50 \text{ mL vinegar}} = 82.3 \text{ g } HC_2H_3O_2/\text{qt}$$

4.72 The balanced equation for the titration is:

$Sr(NO_3)_2(aq) + Na_2CrO_4(aq) \rightarrow SrCrO_4(s) + 2NaNO_3(aq)$

Beginning with a 0.100 L sample, we can do the following conversions:

volume soln → g $Sr(NO_3)_2$ → mol $Sr(NO_3)_2$ → mol Na_2CrO_4 → vol Na_2CrO_4 soln

$$0.100 \text{ L soln} \times \frac{7.52 \text{ g } Sr(NO_3)_2}{0.750 \text{ L soln}} \times \frac{1 \text{ mol } Sr(NO_3)_2}{211.6 \text{ g } Sr(NO_3)_2} \times \frac{1 \text{ mol } Na_2CrO_4}{1 \text{ mol } Sr(NO_3)_2} \times \frac{1 \text{ L soln}}{0.0425 \text{ mol } Na_2CrO_4} = 0.111 \text{ L } Na_2CrO_4 \text{ soln}$$

4.74 (a) $HNO_3(aq) + NaOH(s) \rightarrow NaNO_3(aq) + H_2O(l)$

(b) Determine the limiting reactant, then the identity and concentration of ions remaining in solution. Assume that the $H_2O(l)$ produced by the reaction does **not** increase the total solution volume.

$$12.0 \text{ g NaOH} \times \frac{1 \text{ mol NaOH}}{40.00 \text{ g NaOH}} = 0.300 \text{ mol NaOH}$$

$0.200\ M\ HNO_3 \times 0.0750\ L\ HNO_3 = 0.0150$ mol HNO_3.

The mol ratio is 1:1, so HNO_3 is the limiting reactant. No excess H^+ remains in solution. The remaining ions are: OH^- (excess reactant), Na^+ and NO_3^- (spectators).

OH^-: 0.300 mol OH^- initial - 0.0150 mol OH^- react = 0.285 mol OH^- remain

0.285 mol OH^- / 0.0750 L soln = 3.80 M OH^-(aq)

Na^+: 0.300 mol Na^+ / 0.0750 L soln = 4.00 M Na^+(aq)

NO_3^-: 0.0150 mol NO_3^- / 0.0750 L = 0.200 M NO_3^- aq)

(c) The resulting solution is **basic** because of the large excess of OH^-(aq).

4.76 *Plan.* $CaCO_3(s) + 2HCl(aq) \rightarrow CaCl_2(aq) + H_2O(l) + CO_2(g)$

$HCl(aq) + NaOH(aq) \rightarrow NaCl(aq) + H_2O(l)$

total mol HCl - excess mol HCl = mol HCl reacted; mol $CaCO_3$ = (mol HCl)/2;

g $CaCO_3$ = mol $CaCO_3$ × molar mass; mass % = (g $CaCO_3$/g sample) × 100

Solve:

$$\frac{1.035 \text{ mol HCl}}{1 \text{ L soln}} \times 0.02500 \text{ L} = 0.025875 = 0.02588 \text{ mol HCl total}$$

$$\frac{0.1010 \text{ mol NaOH}}{1 \text{ L soln}} \times 0.01525 \text{ L} = 0.00154025 = 0.001540 \text{ mol HCl excess}$$

0.025875 total - 0.001540 excess = 0.02433475 = 0.02433 mol HCl reacted

$$0.243745 \text{ mol HCl} \times \frac{1 \text{ mol } CaCO_3}{2 \text{ mol HCl}} \times \frac{100.09 \text{ g } CaCO_3}{1 \text{ mol } CaCO_3} = 1.21783 = 1.218 \text{ g } CaCO_3$$

$$\text{mass \% } CaCO_3 = \frac{\text{g } CaCO_3}{\text{g rock}} \times 100 = \frac{1.21783}{1.452} \times 100 = 83.87\%$$

Additional Exercises

4.78 The two precipitates formed are due to AgCl(s) and $SrSO_4(s)$. Since no precipitate forms on addition of hydroxide ion to the remaining solution, the other two possibilities, Ni^{2+} and Mn^{2+}, are absent.

4.79 (a,b) Expt. 1 No reaction

Expt. 2 $2Ag^+(aq) + CrO_4^{2-}(aq) \rightarrow Ag_2CrO_4(s)$ red precipitate

Expt. 3 No reaction

Expt. 4 $2Ag^+(aq) + C_2O_4^{2-}(aq) \rightarrow Ag_2C_2O_4(s)$ white precipitate
Expt. 5 $Ca^{2+}(aq) + C_2O_4^{2-}(aq) \rightarrow CaC_2O_4(s)$ white precipitate
Expt. 6 $Ag^+(aq) + Cl^-(aq) \rightarrow AgCl(s)$ white precipitate

(c) The silver salts of both ions are insoluble, but many silver salts are insoluble (Expt. 6). The calcium salt of CrO_4^{2-} is soluble (Expt. 3), while the calcium salt of $C_2O_4^{2-}(aq)$ is insoluble (Expt. 5). Thus, chromate salts appear more soluble than oxalate salts.

4.81 (a) $2H^+(aq) + SO_3^{2-}(aq) \rightarrow \mathbf{H_2SO_3}(aq)$; sulfurous acid

(b) $H_2SO_3(aq) \rightarrow H_2O(l) + \mathbf{SO_2}(g)$; sulfur dioxide

(c) The boiling point of $SO_2(g)$ is -10°C. It is a gas at room temperature (23°C) and pressure (1 atm).

(d) (i) $Na_2SO_3(aq) + 2HCl(aq) \rightarrow 2NaCl(aq) + H_2O(l) + SO_2(g)$
$SO_3^{2-}(aq) + 2H^+(aq) \rightarrow H_2O(l) + SO_2(g)$

(ii) $Ag_2SO_3(s) + 2HCl(aq) \rightarrow 2AgCl(s) + H_2O(l) + SO_2(g)$
$Ag_2SO_3(s) + 2H^+(aq) + 2Cl^-(aq) \rightarrow 2AgCl(s) + H_2O(l) + SO_2(g)$

(iii) $KHSO_3(s) + HCl(aq) \rightarrow KCl(aq) + H_2O(l) + SO_2(g)$
$KHSO_3(s) + H^+(aq) \rightarrow K^+(aq) + H_2O(l) + SO_2(g)$

(iv) $ZnSO_3(aq) + 2HCl(aq) \rightarrow ZnCl_2(aq) + H_2O(l) + SO_2(g)$
$SO_3^{2-}(aq) + 2H^+(aq) \rightarrow H_2O(l) + SO_2(g)$

4.82 $4\overset{-3}{N}H_3(g) + 5\overset{0}{O_2}(g) \rightarrow 4\overset{+2}{N}O(g) + 6H_2\overset{-2}{O}(g)$. (a) redox reaction
(b) N is oxidized, O is reduced

$2\overset{+2}{N}O(g) + \overset{0}{O_2}(g) \rightarrow 2\overset{+4}{N}\overset{-2}{O_2}(g)$. (a) redox reaction
(b) N is oxidized, O is reduced

$3\overset{+4}{N}O_2(g) + H_2O(l) \rightarrow H\overset{+5}{N}O_3(aq) + \overset{+2}{N}O(g)$. (a) redox reaction

(b) N is oxidized ($NO_2 \rightarrow HNO_3$), N is reduced ($NO_2 \rightarrow NO$). A reaction where the same element is both oxidized and reduced is called disproportionation.

4.84 (a) $2Ti^{4+}(aq) + Zn(s) \rightarrow 2Ti^{3+}(aq) + Zn^{2+}(aq)$
The coefficients are required because the number of electrons lost by Zn ($2e^-$) must equal the number of electrons gained by Ti^{+4} ($2 \times 1e^-$).

(b) This reaction does not indicate the position of Ti on the activity series in Table 4.5. All reactions in Table 4.5 involve oxidation of an elemental metal to a metal ion or compound. This reaction does not produce Ti metal and thus cannot be compared to the other reactions.

4.85 (a)
A : La_2O_3 Metals often react with the oxygen in air to produce metal oxides.
B : $La(OH)_3$ When metals react with water (HOH) to form H_2, OH^- remains.
C : $LaCl_3$ Most chlorides are soluble.
D : $La_2(SO_4)_3$ Sulfuric acid provides SO_4^{2-} ions.

(b)
$4La(s) + 3O_2(g) \rightarrow 2La_2O_3(s)$
$2La(s) + 6HOH(l) \rightarrow 2La(OH)_3(s) + 3H_2(g)$
(There are no spectator ions in either of these reactions.)
molecular: $La_2O_3(s) + 6HCl(aq) \rightarrow 2LaCl_3(aq) + 3H_2O(l)$
net ionic: $La_2O_3(s) + 6H^+(aq) \rightarrow 2La^{3+}(aq) + 3H_2O(l)$
molecular: $La(OH)_3(s) + 3HCl(aq) \rightarrow LaCl_3(aq) + 3H_2O(l)$
net ionic: $La(OH)_3(s) + 3H^+(aq) \rightarrow La^{3+}(aq) + 3H_2O(l)$
molecular: $2LaCl_3(aq) + 3H_2SO_4(aq) \rightarrow La_2(SO_4)_3(s) + 6HCl(aq)$
net ionic: $2La^{3+}(aq) + 3SO_4^{2-}(aq) \rightarrow La_2(SO_4)_3(s)$

(c) La metal is oxidized by water to produce $H_2(g)$, so La is definitely above H on the activity series. In fact, since an acid is not required to oxidize La, it is probably one of the more active metals.

4.87 (a)
$$0.0500 \text{ L soln} \times \frac{0.200 \text{ mol NaCl}}{1 \text{ L soln}} = 1.00 \times 10^{-2} \text{ mol NaCl}$$

$$0.0750 \text{ L soln} \times \frac{0.100 \text{ mol NaCl}}{1 \text{ L soln}} = 7.50 \times 10^{-3} \text{ mol NaCl}$$

Total moles NaCl = 1.75×10^{-2}, total volume = 0.0500 L + 0.0750 L = 0.1250 L

$$\text{Molarity} = \frac{1.75 \times 10^{-2} \text{ mol}}{0.1250 \text{ L}} = 0.140\ M$$

(b)
$$0.025 \text{ L soln} \times \frac{1.50 \text{ mol NaOH}}{1 \text{ L soln}} = 0.03675 = 0.0368 \text{ mol NaOH}$$

$$0.0255 \text{ L soln} \times \frac{0.750 \text{ mol NaOH}}{1 \text{ L soln}} = 0.019125 = 0.0191 \text{ mol NaOH}$$

Total moles NaOH = 0.055875 = 0.0559, total volume = 0.0500 L

$$\text{Molarity} = \frac{0.055875 \text{ mol NaOH}}{0.0500 \text{ L}} = 1.12\ M$$

4.88 (a)
$$\frac{50 \text{ pg}}{1 \text{ mL}} \times \frac{1 \times 10^{-12} \text{ g}}{1 \text{ pg}} \times \frac{1 \times 10^{3} \text{ mL}}{\text{L}} \times \frac{1 \text{ mol Na}}{23.0 \text{ g Na}} = 2.17 \times 10^{-9} = 2.2 \times 10^{-9}\ M$$

(b)
$$\frac{2.17 \times 10^{-9} \text{ mol Na}}{1 \text{ L soln}} \times \frac{1 \text{ L}}{1 \times 10^{3} \text{ cm}^3} \times \frac{6.02 \times 10^{23} \text{ Na atom}}{1 \text{ mol Na}}$$
$$= 1.3 \times 10^{12} \text{ atoms or } Na^+ \text{ ions/cm}^3$$

4.90 $H_2C_4H_4O_6 + 2OH^-(aq) \rightarrow C_4H_4O_6^{2-}(aq) + 2H_2O(l)$

$$0.02262 \text{ L NaOH soln} \times \frac{0.2000 \text{ mol NaOH}}{1 \text{ L}} \times \frac{1 \text{ mol } H_2C_4H_4O_6}{2 \text{ mol NaOH}} \times \frac{1}{0.04000 \text{ L } H_2C_4H_4O_6}$$

$$= 0.05655\ M\ H_2C_4H_4O_6 \text{ soln}$$

4.92 mol OH^- from NaOH(aq) + mol OH^- from $Zn(OH)_2(s)$ = mol H^+ from HBr

mol H^+ = M HBr × L HBr = 0.500 M HBr × 0.400 L HBr = 0.200 mol H^+

mol OH^- from NaOH = M NaOH × L NaOH = 0.500 M NaOH × 0.0985 L NaOH

= 0.04925 = 0.0493 mol OH^-

mol OH^- from $Zn(OH)_2(s)$ = 0.200 mol H^+ - 0.04925 mol OH^- from NaOH = 0.15075

= 0.151 mol OH^- from $Zn(OH)_2$

$$0.15075 \text{ mol } OH^- \times \frac{1 \text{ mol } Zn(OH)_2}{2 \text{ mol } OH^-} \times \frac{99.41 \text{ g } Zn(OH)_2}{1 \text{ mol } Zn(OH)_2} = 7.49 \text{ g } Zn(OH)_2$$

Integrative Exercises

4.94 (a) At the equivalence point of a titration, mol NaOH added = mol H^+ present

$$M_{NaOH} \times L_{NaOH} = \frac{\text{g acid}}{\mathcal{M} \text{ acid}} \text{ (for an acid with 1 acidic hydrogen)}$$

$$\mathcal{M} \text{ acid} = \frac{\text{g acid}}{M_{NaOH} \times L_{NaOH}} = \frac{0.2053 \text{ g}}{0.1008\ M \times 0.0150 \text{ L}} = 136 \text{ g/mol}$$

(b) Assume 100 g of acid.

$$70.6 \text{ g C} \times \frac{1 \text{ mol C}}{12.01 \text{ g C}} = 5.88 \text{ mol C};\ 5.88 / 1.47 \approx 4$$

$$5.89 \text{ g H} \times \frac{1 \text{ mol H}}{1.008 \text{ g H}} = 5.84 \text{ mol H};\ 5.84 / 1.47 \approx 4$$

$$23.5 \text{ g O} \times \frac{1 \text{ mol O}}{16.00 \text{ g O}} = 1.47 \text{ mol O};\ 1.47 / 1.47 = 1$$

The empirical formula is C_4H_4O.

$$\frac{\mathcal{M}}{FW} = \frac{136}{68.1} = 2; \text{ the molecular formula is 2} \times \text{the empirical formula.}$$

The molecular formula is $C_8H_8O_2$.

4.95 $Ba^{2+}(aq) + SO_4^{2-}(aq) \rightarrow BaSO_4(s)$

$$0.4123 \text{ g } BaSO_4 \times \frac{137.3 \text{ g Ba}}{233.4 \text{ g } BaSO_4} = 0.2425 \text{ g Ba}$$

$$\text{mass \%} = \frac{\text{g Ba}}{\text{g sample}} \times 100 = \frac{0.24254 \text{ g Ba}}{6.977 \text{ g sample}} \times 100 = 3.476\% \text{ Ba}$$

4.97 (a) $Mg(OH)_2(s) + 2HNO_3(aq) \rightarrow Mg(NO_3)_2(aq) + 2H_2O(l)$

(b) $5.53 \text{ g } Mg(OH)_2 \times \frac{1 \text{ mol } Mg(OH)_2}{58.32 \text{ g } Mg(OH)_2} = 0.09482 = 0.0948 \text{ mol } Mg(OH)_2$

$0.200\ M\ HNO_3 \times 0.0250 \text{ L} = 0.00500 \text{ mol } HNO_3$

The 0.00500 mol HNO_3 would neutralize 0.00250 mol $Mg(OH)_2$ and much more $Mg(OH)_2$ is present, so HNO_3 is the limiting reactant.

(c) Since HNO_3 limits, 0 mol HNO_3 is present after reaction.

0.00250 mol $Mg(NO_3)_2$ is produced.

0.09482 mol $Mg(OH)_2$ initial - 0.00250 mol $Mg(OH)_2$ react = 0.0923 mol $Mg(OH)_2$ remain

4.98 (a) $Na_2SO_4(aq) + Pb(NO_3)_2(s) \rightarrow PbSO_4(s) + 2NaNO_3(aq)$

(b) Calculate mol of each reactant and compare.

$1.50 \text{ g } Pb(NO_3)_2 \times \frac{1 \text{ mol } Pb(NO_3)_2}{331.2 \text{ g } Pb(NO_3)_2} = 0.004529 = 4.53 \times 10^{-3} \text{ mol } Pb(NO_3)_2$

$0.100\ M\ Na_2SO_4 \times 0.125 \text{ L} = 0.0125 \text{ mol } Na_2SO_4$

Since the reactants combine in a 1:1 mol ratio, $Pb(NO_3)_2$ is the limiting reactant.

(c) $Pb(NO_3)_2$ is the limiting reactant, so no Pb^{2+} remains in solution. The remaining ions are: SO_4^{2-} (excess reactant), Na^+ and NO_3^- (spectators).

SO_4^{2-} : 0.0125 mol SO_4^{2-} initial - 0.00453 mol SO_4^{2-} reacted

= 0.00797 = 0.0080 mol SO_4^{2-} remain

0.00797 mol SO_4^{2-} / 0.125 L soln = 0.064 M SO_4^{2-}

Na^+: Since the total volume of solution is the volume of $Na_2SO_4(aq)$ added, the concentration of Na^+ is unchanged.

$0.100\ M\ Na_2SO_4 \times (2 \text{ mol } Na^+ / 1 \text{ mol } Na_2SO_4) = 0.200\ M\ Na^+$

NO_3^-: 4.53×10^{-3} mol $Pb(NO_3)_2 \times 2$ mol NO_3^- / 1 mol $Pb(NO_3)_2$

$= 9.06 \times 10^{-3}$ mol NO_3^-

9.06×10^{-3} mol NO_3^- / 0.125 L = 0.0725 M NO_3^-

4.100 *Plan.* $M = \frac{\text{mol } Br^-}{\text{L sea water}}$; mg $Br^- \rightarrow$ g $Br^- \rightarrow$ mol Br^-;

1 kg sea water → g $\xrightarrow{\text{density}}$ water mL water → L sea water

Solve. $65 \text{ mg } Br^- \times \frac{1 \text{ g } Br^-}{1000 \text{ mg } Br^-} \times \frac{1 \text{ mol } Br^-}{79.90 \text{ g } Br^-} = 8.135 \times 10^{-4} = 8.1 \times 10^{-4} \text{ mol } Br^-$

$1 \text{ kg sea water} \times \frac{1000 \text{ g}}{1 \text{ kg}} \times \frac{1 \text{ mL water}}{1.025 \text{ g water}} \times \frac{1 \text{ L}}{1000 \text{ mL}} = 0.9756 \text{ L}$

$$M\,Br^- = \frac{8.135 \times 10^{-4}\text{ mol }Br^-}{0.9756\text{ L sea water}} = 8.3 \times 10^{-4}\ M\ Br^-$$

4.101 $Ag^+(aq) + Cl^-(aq) \rightarrow AgCl(s)$

$$\frac{0.2997\text{ mol }Ag^+}{1\text{ L}} \times 0.04258\text{ L} \times \frac{1\text{ mol }Cl^-}{1\text{ mol }Ag^+} \times \frac{35.453\text{ g }Cl^-}{1\text{ mol }Cl^-} = 0.45242 = 0.4524\text{ g }Cl^-$$

$$25.00\text{ mL sea water} \times \frac{1.025\text{ g}}{\text{mL}} = 25.625 = 25.63\text{ g sea water}$$

$$\text{mass \% }Cl^- = \frac{0.45242\text{ g }Cl^-}{25.625\text{ g sea water}} \times 100 = 1.766\%\ Cl^-$$

4.103 (a) mol OH^- in tablet = mol H^+ total - mol H^+ reacted with NaOH

mol H^+ total = 0.500 M HCl × 0.0500 L = 0.0250 mol H^+ total

mol H^+ w/NaOH = 0.255 M NaOH × 0.0309 L = 0.007880 = 0.00788 mol OH^-

= 0.00788 mol H+

mol OH^- in tablet = 0.0250 - 0.00788 = 0.01712 = 0.0171 mol OH^- in tablet

(b) mass [$Mg(OH)_2$ + $Al(OH)_3$] = 500 mg × 0.950 = 475 mg = 0.475 g

g $Mg(OH)_2$ = x; g $Al(OH)_3$ = 0.475 - x

$$\frac{x}{58.32\text{ g }Mg(OH)_2} \times \frac{2\text{ mol }OH^-}{1\text{ mol }Mg(OH)_2} = \text{mol }OH^-\text{ from }Mg(OH)_2$$

$$\frac{0.475 - x}{78.01\text{ g }Al(OH)_3} \times \frac{3\text{ mol }OH^-}{1\text{ mol }Al(OH)_3} = \text{mol }OH^-\text{ from }Al(OH)_3$$

$$\frac{2x}{58.32} + \frac{1.425 - 3x}{78.01} = 0.01712\text{ mol }OH^-$$

$$\frac{156.02x + 83.106 - 174.96x}{58.32(78.01)} = 0.01712$$

-18.94 x = 77.8882 - 83.106 = -5.2178 = -5.2

x = 0.27549 = 0.275 g $Mg(OH)_2$; 0.475 - 0.275 = 0.200 g $Al(OH)_3$

(Strictly speaking, both masses have 2 sig figs because the difference (77.9 - 83.11) has 1 decimal place and 2 sig figs.)

4.104 (a) mol HCl initial - mol NH_3 from air = mol HCl remaining

= mol NaOH required for titration

mol NaOH = 0.0588 M × 0.0131 L = 7.703×10^{-4} = 7.70×10^{-4} mol NaOH

= 7.70×10^{-4} mol HCl remain

mol HCl initial - mol HCl remaining = mol NH_3 from air

(0.0105 M HCl $\times$ 0.100 L) - 7.703 $\times 10^{-4}$ mol HCl = mol NH_3

10.5 $\times 10^{-4}$ mol HCl - 7.703 $\times 10^{-4}$ mol HCl = 2.80 $\times 10^{-4}$ = 2.8 $\times 10^{-4}$ mol NH_3

$$2.8 \times 10^{-4} \text{ mol } NH_3 \times \frac{17.03 \text{ g } NH_3}{1 \text{ mol } NH_3} = 4.77 \times 10^{-3} = 4.8 \times 10^{-3} \text{ g } NH_3$$

(b) ppm is defined as molecules of NH_3/1 $\times 10^6$ molecules in air.
Calculate molecules NH_3 from mol NH_3.

$$2.80 \times 10^{-4} \text{ mol } NH_3 \times \frac{6.022 \times 20^{23} \text{ molecules}}{1 \text{ mol}} = 1.686 \times 10^{20}$$

$$= 1.7 \times 10^{20} \; NH_3 \text{ molecules}$$

Calculate total volume of air processed, then g air using density, then molecules air using molar mass.

$$\frac{10.0 \text{ L}}{1 \text{ min}} \times 10.0 \text{ min} \times \frac{1.20 \text{ g air}}{1 \text{ L air}} \times \frac{1 \text{ mol air}}{29.0 \text{ g air}} \times \frac{6.022 \times 10^{23} \text{ molecules}}{1 \text{ mol}}$$

$$= 2.492 \times 10^{24} = 2.5 \times 10^{24} \text{ air molecules}$$

$$\text{ppm } NH_3 = \frac{1.686 \times 10^{20} \; NH_3 \text{ molecules}}{2.492 \times 10^{24} \text{ air molecules}} \times 1 \times 10^6 = 68 \text{ ppm } NH_3$$

(c) 68 ppm > 50 ppm. The manufacturer is **not** in compliance.

5 Thermochemistry

Nature of Energy

5.2 (a) The kinetic energy of the ball **decreases** as it moves higher. As the ball moves higher and opposes gravity, kinetic energy is changed into potential energy.

(b) The potential energy of the ball **increases** as it moves higher.

(c) The heavier ball would go **half as high** as the tennis ball. At the apex of the trajectory, all initial kinetic energy has been changed into potential energy. The magnitude of the change in potential energy is $m\, g\, \Delta h$, which is equal to the energy initially imparted to the ball. If the same amount of energy is imparted to a ball with twice the mass, m doubles so Δh is half as large.

5.4 (a) *Plan.* Convert lb → kg, mi/hr → m/s.

Solve. $950 \text{ lb} \times \dfrac{1 \text{ kg}}{2.205 \text{ lb}} = 430.84 = 431 \text{ kg}$

$$\frac{68 \text{ mi}}{1 \text{ hr}} \times \frac{1.6093 \text{ km}}{1 \text{ mi}} \times \frac{1000 \text{ m}}{1 \text{ km}} \times \frac{1 \text{ hr}}{60 \text{ min}} \times \frac{1 \text{ min}}{60 \text{ sec}} = 30.398 = 30 \text{ m/s}$$

$$E_k = 1/2\ mv^2 = 1/2 \times 430.84 \text{ kg} \times (30.398)^2 \text{ m}^2/\text{s}^2 = 2.0 \times 10^5 \text{ J}$$

(b) E_k is proportional to v^2, so if speed decreases by a factor of 2, kinetic energy decreases by a factor of 4.

(c) Brakes stop a moving vehicle, so the kinetic energy of the motorcycle is primarily transferred to friction between brakes and wheels, and somewhat to deformation of the tire and friction between the tire and road.

5.6 *Analyze.* Given: 1 kwh; 1 watt = 1 J/s; 1 watt • s = 1 J.

Find: conversion factor for joules and kwh.

Plan. kwh → wh → ws → J

Solve. $1 \text{ kwh} \times \dfrac{1000 \text{ w}}{1 \text{ kw}} \times \dfrac{60 \text{ min}}{\text{h}} \times \dfrac{60 \text{ s}}{\text{min}} \times \dfrac{1 \text{ J}}{1 \text{ w} \cdot \text{s}} = 3.6 \times 10^6 \text{ J}$

$1 \text{ kwh} = 3.6 \times 10^6 \text{ J}$

5.8 The energy source of a 100 watt light bulb is electrical current from household wiring. Current passes through and heats a tungsten filament (thin wire) in the bulb. The energy is radiated in the form of heat and visible light.

The energy source for an adult person is food. When a person eats, the food undergoes a complex series of chemical reactions that release the potential energy stored in chemical bonds. Some of this energy is transferred as electrical impulses that trigger muscle action and become kinetic energy. Some is released as heat.

In both cases, the energy must travel through a network (house wiring and lamp or human body) and undergo several changes in form before it is in the correct location and form to accomplish the desired task. In both cases, the energy given off as heat is wasted; it cannot be applied to the tasks of producing light or motion.

5.10 The change in potential energy equals $m \times g \times \Delta h$. The gravitational force on the moon is much smaller than that on earth, so the change in potential energy is much smaller on the moon, given equal m and Δh.

5.12 (a) The system is not closed, because it is exchanging mass with the surroundings. That is, solution flows into and out of the flask.

(b) If the system is defined as shown, it can be closed by blocking the flow in and out, but leaving the flask full of solution.

5.14 (a) If energy is the capacity to do work or transfer heat, then heat is energy because it can do work. For example, heat causes a gas to expand inside a cylinder and move a piston, doing work.

(b) Heat is transferred from one object (system) to another until the two objects (systems) are at the same temperature.

5.16 (a) Electrostatic attraction; no work is done because the particles are held stationary.

(b) Magnetic attraction; work is done because the nail is moved a distance.

The First Law of Thermodynamics

5.18 (a) $\Delta E_{sys} = -\Delta E_{surr}$; $\Delta E_{sys} = q + w$

(b) In applying the first law, we need only to measure changes in internal energy, not absolute values of E. This is because doing work or transferring heat involves changes in energy, not absolute values. This is convenient, since it is almost impossible to measure the internal energy of a system because it has so many components.

(c) The quantities q and w are negative when the system loses heat to the surroundings (it cools), or does work on the surroundings.

5.20 In each case, evaluate q and w in the expression $\Delta E = q + w$. For an exothermic process, q is negative; for an endothermic process, q is positive.

(a) q is positive and w is negative. $\Delta E = +900\text{ J} - 422\text{ J} = +478\text{ J}$. The process is endothermic.

(b) q is negative and w is essentially zero. $\Delta E = -3140\text{ J}$. The process is exothermic.

(c) q is negative and w is zero. $\Delta E = -8.65\text{ kJ}$. The process is exothermic.

releases heat, w done on it
-ve +ve

5.22 (a) ?

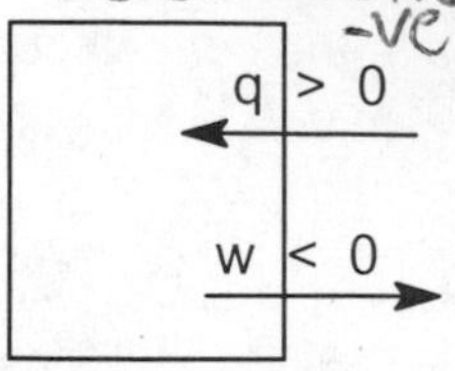

(b) ΔE will be positive for this process if the magnitude of w is greater than the magnitude of q.

(c) ΔE will be negative for this process if the magnitude of q is greater than the magnitude of w.

5.24 $E_{el} = \dfrac{\kappa Q_1 Q_2}{r^2}$. For two oppositely charged particles, the sign of E_{el} is negative; the closer the particles, the greater the magnitude of E_{el}.

(a) The potential energy becomes less negative as the particles are separated (r increases)

(b) ΔE for the process is positive; the internal energy of the system increases as the oppositely charged particles are separated.

(c) Work is done on the system to separate the particles so w is positive. We have no direct knowledge of the change in q, except that it cannot be large and negative, because overall $\Delta E = q + w$ is positive.

5.26 (a) Independent. Potential energy is a state function.

(b) Dependent. Some of the energy released could be employed in performing work, as is done in the body when sugar is metabolized; heat is not a state function.

(c) Dependent. The work accomplished depends on whether the gasoline is used in an engine, burned in an open flame, or in some other manner. Work is not a state function.

Enthalpy

5.28 (a) When a process occurs under constant external pressure, the enthalpy change (ΔH) equals the amount of heat transferred. $\Delta H = q_p$.

(b) State functions are particularly useful because they are totally defined by the current conditions (state) of the system, not the history of how the system arrived at its current state. Changes to state functions, like ΔH can be calculated from knowledge of initial and final states, without details of how the change takes place.

(c) $\Delta H = q_p$. If the system absorbs heat, q and ΔH are positive and the enthalpy of the system increases.

5.30 (a) $ZnCO_3(s) \rightarrow ZnO(s) + CO_2(g)$

$\Delta H = 71.5$ kJ

(b)

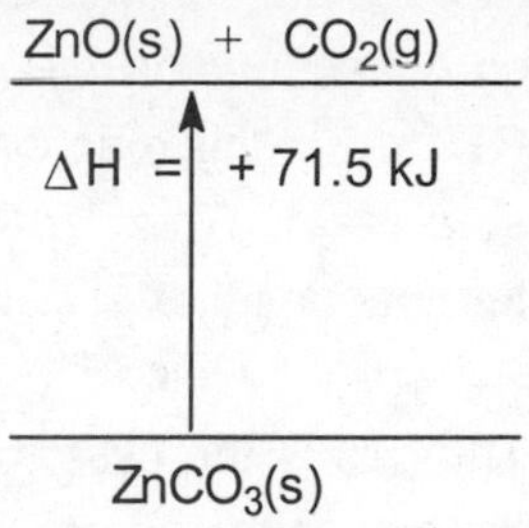

5.32 *Plan*. Consider the sign of an enthalpy change that would convert one of the substances into the other. *Solve*:

(a) $CO_2(s) \rightarrow CO_2(g)$. This change is sublimation, which is endothermic, $+\Delta H$. $CO_2(g)$ has the higher enthalpy.

(b) $H_2 \rightarrow 2H$. Breaking the H–H bond requires energy, so the process is endothermic, $+\Delta H$. Two moles of H atoms have higher enthalpy.

(c) $H_2O(g) \rightarrow H_2(g) + 1/2\ O_2(g)$. Decomposing H_2O into its elements requires energy and is endothermic, $+\Delta H$. One mole of $H_2(g)$ and 0.5 mol $O_2(g)$ at 25°C have the higher enthalpy.

(d) $N_2(g)$ at 100° $\rightarrow N_2(g)$ at 300°. An increase in the temperature of the sample requires that heat is added to the system, +q and $+\Delta H$. $N_2(g)$ at 300° has the higher enthalpy.

5.34 (a) The reaction is endothermic, so heat is absorbed by the system during the course of reaction.

(b) $$1.60 \text{ kg } CH_3OH \times \frac{1000 \text{ g}}{1 \text{ kg}} \frac{1 \text{ mol } CH_3OH}{32.04 \text{ g } CH_3OH} \times \frac{90.7 \text{ kJ}}{1 \text{ mol } CH_3OH}$$
$$= +4.53 \times 10^3 \text{ kJ heat transferred (absorbed)}$$

(c) $$64.7 \text{ kJ} \times \frac{2 \text{ mol } H_2}{90.7 \text{ kJ}} \times \frac{2.016 \text{ g } H_2}{1 \text{ mol } H_2} = 2.88 \text{ g } H_2 \text{ produced}$$

(d) The sign of ΔH is reversed for the reverse reaction: $\Delta H = -90.7$ kJ

$$32.0 \text{ g CO} \times \frac{1 \text{ mol CO}}{28.01 \text{ g CO}} \times \frac{-90.7 \text{ kJ}}{1 \text{ mol CO}} = -104 \text{ kJ heat transferred (evolved)}$$

5.36 (a) $$4.34 \text{ mol } O_2 \times \frac{-89.4 \text{ kJ}}{3 \text{ mol } O_2} = -129.33 = -129 \text{ kJ}$$

(b) $$200.8 \text{ g KCl} \times \frac{1 \text{ mol KCl}}{74.55 \text{ g KCl}} \times \frac{-89.4 \text{ kJ}}{2 \text{ mol KCl}} = -120.40 = -120 \text{ kJ}$$

(c) Since the sign of ΔH is reversed for the reverse reaction, it seems reasonable that other characteristics would be reversed, as well. If the forward reaction proceeds spontaneously, the reverse reaction is probably not spontaneous. Also, we know from experience that KCl(s) does not spontaneously react with atmospheric $O_2(g)$, even at elevated temperature.

5.38 At constant volume ($\Delta V = 0$), $\Delta E = q_v$. According to the definition of enthalpy, $H = E + PV$, so $\Delta H = \Delta E + \Delta(PV)$. For an ideal gas at constant temperature and volume $\Delta PV = V\Delta P = RT\Delta n$. For this reaction, there are 2 mol of gaseous product and 3 mol of gaseous reactants, so $\Delta n = -1$. Thus $V\Delta P$ or $\Delta(PV)$ is negative. Since $\Delta H = \Delta E + \Delta(PV)$, the negative $\Delta(PV)$ term means that ΔH will be smaller or more negative than ΔE.

5.40 The gas is the system. If 518 J of heat is added, q = +518 J. Work done by the system decreases the overall energy of the system, so w = -127 J.

$\Delta E = q + w = +518\text{ J} - 127\text{ J} = +391\text{ J}$. $\Delta H = q = +518\text{ J}$ (at constant pressure).

5.42 (a) $C_2H_2(g) \rightarrow 1/3\ C_6H_6(l)$ $\Delta H = -210$ kJ

(b) $C_6H_6(l) \rightarrow 3C_2H_2(g)$ $\Delta H = 3(+210)\text{ kJ} = +630$ kJ

(c) The exothermic reverse reaction is more likely to be thermodynamically favored.

(d)

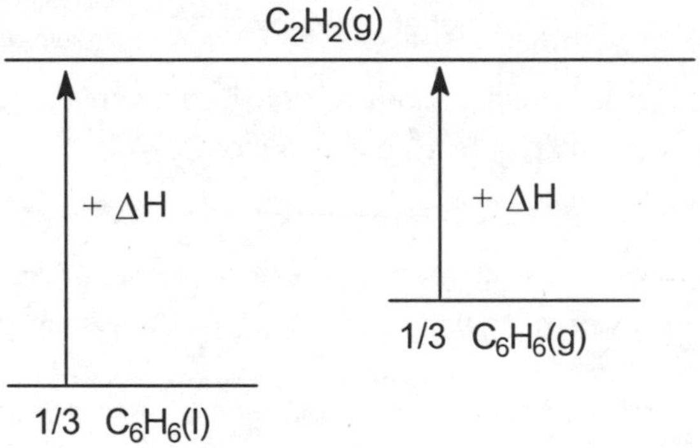

If the reactant is in the higher enthalpy gas phase, the overall ΔH for the reaction has a smaller positive value.

Calorimetry

The specific heat of water to four significant figures, 4.184 J/g•K, will be used in many of the following exercises; temperature units of K and °C will be used interchangeably.

5.44 *Analyze.* Both objects are heated to 100°C. The two hot objects are placed in the same amount of cold water at the same temperature. Object A raises the water temperature more than object B. *Plan.* Apply the definition of heat capacity to heating the water and heating the objects to determine which object has the greater heat capacity. *Solve*:

(a) Both beakers of water contain the same mass of water, so they both have the same heat capacity. Object A raises the temperature of its water more than object B, so more heat was transferred from object A than from object B. Since both objects were heated to the same temperature initially, object A must have absorbed more heat to reach the 100° temperature. The greater the heat capacity of an object, the greater the heat required to produce a given rise in temperature. Thus, object A has the greater heat capacity.

(b) Since no information about the masses of the objects is given, we cannot compare or determine the specific heats of the objects.

5.46 (a) $\frac{4.184 \text{ J}}{1 \text{ g} \bullet {}^\circ\text{C}} \times \frac{18.02 \text{ g } H_2O}{1 \text{ mol } H_2O} = \frac{75.40 \text{ J}}{\text{mol} \bullet {}^\circ\text{C}}$

(b) $8.42 \text{ mol } H_2O \times \frac{75.40 \text{ J}}{\text{mol} \bullet {}^\circ\text{C}} = 635 \text{ J/}^\circ\text{C}$

(c) $2.56 \text{ kg } H_2O \times \frac{1000 \text{ g}}{1 \text{ kg}} \times \frac{4.84 \text{ J}}{\text{g} \bullet {}^\circ\text{C}} \times \frac{1 \text{ kJ}}{1000 \text{ J}} \times (92.0^\circ\text{C} - 44.8^\circ\text{C}) = 505.56 = 506 \text{ kJ}$

5.48 $62.0 \text{ g } C_7H_8 \times \frac{1.13 \text{ J}}{\text{g} \bullet \text{K}} \times (38.8^\circ\text{C} - 16.3^\circ\text{C}) = 1.58 \times 10^3 \text{ J}$

5.50 Since the temperature of the water decreses, the dissolving process is endothermic and ΔH is positive. The total mass of the solution is (60.0 g H_2O + 3.88 g NH_4NO_3) = 63.88 = 63.9 g. The temperature change of the solution is 23.0 - 18.4 = 4.6°C. The heat lost by the water is

$$63.88 \text{ g } H_2O \times \frac{4.184 \text{ J}}{1 \text{ g} \bullet {}^\circ\text{C}} \times 4.6^\circ\text{C} \times \frac{1 \text{ kJ}}{1000 \text{ J}} = 1.229 = 1.2 \text{ kJ}$$

Thus, 1.2 kJ is absorbed when 3.88 g $NH_4NO_3(s)$ dissolves.

$$\frac{+1.229 \text{ kJ}}{3.88 \; NH_4NO_3} \times \frac{80.05 \text{ g } NH_4NO_3}{1 \text{ mol } NH_4NO_3} = +25.36 = +25 \text{ kJ/mol } NH_4NO_3$$

5.52 (a) $C_6H_5OH(s) + 7O_2(g) \rightarrow 6CO_2(g) + 3H_2O(l)$

(b) $q_{bomb} = -q_{rxn}$; $\Delta T = 26.37^\circ\text{C} - 21.36^\circ\text{C} = 5.01^\circ\text{C}$

$$q_{bomb} = \frac{11.66 \text{ kJ}}{1^\circ\text{C}} \times 5.01^\circ\text{C} = 58.417 = 58.4 \text{ kJ}$$

At constant volume, $q_v = \Delta E$. ΔE and ΔH are very similar.

$$\Delta H_{rxn} \approx \Delta E_{rxn} = q_{rxn} = -q_{bomb} = \frac{-58.417 \text{ kJ}}{1.800 \text{ g } C_6H_5OH} = -32.454 = -32.5 \text{ kJ/g } C_6H_5OH$$

$$\Delta H_{rxn} = \frac{-32.454 \text{ kJ}}{1 \text{ g } C_6H_5OH} \times \frac{94.11 \text{ g } C_6H_5OH}{1 \text{ mol } C_6H_5OH} = \frac{-3.054 \times 10^3 \text{ kJ}}{\text{mol } C_6H_5OH}$$

$$= -3.05 \times 10^3 \text{ kJ/mol } C_6H_5OH$$

5.54 (a) $C = 1.640 \text{ g } HC_7H_5O_2 \times \frac{26.38 \text{ kJ}}{1 \text{ g } HC_7H_5O_2} \times \frac{1}{4.95^\circ\text{C}} = 8.740 = 8.74 \text{ kJ/}^\circ\text{C}$

(b) $\frac{8.740 \text{ kJ}}{^\circ\text{C}} \times 4.68^\circ\text{C} \times \frac{1}{1.320 \text{ g sample}} = 30.99 = 31.0 \text{ kJ/g sample}$

(c) If water is lost from the calorimeter, there is less water to heat, so the same amount of heat (kJ) from a reaction would cause a larger increase in the calorimeter temperature. The calorimeter constant, kJ/°C would decrease, because °C is in the denominator of the expression.

Hess's Law

5.56 Hess's Law is a consequence of the fact that enthalpy is a state function. Since ΔH is independent of path, we can describe a process by any series of steps that add up to the overall process and ΔH for the process is the sum of the ΔH values for the steps.

5.58 (a)

$$Y \rightarrow X \quad \Delta H = +35\ kJ$$
$$X \rightarrow Z \quad \Delta H = +90\ kJ$$
$$Y \rightarrow Z \quad \Delta H = +125\ kJ$$

(b)

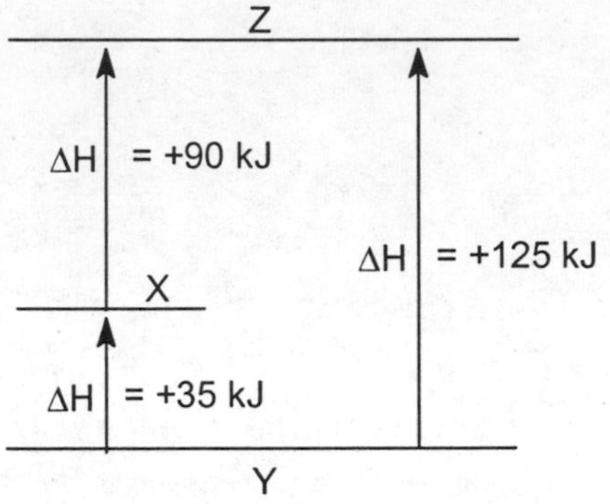

The process of Y forming Z can be described as Y forming X and X forming Z.

(c) No. Any temperature change is accompanied by a change in heat. Comparing reactions and enthalpies of reaction at different temperatures doesn't take into account the change in heat to go from one temperature to the other.

5.60

$3H_2(g) + 3/2\ O_2(g) \rightarrow 3H_2O(g)$	$\Delta H = 3/2(-483.6\ kJ)$
$O_3(g) \rightarrow 3/2\ O_2(g)$	$\Delta H = 1/2(-284.6\ kJ)$
$3H_2(g) + O_3(g) \rightarrow 3H_2O(g)$	$\Delta H = -867.7\ kJ$

5.62

$N_2O(g) \rightarrow N_2(g) + 1/2\ O_2(g)$	$\Delta H = 1/2\ (-163.2\ kJ)$
$NO_2(g) \rightarrow NO(g) + 1/2\ O_2(g)$	$\Delta H = 1/2(113.1\ kJ)$
$N_2(g) + O_2(g) \rightarrow 2NO(g)$	$\Delta H = 180.7\ kJ$
$N_2O(g) + NO_2(g) \rightarrow 3NO(g)$	$\Delta H = 155.7\ kJ$

Enthalpies of Formation

5.64 (a) Tables of ΔH_f° are useful because, according to Hess's law, the standard enthalpy of any reaction can be calculated from the standard enthalpies of formation for the reactants and products.

$$\Delta H_{rxn}^\circ = \sum \Delta H_f^\circ\ (products) - \sum \Delta H_f^\circ\ (reactants)$$

(b) The standard enthalpy of formation for any element in its standard state is zero. Elements in their standard states are the reference point for the enthalpy of formation scale.

5.66 $C_{12}H_{22}O_{11}(s) + H_2O(l) \rightarrow 2C_6H_{12}O_6(s)$

$\Delta H^\circ_{rxn} = 2\Delta H^\circ_f\ C_6H_{12}O_6(s) - \Delta H^\circ_f\ C_{12}H_{22}O_{11}(s) - \Delta H^\circ_f\ H_2O(l)$

$= 2(-1273) - (-2221) - (-285.83) = -39$ kJ

The reaction is slightly exothermic.

5.68 (a) $1/2\ H_2(g) + 1/2\ Br_2(l) \rightarrow HBr(g)$ $\Delta H^\circ_f = -36.23$ kJ

(b) $Ag(s) + 1/2\ N_2(g) + 3/2\ O_2(g) \rightarrow AgNO_3(s)$ $\Delta H^\circ_f = -124.4$ kJ

(c) $2Hg(l) + Cl_2(g) \rightarrow Hg_2Cl_2(s)$ $\Delta H^\circ_f = -264.9$ kJ

(d) $2C(s, gr) + 1/2\ O_2(g) + 3H_2(g) \rightarrow C_2H_5OH(l)$ $\Delta H^\circ_f = -277.7$ kJ

5.70 Use heats of formation to calculate ΔH° for the combustion of butane.

$C_4H_{10}(l) + 13/2\ O_2(g) \rightarrow 4CO_2(g) + 5H_2O(l)$

$\Delta H^\circ_{rxn} = 4\Delta H\ CO_2(g) + 5\Delta H^\circ_f\ H_2O(l) - \Delta H^\circ_f\ C_4H_{10}(l) - 13/2\ \Delta H^\circ_f\ O_2(g)$

$\Delta H^\circ_{rxn} = 4(-393.5\text{ kJ}) + 5(-285.83\text{ kJ}) - (-147.6\text{ kJ}) - 13/2(0) = -2855.6 = -2856\text{ kJ/mol } C_4H_{10}$

$$1.0\text{ g } C_4H_{10} \times \frac{1\text{ mol } C_4H_{10}}{58.123\text{ g } C_4H_{10}} \times \frac{-2855.6\text{ kJ}}{1\text{ mol } C_4H_{10}} = -49\text{ kJ}$$

5.72 (a) $\Delta H^\circ_{rxn} = 2\Delta H^\circ_f\ H_2O(g) + \Delta H^\circ_f\ N_2(g) - \Delta H^\circ_f\ N_2O_4(g) - \Delta H^\circ_f\ H_2(g)$

$= 2(-241.82) + 0 - (9.66) - 0 = -493.30$ kJ

(b) $\Delta H^\circ_{rxn} = \Delta H^\circ_f\ K_2CO_3(s) + \Delta H^\circ_f\ H_2O(g) - 2\Delta H^\circ_f\ KOH(s) - \Delta H^\circ_f\ CO_2(g)$

$= -1150.18\text{ kJ} - 241.82\text{ kJ} - 2(-424.7)\text{ kJ} - (-393.5\text{ kJ}) = -149.1$ kJ

(c) $\Delta H^\circ_{rxn} = 3/8\Delta H^\circ_f\ S_8(s) + 2\Delta H^\circ_f\ H_2O(g) - \Delta H^\circ_f\ SO_2(g) - 2\Delta H^\circ_f\ H_2S(g)$

$= 3/8(0) + 2(-241.82) - (-269.9) - 2(-20.17) = -173.4$ kJ

(d) $\Delta H^\circ_{rxn} = 2\Delta H^\circ_f\ FeCl_3(s) + 3\Delta H^\circ_f\ H_2O(g) - \Delta H^\circ_f\ Fe_2O_3(s) - 6\Delta H^\circ_f\ HCl(g)$

$= 2(-400\text{ kJ}) + 3(-241.82\text{ kJ}) - (-822.16\text{ kJ}) - 6(-92.30\text{ kJ}) = -149.5$ kJ

5.74 $\Delta H^\circ_{rxn} = \Delta H^\circ_f\ Ca(OH)_2(s) + \Delta H^\circ_f\ C_2H_2(g) - 2\Delta H^\circ_f\ H_2O(l) - \Delta H^\circ_f\ CaC_2(s)$

$-127.2\text{ kJ} = -986.2\text{ kJ} + 226.7\text{ kJ} - 2(-285.83\text{ kJ}) - \Delta H^\circ_f\ CaC_2(s)$

ΔH°_f for $CaC_2(s) = -60.6$ kJ

5.76 (a)

$2B(s) + 3/2\ O_2(g) \rightarrow B_2O_3(s)$	$\Delta H^\circ = 1/2(-2509.1\text{ kJ})$
$3H_2(g) + 3/2\ O_2(g) \rightarrow 3H_2O(l)$	$\Delta H^\circ = 3/2(-571.7\text{ kJ})$
$B_2O_3(s) + 3H_2O(l) \rightarrow B_2H_6(g) + 3O_2(g)$	$\Delta H^\circ = -(-2147.5\text{ kJ})$
$2B(s) + 3H_2(g) \rightarrow B_2H_6(g)$	$\Delta H^\circ_f = +35.4$ kJ

(b) If, like B_2H_6, the combustion of B_5H_9 produces B_2O_3 as the boron-containing product, the heat of combustion of B_5H_9 in addition to data given in part (a) would enable calculation of the heat of formation of B_5H_9.

The combustion reaction is: $B_5H_9(l) + 6O_2(g) \rightarrow 5/2\ B_2O_3(s) + 9/2\ H_2O(l)$

$5/4\ [4B(s) + 3O_2(g) \rightarrow 2B_2O_3(s)]$	$\Delta H = 5/4(-2509.1\ kJ)$
$9/4\ [2H_2(g) + O_2(g) \rightarrow 2H_2O(l)]$	$\Delta H = 9/4\ (-571.7\ kJ)$
$5/2\ B_2O_3(s) + 9/2\ H_2O(l) \rightarrow B_5H_9(l) + 6O_2(g)$	ΔH = - (heat of combustion)
$5B(s) + 9/2\ H_2(g) \rightarrow B_5H_9(l)$	ΔH°_f of $B_5H_9(l)$

[$\Delta H^\circ_f\ B_5H_9(l)$ = - [heat of combustion of $B_5H_9(l)$] - 3136.4 kJ - 1286 kJ]

We need to measure the heat of combustion of $B_5H_9(l)$.

5.78 (a) $10C(s) + 4H_2(g) \rightarrow C_{10}H_8(s)$ formation

$C_{10}H_8(s) + 12O_2(g) \rightarrow 10CO_2(g) + 4H_2O(l)$ combustion, $\Delta H^\circ = -5154\ kJ$

(b) $\Delta H^\circ_{rxn} = 10\Delta H^\circ_f\ CO_2(g) + 4\Delta H^\circ_f\ H_2O(l) - \Delta H^\circ_f\ C_{10}H_8 - 12\Delta H^\circ_f\ O_2(g)$

$-5154 = 10(-393.5\ kJ) + 4(-285.83\ kJ) - \Delta H^\circ_f\ C_{10}H_8(s) - 12(0)$

$\Delta H^\circ_f\ C_{10}H_8(s) = 10(-393.5\ kJ) + 4(-285.83\ kJ) + 5154\ kJ = 76\ kJ$

Check. The result has 0 decimal places because the heat of combustion has 0 decimal places.

Foods and Fuels

5.80 (a) Fats are appropriate for fuel storage because they are insoluble in water (and body fluids) and have a high fuel value.

(b) Combustion analysis is a poor measure of the fuel value of proteins, since the products of protein combustion in the body are different than the products of combustion in a calorimeter. That is, we are not measuring ΔH for the reaction that occurs in the body.

(c) $25\text{ g fat} \times \frac{38\text{ kJ}}{\text{g fat}} = x\text{ g protein} \times \frac{17\text{ kJ}}{\text{g protein}}$; $x = 56$ g protein

5.82 Calculate the fuel value in a pound of M&M® candies.

$96\text{ fat} \times \frac{38\text{ kJ}}{1\text{ g fat}} = 3648\text{ kJ} = 3.6 \times 10^3\text{ kJ}$

$320\text{ g carbohydrate} \times \frac{17\text{ kJ}}{1\text{ g carbohydrate}} = 5440\text{ kJ} = 5.4 \times 10^3\text{ kJ}$

$21\text{ g protein} \times \frac{17\text{ kJ}}{1\text{ g protein}} = 357\text{ kJ} = 3.6 \times 10^2\text{ kJ}$

total fuel value = 3648 kJ + 5440 kJ + 357 kJ = 9445 kJ = 9.4×10^3 kJ/lb

$$\frac{9445\ \text{kJ}}{\text{lb}} \times \frac{1\ \text{lb}}{453.6\ \text{g}} \times \frac{42\ \text{g}}{\text{serving}} = 874.5\ \text{kJ} = 8.7 \times 10^2\ \text{kJ/serving}$$

$$\frac{874.5\ \text{kJ}}{\text{serving}} \times \frac{1\ \text{kcal}}{4.184\ \text{kJ}} \times \frac{1\ \text{Cal}}{1\ \text{kcal}} = 209.0\ \text{Cal} = 2.1 \times 10^2\ \text{Cal/serving}$$

Check. 210 Cal is the approximate food value of a candy bar so the result is reasonable.

5.84 $$177\ \text{mL} \times \frac{1.0\ \text{g wine}}{1\ \text{mL}} \times \frac{0.106\ \text{g ethanol}}{1\ \text{g wine}} \times \frac{1\ \text{mol ethanol}}{46.1\ \text{g ethanol}} \times \frac{1367\ \text{kJ}}{1\ \text{mol ethanol}} \times \frac{1\ \text{Cal}}{4.184\ \text{kJ}}$$

$$= 133 = 1.3 \times 10^2\ \text{Cal}$$

Check. A "typical" 6 oz. glass of wine has 150-250 Cal, so this is a reasonable result. Note that alcohol is responsible for most of the food value of wine.

5.86 $$\Delta H^\circ_{rxn} = \Delta H^\circ_f\ CO_2(g) + 2\Delta H^\circ_f\ H_2O(g) - \Delta H^\circ_f\ CH_4(g) - \Delta H^\circ_f\ O_2(g)$$

$$= -393.5\ \text{kJ} + 2(-241.82\ \text{kJ}) - (-74.8\ \text{kJ}) - 0\ \text{kJ} = -802.3\ \text{kJ}$$

$$\Delta H^\circ_{rxn} = \Delta H^\circ_f\ CF_4(g) + 4\Delta H^\circ_f\ HF(g) - \Delta H^\circ_f\ CH_4(g) - 4\Delta H^\circ_f\ F_2(g)$$

$$= -679.9\ \text{kJ} + 4(-268.61\ \text{kJ}) - (-74.8\ \text{kJ}) - 0\ \text{kJ} = -1679.5\ \text{kJ}$$

The second reaction is twice as exothermic as the first. The "fuel values" of hydrocarbons in a fluorine atmosphere are approximately twice those in an oxygen atmosphere. Note that the difference in ΔH° values for the two reactions is in the ΔH°_f for the products, since the ΔH°_f for the reactants are identical.

Additional Exercises

5.88 (a) $E_p = mgh = 52.0\ \text{kg} \times 9.81\ \text{m/s}^2 \times 10.8\ \text{m} = 5509.3\ \text{J} = 5.51\ \text{kJ}$

(b) $E_k = 1/2\ mv^2;\ v = (2E_k/m)^{1/2} = \left(\frac{2 \times 5509\ \text{kg}\cdot\text{m}^2/\text{s}^2}{52.0\ \text{kg}}\right)^{1/2} = 14.6\ \text{m/s}$

(c) Yes, the diver does work on entering (pushing back) the water in the pool.

5.89 In the process described, one mole of solid CO_2 is converted to one mole of gaseous CO_2. The volume of the gas is much greater than the volume of the solid. Thus the system (that is, the mole of CO_2) must work against atmospheric pressure when it expands. To accomplish this work while maintaining a constant temperature requires the absorption of additional heat beyond that required to increase the internal energy of the CO_2. The remaining energy is turned into work.

5.91 Freezing is an exothermic process (the opposite of melting, which is clearly endothermic). When the system, the soft drink, freezes, it releases energy to the surroundings, the can. Some of this energy does the work of splitting the can.

5.92 Equation 5.5 describes energy changes to the system. Specifically, it says any change in the internal energy of the system is manifested as heat transfer or work. The first law requires that an equal but opposite change occur to the surroundings.

$$\Delta E_{sys} = -\Delta E_{surr}$$

$$q_{sys} + w_{sys} = -(q_{surr} + w_{surr})$$

5.94 $\Delta E = q + w = +38.95 \text{ kJ} - 2.47 \text{ kJ} = +36.48 \text{ kJ}$

$\Delta H = q_p = +38.95 \text{ kJ}$

5.95 If a function sometimes depends on path, then it is simply not a state function. Enthalpy is a state function, so ΔH for the two pathways leading to the same change of state pictured in Figure 5.10 must be the same. However, q is not the same for both. Our conclusion must be that $\Delta H \neq q$ for these pathways. The condition for $\Delta H = q_p$ (other than constant pressure) is that the only possible work on or by the system is pressure-volume work. Clearly, the work being done in this scenario is not pressure-volume work, so $\Delta H \neq q$, even though the two changes occur at constant pressure.

5.97 (a) $$q_{Cu} = \frac{0.385 \text{ J}}{\text{g}\bullet\text{K}} \times 121.0 \text{ g Cu} \times (30.1°\text{C} - 100.4°\text{C}) = -3274.9 = -3.27 \times 10^3 \text{ J}$$

The negative sign indicates the 3.27×10^3 J are lost by the Cu block.

(b) $$q_{H_2O} = \frac{4.184 \text{ J}}{\text{g}\bullet\text{K}} \times 150.0 \text{ g } H_2O \times (30.1°\text{C} - 25.1°\text{C}) = 3138 = +3.1 \times 10^3 \text{ J}$$

The positive sign indicates that 3.14×10^3 J are gained by the H_2O.

(c) The difference in the heat lost by the Cu and the heat gained by the water is $3.275 \times 10^3 \text{ J} - 3.138 \times 10^3 \text{ J} = 0.137 \times 10^3 \text{ J} = 1 \times 10^2 \text{ J}$. The temperature change of the calorimeter is 5.0°C. The heat capacity of the calorimeter in J/K is $$0.137 \times 10^3 \text{ J} \times \frac{1}{5.0°\text{C}} = 27.4 = 3 \times 10 \text{ J/K}.$$

Since q_{H_2O} is known to 1 dec. place, the difference has 1 dec. place and the result has 1 sig fig.

If the rounded results from (a) and (b) are used, $$C_{calorimeter} = \frac{0.2 \times 10^3 \text{ J}}{5.0 \text{ °C}} = 4 \times 10 \text{ J/K}.$$

(d) $$q_{H_2O} = 3.275 \times 10^3 \text{ J} = \frac{4.184 \text{ J}}{\text{g}\bullet\text{K}} \times 150.0 \text{ g} \times (\Delta T)$$

$\Delta T = 5.22°\text{C}$; $T_f = 25.1°\text{C} + 5.22°\text{C} = 30.3°\text{C}$

5.98 (a) From the mass of benzoic acid that produces a certain temperature change, we can calculate the heat capacity of the calorimeter.

$$\frac{0.235 \text{ g benzoic acid}}{1.642°\text{C change observed}} \times \frac{26.38 \text{ kJ}}{1 \text{ g benzoic acid}} = 3.7755 = 3.78 \text{ kJ/°C}$$

Now we can use this experimentally determined heat capacity with the data for caffeine.

$$\frac{1.525°\text{C rise}}{0.265\text{ g caffeine}} \times \frac{3.7755\text{ kJ}}{1°\text{C}} \times \frac{194.2\text{ g caffeine}}{1\text{ mol caffeine}} = 4.22 \times 10^3\text{ kJ/mol caffeine}$$

(b) The overall uncertainty is approximately equal to the sum of the uncertainties due to each effect. The uncertainty in the mass measurement is 0.001/0.235 or 0.001/0.265, about 1 part in 235 or 1 part in 265. The uncertainty in the temperature measurements is 0.002/1.642 or 0.002/1.525, about 1 part in 820 or 1 part in 760. Thus the uncertainty in heat of combustion from each measurement is

$$\frac{4220}{235} = 18\text{ kJ};\quad \frac{4220}{265} = 16\text{ kJ};\quad \frac{4220}{820} = 5\text{ kJ};\quad \frac{4220}{760} = 6\text{ kJ}$$

The sum of these uncertainties is 45 kJ. In fact, the overall uncertainty is less than this because independent errors in measurement do tend to partially cancel.

5.99 $\Delta E_p = m\,g\,\Delta h$. Be careful with units. $1\text{ J} = 1\text{ kg} \cdot \text{m}^2/\text{s}^2$

$$200\text{ lb} \times \frac{2.205\text{ kg}}{1\text{ lb}} \times \frac{9.81\text{ m}}{\text{s}^2} \times \frac{45\text{ ft}}{\text{time}} \times \frac{1\text{ yd}}{3\text{ ft}} \times \frac{1\text{ m}}{1.0936\text{ yd}} \times 20\text{ times}$$

$$= 1.87 \times 10^6\text{ kg} \cdot \text{m}^2/\text{s}^2 = 1.187 \times 10^6\text{ J} = 1.2 \times 10^3\text{ kJ}$$

1 Cal = 1 kcal = 4.184 kJ

$$1.187 \times 10^3\text{ kJ} \times \frac{1\text{ Cal}}{4.184\text{ kJ}} = 283.6 = 2.8 \times 10^2\text{ Cal}$$

If all work is used to increase the man's potential energy, 20 rounds of stair-climbing should compensate for one extra order of 245 Cal fries. In fact, more than 280 Cal of work will be required to climb the stairs, because some energy will be lost as heat (see Solution 5.93).

5.101 For nitroethane:

$$\frac{1368\text{ kJ}}{1\text{ mol } C_2H_5NO_2} \times \frac{1\text{ mol } C_2H_5NO_2}{75.072\text{ g } C_2H_5NO_2} \times \frac{1.052\text{ g } C_2H_5NO_2}{1\text{ cm}^3} = 19.17\text{ kJ/cm}^3$$

For ethanol:

$$\frac{1367\text{ kJ}}{1\text{ mol } C_2H_5OH} \times \frac{1\text{ mol } C_2H_5OH}{46.069\text{ g } C_2H_5OH} \times \frac{0.789\text{ g } C_2H_5OH}{1\text{ cm}^3} = 23.4\text{ kJ/cm}^3$$

For methylhydrazine:

$$\frac{1305\text{ kJ}}{1\text{ mol } CH_6N_2} \times \frac{1\text{ mol } CH_6N_2}{46.072\text{ g } CH_6N_2} \times \frac{0.874\text{ g } CH_6N_2}{1\text{ cm}^3} = 24.8\text{ kJ/cm}^3$$

Thus, **methylhydrazine** would provide the most energy per unit volume, with ethanol a close second.

5.102 (a) $3C_2H_2(g) \rightarrow C_6H_6(l)$

$\Delta H^\circ_{rxn} = \Delta H^\circ_f\ C_6H_6(l) - 3\Delta H^\circ_f\ C_2H_2(g) = 49.0\ kJ - 3(226.7\ kJ) = -631.1\ kJ$

(b) Since the reaction is exothermic (ΔH is negative), the product, 1 mole of $C_6H_6(l)$, has less enthalpy than the reactants, 3 moles of $C_2H_2(g)$.

(c) The fuel value of a substance is the amount of heat (kJ) produced when 1 gram of the substance is burned. Calculate the molar heat of combustion (kJ/mol) and use this to find kJ/g of fuel.

$C_2H_2(g) + 5/2\ O_2(g) \rightarrow 2CO_2(g) + H_2O(l)$

$\Delta H^\circ_{rxn} = 2\Delta H^\circ_f\ CO_2(g) + \Delta H^\circ_f\ H_2O(l) - \Delta H^\circ_f\ C_2H_2(g) - 5/2\ \Delta H^\circ_f\ O_2(g)$

$= 2(-393.5\ kJ) + (-285.83\ kJ) - 226.7\ kJ - 5/2\ (0) = -1299.5\ kJ/mol\ C_2H_2$

$$\frac{-1299.5\ kJ}{1\ mol\ C_2H_2} \times \frac{1\ mol\ C_2H_2}{26.036\ g\ C_2H_2} = 49.912 = 50\ kJ/g$$

$C_6H_6(g) + 15/2\ O_2(g) \rightarrow 6CO_2(g) + 3H_2O(l)$

$\Delta H^\circ_{rxn} = 6\Delta H^\circ_f\ CO_2(g) + 3\Delta H^\circ_f\ H_2O(l) - \Delta H^\circ_f\ C_6H_6(l) - 15/2\ \Delta H^\circ_f\ O_2(g)$

$= 6(-393.5\ kJ) + 3(-285.83\ kJ) - 49.0\ kJ - 15/2\ (0) = -3267.5\ kJ/mol\ C_6H_6$

$$\frac{-3267.5\ kJ}{1\ mol\ C_6H_6} \times \frac{1\ mol\ C_6H_6}{78.114\ g\ C_6H_6} = 41.830 = 42\ kJ/g$$

5.104 (a) $C_6H_{12}O_6(s) + 6O_2(g) \rightarrow 6CO_2(g) + 6H_2O(l)$

$\Delta H^\circ_{rxn} = 6\Delta H^\circ_f\ CO_2(g) + 6\Delta H^\circ_f\ H_2O(l) - \Delta H^\circ_f\ C_6H_{12}O_6(s) - 6\Delta H^\circ_f\ O_2(g)$

$= 6(-393.5\ kJ) + 6(-285.83\ kJ) - (-1273\ kJ) - 6(0)$

$= -2803\ kJ/mol\ C_6H_{12}O_6$

$C_{12}H_{22}O_{11}(s) + 12O_2(g) \rightarrow 12CO_2(g) + 11H_2O(l)$

$\Delta H^\circ_{rxn} = 12\Delta H^\circ_f\ CO_2(g) + 11\Delta H^\circ_f\ H_2O(l) - \Delta H^\circ_f\ C_{12}H_{22}O_{11}(s) - 12\Delta H^\circ_f\ O_2(g)$

$= 12(-393.5\ kJ) + 11(-285.83\ kJ) - (-2221\ kJ) -12(0)$

$= -5645\ kJ/mol\ C_{12}H_{22}O_{11}$

(b) $$\frac{-2803\ kJ}{1\ mol\ C_6H_{12}O_6} \times \frac{1\ mol\ C_6H_{12}O_6}{180.2\ g\ C_6H_{12}O_6} = -\frac{15.55\ kJ}{1\ g\ C_6H_{12}O_6} \rightarrow 16\ kJ/g\ C_6H_{12}O_6\ \text{(fuel value)}$$

$$\frac{-5645\ kJ}{1\ mol\ C_{12}H_{22}O_{11}} \times \frac{1\ mol\ C_{12}H_{22}O_{11}}{342.3\ g\ C_{12}H_{22}O_{11}} = -\frac{16.49\ kJ}{1\ g\ C_{12}H_{22}O_{11}} \rightarrow 16\ kJ/g\ C_{12}H_{22}O_{11}\ \text{(fuel value)}$$

(c) The average fuel value of carbohydrates (Section 5.8) is 17 kJ/g. These two carbohydrates have fuel values (16 kJ/g) slightly lower but in line with this average. (More complex carbohydrates supply more energy and raise the average value.)

5.105 (a) $6CO_2(g) + 6H_2O(l) \rightarrow C_6H_{12}O_6(s) + 6O_2(g)$, $\Delta H° = 2803$ kJ

This is the reverse of the combustion of glucose (Section 5.8 and Solution 5.104), so $\Delta H° = -(-2803)$ kJ = +2803 kJ.

$$\frac{5.5 \times 10^{16}\ g\ CO_2}{yr} \times \frac{1\ mol\ CO_2}{44.01\ g\ CO_2} \times \frac{2803\ kJ}{6\ mol\ CO_2} = 5.838 \times 10^{17} = 5.8 \times 10^{17}\ kJ$$

(b) 1 W = 1 J/s; 1 W • s = 1 J

$$\frac{5.838 \times 10^{17}\ kJ}{yr} \times \frac{1000\ J}{kJ} \times \frac{1\ yr}{365\ d} \times \frac{1\ d}{24\ hr} \times \frac{1\ hr}{60\ min} \times \frac{1\ min}{60\ s} \times \frac{1\ W \bullet s}{J}$$

$$\times \frac{1\ MW}{1 \times 10^5\ W} = 1.851 \times 10^7\ MW = 1.9 \times 10^7\ MW$$

$$1.9 \times 10^7\ MW \times \frac{1\ plant}{10^3\ MW} = 1.9 \times 10^4 = 19{,}000 \text{ nuclear power plants}$$

5.106 The reaction for which we want ΔH is:

$$4NH_3(l) + 3O_2(g) \rightarrow 2N_2(g) + 6H_2O(g)$$

Before we can calculate ΔH for this reaction, we must calculate ΔH_f for $NH_3(l)$.

We know that ΔH_f for $NH_3(g)$ is -46.2 kJ, and that for $NH_3(l) \rightarrow NH_3(g)$, ΔH = 23.2 kJ

Thus, $\Delta H_{vap} = \Delta H_f\ NH_3(g) - \Delta H_f\ NH_3(l)$.

$23.2\ kJ = -46.2\ kJ - \Delta H_f\ NH_3(l)$; $\Delta H_f\ NH_3(l) = -69.4$ kJ/mol

Then for the overall reaction, the enthalpy change is:

$\Delta H_{rxn} = 6\Delta H_f\ H_2O(g) + 2\Delta H_f\ N_2(g) - 4\Delta H_f\ NH_3(l) - 3\Delta H_f\ O_2$

$= 6(-241.82\ kJ) + 2(0) - 4(-69.4\ kJ) - 3(0) = -1173.3$ kJ

$$\frac{-1173.3\ kJ}{4\ mol\ NH_3} \times \frac{1\ mol\ NH_3}{17.0\ g\ NH_3} \times \frac{0.81\ g\ NH_3}{1\ cm^3} \times \frac{1000\ cm^3}{1\ L} = \frac{1.4 \times 10^4\ kJ}{L\ NH_3}$$

(This result has 2 significant figures because the density is expressed to 2 figures.)

$2CH_3OH(l) + 3O_2(g) \rightarrow 2CO_2(g) + 4H_2O(g)$

$\Delta H = 2(-393.5\ kJ) + 4(-241.82\ kJ) - 2(-239\ kJ) - 3(0) = -1276$ kJ

$$\frac{-1276\ kJ}{2\ mol\ CH_3OH} \times \frac{1\ mol\ CH_3OH}{32.04\ g\ CH_3OH} \times \frac{0.792\ g\ CH_3OH}{1\ cm^3} \times \frac{1000\ cm^3}{1\ L} = \frac{1.58 \times 10^4\ kJ}{1\ L\ CH_3OH}$$

In terms of heat obtained per unit volume of fuel, methanol is a slightly better fuel than liquid ammonia.

Integrative Exercises

5.108 The situation in Figure 4.3 is a more complex version of that pictured in Exercise 5.24 and discussed in Solution 5.24. An ionic solid is an orderly arrangement of closely spaced ions, oppositely charged particles. The potential energy of any pair of these ions is described as $E_{el} = \kappa\ Q_1Q_2/r^2$. Separating these oppositely charged particles leads to an increase in the energy of the system, + ΔE. Work is done to the NaCl by the water molecules. Since both NaCl and water are part of the system, the net amount of work is zero. Since $\Delta E = q + w$, $\Delta E = q$ and both are positive. The dissolving process typically takes place at constant atmospheric pressure, so $\Delta H = q$ and ΔH is also positive.

To verify this conclusion, carry out the dissolution of NaCl in a constant pressure calorimeter. Begin with 1 L of H_2O, record the temperature, add 0.1 mol NaCl and dissolve completely; record the final temperature. If ΔH is positive, the temperature will increase.

5.109 (a),(b) $Ag^+(aq) + Li(s) \rightarrow Ag(s) + Li^+(aq)$

$\Delta H^\circ = \Delta H_f^\circ\ Li^+(aq) - \Delta H_f^\circ\ Ag^+(aq)$

$= -278.5\ kJ - 105.90\ kJ = -384.4\ kJ$

$Fe(s) + 2Na^+(aq) \rightarrow Fe^{2+}(aq) + 2Na(s)$

$\Delta H^\circ = \Delta H_f^\circ\ Fe^{2+}(aq) - 2\Delta H_f^\circ\ Na^+(aq)$

$= -87.86\ kJ - 2(-240.1\ kJ) = +392.3\ kJ$

$2K(s) + 2H_2O(l) \rightarrow 2KOH(aq) + H_2(g)$

$\Delta H^\circ = 2\Delta H_f^\circ\ KOH(aq) - 2\Delta H_f^\circ\ H_2O(l)$

$= 2(-482.4\ kJ) - 2(-285.83\ kJ) = -393.1\ kJ$

(c) Exothermic reactions are more likely to be favorable, so the first and third reactions should be favorable and the second reaction should be unfavorable.

(d) In the activity series of metals, Table 4.5, any metal can be oxidized by the cation of a metal below it on the table.

Ag^+ is below Li, so the first reaction will occur.
Na^+ is above Fe, so the second reaction will not occur.
H^+ (formally in H_2O) is below K, so the third reaction will occur.
These predictions agree with those in part (c).

5.110 (a) $\Delta H^\circ = \Delta H_f^\circ\ NaNO_3(aq) + \Delta H_f^\circ\ H_2O(l) - \Delta H_f^\circ\ HNO_3(aq) - \Delta H_f^\circ\ NaOH(aq)$

$\Delta H^\circ = -446.2\ kJ - 285.83\ kJ - (-206.6\ kJ) - (-469.6\ kJ) = -55.8\ kJ$

$\Delta H^\circ = \Delta H_f^\circ\ NaCl(aq) + \Delta H_f^\circ\ H_2O(l) - \Delta H_f^\circ\ HCl(aq) - \Delta H_f^\circ\ NaOH(aq)$

$\Delta H^\circ = -407.1\ kJ - 285.83\ kJ - (-167.2\ kJ) - (-469.6\ kJ) = -56.1\ kJ$

$\Delta H^\circ = \Delta H_f^\circ\ NH_3(aq) + \Delta H_f^\circ\ Na^+(aq) + \Delta H_f^\circ\ H_2O(l) - \Delta H_f^\circ\ NH_4^+(aq) - \Delta H_f^\circ\ NaOH(aq)$

$= -80.29\ kJ - 240.1\ kJ - 285.83\ kJ - (-132.5\ kJ) - (-469.6\ kJ) = -4.1\ kJ$

(b) $H^+(aq) + OH^-(aq) \rightarrow H_2O(l)$ is the net ionic equation for both reactions.

(c) The ΔH° values for the first two reactions are nearly identical, -55.9 kJ and -56.2 kJ. The spectator ions by definition do not change during the course of a reaction, so ΔH° is the enthalpy change for the net ionic equation. Since the first two reactions have the same net ionic equation, it is not surprising that they have the same ΔH°.

(d) Strong acids are more likely than weak acids to donate H^+. The neutralization of the two strong acids is energetically favorable, while the third reaction is not. $NH_4^+(aq)$ is probably a weak acid.

5.112 (a) $AgNO_3(aq) + NaCl(aq) \rightarrow NaNO_3(aq) + AgCl(s)$

net ionic equation: $Ag^+(aq) + Cl^-(aq) \rightarrow AgCl(s)$

$\Delta H^\circ = \Delta H^\circ_f\ AgCl(s) - \Delta H^\circ_f\ Ag^+(aq) - \Delta H^\circ_f\ Cl^-(aq)$

$\Delta H^\circ = -127.0\ kJ - (105.90\ kJ) - (-167.2\ kJ) = -65.7\ kJ$

(b) ΔH° for the complete molecular equation will be the same as ΔH° for the net ionic equation. $Na^+(aq)$ and $NO_3^-(aq)$ are spectator ions; they appear on both sides of the chemical equation. Since the overall enthalpy change is the enthalpy of the products minus the enthalpy of the reactants, the contributions of the spectator ions cancel.

(c) $\Delta H^\circ = \Delta H^\circ_f\ NaNO_3(aq) + \Delta H^\circ_f\ AgCl(s) - \Delta H^\circ_f\ AgNO_3(aq) - \Delta H^\circ_f\ NaCl(aq)$

$\Delta H^\circ_f\ AgNO_3(aq) = \Delta H^\circ_f\ NaNO_3(aq) + \Delta H^\circ_f\ AgCl(s) - \Delta H^\circ_f\ NaCl(aq) - \Delta H^\circ$

$\Delta H^\circ_f\ AgNO_3(aq) = -446.2\ kJ + (-127.0\ kJ) - (-407.1\ kJ) - (-65.7\ kJ)$

$\Delta H^\circ_f\ AgNO_3(aq) = -100.4\ kJ/mol$

5.113 (a) $$21.83\ g\ CO_2 \times \frac{1\ mol\ CO_2}{44.01\ g\ CO_2} \times \frac{1\ mol\ C}{1\ mol\ CO_2} \times \frac{12.01\ g\ C}{1\ mol\ C} = 5.9572 = 5.957\ g\ C$$

$$4.47\ g\ H_2O \times \frac{1\ mol\ H_2O}{18.02\ g\ H_2O} \times \frac{2\ mol\ H}{1\ mol\ H_2O} \times \frac{1.008\ g\ H}{mol\ H} = 0.5001 = 0.500\ g\ H$$

The sample mass is (5.9572 + 0.5001) = 6.457 g

(b) $$5.957\ g\ C \times \frac{1\ mol\ C}{12.01\ g\ C} = 0.4960\ mol\ C;\ \ 0.4960/0.496 = 1$$

$$0.500\ g\ H \times \frac{1\ mol\ H}{1.008\ g\ H} = 0.496\ mol\ H;\ \ 0.496/0.496 = 1$$

The empirical formula of the hydrocarbon is CH.

(c) Calculate the ΔH°_f for 6.457 g of the sample.

6.457 g sample + $O_2(g) \rightarrow$ 21.83 g $CO_2(g)$ + 4.47 g $H_2O(g)$, $\Delta H^\circ = -311\ kJ$

$\Delta H^\circ_{comb} = \Delta H^\circ_f\ CO_2(g) + \Delta H^\circ_f\ H_2O(g) - \Delta H^\circ_f\ sample - \Delta H^\circ_f\ O_2(g)$

$\Delta H^\circ_f\ sample = \Delta H^\circ_f\ CO_2(g) + \Delta H^\circ_f\ H_2O(g) - \Delta H^\circ_{comb}$

$$\Delta H^\circ_f\ CO_2(g) = 21.83\ g\ CO_2 \times \frac{1\ mol\ CO_2}{44.01\ g\ CO_2} \times \frac{-393.5\ kJ}{mol\ CO_2} = -195.185 = -195.2\ kJ$$

ΔH°_f $H_2O(g)$ = 4.47 g H_2O × $\frac{1 \text{ mol } H_2O}{18.02 \text{ g } H_2O}$ × $\frac{-241.82 \text{ kJ}}{\text{mol } H_2O}$ = 59.985 = -60.0 kJ

ΔH°_f sample = -195.185 kJ - 59.985 kJ - (-311 kJ) = 55.83 = 56 kJ

$\frac{55.83 \text{ kJ}}{6.457 \text{ g sample}} \times \frac{13.02 \text{ g}}{\text{CH unit}}$ = 112.6 = 1.1 × 10^2 kJ/CH unit

(d) The hydrocarbons in Appendix C with empirical formula CH are C_2H_2 and C_6H_6.

substance	ΔH°_f / mol	ΔH°_f / CH unit
$C_2H_2(g)$	226.7 kJ	113.4 kJ
$C_6H_6(g)$	82.9 kJ	13.8 kJ
$C_6H_6(l)$	49.0 kJ	8.17 kJ
sample	1.1 × 10^2 kJ	

The calculated value of ΔH°_f/CH unit for the sample is a good match with acetylene, $C_2H_2(g)$.

5.114 (a) $CH_4(g) \rightarrow C(g) + 4H(g)$ (i) reaction given

$CH_4(g) \rightarrow C(s) + 2H_2(g)$ (ii) reverse of formation

The differences are: the state of C in the products; the chemical form, atoms or diatomic molecules, of H in the products.

(b) i. $\Delta H^\circ = \Delta H^\circ_f$ C(g) + 4ΔH°_f H(g) - ΔH°_f $CH_4(g)$

= 718.4 kJ + 4(217.94) kJ - (-74.8) kJ = 1665.0 kJ

ii. $\Delta H^\circ = \Delta H^\circ_f$ CH_4 = -(-74.8) kJ = 74.8 kJ

The rather large difference in ΔH° values is due to: the enthalpy difference between isolated gaseous C atoms and the orderly, bonded array of C atoms in graphite, C(s); and the enthalpy difference between isolated H atoms and H_2 molecules. In other words, the difference in the enthalpy stored in chemical bonds in C(s) and $H_2(g)$ versus the corresponding isolated atoms.

(c) $CH_4(g) + 4F_2(g) \rightarrow CF_4(g) + 4HF(g)$ ΔH° = -1679.5 kJ

The ΔH° value for this reaction was calculated in Solution 5.86.

3.45 g CH_4 × $\frac{1 \text{ mol } CH_4}{16.04 \text{ g } CH_4}$ = 0.21509 = 0.215 mol CH_4

1.22 g F_2 × $\frac{1 \text{ mol } F_2}{38.00 \text{ g } F_2}$ = 0.03211 = 0.0321 mol F_2

There are fewer mol F_2 than CH_4, but 4 mol F_2 are required for every 1 mol of CH_4 reacted, so clearly F_2 is the limiting reactant.

0.03211 mol F_2 × $\frac{-1679.5 \text{ kJ}}{4 \text{ mol } F_2}$ = -13.48 = -13.5 kJ heat evolved

6 Electronic Structure of Atoms

Radiant Energy

6.2 (a) Wavelength (λ) and frequency (ν) are inversely proportional; the proportionality constant is the speed of light (c). $\nu = c/\lambda$.

(b) Light in the 210-230 nm range is in the ultraviolet region of the spectrum. These wavelengths are slightly shorter than the 400 nm short-wavelength boundary of the visible region.

6.4 (a) False. Electromagnetic radiation passes through water. See Figure 13.27.
(b) True.
(c) False. Infrared light has lower frequencies than visible light.
(d) False. A foghorn blast is a form of sound waves.

6.6 Wavelength of (a) gamma rays < (d) yellow (visible) light < (e) red (visible) light < (b) 93.1 MHz FM (radio) waves < (c) 680 kHz or 0.680 MHz AM (radio) waves

6.8 (a) $\nu = c/\lambda;\ \dfrac{2.998 \times 10^8\ \text{m}}{\text{s}} \times \dfrac{1}{589\ \text{nm}} \times \dfrac{1\ \text{nm}}{1 \times 10^{-9}\ \text{m}} = 5.10 \times 10^{14}\ \text{s}^{-1}$

(b) $\lambda = c/\nu;\ \dfrac{2.998 \times 10^8\ \text{m}}{\text{s}} \times \dfrac{1\ \text{s}}{1.2 \times 10^{13}} = 2.5 \times 10^{-5}\ \text{m}$

(c) Yes. The radiation in (b) is in the infrared range.

(d) $10\ \mu\text{s} \times \dfrac{1 \times 10^{-6}\ \text{s}}{1\ \mu\text{s}} \times \dfrac{2.998 \times 10^8\ \text{m}}{\text{s}} = 3.0 \times 10^3\ \text{m}$ (3.0 km)

6.10 $\nu = c/\lambda;\ \dfrac{2.998 \times 10^8\ \text{m}}{1\ \text{s}} \times \dfrac{1}{489\ \text{nm}} \times \dfrac{1\ \text{nm}}{1 \times 10^{-9}\ \text{m}} = 6.13 \times 10^{14}\ \text{s}^{-1}$

The laser emits visible light; the color is green to blue-green.

Quantized Energy and Photons

6.12 Planck's original hypothesis was that energy could only be gained or lost in discreet amounts (quanta) with a certain minimum size. The size of the minimum energy change is related to the frequency of the radiation absorbed or emitted, $\Delta E = h\nu$, and energy changes occur only in multiples of $h\nu$.

Einstein postulated that light itself is quantized, that the minimum energy of a photon (a quantum of light) is directly proportional to its frequency, E = hν. If a photon that strikes a metal surface has less than the threshold energy, no electron is emitted from the surface. If the photon has energy equal to or greater than the threshold energy, an electron is emitted and any excess energy becomes the kinetic energy of the electron.

6.14 (a) $E = hc/\lambda = 6.626 \times 10^{-34}\ J\cdot s \times \dfrac{2.998 \times 10^{8}\ m}{1\ s} \times \dfrac{1}{3.80\ mm} \times \dfrac{1\ mm}{1 \times 10^{-3}\ m}$

$= 5.23 \times 10^{-23}\ J$

$Hz = s^{-1}$

(b) $E = h\nu = 6.626 \times 10^{-34}\ J \cdot s \times \dfrac{80.5 \times 10^{6}}{1\ s} = 5.33 \times 10^{-26}\ J$

(c) $\nu = E/h = \dfrac{1.77 \times 10^{-19}\ J}{6.626 \times 10^{-34}\ J\cdot s} = 2.67 \times 10^{14}\ s^{-1}$

$\lambda = hc/E = 1.12 \times 10^{-6}\ m$; the radiation is infrared but near the visible "edge."

6.16 $E = h\nu$

AM: $6.626 \times 10^{-34}\ J\cdot s \times \dfrac{1440 \times 10^{3}}{1\ s} = 9.54 \times 10^{-28}\ J$

FM: $6.626 \times 10^{-34}\ J\cdot s \times \dfrac{94.5 \times 10^{6}}{1\ s} = 6.26 \times 10^{-26}\ J$

The FM photon has about 66 times more energy than the AM photon.

6.18 $\dfrac{495 \times 10^{3}\ J}{mol\ O_2} \times \dfrac{1\ mol}{6.022 \times 10^{23}\ photons} = 8.220 \times 10^{-19} = 8.22 \times 10^{-19}\ J/photon$

$\lambda = hc/E = \dfrac{6.626 \times 10^{-34}\ J\cdot s}{8.220 \times 10^{-19}\ J} \times \dfrac{2.998 \times 10^{8}\ m}{1\ s} = 2.42 \times 10^{-7}\ m = 242\ nm$

According to Figure 6.4, this is ultraviolet radiation.

6.20 $E_{photon} = hc/\lambda = \dfrac{6.626 \times 10^{-34}\ J \cdot s}{1350 \times 10^{-9}\ m} \times \dfrac{2.998 \times 10^{8}\ m}{1\ s} = 1.4715 \times 10^{-19} = 1.47 \times 10^{-19}\ J/photon$

$\dfrac{1.4715 \times 10^{-19}\ J}{1\ photon} \times \dfrac{8 \times 10^{7}\ photons}{1\ s} \times \dfrac{60\ s}{1\ min} \times \dfrac{60\ min}{1\ hr} = 4.24 \times 10^{-8} = 4 \times 10^{-8}\ J/hr$

6.22 (a) $\nu = E/h = \dfrac{4.41 \times 10^{-19}\ J}{6.626 \times 10^{-34}\ J\cdot s} = 6.6556 \times 10^{14} = 6.66 \times 10^{14}\ s^{-1}$

(b) $\lambda = hc/E = \dfrac{6.626 \times 10^{-34}\ J\cdot s}{4.41 \times 10^{-19}\ J} \times \dfrac{2.998 \times 10^{8}\ m}{s} = 4.50 \times 10^{-7}\ m = 450\ nm$

(c) $E_{439} = hc/\lambda = \dfrac{6.626 \times 10^{-34}\ J\cdot s}{439 \times 10^{-9}\ m} \times \dfrac{2.998 \times 10^{8}\ m}{s} = 4.525 \times 10^{-19} = 4.53 \times 10^{-19}\ J$

$E_K = E_{439} - E_{min} = 4.525 \times 10^{-19}\ J - 4.41 \times 10^{-19}\ J = 0.115 \times 10^{-19} = 1.1 \times 10^{-20}\ J$

(d) One electron is emitted per photon. Calculate the number of 439 nm photons in 1.00 μJ. The excess energy in each photon will become the kinetic energy of the electron; it cannot be "pooled" to emit additional electrons.

$$1.00\ \mu J \times \frac{1 \times 10^{-6}\ J}{\mu J} \times \frac{1\ \text{photon}}{4.525 \times 10^{-19}\ J} \times \frac{1\ e^-}{1\ \text{photon}} = 2.21 \times 10^{12}\ \text{electrons}$$

Bohr's Model; Matter Waves

6.24 (a) According to Bohr theory, when hydrogen emits radiant energy, electrons are moving from a higher allowed energy state to a lower one. Since only certain energy states are allowed, only certain energy changes can occur. These allowed energy changes correspond ($\lambda = hc/\Delta E$) to the wavelengths of the lines in the emission spectrum of hydrogen.

(b) When a hydrogen atom changes from the ground state to an excited state, the single electron moves further away from the nucleus, so the atom "expands".

6.26 (a) absorbed (b) emitted (c) absorbed.

6.28 (a) $\Delta E = -2.18 \times 10^{-18}\ J \left[\frac{1}{n_f^2} - \frac{1}{n_i^2}\right] = -2.18 \times 10^{-18}\ J\ (1/1 - 1/25) = -2.093 \times 10^{-18}$

$= -2.09 \times 10^{-18}\ J$

$$\nu = E/h = \frac{2.093 \times 10^{-18}\ J}{6.626 \times 10^{-34}\ J \bullet s} = 3.158 \times 10^{15} = 3.16 \times 10^{15}\ s^{-1}$$

$$\lambda = c/\nu = \frac{2.998 \times 10^{8}\ m}{1\ s} \times \frac{1\ s}{3.158 \times 10^{15}} = 9.49 \times 10^{-8}\ m$$

Since the sign of ΔE is negative, radiation is emitted.

(b) $\Delta E = -2.18 \times 10^{-18}\ J(1/4 - 1/16) = -4.0875 \times 10^{-19} = -4.09 \times 10^{-19}\ J$

$$\nu = \frac{4.0875 \times 10^{-19}\ J}{6.626 \times 10^{-34}\ J \bullet s} = 6.1689 \times 10^{14} = 6.17 \times 10^{14}\ s^{-1}\ ;\ \lambda = \frac{2.998 \times 10^{8}\ m/s}{6.1689 \times 10^{14}/s}$$

$\lambda = 4.86 \times 10^{-7}$ m. Visible radiation is emitted.

(c) $\Delta E = -2.18 \times 10^{-18}\ J\ (1/36 - 1/16) = 7.5694 \times 10^{-20} = 7.57 \times 10^{-20}\ J$

$$\nu = \frac{7.5694 \times 10^{-20}\ J}{6.626 \times 10^{-34}\ J \bullet s} = 1.1424 \times 10^{14} = 1.14 \times 10^{14}\ s^{-1}\ ;\ \lambda = \frac{2.998 \times 10^{8}\ m/s}{1.1424 \times 10^{14}/s}$$

$\lambda = 2.62 \times 10^{-6}$ m. Radiation is absorbed.

6.30 (a) Transitions with $n_f = 1$ have larger ΔE values and shorter wavelengths than those with $n_f = 2$. These transitions will lie in the ultraviolet region.

(b) $n_i = 2, n_f = 1;\ \lambda = hc/E = \dfrac{6.626 \times 10^{-34}\ J\bullet s \times 2.998 \times 10^{8}\ m/s}{-2.18 \times 10^{-18}\ J\,(1/1 - 1/4)} = 1.22 \times 10^{-7}\ m$

$n_i = 3, n_f = 1;\ \lambda = hc/E = \dfrac{6.626 \times 10^{-34}\ J\bullet s \times 2.998 \times 10^{8}\ m/s}{-2.18 \times 10^{-18}\ J\,(1/1 - 1/9)} = 1.03 \times 10^{-7}\ m$

$n_i = 4, n_f = 1;\ \lambda = hc/E = \dfrac{6.626 \times 10^{-34}\ J\bullet s \times 2.998 \times 10^{8}\ m/s}{-2.18 \times 10^{-18}\ J\,(1/1 - 1/16)} = 0.972 \times 10^{-7}\ m$

6.32 (a) $4055\ nm \times \dfrac{1 \times 10^{-9}\ m}{1\ nm} = 4.055 \times 10^{-6}\ m$; this line is in the infrared.

(b) Absorption lines with $n_i = 1$ are in the ultraviolet and with $n_i = 2$ are in the visible. Thus, $n_i \geq 3$, but we do not know the exact value of n_i. Calculate the longest wavelength with $n_i = 3$ ($n_f = 4$). If this is less than 4055 nm, $n_i > 3$.

$$\lambda = hc/E = \frac{6.626 \times 10^{-34}\ J\bullet s \times 2.998 \times 10^{8}\ m/s}{-2.18 \times 10^{-18}\ J\,(1/9 - 1/16)} = 1.875 \times 10^{-6}\ m$$

This wavelength is shorter than 4.055×10^{-6} m, so $n_i > 3$; try $n_i = 4$ and solve for n_f as in Solution 6.31.

$$n_f = \left(\frac{1}{n_i^2} - \frac{hc}{\lambda(2.18 \times 10^{-18}\ J)}\right)^{-1/2} = \left(1/16 - \frac{6.626 \times 10^{-34}\ J\bullet s \times 2.998 \times 10^{8}\ m/s}{4.055 \times 10^{-6}\ m \times 2.18 \times 10^{-18}\ J}\right)^{-1/2} = 5$$

$n_f = 5, n_i = 4$

6.34 $\lambda = h/mv$; change mass to kg and velocity to m/s

mass of muon $= 206.8 \times 9.1094 \times 10^{-28}\ g \times \dfrac{1\ kg}{1000\ g} = 1.8838 \times 10^{-28} = 1.88 \times 10^{-28}\ kg$

$$\lambda = \frac{6.626 \times 10^{-34}\ kg\bullet m^2\bullet s}{1\ s^2} \times \frac{1}{1.8838 \times 10^{-28}\ kg} \times \frac{1\ s}{8.85 \times 10^{3}\ m/s} = 3.97 \times 10^{-10}\ m = 3.97\ Å$$

6.36 $m_e = 9.1094 \times 10^{-31}$ kg (back-inside cover of text)

$$\lambda = \frac{6.626 \times 10^{-34}\ kg\bullet m^2\bullet s}{1\ s^2} \times \frac{1}{9.1094 \times 10^{-31}\ kg} \times \frac{1\ s}{5.93 \times 10^{6}\ m} = 1.23 \times 10^{-10}\ m$$

$$1.23 \times 10^{-10}\ m \times \frac{1\ Å}{1 \times 10^{-10}\ m} = 1.23\ Å$$

Since atomic radii and interatomic distances are on the order of 1-5 Å (Section 2.3), the wavelength of this electron is comparable to the size of atoms.

6.38 $\Delta x \geq = h/4\pi m\Delta v$; use masses in kg, Δv in m/s.

(a) $$\frac{6.626 \times 10^{-34}\ \text{J}\bullet\text{s}}{4\pi(9.109 \times 10^{-31}\ \text{kg})(0.01 \times 10^{5}\ \text{m/s})} = 6 \times 10^{-8}\ \text{m}$$

(b) $$\frac{6.626 \times 10^{-34}\ \text{J}\bullet\text{s}}{4\pi(1.675 \times 10^{-27}\ \text{kg})(0.01 \times 10^{5}\ \text{m/s})} = 3 \times 10^{-11}\ \text{m}$$

(c) For particles moving with the same uncertainty in velocity, the more massive neutron has a much smaller uncertainty in position than the lighter electron. In our model of the atom, we know where the massive particles in the nucleus are located, but we cannot know the location of the electrons with any certainty, if we know their speed.

Quantum Mechanics and Atomic Orbitals

6.40 (a) The square of the wave function has the physical significance of an amplitude, or probability. The quantity ψ^2 at a given point in space is the probability of locating the electron within a small volume element around that point at any given instant. The total probability, that is, the sum of ψ^2 over all the space around the nucleus, must equal 1.

(b) Electron density is a way to express the probability of finding an electron in a region of space. The greater the probability (the value of ψ^2), the greater the electron density.

(c) An orbital is one of the wave functions, ψ, that is a solution to Schrödinger's equation for a particular atom. Each orbital has a distinctive energy and shape or electron density distribution.

6.42 (a) For $n = 3$, there are 3 l values (2, 1, 0) and 9 m_l values ($l = 2$; $m_l = -2, -1, 0, 1, 2$; $l = 1$, $m_l = -1, 0, 1$; $l = 0$, $m_l = 0$).

(b) For $n = 5$, there are 5 l values (4, 3, 2, 1, 0) and 25 m_l values ($l = 4$, $m_l = -4$ to $+4$; $l = 3$, $m_l = -3$ to $+3$; $l = 2$, $m_l = -2$ to $+2$; $l = 1$, $m_l = -1$ to $+1$; $l = 0$, $= 0$).

In general, for each principle quantum number n there are nl -values and n^2 m_l-values. For each shell, there are n kinds of orbitals and n^2 total orbitals.

6.44 (a) 2, 1, 1; 2, 1, 0; 2, 1 -1

(b) 5, 2, 2; 5, 2, 1; 5, 2, 0; 5, 2, -1; 5, 2, -2

6.46 (a) permissible, 2p (b) forbidden, for $l = 0$, m_l can only equal 0

(c) permissible, 4d (d) forbidden, for n = 3, the largest l value is 2

6.48

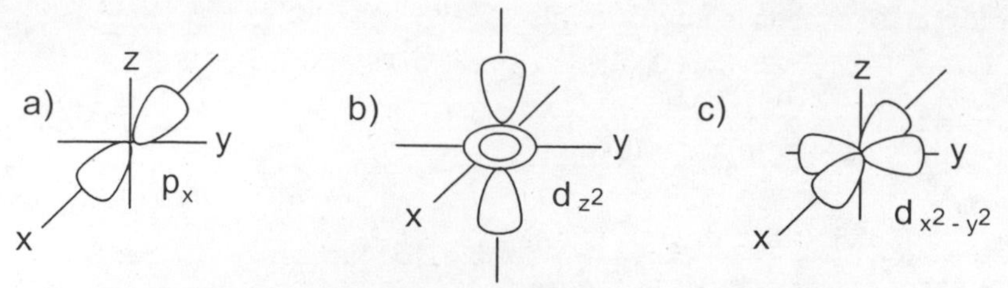

6.50 (a) In an s orbital, there are (n - 1) nodes.

(b) The $2p_x$ orbital has one node (the yz plane passing through the nucleus of the atom). The 3s orbital has 2 nodes.

(c) The nodes in p orbitals are planes.

(d) 2s = 2p < 3s < 4d < 5s. In the hydrogen atom, orbitals with the same n value are degenerate and energy increases with increasing n value.

Many-Electron Atoms and Electron Configurations

6.52 (a) The electron with the greater average distance from the nucleus feels a smaller attraction for the nucleus and is higher in energy. Thus the 3p is higher in energy than 3s.

(b) Because it has a larger n value, a 3s electron has a greater average distance from the chlorine nucleus than a 2p electron. The 3s electron experiences a smaller attraction for the nucleus and requires less energy to remove from the chlorine atom.

6.54 (a) The Pauli exclusion principle states that no two electrons can have the same four quantum numbers.

(b) An alternate statement of the Pauli exclusion principle is that a single orbital can hold a maximum of two electrons. Thus, the Pauli principle limits the maximum number of electrons in a main shell and its subshells, which determines when a new row of the periodic table begins.

6.56 (a) 4 (b) 14 (c) 2 (d) 2

6.58 (a) "Outer-shell electrons" are those beyond the previous noble-gas or core electron configuration.

(b) "Unpaired electrons" are electrons that occupy orbitals singly. That is, when there is only one electron in an orbital, this electron is "unpaired."

(c) A Si atom has 4 outer-shell electrons: $3s^23p^2$. Two of them (those in the degenerate 3p orbitals) are unpaired.

6.60 (a) Al: $[Ne]3s^23p^1$ (b) Sc: $[Ar]4s^23d^1$ (c) Co: $[Ar]4s^23d^7$

(d) Br: $[Ar]4s^23d^{10}4p^5$ (e) Ba: $[Xe]6s^2$ (f) Re: $[Xe]6s^24f^{14}5d^5$

(g) Lu: $[Xe]6s^24f^{14}5d^1$

6.62 (a) Ti: [Ar] 4s: [↑↓] 3d: [↑][↑][ ][ ][ ] 2 unpaired electrons

(b) Ga: [Ar] 4s: [↑↓] 3d: [↑↓][↑↓][↑↓][↑↓][↑↓] 4p: [↑][ ][ ] 1 unpaired electron

(c) Rh: [Kr] 5s: [↑↓] 4d: [↑↓][↑↓][↑][↑][↑] 3 unpaired electrons

(d) I: [Kr] 5s: [↑↓] 4d: [↑↓][↑↓][↑↓][↑↓][↑↓] 5p: [↑↓][↑↓][↑] 1 unpaired electron

(e) Po: [Xe] 6s: [↑↓] 4f: [↑↓][↑↓][↑↓][↑↓][↑↓][↑↓][↑↓] 5d: [↑↓][↑↓][↑↓][↑↓][↑↓] 6p: [↑↓][↑][↑]

2 unpaired electrons

6.64 (a) 7A (halogens) (b) 4B (c) 3A (d) the f-block elements Sm and Pu

6.66 Count the total number of electrons to assign the element.

(a) N: $[He]2s^22p^3$ (b) Se: $[Ar]4s^23d^{10}4p^4$ (c) Rh: $[Kr]5s^24d^7$

Additional Exercises

6.68 (a) Elements that emit in the visible: Ba (dark blue), Ca (dark blue), K (dark blue), Na (yellow/orange). (The other wavelengths are in the ultraviolet.)

(b) Au: shortest wavelength, highest energy

Na: longest wavelength, lowest energy

(c) $\lambda = c/\nu = \dfrac{2.998 \times 10^8 \text{ m/s}}{6.59 \times 10^{14}\text{/s}} \times \dfrac{1 \text{ nm}}{1 \times 10^{-9} \text{ m}} = 455 \text{ nm}$, **Ba**

6.70 (a) $\nu = c/\lambda = \dfrac{2.998 \times 10^8 \text{ m/s}}{320 \text{ nm}} \times \dfrac{1 \text{ nm}}{1 \times 10^{-9} \text{ m}} = 9.37 \times 10^{14} \text{ s}^{-1}$

(b) $E = hc/\lambda = \dfrac{6.626 \times 10^{-34} \text{ J}\bullet\text{s} \times 2.998 \times 10^8 \text{ m/s}}{3.20 \times 10^{-7} \text{ m}} \times \dfrac{1 \text{ kJ}}{1000 \text{ J}} \times \dfrac{6.022 \times 10^{23} \text{ photons}}{\text{mole}}$

$= 374 \text{ kJ/mol}$

(c) UV-B photons have shorter wavelength and higher energy.

(d) Yes. The higher energy UV-B photons would be more likely to cause sunburn.

6.72 E/photon = hc/λ

$$E = \frac{6.626 \times 10^{-34}\ J \cdot s \times 2.998 \times 10^{8}\ m/s}{455 \times 10^{-9}\ m} \times \frac{6.022 \times 10^{23}\ photons}{mol} = 2.63 \times 10^{5}\ J/mol$$

$$= 263\ kJ/mol$$

6.74 (a) $\frac{2.00 \times 10^{5}\ J}{mol} \times \frac{1\ mol\ photons}{6.022 \times 10^{23}\ photons} = 3.321 \times 10^{-19} = 3.32 \times 10^{-19}$ J/photon

(b) $\lambda = \frac{hc}{E} = \frac{6.626 \times 10^{-34}\ J \cdot s \times 2.998 \times 10^{8}\ m/s}{3.321 \times 10^{-19}\ J} = 5.98 \times 10^{-7}\ m$

(c) 5.98×10^{-7} m = 598 nm is well within the visible portion of the electromagnetic spectrum and corresponds to yellow or yellow-orange light. Red light, with wavelengths near or greater than 700 nm, does not have sufficient energy to initiate electron transfer and darken the film.

6.76 (a) He^+ is hydrogen-like because it is a one-electron particle. An He atom has two electrons. The Bohr model is based on the interaction of a single electron with the nucleus, but does not accurately account for additional interactions when two or more electrons are present.

(b) Divide each energy by the smallest value to find the integer relationship.

H: $2.18 \times 10^{-18}/2.18 \times 10^{-18} = 1$; Z = 1

He^+: $8.72 \times 10^{-18}/2.18 \times 10^{-18} = 4$; Z = 2

Li^{2+}: $1.96 \times 10^{-17}/2.18 \times 10^{-18} = 9$; Z = 3

The ground-state energies are in the ratio of 1:4:9, which is also the ratio Z^2, the square of the nuclear charge for each particle.

The ground state energy for hydrogen-like particles is:
$E = R_H Z^2$. (By definition, n = 1 for the ground state of a one-electron particle.)

(c) Z = 6 for C. $E = -2.18 \times 10^{-18}\ J\ (6)^2 = -7.85 \times 10^{-17}\ J$

6.78 *Plan.* Change keV to J/electron. Calculate v from kinetic energy. λ = h/mv. *Solve:*

$$82.4\ keV \times \frac{1000\ eV}{keV} \times \frac{96.485\ kJ}{1\ eV \cdot mol} \times \frac{1000\ J}{1\ kJ} \times \frac{1\ mol}{6.022 \times 10^{23}\ electrons}$$

$$= 1.320 \times 10^{-14} = 1.32 \times 10^{-14}\ J/electron$$

$E_k = mv^2/2$; $v^2 = 2E_k/m$; $v = \sqrt{2E_k/m}$

$$v = \left(\frac{2 \times 1.320 \times 10^{-14}\ kg \cdot m^2/s^2}{9.1094 \times 10^{-31}\ kg}\right)^{1/2} = 1.703 \times 10^{8} = 1.70 \times 10^{8}\ m/s$$

$$\lambda = h/mv = \frac{6.626 \times 10^{-34}\ J \cdot s}{9.1094 \times 10^{-31}\ kg \times 1.703 \times 10^{8}\ m/s} \times \frac{1\ kg \cdot m^2/s^2}{1\ J} = 4.27 \times 10^{-12}\ m = 4.27\ pm$$

6.80 (a) 3p (b) 6g (c) 2s (d) 4f

6.82 What the noble gas elements have in common are completed ns and np subshells. Since the Pauli principle limits the number of electrons per orbital to two, this leads to the first three magic numbers, $2(1s^2)$, $10(1s^22s^22p^6)$ and $18(1s^22s^22p^63s^23p^6)$. In the fourth row, (n-1) d orbitals begin to fill as their energy falls below that of the np orbitals. This leads to the next two magic numbers, $36(1s^22s^22p^63s^23p^64s^23d^{10}4p^6)$ and $54(1s^22s^22p^63s^23p^64s^23d^{10}4p^65s^24d^{10}5p^6)$. In the sixth row, the energy of the 4f orbitals falls below that of the (n-1)d and np subshells, and it fills. This explains the final magic number, $86(1s^22s^22p^63s^23p^64s^23d^{10}4p^65s^24d^{10}5p^66s^24f^{14}5d^{10}6p^6)$.

6.84 (a) Se: [Ar] $4s^23d^{10}4p^4$ (b) Rh: [Kr] $5s^24d^7$ (c) Si: [Ne] $3s^23p^2$

(d) Hg: [Xe] $6s^24f^{14}5d^{10}$ (e) Hf: [Xe] $6s^24f^{14}5d^2$

6.86 The core would be the electron configuration of element 118. If no new subshell begins to fill, the condensed electron configuration of element 126 would be similar to those of elements vertically above it on the periodic chart, Pu and Sm. The condensed configuration would be $[118]8s^26f^6$. On the other hand, the 5g subshell could begin to fill after 8s, resulting in the condensed configuration $[118]8s^25g^6$. Exceptions are also possible.

Integrative Exercises

6.88 $\Delta H^\circ_{rxn} = \Delta H^\circ_f\ O_2(g) + \Delta H^\circ_f\ O(g) - \Delta H^\circ_f\ O_3(g)$

$\Delta H^\circ_{rxn} = 0 + 247.5\text{ kJ} - 142.3\text{ kJ} = +105.2\text{ kJ}$

$$\frac{105.2\text{ kJ}}{\text{mol } O_3} \times \frac{1\text{ mol } O_3}{6.022 \times 10^{23}\text{ molecules}} \times \frac{1000\text{ J}}{1\text{ kJ}} = \frac{1.747 \times 10^{-19}\text{ J}}{O_3\text{ molecule}}$$

$$\Delta E = hc/\lambda;\ \lambda = \frac{hc}{\Delta E} = \frac{6.626 \times 10^{-34}\text{ J}\bullet\text{s} \times 2.998 \times 10^8\text{ m/s}}{1.747 \times 10^{-19}\text{ J}} = 1.137 \times 10^{-6}\text{ m}$$

Radiation with this wavelength is in the infrared portion of the spectrum. (Clearly, processes other than simple photodissociation cause O_3 to absorb ultraviolet radiation.)

6.89 (a) The electron configuration of Zr is [Kr] $5s^24d^2$ and that of Hf is [Xe] $6s^24f^{14}5d^2$. Although Hf has electrons in f orbitals as the rare earth elements do, the 4f subshell in Hf is filled, and the 5d electrons primarily determine the chemical properties of the element. Thus, Hf should be chemically similar to Zr rather than the rare earth elements.

(b) $ZrCl_4(s) + 4Na(l) \rightarrow Zr(s) + 4NaCl(s)$

This is an oxidation-reduction reaction; Na is oxidized and Zr is reduced.

(c) $2ZrO_2(s) + 4Cl_2(g) + 3C(s) \rightarrow 2ZrCl_4(s) + CO_2(g) + 2\ CO(g)$

$$55.4\text{ g } ZrO_2 \times \frac{1\text{ mol } ZrO_2}{123.2\text{ g } ZrO_2} \times \frac{2\text{ mol } ZrCl_4}{2\text{ mol } ZrO_2} \times \frac{233.0\text{ g } ZrCl_4}{1\text{ mol } ZrCl_4} = 105\text{ g } ZrCl_4$$

(d) In ionic-compounds of the type MCl_4 and MO_2, the metal ions have a 4+ charge, indicating that the neutral atoms have lost 4 electrons. Zr, [Kr] $5s^24d^2$, loses the 4 electrons beyond its Kr core configuration. Hf, [Xe]$6s^24f^{14}5d^2$, similarly loses its four 6s and 5d electrons, but not electrons from the "complete" 4f subshell.

6.90 (a) Each oxide ion, O^{2-}, carries a 2- charge. Each metal oxide is a neutral compound, so the metal ion or ions must adopt a total positive charge equal to the total negative charge of the oxide ions in the compound. The table below lists the electron configuration of the neutral metal atom, the positive charge of **each** metal ion in the oxide, and the corresponding electron configuration of the metal ion.

i.	K:	[Ar] $4s^1$	1+	[Ar]
ii.	Ca:	[Ar] $4s^2$	2+	[Ar]
iii.	Sc:	[Ar] $4s^23d^1$	3+	[Ar]
iv.	Ti:	[Ar] $4s^23d^2$	4+	[Ar]
v.	V:	[Ar] $4s^23d^3$	5+	[Ar]
vi.	Cr:	[Ar]$4s^13d^5$	6+	[Ar]

Each metal atom loses all (valence) electrons beyond the Ar core configuration. In K_2O, Sc_2O_3 and V_2O_5, where the metal ions have odd charges, two metal ions are required to produce a neutral oxide.

(b) i. potassium oxide ii. calcium oxide iii. scandium(III) oxide
iv. titanium (IV) oxide v. vanadium (V) oxide vi. chromium(VI) oxide

(Roman numerals are required to specify the charges on the transition metal ions, because more than one stable ion may exist.)

(c) Recall that $\Delta H_f^\circ = 0$ for elements in their standard states. In these reactions, M(s) and H_2(g) are elements in their standard states.

i. $K_2O(s) + H_2(g) \rightarrow 2K(s) + H_2O(g)$

$\Delta H^\circ = \Delta H_f^\circ\ H_2O(g) + 2\Delta H_f^\circ\ K(s) - \Delta H\ K_2O(s) - \Delta H_f^\circ\ H_2(g)$

$\Delta H^\circ = -241.82\text{ kJ} + 2(0) - (-363.2\text{ kJ}) - 0 = 121.4\text{ kJ}$

ii. $CaO(s) + H_2(g) \rightarrow Ca(s) + H_2O(g)$

$\Delta H^\circ = \Delta H_f^\circ\ H_2O(g) + \Delta H_f^\circ\ Ca(s) - \Delta H_f^\circ\ CaO(s) - \Delta H_f^\circ\ H_2(g)$

$\Delta H^\circ = -241.82\text{ kJ} + 0 - (-635.1\text{ kJ}) - 0 = 393.3\text{ kJ}$

iv. $TiO_2(s) + 2H_2(g) \rightarrow Ti(s) + 2H_2O(g)$

$\Delta H^\circ = 2\Delta H_f^\circ\ H_2O(g) + \Delta H_f^\circ\ Ti(s) - \Delta H_f^\circ\ TiO_2(s) - 2\Delta H_f^\circ\ H_2(g)$

$= 2(-241.82) + 0 - (-938.7) - 2(0) = 455.1\text{ kJ}$

v. $V_2O_5(s) + 5H_2(g) \rightarrow 2V(s) + 5H_2O(g)$

$\Delta H^\circ = 5\Delta H_f^\circ\ H_2O(g) + 2\Delta H_f^\circ\ V(s) - \Delta H_f^\circ\ V_2O_5(s) - 5\Delta H_f^\circ\ H_2(g)$

$= 5(-241.82) + 2(0) - (-1550.6) - 5(0) = 341.5\text{ kJ}$

(d) ΔH_f° becomes more negative moving from left to right across this row of the periodic chart. Since Sc lies between Ca and Ti, the median of the two ΔH_f° values is approximately -785 kJ/mol. However, the trend is clearly not linear. Dividing the ΔH_f° values by the positive charge on the pertinent metal ion produces the values -363, -318, -235 and -310. The value between Ca^{2+} (-318) and Ti^{4+} (-235) is Sc^{3+} (-277). Multiplying (-277) by 3, a value of approximately -830 kJ results. A reasonable range of values for ΔH_f° of $Sc_2O_3(s)$ is then -785 to -830 kJ/mol.

6.91 (a) Bohr's theory was based on the Rutherford "nuclear" model of the atom. That is, Bohr theory assumed a dense positive charge at the center of the atom and a diffuse negative charge (electrons) surrounding it. Bohr's theory then specified the nature of the diffuse negative charge. The prevailing theory before the nuclear model was Thomson's plum pudding or watermelon model, with discrete electrons scattered about a diffuse positive charge cloud. Bohr's theory could not have been based on the Thomson model of the atom.

(b) deBroglie's hypothesis is that electrons exhibit both particle and wave properties. Thomson's conclusion that electrons have mass is a particle property, while the nature of cathode rays is a wave property. de Broglie's hypothesis actually rationalizes these two seemingly contradictory observations about the properties of electrons.

7 Periodic Properties of the Elements

Periodic Table; Effective Nuclear Charge

7.2 (a) The verification of the existence of many new elements by accurately measuring their atomic weights spurred interest in a classification scheme. Mendeleev (and Meyer) noted that certain chemical and physical properties recur periodically when the elements are arranged by increasing atomic weight. The accurate atomic weights provided a common property on which to base a classification scheme of the elements.

(b) Moseley realized that the characteristic X-ray frequencies emitted by each element were related to a unique integer that he assigned to each element. We now know this integer as the atomic number, the number of protons in the nucleus of an atom. In general, atomic weight increases as atomic number increases, but there are a few exceptions. If elements are arranged by increasing atomic number, a few seeming contradictions in the Mendelev table (the positions of Ar and K or Te and I) are eliminated.

7.4 (a) Electrostatic attraction for the nucleus lowers the energy of an electron, while electron-electron repulsions increase this energy. The concept of effective nuclear charge allows us to model this increase in the energy of an electron as a smaller net attraction to a nucleus with a smaller positive charge, Z_{eff}.

(b) In Be (or any element), the 1s electrons are not shielded by any core electrons, so they experience a much greater Z_{eff} than the 2s electrons.

7.6 (a) Z_{eff} = Z - # of core electrons = 13 - 10 = +3.

(b) An estimate of Z_{eff} based on the assumption in part (a) will always be lower than the value based on detailed calculations. Because outer electrons have some probability of being in the core, the core electrons are never 100% effective at shielding; the number of core electrons represents an upper limit for S.

7.8 Mg < P < K < Ti < Rh. The shielding of electrons in the n = 3 shell by 1s and 2s core electrons in these elements is approximately equal, so the effective nuclear charge increases as Z increases.

Atomic and Ionic Radii

7.10 (a) Since the quantum mechanical description of the atom does not specify the exact location of electrons, there is no specific distance from the nucleus where the last electron can be found. Rather, the electron density decreases gradually as the distance from the nucleus increases. There is no quantum mechanical "edge" of an atom.

(b) When nonbonded atoms touch, it is their electron clouds that interact. These interactions are primarily repulsive because of the negative charges of electrons. Thus, the size of the electron clouds determines the nuclear approach distance of nonbonded atoms.

7.12 The distance between Si atoms in solid silicon is 2 times the bonding atomic radius from Figure 7.5. the Si-Si distance is 2 × 1.11 Å = 2.22 Å.

7.14 (a) The estimated distances in the table below are the sum of the radii of the group 5A elements and H from Table 7.5.

bonded atoms	estimated distance	measured distance
P – H	1.43	1.419
As – H	1.56	1.519
Sb – H	1.75	1.707

In general, the estimated distances are a bit longer than the measured distances. This probably shows a systematic bias in either the estimated radii or in the method of obtaining the measured values.

(b) The principle quantum number of the outer electrons and thus the average distance of these electrons from the nucleus increases from P ($n = 3$) to As ($n = 4$) to Sb ($n = 5$). This causes the systematic increase in M-H distance.

7.16 (a) The vertical difference in radius is due to a change in principle quantum number of the outer electrons. The horizontal difference in radius is due to the change in electrostatic attraction between the outer electron and a nucleus with one more or one fewer proton. Adding or subtracting a proton has a much smaller radius effect than moving from one principle quantum level to the next.

(b) S < Si < Se < Ge. This order is predicted by the trends in increasing atomic radius moving to the left in a row and down a column of the periodic chart, assuming that changes moving down a column are larger [see part (a)]. That is, the order above assumes that the change from S to Se is larger than the change from S to Si. This order is confirmed by the values in Figure 7.5.

7.18 (a) K < Cs < Rb (b) Te < Sn < In (c) Cl < P < Sr

7.20 (a) As Z stays constant and the number of electrons increases, the electron-electron repulsions increase, the electrons spread apart and the ions become larger. $I^- > I > I^+$

(b) Going down a column, the increasing average distance of the outer electrons from the nucleus causes the size of particles with like charge to increase. $Ca^{2+} > Mg^{2+} > Be^{2+}$

(c) Fe: $[Ar]4s^23d^6$; Fe^{2+}: $[Ar]3d^6$; Fe^{3+}: $[Ar]3d^5$. The 4s valence electrons in Fe are on average further from the nucleus than the 3d electrons, so Fe is larger than Fe^{2+}. Since there are five 3d orbitals, in Fe^{2+} at least one orbital must contain a pair of electrons. Removing one electron to form Fe^{3+} significantly reduces repulsion, increasing the nuclear charge experienced by each of the other d electrons and decreasing the size of the ion. $Fe > Fe^{2+} > Fe^{3+}$

7.22 The order of radii is $Ca > Ca^{2+} > Mg^{2+}$, so the largest sphere is Ca, the intermediate one is Ca^{2+} and the smallest is Mg^{2+}.

7.24 (a) K^+, Ca^{2+} (b) Ca^{2+}, Sc^{3+} (c) S^{2-}, Ar (d) Co^{3+}, Fe^{2+}

7.26 (a) Cl < S < K (b) $K^+ < Cl^- < S^{2-}$

(c) Even though K has the largest Z value, the *n*-value of the outer electron is larger than the *n*-value of valence electrons in S and Cl so K atoms are largest. When the 4s electron is removed, K^+ is isoelectronic with Cl^- and S^{2-}. The larger Z value causes the 3p electrons in K^+ to experience the largest effective nuclear charge and K^+ is the smallest ion.

7.28 (a) Cl^- is larger than Cl because the increase in electron repulsions that accompany addition of an electron cause the electron cloud to expand.

(b) S^{2-} is larger than O^{2-}, because for particles with like charges, size increases going down a family.

(c) K^+ is larger than Ca^{2+} because the two ions are isoelectronic and K^+ has the larger Z.

Ionization Energies; Electron Affinities

7.30 (a) $Ga(g) \rightarrow Ga^+(g) + 1e^-$; $Ga^+(g) \rightarrow Ga^{2+}(g) + 1e^-$ (b) $Rh^{3+}(g) \rightarrow Rh^{4+}(g) + 1e^-$

7.32 (a) The effective nuclear charges of Li and Na are similar, but the outer electron in Li has a smaller *n*-value and is closer to the nucleus than the outer electron in Na. More energy is needed to overcome the greater attraction of the Li electron for the nucleus.

(b) Sc: [Ar] $4s^2 3d^1$; Ti: [Ar] $4s^2 3d^2$. The fourth ionization of titanium involves removing a 4s outer electron, while the fourth ionization of Sc requires removing a 3p electron from the [Ar] core. The effective nuclear charges experienced by the two 4s electrons in Ti are much more similar than the effective nuclear charges of a 4s outer electron and a 3p core electron in Sc. Thus, the difference between the third and fourth ionization energies of Sc is much larger.

(c) The electron configuration of Li^+ is $1s^2$ or [He] and that of Be^+ is [He]$2s^1$. Be^+ has one more valence electron to lose while Li^+ has the stable noble gas configuration of He. It requires much more energy to remove a 1s core electron close to the nucleus of Li^+ than a 2s valence electron further from the nucleus of Be^+.

7.34 (a) Moving from F to I in group 7A, first ionization energies decrease and atomic radii increase. The greater the atomic radius, the smaller the electrostatic attraction of an outer electron for the nucleus and the smaller the ionization energy of the element.

(b) First ionization energies increase slightly going from K to Ar and atomic sizes decrease. As valence electrons are drawn closer to the nucleus (atom size decreases), it requires more energy to completely remove them from the atom (first ionization energy increases). Each trend has a discontinuity at Ga, owing to the increased shielding of the 4p electrons by the filled 3d subshell.

7.36 (a) Cd. As the effective nuclear charge increases in moving from left to right in the fifth row, the energy required to remove an electron increases.

(b) C. Valence electrons in C are closer to the nucleus (n = 2) and are shielded only by the [He] core, so they experience greater attraction for the nucleus and have a higher ionization energy.

(c) I. In and I compare as two elements in the same row, with the effects of increasing effective nuclear charge dominating their periodic properties.

(d) Xe. Sn and Xe are in the same row, so Xe with the larger Z experiences a greater effective nuclear charge and a larger ionization energy.

7.38 (a) Mn^{3+} [Ar]$3d^4$ (b) Se^{2-} [Ar]$4s^2 3d^{10} 4p^6$ = [Kr], noble-gas configuration

(c) Sc^{3+}: [Ar], noble-gas configuration (d) Ru^{2+}: [Kr]$4d^6$

(e) Tl^+: [Xe]$6s^2 4f^{14} 5d^{10}$ (f) Au^+: [Xe]$4f^{14} 5d^{10}$

7.40 (a) Cr^{3+}, 3 unpaired electrons

(b) Sn^{2+}, 0 unpaired electrons

7.42 Electron affinity

Br(g)	+ 1e⁻	→	Br^-(g)
[Ar]$4s^2 3d^{10} 4p^5$			[Ar]$4s^2 3d^{10} 4p^6$

When a Br atom gains an electron, the Br^- ion adopts the stable electron configuration of Kr. Since the electron is added to the same 4p subshell as other outer electrons, it experiences essentially the same attraction for the nucleus. Thus, the energy of the Br^- ion is lower than the total energy of a Br atom and an isolated electron, and electron affinity is negative.

Electron affinity: $Kr(g) + 1e^- \rightarrow Kr^-(g)$

$[Ar]4s^2 3d^{10} 4p^6$ $\quad$ $[Ar]4s^2 3d^{10} 4p^6 5s^1$

Energy is required to add an electron to a Kr atom; Kr^- has a higher energy than the isolated Kr atom and free electron. In Kr^- the added electron would have to occupy the higher energy 5s orbital; a 5s electron is farther from the nucleus and effectively shielded by the spherical Kr core and is not stabilized by the nucleus.

7.44 $Mg^+(g) + 1e^- \rightarrow Mg(g)$

$[Ne]\ 3s^1$ $\quad$ $[Ne]\ 3s^2$

This process is the reverse of the first ionization of Mg. The magnitude of the energy change for this process is the same as the magnitude of the first ionization energy of Mg, 738 kJ/mol.

Properties of Metals and Nonmetals

7.46 P < Sb < Ag. P is a nonmetal, Sb is a metalloid and Ag is a metal. We expect that electrical conductivity increases as metallic character increases. Since metallic character increases going down a column and to the left in a row, the order of increasing electrical conductivity is as shown above.

7.48 (a) In general, ionization energy decreases as metallic character increases. According to Figure 7.10 the ionization energies of the group 5A elements decreases as atomic weight increases (going down the column). Therefore, metallic character of the group 5A elements increases with increasing atomic weight.

(b) Ag < Sn < Se < C < F. Nonmetallic character increases going up and to the right on the periodic chart. Vertical trends dominate the relationship between Se and C.

7.50 (a) metal oxides: $Li_2O(s) + H_2O(l) \rightarrow 2\ LiOH(aq)$

$BaO(s) + H_2O(l) \rightarrow Ba(OH)_2(aq)$

nonmetal oxides: $P_4O_{10}(s) + 6H_2O(l) \rightarrow 4H_3PO_4(aq)$

$SO_3(g) + H_2O(l) \rightarrow H_2SO_4(aq)$

(b) Metals have lower ionization energies than nonmetals, so they tend to form ionic oxides, while nonmetals form molecular oxides. Ionic compounds, in this case oxides, dissociate into ions when they dissolve in water. The reactive oxide ion ends up as hydroxide, separated from the metal ion. Molecular oxides do not ionize upon dissolution, so the oxygen remains bound to the nonmetal.

7.52 The more **nonmetallic** the central atom, the more acidic the oxide. In order of increasing acidity: $CaO < Al_2O_3 < SiO_2 < CO_2 < P_2O_5 < SO_3$

7.54 (a) $K_2O(s) + H_2O(l) \rightarrow 2KOH(aq)$

(b) $P_2O_3(s) + 3H_2O(l) \rightarrow 2H_3PO_3(aq)$

(c) $Cr_2O_3(s) + 6HCl(aq) \rightarrow 2CrCl_3(aq) + 3H_2O(l)$

(d) $SeO_2(s) + 2KOH(aq) \rightarrow K_2SeO_3(aq) + H_2O(l)$

Group Trends in Metals and Nonmetals

7.56 (a) Rb: [Kr] $5s^1$, r = 2.11 Å   Ag: [Kr] $5s^1 4d^{10}$, r = 1.53 Å

The electron configurations both have a [Kr] core and a single 5s electron; Ag has a completed 4d subshell as well. The radii are very different because the 5s electron in Ag experiences a much greater effective nuclear charge. Ag has a much larger Z (47 vs. 37), and although the 4d electrons in Ag shield the 5s electron somewhat, the increased shielding does not compensate for the large increase in Z.

(b) Ag is much less reactive (less likely to lose an electron) because its 5s electron experiences a much larger effective nuclear charge and is more difficult to remove.

7.58 (a) Cs is much more reactive than Li toward H_2O because its valence electron is less tightly held (greater *n* value), and Cs is more easily oxidized.

(b) The purple flame indicates that the metal is potassium (see Figure 7.22).

(c) $K_2O_2(s) + H_2O(l) \rightarrow H_2O_2(aq) + K_2O(aq)$

potassium peroxide   hydrogen peroxide

7.60 (a) $2K(s) + 2H_2O(l) \rightarrow 2KOH(aq) + H_2(g)$

(b) $Ba(s) + 2H_2O(l) \rightarrow Ba(OH)_2(aq) + H_2(g)$

(c) $6Li(s) + N_2(g) \rightarrow 2Li_3N(s)$

(d) $2Mg(s) + O_2(g) \rightarrow 2MgO(s)$

7.62 (a) The reactions of the alkali metals with hydrogen and with a halogen are redox reactions. In both classes of reaction, the alkali metal loses electrons and is oxidized. Both hydrogen and the halogen gain electrons and are reduced. The product is an ionic solid, where either hydride ion, H^-, or a halide ion, X^-, is the anion and the alkali metal is the cation.

(b) $Ca(s) + F_2(g) \rightarrow CaF_2(s)$

$Ca(s) + H_2(g) \rightarrow CaH_2(s)$

Both products are ionic solids containing Ca^{2+} and the corresponding anion in a 1:2 ratio.

7.64 *Plan.* Predict the physical and chemical properties of At based on the trends in properties in the halogen (7A) family. *Solve:*

(a) F, at the top of the column, is a gas; I, immediately above At, is a solid; the melting points of the halogens increase going down the column. At is likely to be a solid at room temperature.

(b) All halogens form ionic compounds with Na; they have the generic formula NaX. The compound formed by At will have the formula NaAt.

7.66 (a) When the noble gases react with fluorine, they (at least partially) lose electrons. This is related to ionization energy; the smaller the ionization energy the more reactive the noble-gas element. Moving down the family, the *n* value and the average distance of the outer electrons from the nucleus increase. Outer electrons experience a smaller attraction for the nucleus, ionization energy decreases and reactivity towards fluorine increases. Xe is most reactive toward F_2, followed by Kr.

(b) Although it has a relatively large negative electron affinity, Cl does not have the same ability to remove electrons from other atoms as F has. At least in part, this is due to the small size of F atoms, which can approach the electron clouds of the noble gases more closely than Cl atoms.

7.68 (a) $Cl_2(g) + H_2O(l) \rightarrow HCl(aq) + HOCl(aq)$

(b) $Ba(s) + H_2(g) \rightarrow BaH_2(s)$

(c) $2Li(s) + S(s) \rightarrow Li_2S(s)$

(d) $Mg(s) + F_2(g) \rightarrow MgF_2(s)$

7.70 (a) $S(s) + 2F_2(g) \rightarrow SF_4(g)$

(b) O_2, oxygen; O_3, ozone

(c) Fluorine can remove electrons from silica glass (SiO_2) according to the reaction $SiO_2(s) + 2F_2(g) \rightarrow SiF_4(g) + O_2(g)$. Thus, fluorine gas would "dissolve" the glass container. This process is also known as etching.

Additional Exercises

7.72 (a) *eka - aluminum* is gallium (Ga), Z = 31.

(b) From the **Handbook of Chemistry and Physics**, 74th edition, the physical properties of Ga are:

atomic weight = 69.92 g/mol	m.p. = 29.78°C
density = 5.904 g/mL (s)	b.p. = 2403°C
= 6.095 g/mL (l)	oxide = Ga_2O_3, Ga_2O

The atomic weight, density and formula of oxide all agree with Mendeleev's predictions. Gallium does have a low melting point and a high boiling point.

7.74 (a) P: (+15 - 10) = +5

(b) The 3s electrons have an approximately spherical distribution and provide additional shielding, beyond the Ne core to the 3p electrons. That is, S is greater for 3p electrons, owing to the presence of the 3s electrons, so Z - S(3p) is less than Z - S(3s).

(c) The electron configuration of P is $[Ne]3s^2 3p^3$. The 3p electrons are the outermost electrons; they experience a smaller Z_{eff} than 3s electrons and thus a smaller attraction for the nucleus, given equal *n*-values. The first electron lost is a 3p electron. Each 3p orbital holds one electron, so there is no preference as to which 3p electron will be lost.

7.75 Moving from left to right across the representative elements, electrons are added to *n*p orbitals. These are valence or outer electrons, so their distance from the nucleus directly determines atomic size.

Moving from left to right across the transition elements, electrons are added to an (*n*-1)d subshell, which is not the outermost shell. These (*n*-1)d electrons modify the shielding experienced by the outer or valence electrons, but this has a much smaller effect on atomic size.

7.77 Ge – H distance $= r_{Ge} + r_H = 1.22 + 0.37 = 1.59$ Å
Ge – Cl distance $= r_{Ge} + r_{Cl} = 1.22 + 0.99 = 2.21$ Å

7.78 Close approach by two positively charged nuclei is impossible because of the large electrostatic repulsion between like-charged particles at small distances. The additional space between the nuclei in a molecule like F_2 is occupied by bonding electrons, which are electrostatically stabilized by attraction to both nuclei. The electrons also provide a buffer between the two nuclei.

7.80 C: $1s^2 2s^2 2p^2$. I_1 through I_4 represent loss of the 2p and 2s electrons in the outer shell of the atom. The values of $I_1 - I_4$ increase as expected. The nuclear charge is constant, but removing each electron reduces repulsive interactions between the remaining electrons, so effective nuclear charge increases and ionization energy increases. I_5 and I_6 represent loss of the 1s core electrons. These 1s electrons are much closer to the nucleus and experience the **full nuclear charge (they are not shielded)**, so the values of I_5 and I_6 are significantly greater than $I_1 - I_4$. I_6 is larger than I_5 because all repulsive interactions have been eliminated.

7.81 (a) Ca: [Ar] $4s^2$; Ca^{2+}: [Ar]. Zn: [Ar] $4s^2 3d^{10}$; Zn^{2+}: [Ar] $3d^{10}$. In both cases, forming ions involves losing the only electrons in the $n = 4$ shell. The average distance from the nucleus of $n = 3$ electrons is less, so the radii of the ions are smaller.

(b) The atomic radius of Ca is greater than that of Zn because Zn has a significantly greater Z and Z_{eff}, which draws the 4s valence electrons closer to the nucleus.

(c) In both Ca and Zn atoms, the outermost electrons are in the 4s subshell. The much larger Z_{eff} for Zn causes it to have a much smaller radius. In the +2 ions, both have lost their 4s electrons. The outermost electrons in Zn are in the 3d sublevel and are significantly shielded by the [Ar] core electrons. Thus, the radius of Zn^{2+} is closer to the radius of Ca^{2+} than the radii of the neutral ions.

7.83 The statement is somewhat true, but more accurate if changed to read: "A negative value for the electron affinity of an atom occurs when the outermost electrons only incompletely shield **the added electron** from the nucleus." This new statement totally explains the negative electron affinity of Br and the positive value for Kr. For Br^-, the electron is added to the 4p subshell and is incompletely shielded by the "other" 4s and 4p electrons. For Kr^-, the electron is added to the 5s subshell, which is effectively shielded by the spherical Kr core.

7.85 (a) P: [Ne] $3s^23p^3$; S: [Ne] $3s^23p^4$. In P, each 3p orbital contains a single electron, while in S one 3p orbital contains a pair of electrons. Removing an electron from S eliminates the need for electron pairing and reduces electrostatic repulsion, so the overall energy required to remove the electron is smaller than in P, even though Z is greater.

(b) C: [He] $2s^22p^2$; N: [He] $2s^22p^3$; O: [He] $2s^22p^4$. An electron added to a N atom must be paired in a relatively small 2p orbital, so the additional electron-electron repulsion more than compensates for the increase in Z and the electron affinity is smaller (less exothermic) than that of C. In an O atom, one 2p orbital already contains a pair of electrons, so the additional repulsion from an extra electron is offset by the increase in Z and the electron affinity is greater (more exothermic). Note from Figure 7.11 that the electron affinity of O is only slightly more exothermic than that of C, although the value of Z has increased by 2.

(c) O^+: [Ne] $2s^22p^3$; O^{2+}: [Ne] $2s^22p^2$; F^+: [Ne] $2s^22p^4$; F^{2+}: [Ne] $2s^22p^3$. The decrease in electron-electron repulsion going from F^+ to F^{2+} energetically favors ionization and causes it to be less endothermic than the corresponding process in O, where there is no significant decrease in repulsion.

(d) Mn^{2+}: [Ar]$3d^5$; Mn^{3+}: [Ar] $3d^4$; Cr^{2+}: [Ar] $3d^4$; Cr^{3+}: [Ar] $3d^3$; Fe^{2+}: [Ar] $3d^6$; Fe^{3+}: [Ar] $3d^5$. The third ionization energy of Mn is expected to be larger than that of Cr because of the larger Z value of Mn. The third ionization energy of Fe is **less** than that of Mn because going from $3d^6$ to $3d^5$ reduces electron repulsions, making the process less endothermic than predicted by nuclear charge arguments.

7.87 (a) For both H and the alkali metals, the added electron will complete an *n*s subshell (1s for H and *n*s for the alkali metals) so shielding and repulsion effects will be similar. For the halogens, the electron is added to an *n*p subshell, so the energy change is likely to be quite different.

(b) True. Only He has a smaller estimated "bonding" atomic radius, and no known compounds of He exist. The electron configuration of H is $1s^1$. The single 1s electron experiences no repulsion from other electrons and feels the full unshielded nuclear charge. It is held very close to the nucleus. The outer electrons of all other elements that form compounds are shielded by a spherical inner core of electrons and are less strongly attracted to the nucleus, resulting in larger atomic radii.

(c) Ionization is the process of removing an electron from an atom. For the alkali metals, the *n*s electron being removed is effectively shielded by the core electrons, so ionization energies are low. For the halogens, a significant increase in nuclear charge occurs as the *n*p orbitals fill, and this is not offset by an increase in shielding. The relatively large effective nuclear charge experienced by *n*p electrons of the halogens is similar to the unshielded nuclear charge experienced by the H 1s electron. Both H and the halogens have large ionization energies.

7.88 Since Xe reacts with F_2, and O_2 has approximately the same ionization energy as Xe, O_2 will probably react with F_2. Possible products would be O_2F_2, analogous to XeF_2, or OF_2.

$$O_2(g) + F_2(g) \rightarrow O_2F_2(g)$$

$$O_2(g) + 2F_2(g) \rightarrow 2OF_2(g)$$

7.90 (a) Li has a relatively small, positive ionization energy while O and F have relatively large negative electron affinities. When Li reacts with the nonmetals, it loses electrons while O and F gain electrons. Two Li atoms are required to provide the two electrons needed by O to complete its 2p subshell and form Li_2O. One Li is required to complete the 2p subshell of F and form LiF.

(b) The radius of F, 0.71 Å, is only slightly smaller than the radius of O, 0.73 Å. Because F has a greater nuclear charge, we might anticipate a larger difference. However, electron-electron repulsions are so great in the relatively cramped 2p orbitals of F that the larger Z does not lead to a significantly smaller radius.

(c) When nonmetals react, they tend to gain electrons, a process related to electron affinity. Fluorine has a more negative (more exothermic) electron affinity, so it is the more reactive nonmetal.

7.92 Fr (1A), Ra (2A), Po (6A), At (7A), Rn (8A)

(a) most metallic character: **Fr** (Metallic character decreases from left to right in a row.)
(b) most nonmetallic character: **Rn**
(c) largest ionization energy: **Rn** (Ionization energy increases from left to right in a row.)
(d) smallest ionization energy: **Fr**
(e) greatest electron affinity: **At** (Electron affinity becomes more exothermic from left to right in a row.)
(f) largest atomic radius: **Fr** (Size decreases from left to right in a row.)
(g) appears least like the element above it: **Fr** (According to the trends in melting point, Fr may be a liquid or a gas at room temperature, while Cs is a solid. The others should be in the same state as the element above them.)
(h) highest melting point: **Ra** (The melting points of the group 2A metals are much higher than those of the other groups, even though the values decrease going down the group.)

(i) react most readily with H_2O: **Fr** (It has the lowest ionization energy.)

7.93 (a) *Plan*. Use qualitative physical (bulk) properties to narrow the range of choices, then match melting point and density to identify the specific element. *Solve*:

Hardness varies widely in metals and nonmetals, so this information is not too useful. The relatively high density, appearance and ductility indicate that the element is probably less metallic than copper. Focus on the block of nine main group elements centered around Sn. Pb is not a possibility because it was used as a comparison standard. The melting point of the five elements closest to Pb are:

Tl, 303.5°C; In, 156.1°C; Sn, 232°C ; Sb, 630.5°C; Bi, 271.3°C

The best match is In. To confirm this identification, the density of In is 7.3 g/cm^3, also a good match to properties of the unknown element.

(b) In order to write the correct balanced equation, determine the formula of the oxide product from the mass data, assuming the unknown is In.

5.08 g oxide - 4.20 g In = 0.88 g O
4.20 g In/114.82 g/mol = 0.0366 mol In; 0.0366/0.0366 = 1
0.88g O/16.00 g/mol = 0.0550 mol O; 0.0550/0.0366 = 1.5

Multiplying by 2 produces an integer ratio of 2 In: 3 O and a formula of In_2O_3. The balanced equation is: $4\ In(s) + 3O_2(g) \rightarrow 2\ In_2O_3(s)$

(c) According to Figure 7.2, the element In was discovered between 1843 –1886. The investigator who first recorded this data in 1822 could have been the first to discover In.

Integrative Exercises

7.95 (a) $\nu = c/\lambda$; $1\ Hz = 1 s^{-1}$

$$\text{Ne: } \nu = \frac{2.998 \times 10^8\ m/s}{14.610\ \text{Å}} \times \frac{1\ \text{Å}}{1 \times 10^{-10}\ m} = 2.052 \times 10^{17}\ s^{-1} = 2.052 \times 10^{17}\ Hz$$

$$\text{Ca: } \nu = \frac{2.998 \times 10^8\ m/s}{3.358 \times 10^{-10}\ m} = 8.928 \times 10^{17}\ Hz$$

$$\text{Zn: } \nu = \frac{2.998 \times 10^8\ m/s}{1.435 \times 10^{-10}\ m} = 20.89 \times 10^{17}\ Hz$$

$$\text{Zr: } \nu = \frac{2.998 \times 10^8\ m/s}{0.786 \times 10^{-10}\ m} = 38.14 \times 10^{17} = 38.1 \times 10^{17}\ Hz$$

$$\text{Sn: } \nu = \frac{2.998 \times 10^8\ m/s}{0.491 \times 10^{-10}\ m} = 61.06 \times 10^{17} = 61.1 \times 10^{17}\ Hz$$

(b)

Element	Z	ν	$\nu^{1/2}$
Ne	10	2.052×10^{17}	4.530×10^{8}
Ca	20	8.928×10^{17}	9.449×10^{8}
Zn	30	20.89×10^{17}	14.45×10^{8}
Zr	40	38.14×10^{17}	19.5×10^{8}
Sn	50	61.06×10^{17}	24.7×10^{8}

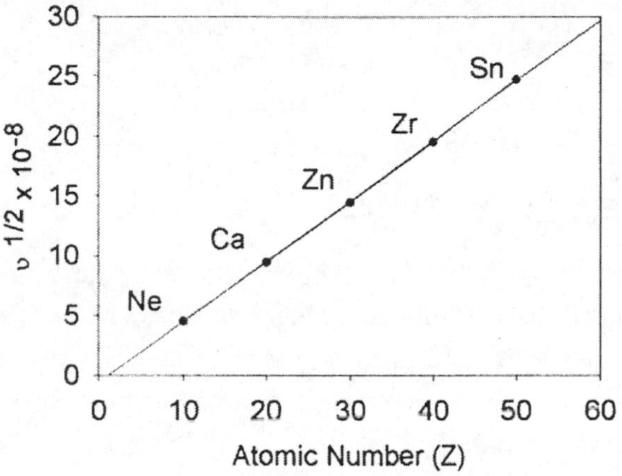

(c) The plot in part (b) indicates that there is a linear relationship between atomic number and the square root of the frequency of the X-rays emitted by an element. Thus, elements with each integer atomic number should exist. This relationship allowed Moseley to predict the existence of elements that filled "holes" or gaps in the periodic table.

(d) For Fe, Z = 26. From the graph, $\nu^{1/2} = 12.5 \times 10^8$, $\nu = 1.56 \times 10^{18}$ Hz.

$$\lambda = c/\nu = \frac{2.998 \times 10^8 \text{ m/s}}{1.56 \times 10^{18} \text{ s}^{-1}} \times \frac{1 \text{ Å}}{1 \times 10^{-10} \text{ m}} = 1.92 \text{ Å}$$

(e) $\lambda = 0.980$ Å $= 0.980 \times 10^{-10}$ m

$$\nu = c/\lambda = \frac{2.998 \times 10^8 \text{ m/s}}{0.980 \times 10^{-10} \text{ m}} = 30.6 \times 10^{17} \text{ Hz}; \quad \nu^{1/2} = 17.5 \times 10^8$$

From the graph, $\nu^{1/2} = 17.5 \times 10^8$, Z = 36. The element is krypton, Kr.

7.97 (a) $E = hc/\lambda$; 1 nm $= 1 \times 10^{-9}$ m; 58.4 nm $= 58.4 \times 10^{-9}$ m;

1 eV = 96.485 kJ/mol, 1 eV • mol = 96.485 kJ

$$E = \frac{6.626 \times 10^{-34} \text{ J•s} \times 2.998 \times 10^8 \text{ m/s}}{58.4 \times 10^{-9} \text{ m}} = 3.4015 \times 10^{-18} = 3.40 \times 10^{-18} \text{ J/photon}$$

$$\frac{3.4015 \times 10^{-18} \text{ J}}{\text{photon}} \times \frac{1 \text{ kJ}}{1000 \text{ J}} \times \frac{6.022 \times 10^{23} \text{ photons}}{\text{mol}} \times \frac{1 \text{ eV•mol}}{96.485 \text{ kJ}} = 21.230$$

$$= 21.2 \text{ eV}$$

(b) $Hg(g) \rightarrow Hg^+(g) + 1e^-$

(c) $I_1 = E_{58.4} - E_K = 21.23\text{ eV} - 10.75\text{ eV} = 10.48 = 10.5\text{ eV}$

$$10.48\text{ eV} \times \frac{96.485\text{ kJ}}{1\text{ eV} \bullet \text{mol}} = 1.01 \times 10^3\text{ kJ/mol}$$

(d) From Figure 7.10, iodine (I) appears to have the ionization energy closest to that of Hg, approximately 1000 kJ/mol.

7.98 (a)

$$Na(g) \rightarrow Na^+(g) + 1e^- \quad \text{(ionization energy of Na)}$$
$$Cl(g) + 1e^- \rightarrow Cl^-(g) \quad \text{(electron affinity of Cl)}$$

$$Na(g) + Cl(g) \rightarrow Na^+(g) + Cl^-(g)$$

(b) $\Delta H = I_1\text{(Na)} + E_1\text{(Cl)} = +496\text{ kJ} - 349\text{ kJ} = +147\text{ kJ}$, endothermic

(c) The reaction $2Na(s) + Cl_2(g) \rightarrow 2NaCl(s)$ involves many more steps than the reaction in part (a). One important difference is the production of NaCl(s) versus NaCl(g). The condensation $NaCl(g) \rightarrow NaCl(s)$ is very exothermic and is the step that causes the reaction of the elements in their standard states to be exothermic, while the gas phase reaction is endothermic.

7.100 (a) $r_{Bi} = r_{BiBr_3} - r_{Br} = 2.63\text{ Å} - 1.14\text{ Å} = 1.49\text{ Å}$

(b) $Bi_2O_3(s) + 6HBr(aq) \rightarrow 2BiBr_3(aq) + 3H_2O(l)$

(c) Bi_2O_3 is soluble in acid solutions because it acts as a base and undergoes acid-base reactions like the one in part (b). It is insoluble in base because it cannot act as an acid. Thus, Bi_2O_3 is a basic oxide, the oxide of a metal. Based on the properties of its oxide, Bi is characterized as a metal.

(d) Bi: $[Xe]6s^2 4f^{14} 5d^{10} 6p^3$. Bi has 5 outer electrons in the 6p and 6s subshells. If all 5 electrons participate in bonding, compounds such as BiF_5 are possible. Also, Bi has a large enough atomic radius (1.49 Å) and low-energy orbitals available to accommodate more than four pairs of bonding electrons.

(e) The high ionization energy and relatively large negative electron affinity of F, coupled with its small atomic radius, make it the most electron withdrawing of the halogens. BiF_5 forms because F has the greatest tendency to attract electrons from Bi. Also, the small atomic radius of F reduces repulsions between neighboring bonded F atoms. The strong electron withdrawing properties of F are also the reason that only F compounds of Xe are known (Solution 7.66).

8 Basic Concepts of Chemical Bonding

Lewis Symbols and Ionic Bonding

Octet rule

8.2 (a) Atoms will gain, lose or share electrons to achieve the nearest noble-gas electron configuration. Except for H and He, this corresponds to eight electrons in the valence shell, thus the term **octet** rule.

(b) S: $[Ne]3s^2 3p^4$ A sulfur atom has 6 valence electrons, so it must gain 2 electrons to achieve an octet.

(c) $1s^2 2s^2 2p^3 = [He]2s^2 2p^3$ The atom (N) has 5 valence electrons and must gain 3 electrons to achieve an octet.

8.4 Sc: $1s^2 2s^2 2p^6 3s^2 3p^6 4s^2 3d^1 = [Ar]4s^2 3d^1$. Scandium has three (3) valence electrons. These valence electrons are available for chemical bonding, while the core electrons do not participate in bonding.

8.6 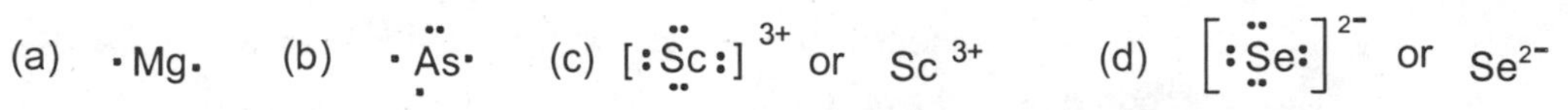

8.8 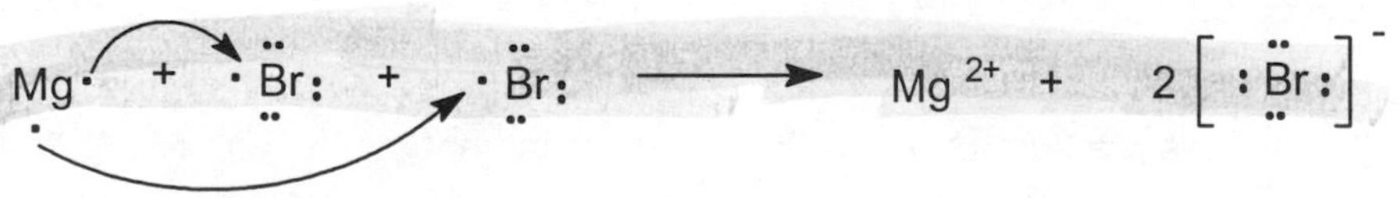

8.10 Bromine does not accept more than one electron, because the additional electron(s) would have a higher principle quantum number than the valence electrons in the completed octet of Br^-. Electrons beyond the n = 4 level in a bromine anion would be substantially shielded from the nucleus by the core electrons and are further from the nucleus than the other electrons. In other words, the energy of the 5s orbital in Br^- is sufficiently high that Br^{2-} or other anions with a negative charge greater than -1 do not form.

8.12 (a) Rb_2O (b) BaI_2 (c) Li_2O (d) $MgCl_2$

8.14 (a) Zn^{2+}: $[Ar]3d^{10}$ (b) Te^{2-}: $[Kr]5s^2 4d^{10} 5p^6$ = [Xe], noble-gas configuration

(c) Se^{3+}: $[Ar]4s^2 3d^{10} 4p^1$ (This is a very unlikely ion. A more stable and commonly-found ion would be Sc^{3+}.) Sc^{3+}: [Ar], noble-gas configuration

(d) Ru^{2+}: $[Kr]4d^6$ (e) Tl^+: $[Xe]6s^2 4f^{14} 5d^{10}$ (f) $Au^+[Xe]4f^{14}5d^{10}$

8.16 (a) NaF, 910 kJ/mol; MgO, 3795 kJ/mol

The two factors that affect lattice energies are charge and ionic radii. The Na–F and Mg–O separations are similar (Na^+ is larger than Mg^{2+}, but F^- is smaller than O^{2-}). The charges on Mg^{2+} and O^{2-} are twice those of Na^+ and F^-, so according to Equation 8.4, the lattice energy of MgO is approximately four times that of NaF.

(b) $MgCl_2$, 2326 kJ/mol; $SrCl_2$, 2127 kJ/mol

The two factors that affect lattice energies are charge and ionic radii. The ionic charges are the same in the two compounds. The ionic radius of Mg^{2+} is smaller than that of Sr^{2+} so the Mg–Cl distance is slightly smaller than the Sr–Cl distance. Since lattice energy is inversely proportional to the ion separation, the lattice energy of $MgCl_2$ is slightly larger than that of $SrCl_2$.

8.18 (a) According to Equation 8.4, electrostatic attraction increases with increasing charges of the ions and decreases with increasing radius of the ions. Thus, lattice energy (i) **increases** as the charges of the ions increase and (ii) **decreases** as the sizes of the ions increase.

(b) KBr < KCl < LiCl < CaO. This order is confirmed by the lattice energies given in Table 8.2. CaO has the highest lattice energy because the ions have 2+ and 2- charges. The other compounds have cations with 1+ charges and anions with 1- charges. They are placed in order of decreasing ionic separation. K^+ and Br^- have the largest radii, Cl^- is smaller than Br^-, and Li^+ is smaller than K^+.

8.20 (a) In MgO, the magnitude of the charges on both ions is 2; in $MgCl_2$, the magnitudes of the charges are 2 and 1. Also, the Cl^- ion is larger than the O^{2-} ion, so the charge separation is greater in $MgCl_2$. Thus, the lattice energy of MgO is greater, because the product of the ionic charges is greater and the ion separation is smaller.

(b) The ions have +1 and -1 charger in all three compounds. In NaCl the cationic and anionic radii are smaller than in the other two compounds, so it has the largest lattice energy. In RbBr and CsBr, the anion is the same, but the Cs cation is larger, so CsBr has the smaller lattice energy.

(c) In BaO, the magnitude of the charges of both ions is 2; in KF, the magnitudes are 1. Charge considerations alone predict that BaO will have the higher lattice energy. The distance effect is less clear; O^{2-} and F^- are isoelectronic, so F^-, with the larger Z, has a slightly smaller radius. Ba^{2+} is two rows lower on the periodic chart than K^+, but it has a greater positive charge, so the radii are probably similar. In any case, the ionic separations in the two compounds are not very different, and the charge effect dominates.

8.22 $Ca(s) \rightarrow Ca(g)$; $Br_2(l) \rightarrow 2Br(g)$; $Ca(g) \rightarrow Ca^+(g) + 1e^-$;
$Ca^+(g) \rightarrow Ca^{2+}(g) + 1e^-$; $2Br(g) + 2e^- \rightarrow 2Br^-(g)$, exothermic;
$Ca^{2+}(g) + 2Br^-(g) \rightarrow CaBr_2(s)$, exothermic

8.24 By analogy to Figure 8.4:

$$\Delta H_{latt} = -\Delta H_f^\circ\ CaCl_2 + \Delta H_f^\circ\ Ca(g) + 2\Delta H_f^\circ\ Cl(g) + I_1\ (Ca) + I_2\ (Ca) + 2E\ (Cl)$$

$$= -(-795.8\ kJ) + 179.3\ kJ + 2(121.7\ kJ) + 590\ kJ + 1145\ kJ + 2(-349\ kJ) = +2256\ kJ$$

From Table 8.2, the lattice energy of NaCl, +788 kJ/mol, is considerably less than that of CaF_2. The 2+ charge of Ca^{2+} leads to much greater electrostatic attractions and a higher lattice energy.

Covalent Bonding, Electronegativity and Bond Polarity

8.26 K and Ar. K is an active metal with one valence electron. It is most likely to achieve an octet by losing this single electron and to participate in ionic bonding. Ar has a stable octet of valence electrons; it is not likely to form chemical bonds of any type.

8.28 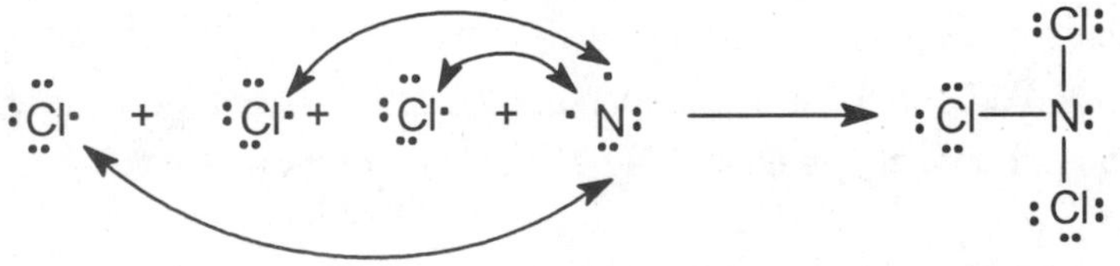

8.30 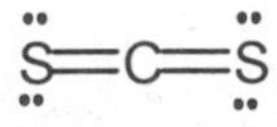

The C–S bonds in CS_2 are double bonds, so the C–S distances will be shorter than a C–S single bond distance.

8.32 (a) The electronegativity of the elements increases going from left to right across a row of the periodic chart.

(b) Electronegativity decreases going down a family of the periodic chart.

(c) Generally, the trends in electronegativity are the same as those in ionization energy and opposite those in electron affinity. That is, the more positive the ionization energy and the more negative the electron affinity (omitting a few exceptions), the greater the electronegativity of an element.

8.34 Electronegativity increases going up and to the right in the periodic table.

(a) O (b) Al (c) Cl (d) F

8.36 The more different the electronegativity values of the two elements, the more polar the bond.

(a) O–F < C–F < Be–F. This order is clear from the periodic trend.

(b) Br–N < P–Br < Br–O. Refer to the electronegativity values in Figure 8.9 to confirm the order of bond polarity. The electronegativity order of the four elements is P < Br < N < O. Br is significantly to the right and below the other three elements, but these directions have conflicting trends. Even though Br and N are farthest apart, their electronegativity values are nearly equal. The Br-N bond is least polar, with Br the less electronegative element.

(c) C–S < N–O < B–F. You might predict that N–O is least polar since the elements are adjacent on the table. However, the big decrease going from the second row to the third means that the electronegativity of S is not only less than that of O, but essentially the same as that of C. C–S is the least polar.

8.38 (a) Non-zero. Cl and F have different electronegativities. In a diatomic molecule, a polar bond means a polar molecule.

(b) Non-zero. C and O have different electronegativities. In a diatomic molecule, a polar bond means a polar molecule.

(c) Zero. Even though the C–O bond is polar in this linear molecule, the two equal C–O bond dipoles lie in opposite directions and cancel each other. This orientation results in a nonpolar molecule.

(d) Non-zero. The two O-H bonds are polar and the molecule is bent (non-linear), so the bond dipoles do not cancel, resulting in a net dipole moment and a polar molecule.

8.40 (a) The more electronegative element, Br, will have a stronger attraction for the shared electrons and adopt a partial negative charge.

(b) Q is the charge at either end of the dipole.

$$Q = \frac{\mu}{r} = \frac{1.21\ \text{D}}{2.49\ \text{Å}} \times \frac{1\ \text{Å}}{1 \times 10^{-10}\ \text{m}} \times \frac{3.34 \times 10^{-30}\ \text{C} \bullet \text{m}}{1\ \text{D}} \times \frac{1\ e}{1.60 \times 10^{-19}\ \text{C}}$$

$$= 0.1014 = 0.101\ e$$

The charges on I and Br are 0.101 *e*.

8.42 Generally, compounds formed by a metal and a nonmetal are described as ionic, while compounds formed from two or more nonmetals are covalent.

(a) MnF_3, ionic (b) CrO_3, ionic

(c) $AsBr_5$, ionic (Although As is a metalloid, use of a roman numeral usually presumes an ionic compound.)

(d) sulfur tetrafluoride, covalent (e) molybdenum(IV) chloride, ionic

(f) scandium(III) chloride, ionic

Lewis Structures; Resonance Structures

8.44 (a) 12 e⁻, 6 e⁻ pairs

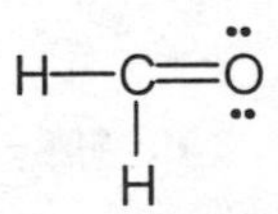

(b) 14 valence e⁻, 7 e⁻ pairs

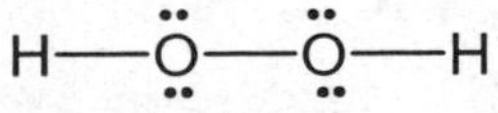

(c) 50 valence e⁻, 25 e⁻ pairs

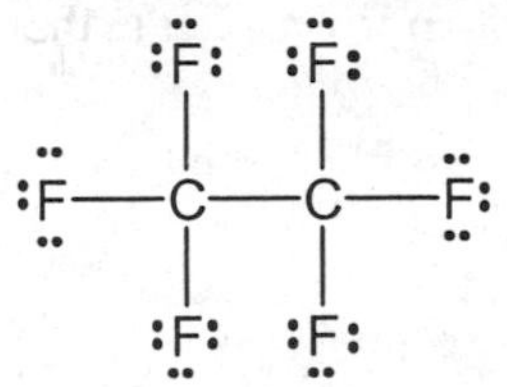

(d) 26 valence e⁻, 13 e⁻ pairs

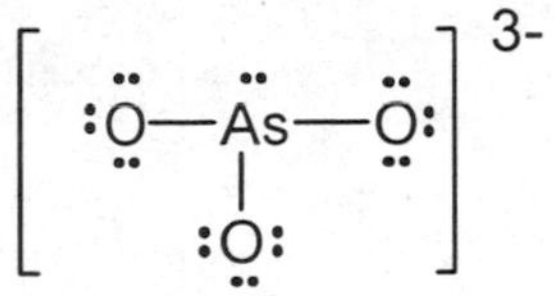

(Choose the Lewis structure that obeys the octet rule, Section 8.7)

(e) 26 valence e⁻ 13 e⁻ pairs

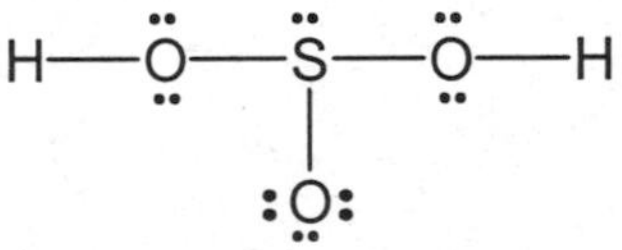

(Choose the Lewis structure that obeys they octet rule, Section 8.7.)

(f) 10 e⁻, 5 e⁻ pairs

H—C≡C—H

8.46 (a) 18 e⁻, 9 e⁻ pairs

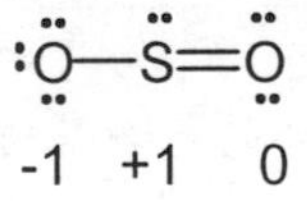

(b) 24 e⁻, 12 e⁻ pairs

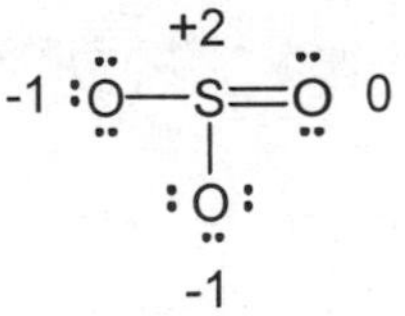

(c) 26 e⁻, 13 e⁻ pairs

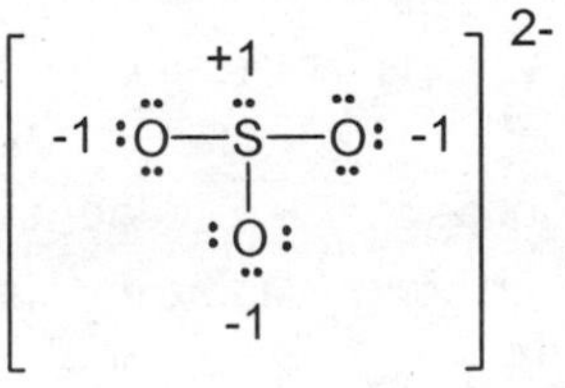

(d) 32 e⁻, 16 e⁻ pairs

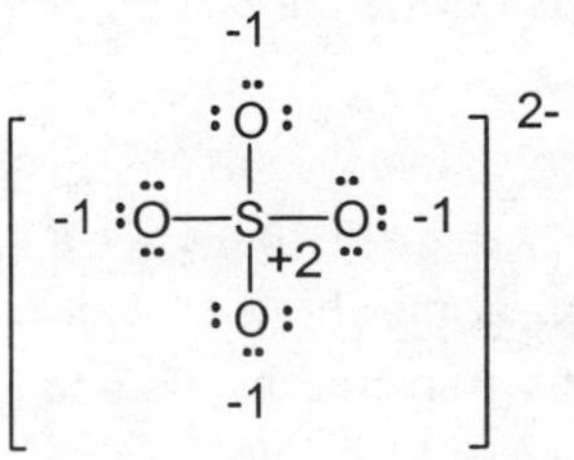

8.48 (a) 16 e^-, 8 e^- pairs

No ē on N?

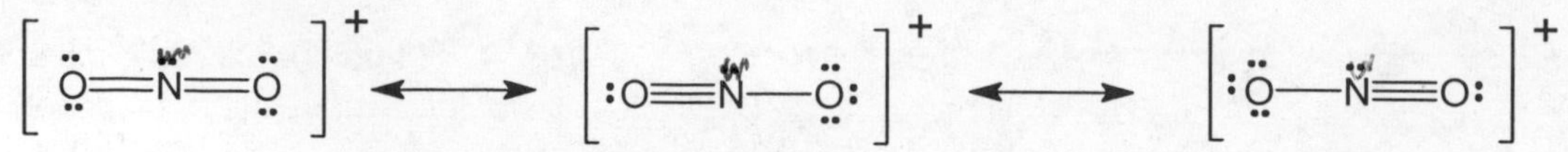

(b) More than one correct Lewis structure can be drawn, so resonance structures are needed to accurately describe the structure.

(c) NO_2^+ has 16 valence electrons. Consider other triatomic molecules involving second-row nonmetallic elements. O_3^{2+} or C_3^{4-} are not 'common' (or stable). CO_2 is common and matches the description (as does N_3^-, azide ion).

8.50 The Lewis structures are as follows:

5 e^- pairs

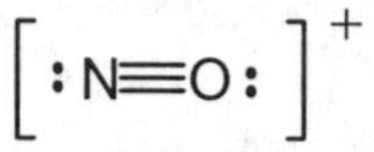

9 e^- pairs

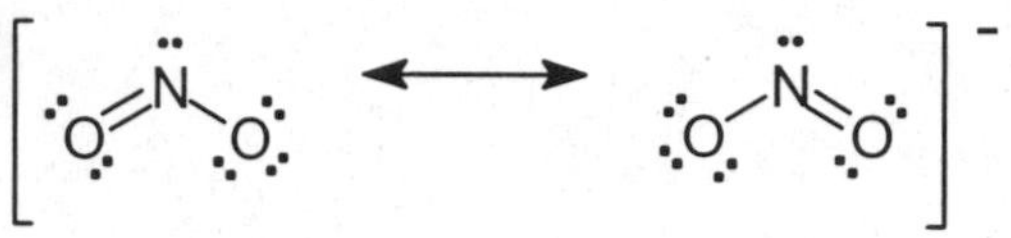

12 e^- pairs

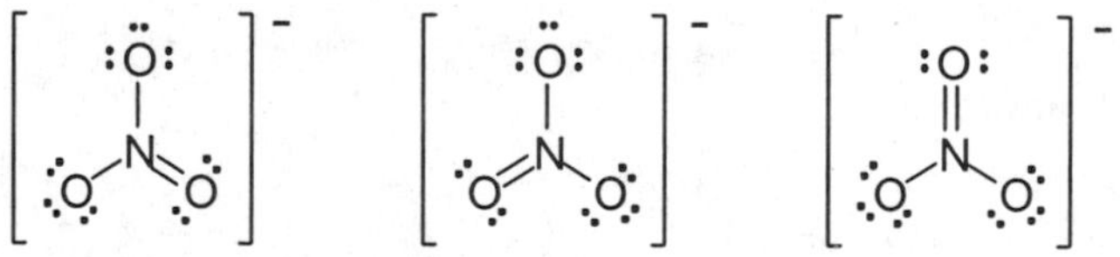

The average number of electron pairs in the N–O bond is 3.0 for NO^+, 1.5 for NO_2^- and 1.33 for NO_3^-. The more electron pairs shared between two atoms, the shorter the bond. Thus the N–O bond lengths vary in the order $NO^+ < NO_2^- < NO_3^-$.

8.52 (a)

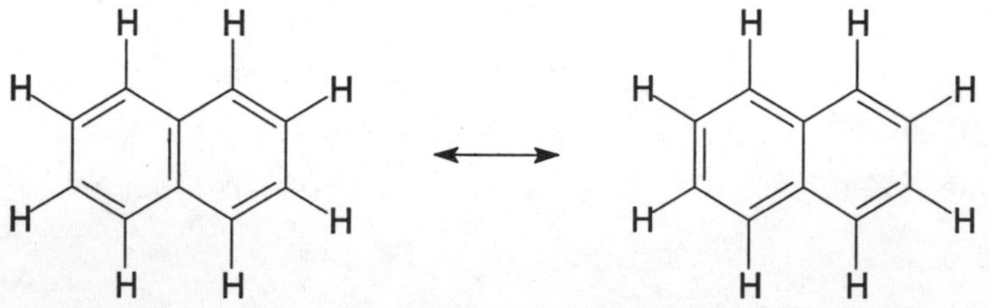

(b) The resonance model of this molecule has bonds that are neither single nor double, but somewhere in between. This results in bond lengths that are intermediate between C–C single and C=C double bond lengths.

(c)

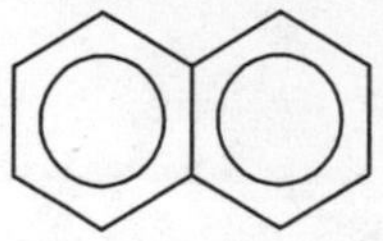

Exceptions to the Octet Rule

8.54 Carbon, in group 14, needs to form four single bonds to achieve an octet, as in CH_4. Nitrogen, in group 15, needs to form three, as in NH_3. If G = group number and n = the number of single bonds, G + n = 18 is a general relationship for the representative non-metals.

Check: O as in H_2O (G = 16) + (n = 2 bonds) = 18

8.56 In the third period, atoms have the space and available orbitals to accommodate extra electrons. Since atomic radius increases going down a family, elements in the third period and beyond are less subject to destabilization from additional electron-electron repulsions. Also, the third shell contains d orbitals that are relatively close in energy to 3s and 3p orbitals (the ones that accommodate the octet) and provide an allowed energy state for the extra electrons.

8.58 (a) 11 e^-, 5.5 e^- pairs;
odd electron molecule

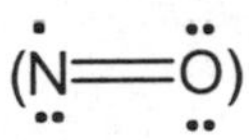

The odd electron is probably on N because it is less electronegative than O.

(b) 22 e^- 11 e^- pairs

10 e^- around central I

(c) 18 e^-, 9 e^- pairs

Structures with expanded octets around S can be drawn, but are not preferred (Section 8.7).

(d) 24 e^-, 12 e^- pairs

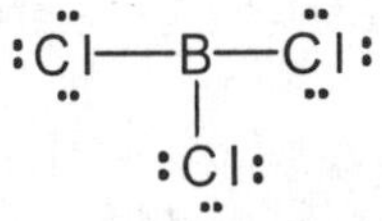

6 e^- around B
Structures such as the one below can be drawn, but are not likely because of high formal charges on B and Cl.

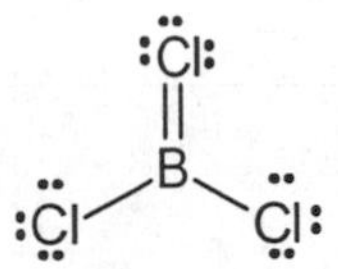

(e) 36 e^-, 18 e^- pairs

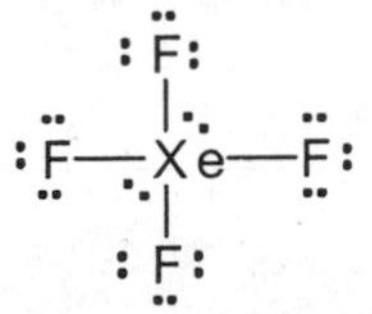

12 e^- around the central Xe
(F cannot expand beyond an octet.)

8.60 (a) 19 e^-, 9.5 e^- pairs, odd electron molecule

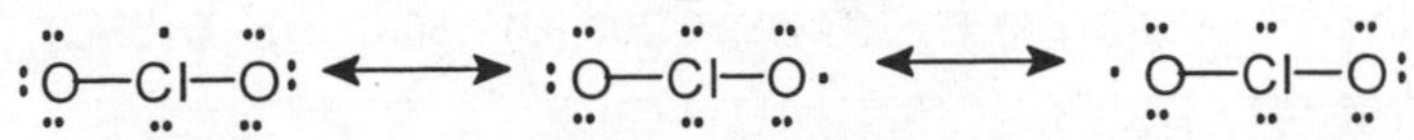

(b) None of the structures satisfies the octet rule. In each structure, one atom has only 7 e^- around it. If a molecule has an odd number of electrons in the valence shell, no Lewis structure can satisfy the octet rule.

(c) 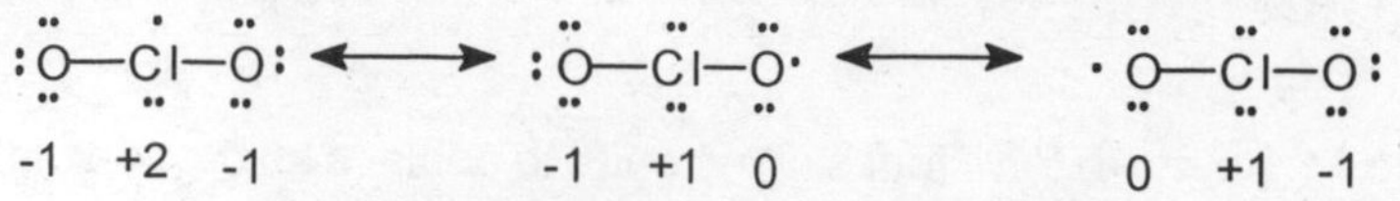

Formal charge arguments predict that the two resonance structures with the odd electron on O are most important. This contradicts electronegativity arguments, which would predict that the less electronegative atom, Cl, would be more likely to have fewer than 8 e^- around it.

Bond Enthalpies

8.62 (a) $\Delta H = 3D(C\text{-}Br) + D(C\text{-}H) + D(Cl\text{-}Cl) - 3D(C\text{-}Br) - (C\text{-}Cl) - D(H\text{-}Cl)$

$= D(C\text{-}H) + D(Cl\text{-}Cl) - D(C\text{-}Cl) - D(H\text{-}Cl)$

$\Delta H = 413 + 242 - 328 - 431 = -104$ kJ

(b) $\Delta H = 4D(C\text{-}H) + 2D(C\text{-}S) + 2D(S\text{-}H) + D(C\text{-}C) + D(H\text{-}Br)$

$-4D(S\text{-}H) - D(C\text{-}C) - 2D(C\text{-}Br) - 4D(C\text{-}H)$

$= 2D(C\text{-}S) + D(H\text{-}Br) - 2D(S\text{-}H) - 2D(C\text{-}Br)$

$\Delta H = 2(259) + 366 - 2(339) - 2(276) = -346$ kJ

(c) $\Delta H = 4D(N\text{-}H) + D(N\text{-}N) + D(Cl\text{-}Cl) - 4D(N\text{-}H) - D(N\text{-}Cl)$

$= D(N\text{-}N) + D(Cl\text{-}Cl) - D(N\text{-}Cl)$

$\Delta H = 163 + 242 - 200 = 205$ kJ

8.64 *Plan*. Draw structural formulas so bonds can be visualized.

(a) 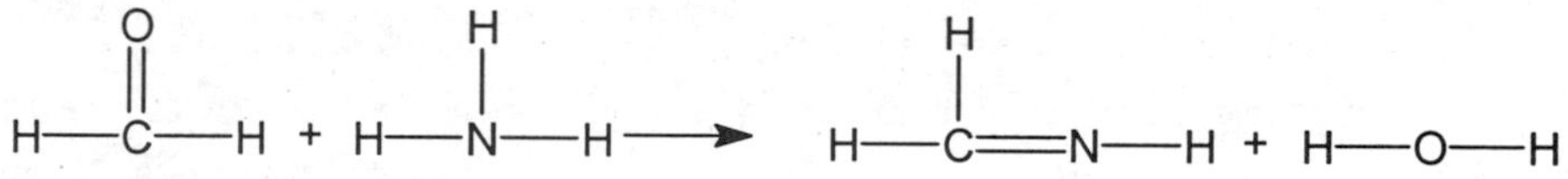

$\Delta H = D(C{=}O) + 2D(C\text{-}H) + 3D(N\text{-}H) - D(C{=}N) - 2D(C\text{-}H) - 2D(N\text{-}H) - 2D(O\text{-}H)$

$= D(C{=}O) + D(N\text{-}H) - D(C{=}N) - 2D(O\text{-}H)$

$\Delta H = 799 + 391 - 615 - 2(463) = -351$ kJ

(b) 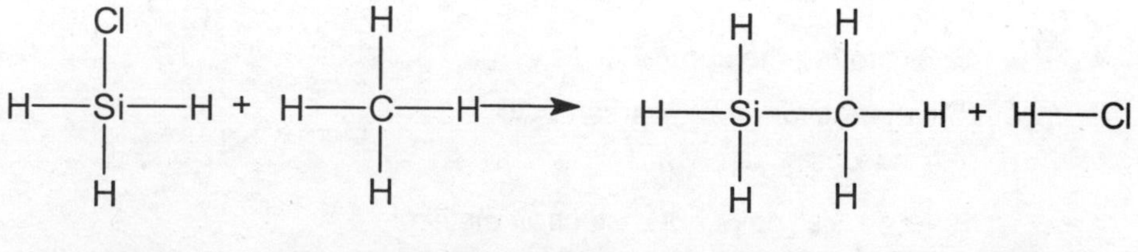

$\Delta H = 3D(Si\text{-}H) + D(Si\text{-}Cl) + 4D(C\text{-}H) - 3D(Si\text{-}H) - 3D(C\text{-}H) - D(Si\text{-}C) - D(H\text{-}Cl)$

$= D(Si\text{-}Cl) + D(C\text{-}H) - D(Si\text{-}C) - D(H\text{-}Cl)$

$\Delta H = (464) + 413 - (301) - 431 = 145$ kJ

(c) *Plan.* Use bond enthalpies to calculate ΔH for the reaction with $S_8(g)$ as a product. Then,

$8H_2S(g) \rightarrow 8H_2(g) + S_8(g)$	ΔH
$S_8(g) \rightarrow S_8(s)$	$-\Delta H^\circ_f$ for $S_8(g)$
$8H_2S(g) \rightarrow 8H_2(g) + S_8(s)$	$\Delta H_{rxn} = [\Delta H - \Delta H^\circ_f\ S_8(g)]$

$\Delta H = 16D(S\text{-}H) - 8(H\text{-}H) - 8(S\text{-}S)$

$= 16(339) - 8(436) - 8(266) = -192$ kJ

$\Delta H_{rxn} = \Delta H - \Delta H^\circ_f\ S_8(g) = -192\text{ kJ} - 102.3\text{ kJ} = -294.3 = -294$ kJ

8.66 (a)

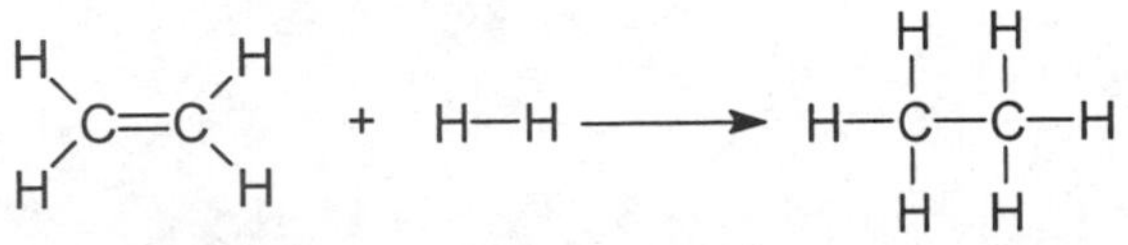

$\Delta H = 4D(C\text{-}H) + D(C{=}C) + D(H\text{-}H) - 6D(C\text{-}H) - D(C\text{-}C)$

$= D(C{=}C) + D(H\text{-}H) - 2D(C\text{-}H) - D(C\text{-}C)$

$\Delta H = 614 + 436 - 2(413) - 348 = -124$ kJ

(b) $\Delta H^\circ = \Delta H^\circ_f\ C_2H_6(g) - \Delta H^\circ_f\ C_2H_4(g) - \Delta H^\circ_f\ H_2(g)$

$= -84.68 - 52.30 - 0 = -136.98$ kJ

The values of ΔH for the reaction differ because the bond enthalpies used in part (a) are average values that can differ from one compound to another. For example, the exact enthalpy of a C–H bond in C_2H_4 is probably not equal to the enthalpy of a C–H bond in C_2H_6. Thus, reaction enthalpies calculated from average bond enthalpies are estimates. On the other hand, standard enthalpies of formation are measured quantities and should lead to accurate reaction enthalpies. The advantage of average bond enthalpies is that they can be used for reactions where no measured enthalpies of formation are available.

8.68 (a) (i)

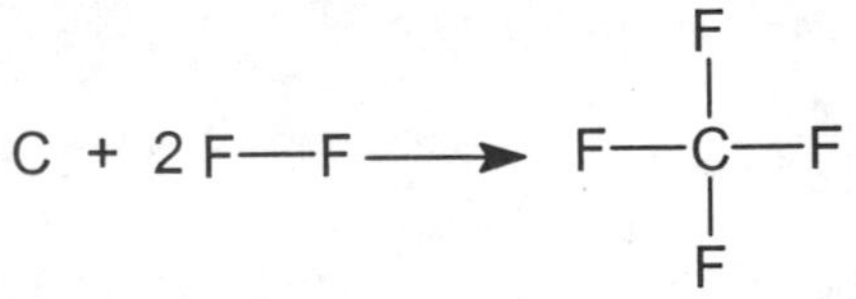

$\Delta H = 2D(F\text{–}F) - 4D(C\text{–}F) = 2(155) - 4(485) = -1630$ kJ

(ii)

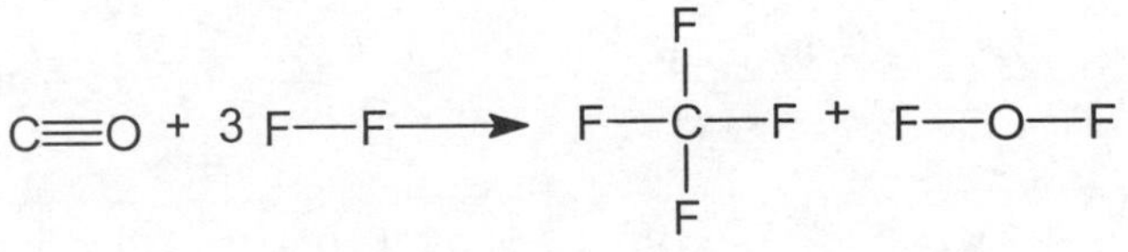

$\Delta H = D(C{\equiv}O) + 3D(F\text{–}F) - 4D(C\text{–}F) - 2D(D\text{–}F)$

$= 1072 + 3(155) - 4(485) - 2(190) = -783$ kJ

(iii) 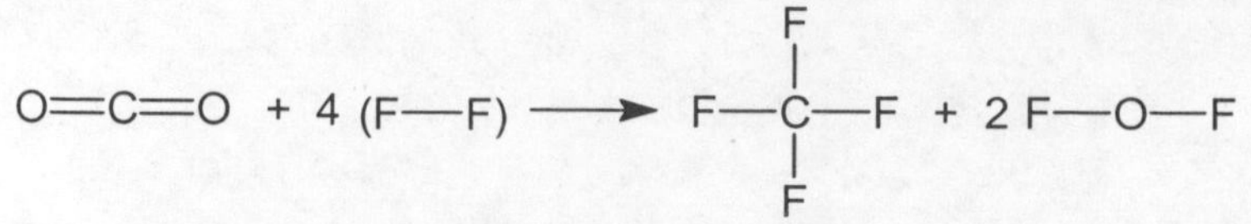

$\Delta H = 2D(C{=}O) + 4D(F{-}F) - 4D(C{-}F) - 4D(O{-}F)$
$= 2(799) + 4(155) - 4(485) - 4(190) = -482$ kJ

(b) The more oxygen atoms bound to carbon, the less exothermic the reaction in this series.

Additional Exercises

8.70 (a) Lattice energy is proportional to Q_1Q_2 / d. For each of these compounds, Q_1Q_2 is the same. The anion H^- is present in each compound, but the ionic radius of the cation increases going from Be to Ba. Thus, the value of d (the cation-anion separation) increases and the ratio Q_1Q_2 / d decreases. This is reflected in the decrease in lattice energy going from BeH_2 to BaH_2.

(b) Again, Q_1Q_2 for ZnH_2 is the same as that for the other compounds in the series and the anion is H^-. The lattice energy of ZnH_2, 2870 kJ, is closest to that of MgH_2, 2791 kJ. The ionic radius of Zn^{2+} is similar to that of Mg^{2+}.

8.72 $E = Q_1Q_2 / d$; $k = 8.99 \times 10^9$ J•m/coul^2

(a) $$E = \frac{-8.99 \times 10^9 \text{ J}\bullet\text{m}}{\text{C}^2} \times \frac{(1.60 \times 10^{-19}\text{ C})^2}{(0.97 + 1.96) \times 10^{-10}\text{ m}} = -7.8547 \times 10^{-19} = -7.85 \times 10^{-19}\text{ J}$$

The sign of E is negative because one of the interacting ions is an anion; this is an attractive interaction.

On a molar basis: $-7.855 \times 10^{-19} \times 6.022 \times 10^{23} = -4.73 \times 10^5$ J = -473 kJ

(b) $$E = \frac{-8.99 \times 10^9 \text{ J}\bullet\text{m}}{\text{C}^2} \times \frac{(1.60 \times 10^{-19}\text{ C})^2}{(1.47 + 1.96) \times 10^{-10}\text{ m}} = -6.71 \times 10^{-19}\text{ J}$$

On a molar basis: -4.04×10^5 J = -404 kJ

(c) $$E = \frac{-8.99 \times 10^9 \text{ J}\bullet\text{m}}{\text{C}^2} \times \frac{(2 \times 1.60 \times 10^{-19}\text{ C})^2}{(1.13 + 1.84) \times 10^{-10}\text{ m}} = -3.10 \times 10^{-18}\text{ J}$$

On a molar basis: -1.87×10^6 J = -1.87×10^3 kJ

8.74 Rh: $[Kr]5s^2 4d^7$. In order to achieve the electron configuration of Kr as a positive ion, Rh would have to lose it's 5s valence electrons and all seven 4d electrons resulting in a Rh^{9+} ion. The 4d electrons are closer to the nucleus than n = 5 electrons and are incompletely shielded from the nucleus by the 4s and 4p electrons. Thus, I_3 through I_9 are likely to be quite large. Even though the lattice energy of an ionic compound involving Rb^{9+} would be large, it could not compensate for the total ionization energy required to form Rh^{9+}. It is unlikely that Rh can adapt the noble-gas configuration of Kr by forming Rh^{9+}.

8.75 (a) 12 + 3 + 15 = 30 valence e^-, 15 e^- pairs.

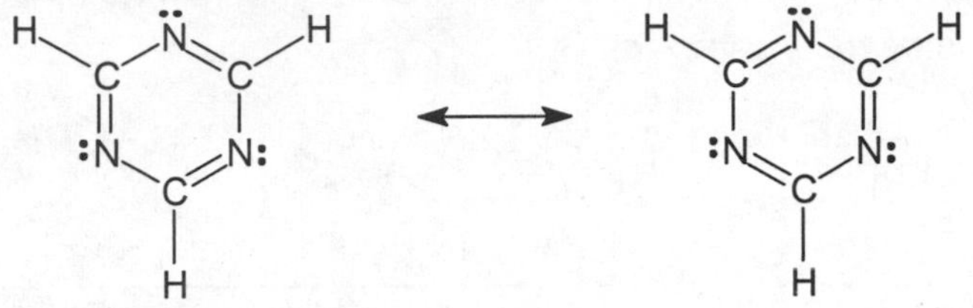

Structures with H bound to N and nonbonded electron pairs on C can be drawn, but the structures above minimize formal charges on the atoms.

(b) The resonance structures indicate that triazine will have six equal C–N bond lengths, intermediate between C–N single and C–N double bond lengths. (See Solutions 8.51 and 8.52). From Table 8.5, an average C–N length is 1.43 Å, a C=N length is 1.38 Å. The average of these two lengths is 1.405 Å. The C–N bond length in triazine should be in the range 1.40 - 1.41 Å.

8.77 (a) B–O. the most polar bond will be formed by the two elements with the greatest difference in electronegativity. Since electronegativity increases moving right and up on the periodic chart, the possibilities are B–O and Te–O. These two bonds are likely to have similar electronegativitiy differences (3 columns apart vs. 3 rows apart). Values from Figure 8.6 confirm the similarity, and show that B–O is slightly more polar.

(b) Te–I. Both are in the fifth row of the periodic chart and have the two largest covalent radii among this group of elements.

(c) TeI_2. Te needs to participate in two covalent bonds to satisfy the octet rule, and each I atom needs to participate in one bond, so by forming a TeI_2 molecule, the octet rule can be satisfied for all three atoms.

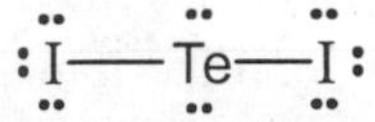

(d) B_2O_3. Although this is probably not a purely ionic compound, it can be understood in terms of gaining and losing electrons to achieve a noble-gas configuration. If each B atom were to lose 3 e^- and each O atom were to gain 2 e^-, charge balance and the octet rule would be satisfied.

P_2O_3. Each P atom needs to share 3 e^- and each O atom 2 e^- to achieve an octet. Although the correct number of electrons seem to be available, a correct Lewis structure is difficult to imagine. In fact, phosphorus (III) oxide exists as P_4O_6 rather than P_2O_3 (Chapter 22).

8.78 Use the method detailed in Section 8.5, *A Closer Look*, to estimate partial charges from electronegativity values. From Figure 8.6, the electronegativity of F is 4.0 and of Cl is 3.0.

F has 4.0 / (3.0 + 4.0) = 0.57 of the charge of the bonding e^- pair.
Cl has 3.0 / (3.0 + 4.0) = 0.43 of the charge of the bonding e^- pair.

This amounts to 0.57 × *2e* = 1.14*e* on F or 0.14*e* more than a neutral F atom. This implies a -0.14 charge on F and +0.14 charge on Cl.

From Figure 7.5, the covalent radius of F is 0.71 Å and of Cl is 0.99 Å. The F–Cl separation is 1.70 Å.

$$\mu = Qr = 0.14e \times \frac{1.60 \times 10^{-19}\ \text{C}}{e} \times 1.70\ \text{Å} \times \frac{1 \times 10^{-10}\ \text{m}}{\text{Å}} \times \frac{1\ \text{D}}{3.34 \times 10^{-30}\ \text{C}\bullet\text{m}} = 1.1\ \text{D}$$

Clearly, this method is approximate. The estimated dipole moment of 1.1 D is within 30% of the measured value of 0.88 D.

8.80 (a) $14e^-$, 7 e^- pairs 32 e^-, 16 e^- pairs

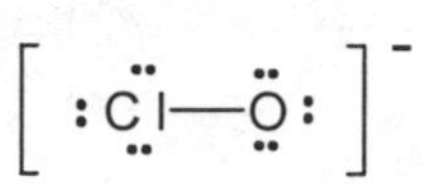

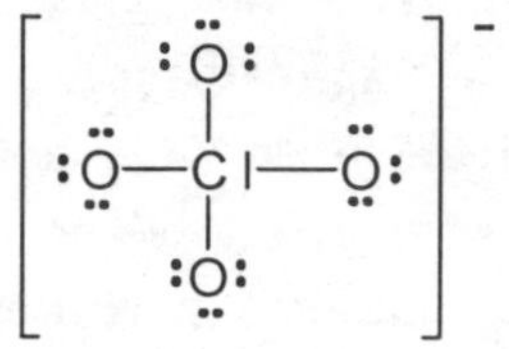

FC on Cl = 7 - [6 + 1/2(2)] = 0 FC on Cl = 7 - [0 + 1/2(8)] = +3

(b) The oxidation number of Cl is +1 in ClO^- and +7 in ClO_4^-.

(c) The definition of formal charge assumes that all bonding pairs of electrons are equally shared by the two bonded atoms, that all bonds are purely covalent. The definition of oxidation number assumes that the more electronegative element in the bond gets all of the bonding electrons, that the bonds are purely ionic. These two definitions represent the two extremes of how electron density is distributed between bonded atoms.

In ClO^- and ClO_4^-, Cl is the less electronegative element, so the oxidation numbers have a higher positive value than the formal charges. The true description of the electron density distribution is somewhere between the extremes indicated by formal charge and oxidation number.

8.82 I_3^- has a Lewis structure with an expanded octet of electrons around the central I.

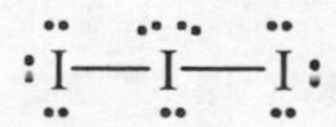

F cannot accommodate an expanded octet because it is too small and has no available d orbitals in its valence shell.

8.84 (a) $\Delta H = 5D(C\text{-}H) + D(C\text{-}C) + D(C\text{-}O) + D(O\text{-}H) - 6D(C\text{-}H) - 2D(C\text{-}O)$

$= D(C\text{-}C) + D(O\text{-}H) - D(C\text{-}H) - D(C\text{-}O)$

$= 348\ kJ + 463\ kJ - 413\ kJ - 358\ kJ$

$\Delta H = +40\ kJ$; ethanol has the lower enthalpy

(b) $\Delta H = 4D(C\text{-}H) + D(C\text{-}C) + 2D(C\text{-}O) - 4D(C\text{-}H) - D(C\text{-}C) - D(C{=}O)$

$= 2D(C\text{-}O) - D(C{=}O)$

$= 2(358\ kJ) - 799\ kJ$

$\Delta H = -83\ kJ$; acetaldehyde has the lower enthalpy

(c) $\Delta H = 8D(C\text{-}H) + 4D(C\text{-}C) + D(C{=}C) - 8D(C\text{-}H) - 2D(C\text{-}C) - 2D(C{=}C)$

$= 2D(C\text{-}C) - D(C{=}C)$

$= 2(348\ kJ) - 614\ kJ$

$\Delta H = +82\ kJ$; cyclopentene has the lower enthalpy

(d) $\Delta H = 3D(C\text{-}H) + D(C\text{-}N) + D(C\equiv N) - 3D(C\text{-}H) - D(C\text{-}C) - D(C\equiv N)$

$= D(C\text{-}N) - D(C\text{-}C)$

$= 293\ kJ - 348\ kJ$

$\Delta H = -55\ kJ$; acetonitrile has the lower enthalpy

8.86

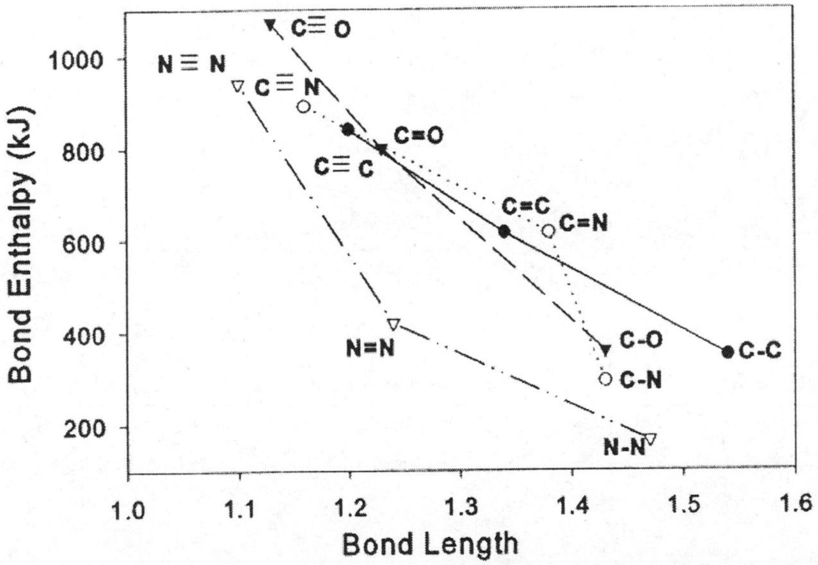

When comparing the same pair of bonded atoms (C–N vs. C=N vs. C≡N), the shorter the bond the greater the bond energy, but the two quantities are not necessarily directly proportional. The plot clearly shows that there are no simple length/strength correlations for single bonds alone, double bonds alone, triple bonds alone, or among different pairs of bonded atoms (all C–C bonds vs. all C–N bonds, etc.).

8.87 (a) S–N ≈ 1.77 Å (sum of the bonding atomic radii from figure 7.5).

(b) S–O ≈ 1.75 Å (the sum of the bonding atomic radii from figure 7.5.) Alternatively, half of the S–S distance in S_8 (1.02) plus half of the O–O distance from Table 8.5 (0.74) is 1.76 Å.

(c) Owing to the resonance structures for SO_2 (see Solution 8.58(c)), we assume that the S–O bond in SO_2 is intermediate between a double and single bond, so the distance of 1.43 Å should be significantly shorter than an S–O single bond distance, 1.75 Å.

(d) 54 e^-, 27 e^- pair

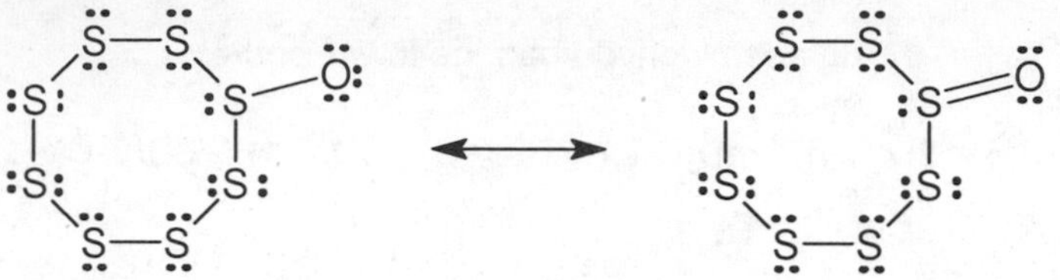

The observed S–O bond distance, 1.48 Å, is similar to that in SO_2, 1.43 Å, which can be described by resonance structures showing both single and double S–O bonds. Thus, S_8O must have resonance structures with both single and double S–O bonds. The structure with the S=O bond has 5 e^- pairs about this S atom. To the extent that this resonance form contributes to the true structure, the S atom bound to O has more than an octet of electrons around it.

Integrative Exercises

8.89 (a)

$Sr(s) \rightarrow Sr(g)$	ΔH_f° Sr(g) [ΔH_{sub}° Sr(s)]
$Sr(g) \rightarrow Sr^+(g) + 1\ e^-$	I_1 Sr
$Sr^+(g) \rightarrow Sr^{2+}(g) + 1\ e^-$	I_2 Sr
$Cl_2(g) \rightarrow 2Cl(g)$	2 ΔH_f° Cl(g) [$D(Cl_2)$]
$2Cl(g) + 2\ e^- \rightarrow 2Cl^-(g)$	$2E_1$ Cl
$SrCl_2(s) \rightarrow Sr(s) + Cl_2(g)$	$-\Delta H_f^\circ$ $SrCl_2$
$SrCl_2(s) \rightarrow Sr^{2+}(g) + 2Cl^-(g)$	ΔH_{latt}

(b) $\Delta H_f^\circ\ SrCl_2(s) = \Delta H_f^\circ\ Sr(g) + I_1(Sr) + I_2(Sr) + 2\Delta H_f^\circ\ Cl(g) + 2E(Cl) - \Delta H_{latt}\ SrCl_2$

$\Delta H_f^\circ\ SrCl_2(s) = 164.4\ kJ + 549\ kJ + 1064\ kJ + 2(121.7)\ kJ + 2(-349)\ kJ - 2127\ kJ$

$= -804\ kJ$

8.91 (a) Assume 100 g.

$$14.52\ g\ C \times \frac{1\ mol}{12.011\ g\ C} = 1.209\ mol\ C;\ 1.209 / 1.209 = 1$$

$$1.83\ g\ H \times \frac{1\ mol}{1.008\ g\ H} = 1.816\ mol\ H;\ 1.816 / 1.209 = 1.5$$

$$64.30\ g\ Cl \times \frac{1\ mol}{35.453\ g\ Cl} = 1.814\ mol\ Cl;\ 1.814 / 1.209 = 1.5$$

$$19.35\ g\ O \times \frac{1\ mol}{15.9994\ g\ O} = 1.209\ mol\ O;\ 1.209 / 1.209 = 1.0$$

Multiplying by 2 to obtain an integer ratio, the empirical formula is $C_2H_3Cl_3O_2$.

(b) The empirical formula weight is 2(12.0) + 3(1.0) + 3(35.5) + 2(16) = 165.5. The empirical formula is the molecular formula.

(c) 44 e^-, 22 e^- pairs

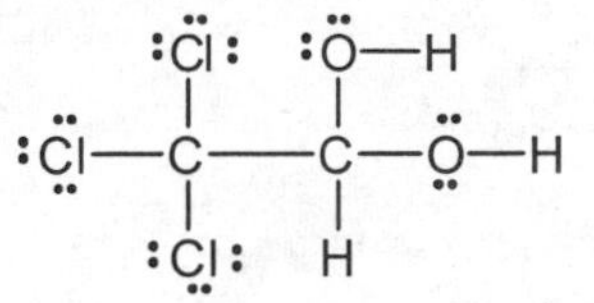

8.92 (a) C_2H_2: 10 e^-, 5 e^- pair N_2: 10 e^-, 5 e^- pair

H—C≡C—H :N≡N:

(b) N_2 is an extremely stable, unreactive compound. Under appropriate conditions, it can be either oxidized (Section 22.7) or reduced (Sections 14.6 and 15.1). C_2H_2 is a reactive gas, used in combination with O_2 for welding and as starting material for organic synthesis (Section 25.4).

(c) $2N_2(g) + 5O_2(g) \rightarrow 2N_2O_5(g)$

$2C_2H_2(g) + 5O_2(g) \rightarrow 4CO_2(g) + 2H_2O(g)$

(d) $\Delta H^\circ_{rxn}(N_2) = 2\Delta H^\circ_f\ N_2O_5(g) - 2\Delta H^\circ_f\ N_2(g) - 5\Delta H^\circ_f\ O_2(g)$

$= 2(11.30) - 2(0) - 5(0) = 22.60$ kJ

$\Delta H^\circ_{ox} = 11.30$ kJ/mol N_2

$\Delta H^\circ_{rxn}(C_2H_2) = 4\Delta H^\circ_f\ CO_2(g) + 2\Delta H^\circ_f\ H_2O(g) - 2\Delta H^\circ_f\ C_2H_2(g) - 5\Delta H^\circ_f\ O_2(g)$

$= 4(-393.5\text{ kJ}) + 2(-241.82\text{ kJ}) - 2(226.7\text{ kJ}) - 5(0)$

$= -2511.0$ kJ

$\Delta H^\circ_{ox}(C_2H_2) = -1255.5$ kJ/mol C_2H_2

The oxidation of C_2H_2 is highly exothermic, which means that the energy state of the combined products is much lower than that of the reactants. The reaction is "down hill" in an energy sense, and occurs readily. The oxidation of N_2 is mildly endothermic (energy of products higher than reactants) and the reaction does not readily occur. This is in agreement with the general reactivities from part (b).

(e) Referring to bond enthalpies in Table 8.4, when the C–H bonds are taken into account, even more energy is required for bond breaking in the oxidation of C_2H_2 than in the oxidation of N_2. The difference seems to be in the enthalpies of formation of the products. $CO_2(g)$ and $H_2O(g)$ have extremely exothermic ΔH°_f values, which cause the oxidation of C_2H_2 to be energetically favorable. $N_2O_5(g)$ has an endothermic ΔH°_f values, which causes the oxidation of N_2 to be energetically unfavorable.

8.93 (a) Assume 100 g.

$$62.04 \text{ g Ba} \times \frac{1 \text{ mol}}{137.33 \text{ g Ba}} = 0.4518 \text{ mol Ba}; \; 0.4518 / 0.4518 = 1.0$$

$$37.96 \text{ g N} \times \frac{1 \text{ mol}}{14.007 \text{ g N}} = 2.710 \text{ mol N}; \; 2.710 / 0.4518 = 6.0$$

The empirical formula is BaN_6. Ba has an ionic charge of 2+, so there must be two 1- azide ions to balance the charge. The formula of each azide ion is N_3^-.

(b) 16 e^-, 8 e^- pairs

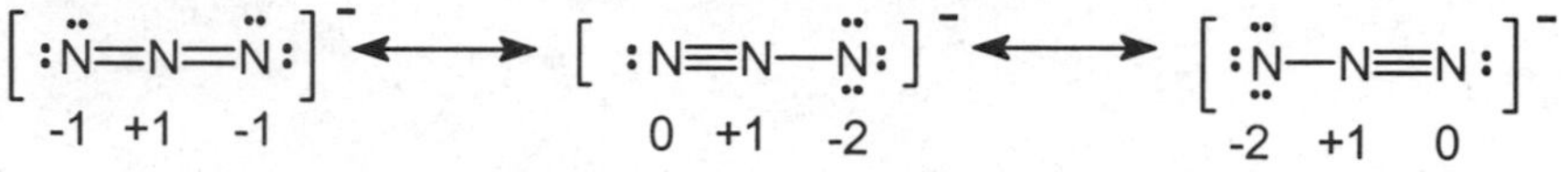

(c) The left structure minimizes formal charges and is probably the main contributor.

(d) The two N–N bond lengths will be equal. The two minor contributors would individually cause unequal N–N distances, but collectively they contribute equally to the lengthening and shortening of each bond. The N–N distance will be approximately 1.24 Å, the average N=N distance.

8.94 (a) Assume 100 g of compound

$$69.6 \text{ g S} \times \frac{1 \text{ mol S}}{32.07 \text{ g}} = 2.17 \text{ mol S}$$

$$30.4 \text{ g N} \times \frac{1 \text{ mol N}}{14.01 \text{ g}} = 2.17 \text{ mol N}$$

S and N are present in a 1:1 mol ratio, so the empirical formula is SN. The empirical formula weight is 46. $\mathcal{M}$/FW = 184.3/46 = 4 The molecular formula is S_4N_4.

(b) 44 e^-, 22 e^- pairs. Because of its small radius, N is unlikely to have an expanded octet. Begin with alternating S and N atoms in the ring. Try to satisfy the octet rule with single bonds and lone pairs. At least two double bonds somewhere in the ring are required.

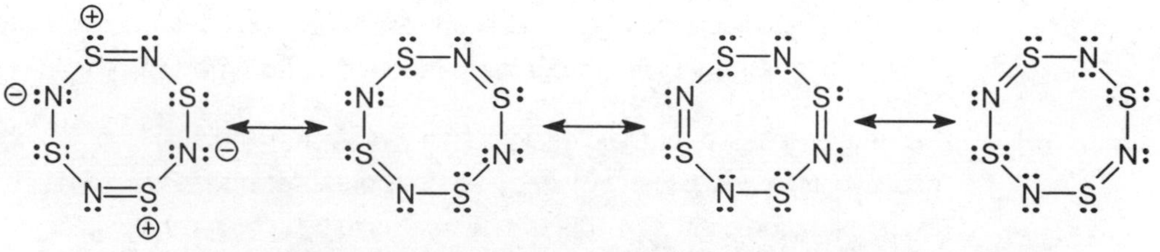

These structures carry formal charges on S and N atoms as shown. Other possibilities include:

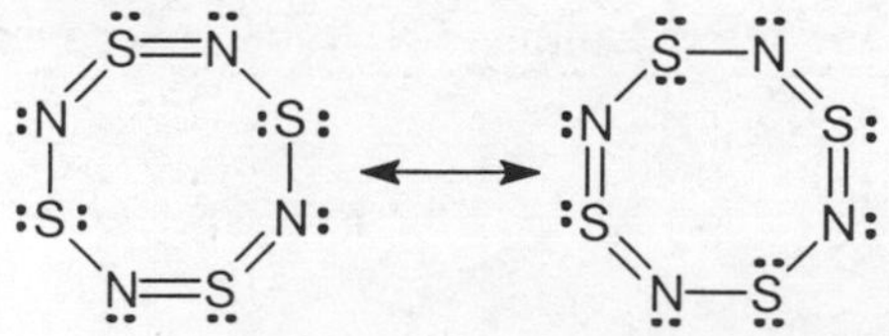

These structures have zero formal charges on all atoms and are likely to contribute to the true structure. Note that the S atoms that are shown with two double bonds are not necessarily linear, because S has an expanded octet. Other resonance structures with four double bonds are.

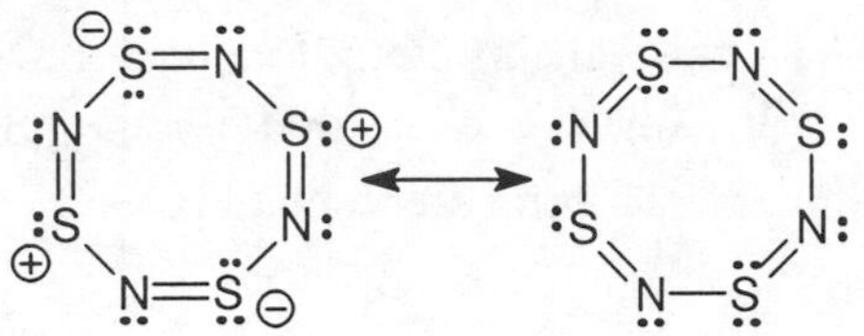

In either resonance structure, the two 'extra' electron pairs can be placed on any pair of S atoms in ring, leading to a total of 10 resonance structures. The sulfur atoms alternately carry formal charges of +1 and -1. Without further structural information, it is not possible to eliminate any of the above structures. Clearly, the S_4N_4 molecule stretches the limits of the Lewis model of chemical bonding.

(c) Each resonance structure has 8 total bonds and more than 8 but less than 16 bonding e^- pairs, so an "average" bond will be intermediate between a S–N single and double bond. We estimate an average S–N single bond length to be 1.77 Å (sum of bonding atomic radii from figure 7.5). We do not have a direct value for a S–N double bond length. Comparing double and single bond lengths for C–C (1.34 Å, 1.54 Å), N–N (1.24 Å, 1.47 Å) and O–O (1.21 Å, 1.48 Å) bonds from Table 8.5, we see that, on average, a double bond is approximately 0.23 Å shorter than a single bond. Applying this difference to the S–N single bond length, we estimate the S–N double bond length as 1.54 Å. Finally, the intermediate S–N bond length in S_4N_4 should be between these two values, approximately 1.60-165 Å. [The measured bond length is 1.62 Å.]

(d) $S_4N_4 \rightarrow 4S(g) + 4N(g)$

$\Delta H = 4\Delta H^\circ_f\ S(g) + 4\Delta H^\circ_f\ N(g) - \Delta H^\circ_f\ S_4N_4$

$\Delta H = 4(222.8\ kJ) + 4(472.7\ kJ) - 480\ kJ = 2302\ kJ$

This energy, 2302 kJ, represents the dissociation of 8 S–N bonds in the molecule; the average dissociation energy of one S-N bond in S_4N_4 is then 2302 kJ/8 bonds = 287.8 kJ.

8.96 (a) $C_6H_6(g) \rightarrow 6H(g) + 6C(g)$

$\Delta H^\circ = 6\Delta H^\circ_f\ H(g) + 6\Delta H^\circ_f\ C(g) - \Delta H^\circ_f\ C_6H_6(g)$

$\Delta H^\circ = 6(217.94)\ kJ + 6(718.4)\ kJ - 82.9\ kJ = 5535\ kJ$

(b) $C_6H_6(g) \rightarrow 6CH(g)$

(c)

$C_6H_6(g) \rightarrow 6H(g) + 6C(g)$ ΔH°		5535 kJ
$6H(g) + 6C(g) \rightarrow 6CH(g)$	-6D(C-H)	-6(413) kJ
$C_6H_6(g) \rightarrow 6CH(g)$		3057 kJ

3057 kJ is the energy required to break the 6 C–C bonds in $C_6H_6(g)$. The average bond dissociation energy for one carbon-carbon bond in $C_6H_6(g)$ is $\frac{3057\ \text{kJ}}{6\,\text{C–C bonds}}$ = 509.5 kJ.

(d) The value of 509.5 kJ is between the average value for a C–C single bond (348 kJ) and a C=C double bond (614 kJ). It is somewhat greater than the average of these two values, indicating that the carbon-carbon bond in benzene is a bit stronger than we might expect.

8.98 (a) Assume 100 g.

A: 87.7 g In / 114.82 = 0.764 mol In; 0.764 / 0.384 ≈ 2
12.3 g S / 32.07 = 0.384 mol S; 0.384 / 0.384 = 1
B: 78.2 g In / 114.82 = 0.681 mol In; 0.681 / 0.680 ≈ 1
21.8 g S / 32.07 = 0.680 mol S; 0.680 / 0.680 = 1
C: 70.5 g In / 114.82 = 0.614 mol In; 0.614 / 0.614 = 1
29.5 g S / 32.07 = 0.920 mol S; 0.920 / 0.614 = 1.5

A: In_2S; B: InS; C: In_2S_3

(b) A: In(I); B: In(II); C: In(III)

(c) In(I) : $[Kr]5s^24d^{10}$; In(II) : $[Kr]5s^14d^{10}$; In(III) : $[Kr]4d^{10}$
None of these are noble-gas configurations.

(d) The ionic radius of In^{3+} in compound C will be smallest. Removing successive electrons from an atom reduces electron repulsion, increases the effective nuclear charge experienced by the valence electrons and decreases the ionic radius. The higher the charge on a cation, the smaller the radius.

(e) Lattice energy is directly related to the charge on the ions and inversely related to the interionic distance. Only the charge and size of the In varies in the three compounds. In(I) in compound A has the smallest charge and the largest ionic radius, so compound A has the smallest lattice energy and the lowest melting point. In(III) in compound C has the greatest charge and the smallest ionic radius, so compound C has the largest lattice energy and highest melting point.

9 Molecular Geometry and Bonding Theories

Molecular Shapes; the VSEPR Model

9.2 In a symmetrical tetrahedron, the four bond angles are equal to each other, with values of 109.5°. The H–C–H angles in CH_4 and the O–Cl–O angles in ClO_4^- will have values close to 109.5°.

9.4 (a) The number of electron domains in a molecule or ion is the number of bonds (double and triple bonds count as one domain) **plus** the number of nonbonding (lone) electron pairs.

(b) A *bonding electron domain* is a region between two bonded atoms that contains one or more pairs of bonding electrons. A *nonbonding electron domain* is localized on a single atom and contains one pair of nonbonding electrons (a lone pair).

9.6 (a) 3 (or 5 if 90° angles are also present)
(b) 2 (or 5 if 120° angles are also present, 6 if more than one 180° angle is present)
(c) 4
(d) 6 (or 5 if 120° angles are also present)

9.8 If the electron-domain geometry is trigonal bipyramidal, there are 5 total electron domains around the central atom. An AB_3 molecule has 3 bonding domains, so there must be 2 nonbonding domains on A.

		Lewis structure	electron-domain geometry	molecular geometry
9.10	(a)	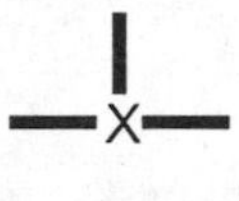	 trigonal planar	 trigonal planar
	(b)		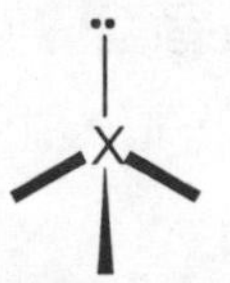 tetrahedral	 trigonal pyramidal

9.10 (continued)

	Lewis structure	electron-domain geometry	molecular geometry
(c)		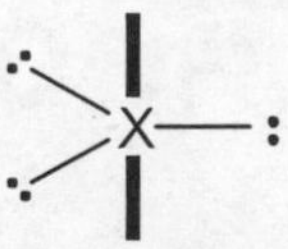 trigonal bipyramidal	 linear

9.12 **bent (b), linear (l), octahedral (oh), seesaw (ss) square pyramidal (sp), square planar (spl), tetrahedral (td), trigonal bipyramidal (tbp), trigonal planar (tr), trigonal pyramidal (tp), T-shaped (T)**

	Molecule or ion	Valence electrons	Lewis structure		Electron-domain geometry	Molecular geometry
(a)	N_2O	16	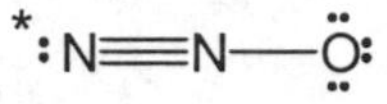		l	l
(b)	SO_3	24	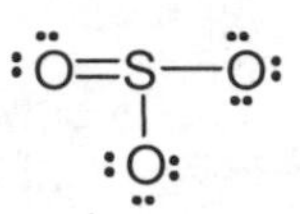	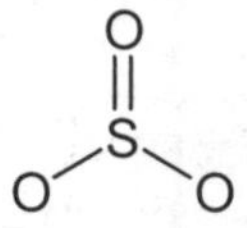	tr	tr
(c)	PCl_3	26	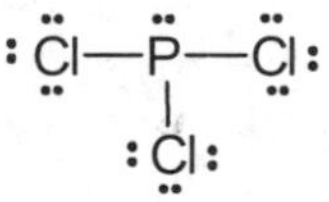	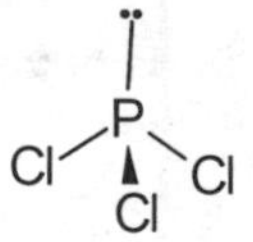	td	tp
(d)	NH_2Cl	14	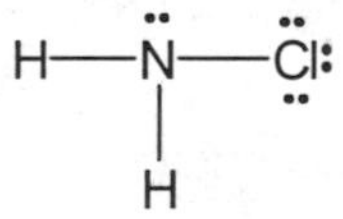	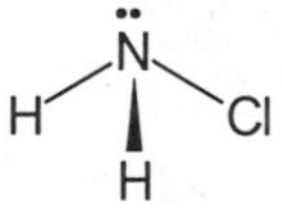	td	tp
(e)	BrF_5	42	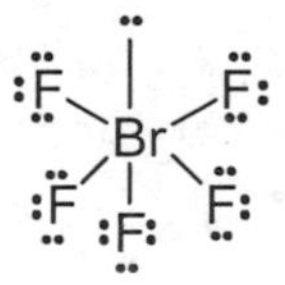	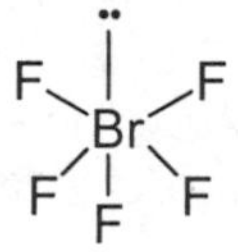	oh	sp
(f)	KrF_2	22	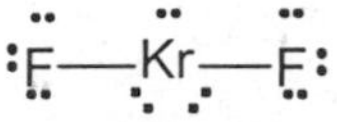	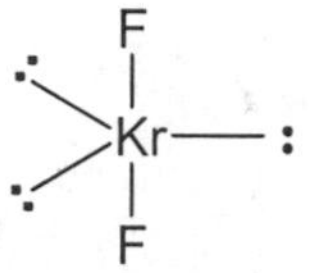	tbp	l

*** More than 1 resonance structure is possible. All equivalent resonance structures predict the same molecular geometry.**

9.14 (a) electron-domain geometries: i, octahedral; ii, tedrahedral; iii, trigonal bipyramidal

(b) nonbonding electron domains: i, 2; ii, 0; iii, 1

(c) S or Se. Shape iii has 5 electron domains, so A must be in or below the third row of the periodic table. This eliminates Be and C. Assuming each F atom has 3 nonbonding electron domains and forms only single bonds with A, A must have 6 valence electrons to produce these electron-domain and molecular geometries.

(d) Xe. (See Table 9.3) Assuming F behaves typically, A must be in or below the third row and have 8 valence electrons. Only Xe fits this description. (Noble gas elements above Xe have not been shown to form molecules of the type AF_4. See Section 7.8.)

9.16 (a) 1 – 109°, 2 – 120° (b) 3 – 109°, 4 – 120°
(c) 5 – 109°, 6 – 109° (d) 7 – 180°, 8 – 109°

9.18 (a) ClO_2^- 20 e^-, 10 e^- pr

NO_2^- 18 e^-, 9 e^- pr

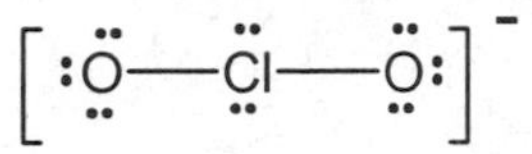

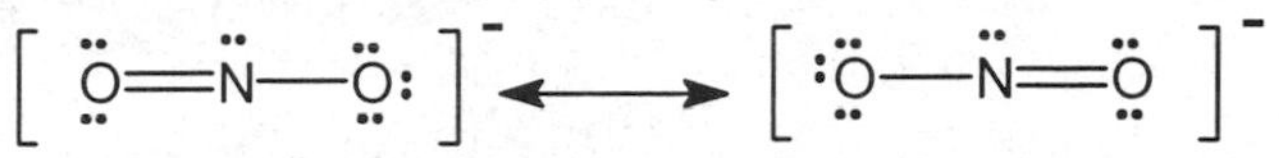

4 e^- domains around Cl
tetrahedral e^- domain geometry
bent molecular geometry
bond angle $\lesssim$109.5°

3 e^- domains about N
(both resonance structures)
trigonal planar e^- domain geometry
bent molecular geometry
bond angle $\lesssim$ 120°

Both molecular geometries are described as 'bent" because both molecules have two nonlinear bonding electron domains. The bond angles (the angle between the two bonding domains) in the two ions are different because the total number of electron domains, and thus the electron domain geometries are different.

(b) XeF_2 22 e^-, 11 e^- pr

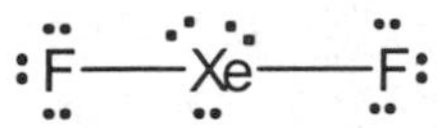

5 e^- domains around Xe
trigonal bipyramidal e^- domain geometry
linear molecular geometry

The question here really is: why do the three nonbonding domains all occupy the equatorial plane of the trigonal bipyramid? In a tbp, there are several different kinds of repulsions, bonding domain-bonding domain (bd-bd), bonding domain-nonbonding domain (bd-nd) and nonbonding domain-nonbonding domain (nd-nd). Each of these can have 90°, 120° or 180° geometry. Since nonbonding domains occupy more space, 90° nd-nd repulsions are most significant and least desirable. The various electron domains arrange themselves to minimize these 90° nd-nd interactions. The arrangement shown above has no 90° nd-nd repulsions. An arrangement with one or two nonbonding domains in axial positions would lead to at least two 90° nd-nd repulsions, a less stable situation. [To convince yourself, tabulate the number and kinds of repulsions for each possible tbp arrangement of 2bd's and 3nd's.]

9.20

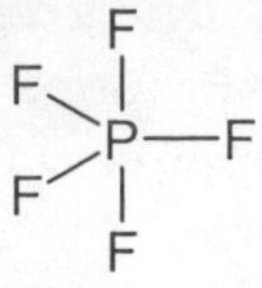
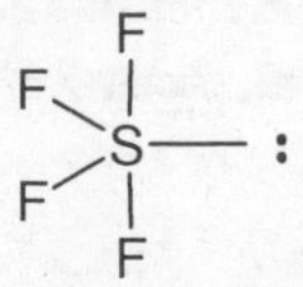
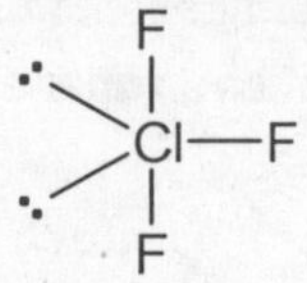

The three nonbonded electron pairs on each F atom have been omitted for clarity.

The F (axial) –A –F (equatorial) angle is largest in PF_5 and smallest in ClF_3. As the number of nonbonding domains in the equatorial plane increases, they push back the axial A–F bonds, decreasing the F (axial) –A –F (equatorial) bond angles.

Polarity of Polyatomic Molecules

9.22 If H_2O were linear, H–O–H, the two O–H bond dipoles would cancel, and the net dipole moment would be zero. Since H_2O is polar, the O–H and dipoles cannot be directly opposed to each other; the molecule cannot be linear.

9.24 (a) For a molecule with polar bonds to be nonpolar, the polar bonds must be (symmetrically) arranged so that the bond dipoles cancel. In most cases, nonbonding e^- domains must be absent from the central atom. Square planar structures may not meet the second condition.

(b) AB_2: linear e^- domain geometry (edg), linear molecular geometry (mg), trigonal bipyramidal edg, linear mg

AB_3: trigonal planar edg, trigonal planar mg

AB_4: tetrahedral edg, tetrahedral mg; octahedral edg, square planar mg

9.26 (a) **Polar**, ΔEN > 0

I-F

(b) **Nonpolar**, the molecule is linear and the bond dipoles cancel.

S=C=S

(c) **Nonpolar,** in a symmetrical trigonal planar structure [Exercise (9.12 (b)], the bond dipoles cancel.

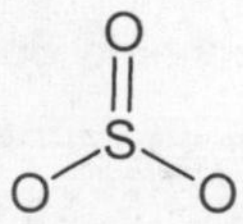

(d) **Polar**, although the bond dipoles are essentially zero, there is an unequal charge distribution due to the nonbonded electron pair on P.

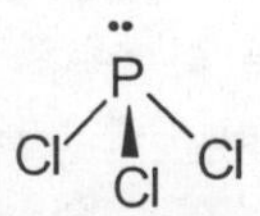

(e) **Nonpolar**, symmetrical octahedron

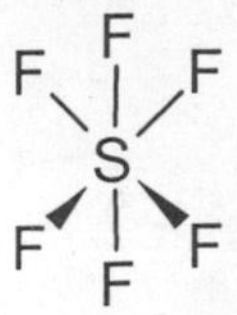

(f) **Polar**, square pyramidal molecular geometry, bond dipoles do not cancel

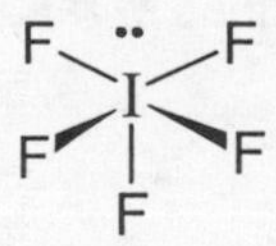

9.28 Each C–Cl bond is polar. The question is whether the vector sum of the C–Cl bond dipoles in each molecule will be nonzero. In the *ortho* and *meta* isomers, the C–Cl vectors are at 60° and 120° angles, respectively, and their resultant dipole moments are nonzero. In the *para* isomer, the C–Cl vectors are opposite, at an angle of 180°, with a resultant dipole moment of zero. The *ortho* and *meta* isomers are polar, the *para* isomer is nonpolar.

Orbital Overlap; Hybrid Orbitals

9.30 (a) (b) (c)

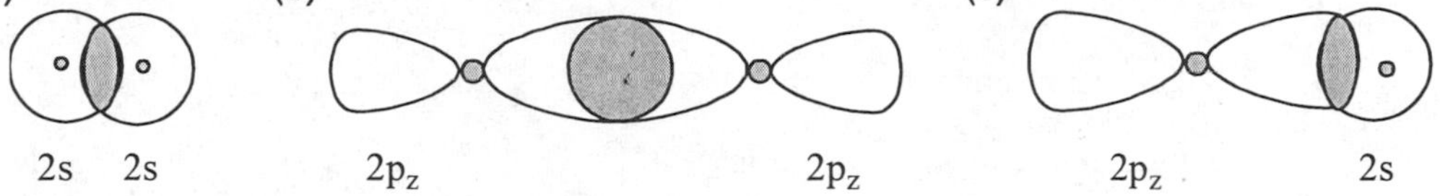

9.32 (a) sp^2 -- 120° angles in a plane
(b) sp^3d -- 90°, 120° and 180° bond angles (trigonal bipyramid)
(c) sp^3d^2 -- 90° and 180° bond angles (octahedron)

9.34 The maximum number of hybrid orbitals on C is 4 (sp^3); the minimum number is 2(sp). Carbon is in the second row of the periodic chart, and has no d-orbitals of sufficiently low energy to allow for an expanded octet or hydrization involving d-orbitals. Thus, the maximum hybridization is when the 2s and all 2p orbitals are involved (sp^3); the minimum is when the 2s and a single 2p are hybridized (sp).

9.36 (a) S: $[Ne]3s^23p^4$

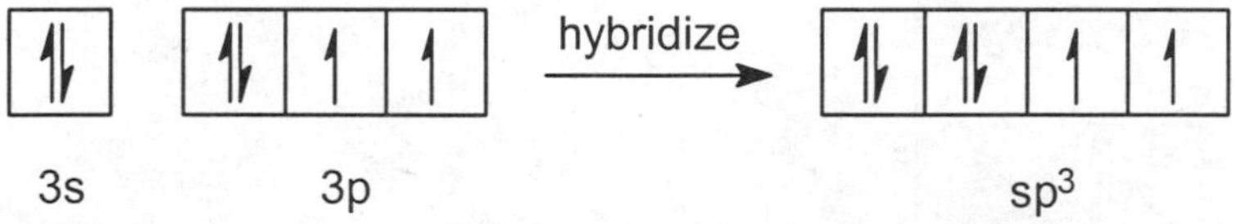

(b) The hybrid orbitals are called sp^3.

(c)

(d) The hybrid orbitals formed in (a) would not be appropriate for SF_4. There are 5 electron domains in SF_4, 4 bonding and one nonbonding, so 5 hybrid orbitals are required. A set of 4 sp^3 hybrid orbitals could not accommodate all the electron pairs around S.

9.38 (a) 32 e^-, 16 e^- pairs

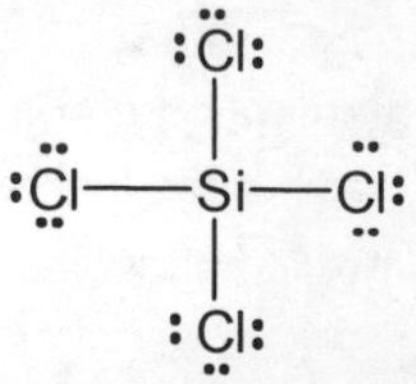

4 e^- pairs around Si
tetrahedral e^- domain geometry
sp^3 hybrid orbitals

(b) 10 e^-, 5 e^- pairs

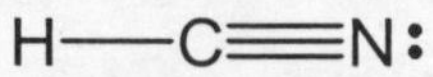

2 e^- domains around C
linear e^- domain geometry
sp hybrid orbitals

(c) 24 e^-, 12 e^- pairs

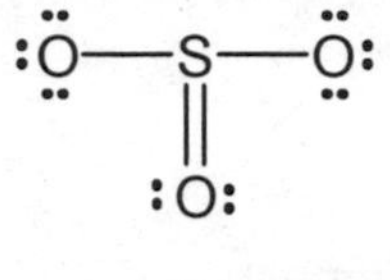

(other resonance structures are possible)

3 e^- domains around S
trigonal planar e^- domain geometry, sp^2 hybrid orbitals

(d) 22 e^-, 11 e^- pairs

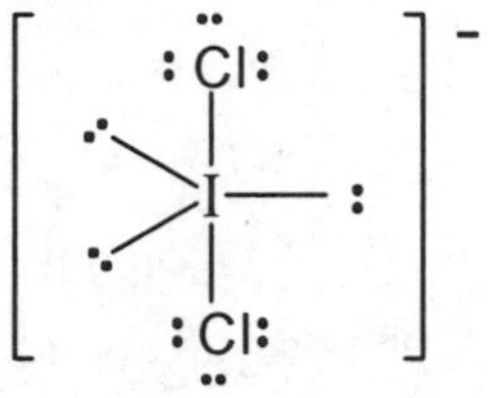

5 e^- domains around I, trigonal bipyramidal e^- domain geometry
sp^3d hybrid orbitals (in a trigonal bipyramid, placing nonbonding e^- pairs in the equatorial position minimizes repulsion

(e) 36 e^-, 18 e^- pairs

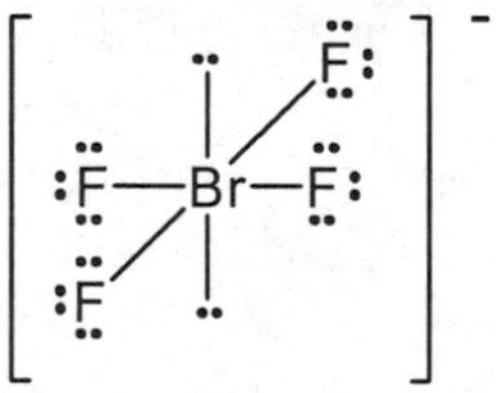

6 e^- domains around Br
octahedral e^- domain geometry, sp^3d^2 hybrid orbitals

Multiple Bonds

9.40 (a) Two unhybridized p orbitals remain, and the atom can form two pi bonds.

(b) A triple bond is composed of 1 σ and 2 π bonds.

(c) There is free rotation of attached groups around a σ bond, but not around a π bond. Rotation about a π bond would require that the bond be broken; the p orbitals would no longer be in the correct orientation for π overlap. The π overlap that is part of all multiple bonds introduces rigidity into molecules.

9.42 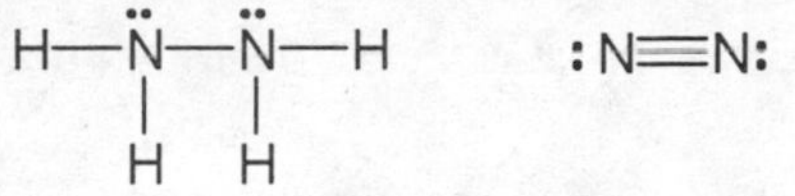

The N atoms in N_2H_4 are sp^3 hybridized; there are no unhybridized p orbitals available for π bonding. In N_2, the N atoms are sp hybridized, with 2 unhybridized p orbitals on each N atom available to form the 2 π bonds in the N≡N triple bond.

9.44 (a) The C bound to H has 3 electron domains and is sp^2 hybridized.
The C bound to O has 2 electron domains and is sp hybridized.

(b) C_2H_2O has 2(4) + 2(1) + 6 = 16 valence electrons.

(c) 4 pairs or 8 total valence electrons form σ bonds

(d) 2 pairs or 4 total valence electrons form π bonds

(e) 2 pairs or 4 total valence electrons are nonbonding

9.46 (a) 1, 120°; 2, 120°; 3, 109° (b) 1, sp^2; 2, sp^2; 3, sp^3 (c) 21 σ bonds

9.48 (a) 24 e^-, 12 e^- pairs (b)

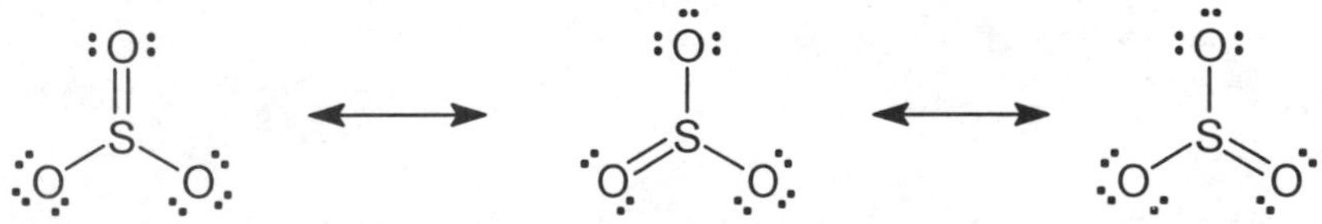

3 electron domains around S, trigonal planar electron-domain geometry, sp^2 hybrid orbitals

(c) The multiple resonance structures indicate delocalized π bonding. All four atoms lie in the trigonal plane of the sp^2 hybrid orbitals. On each atom there is a p atomic orbital perpendicular to this plane in the correct orientation for π overlap. The resulting delocalized π electron cloud is Y-shaped (the shape of the molecule) and has electron density above and below the plane of the molecule.

Molecular Orbitals

9.50 (a) In the σ anti-bonding MO, electron density is concentrated away from the nuclei; an electron in this orbital experiences less stabilization by the nucleus than an electron in an isolated atom.

(b) Yes. The Pauli principle, that no two electrons can have the same 4 quantum numbers, means that an orbital can hold at most 2 electrons. (Since n, l and m_l are the same for a particular orbital and m_s has only 2 possible values, an orbital can hold at most 2 electrons). This is true for atomic and molecular orbitals.

(c) 4. When AOs combine to form MOs, the total number of orbitals is conserved. Combination of 4 AOs must result in formation of 4 MOs. Both can accommodate 8 electrons.

9.52 (a)

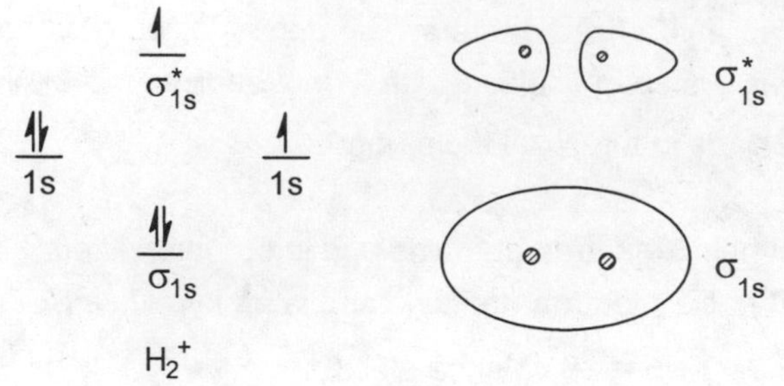

(b)

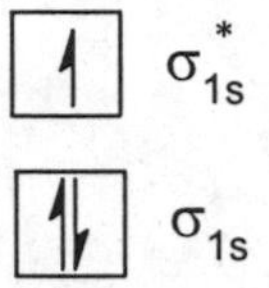

(c) Bond order = 1/2 (2-1) = 1/2

(d) If 1 electron moves from σ_{1s} to σ^*_{1s}, the bond order becomes -1/2. There is a net increase in energy relative to isolated H atoms, so the molecule will decompose.

$$H_2^- \xrightarrow{h\nu} H + H^-.$$

9.54 (a) zero

(b) The 2 π_{2p} molecular orbitals are degenerate; they have the same energy, but they have different spatial orientations 90° apart.

(c) In the bonding MO the electrons are stabilized by both nuclei. In an antibonding MO, the electrons are directed away from the nuclei, so π_{2p} is lower in energy than π^*_{2p}.

9.56 (a) O_2^{2-} has a bond order of 1.0, while O_2^- has a bond order of 1.5. For the same bonded atoms, the greater the bond order the shorter the bond, so O_2^- has the shorter bond.

(b) The two possible orbital energy level diagrams are:

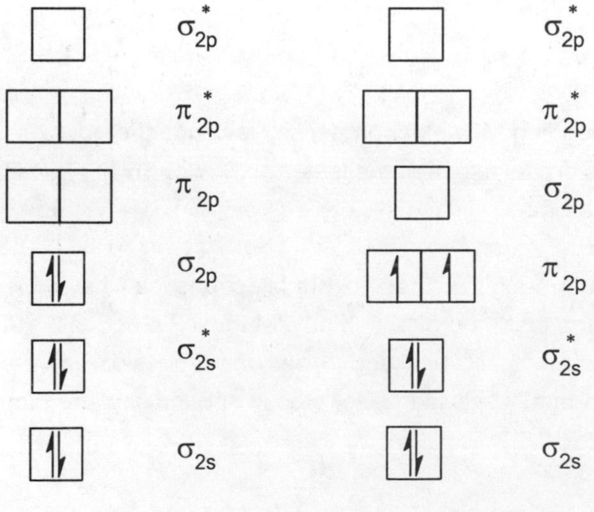

If the σ_{2p} molecular orbital is lower in energy than the π_{2p} orbitals, there are no unpaired electrons, and the molecule is diamagnetic. Switching the order of σ_{2p} and π_{2p} gives 1 unpaired electron in each degenerate π_{2p} orbital and explains the observed paramagnetism of B_2 (see Figure 9.41).

9.58 (a) Substances with unpaired electrons are attracted into a magnetic field. This property is called *paramagnetism*.

(b) Weigh the substance normally and in a magnetic field. Paramagnetic substances appear to have a larger mass when weighed in a magnetic field.

(c) See Figures 9.36 and 9.41. O_2^+, 1 unpaired electron; N_2^{2-}, 2 unpaired electrons; Li_2^+, 1 unpaired electron

9.60 Determine the number of 'valence' (non-core) electrons in each molecule or ion. Use the homonuclear diatomic MO diagram from Figure 9.38 (shown below) to calculate bond order and magnetic properties of each species. The electronegativity difference between heteroatomics increases the energy difference between the 2S AO on one atom and the 2p AO on the other, rendering the 'no interaction' MO diagram in figure 9.38 appropriate.

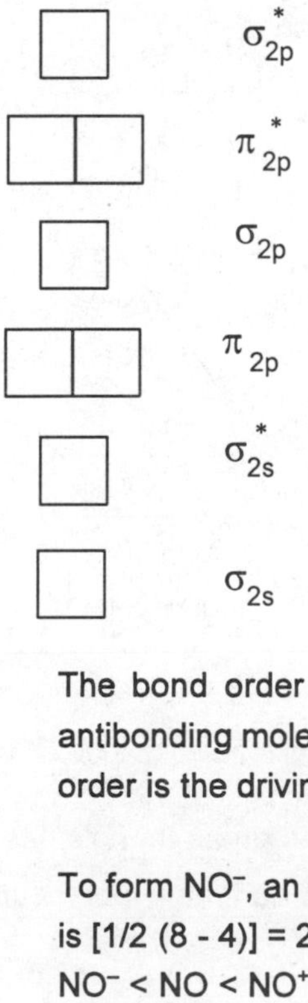

(a) CO: 10 e^-, B.O. = (8-2) / 2 = 3.0, diamagnetic
(b) NO^-: 12 e^-, B.O. = (8-4) / 2 = 2.0, paramagnetic
(c) OF^+: 12 e^-, B.O. = (8-4) / 2 = 2.0, paramagnetic
(d) NeF^+: 14 e^-, B.O. = (8-6) / 2 = 1.0, diamagnetic

9.62 (a) The bond order of NO is [1/2 (8 - 3)] = 2.5. The electron that is lost is in an antibonding molecular orbital, so the bond order in NO^+ is 3.0. The increase in bond order is the driving force for the formation of NO^+.

(b) To form NO^-, an electron is added to an antibonding orbital, and the new bond order is [1/2 (8 - 4)] = 2. The order of increasing bond order and bond strength is: $NO^- < NO < NO^+$.

(c) NO^+ is isoelectronic with N_2, and NO^- is isoelectronic with O_2.

9.64 (a) I: 5s, $5p_x$, $5p_y$, $5p_z$; Br: 4s, $4p_x$, $4p_y$, $4p_z$

(b) By analogy to F_2, the BO of IBr will be 1.

(c) I and Br have valence atomic orbitals with different principle quantum numbers. This means that the radial extensions (sizes) of the valence atomic orbital that contribute to the MO are different. The n = 5 valence AOs on I are larger than the n = 4 valence AOs on Br.

(d) σ^*_{np} (e) none

Additional Exercises

9.66 (a) The physical basis of VSEPR is the electrostatic repulsion of like-charged particles, in this case groups or domains of electrons. That is, owing to electrostatic repulsion, electron domains will arrange themselves to be as far apart as possible.

(b) The σ-bond electrons are localized in the region along the internuclear axes. The positions of the atoms and geometry of the molecule are thus closely tied to the locations of these electron pairs. Because the π-bond electrons are distributed above and below the plane that contains the σ bonds, these electron pairs do not, in effect, influence the geometry of the molecule. Thus, all σ- and π-bond electrons localized between two atoms are located in the same electron domain.

9.68 For any triangle, the law of cosines gives the length of side c as $c^2 = a^2 + b^2 - 2ab \cos\theta$.

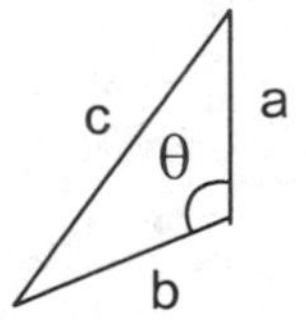

Let the edge length of the cube (uy = vy = vz) = X

The length of the face diagonal (uv) is

$(uv)^2 = (uy)^2 + (vy)^2 - 2(uy)(vy) \cos 90$

$(uv)^2 = X^2 + X^2 - 2(X)(X) \cos 90$

$(uv)^2 = 2X^2;\ \ uv = \sqrt{2}X$

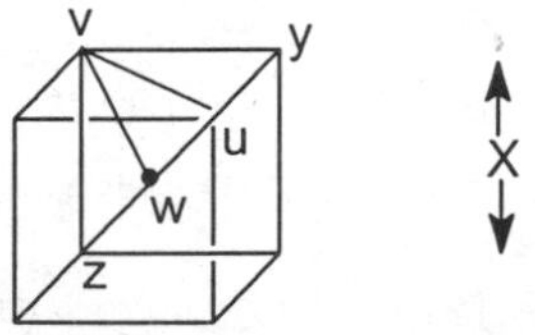

The length of the body diagonal (uz) is

$(uz)^2 = (vz^2) + (uv)^2 - 2(vz)(uv) \cos 90$

$(uz)^2 = X^2 + (\sqrt{2}X)^2 - 2(X)(\sqrt{2}X) \cos 90$

$(uz)^2 = 3X^2;\ \ uz = \sqrt{3}X$

For calculating the characteristic tetrahedral angle, the appropriate triangle has vertices u, v and w. Theta, θ, is the angle formed by sides wu and wv and the hypotenous is side uv.

$wu = wv = uz/2 = \sqrt{3}/2X;\ \ uv = \sqrt{2}X$

$(\sqrt{2}X)^2 = (\sqrt{3}/2X)^2 + (\sqrt{3}/2X)^2 - 2(\sqrt{3}/2X)(\sqrt{3}/2) \cos\theta$

$2X^2 = 3/4\ X^2 + 3/4\ X^2 - 3/2\ X^2 \cos\theta$

$2X^2 = 3/2\ X^2 - 3/2\ X^2 \cos\theta$

$1/2\ X^2 = -3/2\ X^2 \cos\theta$

$\cos\theta = -(1/2\ X^2) / (3/2\ X^2) = -1/3 = -0.3333$

$\theta = 109.47°$

9.70

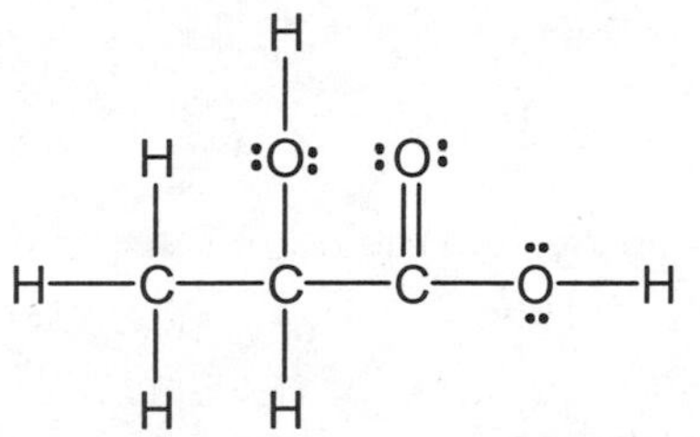

3(4) + 3(6) + 6(1) = 36 e^-, 18 e^- pr
There are 11 σ and 1 π bonds.
The C=O on the right-hand C atom is shortest. This C has 3 e^- domains, so the hybridization is sp^2; bond angles about this C atom are approximately 120°. The middle and left-hand C atoms both have 4 e^- domains, are sp^3 hybridized and have bond angles of approximately 109°.

9.71

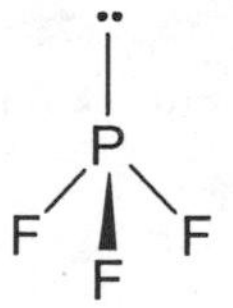

μ = 1.03 D

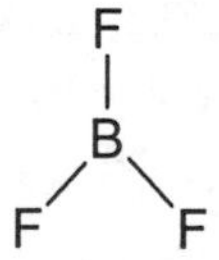

μ = 0

BF_3 is a trigonal planar molecule with the central B atom symmetrically surrounded by the three F atoms (Figure 9.13). The individual B–F bond dipoles cancel, and the molecule has a net dipole moment of zero. PF_3 has tetrahedral electron-domain geometry with one of the positions in the tetrahedron occupied by a nonbonding electron pair. The individual P–F bond dipoles do not cancel and the presence of a nonbonding electron pair ensures an asymmetrical electron distribution; the molecule is polar.

9.73

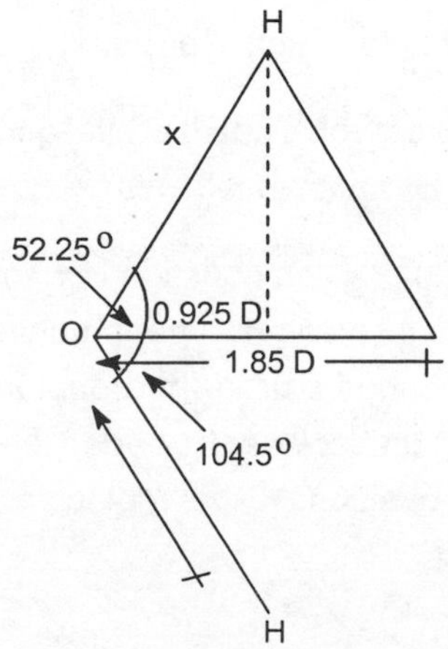

(a) The bond dipoles in H_2O lie along the O–H bonds with the positive end at H and the negative end at O. The dipole moment vector of the H_2O molecule is the resultant (vector sum) of the two bond dipoles. This vector bisects the H–O–H angle and has a magnitude of 1.85 D with the negative end pointing toward O.

(b) Since the dipole moment vector bisects the H-O-H bond angle, the angle between one H–O bond and the dipole moment vector is 1/2 the H–O–H bond angle, 52.25°. Dropping a perpendicular line from H to the dipole moment vector creates the right triangle pictured. If x = the magnitude of the O–H bond dipole, x cos (52.25) = 0.925 D. **x = 1.51 D.**

(c) The X–H bond dipoles (Table 8.3) and the electronegativity values of X (Figure 8.6) are

	Electronegativity	**Bond dipole**
F	4.0	1.82
O	3.5	1.51
Cl	3.0	1.08

Since the electronegativity of O is midway between the values for F and Cl, the O–H bond dipole should be approximately midway between the bond dipoles of HF and HCl. The value of the O–H bond dipole calculated in part (b) is consistent with this prediction.

9.75 (a) XeF_6 50 e^-, 25 e^- pairs

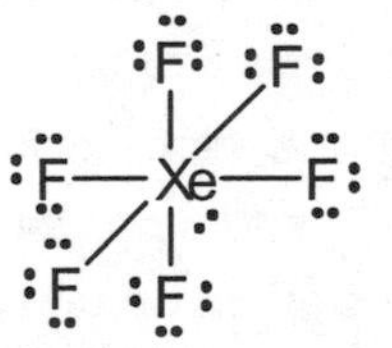

(b) There are 7 VSEPR e^- pairs around Xe, and the maximum number of e^- pairs in Table 9.3 is 6.

(c) Tie 7 balloons together and see what arrangement they adopt (seriously! see Figure 9.5). Alternatively, go to the chemical literature where VSEPR was first proposed and see if there is a preferred orientation for 7 e^- pairs.

(d) Since the hybrid orbitals for 5 VSEPR e^- pairs involve one d orbital and for 6 pairs, two d orbitals, a reasonable suggestion would be sp^3d^3.

(e) One of the 7 VSEPR pairs is a nonbonded pair. The question is whether it occupies an axial or equatorial position. The equatorial plane of a pentagonal bipyramid has F–Xe–F angles of 72°. Placing the nonbonded pair in the equatorial plane would create severe repulsions between it and the adjacent bonded pairs. Thus, the nonbonded pair will reside in the axial position. The molecular structure is a pentagonal pyramid.

9.76 (a) 16 e⁻, 8 e⁻ pairs

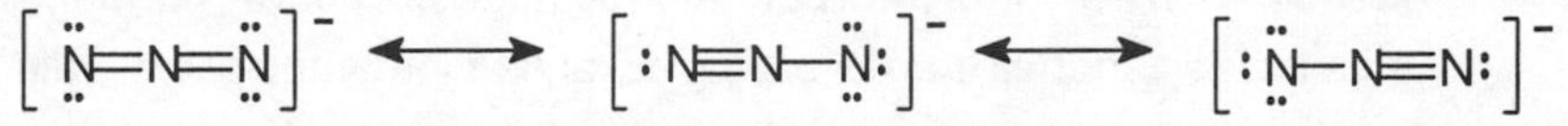

(b) The observed bond length of 1.16 Å is intermediate between the values for N=N, 1.24 Å, and N ≡ N, 1.10 Å. This is consistent with the resonance structures, which indicate contribution from formally double and triple bonds to the true bonding picture in N_3^-.

(c) In each resonance structure, the central N has two electron domains, so it must be sp hybridized. It is difficult to predict the hybridization of terminal atoms in molecules where there are resonance structures because there are a different number of electron domains around the terminal atoms in each structure. Since the "true" electronic arrangement is a combination of all resonance structures, we will assume that the terminal N–N bonds have some triple bond character and that the terminal N atoms are sp hybridized. (There is no experimental measure of hybridization at terminal atoms, since there are no bond angles to observe.)

(d) In each resonance structure, N–N σ bonds are formed by sp hybrids and π bonds are formed by unhybridized p orbitals. Nonbonding e⁻ pairs can reside in sp hybrids or p atomic orbitals.

(e) Recall that electrons in 2s orbitals are on the average closer to the nucleus than electrons in 2p orbitals. Since sp hybrids have greater s orbital character, it is resonable to expect the radial extension of sp orbitals to be smaller than that of sp^2 or sp^3 orbitals and σ bonds formed by sp orbitals to be slightly shorter than those formed by other hybrid orbitals, assuming the same bonded atoms.

There are no solitary σ bonds in N_3^-. That is, the two σ bonds in N_3^- are each accompanied by at least one π bond between the bonding pair of atoms. Sigma bonds that are part of a double or triple bond must be shorter so that the p orbitals can overlap enough for the π bond to form. Thus, the observation is not applicable to this molecule. (Comparison of C–H bond lengths in C_2H_2, C_2H_4, C_2H_6 and related molecules would confirm or deny the observation.)

9.78 (a) Each C atom is surrounded by 3 electron domains (2 single bonds and 1 double bond), so bond angles at each C atom will be approximately 120°.

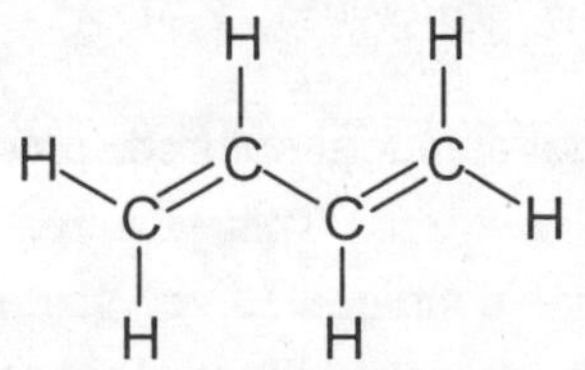

Since there is free rotation around the central C–C single bond, other conformations are possible.

(b) According to Table 8.5, the average C–C length is 1.54 Å, and the average C=C length is 1.34 Å. While the C=C bonds in butadiene appear "normal," the central C–C is significantly shorter than average. Examination of the bonding in butadiene reveals that each C atom is sp^2 hybridized and the π bonds are formed by the remaining unhybridized 2p orbital on each atom. If the central C–C bond is rotated so that all four C atoms are coplanar, the four 2p orbitals are parallel and some delocalization of the π electrons occurs.

9.80

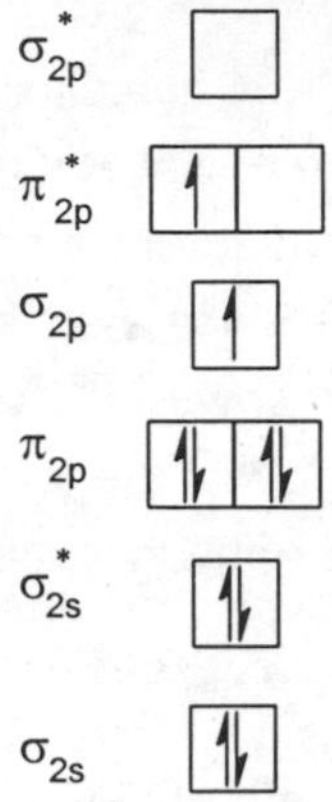

N_2 in the ground state has a B.O. of 3; in the first excited state (at left) it has a B.O. of 2. Owing to the reduction in bond order, N_2 in the first excited state would be more reactive, have a smaller bond energy and a longer N–N separation.

9.81 [We will refer to azo benzene (on the left) as A and hydrazobenzene (on the right) as H.]

(a) A: sp^2; H: sp^3

(b) A: Each N and C atom has one unhybridized p orbital. H: Each C atom has one unhybridized p orbital, but the N atoms have no unhybridized p orbitals.

(c) A: 120°; H: 109°

(d) Since all C and N atoms in A have unhybridized p orbitals, all can participate in delocalized π bonding. The delocalized π system extends over the entire molecule, including both benzene rings and the azo "bridge". In H, the N atoms have no unhybridized p orbitals, so they cannot participate in delocalized π bonding. Each of the benzene rings in H is delocalized, but the network cannot span the N atoms in the bridge.

(e) This is consistent with the answer to (d). In order for the unhybridized p orbitals in A to overlap, they must be parallel. This requires a planar σ bond framework where all atoms in the molecule are coplanar.

(f) In order for a substance to appear colored, it must absorb light in the visible region of the electromagnetic spectrum. This requires a HOMO-LUMO energy gap in the visible region. For organic molecules, the size of the gap is related to the number of conjugated π bonds; the more conjugated π bonds, the smaller the gap and the more likely the molecule is to be colored. Azobenzene has 7 conjugated π bonds (π network delocalized over entire molecule) while hydrazobenzene has only 3 (π network on benzene rings only). Thus, the size of the HOMO-LUMO energy gap is smaller in A, and A is more likely than H to appear colored.

Integrative Exercises

9.83 (a) $2SF_4(g) + O_2(g) \rightarrow 2OSF_4(g)$

(b) 40 e^-, 20 e^- pairs

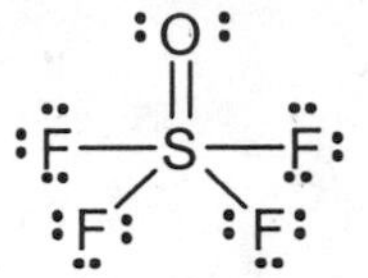

There must be a double bond drawn between O and S in order for their formal charges to be zero.

(c) $\Delta H = 8D(S\text{-}F) + D(O{=}O) - 8D(S\text{-}F) - 2D(S{=}O)$
$\Delta H = D(O{=}O) - 2D(S{=}O) = 495 - 2(523) = -551$ kJ, exothermic

(d) trigonal bipyramidal electron-domain geometry

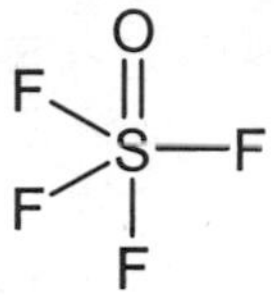

or

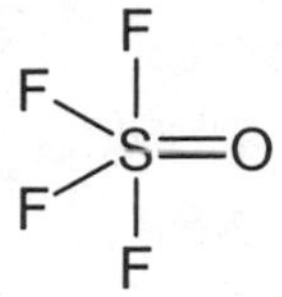

(e) Because F is more electronegative than O, the structure that minimizes S–F repulsions is more likely (see Solution 9.84). That is, the structure with fewer 90° F–S–F angles and more 120° F–S–F angles is favored. The structure on the left, with O in the axial position is more likely. Note that a double bond involving an atom with an expanded octet of electrons, such as the S=O in this molecule, does not have the same geometric implications as a double bond to a first row element.

9.84 (a) PX_3, 26 valence e^-, 13^- pairs

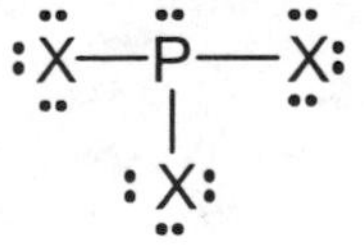

4 electron domains around P
tetrahedral e^- domain geometry
107° bond angles (less than 109° due to repulsion with nonbonded pair)

(b) As electronegativity increases (I < Br < Cl < F), the X–P–X angles decreases.

(c) For P–I, ΔEN is (2.5- 2.1) = 0.4 and the bond dipole is small. For P–F, ΔEN is (4.0 - 2.1) = 1.9 and the bond dipole is large. The greater the ΔEN and bond dipole, the larger the magnitude of negative charge centered on X. The more negative charge centered on X, the greater the repulsion between X and the nonbonding electron pair on P and the smaller the bond angle. (Since electrostatic attractions and repulsions vary as 1/r, the shorter P–F bond may also contribute to this effect.)

(d) $PBrCl_4$, 40 valence electrons, 20 e^- pairs. The molecule will have trigonal bipyramidal electron-domain geometry (similar to PCl_5 in Table 9.3.) Based on the argument in part (c), the P–Br bond will have smaller repulsions with P–Cl bonds than P–Cl bonds have with each other. Therefore, the Br will occupy an axial position in the trigonal bipyramid, so that the more unfavorable P–Cl to P–Cl repulsions can be situated at larger angles in the equatorial plane.

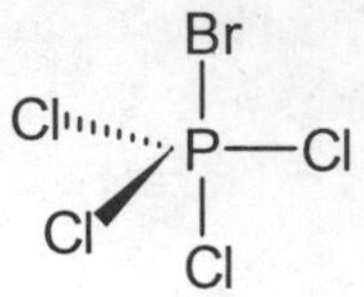

9.86 (a)

C≡C	839 kJ/mol	(1 σ, 2 π)
C=C	614 kJ/mol	(1 σ, 1 π)
C–C	348 kJ/mol	(1 σ)

The contribution from 1 π bond would be (614-348) 266 kJ/mol. From a second π bond, (839 - 614), 225 kJ/mol. An average π bond contribution would be (266 + 225)/2 = 246 kJ/mol.

This is $\dfrac{246\ \text{kJ}/\pi\ \text{bond}}{348\ \text{kJ}/\sigma\ \text{bond}} \times 100 = 71\%$ of the average enthalpy of a σ bond.

(b)

N≡N	941 kJ/mol
N=N	418 kJ/mol
N-N	163 kJ/mol

first π = (418 - 163) = 255 kJ/mol
second π = (941 - 418) = 523 kJ/mol
average π bond enthalpy = (255 + 523) / 2 = 389 kJ/mol

This is $\dfrac{389\ \text{kJ}/\pi\ \text{bond}}{163\ \text{kJ}/\sigma\ \text{bond}} \times 100 = 240\%$ of the average enthalpy of a σ bond.

N–N σ bonds are weaker than C–C σ bonds, while N-N π bonds are stronger than C–C π bonds. The relative energies of C–C σ and π bonds are similar, while N–N π bonds are much stronger than N–N σ bonds.

(c) N_2H_4, 14 valence e^-, 7 e^- pairs

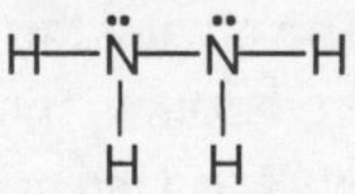

4 electron domains around N, sp^3 hybridization

N_2H_2, 12 valence e^-, 6 e^- pairs

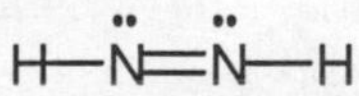

3 electron domains around N, sp^2 hybridization

N_2, 10 valence e^-, 5 e^- pairs

$:N{\equiv}N:$

2 electron domains around N,
sp hybridization

(d) In the three types of N–N bonds, each N atom has a nonbonding or lone pair of electrons. The lone pair to bond pair repulsions are minimized going from 109° to 120° to 180° bond angles, making the π bonds stronger relative to the σ bond. In the three types of C–C bonds, no lone-pair to bond-pair repulsions exist, and the σ and π bonds have more similar energies.

9.88 (a) 1 eV = 96.485 kJ/mol

$$H_2\text{: } 15.4 \text{ eV} \times \frac{96.485 \text{ kJ/mol}}{1 \text{ eV}} = 1486 = 1.49 \times 10^3 \text{ kJ}$$

$$N_2\text{: } 15.6 \text{ eV} \times \frac{96.485 \text{ kJ/mol}}{1 \text{ eV}} = 1505 = 1.51 \times 10^3 \text{ kJ}$$

$$O_2\text{: } 12.1 \text{ eV} \times \frac{96.485 \text{ kJ/mol}}{1 \text{ eV}} = 1167 = 1.17 \times 10^3 \text{ kJ}$$

$$F_2\text{: } 15.7 \text{ eV} \times \frac{96.485 \text{ kJ/mol}}{1 \text{ eV}} = 1515 = 1.52 \times 10^3 \text{ kJ}$$

(b)

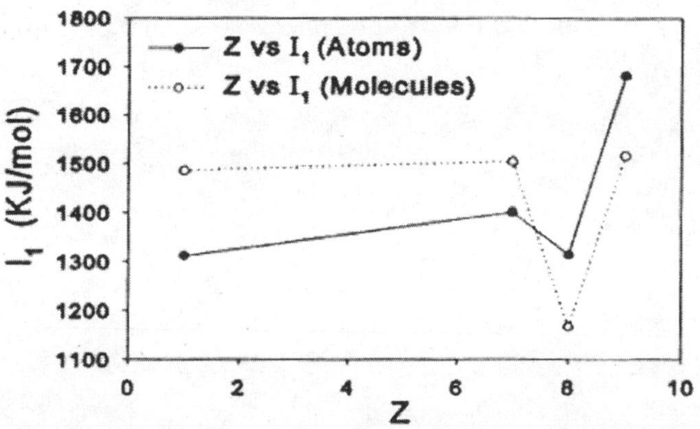

(c) In general, I_1 for atoms and molecules increases going across a row of the periodic chart. In both cases, there is a discontinuity at oxygen. The details of the trends are different. The deviation at O is larger for the molecules than the atoms, while the increase at F is much greater for the atoms than the molecules.

(d) According to Figures 9.32 and 9.39, H_2, N_2 and F_2 are diamagnetic and O_2 is paramagnetic. That is, ionization in H_2, N_2 and F_2 has to overcome spin-pairing energy, while ionization of O_2 removes an already unpaired electron. Thus, the ionization energy of O_2 is much less than I_1 for H_2, N_2 and F_2.

Despite differences in bond order, bond length and the bonding or antibonding nature of the HOMO in H_2, N_2 and F_2, the ionization energies for these molecules are very similar.

9.90 (a) Parentheses around the atomic weight indicate that the element is radioactive. The nuclei of radioactive elements spontaneously decay to form other, lighter nuclei. The difficulty with studying At is that it decays before a reliable set of physical and chemical properties can be measured.

(b) $1s^2 2s^2 2p^6 3s^2 3p^6 4s^2 3d^{10} 4p^6 5s^2 4d^{10} 5p^6 6s^2 4f^{14} 5d^{10} 6p^5$

(c) AtI is expected to have a slightly polar covalent bond, similar to other interhalogen molecules. Since At and I are adjacent in the halogen family, their electronegativities will be very similar, but not equal. When two atoms with similar electronegativies combine, the result is a covalent molecule with a small net dipole moment.

(d) 22 e^-, 11 e^- pairs;

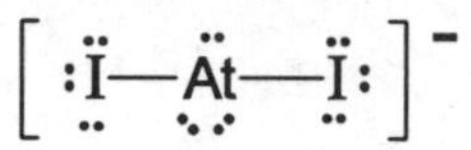

trigonal bipyramidal electron-domain geometry, linear molecular geometry (In a trigonal bipyramid, placing nonbonding electron pairs in the equatorial plane minimizes repulsions.)

(e) By analogy to F_2 in Figure 9.41, the bond order should be 1 and the HOMO is π^*_{6p}.

10 Gases

Gas Characteristics; Pressure

10.2 (a) Because gas molecules are far apart and in constant motion, the gas expands to fill the container. Attractive forces hold liquid molecules together and the volume of the liquid does not change.

(b) H_2O and CCl_4 molecules are too dissimilar to displace each other and mix in the liquid state. All mixtures of gases are homogeneous. (See Solution 10.1 (c)).

(c) Because gas molecules are far apart, the mass present in 1 mL of a gas is very small. The mass of a gas present in 1 L is on the same order of magnitude as the mass of a liquid present in 1 mL.

10.4 The height of the mercury column in a barometer is a direct measure of atmospheric pressure. Atmospheric pressure decreases with increasing altitude (Section 18.1), so atmospheric pressure in Denver, at an altitude of nearly one mile, is measurably lower than atmospheric pressure in Los Angeles, near sea level. Thus, the mercury column in a Denver barometer should be lower than that in a Los Angeles barometer.

10.6 Using the relationship derived in Solution 10.5 for two liquids under the influence of gravity, $(d \times h)_{1id} = (d \times h)_{Hg}$. At 752 torr, the height of a Hg barometer is 752 mm.

$$\frac{1.20\ g}{1\ mL} \times h_{1id} = \frac{13.6\ g}{1\ mL} \times 760\ mm;\ h_{1id} = \frac{13.6\ g/mL \times 752\ mm}{1.20\ g/mL} = 8.52 \times 10^3\ mm = 8.52\ m$$

10.8 The mercury would fill the tube completely; there would be no vacuum at the closed end. This is because atmospheric pressure will support a mercury column higher than 70 cm, while our tube is only 50 cm. No mercury flows from the tube into the dish and no vacuum forms at the top of the tube.

10.10 (a) $2.44\ atm \times \frac{760\ torr}{1\ atm} = 1.85 \times 10^3\ torr$

(b) $682\ torr \times \frac{101.325\ kPa}{760\ torr} = 90.9\ kPa$

(c) $776\ mm\ Hg \times \frac{1\ atm}{760\ mm\ Hg} = 1.02\ atm$

(d) $1.456 \times 10^5 \text{ Pa} \times \dfrac{1 \text{ atm}}{1.01325 \times 10^5 \text{ Pa}} = 1.44 \text{ atm}$

(e) $3.44 \text{ atm} \times \dfrac{1.01325 \times 10^5 \text{ Pa}}{1 \text{ atm}} \times \dfrac{1 \text{ bar}}{1 \times 10^5 \text{ Pa}} = 3.49 \text{ bar}$

10.12 (a) $\dfrac{1.63105 \text{ Pa}}{1 \text{ Titan atm}} \times \dfrac{1 \text{ Earth atm}}{101{,}325 \text{ Pa}} = \dfrac{1.60972 \times 10^{-5} \text{ Earth atm}}{1 \text{ Titan atm}}$

(b) $\dfrac{90 \text{ Earth atm}}{1 \text{ Venus atm}} \times \dfrac{101.3 \text{ kPa}}{1 \text{ Earth atm}} = \dfrac{9.1 \times 10^3 \text{ kPa}}{1 \text{ Venus atm}}$

10.14 $P = m \times a/A$; $1 \text{ Pa} = 1 \text{ kg/m} \bullet \text{s}^2$; $A = 2.2 \text{ cm} \times 30 \text{ cm} \times 2 = 132 \text{ cm}^2$

$$\frac{262 \text{ kg}}{132 \text{ cm}^2} \times \frac{9.81 \text{ m}}{\text{s}^2} \times \frac{(100)^2 \text{ cm}^2}{1 \text{ m}^2} \times \frac{1 \text{ Pa} \bullet \text{m} \bullet \text{s}^2}{\text{kg}} = 1.947 \times 10^5 = 1.9 \times 10^5 \text{ Pa}$$

10.16 (a) The atmosphere is exerting 13.6 cm = 136 mm Hg (torr) more pressure than the gas.

$$P_{gas} = P_{atm} - 136 \text{ torr} = \left(1.05 \text{ atm} \times \frac{760 \text{ torr}}{1 \text{ atm}}\right) - 136 \text{ torr} = 662 \text{ torr}$$

(b) The gas is exerting 12 mm Hg (torr) more pressure than the atmosphere.

$$P_{gas} = P_{atm} + 12 \text{ torr} = \left(0.988 \text{ atm} \times \frac{760 \text{ torr}}{1 \text{ atm}}\right) + 12 \text{ torr} = 763 \text{ torr}$$

The Gas Laws

10.18 (a) P and V are inversely proportional at constant T. If the volume decreases by a factor of 3, the pressure increases by a factor of 3.

(b) P and T are directly proportional at constant V. If T decreases by a factor of 2, P also decreases by a factor of 2.

(c) P and n are directly proportional at constant V. If n decreases by a factor of 2, P also decreases by a factor of 2.

10.20 (a) $P_1V_1 = P_2V_2$; $P_1 = 0.988$ atm, $V_1 = 1248 \text{ ft}^3$, $V_2 = 978 \text{ ft}^3$

$$P_2 = \frac{P_1V_1}{V_2} = \frac{0.988 \text{ atm} \times 1248 \text{ ft}^3}{978 \text{ ft}^3} = 1.26 \text{ atm}$$

(b) $V_1/T_1 = V_2/T_2$; $V_1 = 1248 \text{ ft}^3$ L, $V_2 = 1435 \text{ ft}^3$, $T_1 = 28.0°\text{C} + 273.15 = 301.15$ K

$$T_2 = \frac{V_2T_1}{V_1} = \frac{1435 \text{ ft}^3 \times 301.15 \text{ K}}{1248 \text{ ft}^3} = 346.27 = 346.3 \text{ K};\ 346.27 - 273.15 = 73.1°\text{C}$$

The result in K has 4 sig figs and 1 decimal place. The result in °C then has 1 decimal place (and 3 sig figs).

10.22 According to Avogadro's hypothesis, the mole ratios in the chemical equation will be volume ratios for the gases if they are at the same temperature and pressure.

$$N_2(g) + 3H_2(g) \rightarrow 2NH_3(g)$$

The volumes of H_2 and N_2 are in a stoichiometric $\frac{3.6\ L}{1.2\ L}$ or $\frac{3\ \text{vol}\ H_2}{1\ \text{vol}\ N_2}$ ratio, so either can be used to determine the volume of $NH_3(g)$ produced.

$$1.2\ L\ N_2 \times \frac{2\ \text{mol}\ NH_3}{1\ \text{mol}\ N_2} = 2.4\ L\ NH_3(g)\ \text{produced.}$$

The Ideal-Gas Equation

(In *Solutions to Exercises*, the symbol for molar mass is $\mathcal{M}$.)

10.24 (a) STP stands for standard temperature, 0°C (or 273 K), and standard pressure, 1 atm.

(b) $V = \frac{nRT}{P}$; $V = 1\ \text{mol} \times \frac{0.08206\ L \cdot atm}{K \cdot mol} \times \frac{273\ K}{1\ atm}$

V = 22.4 L for 1 mole of gas at STP

(c) 25°C + 273 = 298 K

$V = \frac{nRT}{P}$; $V = 1\ \text{mol} \times \frac{0.08206\ L \cdot atm}{K \cdot mol} \times \frac{298\ K}{1\ atm}$

V = 24.5 L for 1 mol of gas at 1 atm and 25°C

10.26 $n = g/\mathcal{M}$; $PV = nRT = gRT/\mathcal{M}$; $\mathcal{M} = gRT/PV$.

2-L flask: $\mathcal{M} = 4.8\ T/2.0(X) = 2.4\ T/X$

3-L flask: $\mathcal{M} = 0.36\ T/3.0\ (0.1\ X) = 1.2\ T/X$

The molar masses of the two gases are not equal. The gas in the 2-L flask has a molar mass that is twice as large as the gas in the 3-L flask.

10.28 (a) n = 0.215 mol, V = 338 mL = 0.338 L, T = 32°C = 305 K

$$P = \frac{nRT}{V} = 0.215\ \text{mol} \times \frac{0.08206\ L \cdot atm}{K \cdot atm} \times \frac{305\ K}{0.338\ L} = 15.9\ atm$$

(b) n = 0.0412 mol, V = 3.00 L, P = 1.05 atm

$$T = \frac{PV}{nR} = \frac{1.05\ atm \times 3.00\ L}{0.0412\ mol} \times \frac{K \cdot mol}{0.08206\ L \cdot atm} = 932\ K$$

(c) $V = 98.5\ L,\ T = 236\ K,\ P = 690\ torr \times \frac{1\ atm}{760\ torr} = 0.9079 = 0.908\ atm$

$$n = \frac{PV}{RT} = 0.9079\ atm \times \frac{K \cdot mol}{0.08206\ L \cdot atm} \times \frac{98.5\ L}{236\ K} = 4.62\ mol$$

(d) $n = 5.48 \times 10^{-3}\ mol,\ T = 55°C = 328\ K$

$$P = 3.87\ kPa \times \frac{1\ atm}{101.325\ kPa} = 0.03819 = 0.0382\ atm$$

$$V = \frac{nRT}{P} = 5.48 \times 10^{-3}\ mol \times \frac{0.08206\ L \cdot atm}{K \cdot mol} \times \frac{328\ K}{0.03819\ atm} = 3.86\ L$$

10.30 Find the volume of the tube in cm^3; $1\ cm^3 = 1\ mL$.
$r = d/2 = 4.5\ cm/2 = 2.25 = 2.3\ cm$; $h = 5.3\ m = 5.3 \times 10^2\ cm$
$V = \pi r^2 h = 3.14159 \times (2.25\ cm)^2 \times (5.3 \times 10^2\ cm) = 8.429 \times 10^3\ cm^3 = 8.4\ L$

$$PV = \frac{g}{\mathcal{M}} RT;\ g = \frac{\mathcal{M}PV}{RT};\ P = 2.03\ torr \times \frac{1\ atm}{760\ torr} = 2.621 \times 10^{-3} = 2.62 \times 10^{-3}\ atm$$

$$g = \frac{20.18\ g\ Ne}{1\ mol\ Ne} \times \frac{K \cdot mol}{0.08206\ L \cdot atm} \times \frac{2.67 \times 10^{-3}\ atm \times 8.429\ L}{308\ K} = 0.018\ g\ Ne$$

10.32 (a) $V = 0.456\ L,\ T = 23°C = 296\ K,\ n = 3.18\ g\ C_3H_8 \times \frac{1\ mol\ C_3H_8}{44.1\ g\ C_3H_8} = 0.07211$
$= 0.0721\ mol$

$$P = \frac{nRT}{V} = 0.07211\ mol \times \frac{0.08206\ L \cdot atm}{K \cdot mol} \times \frac{296\ K}{0.456\ L} = 3.84\ atm$$

(b) STP = 1.00 atm, 273 K

$$V = \frac{nRT}{P} = 0.07211\ mol \times \frac{0.08206\ L \cdot atm}{K \cdot mol} \times \frac{273\ K}{1.00 atm} = 1.16154 = 1.62\ L$$

(c) $°C = 5/9\ (°F - 32°)$; $K = °C + 273.15 = 5/9\ (130°F - 32°) + 273.15 = 327.59 = 328\ K$

$$P = \frac{nRT}{V} = 0.07211\ mol \times \frac{0.08206\ L \cdot atm}{K \cdot mol} \times \frac{327.59\ K}{0.456\ L} = 4.251 = 4.25\ atm$$

10.34 (a) $g = \frac{\mathcal{M}\ PV}{RT}$; $V = 68.0\ L,\ T = 23°C = 296\ K,\ P = 15{,}900\ kPa \times \frac{1\ atm}{101.325} = 156.92$
$= 157\ atm$

$$g = \frac{32.0\ g\ O_2}{1\ mol\ O_2} \times \frac{K \cdot mol}{0.08206\ L \cdot atm} \times \frac{156.92\ atm}{296\ K} \times 68.0\ L = 1.406 \times 10^4\ g\ O_2$$
$= 14.1\ kg\ O_2$

(b) $$V_2 = \frac{P_1V_1T_2}{T_1P_2} = \frac{15{,}900\ kPa \times 68.0\ L \times 273\ K}{296\ K \times 101.325\ kPa} = 9.84 \times 10^3\ L$$

(c) $$T_2 = \frac{P_2T_1}{P_1} = \frac{170\ atm \times 296\ K}{15{,}900\ kPa} \times \frac{101.325\ kPa}{1\ atm} = 321\ K$$

(d) $$P_2 = \frac{P_1V_1T_2}{V_2T_1} = \frac{15{,}900\ kPa \times 68.0\ L \times 297\ K}{52.6\ L \times 296\ K} = 20{,}625 = 2.06 \times 10^4\ kPa$$

10.36 (a) $P = \dfrac{gRT}{\mathcal{M}V}$; mass = 1800 × 10^{-9} g = 1.8 × 10^{-6} g; V = 1 m^3 = 1 × 10^3 L

$$P = \frac{1.8 \times 10^{-6}\,\text{g Hg} \times 1\,\text{mol Hg}}{200.6\,\text{g Hg}} \times \frac{0.08206\,\text{L•atm}}{\text{K•mol}} \times \frac{283\,\text{K}}{1 \times 10^3\,\text{L}} = 2.1 \times 10^{-10}\,\text{atm}$$

(b) $$\frac{1.8 \times 10^{-6}\,\text{g Hg}}{1\,\text{m}^3} \times \frac{1\,\text{mol Hg}}{200.6\,\text{g Hg}} \times \frac{6.022 \times 10^{23}\,\text{Hg atoms}}{1\,\text{mol Hg}} = 5.4 \times 10^{15}\,\text{Hg atoms/m}^3$$

(c) $$1600\,\text{km}^3 \times \frac{1000^3\,\text{m}^3}{1\,\text{km}^3} \times \frac{1.8 \times 10^{-6}\,\text{g Hg}}{1\,\text{m}^3} = 2.9 \times 10^6\,\text{g Hg/day}$$

Further Applications of the Ideal-Gas Equation

10.38 (b) HCl(g) is least dense. For gases at the same conditions, density is directly proportional to molar mass, and HCl has the smallest molar mass.

10.40 (b) Xe atoms have a higher mass than N_2 molecules. Because both gases at STP have the same number of molecules per unit volume, the Xe gas must be denser.

10.42 (a) $d = \dfrac{\mathcal{M}P}{RT}$; $\mathcal{M}$ = 146.1 g/mol, T = 32°C = 305 K, P = 455 torr

$$d = \frac{146.1\,\text{g}}{1\,\text{mol}} \times \frac{\text{K•mol}}{0.08206\,\text{L•atm}} \times \frac{455\,\text{torr}}{305\,\text{K}} \times \frac{1\,\text{atm}}{760\,\text{torr}} = 3.49\,\text{g/L}$$

(b) $$\mathcal{M} = \frac{dRT}{P} = \frac{6.345\,\text{g}}{1\,\text{L}} \times \frac{0.08206\,\text{L•atm}}{\text{K•mol}} \times \frac{295\,\text{K}}{743\,\text{torr}} \times \frac{760\,\text{torr}}{1\,\text{atm}} = 157\,\text{g/mol}$$

10.44 $$\mathcal{M} = \frac{gRT}{PV} = \frac{0.963\,\text{g}}{0.418\,\text{L}} \times \frac{0.08206\,\text{L•atm}}{\text{K•atm}} \times \frac{373\,\text{K}}{752\,\text{torr}} \times \frac{760\,\text{torr}}{1\,\text{atm}} = 71.3\,\text{g/mol}$$

10.46 $n_{H_2} = \dfrac{P_{H_2}V}{RT}$; $P = 814\,\text{torr} \times \dfrac{1\,\text{atm}}{760\,\text{torr}} = 1.071 = 1.07\,\text{atm}$

$$n_{H_2} = 1.071\,\text{atm} \times \frac{\text{K•mol}}{0.08206\,\text{L•atm}} \times \frac{64.5\,\text{L}}{305\,\text{K}} = 2.760 = 2.76\,\text{mol H}_2$$

$$2.760\,\text{mol H}_2 \times \frac{1\,\text{mol CaH}_2}{2\,\text{mol H}_2} \times \frac{42.10\,\text{g CaH}_2}{1\,\text{mol CaH}_2} = 58.1\,\text{g CaH}_2$$

10.48 g glucose → mol glucose → mol CO_2 → V CO_2

$$24.5\,\text{g} \times \frac{1\,\text{mol glucose}}{180.1\,\text{g}} \times \frac{6\,\text{mol CO}_2}{1\,\text{mol glucose}} = 0.8162 = 0.816\,\text{mol CO}_2$$

$$V = \frac{nRT}{P} = 0.8162\,\text{mol} \times \frac{0.08206\,\text{L•atm}}{\text{K•mol}} \times \frac{310\,\text{K}}{0.970\,\text{atm}} = 21.4\,\text{L CO}_2$$

10.50 The gas sample is a mixture of $C_2H_2(g)$ and $H_2O(g)$. Find the partial pressure of C_2H_2, then moles CaC_2 and C_2H_2.

P_t = 726 torr = $P_{C_2H_2} + P_{H_2O}$. P_{H_2O} at 21°C = 18.65 torr

$$P_{C_2H_2} = (748 \text{ torr} - 18.65 \text{ torr}) \times \frac{1 \text{ atm}}{760 \text{ torr}} = 0.9597 = 0.960 \text{ atm}$$

$$3.26 \text{ g } CaC_2 \times \frac{1 \text{ mol } CaC_2}{64.10 \text{ g}} \times \frac{1 \text{ mol } C_2H_2}{1 \text{ mol } CaC_2} = 0.050858 = 0.0509 \text{ mol } C_2H_2$$

$$V = 0.050858 \text{ mol} \times \frac{0.08206 \text{ L}\cdot\text{atm}}{\text{K}\cdot\text{mol}} \times \frac{294 \text{ K}}{0.9597 \text{ atm}} = 1.28 \text{ L}$$

Partial Pressures

10.52 (a) The partial pressure of gas A is **not affected** by the addition of gas C. The partial pressure of A depends only on moles of A, volume of container and conditions; none of these factors change when gas C is added.

(b) The total pressure in the vessel **increases** when gas C is added, because the total number of moles of gas increases.

(c) The mole fraction of gas B **decreases** when gas C is added. The moles of gas B stay the same, but the total moles increase, so the mole fraction of B (n_B/n_t) decreases.

10.54 (a)

$$3.15 \text{ g } CH_4 \times \frac{1 \text{ mol } CH_4}{16.04 \text{ g } CH_4} = 0.1964 = 0.196 \text{ mol } CH_4$$

$$P_{CH_4} = \frac{nRT}{V} = 0.1964 \text{ mol} \times \frac{0.08206 \text{ L}\cdot\text{atm}}{\text{K}\cdot\text{mol}} \times \frac{337 \text{ K}}{2.00 \text{ L}} = 2.715 = 2.72 \text{ atm}$$

$$3.15 \text{ g } C_2H_4 \times \frac{1 \text{ mol } C_2H_4}{28.05 \text{ g } C_2H_4} = 0.1123 = 0.112 \text{ mol } C_2H_4$$

$$P_{C_2H_4} = \frac{nRT}{V} = 0.1123 \text{ mol } C_2H_4 \times \frac{0.08206 \text{ L}\cdot\text{atm}}{\text{K}\cdot\text{mol}} \times \frac{337 \text{ K}}{2.00 \text{ L}} = 1.553 = 1.55 \text{ atm}$$

$$3.15 \text{ g } C_4H_{10} \times \frac{1 \text{ mol } C_4H_{10}}{58.12 \text{ g } C_4H_{10}} = 0.05420 = 0.0542 \text{ mol } C_4H_{10}$$

$$P_{C_4H_{10}} = \frac{nRT}{V} = 0.05420 \text{ mol} \times \frac{0.08206 \text{ L}\cdot\text{atm}}{\text{K}\cdot\text{mol}} \times \frac{337 \text{ K}}{2.00 \text{ L}} = 0.7494 = 0.749 \text{ atm}$$

(b) P_t = 2.715 atm + 1.553 atm + 0.749 atm = 5.017 = 5.02 atm

10.56 $$n_{N_2} = 12.47 \text{ g } N_2 \times \frac{1 \text{ mol}}{28.02 \text{ g}} = 0.4450 \text{ mol}; \quad n_{H_2} = 1.98 \text{ g } H_2 \times \frac{1 \text{ mol}}{2.016 \text{ g}} = 0.982 \text{ mol}$$

$$n_{NH_3} = 8.15 \text{ g } NH_3 \times \frac{1 \text{ mol}}{17.03 \text{ g}} = 0.479 \text{ mol}; \quad n_t = 0.4450 + 0.982 + 0.479 = 1.906 \text{ mol}$$

$$P_{N_2} = \frac{n_{N_2}}{n_t} \times P_t = \frac{0.4450}{1.906} \times 2.35 \text{ atm} = 0.549 \text{ atm}$$

$$P_{H_2} = \frac{0.982}{1.906} \times 2.35 \text{ atm} = 1.21 \text{ atm}; \; P_{NH_3} = \frac{0.479}{1.906} \times 2.35 \text{ atm} = 0.591 \text{ atm}$$

10.58 (a) $n_{O_2} = 6.55 \text{ g } O_2 \times \frac{1 \text{ mol}}{32.00 \text{ g}} = 0.205 \text{ mol}; \; n_{N_2} = 4.92 \text{ g } N_2 \times \frac{1 \text{ mol}}{28.02 \text{ g}} = 0.176 \text{ mol}$

$$n_{H_2} = 1.32 \text{ g } H_2 \times \frac{1 \text{ mol}}{2.016 \text{ g}} = 0.655 \text{ mol}; \; n_t = 0.205 + 0.176 + 0.655 = 1.036 \text{ mol}$$

$$\chi_{O_2} = \frac{n_{O_2}}{n_t} = \frac{0.205}{1.036} = 0.198; \; \chi_{N_2} = \frac{n_{N_2}}{n_t} = \frac{0.176}{1.036} = 0.170$$

$$\chi_{H_2} = \frac{0.655}{1.036} = 0.632$$

(b) $P_{O_2} = n \times \frac{RT}{V}; \; P_{O_2} = 0.205 \text{ mol} \times \frac{0.08206 \text{ L} \cdot \text{atm}}{\text{K} \cdot \text{mol}} \times \frac{288 \text{ K}}{12.40 \text{ L}} = 0.391 \text{ atm}$

$$P_{N_2} = 0.176 \text{ mol} \times \frac{0.08206 \text{ L} \cdot \text{atm}}{\text{K} \cdot \text{mol}} \times \frac{288 \text{ K}}{12.40 \text{ L}} = 0.335 \text{ atm}$$

$$P_{H_2} = 0.655 \text{ mol} \times \frac{0.08206 \text{ L} \cdot \text{atm}}{\text{K} \cdot \text{mol}} \times \frac{288 \text{ K}}{12.40 \text{ L}} = 1.25 \text{ atm}$$

10.60 Calculate the pressure of the gas in the second vessel directly from mass and conditions using the ideal-gas equation.

(a) $P_{SO_2} = \frac{gRT}{\mathcal{M}V} = \frac{5.25 \text{ g } SO_2}{64.07 \text{ g } SO_2/\text{mol}} \times \frac{0.08206 \text{ L} \cdot \text{atm}}{\text{K} \cdot \text{mol}} \times \frac{298 \text{ K}}{13.6 \text{ L}} = 0.14734$

$= 0.147 \text{ atm}$

(b) $P_{N_2} = \frac{gRT}{\mathcal{M}V} = \frac{2.35 \text{ g } N_2}{28.01 \text{ g } N_2/\text{mol}} \times \frac{0.08206 \text{ L} \cdot \text{atm}}{\text{K} \cdot \text{mol}} \times \frac{298 \text{ K}}{13.6 \text{ L}} = 0.15086$

$= 0.151 \text{ atm}$

(c) $P_T = P_{SO_2} + P_{N_2} = 0.14734 \text{ atm} + 0.15086 \text{ atm} = 0.298 \text{ atm}$

Kinetic - Molecular Theory; Graham's Law

10.62 (a) False. The average kinetic energy per molecule in a collection of gas molecules is the same for all gases at the same temperature. (b) True. (c) False. The molecules in a gas sample at a given temperature exhibit a distribution of kinetic energies. (d) True.

10.64 Newton's model provides no explanation of the effect of a change in temperature on the pressure of a gas at constant volume or on the volume of a gas at constant pressure. On the other hand, the assumption that the average kinetic energy of gas molecules increases with increasing temperature explains Charles Law, that an increase in temperature requires an increase in volume to maintain constant pressure.

10.66 (a) They have the same number of molecules (equal volumes of gases at the same temperature and pressure contain equal numbers of molecules).

(b) N_2 is more dense because it has the larger molar mass. Since the volumes of the samples and the number of molecules are equal, the gas with the larger molar mass will have the greater density.

(c) The average kinetic energies are equal (statement 5, section 10.7).

(d) CH_4 will effuse faster. The lighter the gas molecules, the faster they will effuse (Graham's Law).

10.68 (a) The larger the molar mass, the slower the average speed (at constant temperature). In order of increasing speed (and decreasing molar mass):
$HBr < NF_3 < SO_2 < CO < Ne$

(b) $$u = \sqrt{\frac{3RT}{\mathcal{M}}} = \left(\frac{3 \times 8.314\ \text{kg}\bullet\text{m}^2/\text{s}^2\bullet\text{K}\bullet\text{mol} \times 298\ \text{K}}{71.0 \times 10^{-3}\ \text{kg/mol}}\right)^{1/2} = 324\ \text{m/s}$$

10.70 $$\frac{\text{rate}\ ^{235}\text{U}}{\text{rate}\ ^{238}\text{U}} = \sqrt{\frac{238.05}{235.04}} = \sqrt{1.0128} = 1.0064$$

There is a slightly greater rate enhancement for $^{235}U(g)$ atoms than $^{235}UF_6(g)$ molecules (1.0043), because ^{235}U is a greater percentage (100%) of the mass of the diffusing particles than in $^{235}UF_6$ molecules. The masses of the isotopes were taken from *The Handbook of Chemistry and Physics.*

10.72 The time required is proportional to the reciprocal of the effusion rate.

$$\frac{\text{rate (X)}}{\text{rate (O}_2)} = \frac{105\ \text{s}}{31\ \text{s}} = \left[\frac{32\ \text{g O}_2}{\mathcal{M}_x}\right]^{1/2}; \quad \mathcal{M}_x = 32\ \text{g O}_2 \times \left[\frac{105}{31}\right]^2 = 370\ \text{g/mol (two sig figs)}$$

Nonideal-Gas Behavior

10.74 Ideal-gas behavior is most likely to occur at high temperature and low pressure, so the atmosphere on Mercury is more likely to obey the ideal gas law. The higher temperature on Mercury means that the kinetic energies of the molecules will be larger relative to intermolecular attractive forces. Further, the gravitational attractive forces on Mercury are lower because the planet has a much smaller mass. This means that for the same column mass of gas (Figure 10.1), atmospheric pressure on Mercury will be lower.

10.76 (a) The initial drop in the value of PV/RT is due to attractive forces between molecules. These intermolecular forces cause the molecules to "stick" together and behave as if there are fewer net particles in the sample. At lower pressures, this is the dominant effect. At the same time, the real volume of gas molecules causes the amount of free space in the gas sample to be less than the container volume. Using the container volume to calculate PV/RT gives a value larger than that for an ideal gas (which assumes that the total container volume is free space). At higher pressures, this effect more than compensates for molecular attraction, and PV/RT is greater than 1.

(b) As the temperature of a gas increases, the average kinetic energy of the particles increases. The increased kinetic energy overcomes the attractive forces between molecules and keeps them separate.

10.78 The constant *a* is a measure of the strength of intermolecular attractions among gas molecules; *b* is a measure of molecular volume. Both increase with increasing molecular mass and structural complexity.

10.80 (a) At STP, the molar volume = $1 \text{ mol} \times \frac{0.08206 \text{ L}\bullet\text{atm}}{\text{K}\bullet\text{mol}} \times \frac{273 \text{ K}}{1 \text{ atm}} = 22.4 \text{ L}$

Dividing the value for *b*, 0.0322 L/mol, by 4, we obtain 0.0080 L. Thus, the volume of the Ar atoms is (0.0080/22.4)100 = 0.036% of the total volume.

(b) At 100 atm pressure the molar volume is 0.224 L, and the volume of the Ar atoms is 3.6% of the total volume.

Additional Exercises

10.82 A mercury barometer with water trapped in its tip would not read the correct pressure. The standard relationship between height of an Hg column and atmospheric pressure (760 mm Hg = 1 atm) assumes that there is a vacuum in the closed end of the barometer and that gravity is the only downward force on the Hg column. Water at the top of the Hg column would establish a vapor pressure which would exert additional downward pressure and partially counterbalance the pressure of the atmosphere. The Hg column would read lower than the actual atmospheric pressure.

10.84 $P = \frac{nRT}{V}$; $n = 1.4 \times 10^{-5}$ mol, V = 0.600 L, T = 23°C = 296 K

$$P = 1.4 \times 10^{-5} \text{ mol} \times \frac{0.08206 \text{ L}\bullet\text{atm}}{\text{K}\bullet\text{mol}} \times \frac{296 \text{ K}}{0.600 \text{ L}} = 5.7 \times 10^{-4} \text{ atm} = 0.43 \text{ mm Hg}$$

10.85 (a) $n = \frac{PV}{RT} = 3.00 \text{ atm} \times \frac{\text{K}\bullet\text{mol}}{0.08206 \text{ L}\bullet\text{atm}} \times \frac{110 \text{ L}}{300 \text{ K}} = 13.4 \text{ mol } C_3H_8(g)$

(b) $\frac{0.590 \text{ g } C_3H_8 (l)}{1 \text{ mL}} \times 110 \times 10^3 \text{ mL} \times \frac{1 \text{ mol } C_3H_8}{44.094 \text{ g}} = 1.47 \times 10^3 \text{ mol } C_3H_8 (l)$

(c) Using C_3H_8 in a 110 L container as an example, the ratio of moles liquid to moles gas that can be stored in a certain volume is $\frac{1.47 \times 10^3 \text{ mol liquid}}{13.4 \text{ mol gas}} = 110$.

A container with a fixed volume holds many more moles (molecules) of $C_3H_8(l)$ because in the liquid phase the molecules are touching. In the gas phase, the molecules are far apart (statement 2, section 10.7) and many fewer molecules will fit in the container.

10.87 Volume of laboratory = $54\ m^2 \times 3.1\ m \times \frac{1000\ L}{1\ m^3} = 1.674 \times 10^5 = 1.7 \times 10^5\ L$

Calculate the **total** moles of gas in the laboratory at the conditions given.

$$n_t = \frac{PV}{RT} = 1.00\ atm \times \frac{K \cdot mol}{0.08206\ L \cdot atm} \times \frac{1.674 \times 10^5\ L}{297\ K} = 6.869 \times 10^3 = 6.9 \times 10^3\ mol\ gas$$

An $Ni(CO)_4$ concentration of 1 part in 10^9 means 1 mol $Ni(CO)_4$ in 1×10^9 total moles of gas.

$$\frac{x\ mol\ Ni(CO)_4}{6.869 \times 10^3\ mol\ gas} = \frac{1}{10^9} = 6.869 \times 10^{-6}\ mol\ Ni(CO)_4$$

$$6.869 \times 10^{-6}\ mol\ Ni(CO)_4 \times \frac{170.74\ g\ Ni(CO)_4}{1\ mol\ Ni(CO)_4} = 1.2 \times 10^{-3}\ g\ Ni(CO)_4$$

10.88 It is simplest to calculate the partial pressure of each gas as it expands into the total volume, then sum the partial pressures.

$P_2 = P_1V_1 / V_2$; $P_{N_2} = 265\ torr\ (1.0\ L / 2.5\ L) = 106 = 1.1 \times 10^2\ torr$

$P_{Ne} = 800\ torr\ (1.0\ L / 2.5\ L) = 320 = 3.2 \times 10^2\ torr$; $P_{H_2} = 532\ torr\ (0.5\ L / 2.5\ L)$

$= 106 = 1.1 \times 10^2\ torr$

$P_t = P_{N_2} + P_{Ne} + P_{H_2} = (106 + 320 + 106)\ torr = 532 = 5.3 \times 10^2\ torr$

10.89 (a) $$n = \frac{PV}{RT} = 0.980\ atm \times \frac{K \cdot mol}{0.08206\ L \cdot atm} \times \frac{0.524\ L}{347\ K} = 0.018034 = 0.0180\ mol\ air$$

$$mol\ O_2 = 0.018034\ mol\ air \times \frac{0.2095\ mol\ O_2}{1\ mol\ air} = 0.003778 = 0.00378\ mol\ O_2$$

(b) $C_8H_{18}(l) + 25/2\ O_2(g) \rightarrow 8CO_2(g) + 9H_2O(g)$

(The H_2O produced in an automobile engine is in the gaseous state.)

$$0.003778\ mol\ O_2 \times \frac{1\ mol\ C_8H_{18}}{12.5\ mol\ O_2} \times \frac{114.2\ g\ C_8H_{18}}{1\ mol\ C_8H_{18}} = 0.0345\ g\ C_8H_{18}$$

10.91 V and T are the same for He and O_2.

$P_{He}V = n_{He}RT$, $P_{He}/n_{He} = RT/V$; $P_{O_2}/n_{O_2} = RT/V$

$$\frac{P_{He}}{n_{He}} = \frac{P_{O_2}}{n_{O_2}} = n_{O_2} = \frac{P_{O_2} \times n_{He}}{P_{He}};\quad n_{He} = 1.42\ g\ He \times \frac{1\ mol\ He}{4.003\ g\ He} = 0.3547 = 0.355\ mol\ He$$

$$n_{O_2} = \frac{158\ torr}{42.5\ torr} \times 0.355\ mol = 1.3188 = 1.32\ mol\ O_2;\ 1.3188\ mol\ O_2 \times \frac{32.00\ g\ O_2}{1\ mol\ O_2} = 42.2\ g\ O_2$$

10.93 Calculate the number of moles of Ar in the vessel:
n = (339.854 - 337.428)/39.948 = 0.060729 = 0.06073 mol

The total number of moles of the mixed gas is the same (Avogadro's Law). Thus, the average atomic weight is (339.076 - 337.428)/0.060729 = 27.137 = 27.14. Let the mole fraction of Ne be χ. Then,

χ (20.183) + (1 - χ) (39.948) = 27.137; 12.811 = 19.765 χ; χ = 0.6482

Neon is thus 64.82 mole percent of the mixture.

10.94 (a) The quantity d/P = $\mathcal{M}$/RT should be a constant at all pressures for an ideal gas. It is not, however, because of nonideal behavior. If we graph d/P vs P, the ratio should approach ideal behavior at low P. At P = 0, d/P = 2.2525. Using this value in the formula $\mathcal{M}$ = d/P × RT, $\mathcal{M}$ = 50.46 g/mol.

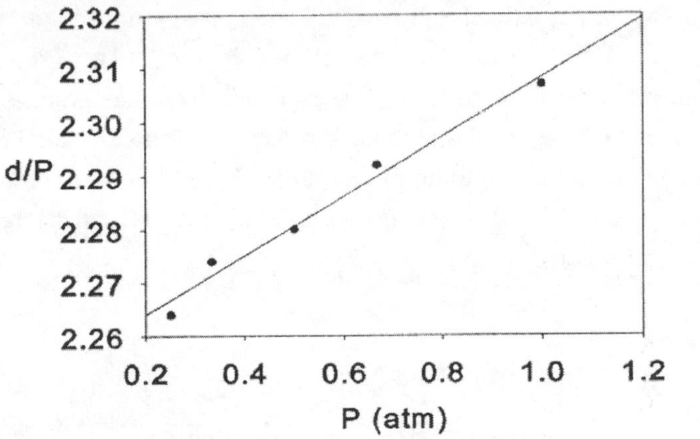

(b) The ratio d/P varies with pressure because of the finite volumes of gas molecules and attractive intermolecular forces.

10.96 In the expanded container volume, there are fewer collisions with the walls and with other gas particles. Attractive and repulsive forces which might change the speed of the particles become less important, and the particles maintain essentially the same average speed, kinetic energy and temperature after the expansion.

10.97

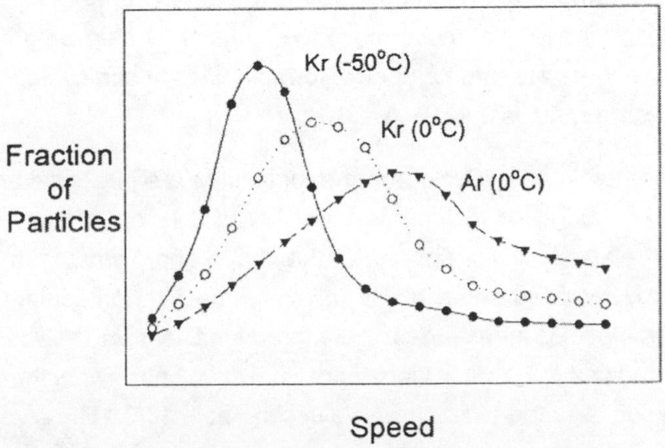

10.99 (a) $120.00 \text{ kg } N_2(g) \times \frac{1000 \text{ g}}{1 \text{ kg}} \times \frac{1 \text{ mol } N_2}{28.0135 \text{ g N}} = 4283.6 \text{ mol } N_2$

$$P = \frac{nRT}{V} = 4283.6 \text{ mol} \times \frac{0.08206 \text{ L}\cdot\text{atm}}{\text{K}\cdot\text{mol}} \times \frac{553 \text{ K}}{1100.0 \text{ L}} = 176.72 = 177 \text{ atm}$$

(b) According to Equation 10.26,

$$P = \frac{nRT}{V - nb} - \frac{n^2 a}{V^2}$$

$$P = \frac{(4283.6 \text{ mol})(0.08206 \text{ L}\cdot\text{atm/K}\cdot\text{mol})(553 \text{ K})}{1100.0 \text{ L} - (4283.6 \text{ mol})(0.0391 \text{ L/mol})} - \frac{(4283.6 \text{ mol})^2 (1.39 \text{ L}^2\cdot\text{atm/mol}^2)}{(1100.0 \text{ L})^2}$$

$$P = \frac{194{,}388 \text{ L}\cdot\text{atm}}{1100.0 \text{ L} - 167.5 \text{ L}} - 21.1 \text{ atm} = 208.5 \text{ atm} - 21.1 \text{ atm} = 187.4 \text{ atm}$$

(c) The pressure corrected for the real volume of the N_2 molecules is 208.5 atm, 31.8 atm higher than the ideal pressure of 176.7 atm. The 21.1 atm correction for intermolecular forces reduces the calculated pressure somewhat, but the "real" pressure is still higher than the ideal pressure. The correction for the real volume of molecules dominates. Even though the value of *b* is small, the number of moles of N_2 is large enough so that the molecular volume correction is larger than the attractive forces correction.

Integrative Exercises

10.100 (a) $\mathcal{M} = \frac{gRT}{VP} = \frac{1.56 \text{ g}}{1.00 \text{ L}} \times \frac{0.08206 \text{ L}\cdot\text{atm}}{\text{K}\cdot\text{mol}} \times \frac{323 \text{ K}}{0.984 \text{ atm}} = 42.0 \text{ g/mol}$

Assume 100 g cyclopropane

$$100 \text{ g} \times 0.857 \text{ C} = 85.7 \text{ g C} \times \frac{1 \text{ mol C}}{12.01 \text{ g}} = \frac{7.136 \text{ mol C}}{7.136} = 1 \text{ mol C}$$

$$100 \text{ g} \times 0.143 \text{ H} = 14.3 \text{ g H} \times \frac{1 \text{ mol H}}{1.008 \text{ g}} = \frac{14.19 \text{ mol H}}{7.136} = 2 \text{ mol H}$$

The empirical formula of cyclopropane is CH_2 and the empirical formula weight is 12 + 2 = 14 g. The ratio of molar mass to empirical formula weight, 42.0 g/14 g, is 3; therefore, there are three empirical formula units in one cyclopropane molecule. The molecular formula is $3 \times (CH_2) = C_3H_6$.

(b) Ar is a monoatomic gas. Cyclopropane molecules are larger and more structurally complex, even though the molar masses of Ar and C_3H_6 are similar. If both gases are at the same relatively low temperature, they have approximately the same average kinetic energy, and the same ability to overcome intermolecular attractions. We expect intermolecular attractions to be more significant for the more complex C_3H_6 molecules, and that C_3H_6 will deviate more from ideal behavior at the conditions listed. This conclusion is supported by the <u>a</u> values in Table 10.3. The <u>a</u> values for CH_4 and

CO_2, more complex molecules than Ar atoms, are larger than the value for Ar. If the pressure is high enough for the volume correction in the van der Waals equation to dominate behavior, the larger C_3H_6 molecules definitely deviate more than Ar atoms from ideal behavior.

10.102 (a) *Analyze/Plan.* $AgF + S_8 \xrightarrow{\Delta}$ unknown gas

The gas probably contains the elements S and F in an unknown mole ratio. (Most compounds containing Ag are ionic and therefore solids.) Calculate the molar mass of the gas from its density at the given conditions. Determine the relative amount of F from the data on the reaction of the gas with water to produce HF. *Solve*:

$$\mathcal{M} = \frac{dRT}{P} = \frac{0.803\text{ g}}{\text{L}} \times \frac{0.08206\text{ L}\bullet\text{atm}}{\text{K}\bullet\text{mol}} \times \frac{305\text{ K}}{150\text{ mm}} \times \frac{760\text{ mm}}{1\text{ atm}} = 101.83 = 102\text{ g/mol}$$

mol F in 480 mL sample: $M \times L$ = mol

0.081 M HF × 0.080 L = 0.00648 = 0.0065 mol HF = 0.0065 mol F in the sample

total mol gas in 480 mL sample: n = PV/RT

$$n = 126\text{ mm} \times \frac{1\text{ atm}}{760\text{ mm}} \times \frac{0.480\text{ L}}{301\text{ K}} \times \frac{\text{K}\bullet\text{mol}}{0.08206\text{ L}\bullet\text{atm}} = 3.222 \times 10^{-3} = 3.22 \times 10^{-3}\text{ mol}$$

mole ratio of S and F:

total g gas = 3.222×10^{-3} mol gas × 101.83 g/mol; = 0.32808 = 0.328 g gas

g F = 6.48×10^{-3} mol F × 18.998 g/mol F = 0.12311 = 0.123 g F

g S = 0.32808 - 0.12311 = 0.20497 = 0.205 g S

mol S = 0.205 g S/32.07 g/mol = 0.0639 mol S

0.00639 mol S/0.00648 mol F = 1:1 mole ratio of S:F

The empirical formula is SF; empirical FW = 32.07 + 19.00 = 51.07; since $\mathcal{M}$ = 102

The empirical formula is S_2F_2

Check. The empirical and molecular formula weights are in an integer ratio, so the result is reasonable.

(b) 26 valence e^-, 13 e^- pairs

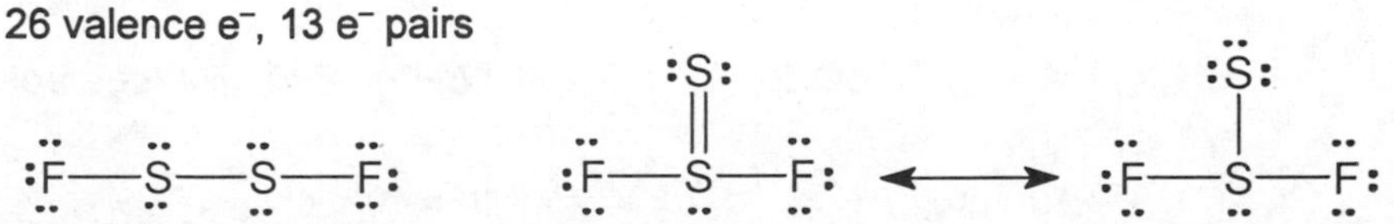

(c) According to VSEPR the electron domain geometry about S in each of the molecules will be tetrahedral, with bond angles of 109° or less. The left molecule will have a structure similar to hydrogen peroxide, H_2O_2; the 4 atoms are not necessarily coplanar, and in fact we expect a dihedral angle of approximately 110°. Since the right molecule has a single central atom, we can describe the molecular geometry as trigonal pyramidal.

From the given bond distances, we expect the single-bond covalent radii to be S = 1.02 Å, F = 0.72 Å. The simple conclusion is that the S–S distances will be ~2.04 Å and the S-F distances ~1.74 Å. In fact, the S–S distance in the left compound is 1.89 Å and in the right it is 1.86 Å. Clearly each of these bonds has some double bond character, as indicated by one of the resonance structures for the right molecule. The actual S-F distances are 1.63 Å (left) and 1.60 Å (right), also shorter than the predicted S-F single bond distance. One possible conclusion is that each of the bonds has some double bond character, that some of the "nonbonding" electron density is incorporated into a delocalized π-bonding network in the molecules.

10.103 (a) 19 e^-, 9.5 e^- pairs

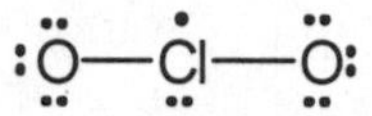

Resonance structures can be drawn with the odd electron on O, but electronegativity considerations predict that it will be on Cl for most of the time.

(b) ClO_2 is very reactive because it is an odd-electron molecule. Adding an electron (reduction), both pairs the odd electron and completes the octet of Cl. Thus, ClO_2 has a strong tendency to gain an electron and be reduced.

10.104 (a) $ft^3\ CH_4 \rightarrow L\ CH_4 \rightarrow mol\ CH_4 \rightarrow mol\ CH_3OH \rightarrow g\ CH_3OH \rightarrow L\ CH_3OH$

$$10.7 \times 10^9\ ft\ CH_4 \times \frac{1\ yd^3}{3^3\ ft^3} \times \frac{1\ m^3}{(1.0936)^3\ yd^3} \times \frac{1\ L}{1 \times 10^{-3}\ m^3} = 3.03001 \times 10^{11}$$

$$= 3.03 \times 10^{11}\ L\ CH_4$$

$$n = \frac{PV}{RT} = \frac{3.03 \times 10^{11}\ L \times 1.00\ atm}{298\ K} \times \frac{K \bullet mol}{0.08206\ L \bullet atm} = 1.2391 \times 10^{10}$$

$$= 1.24 \times 10^{10}\ mol\ CH_4$$

1 mol CH_4 = 1 mol CH_3OH

$$1.2391 \times 10^{10}\ mol\ CH_3OH \times \frac{32.04\ g\ CH_3OH}{mol\ CH_3OH} \times \frac{1\ mL\ CH_3OH}{0.791\ g} \times \frac{1\ L}{1000\ mL}$$

$$= 5.0189 \times 10^8 = 5.02 \times 10^8\ L\ CH_3OH$$

(b) $CH_4(g) + 2O_2(g) \rightarrow CO_2(g) + 2H_2O(l)$ $\Delta H° = -890.4$ kJ (see Solution 10.101)

$$1.2391 \times 10^{10}\ mol\ CH_4 \times \frac{-890.4\ kJ}{1\ mol\ CH_4} = -1.10 \times 10^{13}\ kJ$$

$CH_3OH(l) + 3/2\ O_2(g) \rightarrow CO_2(g) + 2H_2O(l)$ $\Delta H° = -726.6$ kJ

$$\Delta H° = \Delta H_f^\circ\ CO_2(g) + 2\Delta H_f^\circ\ H_2O(l) - \Delta H_f^\circ\ CH_3OH(l) - 3/2\ \Delta H_f^\circ\ O_2(g)$$

$$= -393.5\ kJ + 2(-285.83\ kJ) - (-238.6\ kJ) - 0 = -726.6\ kJ$$

$$1.2391 \times 10^{10}\ mol\ CH_3OH \times \frac{-726.6\ kJ}{1\ mol\ CH_3OH} = -9.00 \times 10^{12}\ kJ$$

(c) Assume a volume of 1.00 L of each liquid. The densities stated in the Exercise should be 0.466 g/mL or 466 g/L for $CH_4(l)$ and 0.786 g/mL or 786 g/L for $CH_3OH(l)$. This is a slightly different density for $CH_3OH(l)$ than the value given in part (a).

$$1.00 \text{ L } CH_4(l) \times \frac{466 \text{ g}}{1 \text{ L}} \times \frac{1 \text{ mol}}{16.04 \text{ g}} \times \frac{-890.4 \text{ kJ}}{\text{mol } CH_4} = -2.59 \times 10^4 \text{ kJ/L } CH_4$$

$$1.00 \text{ L } CH_3OH \times \frac{786 \text{ g}}{1 \text{ L}} \times \frac{1 \text{ mol}}{32.04 \text{ g}} \times \frac{-726.6 \text{ kJ}}{\text{mol } CH_3OH} = -1.78 \times 10^4 \text{ kJ/L } CH_3OH$$

(Using 0.791 g/mL as the density of $CH_3OH(l)$ gives -1.79×10^4 kJ/L)

Clearly $CH_4(l)$ has the higher enthalpy of combustion per unit volume.

10.106 (a) $MgCO_3(s) + 2HCl(aq) \rightarrow MgCl_2(aq) + H_2O(l) + CO_2(g)$

$CaCO_3(s) + 2HCl(aq) \rightarrow CaCl_2(aq) + H_2O(l) + CO_2(g)$

(b) $$n = \frac{PV}{RT} = 743 \text{ torr} \times \frac{1 \text{ atm}}{760 \text{ torr}} \times \frac{\text{K} \cdot \text{mol}}{0.08206 \text{ L} \cdot \text{atm}} \times \frac{1.72 \text{ L}}{301 \text{ K}}$$

$$= 0.06808 = 0.0681 \text{ mol } CO_2$$

(c) x = g $MgCO_3$, y = g $CaCO_3$, x + y = 6.53 g

mol $MgCO_3$ + mol $CaCO_3$ = mol CO_2 total

$$\frac{x}{84.32} + \frac{y}{100.09} = 0.06808; \quad y = 6.53 - x$$

$$\frac{x}{84.32} + \frac{6.53 - x}{100.09} = 0.06808$$

$$100.09x - 84.32x + 84.32(6.53) = 0.06808 (84.32)(100.09)$$

$$15.77x + 550.610 = 574.549; \quad x = 1.52 \text{ g } MgCO_3$$

$$\text{mass \% } MgCO_3 = \frac{1.52 \text{ g } MgCO_3}{6.53 \text{ g sample}} \times 100 = 23.3\%$$

[By strict sig fig rules, the answer has 2 sig figs: 15.77x + 551 (3 digits from 6.53) = 575; 575 - 551 = 24 (no decimal places, 2 sig figs) leads to 1.5 g $MgCO_3$.]

11 Intermolecular Forces, Liquids and Solids

Kinetic-Molecular Theory

11.2 Liquids are fluid and take the shape of their container. Solids are rigid, they have their own volume and do not flow. Solids are usually denser than liquids, indicating less empty space and a higher degree of order. Water is a notable exception.

11.4 (a) The average distance between molecules is greater in the liquid state. Density is the ratio of the mass of a substance to the volume it occupies. For the same substance in different states, mass will be the same. The smaller the density, the greater the volume occupied, and the greater the distance between molecules. The liquid at 130° has the lower density (1.08 g/cm^3), so the average distance between molecules is greater.

(b) As the temperature of a substance increases, the average kinetic energy and speed of the molecules increases. At the melting point the molecules, on average, have enough kinetic energy to break away from the very orderly array that was present in the solid. As the translational motion of the molecules increases, the occupied volume increases and the density decreases. Thus, the density 1.266 g/cm^3 at 15°C is greater than the density 1.08 g/cm^3 at 130°C.

11.6 (a) At constant temperature, the average kinetic energy of a collection of particles is constant. Compression brings particles closer together and increases the number of particle-particle collisions. With more collisions, the likelihood of intermolecular attractions causing the particles to coalesce (liquefy) is greater.

(b) In both liquids and solids, the component particles are touching. Most of the empty space in the sample volume has been eliminated and the sample is condensed.

Intermolecular Forces

11.8 (a) London-dispersion forces (b) dipole-dipole and London-dispersion forces
(c) hydrogen bonding

11.10 (a) CH_3OH experiences hydrogen bonding, but CH_3SH does not.

(b) Both gases are influenced by London-dispersion forces. The heavier the gas particles, the stronger the London-dispersion forces. The heavier Xe is a liquid at the specified conditions, while the lighter Ar is a gas.

(c) Both gases are influenced by London-dispersion forces. The larger, diatomic Cl_2 molecules are more polarizable, experience stronger dispersion forces and have the higher boiling point.

(d) Acetone and 2-methyl propane are molecules with similar molar masses and London-dispersion forces. Acetone also experiences dipole-dipole forces and has the higher boiling point.

11.12 (a) A more polarizable molecule can develop a larger transient dipole, increasing the strength of electrostatic attractions among polarized molecules.

(b) The noble gases are all monoatomic. Going down the column, the atomic radius and the size of the electron cloud increases. The larger the electron cloud, the more polarizable the atom, the stronger the London-disperson forces and the higher the boiling point.

(c) It is generally true that the greater the molecular weight, the stronger the dispersion forces experienced by a molecule. This is true because trends in molecular size and molecular weight are usually parallel.

(d) It is usually true that as the number of electrons in a molecule increases, the size of the molecule increases. Larger molecules tend to have diffuse electron clouds, which leads to greater polarizability. Thus, the statement that more electrons lead to increased dispersion forces (and greater polarizability) is correct.

11.14 For molecules with similar structures, the strength of dispersion forces increases with molecular size (molecular weight and number of electrons in the molecule).

(a) Br_2 (b) $CH_3CH_2CH_2SH$

(c) $CH_3CH_2CH_2Cl$. These two molecules have the same molecular formula and molecular weight (C_3H_7Cl, molecular weight = 78.5 amu), so the shapes of the molecules determine which has the stronger dispersion forces. According to Figure 11.6, the cylindrical (not branched) molecule will have stronger dispersion forces.

11.16 Both molecules experience hydrogen bonding through their –OH groups and dispersion forces between their hydrocarbon portions. The position of the –OH group in isopropyl alcohol shields it somewhat from approach by other molecules and slightly decreases the extent of hydrogen bonding. Also, isopropyl alcohol is less rod-like (it has a shorter chain) than propyl alcohol, so dispersion forces are weaker. Since hydrogen bonding and dispersion forces are weaker in isopropyl alcohol, it has the lower boiling point.

11.18 (a) Replacing a hydroxyl hydrogen with a CH_3 group eliminates hydrogen bonding in that part of the molecule. This reduces the strength of intermolecular forces and leads to a (much) lower boiling point.

(b) $CH_3OCH_2CH_2OCH_3$ is a larger, more polarizable molecule with stronger London-dispersion forces and thus a higher boiling point.

11.20 (a) C_6H_{14} – dispersion; C_8H_{18} – dispersion. C_8H_{18} has the higher boiling point due to greater molar mass and similar strength of forces.

(b) C_3H_8 – dispersion; CH_3OCH_3 – dipole-dipole and dispersion. CH_3OCH_3 has the higher boiling point due to stronger intermolecular forces and similar molar mass.

(c) CH_3OH – hydrogen bonding, dipole-dipole and dispersion; CH_3SH – dipole-dipole and dispersion. CH_3OH has the higher boiling point due to the influence of hydrogen bonding (Figure 11.7).

(d) NH_2NH_2 – hydrogen bonding, dipole-dipole and dispersion; CH_3CH_3 – dispersion. NH_2NH_2 has the higher boiling point due to much stronger intermolecular forces.

11.22 (a) In the solid state, NH_3 molecules are arranged so as to form the maximum number of hydrogen bonds. At the melting point, the average kinetic energy of the molecules is large enough so that they are free to move relative to each other. As they move, old hydrogen bonds break and new ones form, but the strict relative order required for maximum hydrogen bonding is no longer present.

(b) In the liquid state, molecules are moving relative to one another while touching, which makes some hydrogen bonding possible. When molecules achieve enough kinetic energy to vaporize, the distance between them increases beyond the point where hydrogen bonds can form.

Viscosity and Surface Tension

11.24 (a) *Cohesive* forces bind molecules to each other.
Adhesive forces bind molecules to surfaces.

(b) Viscosity and surface tension reflect attractive forces among molecules in a liquid. That is, they reflect cohesive forces.

(c) The shape of a meniscus depends on the strength of the cohesive forces within a liquid relative to the adhesive forces between the walls of the tube and the liquid. Adhesive forces between polar water molecules and silicates in glass (Figure 11.16) are even stronger than cohesive hydrogen-bonding forces among water molecules, so the meniscus is U-shaped (concave-upward).

(d) Water travels through the paper towel by capillary action. The stronger the adhesive forces between the cellulose fibers in the towel and the water molecules, the greater the capillary action. Also, the number and orientation of the capillaries in the towel affect the absorbency of the towel.

11.26 (a)

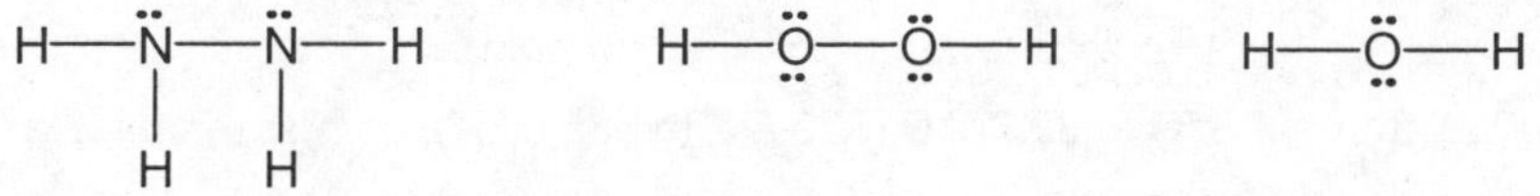

(b) All have bonds (N-H or O-H, respectively) capable of forming hydrogen bonds. Hydrogen bonding is the strongest intermolecular interaction between neutral molecules and leads to very strong cohesive forces in liquids. The stronger the cohesive forces in a liquid, the greater the surface tension.

Changes of State

11.28 (a) Condensation, exothermic (b) sublimation, endothermic
(c) vaporization (evaporation), endothermic (d) freezing, exothermic

11.30 (a) Liquid ethyl chloride at room temperature is far above its boiling point. When the liquid contacts the metal surface, heat sufficient to vaporize the liquid is transferred from the metal to the ethyl chloride, and the heat content of the molecules increases. At constant atmospheric pressure, $\Delta H = q$, so the heat content and the enthalpy content of $C_2H_5Cl(g)$ is higher than that of $C_2H_5Cl(l)$.

(b) Attractive intermolecular forces hold the C_2H_5Cl molecules in close contact in the liquid phase. In order to overcome these attractive forces and maintain separation in the gas phase, the enthalpy content of the C_2H_5Cl molecules must increase when they change from the liquid to the gaseous state.

11.32 Energy released when 100 g of H_2O is cooled from 18°C to 0°C:

$$\frac{4.184\ \text{J}}{\text{g}\bullet\text{K}} \times 100\ \text{g H}_2\text{O} \times 18°\text{C} = 7.53 \times 10^3\ \text{J} = 7.5\ \text{kJ}$$

Energy released when 100 g of H_2O is frozen (there is no change in temperature during a change of state):

$$\frac{334\ \text{J}}{\text{g}} \times 100\ \text{g H}_2\text{O} = 3.34 \times 10^4\ \text{J} = 33.4\ \text{kJ}$$

Total energy released = 7.53 kJ + 33.4 kJ = 40.93 = 40.9 kJ

Mass of freon that will absorb 40.9 kJ when vaporized:

$$40.93\ \text{kJ} \times \frac{1 \times 10^3\ \text{J}}{1\ \text{kJ}} \times \frac{1\ \text{g CCl}_2\text{F}_2}{289\ \text{J}} = 142\ \text{g CCl}_2\text{F}_2$$

11.34 Consider the process in steps, using the appropriate thermochemical constant.

Heat the liquid from 5.00°C to 47.6°C (278.00 K to 320.6 K), using the specific heat of the liquid.

$$25.0 \text{ g } C_2Co_3F_3 \times \frac{0.91 \text{ J}}{\text{g}\bullet\text{K}} \times 42.6 \text{ K} \times \frac{1 \text{ kJ}}{1000 \text{ J}} = 0.969 = 0.97 \text{ kJ}$$

Boil the liquid at 47.6°C (320.6 K), using the enthalpy of vaporization.

$$25.0 \text{ g } C_2Cl_3F_3 \times \frac{1 \text{ mol } C_2Cl_3F_3}{187.4 \text{ g } C_2Cl_3F_3} \times \frac{27.49 \text{ kJ}}{\text{mol}} = 3.667 = 3.67 \text{ kJ}$$

Heat the gas from 47.6°C to 82.00°C (320.6 K to 355.00 K), using the specific heat of the gas.

$$25.0 \text{ g } C_2Cl_3F_3 \times \frac{0.67 \text{ J}}{\text{g}\bullet\text{K}} \times 34.4 \text{ K} \times \frac{1 \text{ kJ}}{1000 \text{ J}} = 0.576 = 0.58 \text{ kJ}$$

The total energy required is 0.969 kJ + 3.667 kJ + 0.576 kJ = 5.21 kJ.

11.36 (a) According to Solution 11.35(b), the higher the critical temperature, the stronger the intermolecular forces of a substance. Therefore, the strength of intermolecular forces decreases moving from left to right across the series and as molecular weight decreases.

(b) The molecules in this series experience London-dispersion forces and, except for CF_4, dipole-dipole forces. We expect the strength of dispersion forces to increase with increasing molecular weight, which agrees with the trends in critical temperature and pressure.

Vapor Pressure and Boiling Point

11.38 (a) The pressure difference is 130 mm Hg and the gas is essentially 100% molecules of the substance in the vapor phase. When the vessel is evacuated, essentially all air is removed.

(b) The pressure difference is 1 atm. The gas is 130 mm Hg of the molecular vapor and the rest is air. The liquid vaporizes in contact with the atmosphere, so atmospheric pressure is maintained above the liquid, but the equilibrium gas composition reflects the amount of vapor necessary to maintain 130 mm pressure, plus enough air to maintain a total pressure of 1 atm.

(c) The pressure difference is 890 mm Hg (1 atm + 130 mm Hg) and the gas is a mixture of 130 mm vapor and 1 atm air. The initial air pressure in the flask is 1 atm and no air is allowed to escape. The gas in the flask is not in equilibrium with the atmosphere and the final pressure in the flask does not equal atmospheric pressure. After the liquid vaporizes, the total gas pressure is the result of 130 mm vapor and 1 atm air.

11.40 Both molecules are pyramidal, with a nonbonding electron pair on the central atom. Even though they are polar covalent, the intermolecular forces and physical properties are likely to be dominated by dispersion forces.

(a) PCl_3 (b) $AsCl_3$

(c) At the same temperature, the average kinetic energy of molecules of the two substances is equal.

(d) The strength of dispersion forces increases with increasing molecular weight, so $AsCl_3$ will experience stronger intermolecular forces. This is the basis of predictions in parts (a) and (b) above.

11.42 (a) On a humid day, there are more gaseous water molecules in the air and more are recaptured by the surface of the liquid, making evaporation slower.

(b) At high altitude, atmospheric pressure is lower and water boils at a lower temperature. The eggs must be cooked longer at the lower temperature.

11.44 (a) A pressure of 1.2 atm corresponds to 1.4 atm $\times \frac{760 \text{ torr}}{1 \text{ atm}} = 912 = 9.1 \times 10^2$ torr. According to Appendix B, the vapor pressure of water reaches 912 torr somewhere between 104-106°C. By linear interpolation, the boiling point should be near

$$104°\text{C} + \left[\frac{(912 - 875)\text{torr}}{(938 - 875)\text{torr}} \times 2°\text{C}\right] = 105.2°\text{C} = 105°\text{C}$$

(b) The vapor pressure of ethyl alcohol at 70°C is approximately 510 torr. Thus, at 70°C ethyl alcohol would boil at an external pressure of 510 torr.

11.46 (a) The boiling point of a liquid is the temperature at which its vapor pressure equals atmospheric pressure. According to Appendix B, the vapor pressure of water is 680 torr at approximately 97°C.

(b) The temperature at which the vapor pressure of water is 752 mm Hg is almost 100°C, greater than the boiling temperature at 680 mm Hg. The average kinetic energy of the H_2O molecules at the boiling temperature in Chicago is greater than the average kinetic energy of the molecules at the boiling temperature in Reno. A liquid boils when its vapor pressure equals the external pressure acting on the liquid. If the external pressure acting on the liquid molecules is smaller (as is the atmospheric pressure in Reno), a smaller average kinetic energy is required for boiling (bubble formation within the liquid).

Phase Diagrams

11.48 (a) The triple point on a phase diagram represents the temperature at which the gas, liquid and solid phases are in equilibrium.

(b) No. A phase diagram represents a closed system, one where no matter can escape and no substance other than the one under consideration is present; air cannot be present in the system. Even if air is excluded, at 1 atm of external pressure, the triple point of water is inaccessible, regardless of temperature [see Sample Exercise 11.6(b)].

11.50 (a) Solid CO_2 sublimes to form $CO_2(g)$ at a temperature of about -60°C.

(b) Solid CO_2 melts to form $CO_2(l)$ at a temperature of about -50°C. The $CO_2(l)$ boils when the temperature reaches approximately -40°C.

11.52 (a)

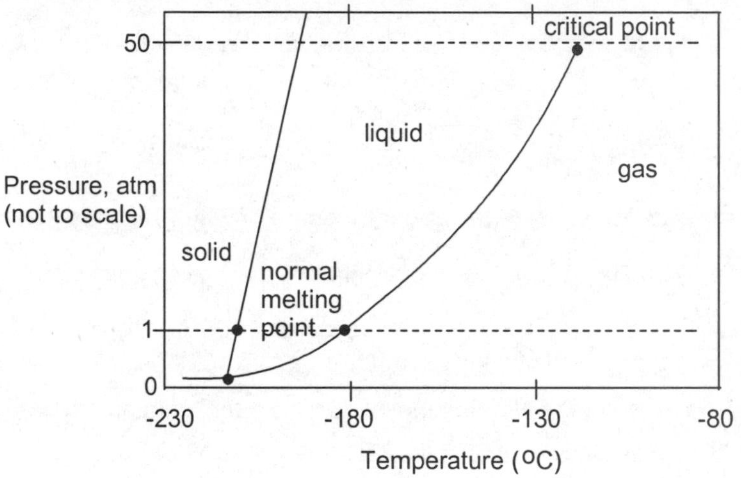

(b) $O_2(s)$ will not float on $O_2(l)$. $O_2(s)$ is denser than $O_2(l)$ because the solid-liquid line on the phase diagram is normal. That is, as pressure increases, the melting temperature increases. [Note that the solid-liquid line for O_2 is nearly vertical, indicating a small difference in the densities of $O_2(s)$ and $O_2(l)$].

(c) $O_2(s)$ will melt when heated at a pressure of 1 atm, since this is a much greater pressure than the pressure at the triple point.

Structures of Solids

11.54 In amorphous silica (SiO_2) the regular structure of quartz is disrupted; the loose, disordered structure, Figure 11.30(b), has many vacant "pockets" throughout. There are fewer SiO_2 groups per volume in the amorphous solid; the packing is less efficient and less dense.

11.56 Ca: Ca atoms occupy the 8 corners of the cube. 8 corners × 1/8 sphere/corner = 1 Ca atom

O: O atoms occupy the centers of the 6 faces of the cube.
6 faces × 1/2 atom/face = 3 O atoms

Ti: There is 1 Ti atom at the body center of the cube.

Formula: $CaTiO_3$

11.58 (a) Ti: 8 corners × 1/8 sphere/corner + [1 center × 1 sphere/center] = 2 Ti atoms

O: 4 faces × 1/2 sphere/face + [2 interior × 1 sphere/interior] = 4 O atoms

Formula: Ti_2O_4

(b) Rutile is an ionic solid; ion-ion forces among Ti^{4+} cations and O^{2-} anions are quite strong, owing to the magnitudes of the charges, and lead to the ordered structure.

11.60 (a) 8 corners × 1/8 atom/corner + 6 faces × ½ atom/face = 4 atoms

(b) Each aluminum atom is in contact with 12 nearest neighbors, 6 in one plane, 3 above that plane, and 3 below. Its coordination number is thus 12.

(c) The length of the face diagonal of a face-centered cubic unit cell is four times the radius of the metal and $\sqrt{2}$ times the unit cell dimension (usually designated *a* for cubic cells).

$$4 \times 1.43 \text{ Å} = \sqrt{2} \times a; \quad a = \frac{4 \times 1.43 \text{ Å}}{\sqrt{2}} = 4.0447 = 4.04 \text{ Å} = 4.04 \times 10^{-8} \text{ cm}$$

(d) The density of the metal is the mass of the unit cell contents divided by the volume of the unit cell.

$$\text{density} = \frac{4 \text{ Al atoms}}{(4.0447 \times 10^{-8} \text{ cm})^3} \times \frac{26.98 \text{ g Al}}{6.022 \times 10^{23} \text{ Al atoms}} = 2.71 \text{ g/cm}^3$$

11.62 Avogadro's number is the number of KCl formula units in 74.55 g of KCl.

$$74.55 \text{ g KCl} \times \frac{1 \text{ cm}^3}{1.984 \text{ g}} \times \frac{(1 \times 10^{10} \text{ pm})^3}{1 \text{ cm}^3} \times \frac{4 \text{ KCl units}}{628^3 \text{ pm}^3} = 6.07 \times 10^{23} \text{ KCl formula units}$$

11.64 (a) Na^+, 6 (b) Zn^{2+}, 4 (c) Ca^{2+}, 8

11.66 In the face-centered cubic structure, there are four CaS units in the unit cell. Density is the mass of the unit cell contents divided by the unit cell volume (a^3).

$$\text{density} = \frac{4 \text{ CaS units}}{(5.689 \text{ Å})^3} \times \frac{72.144 \text{ g NiO}}{6.022 \times 10^{23} \text{ NiO units}} \times \left(\frac{1 \text{ Å}}{1 \times 10^{-8} \text{ cm}}\right)^3 = 2.603 \text{ g/cm}^3$$

11.68 (a) According to Figure 11.42(b), there are 4 HgS units in a unit cell with the zinc blende structure. [4 complete Hg^{2+} ions, 6(1/2) + 8(1/8) S^{2-} ions]

$$\text{density} = \frac{4 \text{ HgS units}}{(5.852 \text{ Å})^3} \times \frac{232.656 \text{ g}}{6.022 \times 10^{23} \text{ HgS units}} \times \left(\frac{1 \text{ Å}}{1 \times 10^{-8} \text{ cm}}\right)^3 = 7.711 \text{ g/cm}^3$$

(b) We expect Se^{2-} to have a larger ionic radius than S^{2-}, since Se is below S in the chalcogen family and both ions have the same charge. Thus, HgSe will occupy a larger volume and the unit cell edge will be longer.

(c) For HgSe:

$$\text{density} = \frac{4 \text{ HgSe units}}{(6.085 \text{ Å})^3} \times \frac{279.55 \text{ g HgSe}}{6.022 \times 10^{23} \text{ HgSe units}} \times \left(\frac{1 \text{ Å}}{1 \times 10^{-8} \text{ cm}}\right)^3 = 8.241 \text{ g/cm}^3$$

Even though HgSe has a larger unit cell volume than HgS, it also has a larger molar mass. The mass of Se is more than twice that of S, while the radius of Se^{2-} is only slightly larger than that of S (Figure 7.6). The greater mass of Se accounts for the greater density of HgSe.

Bonding in Solids

11.70 (a) ionic (b) metallic (c) covalent-network
(d) molecular (e) molecular (f) molecular

11.72 (a) metallic (b) molecular or metallic (physical properties of metals vary widely)
(c) covalent-network (d) covalent-network (e) ionic

11.74 According to Table 11.7, the solid could be either ionic with low water solubility or network covalent. Due to the extremely high sublimation temperature, it is probably covalent-network.

11.76 (a) Xe – greater atomic weight, stronger dispersion forces

(b) SiO_2 – covalent-network lattice versus weak dispersion forces

(c) KBr – strong ionic versus weak dispersion forces

(d) C_6Cl_6 – both are influenced by dispersion forces, C_6Cl_6 has the higher molar mass.

Additional Exercises

11.77 In intramolecular covalent or ionic bonding, the bonded atoms are closer together and the magnitudes of the interacting charges are greater. Intermolecular interactions are the result of weaker attractive forces between molecules with net partial or transient charges.

11.79 (a) Correct

(b) The lower boiling liquid must experience less total intermolecular forces.

(c) If both liquids are structurally-similar nonpolar molecules, the lower boiling liquid has a lower molecular weight than the higher boiling liquid.

(d) Correct

(e) Correct

11.81 (a) In dibromomethane, CH_2Br_2, the dispersion force contribution will be larger than for CH_2Cl_2, because bromine is more polarizable than the lighter element chlorine. At the same time, the dipole-dipole contribution for CH_2Cl_2 is greater than for CH_2Br_2 because CH_2Cl_2 has a larger dipole moment.

(b) Just the opposite comparisons apply to CH_2F_2, which is less polarizable and has a higher dipole moment than CH_2Cl_2.

11.82 (a) The ability to flow is determined by factors that hold molecules in the same position relative to one another. These include strength of intermolecular forces and structural features such as chain length or branching that cause molecules to become entangled.

(b) The tendency of a liquid to bead is caused by an imbalance of intermolecular forces at the surface of a liquid. If the liquid has no appreciable adhesive forces with the surface, the stronger the cohesive forces among liquid molecules, the greater the tendency to bead.

(c) The strength of intermolecular forces determines boiling point. Hydrogen bonding, dipole moment, molecular weight and shape are important molecular properties that contribute to the overall strength of intermolecular forces.

(d) The strength of intermolecular forces determines heat of vaporization. Hydrogen bonding, dipole moment, molecular weight and shape are important molecular properties that contribute to the overall strength of intermolecular forces.

11.84 When a halogen atom (Cl or Br) is substituted for H in benzene, the molecule becomes polar. These molecules experience dispersion forces similar to those in benzene plus dipole-dipole forces, so they have higher boiling points than benzene. C_6H_5Br has a higher molar mass and is more polarizable than C_6H_5Cl so it has the higher boiling point. C_6H_5OH experiences hydrogen bonding, the strongest force between neutral molecules, so it has the highest boiling point.

11.85 (a) Propylamine experiences hydrogen bonding interactions while trimethylamine, with no N-H bonds, does not. Also, the rod-like shape of propylamine (see Solution 11.15) leads to stronger dispersion forces than in pyramidal trimethylamine. The stronger intermolecular forces in propylamine lead to the higher boiling point.

(b) Propylamine is most soluble in water by virtue of its $-NH_2$ group, which can act as both a donor and acceptor in hydrogen bonding. Trimethylamine is much more soluble than the structurally similar isobutane, because the pyramidal $\ddot{N}$ atom can act as a hydrogen bond acceptor. Trimethylamine is less soluble than propylamine because its participation in hydrogen bonding is less extensive.

11.87 The more carbon atoms in the hydrocarbon, the longer the chain, the more polarizable the electron cloud, the higher the boiling point. A plot of the number of carbon atoms versus boiling point is shown below. For 8 C atoms, the boiling point is approximately 130°C.

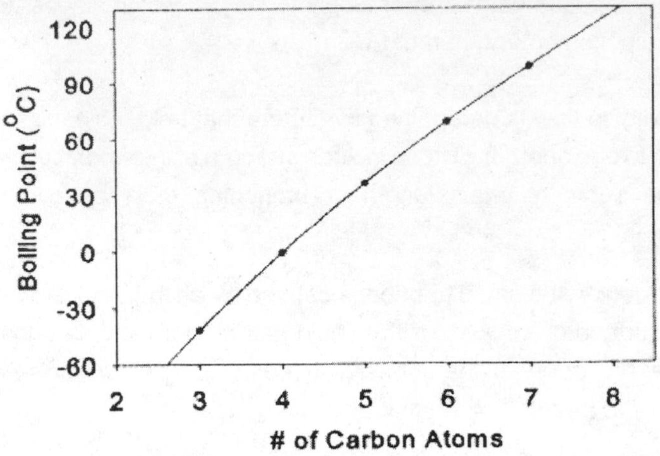

11.89 According to Figure 11.23, as the pressure of a gas above its critical temperature increases beyond critical pressure, the solubility of a solute increases. The solubility of the solute is essentially zero below critical pressure. Supercritical CO_2 at very high pressure dissolves caffeine and the solution leaves the extractor. The pressure reduction value reduces the pressure of CO_2 enough so that the caffeine becomes insoluble. The solid caffeine is deposited in the separator and the low pressure CO_2 gas is recycled.

11.90 (a) If the Clausius-Clapeyron equation is obeyed, a graph of ln P vs 1/T(K) should be linear. Here are the data in a form

T(K)	1/T	P(torr)	ln P
280.0	3.571×10^{-3}	32.42	3.479
300.0	3.333×10^{-3}	92.47	4.527
320.0	3.125×10^{-3}	225.1	5.417
330.0	3.030×10^{-3}	334.4	5.812
340.0	2.941×10^{-3}	482.9	6.180

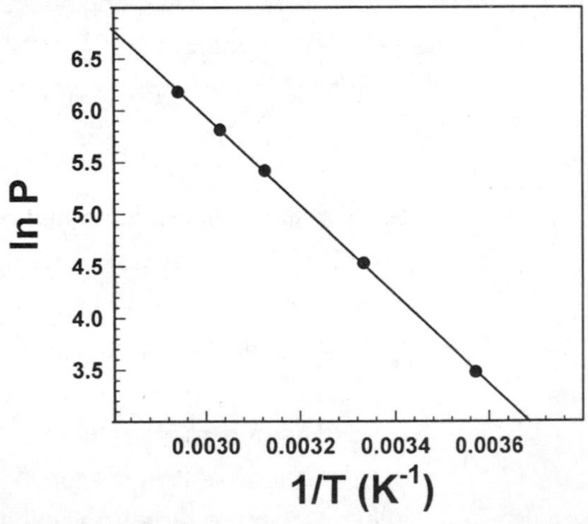

According to the graph, the Clausius-Clape equation is obeyed, to a first approximation

$$\Delta H_{vap} = \text{-slope} \times R;\ \text{slope} = \frac{3.479 - 6.180}{(3.571 - 2.941) \times 10^{-3}} = -\frac{2.701}{0.630 \times 10^{-3}} = -4.29 \times 10^3$$

$$\Delta H_{vap} = -(-4.29 \times 10^3) \times 8.314 \text{ J/K} \bullet \text{mol} = 35.7 \text{ kJ/mol}$$

(b) The normal boiling point is the temperature at which the vapor pressure of the liquid equals atmospheric pressure, 760 torr. From the graph,

ln 760 = 6.63, 1/T for this vapor pressure = 2.828×10^{-3}; T = 353.6 K

11.91 (a) The Clausius-Clapeyron equation is $\ln P = \frac{-\Delta H_{vap}}{RT} + C$.

For two vapor pressures, P_1 and P_2, measured at corresponding temperatures T_1 and

T_2, the relationship is

$$\ln P_1 - \ln P_2 = \left(\frac{-\Delta H_{vap}}{RT_1} + C\right) - \left(\frac{-\Delta H_{vap}}{RT_2} + C\right)$$

$$\ln P_1 - \ln P_2 = \frac{-\Delta H_{vap}}{R}\left(\frac{1}{T_1} - \frac{1}{T_2}\right) + C - C;\ \ln\frac{P_1}{P_2} = \frac{-\Delta H_{vap}}{R}\left(\frac{1}{T_1} - \frac{1}{T_2}\right)$$

(b) P_1 = 10.00 torr, T_1 = 716 K; P_2 = 400.0 torr, T_2 = 981 K

$$\ln\frac{10.00}{400.0} = \frac{-\Delta H_{vap}}{8.314\ \text{J/K}\bullet\text{mol}}\left(\frac{1}{716} - \frac{1}{981}\right)$$

$-3.6889\ (8.314\ \text{J/K} \bullet \text{mol}) = -\Delta H_{vap}(3.773 \times 10^{-4}/\text{K})$

$\Delta H_{vap} = 8.129 \times 10^4 = 8.13 \times 10^4$ J/mol = 81.3 kJ/mol

(c) The normal boiling point of a liquid is the temperature at which the vapor pressure of the liquid is 760 torr.

P_1 = 400.0 torr, T_1 = 981 K; P_2 = 760 torr, T_2 = b.p. of potassium

$$\ln\left(\frac{400.0}{760.0}\right) = \frac{-8.129 \times 10^4\ \text{J/mol}}{8.314\ \text{J/K}\bullet\text{mol}}\left(\frac{1}{981\ \text{K}} - \frac{1}{T_2}\right)$$

$$\frac{-0.64185}{-9.7775 \times 10^3} = 1.0194 \times 10^{-3} - \frac{1}{T_2};\ \frac{1}{T_2} = 1.0194 \times 10^{-3} - 6.565 \times 10^{-5}$$

$\frac{1}{T_2} = 9.5375 \times 10^{-4}$; T_2 = 1048 K (775°C)

(d) P_1 = VP of K(l) at 100°C, T_1 = 373 K; P_2 = 10.00 torr, T_2 = 716 K

$$\ln\frac{P_1}{10.00\ \text{torr}} = \frac{-8.129 \times 10^4\ \text{J/mol}}{8.314\ \text{J/K}\bullet\text{mol}}\left(\frac{1}{373} - \frac{1}{716}\right)$$

$$\ln\frac{P_1}{10.00\ \text{torr}} = \frac{-8.129 \times 10^4\ \text{J/mol}}{8.314\ \text{J/K}\bullet\text{mol}} \times 1.284 \times 10^{-3} = -12.5543$$

$$\frac{P_1}{10.00\ \text{torr}} = e^{-12.5543} = 3.530 \times 10^{-6};\ P_1 = 3.53 \times 10^{-5}\ \text{torr}$$

11.92 (a) The face diagonal of a face-centered cubic unit cell has length $a\sqrt{2}$ and also 4 r, where a is the cubic cell dimension and r is the atomic radius.

$4\,r = a\sqrt{2}$; $r = (a\sqrt{2})/4 = (4.078\ \text{Å})(\sqrt{2})/4 = 1.44179 = 1.442$ Å

(b) Density is the mass of the unit cell contents divided by the unit cell volume (a^3). In a face-centered cubic unit cell, there are 4 Au atoms.

$$\text{density} = \frac{4\ \text{Au atoms}}{(4.078\ \text{Å})^3} \times \frac{196.97\ \text{g}}{6.0221 \times 10^{23}\ \text{Au atoms}} \times \left(\frac{1\ \text{Å}}{1 \times 10^{-8}\ \text{cm}}\right)^3 = 19.29\ \text{g/cm}^3$$

11.94 Physical data for the two compounds from the *Handbook of Chemistry and Physics*:

	$\mathcal{M}$	dipole moment	boiling point
CH_2Cl_2	85 g/mol	1.60 D	40.0°C
CH_3I	142 g/mol	1.62 D	42.4°C

(a) The two substances have very similar molecular structures; each is an unsymmetrical tetrahedron with a single central carbon atom and no hydrogen bonding. Since the structures are very similar, the magnitudes of the dipole-dipole forces should be similar. This is verified by their very similar dipole moments. The heavier compound, CH_3I, will have slightly stronger London dispersion forces. Since the nature and magnitude of the intermolecular forces in the two compounds are nearly the same, it is very difficult to predict which will be more volatile (or which will have the higher boiling point as in part (b)).

(b) Given the structural similarities discussed in part (a), one would expect the boiling points to be very similar, and they are. Based on its larger molar mass (and dipole-dipole forces being essentially equal) one might predict that CH_3I would have a slightly higher boiling point; this is verified by the known boiling points.

(c) According to Equation 11.1, $\ln P = \frac{-\Delta H_{vap}}{RT} + C$

A plot of ln P vs. 1/T for each compound is linear. Since the order of volatility changes with temperature for the two compounds, the two lines must cross at some temperature; the slopes of the two lines, ΔH_{vap} for the two compounds, and the y-intercepts, C, must be different.

(d)

CH_2Cl_2

ln P	T(K)	1/T
2.303	229.9	4.351×10^{-3}
3.689	250.9	3.986×10^{-3}
4.605	266.9	3.747×10^{-3}
5.991	297.3	3.364×10^{-3}

CH_3I

ln P	T(K)	1/T
2.303	227.4	4.398×10^{-3}
3.689	249.0	4.016×10^{-3}
4.605	266.2	3.757×10^{-3}
5.991	298.5	3.350×10^{-3}

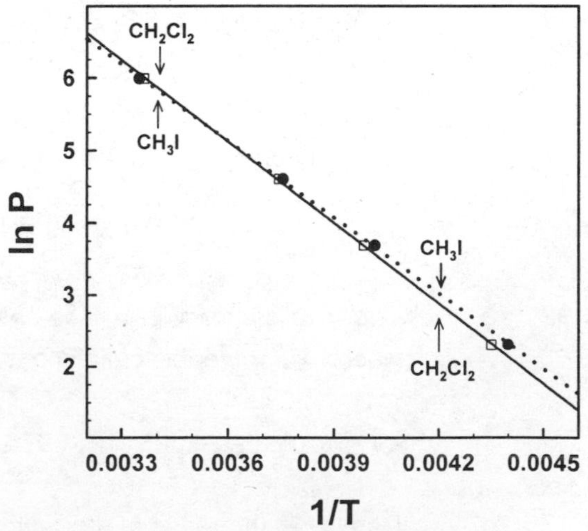

For CH_2Cl_2, $-\Delta H_{vap}/R = \text{slope} = \frac{(5.991 - 2.303)}{(3.364 \times 10^{-3} - 4.350 \times 10^{-3})} = \frac{-3.688}{0.987 \times 10^{-3}}$

$= -3.74 \times 10^3 = -\Delta H_{vap}/R$

$\Delta H_{vap} = 8.314\ (3.74 \times 10^3) = 3.107 \times 10^4$ J/mol = 31.1 kJ/mol

For CH_3I, $-\Delta H_{vap}/R = \text{slope} = \dfrac{(5.991 - 2.303)}{(3.350 \times 10^{-3} - 4.398 \times 10^{-3})} = \dfrac{-3.688}{1.048 \times 10^{-3}} = -3.519 \times 10^3$

$= -\Delta H_{vap}/R$

$\Delta H_{vap} = 8.314\ (3.519 \times 10^3) = 2.926 \times 10^4$ J/mol = 29.3 kJ/mol

11.96 (a) Both diamond (d = 3.5 g/cm^3) and graphite (d = 2.3 g/cm^3) are covalent-network solids with efficient packing arrangements in the solid state; there is relatively little empty space in their respective crystal lattices. Diamond, with bonded C–C distances of 1.54 Å in all directions, is more dense than graphite, with shorter C–C distances within carbon sheets but longer 3.41 Å separations between sheets (Figure 11.40). Buckminsterfullerene has much more empty space, both inside each C_{60} "ball" and between balls, than either diamond or graphite, so its density will be considerably less than 2.3 g/cm^3.

(b) In a face-centered-cubic unit cell, there are 4 complete C_{60} units.

$$\frac{4\,C_{60}\text{ units}}{(14.2\text{ Å})^3} \times \frac{720.66\text{ g}}{6.022 \times 10^{23}\,C_{60}\text{ units}} \times \left(\frac{1\text{ Å}}{1 \times 10^{-8}\text{ cm}}\right)^3 = 1.67\text{ g/cm}^3$$

(1.67 g/cm^3 is the smallest density of the three allotropes, diamond, graphite and buckminsterfullerene.)

Integrative Exercises

11.97 (a) In Table 11.4, viscosity increases as the length of the carbon chain increases. Longer molecular chains become increasingly entangled, increasing resistance to flow.

(b) Whereas viscosity depends on molecular chain length in a critical way, surface tension depends on the strengths of intermolecular interactions between molecules. These dispersion forces do not increase as rapidly with increasing chain length and molecular weight as viscosity does.

(c) The –OH group in n-octyl alcohol gives rise to hydrogen bonding among molecules, which increases molecular entanglement and leads to greater viscosity and higher boiling point.

11.98 (a) 24 valence e^-, 12 e^- pairs

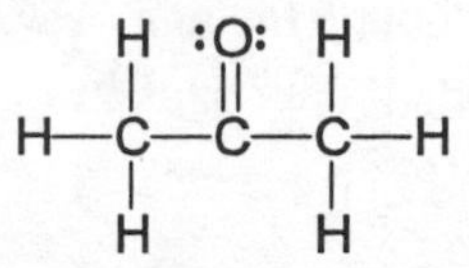

The geometry around the central C atom is trigonal planar, and around the two terminal C atoms, tetrahedral.

(b) Polar. The C=O bond is quite polar and the dipoles in the trigonal plane around the central C atom do not cancel.

(c) Dipole-dipole and London-dispersion forces

(d) Since the molecular weights of acetone and 1-propanol are similar, the strength of the London-dispersion forces in the two compounds is also similar. The big difference is that 1-propanol has hydrogen bonding, while acetone does not. These relatively strong attractive forces lead to the higher boiling point for 1-propanol.

11.99

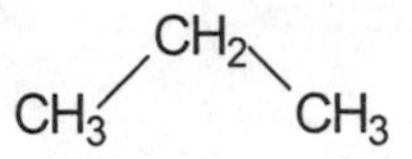

(i) $\mathcal{M} = 44$

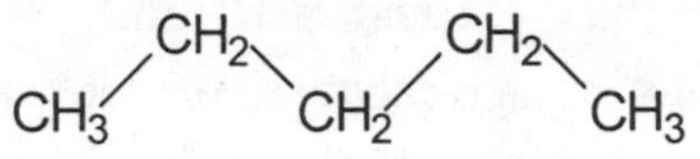

(ii) $\mathcal{M} = 72$

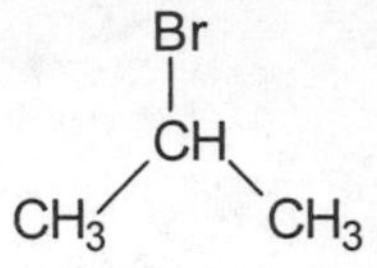

(iii) $\mathcal{M} = 123$

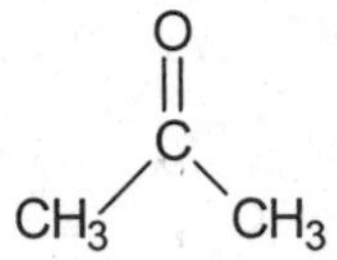

(iv) $\mathcal{M} = 58$

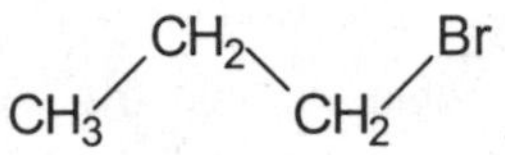

(v) $\mathcal{M} = 123$

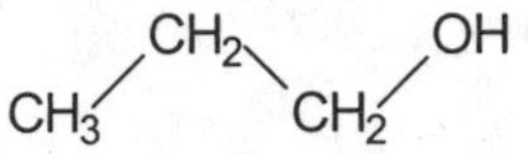

(vi) $\mathcal{M} = 60$

It is useful to draw the structural formulas because intermolecular forces are determined by the size and shape (structure) of molecules.

(a) *Molar mass*: compounds (i) and (ii) have similar rod-like structures; (ii) has a longer rod. The longer chain leads to greater molar mass, stronger London-dispersion forces and higher heat of vaporization.

(b) *Molecular shape*: compounds (iii) and (v) have the same chemical formula and molar mass but different molecular shapes (they are structural isomers). The more rod-like shape of (v) leads to more contact between molecules, stronger dispersion forces and higher heat of vaporization.

(c) *Molecular polarity*: rod-like hydrocarbons (i) and (ii) are essentially nonpolar, owing to free rotation about C-C σ bonds, while (iv) is quite polar, owing to the C=O group. (iv) has a smaller molar mass than (ii) but a larger heat of vaporization, which must be due to the presence of dipole-dipole forces in (iv). [Note that (iii) and (iv), with similar shape and molecular polarity, have very similar heats of vaporization.]

(d) *Hydrogen-bonding interactions*: molecules (v) and (vi) have similar structures, but (vi) has hydrogen bonding and (v) does not. Even though molar mass and thus dispersion forces are larger for (v), (vi) has the higher heat of vaporization. This must be due to hydrogen bonding interactions.

11.101 *Plan*:

(i) Using thermochemical data from Appendix B, calculate the energy (enthalpy) required to melt and heat the H_2O.

(ii) Using Hess's Law, calculate the enthalpy of combustion, ΔH_{comb}, for C_3H_8.

(iii) Solve the stoichiometry problem.

Solve:

(i) Heat $H_2O(s)$ from -14.0°C to 0.0°C; $2500 \text{ g } H_2O \times \frac{2.092 \text{ J}}{\text{g} \bullet {}^\circ\text{C}} \times 14.0\,^\circ\text{C} = 73.22$

$= 73.2$ kJ

Melt $H_2O(s)$; $2500 \text{ g } H_2O \times \frac{6.008 \text{ kJ}}{\text{mol } H_2O} \times \frac{1 \text{ mol } H_2O}{18.02 \text{ g } H_2O} = 833.52 = 834.4 \text{ kJ}$

Heat $H_2O(l)$ from 0.0°C to 60.0°C; $2500 \text{ g } H_2O \times \frac{4.184 \text{ J}}{\text{g} \bullet {}^\circ\text{C}} \times 60.0\,^\circ\text{C} = 627.6$

$= 628$ kJ

Total energy = 73.22 kJ + 833.52 kJ + 627.6 kJ = 1534.3 = 1.53×10^3 kJ

(The result has zero decimal places because 628 kJ has zero decimal places.)

(ii) $C_3H_8(g) + 5O_2(g) \rightarrow 3CO_2(g) + 4H_2O(l)$

Assume that one product is $H_2O(l)$, since this leads to a more negative ΔH_{comb} and fewer grams of $C_3H_8(g)$ required.

$$\Delta H_{comb} = 3\Delta H_f^\circ\ CO_2(g) + 4\Delta H_f^\circ\ H_2O(l) - \Delta H_f^\circ\ C_3H_8(g) - 5\Delta H_f^\circ\ O_2(g)$$

$$= 3(-393.5 \text{ kJ}) + 4(-285.83 \text{ kJ}) - (-103.85 \text{ kJ}) - 5(0) = -2219.97 = -2220 \text{ kJ}$$

(iii) $1.5343 \times 10^3 \text{ kJ required} \times \frac{1 \text{ mol } C_3H_8}{2219.97 \text{ kJ}} \times \frac{44.094 \text{ g } C_3H_8}{1 \text{ mol } C_3H_8} = 30.5 \text{ g } C_3H_8$

(1.53×10^3 kJ required has 3 sig figs and so does the result)

11.02 (a) Low viscosity, low surface tension, and especially, high thermal conductivity owing to metallic properties.

(b) Metallic bonding between sodium atoms, which persists in the liquid state, is probably the main inhibitor of movement of atoms relative to one another. As temperature increases, thermal motion of the atoms increases and the liquid expands, weakening bonding interactions relative to thermal energies.

11.104 *Plan*: relative humidity and v.p. of H_2O at 23°C → P_{H_2O}

ideal-gas law → mol $H_2O(g)$ → H_2O molecules

r.h. = (P_{H_2O} in air / v.p. of H_2O) × 100; From Appendix B, v.p. of H_2O at 23°C = 21.07 torr

P_{H_2O} in air = r.h. × v.p. of H_2O/100 = 45 × 21.07 torr/100 = 9.4815 = 9.5 torr

$n = PV/RT$; $V = 14 \text{ m} \times 9.0 \text{ m} \times 8.6 \text{ m} \times \frac{1 \text{ dm}^3}{(0.1)^3 \text{ m}^3} \times \frac{1 \text{ L}}{\text{dm}^3} = 1.0836 \times 10^6 = 1.1 \times 10^6 \text{ L}$

$$n = 9.4815 \text{ torr} \times \frac{1 \text{ atm}}{760 \text{ torr}} \times \frac{\text{mol} \bullet \text{K}}{0.08206 \text{ L} \bullet \text{atm}} \times \frac{1.0836 \times 10^6 \text{ L}}{296 \text{ K}} = 556.6 = 5.6 \times 10^2 \text{ mol } H_2O$$

$$556.6 \text{ mol } H_2O \times \frac{6.022 \times 10^{23} \text{ molecules}}{1 \text{ mol}} = 3.4 \times 10^{26} \text{ } H_2O \text{ molecules}$$

11.105 Data are taken from the 74th edition of the *Handbook of Chemistry and Physics*. T_m = melting point, T_b = boiling point

(a) W: T_m = 3410°C, T_b = 5660 °C; WF_6: T_m = 2.5°C, T_b = 17.5°C

W is a metal, with strong metallic bonding, and very high T_m and T_b. WF_6 is an octahedral, nonpolar molecule. Even though it has high molar mass, the spherical shape of the molecule prevents extensive molecular contacts. The resulting London-dispersion forces are very weak, which leads to the low T_m and T_b.

(b) SO_2: T_m = -72.7°C, T_b = -10°C; SF_4: T_m = -124°C, T_b = -40°C (sublimes)

Both SO_2 and SF_4 are polar covalent molecules with a nonbonding electron pair on the central S atom. The electron-domain geometry in SO_2 is trigonal planar and the molecule shape is bent. The electron-domain geometry in SF_4 is trigonal bipyramidal and the molecular shape is see-saw. Both are gases at ambient temperature and pressure. SF_4 has higher molar mass but lower melting and boiling points than SO_2. This indicates that dipole-dipole forces are more influential on the properties of these molecules and that SF_4 has a smaller dipole moment than SO_2.

(c) SiO_2: T_m = 1723°C, T_b = 2230°C, $\mathcal{M}$ = 60 g/mol

$SiCl_4$: T_m = -70°C, T_b = 57.57°C, $\mathcal{M}$ = 170 g/mol

SiO_2 is a covalent-network substance, with high T_m and T_b. Covalent bonds hold SiO_2 units in a rigid lattice, and high energy is required to break these bonds and melt or boil the substance. $SiCl_4$ is a tetrahedral, nonpolar molecule. Weak dispersion forces between the approximately spherical molecules result in predictably low T_m and T_b.

12 Modern Materials

Liquid Crystals

12.2 In an ordinary liquid, molecules are oriented randomly and their relative orientations are continuously changing. In liquid crystals, the molecules are aligned in at least one dimension. The relative orientations in the other two dimensions may change, but alignment in the oriented direction is maintained.

12.4 Reinitzer observed that cholesteryl benzoate has a phase that exhibits properties intermediate between those of the solid and liquid phases. This "liquid-crystalline" phase, formed by melting at 145°C, is opaque, changes color as the temperature increases, and becomes clear at 179°C.

12.6 Because order is maintained in at least one dimension, the molecules in a liquid-crystalline phase are not totally free to change orientation. This makes the liquid-crystalline phase more resistant to flow, more viscous, than the isotropic liquid.

12.8 The "LCD molecule" is long relative to its thickness. It has C=C and C≡N groups that promote rigidity and polarizability along the length of the molecule. The C≡N group also provides dipole-dipole interactions that encourage alignment. Unlike the molecules in Figure 12.4, which contain planar phenyl rings, the LCD molecule contains nonaromatic, nonplanar six-membered rings. These rings could contribute to specific physical properties such as the liquid crystal temperature range that make this molecule particularly functional in LCD displays.

12.10 As the temperature of a substance increases, the average kinetic energy of the molecules increases. More molecules have sufficient kinetic energy to overcome intermolecular attractive forces, so overall ordering of the molecules decreases as temperature increases. Melting provides kinetic energy sufficient to disrupt alignment in one dimension in the solid, producing a smectic phase with ordering in two dimensions. Additional heating of the smectic phase provides kinetic energy sufficient to disrupt alignment in another dimension, producing a nematic phase with one-dimensional order.

Polymers

12.12 Monomers are small molecules with low molecular mass that are joined together to form polymers. They are the repeating units of a polymer. Three monomers mentioned in this chapter are

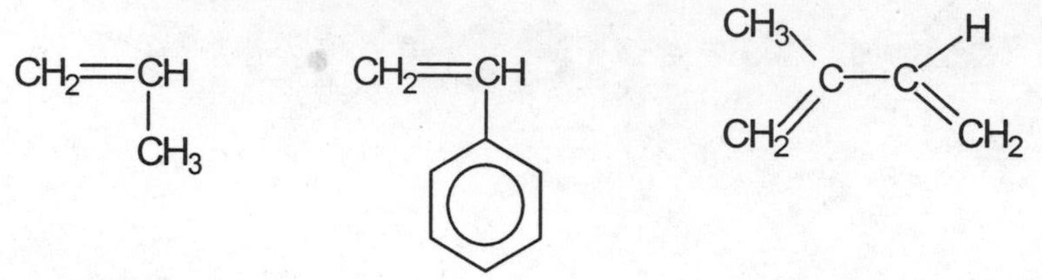

propylene (propene) | styrene (phenyl ethene) | isoprene (2-methyl-1,3-butadiene)

12.14

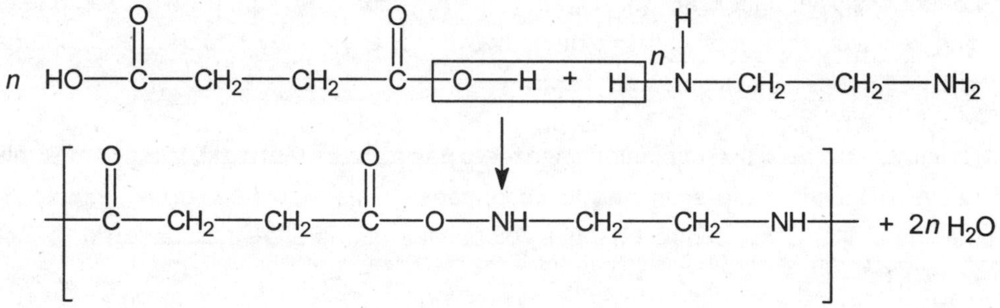

12.16 (a) By analogy to polyisoprene, Table 12.1,

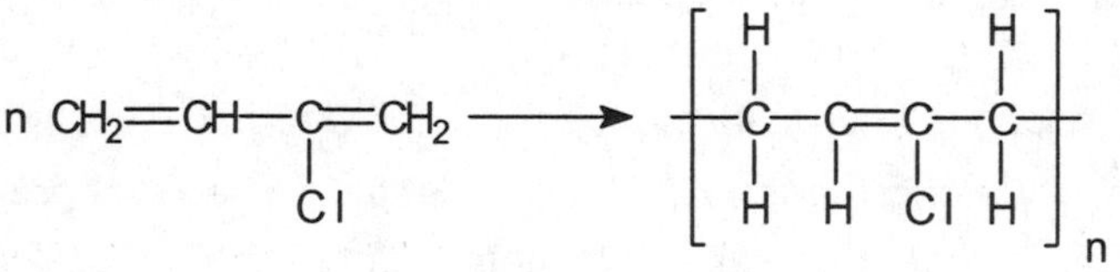

(b)

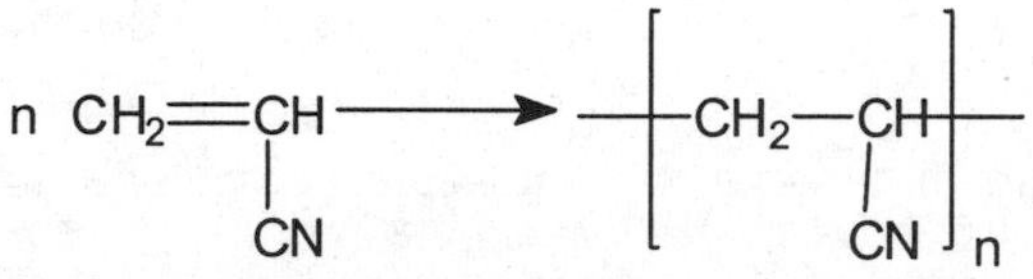

12.18

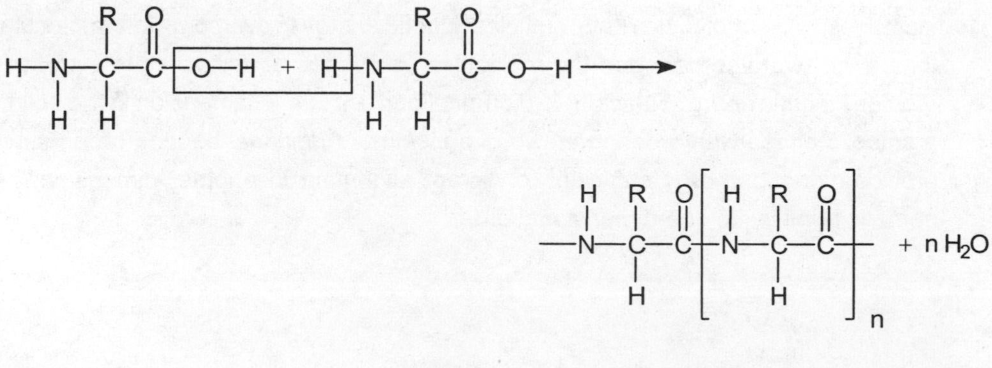

12.20 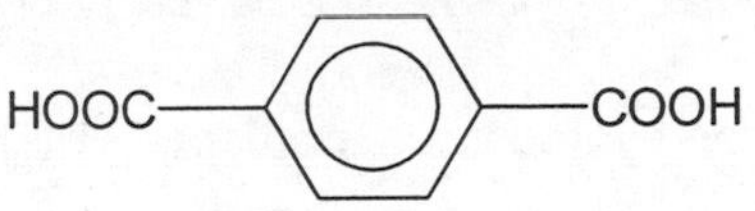

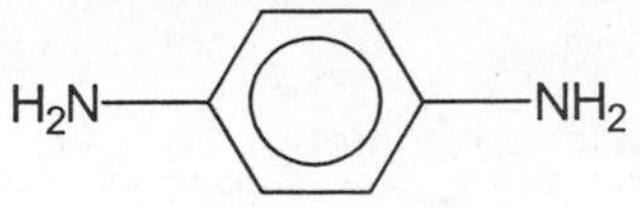

diacid
terephthalic acid

diamine
p-diaminobenzene

Note that these monomers are the same as those in Nomex (Solution 12.19) except for the orientation of the functional groups on the benzene rings. Clearly monomer structure strongly impacts polymer structure.

12.22 At the molecular level, the longer, unbranched chains of HDPE fit closer together and have more crystalline (ordered, aligned) regions than the shorter, branched chains of LDPE. Closer packing leads to higher density.

12.24 (a) An *elastomer* is a polymer material that recovers its shape when released from a distorting force. A typical elastomeric polymer can be stretched to at least twice its original length and return to its original dimensions upon release.

(b) A *thermoplastic* material can be shaped and reshaped by application of heat and/or pressure.

(c) A *thermosetting plastic* can be shaped once, through chemical reaction in the shape-forming process, but cannot easily be reshaped, due to the presence of chemical bonds that crosslink the polymer chains.

(d) A *plasticizer* is a substance of relatively low molar mass added to a polymer material to soften it.

Biomaterials

12.26 One structural characteristic of polymers that forms effective interfaces with biological systems is the presence of polar functional groups in the polymer backbone or as substituents. Polystyrene is a hydrocarbon; it has no polar functional groups and is a nonpolar substance. Polyurethane has polar carbon-oxygen, carbon-nitrogen and nitrogen-hydrogen functional groups. The N–H groups mean that it can act as a hydrogen-bond donor as well as an acceptor. In fact, the polyurethane backbone is very similar to the protein backbone shown in this section. We expect polyurethane to be the superior biointerface.

12.28 Surface roughness in synthetic heart valves causes *hemolysis*, the breakdown of red blood cells. The surface of the valve implant was probably not smooth enough.

12.30 Polystyrene is an essentially nonpolar hydrocarbon, while polyethyleneterephthalate (PET) contains polar ester groups, as well as nonpolar hydrocarbon portions. PET is more appropriate, because it provides polar ester groups $\left(-\overset{\overset{\displaystyle O}{\|}}{C}-O-C-\right)$ with hydrogen bonding capabilities where the cells can attach. Also, the ester linkages are susceptible to hydrolysis (the reverse of condensation); this renders the synthetic matrix biodegradable when employed in the body.

Ceramics

12.32 (a) The object that shatters is ceramic; the one that dents is metal.

(b) The two materials differ in their behavior because of their different solid state bonding characteristics. Ceramics are formed from inorganic materials linked by ionic or highly polar covalent bonds into three-dimensional bonding networks. During catastrophic failure (dropping 10 feet onto cement), the network structure prevents atoms from sliding over one-another and the ceramic shatters. A series of bond ruptures occurs, often along planes in the three-dimensional structure, leading to fragments with sharp edges.

Metallic bonding is characterized by delocalization of loosely-held valence electrons among metal atoms. Unlike the covalent or ionic network bonding in ceramics, metallic bonding is multidirectional. This allows metal atoms to slide over each other during deformation, resulting in dents and cracks rather than shattering.

12.34 Since Zr and Ti are in the same family, assume that the stoichiometry of the compounds in a sol-gel process will be the same for the two metals.

i. Alkoxide formation: oxidation-reduction reaction

$$Zr(s) + 4CH_3CH_2OH(l) \rightarrow \underset{\text{alkoxide}}{Zr(OCH_2CH_3)_4(s)} + 2H_2(g)$$

ii. Sol formation: metathesis reaction

$$Zr(OCH_2CH_3)_4(soln) + 4H_2O(l) \rightarrow \underset{\substack{\text{"precipitate"} \\ \text{sol}}}{Zr(OH)_4(s)} + \underset{\text{nonelectrolyte}}{4CH_3CH_2OH(l)}$$

$Zr(OCH_2CH_3)_4(s)$ is dissolved in an alcohol solvent and then reacted with water. In general, reaction with water is called *hydrolysis*. The alkoxide anions ($CH_3CH_2O^-$) combine with H^+ from H_2O to form the nonelectrolyte $CH_3CH_2OH(l)$, and Zr^{4+} cations combine with OH^- to form the $Zr(OH)_4$ solid. The product $Zr(OH)_4(s)$ is not a traditional coagulated precipitate, but a finely divided evenly dispersed collection of particles called a sol.

iii. Gel formation: condensation reaction

$$(OH)_3Zr\text{–}O\text{–}H(s) + H\text{–}O\text{–}Zr(OH)_3(s) \rightarrow \underset{\text{gel}}{(HO)_3Zr\text{–}O\text{–}Zr(OH)_3(s)} + H_2O(l)$$

Adjusting the acidity of the $Zr(OH)_4$ sol initiates condensation, the splitting-out of $H_2O(l)$ and formation of a zirconium-oxide network solid. The solid remains suspended in the solvent mixture and is called a gel.

iv. Processing: physical changes
The gel is heated to drive off solvent and the resulting solid consists of dry, uniform and finely divided ZrO_2 particles.

12.36 The ceramics are: MgO, soda lime glass, ZrB_2, Al_2O_3 and TaC. The criteria are a combination of chemical formula (with corresponding bonding characteristics) and Knoop values. Ceramics are ionic or covalent-network solids with fairly large hardness values. $CaCO_3$ is ionic, but carbonates are not one of the typical types of ceramics listed in Section 12.4. Ag and Cr are metals.

Hardness alone is not a sufficient criteria for ceramics. The range of hardness values for the ceramics in this group is large; Cr, a metal, lies in the middle of the range, as could other metals. Nonetheless, ceramics as a group are hard materials; hardness is a necessary, but not a sufficient condition for classification as a ceramic.

12.38 The four ceramics in Table 12.4 are Al_2O_3, SiC, ZrO_2 and BeO. All are network solids with some ionic and some covalent bonding character. They have a higher modulus of elasticity, which is to say they are more rigid than the metals listed. The high melting points, hardness and rigidity of the these four solids are due to the rigid, highly ordered, three-dimensional network structure of the solids. These network structures resist deformation (hardness) and require a great deal of energy (high melting point) to break the chemical bonds that form the network.

Superconductivity

12.40 A conductive metal such as Ag conducts electricity with a characteristic resistance to the flow of electrons given by Ohm's law, E = IR. A superconducting substance such as Nb_3Sn below its transition temperature conducts electricity with **no** resistance to the flow of electrons. Such a superconductor can transfer energy with no net loss, while a metallic conductor cannot be 100% efficient.

12.42 (a) The superconducting transition temperature, T_c, is the temperature at which a material loses all resistance to the flow of electrical current, the temperature below which the material becomes superconducting.

(b) The temperature 77 K is significant because that is the temperature of liquid nitrogen, a readily-available, inexpensive and safe coolant. Materials with T_c temperatures above 77 K produce more financially viable devices than materials which must be cooled with liquid helium below 77 K to achieve superconductivity.

12.44 Superconductivity acts on electrons that are conduction electrons. Thus you need to have electrons available to be conductors. Insulators have no electrons available for conduction.

Thin Films

12.46 In general, a useful thin film should:

(a) be chemically stable in its working environment
(b) adhere to its substrate
(c) have a uniform thickness
(d) have an easily controllable composition
(e) be nearly free of imperfections

12.48 There are three major methods of producing thin films.

(i) In *vacuum deposition*, a substance is vaporized or evaporated by heating under vacuum and then deposited on the desired substrate. No chemical change occurs.

(ii) In *sputtering*, ions accelerated to high energies by applying a high voltage are allowed to strike the target material, knocking atoms from its surface. These target material atoms are further accelerated toward the substrate, forming a thin film. No net chemical change occurs, because the material in the film is the target material.

(iii) In *chemical vapor deposition*, two gas phase substances react at the substrate surface to form a stable product which is deposited as a thin film. This involves a net chemical change.

Additional Exercises

12.50

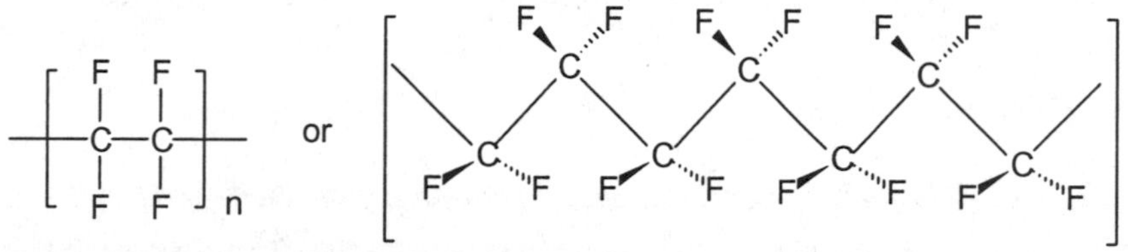

Teflon™ is formed by addition polymerization.

12.51 (a) Polymer (b) ceramic (c) ceramic (d) polymer (e) liquid crystal (an organic molecule with a characteristic long axis and the kinds of functional groups often found in compounds with liquid-crystalline phases (Figure 12.1); not enough repeating units to be a polymer)

12.53 Ceramics are usually three-dimensional network solids, whereas plastics most often consist of large, chain-like molecules (the chain may be branched) held loosely together by relatively weak van der Waals forces. Ceramics are rigid precisely because of the many strong bonding interactions intrinsic to the network. Once a crack forms, atoms near the defect are subject to great stress, and the crack is propagated. They are stable to high temperatures because tremendous kinetic energy (temperature) is required for an atom to break free from the bonding network. On the other hand, plastics are flexible because the molecules themselves are flexible (free rotation around the sigma bonds in the polymer chain), and it is easy for the molecules to move relative to one another (weak intermolecular forces). (However, recall that rigidity of the plastic increases as crosslinking of the polymer chain increases. The melamine-formaldehyde polymer in Figure 12.17 is a very rigid, brittle polymer.) Plastics are not thermally stable because their largely organic molecules are subject to oxidation and/or bond breaking at high temperatures.

12.55 This phenomenon is similar to supercooling, Section 11.4. When the isotropic liquid is cooled below the liquid crystal-liquid transition temperature, the kinetic energy of the molecules has been decreased enough so that formation of the liquid crystalline phase is energetically favorable. However, the molecules may not be correctly organized so that long range ordering can take place.

12.56 Both metals and ceramics have highly ordered three-dimensional structures or lattices, but the bonding characteristics of these lattices are different. Many metals adopt close-packed structures where each metal has 12 nearest neighbors (Section 11.7). Since each metal atom has too few electrons to form a covalent (electron-pair) bond with each of its nearest neighbors, the bonding electrons are delocalized and free to move throughout the lattice. This provides a mechanism for stress relief without catastrophic fracture. Metal atoms or planes of metal atoms can slip relative to each other without significant damage to the metallic bonding network.

In the three dimensional lattices of ceramics, bonding electrons are localized. In ionic solids such as Al_2O_3 they are localized on the ions; in network covalent solids such as SiC (Solution 12.37), the electrons are localized in the covalent bonds between the atoms. In either case, atoms or ions cannot move without breaking chemical bonds. Localized (ionic or covalent) bonding in ceramics renders them harder than metals, which have delocalized bonding throughout the crystal lattice.

12.57 The degree of crystallinity of polyethylene increases with increasing molecular weight. Following the trends in Table 12.3, ultra high molecular weight polyethylene will be dense, mechanically strong and high melting. The important properties in this application are density and mechanical strength, so that the coating does not deform or wear down under load. Movement of the metal ball around the polymer surface should be essentially frictionless; adhesive forces between metal and polymer should be minimal. The high density polymer has no pockets of empty space, so it forms a smooth surface. Attractive interactions between the nonpolar hydrocarbon polymer and the metallic ball are essentially absent, facilitating frictionless movement of the ball.

12.59

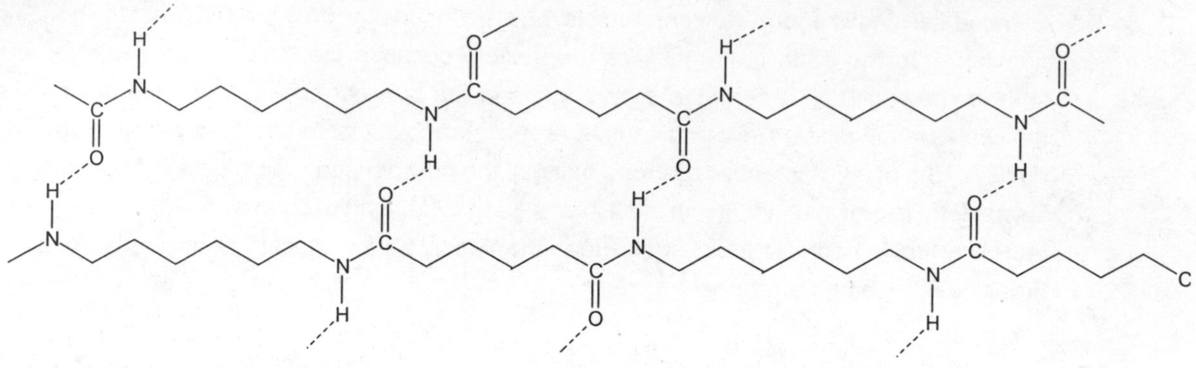

Hydrogen bonding occurs between 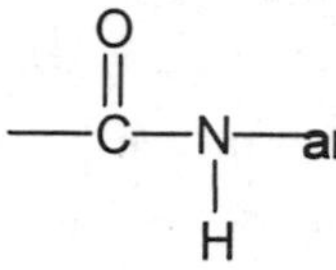 amide groups of adjacent chains.

12.60

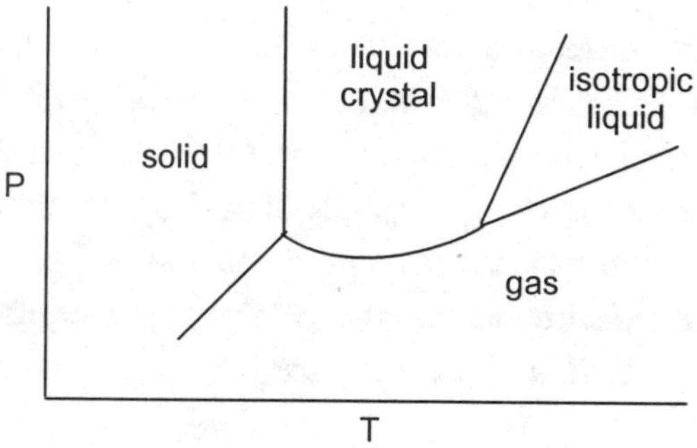

12.61 $TiCl_4(g) + 2SiH_4(g) \rightarrow TiSi_2(s) + 4HCl(g) + 2H_2(g)$

As a ceramic, $TiSi_2$ will have a three dimensional network structure similar to that of Si. (Si(s) has a diamond-like covalent-network structure, Figure 11.41). At the surface of the thin film there will be Ti atoms and Si atoms with incomplete valences that can and will chemically bond with Si atoms on the surface of the substrate. This kind of bonding would not be possible with a Cu thin film. Strong adherence to the surface is an essential component of thin film performance.

Integrative Exercises

12.63 These compounds cannot be vaporized without destroying their chemical identities. Anions with names ending in "ite" or "ate" are oxyanions with nonmetallic elements as central atoms. Under the conditions of vacuum deposition, high temperatures and low pressures, these anions tend to chemically decompose to form gaseous nonmetal oxides. For example:

$$MnSO_4(s) \rightarrow MnO(s) + SO_3(g)$$

12.65 (a) sp^3 hybrid orbitals at C, 109° bond angles around C

(b)

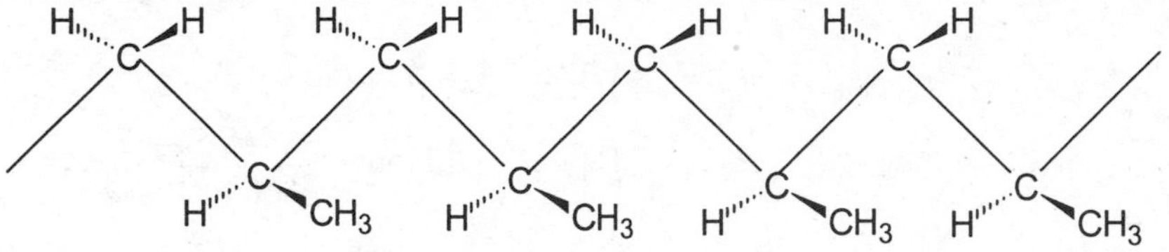

isotactic

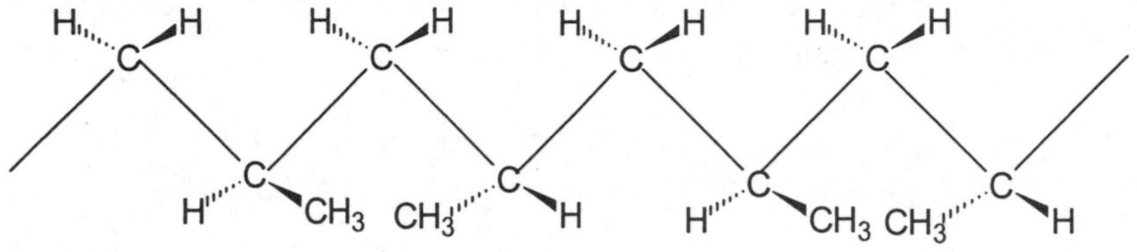

syndiotactic

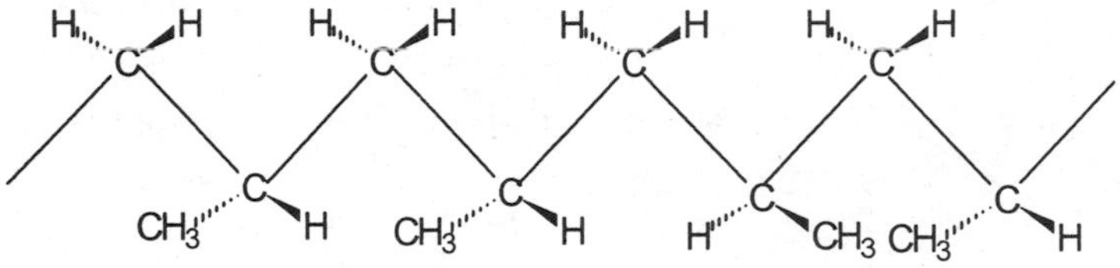

atactic

Isotactic polypropylene has the highest degree of crystallinity and highest melting point. The regular shape of the polymer backbone allows for close, orderly (almost zipper like) contact between chains. This maximizes dispersion forces between chains and produces higher order (crystallinity) and melting point. Atactic polypropylene has the least order and the lowest melting point.

(c) Cotton, with 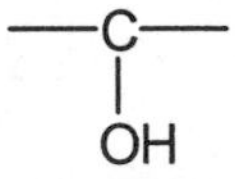 groups and polyester, with 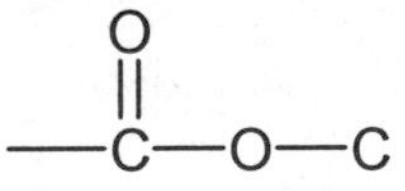 groups, both participate in hydrogen bonding interactions with H_2O molecules. These are strong intermolecular forces that hold the "moisture" at the surface of the fabric next to the skin. Polypropylene has no strong interactions with water and capillary action "wicks" the moisture away from the skin.

12.66 If the expected oxidation states on Y and Ba are +3 and +2, respectively, the **average** oxidation state of Cu is +2 1/3. That is, two Cu ions are in the +2 state and one is in the +3 state. Y^{3+} and Ba^{2+} have the stable electron configurations of their nearest noble gases, while Cu has an incomplete d orbital set. Cu(II) is d^9, Cu(III) is d^8 and both have unpaired electrons. Although the mechanism by which the copper 3d electrons interact through the bridging oxygen atoms to form a superconducting state is still not clear, it is evident that the electronic structure of the copper ions is essential to the observed superconductivity.

12.67 (a) The average molar mass ($\mathcal{M}_{avg}$) of the gas is the average of the individual molar masses weighted for their relative abundances.

$$\mathcal{M}_{avg} = (40/41)(16.04) + (1/41)(2.016) = 15.70 \text{ g} = 16 \text{ g}$$

$$\text{gas density (g/L)} = \mathcal{M}_{avg}\ P/RT;\quad P = 90 \text{ torr} \times \frac{1 \text{ atm}}{760 \text{ torr}} = 0.1184 \text{ atm} = 0.12 \text{ atm}$$

$$\rho = 15.70 \text{ g/mol} \times 0.1184 \text{ atm} \times \frac{\text{K}\bullet\text{mol}}{0.08206 \text{ L}\bullet\text{atm}} \times \frac{1}{1123 \text{ K}} = 0.020 \text{ g/L}$$

(b) The density of diamond, C(s,d), is 3.51 g/mL. Calculate the volume of the diamond film, and then its mass.

$$V = 1 \text{ cm}^2 \times 2.5\ \mu\text{m} \times \frac{1 \times 10^{-6} \text{ m}}{1\ \mu\text{m}} \times \frac{100 \text{ cm}}{\text{m}} \times \frac{1 \text{ mL}}{1 \text{ cm}^3} = 2.5 \times 10^{-4} \text{ mL}$$

$V = 3 \times 10^{-4}$ mL (to 1 sig fig)

$$\frac{3.51 \text{ g C(s,d)}}{1 \text{ mL}} \times 2.5 \times 10^{-4} \text{ mL} = 8.775 \times 10^{-4} \text{ g} = 9 \times 10^{-4} \text{ g C (s, d)}$$

Calculate how many grams of gas are needed to deposit 9×10^{-4} g of film, and the volume of this amount of gas.

$$8.775 \times 10^{-4} \text{ g C (s, d)} \times \frac{15.70 \text{ g gas}}{12.01 \text{ g C(s,d)}} = 1.147 \times 10^{-3} \text{ g gas contains the amount of C(s,d) in the film.}$$

But the process is only 0.5% efficient.

$$\frac{1.147 \times 10^{-3} \text{ g gas needed}}{\text{total of gas}} \times 100 = 0.5;\quad \text{total g gas} = 0.2294 \text{ g} = 0.23 \text{ g gas}$$

$$V = \frac{\text{g RT}}{\mathcal{M}_{avg}\ P} = \frac{0.2294 \text{ g}}{15.70 \text{ g/mol}} \times \frac{0.08206 \text{ L}\bullet\text{atm}}{\text{K}\bullet\text{mol}} \times \frac{1123 \text{ K}}{0.1184 \text{ atm}} = 11.37 \text{ L} = 11 \text{ L}$$

12.69 (a)

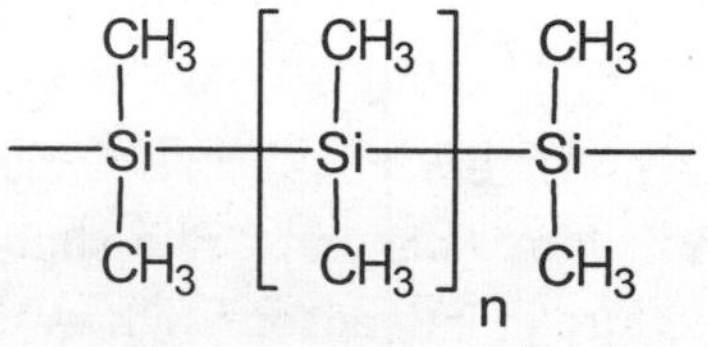

Si-Si 226 kJ ← lowest
Si-C 301 kJ
C-H 413 kJ

(b) Si-Si bonds are weakest, so they are most likely to break upon heating.

(c) At this point, a C–H bond must be broken, because the product polymer has $-CH_2-$ in the backbone, while only terminal $-CH_3$ groups are present in the reactant polymer.

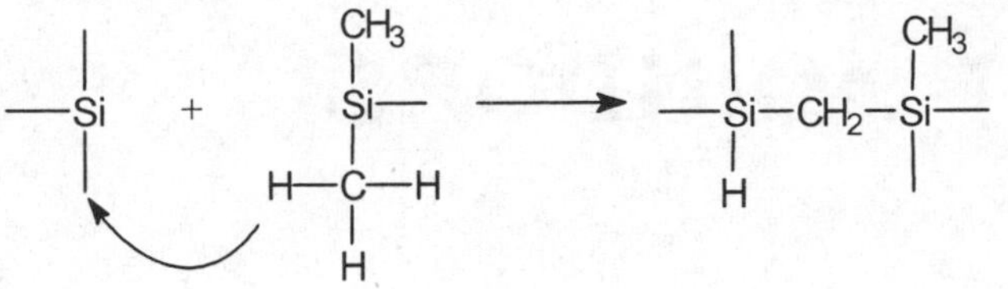

$$\Delta H = D(C\text{-}H) - D(Si\text{-}C) - D(Si\text{-}H) = 413 - 301 - 323 = -211 \text{ kJ/mol}$$

12.70 (a)

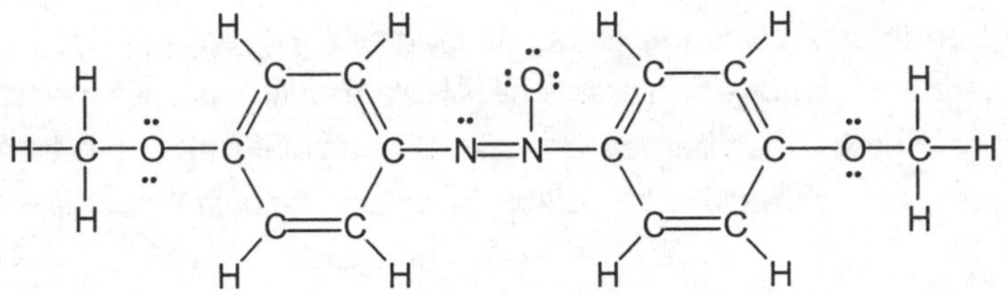

There are several other resonance structures involving alternate placement of the double bonds in the benzene rings.

(b) Both N atoms are surrounded by 3 VSEPR electron domains, so the hybridization at both atoms is sp^2. The bond angles around the N attached to O will be approximately 120°.

(c) When the $-OCH_3$ group is replaced by the $-CH_2CH_2CH_2CH_3$ group, a small rather compact group with some polarity is replaced by a larger, more flexible, nonpolar group. Thus, the molecules don't line up as well in the solid, and the melting point and liquid crystal temperature range are lower.

(d) The density decreases going from solid to nematic liquid crystal to isotropic liquid. In the nematic liquid crystal, most of the long range order of the solid state is lost. The molecules are moving relative to one another with their long axes more or less aligned. The result is more empty space and a lower density than the solid. There is a further small decrease in density when the last degree of order is lost and the substance becomes an isotropic liquid.

13 Properties of Solutions

The Solution Process

13.2 (a) For the same solute, NaCl, in different solvents, solute-solute interactions (ΔH_1) are the same. Because water experiences hydrogen bonding while benzene has only dispersion forces, solvent-solvent interactions (ΔH_2) are greater for water. On the other hand, solute-solvent interactions (ΔH_3) are much weaker between ionic NaCl and nonpolar benzene than between ionic NaCl and polar water. It is the large difference in ΔH_3 that causes NaCl to be soluble in water but not in benzene.

(b) Lattice energy is the main component of ΔH_1, the enthalpy required to separate solute particles. If ΔH_1, is too large, the dissolving process is prohibitively endothermic, and the substance is not very soluble.

(c) Ion-dipole forces between cations and water molecules and relatively small lattice energies (ion-ion forces between cations and anions) lead to strongly hydrated cations.

13.4 From weakest to strongest solvent-solute interactions:
(b), dispersion forces < (c), hydrogen bonding < (a), ion-dipole

13.6 Separation of solvent molecules, ΔH_2, will be smallest in this case, because hydrogen bonding is the weakest of the intermolecular forces involved. ΔH_1 involves breaking ionic bonds, and ΔH_3 involves formation of ion-dipole interactions, both stronger forces than hydrogen bonding.

13.8 KBr is quite soluble in water because of the sizeable increase in disorder of the system (ordered KBr lattice → freely moving hydrated ions) associated with the dissolving process. An increase in disorder or randomness in a process tends to make that process spontaneous.

Saturated Solutions; Factors Affecting Solubility

13.10 (a)
$$\frac{1.22 \text{ mol } MnSO_4 \bullet H_2O}{1 \text{ L soln}} \times \frac{169.0 \text{ g } MnSO_4 \bullet H_2O}{1 \text{ mol}} \times 0.100 \text{ L} = 20.6 \text{ g } MnSO_4 \bullet H_2O / 100 \text{ mL}$$

The 1.22 *M* solution is unsaturated.

(b) Add a known mass, say 5.0 g, of $MnSO_4 \cdot H_2O$ to the unknown solution. If the solid dissolves, the solution is unsaturated. If there is undissolved $MnSO_4 \cdot H_2O$, filter the solution and weigh the solid. If there is less than 5.0 g of solid, some of the added $MnSO_4 \cdot H_2O$ dissolved and the unknown solution is unsaturated. If there is exactly 5.0 g, no additional solid dissolved and the unknown is saturated. If there is more than 5.0 g, excess solute has precipitated and the solution is supersaturated.

13.12 (a) at 30°C, $\frac{10 \text{ g } KClO_3}{100 \text{ g } H_2O} \times 250 \text{ g } H_2O = 25 \text{ g } KClO_3$

(b) $\frac{66 \text{ g } Pb(NO_3)_2}{100 \text{ g } H_2O} \times 250 \text{ g } H_2O = 165 = 1.7 \times 10^2 \text{ g } Pb(NO_3)_2$

(c) $\frac{3 \text{ g } Ce_2(SO_4)_3}{100 \text{ g } H_2O} \times 250 \text{ g } H_2O = 7.5 = 8 \text{ g } Ce_2(SO_4)_3$

13.14 Immiscible means that oil and water do not mix homogeneously; they do not dissolve. Many substances are called 'oil', but they are typically nonpolar carbon-based molecules with fairly high molecular weights. As such, there are fairly strong dispersion forces among oil molecules. The properties of water are dominated by its strong hydrogen bonding. The dispersion-dipole interactions between water and oil are likely to be weak. Thus, ΔH_1 and ΔH_2 are large and positive, while ΔH_3 is small and negative. The net ΔH_{soln} is large and positive, and mixing does not occur.

13.16 (a) Dispersion interactions among nonpolar $CH_3(CH_2)_{16}$–chains dominate the properties of stearic acid. It is more soluble in nonpolar CCl_4 than polar (hydrogen bonding) water, despite the presence of the –COOH group.

(b)

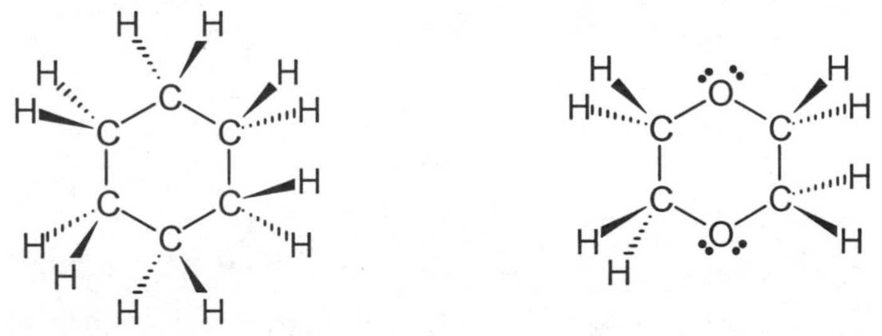

cyclohexane dioxane

Dioxane can act as a hydrogen bond acceptor, so it will be more soluble than cyclohexane in water.

13.18 Hexane is a nonpolar hydrocarbon that experiences dispersion forces with other C_6H_{14} molecules. Solutes that primarily experience dispersion forces will be more soluble in hexane.

(a) Cyclohexane, C_6H_{12}, is also a nonpolar hydrocarbon and will be more soluble in hexane. Glucose experiences hydrogen bonding with itself; these solute-solute interactions are less likely to be overcome by weak solute-solvent interactions.

(b) Propionic acid, which experiences hydrogen bonding, will be more soluble than sodium propionate, which experiences ion-ion forces. The hydrogen bonding is weaker (relatively speaking) and more likely to be overcome by dispersion forces with hexane.

(c) Ethyl chloride, which has a $-CH_2CH_3$ group capable of dispersion forces, will be more soluble. HCl experiences dipole-dipole forces less likely to be disrupted by dispersion forces with hexane.

13.20 Pressure has an effect on O_2 solubility in water because, at constant temperature and volume, pressure is directly related to the amount of O_2 available to dissolve. The greater the partial pressure of O_2 above water, the more O_2 molecules are available for dissolution, and the more molecules that strike the surface of the liquid.

Pressure does not affect the amount or physical properties of NaCl, or ionic solids in general, so it has little influence on the dissolving of NaCl in water.

13.22 $665 \text{ torr} \times \frac{1 \text{ atm}}{760 \text{ torr}} = 0.875 \text{ atm}$; $P_{O_2} = \chi_{O_2}(P_t) = 0.21(0.875 \text{ atm}) = 0.1838 = 0.18 \text{ atm}$

$$S_{O_2} = kP_{O_2} = \frac{1.38 \times 10^{-3} \text{mol}}{\text{L} \bullet \text{atm}} \times 0.1838 \text{ atm} = 2.5 \times 10^{-4}\ M$$

Concentrations of Solutions

13.24 (a) $$\text{mass \%} = \frac{\text{mass solute}}{\text{total mass solution}} \times 100$$

$$\text{mass solute} = 0.045 \text{ mol } I_2 \times \frac{253.8 \text{ g } I_2}{1 \text{ mol } I_2} = 11.421 = 11 \text{ g } I_2$$

$$\text{mass \% } I_2 = \frac{11.421 \text{ g } I_2}{11.421 \text{ g } I_2 + 115 \text{ g } CCl_4} \times 100 = 9.034 = 9.0\% \ I_2$$

(b) $$\text{ppm} = \frac{\text{mass solute}}{\text{total mass solution}} \times 10^6 = \frac{0.0079 \text{ g } Sr^{2+}}{1 \times 10^3 \text{ g } H_2O} \times 10^6 = 7.9 \text{ ppm } Sr^{2+}$$

13.26 (a) $$\frac{25.5 \text{ g } C_6H_5OH}{94.11 \text{ g/mol}} = 0.2710 = 0.271 \text{ mol } C_6H_5OH$$

$$\frac{495 \text{ g } CH_3CH_2OH}{46.07 \text{ g/mol}} = 10.7445 = 10.7 \text{ mol } CH_3CH_2OH$$

$$\chi_{C_6H_5OH} = \frac{0.2710}{0.2710 + 10.7445} = 0.02460 = 0.0246$$

(b) $\text{mass \%} = \dfrac{25.5\text{ g } C_6H_5OH}{25.5\text{ g } C_6H_5OH + 495\text{ g } CH_3CH_2OH} \times 100 = 4.90\%\ C_6H_5OH$

(c) $m = \dfrac{0.2710\text{ mol } C_6H_5OH}{0.495\text{ kg } CH_3CH_2OH} = 0.54747 = 0.547\ m\ C_6H_5OH$

13.28 (a) $M = \dfrac{\text{mol solute}}{\text{L soln}};\ \dfrac{15.0\text{ g } Al_2(SO_4)_3}{0.350\text{ L soln}} \times \dfrac{1\text{ mol } Al_2(SO_4)_3}{342.2\text{ g } Al_2(SO_4)_3} = 0.125\ M\ Al_2(SO_4)_3$

(b) $\dfrac{5.25\text{ g } Mn(NO_3)_2 \bullet 2H_2O}{0.175\text{ L soln}} \times \dfrac{1\text{ mol } Mn(NO_3)_2 \bullet 2H_2O}{215.0\text{ g } Mn(NO_3)_2 \bullet 2H_2O} = 0.140\ M\ Mn(NO_3)_2$

(c) $M_c \times L_c = M_d \times L_d;\ 9.00\ M\ H_2SO_4 \times 0.0350\text{ L} = ?M\ H_2SO_4 \times 0.500\text{ L}$

500 mL of 0.630 $M\ H_2SO_4$

13.30 (a) $16.0\text{ mol } H_2O \times \dfrac{18.02\text{ g } H_2O}{1\text{ mol } H_2O} = 288.3\text{ g } H_2O = 0.288\text{ kg } H_2O$

$m = \dfrac{1.50\text{ mol KCl}}{0.2883\text{ kg } H_2O} = 5.2026 = 5.20\ m\text{ KCl}$

(b) $m = \dfrac{\text{mol solute}}{\text{kg solvent}};\ \text{mol } S_8 = m \times \text{kg } C_{10}H_8 = 0.12\ m \times 0.1000\text{ kg } C_{10}H_8 = 0.012\text{ mol}$

$0.012\text{ mol } S_8 \times \dfrac{256.5\text{ g } S_8}{1\text{ mol } S_8} = 3.078 = 3.1\text{ g } S_8$

13.32 (a) $\text{mass \%} = \dfrac{\text{mass } C_6H_8O_6}{\text{total mass solution}} \times 100;$

$\dfrac{80.5\text{ g } C_6H_8O_6}{80.5\text{ g } C_6H_8O_6 + 210\text{ g } H_2O} \times 100 = 27.71 = 27.7\%\ C_6H_8O_6$

(b) $\text{mol } C_6H_8O_6 = \dfrac{80.5\text{ g } C_6H_8O_6}{176.1\text{ g/mol}} = 0.4571 = 0.457\text{ mol } C_6H_8O_6$

$\text{mol } H_2O = \dfrac{210\text{ g } H_2O}{18.02\text{ g/mol}} = 11.654 = 11.7\text{ mol } H_2O$

$\chi_{C_6H_8O_6} = \dfrac{0.4571\text{ mol } C_6H_8O_6}{0.4571\text{ mol } C_6H_8O_6 + 11.654\text{ mol } H_2O} = 0.0377$

(c) $m = \dfrac{0.4571 \text{ mol } C_6H_8O_6}{0.210 \text{ kg } H_2O} = 2.18\ m\ C_6H_8O_6$

(d) $M = \dfrac{\text{mol } C_6H_8O_6}{\text{L solution}}$; $290.5 \text{ g soln} \times \dfrac{1 \text{ mL}}{1.22 \text{ g}} \times \dfrac{1 \text{ L}}{1000 \text{ mL}} = 0.2381 = 0.238 \text{ L}$

$M = \dfrac{0.4571 \text{ mol } C_6H_8O_6}{0.2381 \text{ L soln}} = 1.92\ M\ C_6H_8O_6$

13.34 **Given: 10.0 g C_4H_4S, 1.065 g/mL; 105.0 mL C_7H_8, 0.897 g/mL**

(a) mol $C_4H_4S = 10.0 \text{ g } C_4H_4S \times \dfrac{1 \text{ mol } C_4H_4S}{84.15 \text{ g } C_4H_4S} = 0.1188 = 0.119 \text{ mol } C_4H_4S$

mol $C_7H_8 = \dfrac{0.867 \text{ g}}{1 \text{ mL}} \times 250.0 \text{ mL} \times \dfrac{1 \text{ mol } C_7H_8}{92.14 \text{ g } C_7H_8} = 2.352 = 2.35 \text{ mol}$

$\chi_{C_4H_4S} = \dfrac{0.1188 \text{ mol } C_4H_4S}{0.1188 \text{ mol } C_4H_4S + 2.352 \text{ mol } C_7H_8} = 0.04809 = 0.0481$

(b) $m_{C_4H_4S} = \dfrac{\text{mol } C_4H_4S}{\text{kg } C_7H_8}$; $250.0 \text{ mL} \times \dfrac{0.867 \text{ g}}{1 \text{ mL}} \times \dfrac{1 \text{ kg}}{1000 \text{ g}} = 0.2168 = 0.217 \text{ kg } C_7H_8$

$m_{C_4H_4S} = \dfrac{0.1188 \text{ mol } C_4H_4S}{0.2168 \text{ kg } C_7H_8} = 0.548\ m\ C_4H_4S$

(c) $10.0 \text{ g } C_4H_4S \times \dfrac{1 \text{ mL}}{1.065 \text{ g}} = 9.390 = 9.39 \text{ mL } C_4H_4S$;

$V_{soln} = 9.39 \text{ mL } C_4H_4S + 250.0 \text{ mL } C_7H_8 = 259.4 \text{ mL}$

$M_{C_4H_4S} = \dfrac{0.1188 \text{ mol } C_4H_4S}{0.2594 \text{ L soln}} = 0.458\ M\ C_4H_4S$

13.36 (a) $\dfrac{1.50 \text{ mol } HNO_3}{1 \text{ L soln}} \times 0.245 \text{ L} = 0.3675 = 0.368 \text{ mol } HNO_3$

(b) Assume that for dilute aqueous solutions, the mass of the solvent is the mass of solution.

$\dfrac{0.125 \text{ mol NaCl}}{1 \text{ kg } H_2O} = \dfrac{x \text{ mol}}{50.0 \times 10^{-6} \text{ kg}}$; $x = 6.25 \times 10^{-5}$ mol NaCl

(c) $\frac{1.50\text{ g } C_{12}H_{22}O_{11}}{100\text{ g soln}} = \frac{x\text{ g } C_{12}H_{22}O_{11}}{75.0\text{ g soln}}$; $x = 1.125 = 1.13\text{ g } C_{12}H_{22}O_{11}$

$$1.125\text{ g } C_{12}H_{22}O_{11} \times \frac{1\text{ mol } C_{12}H_{22}O_{11}}{342.3\text{ g } C_{12}H_{22}O_{11}} = 3.287 \times 10^{-3} = 3.29 \times 10^{-3}\text{ mol } C_{12}H_{22}O_{11}$$

13.38 (a) $\frac{0.110\text{ mol } (NH_4)_2SO_4}{1\text{ L soln}} \times 1.50\text{ L} \times \frac{132.2\text{ g } (NH_4)_2SO_4}{1\text{ mol } (NH_4)_2SO_4} = 21.81 = 21.8\text{ g } (NH_4)_2SO_4$

Weigh 21.8 g $(NH_4)_2SO_4$, dissolve in a small amount of water, continue adding water with thorough mixing up to a total solution volume of 1.50 L.

(b) Determine the mass fraction of Na_2CO_3 in the solution:

$$\frac{0.65\text{ mol } Na_2CO_3}{1000\text{ g } H_2O} \times \frac{106.0\text{ g } Na_2CO_3}{1\text{ mol } Na_2CO_3} = 68.9\text{ g} = \frac{69\text{ g } Na_2CO_3}{1000\text{ g } H_2O}$$

$$\text{mass fraction} = \frac{68.9\text{ g } Na_2CO_3}{1000\text{ g } H_2O + 68.9\text{ g } Na_2CO_3} = 0.06446 = 0.064$$

In 120 g of solution, there are 0.06446(120) = 7.735 = 7.7 g Na_2CO_3.

Weigh out 7.7 g Na_2CO_3 and dissolve it in 120 - 7.7 = 112.3 g H_2O to make exactly 120 g of solution.

(112.3 g H_2O/0.997 g H_2O/mL @ 25° = 112.6 mL H_2O)

(c) $1.20\text{ L} \times \frac{1000\text{ mL}}{1\text{ L}} \times \frac{1.16\text{ g}}{1\text{ mL}} = 1392\text{ g solution}$; $0.150(1392\text{ g soln}) = 209\text{ g } Pb(NO_3)_2$

Weigh 209 g $Pb(NO_3)$ and add (1392 - 209) = 1183 g H_2O to make exactly ($1392 = 1.39 \times 10^3$) g or 1.20 L of solution.

(1183 g H_2O/0.997 g/mL @ 25°C = 1187 mL H_2O)

(d) Calculate the mol HCl necessary to neutralize 5.5 g $Ba(OH)_2$.

$Ba(OH)_2(s) + 2HCl(aq) \rightarrow BaCl_2(aq) + 2H_2O(l)$

$$5.5\text{ g } Ba(OH)_2 \times \frac{1\text{ mol } Ba(OH)_2}{171\text{ g } Ba(OH)_2} \times \frac{2\text{ mol HCl}}{1\text{ mol } Ba(OH)_2} = 0.0643 = 0.064\text{ mol HCl}$$

$$M = \frac{\text{mol}}{\text{L}};\ \text{L} = \frac{\text{mol}}{M} = \frac{0.0643\text{ mol HCl}}{0.50\ M\text{ HCl}} = 0.1287 = 0.13\text{ L} = 130\text{ mL}$$

130 mL of 0.50 M HCl are needed.

$M_c \times L_c = M_d \times L_d$; $6.0\ M \times L_c = 0.50\ M \times 0.1287\text{ L}$; $L_c = 0.01072\text{ L} = 11\text{ mL}$

Using a pipette, measure exactly 11 mL of 6.0 M HCl and dilute with water to a total volume of 130 mL.

13.40 Assume a solution volume of 1.00 L. Calculate the mass of 1.00 L of solution and the mass of HNO_3 in 1.00 L of solution.

$$1.00\ L \times \frac{1000\ mL}{1\ L} \times \frac{1.42\ g\ soln}{mL\ soln} = 1.42 \times 10^3\ g\ soln$$

$$16\ M = \frac{16\ mol\ HNO_3}{1\ L\ soln} \times \frac{63.02\ g\ HNO_3}{1\ mol\ HNO_3} = 1008 = 1.0 \times 10^3\ g\ HNO_3$$

$$\text{mass \%} = \frac{1008\ g\ HNO_3}{1.42 \times 10^3\ g\ soln} \times 100 = 71\%\ HNO_3$$

13.42 (a) $\frac{0.0750\ mol\ C_8H_{10}N_4O_2}{1\ kg\ CHCl_3} \times \frac{194.2\ g\ C_8H_{10}N_4O_2}{1\ mol\ C_8H_{10}N_4O_2} = 14.565$

$= 14.6\ g\ C_8H_{10}N_4O_2\ /\ kg\ CHCl_3$

$$\frac{14.565\ g\ C_8H_{10}N_4O_2}{14.565\ g\ C_8H_{10}N_4O_2 + 1000.00\ g\ CHCl_3} \times 100 = 1.436 = 1.44\%\ C_8H_{10}N_4O_2 \text{ by mass}$$

(b) $1000\ g\ CHCl_3 \times \frac{1\ mol\ CHCl_3}{119.4\ CHCl_3} = 8.375 = 8.38\ mol\ CHCl_3$

$$\chi_{C_8H_{10}N_4O_2} = \frac{0.0750}{0.0750 + 8.375} = 0.00888$$

Colligative Properties

13.44 (a) decrease (b) decrease (c) increase (d) increase

13.46 The vapor pressure over the sucrose solution is higher than the vapor pressure over the glucose solution. Since sucrose has a greater molar mass, 10 g of sucrose contains fewer particles than 10 g of glucose. The solution that contains fewer particles, the sucrose solution, will have the higher vapor pressure.

13.48 (a) H_2O vapor pressure will be determined by the mole fraction of H_2O in the solution. The vapor pressure of pure H_2O at 343 K (70°C) = 233.7 torr.

$$\frac{35.0\ g\ C_3H_8O_3}{92.10\ g/mol} = 0.3800 = 0.380\ mol; \quad \frac{125\ g\ H_2O}{18.02\ g/mol} = 6.937 = 6.94\ mol$$

$$P_{H_2O} = \frac{6.937\ mol\ H_2O}{6.937 + 0.380} \times 233.7\ torr = 221.6 = 222\ torr$$

(b) Calculate χ_B by vapor pressure lowering; $\chi_B = \Delta P_A / P_A^\circ$ (see Solution 13.47(b)). Given moles solvent, calculate moles solute from the definition of mole fraction.

$$\chi_{C_2H_6O_2} = \frac{10.0\ torr}{100\ torr} = 0.100$$

$$\frac{1.00 \times 10^3 \text{ g } C_2H_5OH}{46.07 \text{ g/mol}} = 21.71 = 21.7 \text{ mol } C_2H_5OH; \text{ let y = mol } C_2H_6O_2$$

$$\chi_{C_2H_6O_2} = \frac{\text{y mol } C_2H_6O_2}{\text{y mol } C_2H_6O_2 + 21.71 \text{ mol } C_2H_5OH} = 0.100 = \frac{y}{y + 21.71}$$

$0.100 \text{ y} + 2.171 = \text{y}; \ 0.900 \text{ y} = 2.171; \ \text{y} = 2.412 = 2.41 \text{ mol } C_2H_6O_2$

$$2.412 \text{ mol } C_2H_6O_2 \times \frac{62.07 \text{ g}}{1 \text{ mol}} = 150 \text{ g } C_2H_6O_2$$

13.50 (a) Since C_6H_6 and C_7H_8 form an ideal solution, we can use Raoult's Law. Since both components are volatile, both contribute to the total vapor pressure of 35 torr.

$P_T = P_{C_6H_6} + P_{C_7H_8}; \ P_{C_6H_6} = \chi_{C_6H_6} P^o_{C_6H_6}; \ P_{C_7H_8} = \chi_{C_7H_8} P^o_{C_7H_8}$

$\chi_{C_7H_8} = 1 - \chi_{C_6H_6}; \ P_T = \chi_{C_6H_6} P^o_{C_6H_6} + (1 - \chi_{C_6H_6}) P^o_{C_7H_8}$

$35 \text{ torr} = \chi_{C_6H_6}(75 \text{ torr}) + (1 - \chi_{C_6H_6})22 \text{ torr}$

$13 \text{ torr} = 53 \text{ torr } (\chi_{C_6H_6}); \ \chi_{C_6H_6} = \frac{13 \text{ torr}}{53 \text{ torr}} = 0.2453 = 0.25; \ \chi_{C_7H_8} = 0.7547 = 0.75$

(b) $P_{C_6H_6} = 0.2453(75 \text{ torr}) = 18.4 \text{ torr}; \ P_{C_7H_8} = 0.7547(22 \text{ torr}) = 16.6 \text{ torr}$

In the vapor, $\chi_{C_6H_6} = \frac{P_{C_6H_6}}{P_T} = \frac{18.4 \text{ torr}}{35 \text{ torr}} = 0.53; \ \chi_{C_7H_8} = 0.47$

13.52 *Analyze/Plan*. ΔT_b depends on mol dissolved particles. Assume 100 g of each solution, calculate mol solute and mol dissolved particles. Glucose and sucrose are molecular solutes, but $NaNO_3$ dissociates into 2 mol particles per mol solute. *Solve*:

10% by mass means 10 g solute in 100 g solution. If we have 10 g of each solute, the one with the smallest molar mass will have the largest mol solute. The molar masses are: glucose, 180.2 g/mol; sucrose, 342.3 g/mol; $NaNO_3$, 85.0 g/mol. $NaNO_3$ has most mol solute, and twice as many dissolved particles, so it will have the highest boiling point. Sucrose has least mol solute and lowest boiling point. Glucose is intermediate.

In order of increasing boiling point: 10% sucrose < 10% glucose < 10% $NaNO_3$.

13.54 For dilute aqueous solutions such as these, *M* is essentially equal to *m*. For the purposes of comparison, assume we can use *M*.

The more solute particles, the higher the boiling point. Since LiBr and $Zn(NO_3)_2$ are electrolytes, the particle concentrations in these solutions are 0.10 *M* and 0.15 *M*, respectively (although ion-ion attractive forces may decrease the real concentrations somewhat). Thus, the order of increasing boiling points is:

0.050 *M* LiBr < 0.120 *M* glucose < 0.050 *M* $Zn(NO_3)_2$

13.56 $\Delta T = K(m)$; first calculate the **molality** of the solute particles.

(a) 0.40 *m* (b) $\frac{20.0 \text{ g } C_{10}H_{22}}{0.455 \text{ kg } CHCl_3} \times \frac{1 \text{ mol } C_{10}H_{22}}{142.3 \text{ g } C_{10}H_{22}} = 0.3089 = 0.309\ m$

(c) $m = \frac{0.45 \text{ mol eg} + 2(0.15) \text{ mol KBr}}{0.150 \text{ kg } H_2O} = \frac{0.75 \text{ mol particles}}{0.150 \text{ kg } H_2O} = 5.0\ m$

Then, f.p. = $T_f - K_f(m)$; b.p. = $T_b + K_b(m)$; T in °C

	m	T_f	$-K_f(m)$		f.p.	T_b	$+K_b(m)$		b.p.
(a)	0.40	-114.6	-1.99(0.40)	= -0.80	-115.4	78.4	1.22(0.40)	= 0.49	78.9
(b)	0.309	-63.5	-4.68(0.309)	= -1.45	-65.0	61.2	3.63(0.309)	= 1.12	62.3
(c)	5.0	0.0	-1.86(5.0)	= -9.3	-9.3	100.0	0.51(5.0)	= 2.6	102.6

13.58 $\pi = MRT$; T = 20°C + 273 = 293 K

$$M \text{ (of ions)} = \frac{\text{mol NaCl} \times 2}{\text{L soln}} = \frac{3.4 \text{ g NaCl}}{1 \text{ L soln}} \times \frac{1 \text{ mol NaCl}}{58.4 \text{ g NaCl}} \times \frac{2 \text{ mol ions}}{1 \text{ mol NaCl}} = 0.116 = 0.12\ M$$

$$\pi = \frac{0.116 \text{ mol}}{\text{L}} \times \frac{0.08206 \text{ L} \bullet \text{atm}}{\text{K} \bullet \text{mol}} \times 293 \text{ K} = 2.8 \text{ atm}$$

13.60 $\Delta T_f = 5.5 - 4.1 = 1.4$; $m = \frac{\Delta T_f}{K_f} = \frac{1.4}{5.12} = 0.273 = 0.27\ m$

$$\mathcal{M} \text{ lauryl alcohol} = \frac{\text{g lauryl alcohol}}{m \times \text{kg } C_6H_6} = \frac{5.00 \text{ g lauryl alcohol}}{0.273 \times 0.100 \text{ kg } C_6H_6}$$

$= 1.8 \times 10^2$ g/mol lauryl alcohol

13.62 $M = \pi/RT = \frac{0.605 \text{ atm}}{298 \text{ K}} \times \frac{\text{mol} \bullet \text{K}}{0.08206 \text{ L} \bullet \text{atm}} = 0.02474 = 0.0247\ M$

$$\mathcal{M} = \frac{\text{g}}{M \times \text{L}} = \frac{2.35 \text{ g}}{0.02474\ M \times 0.250 \text{ L}} = 380 \text{ g/mol}$$

13.64 If these were ideal solutions, they would have equal ion concentrations and equal ΔT_f values. Data in Table 13.5 indicates that the van't Hoff factors (*i*) for both salts are less than the ideal values. For 0.030 *m* NaCl, *i* is between 1.87 and 1.94, about 1.92. For 0.020 *m* K_2SO_4, *i* is between 2.32 and 2.70, about 2.62. From Equation 13.14,

ΔT_f (measured) = $i \times \Delta T_f$ (calculated for nonelectrolyte)

NaCl: ΔT_f (measured) = $1.92 \times 0.030\ m \times 1.86$ °C/*m* = 0.11 °C

K_2SO_4: ΔT_f (measured) = $2.62 \times 0.020\ m \times 1.86$°C/*m* = 0.097 °C

0.030 *m* NaCl would have the larger ΔT_f.

The deviations from ideal behavior are due to ion-pairing in the two electrolyte solutions. K_2SO_4 has more extensive ion pairing and a larger deviation from ideality because of the higher charge on SO_4^{2-} relative to Cl^-.

Colloids

13.66 (a) Suspensions are classified as solutions or colloids according to the size of the dispersed particles. Solute particles have diameters less than 10 Å. Clearly a protein with a molecular mass of 30,000 amu will be longer than 10 Å. The aqueous suspensions are colloids because of the size of protein molecules.

(b) Emulsion. An emulsifying agent is one that aids in the formation of an emulsion. It usually has a polar part and a nonpolar part, to facilitate mixing of immiscible liquids with very different molecular polarities.

13.68 (a) When the colloid particle mass becomes large enough so that gravitational and interparticle attractive forces are greater than the kinetic energies of the particles, settling and aggregation can occur.

(b) Hydrophobic colloids do not attract a sheath of water molecules around them and thus tend to aggregate from aqueous solution. They can be stabilized as colloids by adsorbing charges on their surfaces. The charged particles interact with solvent water, stabilizing the colloid.

(c) Charges on colloid particles can stabilize them against aggregation. Particles carrying like charges repel one another and are thus prevented from aggregating and settling out.

13.70 (a) The nonpolar hydrophobic tails of soap particles (the hydrocarbon chain of stearate ions) establish attractive intermolecular dispersion forces with the nonpolar oil molecules, while the charged hydrophilic head of the soap particles interacts with H_2O to keep the oil molecules suspended. (This is the mechanism by which laundry detergents remove greasy dirt from clothes.)

(b) Electrolytes from the acid neutralize surface charges of the suspended particles in milk, causing the colloid to coagulate.

Additional Exercises

13.72 In this equilibrium system, molecules move from the surface of the solid into solution, while molecules in solution are deposited on the surface of the solid. As molecules leave the surface of the small particles of powder, the reverse process preferentially deposits other molecules on the surface of a single crystal. Eventually, all molecules that were present in the 50 g of powder are deposited on the surface of a 50 g crystal; this can only happen if the dissolution and deposition processes are ongoing.

13.74 $P_{Rn} = \chi_{Rn} P_{total}$; $P_{Rn} = 3.5 \times 10^{-6}$ (32 atm) $= 1.12 \times 10^{-4} = 1.1 \times 10^{-4}$ atm

$$S_{Rn} = k\,P_{Rn};\ S_{Rn} = \frac{7.27 \times 10^{-3}\,M}{1\text{ atm}} \times 1.12 \times 10^{-4}\text{ atm} = 8.1 \times 10^{-7}\,M$$

13.75 0.10% by mass means 0.10 g glucose/100 g blood.

(a) $\text{ppm glucose} = \frac{\text{g glucose}}{\text{g solution}} \times 10^6 = \frac{0.10 \text{ g glucose}}{100 \text{ g blood}} \times 10^6 = 1000 \text{ ppm glucose}$

(b) *m* = mol glucose/kg solvent. Assume that the mixture of nonglucose components is the 'solvent'.

mass solvent = 100 g blood - 0.10 g glucose = 99.9 g solvent = 0.0999 kg solvent

$$\text{mol glucose} = 0.10 \text{ g} \times \frac{1 \text{ mol}}{180.2 \text{ g } C_6H_{12}O_6} = 5.55 \times 10^{-4} = 5.6 \times 10^{-4} \text{ mol glucose}$$

$$m = \frac{5.55 \times 10^{-4} \text{ mol glucose}}{0.0999 \text{ kg solvent}} = 5.6 \times 10^{-3}\ m \text{ glucose}$$

In order to calculate molarity, volume solution must be known. The density of blood is needed to relate mass and volume.

13.77 Assume 1.00 L of solution. 1000 mL soln × 0.945 g/mL = 945 g solution

$$\frac{945 \text{ g soln}}{1.0 \text{ L soln}} \times \frac{32.0 \text{ g } C_3H_7OH}{100 \text{ g soln}} \times \frac{1 \text{ mol } C_3H_7OH}{60.09 \text{ g } C_3H_7OH} = 5.032 = 5.03\ M$$

$$945 \text{ g soln} \times \frac{32.0 \text{ g } C_3H_7OH}{100 \text{ g soln}} = 302.4 = 302 \text{ g } C_3H_7OH;\ 945 \text{ g} - 302.4 \text{ g} = 642.6 = 643 \text{ g } H_2O$$

$$\frac{302.4 \text{ g } C_3H_7OH}{0.6426 \text{ kg } H_2O} \times \frac{1 \text{ mol } C_3H_7OH}{60.09 \text{ g } C_3H_7OH} = 7.831 = 7.83\ m$$

13.78 (a) $\frac{1.80 \text{ mol LiBr}}{1 \text{ L soln}} \times \frac{86.85 \text{ g LiBr}}{1 \text{ mol LiBr}} = 156.3 = 156 \text{ g LiBr}$

1 L soln = 826 g soln; g CH_3CN = 826 - 156.3 = 669.7 = 670 g CH_3CN

$$m \text{ LiBr} = \frac{1.80 \text{ mol LiBr}}{0.6697 \text{ kg } CH_3CN} = 2.69\ m$$

(b) $\frac{669.7 \text{ g } CH_3CN}{41.05 \text{ g/mol}} = 16.31 = 16.3 \text{ mol } CH_3CN;\ \chi_{LiBr} = \frac{1.80}{1.80 + 16.31} = 0.0994$

(c) $\text{mass \%} = \frac{669.7 \text{ g } CH_3CN}{826 \text{ g soln}} \times 100 = 81.1\% \ CH_3CN$

13.80 Mole fraction ethylalcohol, $\chi_{C_2H_5OH} = \frac{P_{C_2H_5OH}}{P^o_{C_2H_5OH}} = \frac{8 \text{ torr}}{100 \text{ torr}} = 0.08$

$$\frac{620 \times 10^3 \text{ g } C_{24}H_{50}}{338.6 \text{ g/mol}} = 1.83 \times 10^3 \text{ mol } C_{24}H_{50};\ \text{ let y = mol } C_2H_5OH$$

$$\chi_{C_2H_5OH} = 0.08 = \frac{y}{y + 1.83 \times 10^3};\ 0.92\,y = 146.4;\ y = 1.6 \times 10^2 \text{ mol } C_2H_5OH$$

(Strictly speaking, y should have 1 sig fig because 0.08 has 1 sig fig, but this severely limits the calculation.)

$$1.6 \times 10^2 \text{ mol } C_2H_5OH \times \frac{46 \text{ g } C_2H_5OH}{1 \text{ mol}} = 7.4 \times 10^3 \text{ g or } 7.4 \text{ kg } C_2H_5OH$$

13.81 The solvent vapor pressure over each solution is determined by the total particle concentrations present in the solutions. When the particle concentrations are equal, the vapor pressures will be equal and equilibrium established. The particle concentration of the nonelectrolyte is just 0.060 *M*, the ion concentration of the NaCl is 2 × 0.040 *M* = 0.080 *M*. Solvent will diffuse from the less concentrated nonelectrolyte solution. Let x = volume of solvent transferred.

$$\frac{0.060\ M \times 20.0 \text{ mL}}{(20 - x) \text{ mL}} = \frac{0.080\ M \times 20.0 \text{ mL}}{(20 + x) \text{ mL}};\ 1.2(20.0 + x) = 1.6(20.0 - x)$$

2.8 x = 8, x = 2.86 = 3 mL transferred

13.83 Assume the radiator solution is prepared by mixing 1.00 L of each of the liquids. To calculate the freezing and boiling points, we need the molality of this solution. Assume H_2O is the solvent.

$$m = \frac{\text{mol } C_2H_6O_2}{\text{kg } H_2O};\ \text{kg } H_2O = 1.00 \text{ L} \times \frac{1000 \text{ mL}}{1 \text{ L}} \times \frac{1.00 \text{ g}}{\text{mL}} = 1.00 \text{ kg}$$

$$\text{mol } C_2H_6O_2 = 1.00 \text{ L} \times \frac{1000 \text{ mL}}{1 \text{ L}} \times \frac{1.12 \text{ g}}{1 \text{ mL}} \times \frac{1 \text{ mol } C_2H_6O_2}{62.07 \text{ g } C_2H_6O_2} = 18.04 = 18.0 \text{ mol } C_2H_6O_2$$

$$m = \frac{18.04 \text{ mol } C_2H_6O_2}{1.00 \text{ kg } H_2O} = 18.04\ m$$

$\Delta T_f = K_f m = -1.86(18.04) = -33.6°C$; f.p. = 0.0 - 33.6 = -33.6°C

$\Delta T_b = K_b m = 0.52(18.04) = 9.4°C$; b.p. = 100.0 + 9.4 = +109.4°C

13.84 The compound with the larger *i* value is the stronger electrolyte.

$$i = \frac{\Delta T_f \text{ (measured)}}{\Delta T_f \text{ (calculated)}}$$ The idealized value is 3 for both salts.

$$Hg(NO_3)_2\text{:}\quad m = \frac{10.0 \text{ g } Hg(NO_3)_2}{1.00 \text{ kg } H_2O} \times \frac{1 \text{ mol } Hg(NO_3)_2}{324.6 \text{ g } Hg(NO_3)_2} = 0.0308\ m$$

ΔT_f (nonelectrolyte) = -1.86(0.0308) = -0.0573°C

$$i = \frac{-0.162°C}{-0.0573°C} = 2.83$$

$HgCl_2$: $m = \dfrac{10.0 \text{ g } HgCl_2}{1.00 \text{ kg } H_2O} \times \dfrac{1 \text{ mol } HgCl_2}{271.5 \text{ g } HgCl_2} = 0.0368\ m$

ΔT_f (nonelectrolyte) = -1.86(0.0368) = -0.0685°C

$i = \dfrac{-0.0685}{-0.0685} = 1.00$

With an i value of 2.83, $Hg(NO_3)_2$ is almost completely dissociated into ions; with an i value of 1.00, the $HgCl_2$ behaves essentially like a nonelectrolyte. Clearly, $Hg(NO_3)_2$ is the stronger electrolyte.

13.86 (a) Assume 1000 g of solution. 1000 g soln × $\dfrac{1 \text{ mL}}{1.22 \text{ g}}$ = 819.7 = 820 mL

1000 g soln × $\dfrac{40.0 \text{ g KSCN}}{100 \text{ g soln}}$ = 400 g KSCN; 1000 g soln - 400 g KSCN = 600 g H_2O

$\dfrac{400 \text{ g KSCN}}{97.19 \text{ g/mol}} = 4.116 = 4.12$ mol KSCN; $\dfrac{600 \text{ g } H_2O}{18.02 \text{ g/mol}} = 33.30 = 33.3$ mol H_2O

$\chi_{KSCN} = \dfrac{4.116}{4.116 + 33.30} = 0.110$; $m = \dfrac{4.116 \text{ mol KSCN}}{0.600 \text{ kg } H_2O} = 6.86\ m$

$M = \dfrac{4.116 \text{ mol KSCN}}{0.8197 \text{ L}} = 5.02\ M$

(b) If there are 4.12 mol of KSCN, there are 8.24 moles of ions. There are then 33.3 mol H_2O/8.24 mol ions ≈ 4 mol H_2O for each mol of ions, or 4 water molecules for each ion. This is too few water molecules to completely hydrate the anions and cations in the solution.

For a solution that is this concentrated, one would expect significant ion-pairing, because the ions are not completely surrounded and separated by H_2O molecules. Because of ion-pairing, the effective number of particles will be less than that indicated by m and M, so the observed colligative properties will be significantly different from those predicted by formulas for ideal solutions. The observed freezing point will be higher, the boiling point lower and the osmotic pressure lower than predicted.

13.87 $M = \dfrac{\pi}{RT} = \dfrac{6.41 \text{ atm}}{298 \text{ K}} \times \dfrac{\text{K} \cdot \text{mol}}{0.08206 \text{ L} \cdot \text{atm}} = 0.2621 = 0.262\ M$

There are 0.262 mol of **particles** per liter of solution and 0.131 mol particles in 500 mL. Each mole of sucrose provides 1 mol of particles and each mole of NaCl provides 2.

Let x = g $C_{12}H_{22}O_{11}$, 15.0 - x = g NaCl

$$\frac{x \text{ g } C_{12}H_{22}O_{11}}{342.3 \text{ g } C_{12}H_{22}O_{11}} + \frac{2(15.0 - x)}{58.44 \text{ g NaCl}} = 0.131$$

$58.44x + 2(342.3)(15.0 - x) = 0.131(58.44)(342.3)$

$58.44x - 684.6x + 10{,}269 = 2{,}621$

$-626.2x = -7648;\ x = 12.2\ g\ C_{12}H_{22}O_{11}$

$$\frac{12.2\ g\ C_{12}H_{22}O_{11}}{15.0\ g\ mixture} \times 100 = 81.3\%\ \text{sucrose},\ 18.7\%\ \text{NaCl}$$

13.88 $$M = \frac{\pi}{RT} = \frac{57.1\ torr}{298\ K} \times \frac{1\ atm}{760\ torr} \times \frac{K \bullet mol}{0.08206\ L \bullet atm} = 3.072 \times 10^{-3} = 3.07 \times 10^{-3}\ M$$

$$\frac{0.036\ g\ solute}{100\ g\ H_2O} \times \frac{1000\ g\ H_2O}{1\ kg\ H_2O} = 0.36\ g\ solute/kg\ H_2O$$

Assuming molarity and molality are the same in this dilute solution, we can then say 0.36 g solute = 3.072×10^{-3} mol; $\mathcal{M}$ = 117 g/mol. Because the salt is completely ionized, the formula weight of the lithium salt is **twice** this calculated value, or **234 g/mol**. The organic portion, $C_nH_{2n-1}O_2^-$, has a formula weight of 234-7 = 227 g. Subtracting 32 for the oxygens, and adding 1 to make the formula C_nH_{2n}, we have C_nH_{2n}, $\mathcal{M}$ = 196 g/mol. Since each CH_2 unit has a mass of 14, n = 196/14 = 14. Thus the formula for our salt is $LiC_{14}H_{27}O_2$.

Integrative Exercises

13.90 $$\frac{0.015\ g\ N_2}{1\ L\ blood} \times \frac{1\ mol\ N_2}{28.01\ g\ N_2} = 5.355 \times 10^{-4} = 5.4 \times 10^{-4}\ mol\ N_2/L\ blood$$

At 100 ft, the partial pressure of N_2 in air is 0.78 (4.0 atm) = 3.12 atm. This is just four times the partial pressure of N_2 at 1.0 atm air pressure. According to Henry's law, $S_g = kP_g$, a 4-fold increase in P_g results n a 4-fold increase in S_g, the solubility of the gas. Thus, the solubility of N_2 at 100 ft is $4(5.355 \times 10^{-4}\ M) = 2.142 \times 10^{-3} = 2.1 \times 10^{-3}\ M$. If the diver suddenly surfaces, the amount of N_2/L blood released is the difference in the solubilities at the two depths: $(2.142 \times 10^{-3}\ mol/L - 5.355 \times 10^{-4}\ mol/L) = 1.607 \times 10^{-3} = 1.6 \times 10^{-3}\ mol\ N_2/L$ blood.

At surface conditions of 1.0 atm external pressure and 37°C = 310 K,

$$V = \frac{nRT}{P} = 1.607 \times 10^{-3}\ mol \times \frac{310\ K}{1.0\ atm} \times \frac{0.08206\ L \bullet atm}{mol \bullet K} = 0.041\ L$$

That is, 41 mL of tiny N_2 bubbles are released from each L of blood.

13.91 The stronger the intermolecular forces, the higher the heat (enthalpy) of vaporization.

(a) None of the substances are capable of hydrogen bonding in the pure liquid, and they have similar molar masses. All intermolecular forces are van der Waals forces, dipole-dipole and dispersion forces. In decreasing order of strength of forces:

acetonitrile > acetone > acetaldehyde > ethylene oxide > cyclopropane > propane

The first four compounds have dipole-dipole and dispersion forces, the last two only dispersion forces.

(b) The order of solubility in hexane should be the reverse of the order above. The least polar substance, propane, will be most soluble in hexane. Ethanol, CH_3CH_2OH, is capable of hydrogen bonding with the four polar compounds. Thus, acetonitrile, acetaldehyde, acetone and ethylene oxide should be more soluble than propane and cyclopropane, but without further information we cannot distinguish among the polar molecules.

13.92 For ionic solids, the exothermic part of the solution process is step (3), surrounding the separated ions by solvent molecules. The released energy comes from the attractive interaction of the solvent with the separated ions. In the hydrates, one water molecule is already associated with the cation, reducing the total energy released during solvation.

13.94 (a) $Zn(s) + H_2SO_4(aq) \rightarrow ZnSO_4(aq) + H_2(g)$

$$2.050 \text{ g Zn} \times \frac{1 \text{ mol Zn}}{65.39 \text{ g Zn}} = 0.03135 \text{ mol Zn}$$

$$1.00\ M\ H_2SO_4 \times 0.0150 \text{ L} = 0.0150 \text{ mol } H_2SO_4$$

Since Zn and H_2SO_4 react in a 1:1 mole ratio, H_2SO_4 is the limiting reactant; 0.0150 mol of $H_2(g)$ are produced.

(b)
$$P = \frac{nRT}{V} = \frac{0.0150 \text{ mol}}{0.122 \text{ L}} \times \frac{0.08206 \text{ L} \cdot \text{atm}}{\text{mol} \cdot \text{K}} \times 298 \text{ K} = 3.0066 = 3.01 \text{ atm}$$

(c)
$$S_{H_2} = kP_{H_2} = \frac{7.8 \times 10^{-4} \text{ mol}}{\text{L} \cdot \text{atm}} \times 3.0066 \text{ atm} = 0.002345 = 2.3 \times 10^{-3}\ M$$

$$\frac{0.002345 \text{ mol } H_2}{\text{L soln}} \times 0.0150 \text{ L} = 3.518 \times 10^{-5} = 3.5 \times 10^{-5} \text{ mol dissolved } H_2$$

$$\frac{3.5 \times 10^{-5} \text{ mol dissolved } H_2}{0.0150 \text{ mol } H_2 \text{ produced}} \times 100 = 0.23\% \text{ dissolved } H_2$$

This is approximately 2.3 ppt; for every 10,000 H_2 molecules, 23 are dissolved. It was reasonable to ignore dissolved $H_2(g)$ in part (b).

13.95 (a)
$$\frac{1.3 \times 10^{-3} \text{ mol } CH_4}{\text{L soln}} \times 4.0 \text{ L} = 5.2 \times 10^{-3} \text{ mol } CH_4$$

$$V = \frac{nRT}{P} = \frac{5.2 \times 10^{-3} \text{ mol} \times 273 \text{ K}}{1.0 \text{ atm}} \times \frac{0.08206 \text{ L} \cdot \text{atm}}{\text{K} \cdot \text{mol}} = 0.12 \text{ L}$$

(b) All three hydrocarbons are nonpolar; they have zero net dipole moment. In CH_4 and C_2H_6, the C atoms are tetrahedral and all bonds are σ bonds. C_2H_6 has a higher molar mass than CH_4, which leads to stronger dispersion forces and greater water solubility. In C_2H_4, the C atoms are trigonal planar and the π electron cloud is symmetric above and below the plane that contains all the atoms. The π cloud in C_2H_4 is an area of concentrated electron density that experiences attractive forces with the positive ends of H_2O molecules. These forces increase the solubility of C_2H_4 relative to the other hydrocarbons.

(c) The molecules have similar molar masses. NO is most soluble because it is polar. The triple bond in N_2 is shorter than the double bond in O_2. It is more difficult for H_2O molecules to surround the smaller N_2 molecules, so they are less soluble than O_2 molecules.

(d) H_2S and SO_2 are polar molecules capable of hydrogen bonding with water. Hydrogen bonding is the strongest force between neutral molecules and causes the much greater solubility. H_2S is weakly acidic in water. SO_2 reacts with water to form H_2SO_3, a weak acid. The large solubility of SO_2 is a sure sign that a chemical process has occurred.

(e) N_2 and C_2H_4. N_2 is too small to be easily hydrated so C_2H_4 is more soluble in H_2O.

NO (31) and C_2H_6 (30). The structures of these two molecules are very different, yet they have similar solubilities. NO is slightly polar, but too small to be easily hydrated. The larger C_2H_6 is nonpolar, but more polarizable (stronger dispersion forces).

NO (31) and O_2 (32). The slightly polar NO is more soluble than the slightly larger (longer O=O bond than $N \equiv O$ bond) but nonpolar O_2.

13.97 (a) $$\Delta T_f = K_f m = K_f \times \frac{\text{mol } C_7H_6O_2}{\text{kg } C_6H_6} = K_f \times \frac{\text{g } C_7H_6O_2}{\text{kg } C_6H_6 \times \mathcal{M}\ C_7H_6O_2}$$

$$\mathcal{M} = \frac{K_f \times \text{g } C_7H_6O_2}{\Delta T_f \times \text{kg } C_6H_6} = \frac{5.12 \times 0.55}{0.360 \times 0.032} = 244.4 = 2.4 \times 10^2 \text{ g/mol}$$

(b) The formula weight of $C_7H_6O_2$ is 122 g/mol. The experimental molar mass is twice this value, indicating that benzoic acid is associated into dimers in benzene solution. This is reasonable, since the carboxyl group, -COOH, is capable of strong hydrogen bonding with itself. Many carboxylic acids exist as dimers in solution. The structure of benzoic acid dimer in benzene solution is:

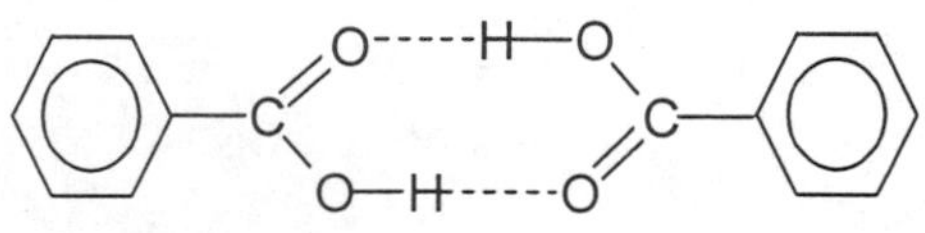

13.98 $\chi_{CHCl_3} = \chi_{C_3H_6O} = 0.500$

(a) For an ideal solution, Raoult's Law is obeyed.

$P_T = P_{CHCl_3} + P_{C_3H_6O}$; $P_{CHCl_3} = 0.5(300 \text{ torr}) = 150$ torr

$P_{C_3H_6O} = 0.5(360 \text{ torr}) = 180$ torr; $P_T = 150 \text{ torr} + 180 \text{ torr} = 330$ torr

(b) The real solution has a lower vapor pressure, 250 torr, than an ideal solution of the same composition, 330 torr. Thus, fewer molecules escape to the vapor phase from the liquid. This means that fewer molecules have sufficient kinetic energy to overcome intermolecular attractions. Clearly, even weak hydrogen bonds such as this one are stronger attractive forces than dipole-dipole or dispersion forces. These hydrogen bonds prevent molecules from escaping to the vapor phase and result in a lower than ideal vapor pressure for the solution. There is essentially no hydrogen bonding in the individual liquids.

(c) According to Coulomb's law, electrostatic attractive forces lead to an overall lowering of the energy of the system. Thus, when the two liquids mix and hydrogen bonds are formed, the energy of the system is decreased and $\Delta H_{soln} < 0$; the solution process is exothermic.

14 Chemical Kinetics

Reaction Rates

14.2 (a) M/s

(b) The hotter the oven, the faster the cake bakes. Milk sours faster in hot weather than cool weather.

(c) The *average rate* is the rate over a period of time, while the *instantaneous rate* is the rate at a particular time.

14.4

Time(s)	Mol A	(a) Mol B	Δ Mol A	(b) Rate (Δ mol A/s)
0	0.100	0.000		
40	0.067	0.033	0.033	8.3×10^{-4}
80	0.045	0.055	-0.022	5.5×10^{-4}
120	0.030	0.070	-0.015	3.8×10^{-4}
160	0.020	0.080	-0.010	2.5×10^{-4}

(c) The volume of the container must be known to report the rate in units of concentration (mol/L) per time.

14.6

Time (min)	Time Interval (min)	Concentration (M)	Δ M	Rate (M/s)
0.0		1.85		
54.0	54.0	1.58	-0.27	8.3×10^{-5}
107.0	53.0	1.36	-0.22	6.9×10^{-5}
215.0	108	1.02	-0.34	5.3×10^{-5}
430.0	215	0.580	-0.44	3.4×10^{-5}

14.8 From the slopes of the lines in the figure at right, the rates are: at t = 75.0 min, -4.2×10^{-3} *M*/min or -7.0×10^{-5} *M*/s; at 250 min, -2.1×10^{-3} *M*/min or -3.5×10^{-5} M/s.

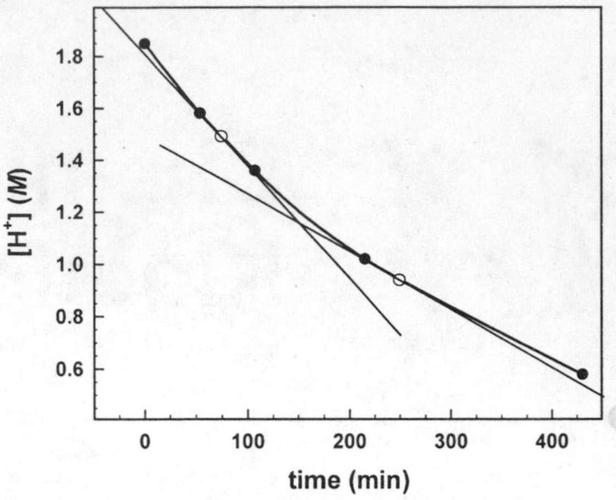

14.10 (a) rate = $-\Delta[HBr]/2\Delta t = \Delta[H_2]/\Delta t = \Delta[Br_2]/\Delta t$

(b) rate = $-\Delta[SO_2]/2\Delta t = -\Delta[O_2]/\Delta t = \Delta[SO_3]/2\Delta t$

(c) rate = $-\Delta[NO]/2\Delta t = -\Delta[H_2]/2\Delta t = \Delta[N_2]/\Delta t = \Delta[H_2O]/2\Delta t$

14.12 (a) $-\Delta[C_2H_4]/\Delta t = \Delta[CO_2]/2\Delta t = \Delta[H_2O]/2\Delta t$

$-2\Delta[C_2H_4]/\Delta t = \Delta[CO_2]/\Delta t = \Delta[H_2O]/\Delta t$

C_2H_4 is burning, $-\Delta[C_2H_4]/\Delta t = 0.23$ *M*/s

CO_2 and H_2O are produced, at twice the rate that C_2H_4 is consumed.

$\Delta[CO_2]/\Delta t = \Delta[H_2O]/\Delta t = 2(0.23)$ *M*/s = 0.46 *M*/s

(b) In this reaction, pressure is a measure of concentration.

$-\Delta[N_2H_4]/\Delta t = -\Delta[H_2]/\Delta t = \Delta[NH_3]/2\Delta t$

N_2H_4 is consumed, $-\Delta[N_2H_4]/\Delta t = 45$ torr/hr

H_2 is consumed, $-\Delta[H_2]/\Delta t = 45$ torr/hr

NH_3 is produced at twice the rate that N_2H_4 and H_2 are consumed,

$\Delta[NH_3]/\Delta t = -2\Delta[N_2H_4]/\Delta t = 2(45)$ torr/hr = 90 torr/hr

$\Delta P_T/\Delta t$ = (+90 torr/hr - 45 torr/hr - 45 torr/hr) = 0 torr/hr

Rate Laws

14.14 (a) If [A] is doubled, there will be no change in the rate or the rate constant. The overall rate is unchanged because [A] does not appear in the rate law; the rate constant changes only with a change in temperature.

(b) The reaction is zero order in A, second order in B and second order overall.

(c) Units of k = $\frac{M/s}{M^2} = M^{-1}\ s^{-1}$

14.16 (a) rate = $k[H_2][NO]^2$

(b) rate = $(6.0 \times 10^4\ M^{-2}\,s^{-1})(0.050\ M)^2(0.010\ M) = 1.5\ M/s$

(c) rate = $(6.0 \times 10^4\ M^{-2}\,s^{-1})(0.10\ M)^2(0.010\ M) = 6.0\ M/s$

(Note that doubling [NO] causes a quadrupling in rate.)

14.18 (a, b) rate = $k[C_2H_5Br][OH^-]$; $k = \dfrac{\text{rate}}{[C_2H_5Br][OH^-]}$

at 298 K, $k = \dfrac{1.7 \times 10^{-7}\ M/s}{[0.0477\ M][0.100\ M]} = 3.6 \times 10^{-5}\ M^{-1}\,s^{-1}$

(c) Adding an equal volume of ethyl alcohol reduces both $[C_2H_5Br]$ and $[OH^-]$ by a factor of two. new rate = (1/2)(1/2) = 1/4 of old rate

14.20 (a) Experiments 1 and 2 show the effect of a change in [A] on the rate while holding [B] constant. Experiment 3 must show the effect of changing [B] while holding [A] constant. The only restrictions on Experiment 3 are that [B] cannot be 1.0 *M* and [A] must be either 1.0 *M* or 2.0 *M*. Two (of the many) possibilities are [A] = 1.0 M, [B] = 2.0 *M* or [A] = 2.0 *M*, [B] = 2.0 *M*.

(b) Based on the observations, the rate law is: rate = $k[A][C]^2$. If all concentrations are half of their original values, rate = $k(1/2)(1/2)^2 = k(1/8)$; the rate is 1/8 of the original rate.

14.22 (a) From the data given, when $[ClO_2]$ increases by a factor of 3 (Expt. 2 to Expt. 1), the rate increases by a factor of 9. When $[OH^-]$ increases by a factor of 3 (Expt. 2 to Expt. 3), the rate increases by a factor of 3. The reaction in second order is $[ClO_2]$ and first order is $[OH^-]$. rate = $k[ClO_2]^2[OH^-]$.

(b) Using data from Expt 2:

$$k = \frac{\text{rate}}{[ClO_2]^2[OH^-]} = \frac{0.00276\ M/s}{(0.020\ M)^2(0.030\ M)} = 2.3 \times 10^2\ M^{-2}\,s^{-1}$$

(c) rate = $2.3 \times 10^2\ M^{-2}\,s^{-1}\ (0.010\ M)^2(0.015\ M) = 3.45 \times 10^{-4} = 3.5 \times 10^{-4}\ M/s$

14.24 (a) Doubling $[NH_3]$ while holding $[BF_3]$ constant doubles the rate (experiments 1 and 2). Doubling $[BF_3]$ while holding $[NH_3]$ constant doubles the rate (experiments 4 and 5). Thus, the reaction is first order in both BF_3 and NH_3; rate = $k[BF_3][NH_3]$.

(b) The reaction is second order overall.

(c) From experiment 1: $k = \dfrac{0.2130\ M/s}{(0.250\ M)(0.250\ M)} = 3.41\ M^{-1}\,s^{-1}$

(Any of the five sets of initial concentrations and rates could be used to calculate the rate constant k. The average of these 5 values is $k_{avg} = 3.41\ M^{-1}\,s^{-1}$)

14.26 (a) Increasing $[S_2O_8^{2-}]$ by a factor of 1.5 while holding $[I^-]$ constant increases the rate by a factor of 1.5 (Experiments 1 and 2). Doubling $[S_2O_8^{2-}]$ and increasing $[I^-]$ by a factor of 1.5 triples the rate (2 × 1.5 = 3, experiments 1 and 3). Thus the reaction is first order in both $[S_2O_8^{2-}]$ and $[I^-]$; rate = k $[S_2O_8^{2-}][I^-]$.

(b) $k = \text{rate}/[S_2O_8^{2-}][I^-]$

$k_1 = 2.6 \times 10^{-6}\ M/s\ /\ (0.018\ M)(0.036\ M) = 4.01 \times 10^{-3} = 4.0 \times 10^{-3}\ M^{-1}\ s^{-1}$

$k_2 = 3.9 \times 10^{-6}/(0.027)(0.036) = 4.01 \times 10^{-3} = 4.01 \times 10^{-3} = 4.0 \times 10^{-3}\ M^{-1}\ s^{-1}$

$k_3 = 7.8 \times 10^{-6}/(0.036)(0.054) = 4.01 \times 10^{-3} = 4.01 \times 10^{-3} = 4.0 \times 10^{-3}\ M^{-1}\ s^{-1}$

$k_4 = 1.4 \times 10^{-5}/(0.050)(0.072) = 3.89 \times 10^{-3} = 3.9 \times 10^{-3}\ M^{-1}\ s^{-1}$

$k_{avg} = 3.98 \times 10^{-3} = 4.0 \times 10^{-3}\ M^{-1}\ s^{-1}$

(c) $-\Delta[S_2O_8^{2-}]/\Delta t = -\Delta[I^-]/3\Delta t$; the rate of disappearance of $S_2O_8^{2-}$ is one-third the rate of disappearance of I^-.

(d) Note that the data is given in terms of disappearance of $S_2O_8^{2-}$.

$$\frac{-\Delta[I^-]}{\Delta t} = \frac{-3\Delta[S_2O_8^{2-}]}{\Delta t} = 3(3.98 \times 10^{-3}\ M^{-1}\ s^{-1})(0.015\ M)(0.040\ M) = 7.2 \times 10^{-6}\ M/s$$

Change of Concentration with Time

14.28 (a) A graph of 1/[A] vs time yields a straight line for a second-order reaction.

(b) The half-life of a first-order reaction is independent of $[A]_0$, $t_{1/2} = 0.693/k$. Whereas, the half-life of a second-order reaction does depend on $[A]_0$, $t_{1/2} = 1/k[A]_0$.

14.30 (a) $t_{1/2} = 0.693/k = 0.693/7.0 \times 10^{-4}\ s^{-1} = 990 = 9.9 \times 10^2\ s$

(b) $$k = \frac{0.693}{t_{1/2}} = \frac{0.693}{56.3\ \text{min}} \times \frac{1\ \text{min}}{60\ \text{s}} = 2.052 \times 10^{-4} = 2.05 \times 10^{-4}\ s^{-1}$$

14.32 (a) Using Equation 14.13 for a first order reaction: $\ln[A]_t = -kt + \ln[A]_0$

2.5 min = 150 s; $[N_2O_5]_0 = (0.0250\ \text{mol}/2.0\ \text{L}) = 0.0125 = 0.013\ M$

$\ln[N_2O_5]_{150} = -(6.82 \times 10^{-3}\ s^{-1})(150\ s) + \ln(0.0125)$

$\ln[N_2O_5]_{150} = -1.0230 + (-4.3820) = -5.4050 = -5.41$

$[N_2O_5]_{150} = 4.494 \times 10^{-3} = 4.5 \times 10^{-3}\ M$; mol $N_2O_5 = 4.494 \times 10^{-3}\ M \times 2.0\ \text{L}$

$= 9.0 \times 10^{-3}$ mol

(b) $[N_2O_5]_t = 0.010\ \text{mol}/2.0\ \text{L} = 0.0050\ M$; $[N_2O_5]_0 = 0.0125\ M$

$\ln(0.0050) = -(6.82 \times 10^{-3}\ s^{-1})(t) + \ln(0.0125)$

$$t = \frac{-[\ln(0.0050) - \ln(0.0125)]}{(6.82 \times 10^{-3}\ s^{-1})} = 134.35 = 1.3 \times 10^2\ s \times \frac{1\ \text{min}}{60\ \text{s}} = 2.24 = 2.2\ \text{min}$$

(c) $t_{1/2} = 0.693/k = 0.693/6.82 \times 10^{-3}\ s^{-1} = 101.6 = 102$ s or 1.69 min

14.34

t(s)	P_{CH_3NC}	$\ln P_{CH_3NC}$
0	502	6.219
2000	335	5.814
5000	180	5.193
8000	95.5	4.559
12000	41.7	3.731
15000	22.4	3.109

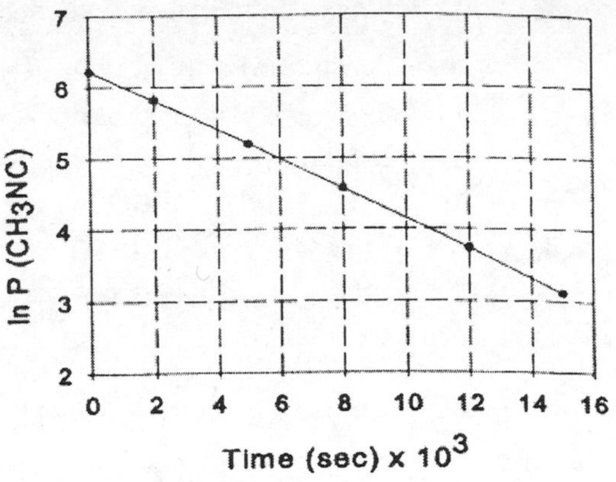

A graph of ln P vs t is linear with a slope of -2.08×10^{-4} s^{-1}. The rate constant k = -slope = 2.08×10^{-4} s^{-1}. Half-life = $t_{1/2} = 0.693/k = 3.33 \times 10^3$ s.

14.36 (a) Make both first- and second-order plots to see which is linear. Moles is a satisfactory concentration unit, since volume is constant.

time(s)	mol A	ln (mol A)	1/mol A
0	0.1000	-2.303	10.00
40	0.067	-2.70	14.9
80	0.045	-3.10	22.2
120	0.030	-3.51	33.3
160	0.020	-3.91	50.0

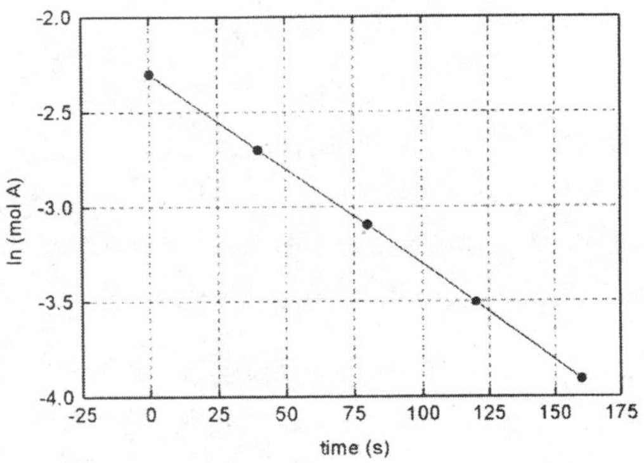

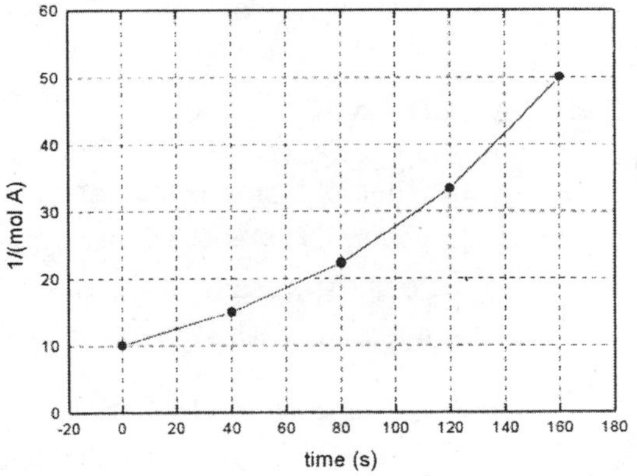

The plot of ln (mol A) vs time is linear, so the reaction is first-order in A.

(b) $k = -\text{slope} = -[-3.91 - (-2.70)]/120 = 0.010083 = 0.0101$ s^{-1}
(The best fit to this line yields the same value for the slope, 0.01006 = 0.0101 s^{-1})

(c) $t_{1/2} = 0.693/k = 0.693/0.010083$ s^{-1} = 68.7 s

14.38 (a) Make both first- and second-order plots to see which is linear.

time(min)	$[C_{12}H_{22}O_{11}]$ (*M*)	$\ln[C_{12}H_{22}O_{11}]$	$1/[C_{12}H_{22}O_{11}]$
0	0.316	-1.152	3.16
39	0.274	-1.295	3.65
80	0.238	-1.435	4.20
140	0.190	-1.661	5.26
210	0.146	-1.924	6.85

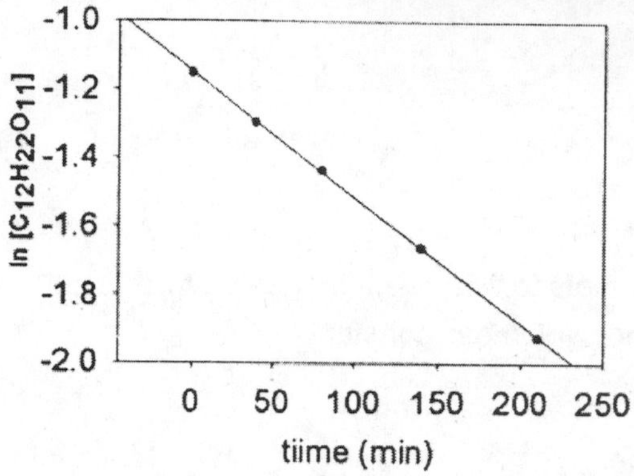

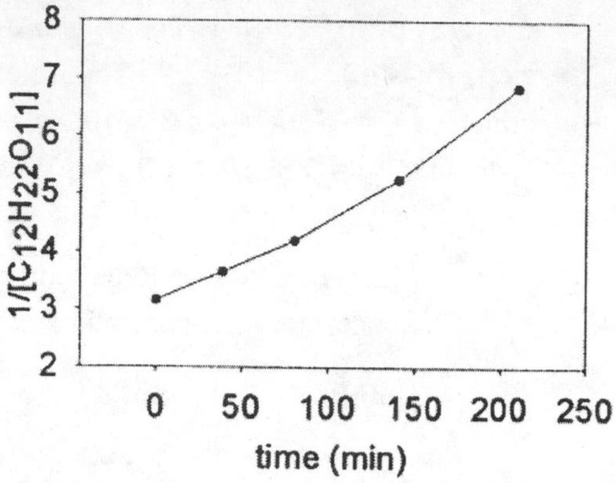

The plot of ln $[C_{12}H_{22}O_{11}]$ in linear, so the reaction is first order in $C_{12}H_{22}O_{11}$.

(b) $k = -\text{slope} = -[-1.924 - (-1.295)] / 171 \text{ min} = 3.68 \times 10^{-3} \text{ min}^{-1}$

(The slope of the best-fit line is $-3.67 \times 10^{-3} \text{ min}^{-1}$.)

Temperature and Rate

14.40 (a) In order for isomerization of methyl isonitrile to acetonitrile ($CH_3N\equiv C \rightarrow CH_3C\equiv N$) to occur, $CH_3N\equiv C$ molecules must collide with each other. The more $CH_3N\equiv C$ molecules present, the more collisions and the faster the rate. The higher the temperature of the sample, the more collisions and the faster the rate.

(b) No. Not only must collisions of A and B be sufficiently energetic, A and B must collide in the correct orientation for the activated complex to form.

(c) The kinetic molecular theory tells us that at some temperature T, there will be a distribution of molecular speeds and kinetic energies, and that the average kinetic energy of the sample is proportional to temperature. That is, as temperature of the sample increases, the average speed and kinetic energy of the molecules increases. At higher temperatures, there will be more molecular collisions (owing to greater speeds) and more energetic collisions (owing to greater kinetic energies). Overall there will be more collisions that have sufficient energy to form an activated complex, and the reaction rate will be greater.

14.42 (a) $f = e^{-E_a/RT}$ E_a = 160 kJ/mol = 1.60 × 10^5 J/mol, T = 500 K

$$-E_a/RT = -\frac{1.60 \times 10^5 \text{ J/mol}}{500 \text{ K}} \times \frac{\text{mol} \bullet \text{K}}{8.314 \text{ J}} = -38.489 = -38.5$$

$$f = e^{-38.489} = 1.924 \times 10^{-17} = 1.92 \times 10^{-17}$$

(b)

$$-E_a/RT = -\frac{1.60 \times 10^5 \text{ J/mol}}{510 \text{ K}} \times \frac{\text{mol} \bullet \text{K}}{8.314 \text{ J}} = -37.735 = -37.7$$

$$f = e^{-37.735} = 4.093 \times 10^{-17} = 4.09 \times 10^{-17}$$

$$\frac{f \text{ at } 510 \text{ K}}{f \text{ at } 500 \text{ K}} = \frac{4.09 \times 10^{-17}}{1.92 \times 10^{-17}} = 2.13$$

An increase of 10 K means that 2.13 times more molecules have this energy.

14.44 (a)

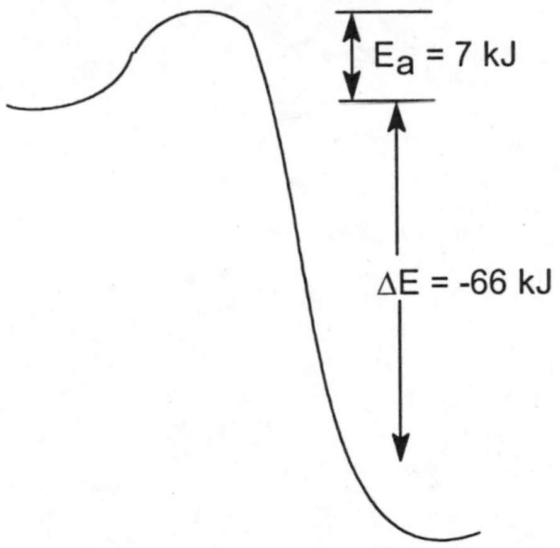

(b) E_a(reverse) = 73 kJ

14.46 E_a for the reverse reactions is:

(a) 45 - (-25) = 70 kJ (b) 35 - (-10) = 45 kJ (c) 55 - 10 = 45 kJ

Based on the magnitude of E_a, the reverse of reactions (b) and (c) occur at the same rate, which is faster than the reverse of reaction (a).

14.48 T_1 = 30°C + 273 = 303 K; T_2 = 60°C + 273 = 333 K

For reaction A, E_a = 45.5 kJ/mol = 4.55 × 10^4 J/mol

$$\ln\left(\frac{k_{30}}{k_{60}}\right) = \frac{E_a}{R}\left[\frac{1}{T_2} - \frac{1}{T_1}\right] = \frac{4.55 \times 10^4 \text{ J/mol}}{8.314 \text{ J/mol}}\left(\frac{1}{333} - \frac{1}{303}\right) = -1.6272 = -1.63$$

$$\left(\frac{k_{A30}}{k_{A60}}\right) = e^{-1.6272} = 0.1965;\ k_{A30} = 0.1965\ k_{A60}$$

For reaction B, E_a = 25.2 kJ/mol = 2.52×10^4 J/mol

$$\ln\left(\frac{k_{30}}{k_{60}}\right) = \frac{2.52 \times 10^4 \text{ J/mol}}{8.314 \text{ J/mol}}\left(\frac{1}{333} - \frac{1}{303}\right) = -0.9012 = -0.901$$

$$\left(\frac{k_{B30}}{k_{B60}}\right) = e^{-0.9012} = 0.4061;\ k_{B30} = 0.4061\ k_{B60}$$

$k_{A30} = k_{B30}$; $0.1965\ k_{A60} = 0.4061\ k_{B60}$

$k_{A60} / k_{B60} = 0.4061 / 0.1965 = 2.067 = 2.07$

For reaction B, E_a = 25.2 kJ/mol = 2.52×10^4 J/mol

$$\ln\left(\frac{k_{30}}{k_{60}}\right) = \frac{2.52 \times 10^4 \text{ J/mol}}{8.314 \text{ J/mol}}\left(\frac{1}{333} - \frac{1}{303}\right) = -0.9012 = -0.901$$

$$\left(\frac{k_{B30}}{k_{B60}}\right) = e^{-0.9012} = 0.4061;\ k_{B30} = 0.4061\ k_{B60}$$

$k_{A30} = k_{B30}$; $0.1965\ k_{A60} = 0.4061\ k_{B60}$

$k_{A60} / k_{B60} = 0.4061 / 0.1965 = 2.067 = 2.07$

14.50

k	ln k	T(K)	1/T(× 10^3)
0.028	-3.58	600	1.67
0.22	-1.51	650	1.54
1.3	0.26	700	1.43
6.0	1.79	750	1.33
23	3.14	800	1.25

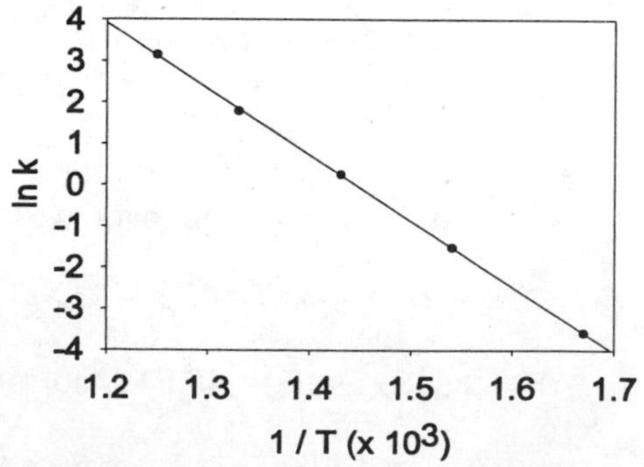

Using the relationship $\ln k = \ln A - E_a/RT$, the slope, $-15.94 \times 10^3 = -16 \times 10^3$, is $-E_a/R$.
$E_a = 15.94 \times 10^3 \times 8.314$ J/mol = 1.3×10^2 kJ/mol.
To calculate A, we will use the rate data at 700 K.
From the equation given above, 0.262 =
$\ln A - 15.94 \times 10^3/700$; $\ln A = 0.262 + 22.771$.
$A = 1.0 \times 10^{10}$.

14.52 (a) $T_1 = 77°F$; $°C = 5/9\,(°F - 32) = 5/9\,(77 - 32) = 25°C = 298\ K$

$T_2 = 59°F$; $°C = 5/9\,(59-32) = 15°C = 288\ K$; $k_1/k_2 = 6$

$$\ln\left(\frac{k_1}{k_2}\right) = \frac{E_a}{R}\left[\frac{1}{T_2} - \frac{1}{T_1}\right];\ \ln(6) = \frac{E_a}{8.314\ J/mol}\left[\frac{1}{288} - \frac{1}{298}\right]$$

$$E_a = \frac{\ln(6)(8.314\ J/mol)}{1.165 \times 10^{-4}} = 1.28 \times 10^5\ J = 1.3 \times 10^2\ kJ/mol$$

$T_1 = 77°F = 25°C = 298\ K$; $T_2 = 41°F = 5°C = 278\ K$, $k_1/k_2 = 40$

$$\ln(40) = \frac{E_a}{8.314\ J/mol}\left[\frac{1}{278} - \frac{1}{298}\right];\ E_a = \frac{\ln(40)(8.314\ J/mol)}{2.414 \times 10^{-4}}$$

$E_a = 1.27 \times 10^5\ J = 1.3 \times 10^2\ kJ/mol$

The values are amazingly consistent, considering the precision of the data.

(b) For a first order reaction, $t_{1/2} = 0.693/k$, $k = 0.693/t_{1/2}$

k_1 at 298 K = 0.693/2.7 yr = 0.257 = 0.26 yr^{-1}

$T_1 = 298\ K$, $T_2 = 273 - 15°C = 258\ K$

$$\ln\left(\frac{0.257}{k_2}\right) = \frac{1.27 \times 10^5\ J}{8.314\ J/mol}\left[\frac{1}{258} - \frac{1}{298}\right] = 7.9497$$

$0.257/k_2 = e^{7.9497} = 2.835 \times 10^3$; $k_2 = 0.257/2.835 \times 10^3 = 9.066 \times 10^{-5} = 9.1 \times 10^{-5}\ yr^{-1}$

$t_{1/2} = 0.693/k = 0.693/9.066 \times 10^{-5} = 7.64 \times 10^3\ yr = 7.6 \times 10^3\ yr$

Reaction Mechanisms

14.54 (a) The *molecularity* of a process indicates the number of molecules that participate as reactants in the process. A unimolecular process has one reactant molecule, a bimolecular process has two reactant molecules and a termolecular process has three reactant molecules.

(b) Termolecular processes are rare because it is highly unlikely that three molecules will simultaneously collide with the correct energy and orientation to form an activated complex.

(c) An *intermediate* is a substance that is produced and then consumed during a chemical reaction. It does not appear in the balanced equation for the overall reaction.

14.56 (a) bimolecular, rate = $k[NO]^2$

(b) unimolecular, rate = $k[C_3H_6]$

(c) unimolecular, rate = $k[SO_3]$

14.58 Two intermediates, three transition states, the C → D step is fastest, the overall reaction is endothermic.

14.60 (a)

$$NO(g) + NO(g) \rightarrow N_2O_2(g)$$
$$N_2O_2(g) + H_2(g) \rightarrow N_2O(g) + H_2O(g)$$
$$\overline{2NO(g) + N_2O_2(g) + H_2(g) \rightarrow N_2O_2(g) + N_2O(g) + H_2O(g)}$$
$$2NO(g) + H_2(g) \rightarrow N_2O(g) + H_2O(g)$$

(b) First step: $-\Delta[NO]/\Delta t = k[NO]\,[NO] = k[NO]^2$

Second step: $-\Delta[H_2]/\Delta t = k[H_2][N_2O_2]$

(c) N_2O_2 is the intermediate; it is produced in the first step and consumed in the second.

(d) Since $[H_2]$ appears in the rate law, the second step must be slow relative to the first.

14.62 (a)

i. $HBr + O_2 \rightarrow HOOBr$

ii. $HOOBr + HBr \rightarrow 2HOBr$

iii. $2HOBr + 2HBr \rightarrow 2H_2O + 2Br_2$

$$4HBr + O_2 \rightarrow 2H_2O + 2Br_2$$

(b) The observed rate law is: rate = $k[HBr][O_2]$, the rate law for the first elementary step. The first step must be rate-determining.

(c) HOOBr and HOBr are both intermediates; HOOBr is produced in i and consumed in ii and HOBr is produced in ii and consumed in iii.

(d) Since the first step is rate-determining, it is possible that neither of the intermediates accumulates enough to be detected. This does not disprove the mechanism, but indicates that steps ii and iii are very fast, relative to step i.

Catalysis

14.64 (a) The smaller the particle size of a solid catalyst, the greater the surface area. The greater the surface area, the more active sites and the greater the increase in reaction rate.

(b) *Adsorption* is the binding of reactants onto the surface of the heterogeneous catalyst. It is usually the first step in the catalyzed reaction.

14.66 (a)

$$2[NO(g) + N_2O(g) \rightarrow N_2(g) + NO_2(g)]$$
$$2NO_2(g) \rightarrow 2NO(g) + O_2(g)$$
$$\overline{2N_2O(g) \rightarrow 2N_2(g) + O_2(g)}$$

(b) An intermediate is produced and then consumed during the course of the reaction. A catalyst is consumed and then reproduced. In other words, the catalyst is present when the reaction sequence begins and after the last step is completed. In this reaction, NO is the catalyst and NO_2 is an intermediate.

(c) No. The proposed mechanism cannot be ruled out, based on the behavior of NO_2. NO_2 functions as an intermediate; it is produced and then consumed during the reaction. That there is no measurable build-up of NO_2 indicates the first step is slow relative to the second; as soon as NO_2 is produced by the slow first step, it is consumed by the faster second step.

14.68 (a) Catalytic converters are heterogeneous catalysts that adsorb gaseous CO and hydrocarbons and speed up their oxidation to $CO_2(g)$ and $H_2O(g)$. They also adsorb nitrogen oxides, NO_x, and speed up their reduction to $N_2(g)$ and $O_2(g)$. If a catalytic converter is working effectively, the exhaust gas should have very small amounts of the undesirable gases CO, $(NO)_x$ and hydrocarbons.

(b) The high temperatures could increase the rate of the desired catalytic reactions given in part (a). It could also increase the rate of undesirable reactions such as corrosion, which decrease the lifetime of the catalytic converter.

(c) The rate flow of exhaust gases over the converter will determine the rate of adsorption of CO, $(NO)_x$ and hydrocarbons onto the catalyst and thus the rate of conversion to desired products. Too fast an exhaust flow leads to less than maximum adsorption. A very slow flow leads to back pressure and potential damage to the exhaust system. Clearly the flow rate must be adjusted to balance chemical and mechanical efficiency of the catalytic converter.

14.70 Just as the π electrons in C_2H_4 are attracted to the surface of a hydrogenation catalyst, the nonbonding electron density on S causes compounds of S to be attracted to these same surfaces. Strong interactions could cause the sulfur compounds to be permanently attached to the surface, blocking active sites and reducing adsorption of alkenes for hydrogenation.

14.72 The individual structure of each enzyme molecule leads to a unique coiling and folding pattern. The resulting shape and electronic properties of the active site in each enzyme leads to its substrate specificity.

14.74 Let k and E_a equal the rate constant and activation energy for the uncatalyzed reaction. Let k_c and E_{ac} equal the rate constant and activation energy of the catalyzed reaction. A is the same for the uncatalyzed and catalyzed reactions. $k_c / k = 1 \times 10^5$, T = 37°C = 310 K.

According to Equation [14.20], ln k = E_a/RT + ln A. Subtracting ln k from ln k_c

$$\ln k_c - \ln k = \left[\frac{-E_{ac}}{RT}\right] + \ln A - \left[\frac{-E_a}{RT}\right] - \ln A$$

$$\ln (k_c/k) = \frac{E_a - E_{ac}}{RT}; \quad E_a - E_{ac} = RT \ln (k_c / k)$$

$$E_a - E_{ac} = \frac{8.314\ J}{K \cdot mol} \times 310\ K \times \ln(1 \times 10^5) = 2.966 \times 10^4\ J = 29.7\ kJ$$

The enzyme must lower the activation energy by 29.7 kJ in order to achieve a 1×10^5 -fold increase in reaction rate.

Additional Exercises

14.76 (a) rate $= \frac{-\Delta[NO]}{2\Delta t} = \frac{-\Delta[O_2]}{\Delta t} = \frac{9.3 \times 10^{-5}\ M/s}{2} = 4.7 \times 10^{-5}\ M/s$

(b,c) rate $= k[NO]^2[O_2]$; $k = rate/[NO]^2[O_2]$

$$k = \frac{9.3 \times 10^{-5}\ M/s}{(0.040\ M)^2(0.035\ M)} = 1.7\ M^{-2}\ s^{-1}$$

(d) Since the reaction is second order in NO, if the [NO] is increased by a factor of 1.8, the rate would increase by a factor of 1.8^2, or (3.24) = 3.2.

14.77 (a) rate $= k[I^-][OCl^-]/[OH^-]$

(b) Since the reaction is first order in $[I^-]$, tripling $[I^-]$ triples the rate.

(c) Since the rate is inversely proportional to $[OH^-]$, doubling $[OH^-]$ cuts the rate in half.

14.79 The units of rate are *M*/s. The reaction must be second order overall if the units of the rate constant are $M^{-1}\ s^{-1}$. If rate $= k[NO_2]^x$, then the cumulative units of $[NO_2]^x$ must be M^2, and x = 2.

If $[NO_2]_o = 0.100\ M$ and $[NO_2]_t = 0.025\ M$, use the integrated form of the second order rate equation, $\frac{1}{[A]_t} = kt + \frac{1}{[A]_o}$, Equation 14.14, to solve for t.

$$\frac{1}{0.025\ M} = 0.63\ M^{-1}\ s^{-1}\ (t) + \frac{1}{0.100\ M}; \quad \frac{(40 - 10)\ M^{-1}}{0.63\ M^{-1}\ s^{-1}} = t = 47.62 = 48\ s.$$

14.81 (a) A = abc, Equation 14.5. A = 0.605, a = $5.60 \times 10^3\ cm^{-1}\ M^{-1}$, b = 1.00 cm

$$c = \frac{A}{a\,b} = \frac{0.605}{(5.60 \times 10^3\ cm^{-1}\ M^{-1})(1.00\ cm)} = 1.080 \times 10^{-4} = 1.08 \times 10^{-4}\ M$$

(b) Calculate $[c]_t$ using Beer's law. We calculated $[c]_o$ in part (a). Use Equation [14.13] to calculate k.

$$A_{30} = abc_{30};\ c_{30} = \frac{A_{30}}{ab} = \frac{0.250}{(5.60 \times 10^3\ cm^{-1}\ M^{-1})(1.00\ cm)} = 4.464 \times 10^{-5}\ M$$

$$\ln[c]_t = -kt + \ln[c]_o; \quad \frac{\ln[c]_o - \ln[c]_t}{t} = k;\ t = 30\ min \times \frac{60\ s}{min} = 1800\ s$$

$$k = \ln(1.080 \times 10^{-4}) - \ln(4.464 \times 10^{-5})\,/\,1800\ s = 4.910 \times 10^{-4} = 4.91 \times 10^{-4}\ s^{-1}$$

(c) For a first order reaction, $t_{1/2} = 0.693/k$.

$t_{1/2} = 0.693/4.910 \times 10^{-4}\ s^{-1} = 1.411 \times 10^3 = 1.41 \times 10^3\ s = 23.5\ min$

(d) $A_t = 0.100$; calculate c_t using Beer's law, then t from the first order integrated rate equation.

$$c_t = \frac{A}{a\,b} = \frac{0.100}{(5.60 \times 10^3\ cm^{-1}\ M^{-1})(1.00\ cm)} = 1.786 \times 10^{-5} = 1.79 \times 10^{-5}\ M$$

$$t = \frac{\ln[c]_0 - \ln[c]_t}{k} = \frac{\ln(1.080 \times 10^{-4}) - \ln(1.786 \times 10^{-5)}}{4.910 \times 10^{-4}\ s^{-1}}$$

$t = 3.666 \times 10^3 = 3.67 \times 10^3\ s = 61.1\ min$

14.82

Time (s)	$[C_5H_6]$ (*M*)	$\ln[C_5H_6]$	$1/[C_5H_6]$
0	0.0400	-3.219	25.0
50	0.0300	-3.507	33.3
100	0.0240	-3.730	41.7
150	0.0200	-3.912	50.0
200	0.0174	-4.051	57.5

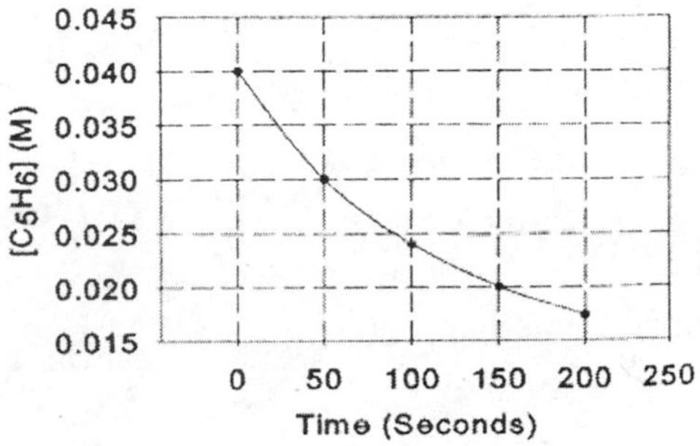

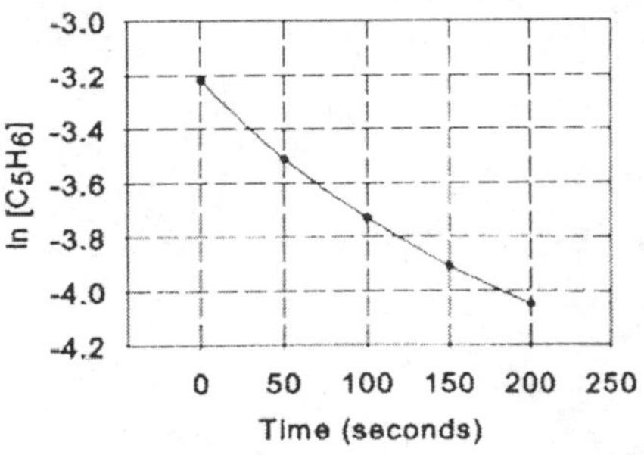

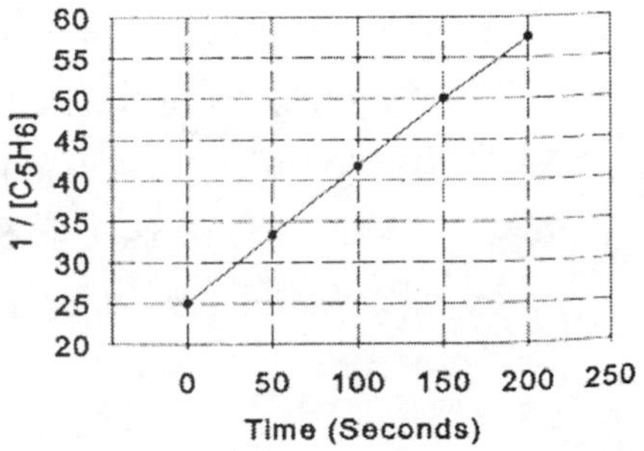

The plot of $1/[C_5H_6]$ vs time is linear and the reaction is second order.

The slope of this line is k. k = slope = $(50.0 - 25.0)\ M^{-1} / (150-0)s = 0.167\ M^{-1}\ s^{-1}$

(The best-fit slope and k value is $0.163\ M^{-1}\ s^{-1}$.)

14.83 (a) No. The value of A, which is related to frequency and effectiveness of collisions, can be different for each reaction and k is proportional to A.

(b) From Equation 14.21, reactions with different variations of k with respect to temperature have different activation energies, E_a. The fact that k for the two reactions is the same at a certain temperature is coincidental. The reaction with the higher rate at 35°C has the larger activation energy, because it was able to use the increase in energy more effectively.

14.85 (a) rate = $k[H_2O_2][I^-]$

(b) $2H_2O_2(aq) \rightarrow 2H_2O(l) + O_2(g)$

(c) $IO^-(aq)$ is the intermediate.

14.86 (a)

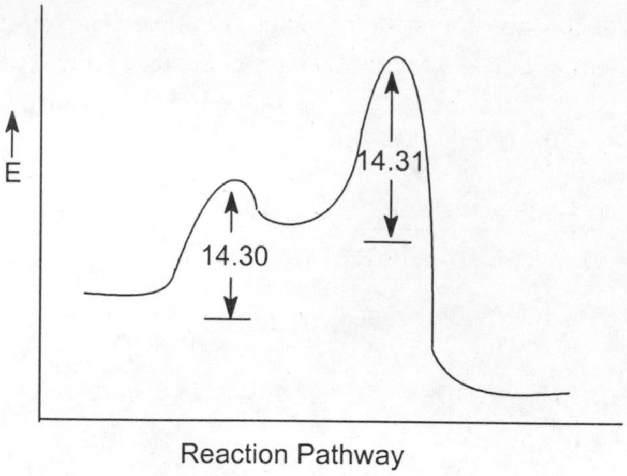

14.30 = E_a for reaction [14.30]

14.31 = E_a for reaction [14.31]

(b) The fact that Br_2 builds up during the reaction tells us that the appearance of Br_2 (reaction [14.30]) is faster than the disappearance of Br_2 (reaction [14.31]). This is the reason that E_a of [14.31] in the energy profile above is larger than E_a of [14.30].

14.88 (a) $(CH_3)_3AuPH_3 \rightarrow C_2H_6 + (CH_3)AuPH_3$

(b) $(CH_3)_3Au$, $(CH_3)Au$ and PH_3 are intermediates.

(c) Step 1 is unimolecular, Step 2 is unimolecular, Step 3 is bimolecular.

(d) Step 2, the slow step, is rate determining.

(e) If Step 2 is rate determining, rate = $k_2[(CH_3)_3Au]$.

$(CH_3)_3Au$ is an intermediate formed in Step 1, an equilibrium. By definition, the rates of the forward and reverse processes in Step 1 are equal:

$k_1[(CH_3)_3\,AuPH_3] = k_{-1}\,[(CH_3)_3Au][PH_3]$; solving for $[(CH_3)_3Au]$,

$$[(CH_3)_3\,Au] = \frac{k_1[(CH_3)_3AuPH_3]}{k_{-1}[PH_3]}$$

Substituting into the rate law

$$\text{rate} = \left(\frac{k_2k_1}{k_{-1}}\right)\frac{[(CH_3)_3AuPH_3]}{[PH_3]} = \frac{k[(CH_3)_3AuPH_3]}{[PH_3]}$$

(f) The rate is inversely proportional to $[PH_3]$, so adding PH_3 to the $(CH_3)_3AuPH_3$ solution would decrease the rate of the reaction.

14.90 (a) The fact that the rate doubles with a doubling of the concentration of sugar tells us that the fraction of enzyme tied up in the form of an enzyme-substrate complex is small. A doubling of the substrate concentration leads to a doubling of the concentration of enzyme-substrate complex, because most of the enzyme molecules are available to bind substrates.

(b) The behavior of inositol suggests that it acts as a competitor with sucrose for binding at the active sites of the enzyme system. Such a competition results in a lower effective concentration of active sites for binding of sucrose, and thus results in a lower reaction rate.

Integrative Exercises

14.92 (a) $\ln k = -E_a/RT + \ln A$; $E_a = 86.8$ kJ/mol $= 8.68 \times 10^4$ J/mol;

$T = 35°C + 273 = 308$ K; $A = 2.10 \times 10^{11}\ M^{-1}\ s^{-1}$

$$\ln k = \frac{-8.68 \times 10^4 \text{ J/mol}}{308 \text{ K}} \times \frac{\text{mol} \bullet \text{K}}{8.314 \text{ J}} + \ln(2.10 \times 10^{11}\ M^{-1}\ s^{-1})$$

$\ln k = -33.8968 + 26.0704 = -7.8264$; $k = 3.99 \times 10^{-4}\ M^{-1}\ s^{-1}$

(b) $$\frac{0.335 \text{ g KOH}}{0.250 \text{ L soln}} \times \frac{1 \text{ mol KOH}}{56.1 \text{ g KOH}} = 0.02389 = 0.0239\ M \text{ KOH}$$

$$\frac{1.453 \text{ g } C_2H_5I}{0.250 \text{ L soln}} \times \frac{1 \text{ mol } C_2H_5I}{156.0 \text{ g } C_2H_5I} = 0.03726 = 0.0373\ M\ C_2H_5I$$

If equal volumes of the two solutions are mixed, the initial concentrations in the reaction mixture are 0.01194 *M* KOH and 0.01863 M C_2H_5I. Assuming the reaction is first order in each reactant:

rate $= k[C_2H_5I][OH^-] = 3.99 \times 10^{-4}\ M^{-1}\ s^{-1}\ (0.01194\ M)(0.01863\ M) = 8.88 \times 10^{-8}\ M/s$

(c) Since C_2H_5I and OH^- react in a 1 : 1 mole ratio and equal volumes of the solutions are mixed, the reactant with the smaller concentration, KOH, is the limiting reactant.

14.94 (a) $\ln k = -E_a/RT + \ln A$, Equation 14.20. $E_a = 6.3$ kJ/mol $= 6.3 \times 10^3$ J/mol

$T = 100°C + 273 = 373$ K

$$\ln k = \frac{-6.3 \times 10^3 \text{ J/mol}}{8.314 \text{ J/K} \bullet \text{mol} \times 373 \text{ K}} + \ln(6.0 \times 10^8\ M^{-1}\ s^{-1})$$

$\ln k = -2.032 + 20.212 = 18.181 = 18.2$; $k = 7.87 \times 10^7 = 8 \times 10^7\ M^{-1}\ s^{-1}$

(b) NO, 11 valence e^-, 5.5 e^- pair (Assume the less electronegative N atom will be electron deficient.)

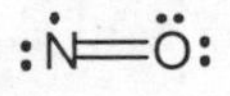

ONF, 18 valence e^-, 9 e^- pr

The resonance form on the right is a very minor contributor to the true bonding picture, due to high formal charges and the unlikely double bond involving F.

(c) ONF has trigonal planar electron domain geometry, which leads to a "bent" structure with a bond angle of approximately 120°.

(d) 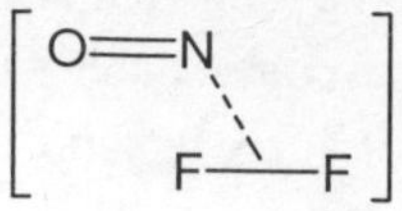

(e) The electron deficient NO molecule is attracted to electron-rich F_2, so the driving force for formation of the transition state is greater than simple random collisions.

14.95 (a) $\Delta H^\circ_{rxn} = 2\Delta H^\circ_f\ H_2O(g) + 2\Delta H^\circ_f\ Br_2(g) - 4\Delta H^\circ_f\ HBr(g) - \Delta H^\circ_f\ O_2(g)$

$\Delta H^\circ_{rxn} = 2(-241.82) + 2(30.71) - 4(-36.23) - (0) = -277.30$ kJ

(b) Since the rate of the uncatalyzed reaction is very slow at room temperature, the magnitude of the activation energy for the rate-determining first step must be quite large. At room temperature, the reactant molecules have a distribution of kinetic energies (Chapter 10), but very few molecules even at the high end of the distribution have sufficient energy to form an activated complex. E_a for this step must be much greater than 3/2 RT, the average kinetic energy of the sample.

(c) 20 e^-, 10 e^- pr

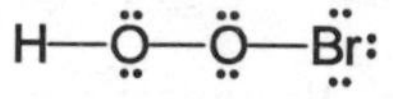

The intermediate resembles hydrogen peroxide, H_2O_2.

14.97 (a) If the reaction proceeds in a single elementary step, the coefficients in the balanced equation are the reaction orders for the respective reactants.

rate $= k[Ce^{4+}]^2\ [Tl^+]$

(b) If the uncatalyzed reaction occurs in a single step, it is *termolecular*. The activated complex requires collision of three particles with the correct energy and orientation for reaction. The probability of an effective three-particle collision is low and the rate is slow.

(c) The first step is rate-determining.

(d) The ability of Mn to adopt every oxidation state from +2 to +7 makes it especially suitable to catalyze this (and many other) reactions.

14.98 (a) D(Cl–Cl) = 242 kJ/mol Cl_2

$$\frac{242\ \text{kJ}}{\text{mol } Cl_2} \times \frac{1000\ \text{J}}{\text{kJ}} \times \frac{1\ \text{mol}}{6.022 \times 10^{23}\ \text{molecules}} = 4.019 \times 10^{-19} = 4.02 \times 10^{-19}\ \text{J}$$

$$\lambda = hc/E = \frac{6.626 \times 10^{-34}\ \text{J}\cdot\text{s} \times 2.998 \times 10^{8}\ \text{m/s}}{4.019 \times 10^{-19}\ \text{J}} = 4.94 \times 10^{-7}\ \text{m}$$

This wavelength, 494 nm, is in the visible portion of the spectrum.

(b)

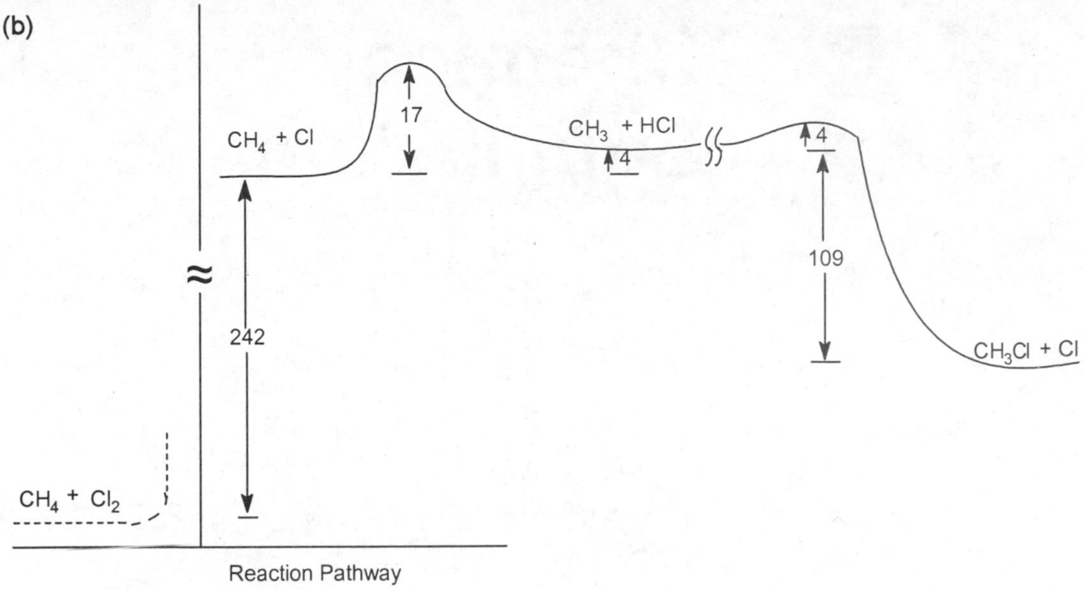

(c) Since D(Cl-Cl) is 242 kJ/mol, $CH_4(g) + Cl_2(g)$ should be about 242 kJ below the starting point on the diagram. For the reaction $CH_4(g) + Cl_2(g) \rightarrow CH_3(g) + HCl(g) + Cl(g)$, E_a is 242 + 17 = 259 kJ. (From bond dissociation enthalpies, ΔH for the overall reaction $CH_4(g) + Cl_2(g) \rightarrow CH_3Cl(g) + Cl(g)$ is -104 kJ, so the graph above is simply a sketch of the relative energies of some of the steps in the process.)

(d) CH_3, 7 valence e^-, odd electron species 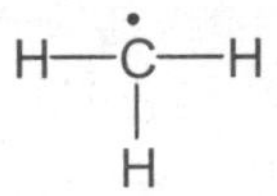

(e) This sequence is called a chain reaction because Cl• radicals are regenerated in Reaction 4, perpetuating the reaction. Absence of Cl• terminates the reaction, so Cl•+Cl• $\rightarrow Cl_2$ is a termination step.

15 Chemical Equilibrium

The Concept of Equilibrium; Equilibrium - Constant Expressions

15.2 (a) At equilibrium the forward and reverse reactions proceed at equal rates. Reactants are continually transformed into products, but products are also transformed into reactants at the same rate, so the net concentrations of reactants and products are constant at equilibrium.

(b) At equilibrium, it is the forward and reverse rates, not the rate constants, that are equal. It is true that the ratio of the two rate constants is constant at equilibrium, but this ratio is not constrained to have a value of 1.

(c) At equilibrium, the net concentrations of reactants and products are *constant* (see part (a)), but not necessarily equal. The relative concentrations of reactants and products at equilibrium are determined by their initial concentrations and the value of the equilibrium constant.

15.4 (a) $K_{eq} = \frac{[C][D]}{[A][B]}$; if K_{eq} is large, the numerator of the K_{eq} expression is much greater than the denominator and products will predominate at equilibrium.

(b) $K_{eq} = k_f/k_r$; if K_{eq} is large, k_f is larger than k_r and the forward reaction has the greater rate constant.

15.6 (a) Yes. The algebraic form of the law of mass action depends only on the coefficients of a chemical equation, not on the reaction mechanism.

(b) $N_2(g) + 3H_2(g) \rightleftharpoons 2NH_3(g)$. The *Haber process* is the primary industrial method of nitrogen fixation, that is, of converting $N_2(g)$ into usable forms. The major use of $NH_3(g)$ from the Haber process is for fertilizer.

(c) $$K_{eq} = \frac{P^2_{NH_3}}{P_{N_2} \times P^3_{H_2}}$$

15.8 (a) $K_{eq} = \frac{P^2_{NO}}{P_{N_2} \times P_{O_2}}$ (b) $K_{eq} = \frac{1}{P^2_{Cl_2}}$ (c) $K_{eq} = \frac{P^2_{C_2H_6} \times P_{O_2}}{P^2_{C_2H_4} \times P^2_{H_2O}}$

(d) $K_{eq} = \frac{[Co^{2+}] \times P_{H_2}}{[H^+]^2}$ (e) $k_{eq} = \frac{[NH_4^+][OH^-]}{[NH_3]}$

homogeneous: (a), (c), (e); heterogeneous: (b), (d)

Note: Categorizing reaction (e) as homogeneous or heterogeneous is problematic. It contains a pure liquid, H_2O, that doesn't appear in the equilibrium expression. However, an aqueous solution of these components is perfectly mixed, with no phase barriers or distinct domains. I have listed it as homogeneous.

15.10 (a) equilibrium lies to right, favoring products (K_{eq} >> 1)

(b) equilibrium lies to left, favoring reactants (K_{eq} << 1)

15.12 (a) $2NOBr(g) \rightleftharpoons 2NO(g) + Br_2(g)$ is the reverse of the reaction given.

$K_{eq}' = (K_{eq})^{-1} = 1/1.3 \times 10^{-2} = 76.92 = 77$

(b) $K_{eq} < 1$ when NOBr is the product, and $K_{eq}' > 1$ when NOBr is the reactant. At this temperature, the equilibrium favors NO and Br_2.

15.14 (a) $K_{eq}' = 1/K_{eq} = 1/0.0752 = 13.3$

(b) $K_{eq}' = (K_{eq})^{1/2} = (0.0752)^{1/2} = 0.274$

(c) $K_{eq}' = 1/K_{eq}^{1/2} = 1/(0.0752)^{1/2} = 3.65$

15.16 According to Hess's law, Section 5.6:

$$A(aq) + B(aq) \rightleftharpoons C(aq) \qquad K_1 = 1.9 \times 10^{-4}$$

$$C(aq) + D(aq) \rightleftharpoons E(aq) + A(aq) \qquad K_2 = 8.5 \times 10^{2}$$

$$A(aq) + B(aq) + C(aq) + D(aq) \rightleftharpoons A(aq) + C(aq) + E(aq)$$

$$B(aq) + D(aq) \rightleftharpoons E(aq) \qquad K_{eq} = K_1 \times K_2 = 0.16$$

$K_{eq} = (1.9 \times 10^{-4})(8.5 \times 10^2) = 0.162 = 0.16$

15.18 (a) $K_{eq} = \frac{[Na_2SO_3]}{[Na_2O]P_{SO_2}}$

(b) The molar concentration, the ratio of moles of a substance to volume occupied by the substance, is a constant for pure solids and liquids.

(c) $K_{eq} = 1/P_{SO_2}$

Calculating Equilibrium Constants

15.20 $K_{eq} = P_{CH_3OH}/P_{CO} \times P^2_{H_2}$; P = nRT/V; RT/V is the same for all gases.

$$RT/V = \frac{0.08206\ L \bullet atm}{mol \bullet K} \times \frac{500\ K}{2.00\ L} = 20.515 = 20.5\ atm/mol$$

$$K_{eq} = \frac{0.0406\ mol\ (20.5\ atm/mol)}{0.170\ mol\ (20.5\ atm/mol) \times [0.302\ mol\ (20.5\ atm/mol)]^2}$$

$$= \frac{0.0406}{0.170[0.302(20.515)]^2} = 0.006222 = 6.22 \times 10^{-3}$$

15.22 (a) $$K_{eq} = \frac{P_{PCl_5}}{P_{PCl_3} \times P_{Cl_2}} = \frac{1.30\ atm}{0.124\ atm \times 0.157\ atm} = 66.8$$

(b) Since $K_{eq} > 1$, products (the numerator of the K_{eq} expression) are favored over reactants (the denonimator of the K_{eq} expression).

15.24 (a) Calculate the initial partial pressures of $H_2(g)$ and $Br_2(g)$ and the equilibrium partial pressure of $H_2(g)$. $P = gRT/\mathcal{M}V$.

$$P_{H_2} = \frac{1.374\ g}{2.016\ g/mol} \times \frac{0.08206\ L \bullet atm}{mol \bullet K} \times \frac{700\ K}{2.00\ L} = 19.5747 = 19.57\ atm$$

$$P_{Br_2} = \frac{70.31\ g}{159.8\ g/mol} \times \frac{0.08206\ L \bullet atm}{mol \bullet K} \times \frac{700\ K}{2.00\ L} = 12.6369 = 12.64\ atm$$

$$P_{H_2} = \frac{0.566\ g}{2.016\ g/mol} \times \frac{0.08206\ L \bullet atm}{mol \bullet K} \times \frac{700\ K}{2.00\ L} = 8.0635 = 8.06\ atm$$

	$H_2(g)$	+ $Br_2(g)$	$\rightleftharpoons$ $2HBr(g)$
initial	19.57atm	12.64 atm	0
change	-11.51 atm	-11.51 atm	+2(11.51 atm)
equil.	8.06 atm	1.13 atm	23.02 atm

The change in P_{H_2} is (19.57 atm - 8.06 atm = 11.51 atm). The changes in P_{Br_2} and P_{HBr} are set by stoichiometry, resulting in the equilibrium concentrations shown in the table.

(b) $$K_{eq} = \frac{P^2_{HBr}}{P_{H_2} \times P_{Br_2}} = \frac{(23.02)^2}{(8.06)(1.13)} = 58.2$$

15.26 (a)

	$N_2O_4(g)$	$\rightleftharpoons$	$2NO_2(g)$
initial	1.500 atm		1.000 atm
change	+0.244 atm		-0.488 atm
equil	1.744 atm		0.512 atm

The change in P_{NO_2} is (1.000 - 0.512) = -0.488 atm, so the change in $P_{N_2O_4}$ is +(0.488/2) = +0.244 atm.

(b) $K_{eq} = \dfrac{P^2_{NO_2}}{P_{N_2O_4}} = \dfrac{(0.512)^2}{(1.744)} = 0.1503 = 0.150$

Applications of Equilibrium Constants

15.28 (a) If the value of Q equals the value of K, the system is at equilibrium.

(b) In the direction of less products (more reactants), to the left.

(c) Q = 0 if the concentration of any product is zero.

15.30 Calculate the reaction quotient in each case, compare with $K_{eq} = \dfrac{P^2_{NH_3}}{P_{N_2} \times P^3_{H_2}} = 4.51 \times 10^{-5}$

(a) $Q = \dfrac{(105)^2}{(35)(495)^3} = 2.6 \times 10^{-6}$

Since $Q < K_{eq}$, the reaction will shift to the right to attain equilibrium.

(b) $Q = \dfrac{(35)^2}{(0)(595)^3} = \infty$

Since $Q > K_{eq}$, reaction must shift to the left to attain equilibrium. There must be **some** N_2 present to attain equilibrium. In this example, the only source of N_2 is the decomposition of NH_3.

(c) $Q = \dfrac{(26)^2}{(42)^3(202)} = 4.52 \times 10^{-5}$; $Q = K_{eq}$ Reaction is at equilibrium.

(d) $Q = \dfrac{(105)^2}{(5.0)(55)^3} = 1.3 \times 10^{-2}$; $Q > K_{eq}$

The reaction will proceed to the left to attain equilibrium.

15.32 $K_{eq} = \dfrac{P^2_{SO_3}}{P^2_{SO_2} \times P_{O_2}}$; $P_{SO_3} = \left(K_{eq} \times P^2_{SO_2} \times P_{O_2}\right)^{1/2} = [(0.345)(0.165)^2(0.755)]^{1/2} = 0.0842$ atm

15.34 (a) $K_{eq} = P_I^2 / P_{I_2}$. $P_I = \dfrac{gRT}{\mathcal{M}V} = \dfrac{3.22 \times 10^{-2}\ g}{126.9\ g/mol} \times \dfrac{0.08206\ L \bullet atm}{mol \bullet K} \times \dfrac{800\ K}{10.0\ L}$

$= 1.666 \times 10^{-3} = 1.67 \times 10^{-3}$ atm

$P_{I_2} = P_I^2/K_{eq} = (1.666 \times 10^{-3})^2 / 2.04 \times 10^{-3} = 1.360 \times 10^{-3} = 1.36 \times 10^{-3}$ atm

$$g_{I_2} = \frac{\mathcal{M}PV}{RT} = \frac{253.8 \text{ g } I_2}{\text{mol } I_2} \quad \frac{\text{K}\bullet\text{mol}}{0.08206 \text{ L}\bullet\text{atm}} \times \frac{1.360 \times 10^{-3} \text{ atm} \times 10.0 \text{ L}}{800 \text{ K}}$$

$$= 0.0526 \text{ g } I_2$$

(b) $PV = nRT;\ P = \dfrac{gRT}{\mathcal{M}V}$

$$P_{SO_3} = \frac{2.65 \text{ g } SO_3}{80.06 \text{ g/mol}} \times \frac{0.08206 \text{ L}\bullet\text{atm}}{\text{K}\bullet\text{mol}} \times \frac{700 \text{ K}}{2.00 \text{ L}} = 0.9507 = 0.951 \text{ atm}$$

$$P_{O_2} = \frac{1.08 \text{ g } O_2}{32.00 \text{ g/mol}} \times \frac{0.08206 \text{ L}\bullet\text{atm}}{\text{K}\bullet\text{mol}} \times \frac{700 \text{ K}}{2.00 \text{ L}} = 0.9693 = 0.969 \text{ atm}$$

$$K_{eq} = 3.0 \times 10^4 = \frac{P^2_{SO_3}}{P^2_{SO_2} \times P_{O_2}}\ ;\ P_{SO_2} = \left[P^2_{SO_3}/(K_{eq})(P_{O_2})\right]^{1/2}$$

$P_{SO_2} = [(0.9507)^2/(3.0 \times 10^4)(0.9693)]^{1/2} = 5.575 \times 10^{-3} = 5.58 \times 10^{-3}$ atm

$$g\ SO_2 = \frac{\mathcal{M}PV}{RT} = \frac{64.06 \text{ g } SO_2}{\text{mol } SO_2} \times \frac{\text{K}\bullet\text{mol}}{0.08206 \text{ L}\bullet\text{atm}} \times \frac{5.575 \times 10^{-3} \text{ atm} \times 2.00 \text{ L}}{700 \text{ K}}$$

$$= 0.01243 = 0.0124 \text{ g } SO_2$$

15.36 $P_{Br_2} = P_{Cl_2} = \dfrac{nRT}{V} = 0.30 \text{ mol} \times \dfrac{0.08206 \text{ L}\bullet\text{atm}}{\text{K}\bullet\text{mol}} \times \dfrac{400 \text{ K}}{1.0 \text{ L}} = 9.847 = 9.8$ atm

	$Br_2(g)$	+ $Cl_2(g)$	$\rightleftharpoons$ $2BrCl(g)$
initial	9.8 atm	9.8 atm	0
change	-x	-x	+2x
equil.	(9.8-x) atm	(9.8-x) atm	+2x

$$K_{eq} = \frac{P^2_{BrCl}}{P_{Br_2} \times P_{Cl_2}} = 7.0$$

$7.0 = \dfrac{(2x)^2}{(9.8-x)^2}$ (Assuming x is small leads to x = 13 atm, P_{BrCl} = 26 atm. Clearly x is not small compared to 9.8 atm.)

$(7.0)^{1/2} = \dfrac{2x}{9.847-x}$, 2.646(9.847-x) = 2x, 26.056 = 4.646x, x = 5.608 = 5.6 atm

P_{BrCl} = 2x = 11.216 = 11 atm

15.38 $K_{eq} = P_{H_2S} \times P_{NH_3} = 7.0 \times 10^{-2}$. The equilibrium pressures of H_2S and NH_3 will be equal; call this quantity y. Then, $y^2 = 7.0 \times 10^{-2}$, y = 0.2646 = 0.26 atm.

15.40 (a) $CaSO_4(s) \rightleftharpoons Ca^{2+}(aq) + SO_4^{2-}(aq)$ $K_{eq} = [Ca^{2+}][SO_4^{2-}] = 2.4 \times 10^{-5}$

At equilibrium, $[Ca^{2+}] = [SO_4^{2-}] = x$

$K_{eq} = 2.4 \times 10^{-5} = x^2$; $x = 4.9 \times 10^{-3}$ *M* Ca^{2+} and SO_4^{2-}

(b) A saturated solution of $CaSO_4(aq)$ is 4.9×10^{-3} *M*.
3.0 L of this solution contain:

$$4.9 \times 10^{-3}\ \frac{\text{mol}}{\text{L}} \times 3.0\ \text{L} \times \frac{136.14\ \text{g}\ CaSO_4}{\text{mol}} = 2.001 = 2.0\ \text{g}\ CaSO_4$$

A bit more than 2.0 g $CaSO_4$ is needed in order to have some undissolved $CaSO_4(s)$ in equilibrium with 3.0 L of saturated solution.

15.42 $CaCrO_4(s) \rightleftharpoons Ca^{2+}(aq) + CrO_4^{2-}(aq)$ $\quad K_{eq} = [Ca^{2+}][CrO_4^{2-}] = 7.1 \times 10^{-4}$

At equilibrium, $[Ca^{2+}] = [CrO_4^{2-}] = x$

$K_{eq} = 7.1 \times 10^{-4} = x^2$, $x = 0.0266 = 0.027$ *M* Ca^{2+} and CrO_4^{2-}

LeChâtelier's Principle

15.44 (a) Increase (b) increase (c) decrease (d) no effect (e) no effect
(f) no effect

15.46 (a) The reaction must be endothermic ($+\Delta H$) if heating increases the fraction of products.

(b) There must be more moles of gas in the products if increasing the volume of the vessel increases the fraction of products.

15.48 (a)
$$\begin{aligned}\Delta H^\circ &= \Delta H_f^\circ\ CH_3OH(g) - \Delta H_f^\circ\ CO(g) - 2\Delta H_f^\circ\ H_2(g)\\ &= -201.2\ \text{kJ} - (-110.5\ \text{kJ}) - 0\ \text{kJ}\\ &= -90.7\ \text{kJ}\end{aligned}$$

(b) The reaction is exothermic; an increase in temperature would decrease the value of K_{eq} and decrease the yield. A *low temperature* is needed to maximize yield.

(c) Increasing total pressure would increase the partial pressure of each gas, shifting the equilibrium toward products. The extent of conversion to CH_3OH increases as the total pressure increases.

Additional Exercises

15.50 $$K_{eq} = \frac{P_{CO} \times P_{H_2}^3}{P_{CH_4} \times P_{H_2O}};\ P = \frac{g\,RT}{\mathcal{M}\,V};\ T = 1000\ \text{K}$$

$$P_{CO} = \frac{8.62\ \text{g}}{28.01\ \text{g/mol}} \times \frac{0.08206\ \text{L}\bullet\text{atm}}{\text{mol}\bullet\text{K}} \bullet \frac{1000\ \text{K}}{5.00\ \text{L}} = 5.0507 = 5.05\ \text{atm}$$

$$P_{H_2} = \frac{2.60\ \text{g}}{2.016\ \text{g/mol}} \times \frac{0.08206\ \text{L}\bullet\text{atm}}{\text{mol}\bullet\text{K}} \times \frac{1000\ \text{K}}{5.00\ \text{L}} = 21.1663 = 21.2\ \text{atm}$$

$$P_{CH_4} = \frac{43.0\text{ g}}{16.04\text{ g/mol}} \times \frac{0.08206\text{ L}\bullet\text{atm}}{\text{mol}\bullet\text{K}} \bullet \frac{1000\text{ K}}{5.00\text{ L}} = 43.9973 = 44.0\text{ atm}$$

$$P_{H_2O} = \frac{48.4\text{ g}}{18.02\text{ g/mol}} \times \frac{0.08206\text{ L}\bullet\text{atm}}{\text{mol}\bullet\text{K}} \bullet \frac{1000\text{ K}}{5.00\text{ L}} = 44.0811 = 44.1\text{ atm}$$

$$K_{eq} = \frac{(5.0507)(21.1663)^3}{(43.9973)(44.0811)} = 24.6949 = 24.7$$

15.52 (a) $H_2(g) + S(s) \rightleftharpoons H_2S(g)$ $K_{eq} = P_{H_2S} / P_{H_2}$

(b) Calculate the partial pressures of H_2S and H_2. $P = \frac{gRT}{\mathcal{M}V}$; T = 90°C + 273 = 363 K

$$P_{H_2S} = \frac{0.46\text{ g}}{34.1\text{ g/mol}} \times \frac{0.08206\text{ L}\bullet\text{atm}}{\text{K}\bullet\text{mol}} \times \frac{363\text{ K}}{1.0\text{ L}} = 0.4018 = 0.40\text{ atm}$$

$$P_{H_2} = \frac{0.40\text{ g}}{2.02\text{ g/mol}} \times \frac{0.08206\text{ L}\bullet\text{atm}}{\text{K}\bullet\text{mol}} \times \frac{363\text{ K}}{1.0\text{ L}} = 5.899 = 5.9\text{ atm}$$

K_{eq} = 0.4018/5.899 = 0.06811 = 0.068

(c) Since S is a pure solid, its 'partial pressure' doesn't change during the reaction, so P_S does not appear in the equilibrium expression.

15.53 (a) $K_{eq} = \frac{P_{Br_2} \times P_{NO}^2}{P_{NOBr}^2}$; $P = \frac{gRT}{PV}$; T = 100°C + 273 = 373

$$P_{Br_2} = \frac{4.19\text{ g}}{159.8\text{ g/mol}} \times \frac{0.08206\text{ L}\bullet\text{atm}}{\text{K}\bullet\text{mol}} \times \frac{373}{5.0\text{ L}} = 0.16051 = 0.161\text{ atm}$$

$$P_{NO} = \frac{3.08\text{ g}}{30.01\text{ g/mol}} \times \frac{0.08206\text{ L}\bullet\text{atm}}{\text{K}\bullet\text{mol}} \times \frac{373}{5.0\text{ L}} = 0.62828 = 0.628\text{ atm}$$

$$P_{NOBr} = \frac{3.22\text{ g NOBr}}{109.9\text{ g/mol}} \times \frac{0.08206\text{ L}\bullet\text{atm}}{\text{K}\bullet\text{mol}} \times \frac{373}{5.0\text{ L}} = 0.17936 = 0.179\text{ atm}$$

$$K_{eq} = \frac{(0.16051)(0.62828)^2}{(0.17936)^2} = 1.9695 = 1.97$$

(b) $P_t = P_{Br_2} + P_{NO} + P_{NOBr}$ = 0.16051 + 0.62828 + 0.17936 = 0.96815 = 0.968 atm

15.55 (a) $K_{eq} = \frac{P_{NH_3}^2}{P_{N_2} \times P_{H_2}^3} = 4.34 \times 10^{-3}$; T = 300°C + 273 = 573 K

$$P_{NH_3} = \frac{gRT}{\mathcal{M} \times V} = \frac{1.05\text{ g}}{17.03\text{ g/mol}} \times \frac{0.08206\text{ L}\bullet\text{atm}}{\text{K}\bullet\text{mol}} \times \frac{573\text{ K}}{1.00\text{ L}} = 2.899 = 2.90\text{ atm}$$

	$N_2(g)$ +	$3H_2(g)$ $\rightleftharpoons$	$2NH_3(g)$
initial	0 atm	0 atm	?
change	x	3x	-2x
equil.	x atm	3x atm	2.899 atm

(Remember, only the change line reflects the stoichiometry of the reaction.)

$$K_{eq} = \frac{(2.899)^2}{(x)(3x)^3} = 4.34 \times 10^{-3};\ 27\,x^4 = \frac{(2.899)^2}{4.34 \times 10^{-3}};\ x^4 = 71.725$$

$x = 2.910 = 2.91$ atm $= P_{N_2}$; $P_{H_2} = 3x = 8.730 = 8.73$ atm

$$g_{N_2} = \frac{\mathcal{M} \times PV}{RT} = \frac{28.02\text{ g }N_2}{\text{mol }N_2} \times \frac{\text{K}\bullet\text{mol}}{0.08206\text{ L}\bullet\text{atm}} \times \frac{2.910\text{ atm} \times 1.000\text{ L}}{573\text{ K}} = 1.73\text{ g }N_2$$

$$g_{H_2} = \frac{2.016\text{ g }H_2}{\text{mol }H_2} \times \frac{\text{K}\bullet\text{mol}}{0.08206\text{ L}\bullet\text{atm}} \times \frac{8.730\text{ atm} \times 1.00\text{ L}}{573\text{ K}} = 0.374\text{ g }N_2$$

(b) The initial $P_{NH_3} = 2.899$ atm + 2(2.910 atm) = 8.719 = 8.72 atm

$$g_{NH_3} = = \frac{17.03\text{ g }NH_3}{\text{mol }NH_3} \times \frac{\text{K}\bullet\text{mol}}{0.08206\text{ L}\bullet\text{atm}} \times \frac{8.719\text{ atm} \times 1.000\text{ L}}{573\text{ K}} = 3.16\text{ g }NH_3$$

(c) $P_t = P_{N_2} + P_{H_2} + P_{NH_3} = 2.910$ atm + 8.730 atm + 8.719 atm = 20.36 atm

15.56 $$P_{IBr} = \frac{nRT}{V} = 0.025\text{ mol} \times \frac{0.08206\text{ L}\bullet\text{atm}}{\text{mol}\bullet\text{K}} \times \frac{423\text{ K}}{2.0\text{ L}} = 0.4339 = 0.43\text{ atm}$$

	$2IBr$ $\rightleftharpoons$	I_2 +	Br_2
initial	0.43 atm	0	0
change	-2x	x	x
equil.	(0.43-2x) atm	x	x

$$K_{eq} = 8.5 \times 10^{-3} = \frac{P_{I_2} \times P_{Br_2}}{P_{IBr}} = \frac{x^2}{(0.43-2x)^2};$$ Taking the square root of both sides

$$\frac{x}{0.4339-2x} = (8.5 \times 10^{-3})^{1/2} = 0.0922;\ x = 0.0922(0.4339 - 2x)$$

$x + 0.184x = 0.04001$; $1.184x = 0.04001$, $x = 0.03379 = 0.034$ atm

P_{IBr} at equilibrium = 0.04339 - 2(0.03379) = 0.3663 = 0.37 atm

15.58 $K_{eq} = P_{NH_3} \times P_{H_2S}$; $P_t = 0.614$ atm

If the equilibrium amounts of NH_3 and H_2S are due solely to the decomposition of $NH_4HS(s)$, the equilibrium pressures of the two gases are equal, and each is 1/2 of the total pressure.

$P_{NH_3} = P_{H_2S} = 0.614$ atm/2 = 0.307 atm

$K_{eq} = (0.307)^2 = 0.0943$

15.59 Initial $P_{SO_3} = \frac{gRT}{\mathcal{M}V} = \frac{0.831\text{ g}}{80.07\text{ g/mol}} \times \frac{0.08206\text{ L}\bullet\text{atm}}{\text{K}\bullet\text{mol}} \times \frac{1100\text{ K}}{1.00\text{ L}} = 0.9368 = 0.937\text{ atm}$

	$2SO_3$	$\rightleftharpoons$	$2SO_2$	+	O_2
initial	0.9368 atm		0		0
change	-2x		+2x		+x
equil.	0.9368-2x		2x		x
[equil.]	0.2104 atm		0.7264 atm		0.3632 atm

$P_t = (0.9368\text{-}2x) + 2x + x;\ 0.9368 + x = 1.300\text{ atm};\ x = 1.300 - 0.9368 = 0.3632 = 0.363\text{ atm}$

$$K_{eq} = \frac{P^2_{SO_2} \times P_{O_2}}{P^2_{SO_3}} = \frac{(0.7264)^2(0.3632)}{(0.2104)^2} = 4.33$$

15.61 $K_{eq} = P_{CO_2} = 0.0108;\ P_{CO_2} = \frac{gRT}{\mathcal{M}V};\ T = 900°C + 273 = 1173\text{ K}$

In each case, calculate P_{CO_2} and determine the position of the equilibrium.

(a) $P_{CO_2} = \frac{4.25\text{ g}}{44.01\text{ g/mol}} \times \frac{0.08206\text{ L}\bullet\text{atm}}{\text{mol}\bullet\text{K}} \times \frac{1173\text{ K}}{10.0\text{ L}} = 0.92954 = 0.930\text{ atm}$

$Q = 0.930 > K_{eq}$. The reaction proceeds to the left to achieve equilibrium and the amount of $CaCO_3(s)$ increases.

(b) 5.66 g CO_2 means $P_{CO_2} > 0.930$ atm; $Q > 0.930 >> K_{eq}$, the amount of $CaCO_3$ increases.

(c) 6.48 g CO_2 means $P_{CO_2} > 0.930$ atm; $Q > 0.930 >> K_{eq}$, the amount of $CaCO_3$ increases.

15.62 (a) $K_{eq} = \frac{P_{Ni(CO)_4}}{P^4_{CO}}$

(b) Increasing the temperature to 200°C favors the reverse process (decomposition of $Ni(CO)_4(g)$) and thus the value of K_{eq} is smaller at the higher temperature. This is the behavior expected from an **exothermic** reaction (heat is a product).

(c) At the temperature of the exhaust pipe, the $Ni(CO)_4$ product is a gas and is carried into the atmosphere with other exhaust gases. Thus, equilibrium is never established (we do not have a closed system) and the reaction proceeds to the right as $Ni(CO)_4$ product is removed.

15.64 (a)

	$CCl_4(g)$	$\rightleftharpoons$	C(s)	+	$2Cl_2(g)$
initial	2.00 atm				0 atm
change	-x atm				+2x atm
equil.	(2.00-x) atm				2x atm

$$K_{eq} = 0.76 = \frac{P^2_{Cl_2}}{P_{CCl_4}} = \frac{(2x)^2}{(2.00-x)}$$

$1.52 - 0.76x = 4x^2$; $4x^2 + 0.76x - 1.52 = 0$

Using the quadratic formula, a = 4, b = 0.76, c = -1.52

$$x = \frac{-0.76 \pm \sqrt{(0.76)^2 - 4(4)(-1.52)}}{2(4)} = \frac{-0.76 + 4.99}{8} = 0.5287 = 0.53 \text{ atm}$$

$$\text{Fraction } CCl_4 \text{ reacted} = \frac{x \text{ atm}}{2.00 \text{ atm}} = \frac{0.53}{2.00} = 0.264 = 26\%$$

(b) $P_{Cl_2} = 2x = 2(0.5287) = 1.06$ atm

$P_{CCl_4} = 2.00 - x = 2.00 - 0.5287 = 1.47$ atm

15.65 (a) $$Q = \frac{P_{PCl_5}}{P_{PCl_3} \times P_{Cl_2}} = \frac{(0.20)}{(0.50)(0.50)} = 0.80$$

0.80 (Q) > 0.0870 (K), the reaction proceeds to the left.

(b)

	$PCl_3(g)$	+	$Cl_2(g)$	$\rightleftharpoons$	$PCl_5(g)$
initial	0.50 atm		0.50 atm		0.20 atm
change	+x atm		+x atm		-x atm
equil.	(0.50 + x) atm		(0.50 + x) atm		(0.20 - x) atm

(Since the reaction proceeds to the left, P_{PCl_5} must decrease and P_{PCl_3} and P_{Cl_2} must increase.)

$$K_{eq} = 0.0870 = \frac{(0.20 - x)}{(0.50 + x)(0.50 + x)}; \quad 0.0870 = \frac{(0.20 - x)}{(0.250 + 1.00x + x^2)}$$

$0.0870(0.250 + 1.00x + x^2) = 0.20 - x$; $-0.17825 + 1.0870x + 0.0870x^2 = 0$

$$x = \frac{-1.0870 \pm \sqrt{(1.0870)^2 - 4(0.0870)(-0.17825)}}{2(0.0870)} = \frac{-1.0870 + 1.1152}{0.174} = 0.162$$

$P_{PCl_3} = (0.50 + 0.162)$ atm = 0.662 $P_{Cl_2} = (0.50 + 0.162)$ atm = 0.662 atm

$P_{PCl_5} = (0.20 - 0.162)$ atm = 0.038 atm

To 2 decimal places, the pressures are 0.66, 0.66 and 0.04 atm, respectively. When substituting into the K_{eq} expression, pressures to 3 decimal places yield a result much closer to 0.0870.

(c) Increasing the volume of the container favors the process where more moles of gas are produced, so the reverse reaction is favored and the equilibrium shifts to the left; the mole fraction of Cl_2 increases.

(d) For an exothermic reaction, increasing the temperature decreases the value of K; more reactants and fewer products are present at equilibrium and the mole fraction of Cl_2 increases.

15.67 (a) Since the volume of the vessel = 1.00 L, mol = *M*. The reaction will proceed to the left to establish equilibrium.

	A(g)	+ 2B(g)	$\rightleftharpoons$ 2C(g)
initial	0 *M*	0 *M*	1.00 *M*
change	+x *M*	+2x *M*	-2x *M*
equil.	x *M*	2x *M*	(1.00 - 2x) *M*

At equilibrium, [C] = (1.00 - 2x) *M*, [B] = 2x *M*.

(b) x must be less than 0.50 *M* (so that [C], 1.00 -2x, is not less than zero).

(c) $K_{eq} = \dfrac{[C]^2}{[A][B]^2}$; $\dfrac{(1.00-2x)^2}{(x)(2x)^2} = 0.25$

$1.00 - 4x + 4x^2 = 0.25(4x)^3$; $x^3 - 4x^2 + 4x - 1 = 0$

(d)

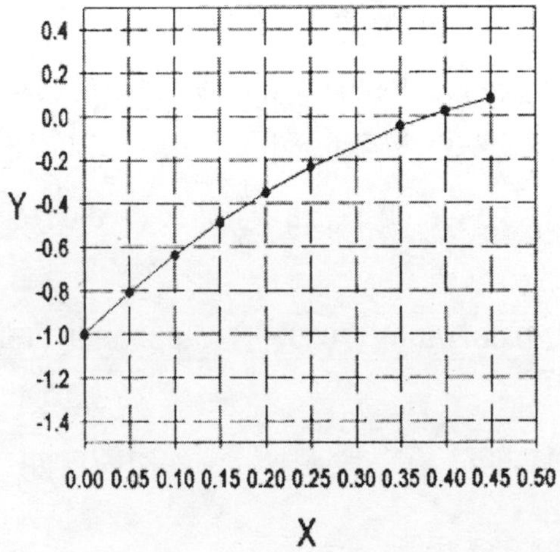

x	y
0.0	-1.000
0.05	-0.810
0.10	-0.639
0.15	-0.487
0.20	-0.352
0.25	-0.234
0.35	-0.047
0.40	+0.024
0.45	+0.081
~0.383	0.00

(e) From the plot, x ≈ 0.383 *M*

$[A] = x = 0.383\ M$; $[B] = 2x = 0.766\ M$

$[C] = 1.00 - 2x = 0.234\ M$

Using the K_{eq} expression as a check:

$K_{eq} = 0.25$; $\dfrac{(0.234)^2}{(0.383)(0.766)^2} = 0.24$; the estimated values are reasonable.

15.68 $K_{eq} = \dfrac{P_{O_2} \times P_{CO}^2}{P_{CO_2}^2} = 1 \times 10^{-13}$; $P_{O_2} = (0.03)(1\text{ atm}) = 0.03\text{ atm}$

$P_{CO} = (0.002)(1\text{ atm}) = 0.002\text{ atm}$; $P_{CO_2} = (0.12)(1\text{ atm}) = 0.12\text{ atm}$

$Q = \dfrac{(0.03)(0.002)^2}{(0.12)^2} = 8.3 \times 10^{-6} = 8 \times 10^{-6}$

Since $Q > K_{eq}$, the system will shift to the left to attain equilibrium. Thus a catalyst that promoted the attainment of equilibrium would result in a lower CO content in the exhaust.

Integrative Exercises

15.71 (a) $AgCl(s) \rightarrow Ag^+(aq) + Cl^-(aq)$

(b) $K_{eq} = [Ag^+][Cl^-]$

(c) Using thermodynamic data from Appendix C, calculate ΔH for the reaction in part (a).

$\Delta H^\circ = \Delta H_f^\circ\ Ag^+(aq) + \Delta H_f^\circ\ Cl^-(aq) - \Delta H_f^\circ\ AgCl(s)$

$\Delta H^\circ = +105.90\text{ kJ} - 167.2\text{ kJ} - (-127.0\text{ kJ}) = +65.7\text{ kJ}$

The reaction is endothermic (heat is a reactant), so the solubility of AgCl(s) in $H_2O(l)$ will increase with increasing temperature.

15.73 Consider the energy profile for an exothermic reaction.

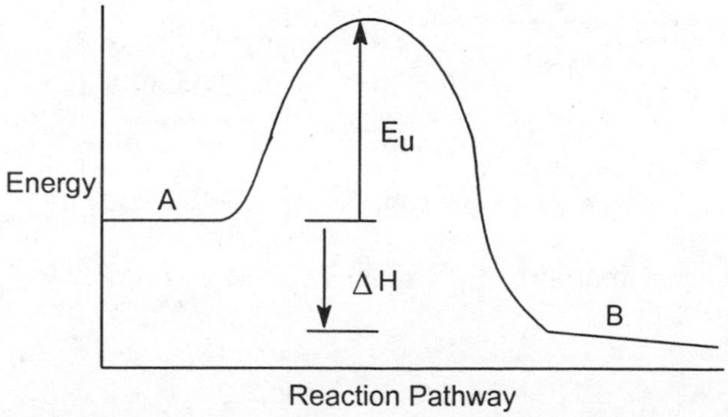

The activation energy in the forward direction, E_{af}, equals E_u, and the activation energy in the reverse reaction, E_{ar}, equals $E_u - \Delta H$. (The same is true for an endothermic reaction because the sign of ΔH is the positive and $E_{ar} < E_{af}$). For the reaction in question,

$$K = \frac{k_f}{k_r} = \frac{A_f e^{-E_{af}/RT}}{A_r e^{-E_{ar}/RT}}$$

Since the ln form of the Arrhenius equation is easier to manipulate, we will consider ln K.

$$\ln K = \ln\left(\frac{k_f}{k_r}\right) = \ln k_f - \ln k_r = \frac{-E_{af}}{RT} + \ln A - \left[\frac{-E_{ar}}{RT} + \ln A_r\right]$$

Substituting E_u for E_{af} and $(E_u - \Delta H)$ for E_{ar}

$$\ln K = \frac{-E_u}{RT} + \ln A_f - \left[\frac{-(E_u - \Delta H)}{RT} + \ln Ar\right]; \ \ln K = \frac{-E_u + (E_u - \Delta H)}{RT} + \ln A_f - \ln A_r$$

$$\ln K = \frac{-\Delta H}{RT} + \ln\frac{A_f}{A_r}$$

For the catalyzed reaction, $E_c < E_u$ and $E_{af} = E_c$, $E_{ar} = E_c - \Delta H$. The catalyst does not change the value of ΔH.

$$\ln K_c = \frac{-E_c + (E_c - \Delta H)}{RT} + \ln A_f - \ln A_r$$

$$\ln K_c = \frac{-\Delta H}{RT} + \frac{\ln A_f}{A_r}$$

Thus, assuming A_f and A_r are not changed by the catalyst, $\ln K = \ln K_c$ and $K = K_c$.

15.74 (a) $$P = \frac{gRT}{\mathcal{M}V} = \frac{0.300 \text{ g } H_2S}{34.08 \text{ g/mol } H_2S} \times \frac{298 \text{ K}}{5.00 \text{ L}} \times \frac{0.08206 \text{ L} \cdot \text{atm}}{\text{mol} \cdot \text{K}} = 0.043053$$

$$= 0.0431 \text{ atm}$$

(b) $K_{eq} = P_{NH_3} \times P_{H_2S}$. Before solid is added, $Q = P_{NH_3} \times P_{H_2S} = 0 \times 0.0431 = 0$. $Q < K$ and the reaction will proceed to the right. However, no $NH_4SH(s)$ is present to produce $NH_3(g)$, so the reaction cannot proceed.

(c)

	$NH_4HS(s) \rightleftharpoons$	$NH_3(g)$	+	$H_2S(g)$
initial		0 atm		0.043053 atm
change		+x atm		+x atm
equil.		+x atm		(0.043053+x) atm

Since $Q < K$ initially (part (a)), P_{H_2S} must increase along with P_{NH_3} until equilibrium is established.

$K_{eq} = P_{NH_3} \times P_{H_2S}$; $0.120 = (x)(0.043053 + x)$; $0 = x^2 + 0.043053\,x - 0.120$

Solve for x using the quadratic formula.

$$x = \frac{-0.043053 \pm \sqrt{(0.043053)^2 - 4(1)(-0.120)}}{2}; \quad x = 0.3256 = 0.326 \text{ atm}$$

$P_{NH_3} = 0.326$ atm; $P_{H_2S} = (0.043053 + 0.3256)$ atm $= 0.3686 = 0.369$ atm

(d) $$\chi_{H_2S} = \frac{P_{H_2S}}{P_t} = \frac{0.3686 \text{ atm}}{(0.3256 + 0.3686) \text{ atm}} = 0.531$$

(e) The minimum amount of $NH_4HS(s)$ required is slightly greater than the number of moles NH_3 present at equilibrium. We can calculate the mol NH_3 present at equilibrium using the ideal-gas equation.

$$n_{NH_3} = \frac{P_{NH_3}V}{RT} = 0.3256 \text{ atm} \times \frac{\text{K} \bullet \text{mol}}{0.08206 \text{ L} \bullet \text{atm}} \times \frac{5.00 \text{ L}}{298 \text{ K}} = 0.06657$$

$$= 0.0666 \text{ mol } NH_3$$

$$0.06657 \text{ mol } H_2S \times \frac{1 \text{ mol } NH_4SH}{1 \text{ mol } H_2S} \times \frac{51.12 \text{ g } NH_4SH}{1 \text{ mol } NH_4SH} = 3.40 \text{ g } NH_4SH$$

The minimum amount is slightly greater than 3.40 g NH_4HS.

15.76 (a) $H_2O(l) \rightleftharpoons H_2O(g)$; $K_{eq} = P_{H_2O}$

(b) At 30°C, the vapor pressure of $H_2O(l)$ is 31.82 torr. $K_{eq} = P_{H_2O} = 31.82$ torr

$K_{eq} = 31.82 \text{ torr} \times 1 \text{ atm}/760 \text{ torr} = 0.041868 = 0.04187$ atm

(c) From part (b), the value of K_{eq} is the vapor pressure of the liquid at that temperature. By definition, vapor pressure = atmospheric pressure = 1 atm at the normal boiling point. $K_{eq} = 1$ atm

15.77 (a)

C-C B.O. = 1 C=C B.O. = 2

(b) ΔH = D(bond breaking) - D (bond making)

E1: ΔH = D(C=C) + D(Cl-Cl) - D(C-C) - 2D (C-Cl)

ΔH = 614 + 242 - 348 - 2(328) = -148 kJ

E2: ΔH = D(C-C) + D(C-H) + D(C-Cl) - D(C=C) - D(H-Cl)

= 348 + 413 + 328 - 614 - 431 = +44 kJ

(c) E1 is exothermic with Δn = -1. The yield of $C_2H_4Cl_2(g)$ would decrease with increasing temperature and with increasing container volume.

(d) E2 is endothermic with $\Delta n = 1$. The yield of C_2H_3Cl would increase with increasing temperature and with increasing container volume.

(e) The boiling points of the reactants and products are: C_2H_4, -103.7°C; Cl_2, -34.6°C, $C_2H_4Cl_2$, +83.5°C; C_2H_3Cl, -13.4°C; HCl, -84.9°C.

Because the products of E1 and E2 are optimized by different conditions, carry out the two equilibria in separate reactors. Since E1 is exothermic and $\Delta n = -1$, the reactor on the left should be as small and cold as possible to maximize yield of $C_2H_4Cl_2$. At temperatures below 83.5°C, $C_2H_4Cl_2$ will condense to the liquid and it can be easily transferred to the second (right) reactor.

Since E_2 is endothermic, the reactor on the right should be as large and hot as possible to optimize production of C_2H_3Cl. The outlet stream will be a mixture of $C_2H_3Cl(g)$, $C_2H_4Cl_2(g)$ and HCl(g). This mixture could be run through a heat exchanger to condense and subsequently recycle $C_2H_4Cl_2(l)$. Since HCl has a lower boiling point than C_2H_3Cl, it cannot be removed by condensation. The $C_2H_3Cl(g)$ / HCl(g) mixture could be bubbled through a basic aqueous solution such as $NaHCO_3(aq)$ or NaOH(aq) to remove HCl(g), leaving pure $C_2H_3Cl(g)$.

Other details of reactor design such as the use of catalysts to speed up these reactions, the exact costs and benefits of heat exchange, recycling unreacted components and separation and recovery of products are issues best resolved by chemical engineers.

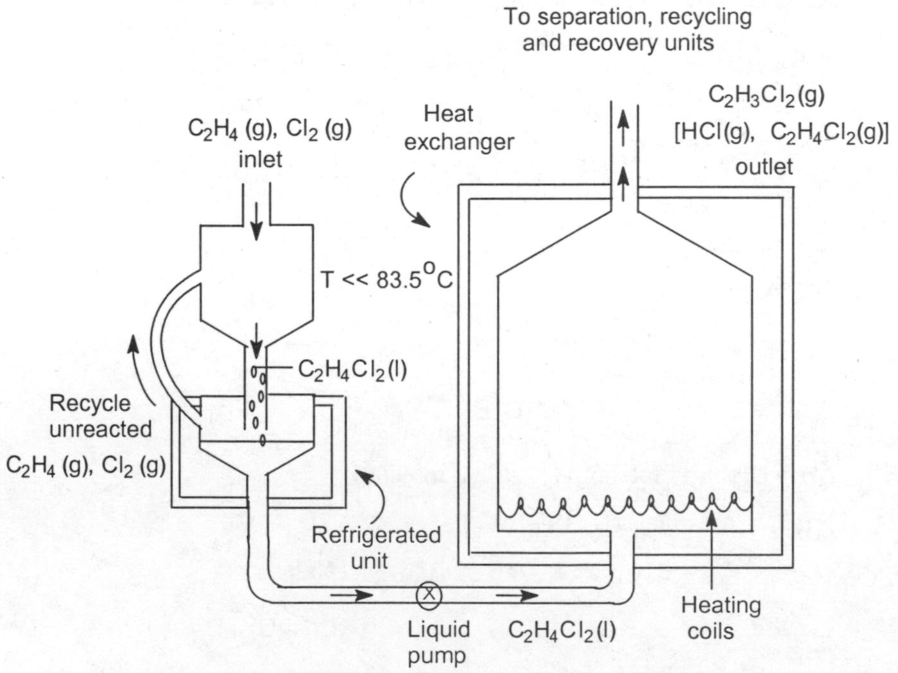

16 Acid-Base Equilibria

Arrhenius and Brønsted-Lowry Acids and Bases

16.2 When NaOH dissolves in water, it completely dissociates to form $Na^+(aq)$ and $OH^-(aq)$. CaO is the oxide of a metal; it dissolves in water according to the following process: $CaO(s) + H_2O(l) \rightarrow Ca^{2+}(aq) + 2OH^-(aq)$. Thus, the properties of both solutions are dominated by the presence of $OH^-(aq)$. Both solutions taste bitter, turn litmus paper blue (are basic), neutralize solutions of acids and conduct electricity.

16.4 (a) According to the Arrhenius definition, a base when dissolved in water increases $[OH^-]$. According to the Brønsted-Lowry theory, a base is an H^+ acceptor regardless of physical state. A Brønsted-Lowry base is not limited to aqueous solution and need not contain OH^- or produce it in aqueous solution.

(b) $NH_3(g) + H_2O(l) \rightleftharpoons NH_4^+(aq) + OH^-(aq)$ When NH_3 dissolves in water, it accepts H^+ from H_2O (B-L definition). In doing so, OH^- is produced (Arrhenius definition).

Note that the OH^- produced was originally part of the H_2O molecule, not part of the NH_3 molecule.

16.6 A conjugate acid has one more H^+ than its conjugate base.

(a) $H_2AsO_4^-$ (b) $CH_3NH_3^+$ (c) HSO_4^- (d) H_3PO_4

16.8

	B-L acid	+	B-L base	$\rightleftharpoons$	Conjugate acid	+	Conjugate base
(a)	$H_2O(l)$		$CHO_2^-(aq)$		$HCHO_2(aq)$		$OH^-(aq)$
(b)	$HSO_4^-(aq)$		$HCO_3^-(aq)$		$H_2CO_3(aq)$		$SO_4^{2-}(aq)$
(c)	$H_3O^+(aq)$		$HSO_3^-(aq)$		$H_2SO_3(aq)$		$H_2O(l)$

16.10 (a) $H_2C_6H_7O_5^-(aq) + H_2O(l) \rightleftharpoons H_3C_6H_7O_5(aq) + OH^-(aq)$

(b) $H_2C_6H_7O_5^-(aq) + H_2O(l) \rightleftharpoons HC_6H_7O_5^{2-}(aq) + H_3O^+(aq)$

(c) $H_3C_6H_7O_5$ is the conjugate acid of $H_2C_6H_7O_5^-$

$HC_6H_7O_5^{2-}$ is the conjugate base of $H_2C_6H_7O_5^-$

16.12 (a) weak, $HC_2H_3O_2$ (b) weak, H_2CO_3 (c) strong, OH^-

(d) negligible, HCl (e) weak, NH_4^+

16.14 (a) HNO_3. It is one of the seven strong acids (Section 16.5). Also, in a series of oxyacids with the same central atom (N), the acid with more O atoms is stronger (Section 16.10).

(b) NH_3. When NH_3 and H_2O are combined, as in $NH_3(aq)$, NH_3 acts as the B-L base, accepting H^+ from H_2O. NH_3 has the greater tendency to accept H^+. For binary hydrides, base strength increases going to the left across a row of the periodic chart (Section 16.10).

16.16 Acid-base equilibria favor formation of the weaker acid and base. Compare the relative strengths of the substances acting as acids on opposite sides of the equation. (Bases can also be compared; the conclusion should be the same.)

	Base	+	Acid	$\rightleftharpoons$	Conjugate acid	+	Conjugate base
(a)	$Cl^-(aq)$	+	$H_3O^+(aq)$		$HCl(aq)$	+	$H_2O(l)$

HCl is a stronger acid than H_3O^+ (Figure 16.4) , so the equilibrium lies to the left.

(b) $H_2O(l) + HNO_2(aq) \rightleftharpoons H_3O^+(aq) + NO_2^-(aq)$

H_3O^+ is a stronger acid than HNO_2, so the equilibrium lies to the left.

(c) $NO_3^-(aq) + H_2O(l) \rightleftharpoons HNO_3(aq) + OH^-(aq)$

HNO_3 is a stronger acid than H_2O (Solution 16.14), so the equilibrium lies to the right.

Autoionization of Water

16.18 (a) $H_2O(l) \rightleftharpoons H^+(aq) + OH^-(aq)$

(b) $K_w = [H^+][OH^-]$. The $[H_2O(l)]$ is omitted because water is a pure liquid. The molarity (mol/L) of pure solids or liquids does not change as equilibrium is established, so it is usually omitted from equilibrium expressions.

(c) If a solution is *basic*, it contains more OH^- than H^+ ($[OH^-] > [H^+]$).

16.20 In pure water at 25°C, $[H^+] = [OH^-] = 1 \times 10^{-7}$ *M*. If $[OH^-] > 1 \times 10^{-7}$ *M*, the solution is basic; if $[OH^-] < 1 \times 10^{-7}$ *M*, the solution is acidic.

(a) $[OH^-] = \dfrac{K_w}{[H^+]} = \dfrac{1.0 \times 10^{-14}}{4.1 \times 10^{-3}\ M} = \mathbf{2.4 \times 10^{-12}\ M} < 1 \times 10^{-7}\ M$; acidic

(b) $[OH^-] = \dfrac{K_w}{[H^+]} = \dfrac{1.0 \times 10^{-14}}{3.5 \times 10^{-9}\ M} = \mathbf{2.9 \times 10^{-6}\ M} < 1 \times 10^{-7}\ M$; basic

(c) $[H^+] = 10[OH^-]$; $K_w = 10[OH^-][OH^-] = 10[OH^-]^2$

$[OH^-] = (K_w / 10)^{1/2} = \mathbf{3.2 \times 10^{-8}\ M} < 1 \times 10^{-7}\ M$; acidic

16.22 $K_w = [D^+][OD^-]$; for pure D_2O, $[D^+] = [OD^-]$; $8.9 \times 10^{-16} = [D^+]^2$; $[D^+] = [OD^-] = 3.0 \times 10^{-8}\ M$

The pH Scale

16.24 $[H^+]_A = 500\,[H^+]_B$ From Solution 16.23, $\Delta pH = -\log \dfrac{[H^+]_B}{[H^+]_A}$

$$\Delta pH = -\log \frac{[H^+]_B}{500\,[H^+]_B} = -\log\left(\frac{1}{500}\right) = 2.70$$

The pH of solution A is 2.70 pH units lower than the pH of solution B, because $[H^+]_A$ is 500 times greater than $[H^+]_B$. The greater $[H^+]$, the lower the pH of the solution.

16.26 (a) $K_w = [H^+][OH^-]$. If HNO_3 is added to water, it ionizes to form $H^+(aq)$ and $NO_3^-(aq)$. This increases $[H^+]$ and necessarily decreases $[OH^-]$. When $[H^+]$ increases, pH decreases.

(b) On Figure 16.5, 1.4×10^{-2} *M* OH^- is between pH = 12 (1×10^{-2} *M* OH^-) and pH 13 (1×10^{-2} *M* OH^-), slightly higher than pH = 12, so we estimate pH = 12.1. By calculation:

$[H^+] = K_w / [OH^-] = 10 \times 10^{-14} / 1.4 \times 10^{-2}\ M = 7.1 \times 10^{-13}\ M$

$pH = -\log(7.1 \times 10^{-13}) = 12.15$. If pH > 7, the solution is basic.

(c) pH = 6.6 is midway between pH 6 and pH 7 on Figure 16.5.

At pH = 7, $[H^+] = 1 \times 10^{-7}$; at pH = 6, $[H^+] = 1 \times 10^{-6} = 10 \times 10^{-7}$.

A reasonable estimate is 5×10^{-7} *M* H^+. By calculation:

pH = 6.6, $[H^+] = 10^{-pH} = 10^{-6.6} \times 10^{-7} = 3 \times 10^{-7}$

At pH = 6 $[OH^-] = 1 \times 10^{-7}$; at pH = 7, $[OH^-] = 1 \times 10^{-7} = 1 \times 10^{-8}$.

A reasonable estimate 5×10^{-7} M OH^-. By calculation:

$pOH = 14.0 - 6.6 = 7.4$; $[OH^-] = 10^{-pOH} = 10^{-7.4} = 4 \times 10^{-8}\ M\ OH^-$.

16.28

pH	pOH	$[H^+]$	$[OH^-]$	acidic or basic
6.21	7.79	$6.2 \times 10^{-7}\ M$	$1.6 \times 10^{-8}\ M$	acidic
3.87	10.13	$1.3 \times 10^{-4}\ M$	$7.4 \times 10^{-11}\ M$	acidic
2.46	11.54	$3.5 \times 10^{-3}\ M$	$2.9 \times 10^{-12}\ M$	acidic
10.75	3.25	$1.8 \times 10^{-11}\ M$	$5.6 \times 10^{-4}\ M$	basic

16.30 The pH ranges from 5.2-5.6; pOH ranges from (14.9-5.2 =) 8.8 to (14.0-5.6 =) 8.4.

$[H^+] = 10^{-pH}$, $[OH^-] = 10^{-pOH}$

$[H^+] = 10^{-5.2} = 6.31 \times 10^{-6} = 6 \times 10^{-6}\ M$; $[H^+] = 10^{-5.6} = 2.51 \times 10^{-6} = 3 \times 10^{-6}\ M$

The range of $[H^+]$ is 6×10^{-6} *M* to 3×10^{-6} *M*.

$[OH^-] = 10^{-8.8} = 1.58 \times 10^{-9} = 2 \times 10^{-9}\ M$; $[OH^-] = 10^{-8.4} = 3.98 \times 10^{-9} = 4 \times 10^{-9}\ M$.

The range of $[OH^-]$ is 2×10^{-9} *M* to 4×10^{-9} *M*.

[The pH has one decimal place, so concentrations are reported to one sig fig.]

Strong Acids and Bases

16.32 (a) A *strong* base is completely dissociated in aqueous solution; a strong base is a strong electrolyte.

(b) $Sr(OH)_2$ is a soluble strong base.

$Sr(OH)_2(aq) \rightarrow Sr^{2+}(aq) + 2OH^-(aq)$

0.125 *M* $Sr(OH)_2(aq)$ = 0.250 *M* OH^-

(c) Base strength should not be confused with solubility. Base strength describes the tendency of a dissolved molecule (formula unit for ionic compounds such as $Mg(OH)_2$) to dissociate into cations and hydroxide ions. $Mg(OH)_2$ is a strong base because each $Mg(OH)_2$ unit that dissolves also dissociates into $Mg^{2+}(aq)$ and $OH^-(aq)$. $Mg(OH)_2$ is not very soluble, so relatively few $Mg(OH)_2$ units dissolve when the solid compound is added to water.

16.34 For a strong acid, which is completely ionized, $[H^+]$ = the initial acid concentration.

(a) 0.0575 *M* HNO_3 = 0.0575 *M* H^+; pH = -log (0.0575) = 1.24

(b) $$\frac{0.723 \text{ g } HClO_4}{2.00 \text{ L soln}} \times \frac{1 \text{ mol } HClO_4}{100.5 \text{ g } HClO_4} = 3.597 \times 10^{-3} = 3.60 \times 10^{-3}\ M\ HClO_4$$

$[H^+] = 3.60 \times 10^{-3}$ *M*; pH = -log (3.60×10^{-3}) = 2.444

(c) $M_c \times V_c = M_d \times V_d$

1.00 *M* HCl × 5.00 mL HCl = M_d HCl × 750 mL HCl

$$M_d\ HCl = \frac{1.00\ M \times 5.00 \text{ mL}}{750 \text{ mL}} = 6.67 \times 10^{-3}\ M\ HCl = 6.67 \times 10^{-3}\ M\ H^+$$

pH = -log (6.67×10^{-3}) = 2.176

(d) $$[H^+]_{total} = \frac{\text{mol } H^+ \text{ from HCl} + \text{mol } H^+ \text{ from HI}}{\text{total L solution}}; \quad \text{mol} = M \times L$$

$$[H^+]_{total} = \frac{(0.020\ M\ HCl \times 0.0500 \text{ L}) + (0.010\ M\ HI \times 0.125 \text{ L})}{0.175 \text{ L}}$$

$$[H^+]_{total} = \frac{1.0 \times 10^{-3} \text{ mol } H^+ + 1.25 \times 10^{-3} \text{ mol } H^+}{0.175 \text{ L}} = 0.01286 = 0.013\ M$$

pH = -log (0.01286) = 1.89

16.36 For a strong base, which is completely dissociated, $[OH^-]$ = the initial base concentration. Then, pOH = -log $[OH^-]$ and pH = 14 - pOH.

(a) 0.0050 *M* KOH = 0.0050 *M* OH^-; pOH = -log (0.0050) = 2.30;

pH = 14 - 1.30 = 11.70

(b) $$\frac{2.055 \text{ g KOH}}{0.5000 \text{ L}} \times \frac{1 \text{ mol KOH}}{56.106 \text{ g KOH}} = 0.073254 = 0.07325\ M = [OH^-]$$

pOH = -log (0.073254) = 1.1352; pH = 14 - pOH = 12.8648

(c) $M_c \times V_c = M_d \times V_d$

0.250 *M* $Ca(OH)_2$ × 10.0 mL = M_d $Ca(OH)_2$ × 500 mL

$$M_d\ Ca(OH)_2 = \frac{0.250\ M\ Ca(OH)_2 \times 10.0 \text{ mL}}{500.0 \text{ mL}} = 0.00500\ M\ Ca(OH)_2$$

$Ca(OH)_2(aq) \rightarrow Ca^{2+}(aq) + 2OH^-(aq)$

$[OH^-] = 2[Ca(OH)_2] = 2(5.00 \times 10^{-3}\ M) = 0.0100\ M$

pOH = -log (0.0100) = 2.000; pH = 14 - pOH = 12.00

(d) $$[OH^-]_{total} = \frac{\text{mol } OH^- \text{ from NaOH} + \text{mol } OH^- \text{ from } Ba(OH)_2}{\text{total L solution}}$$

$$\frac{(7.5 \times 10^{-3}\ M \times 0.0300 \text{ L}) + 2(0.015\ M \times 0.0100 \text{ L})}{0.0400 \text{ L}}$$

$$[OH^-]_{total} = \frac{2.25 \times 10^{-4} \text{ mol } OH^- + 3.0 \times 10^{-4} \text{ mol } OH^-}{0.0400 \text{ L}} = 0.0131 = 0.013\ M\ OH^-$$

pOH = -log (0.0131) = 1.88; pH = 14 - pOH = 12.12

16.38 pOH = 14 - pH = 14.00 - 12.00 = 2.00

pOH = 2.00 = -log$[OH^-]$; $[OH^-] = 10^{-2.00} = 1.0 \times 10^{-2}\ M$

$[OH^-] = 2[Ca(OH)_2]$; $[Ca(OH)_2] = [OH^-] / 2 = 1.0 \times 10^{-2} / 2 = 5.0 \times 10^{-3}\ M$

16.40 Upon dissolving, Li_2O dissociates to form Li^+ and O^{2-}. According to Equation 16.19, O^{2-} is completely protonated in aqueous solution.

Thus, initial $[Li_2O] = [O_2^-]$; $[OH^-] = 2[O^{2-}] = 2[Li_2O]$

$$[Li_2O] = \frac{\text{mol } Li_2O}{\text{L solution}} = 2.50 \text{ g } Li_2O \times \frac{1 \text{ mol } Li_2O}{29.88 \text{ g } Li_2O} \times \frac{1}{1.20 \text{ L}} = 0.06972 = 0.697\ M$$

$[OH^-] = 0.1394 = 0.139\ M$; pOH = 0.856 pH = 14.00 - pOH = 13.144

Weak Acids

16.42 (a) $HC_6H_5O(aq) \rightleftharpoons H^+(aq) + C_6H_5O^-(aq)$; $K_a = \frac{[H^+][C_6H_5O^-]}{[HC_6H_5O]}$

$HC_6H_5O(aq) + H_2O(l) \rightleftharpoons H_3O^+(aq) + C_6H_5O^-(aq)$; $K_a = \frac{[H_3O^+][C_6H_5O^-]}{[HC_6H_5O]}$

(b) $HCO_3^-(aq) \rightleftharpoons H^+(aq) + CO_3^{2-}(aq)$; $K_a = \frac{[H^+][CO_3^{2-}]}{[HCO_3^-]}$

$HCO_3^-(aq) + H_2O(aq) \rightleftharpoons H_3O^+(aq) + CO_3^{2-}(aq)$; $K_a = \frac{[H_3O^+][CO_3^{2-}]}{[HCO_3^-]}$

16.44 $HC_8H_7O_2(aq) \rightleftharpoons H^+(aq) + C_8H_7O_2^-(aq)$; $K_a = \frac{[H^+][C_8H_7O_2^-]}{[HC_8H_7O_2]}$

$[H^+] = [C_8H_7O_2^-] = 10^{-2.68} = 2.09 \times 10^{-3} = 2.1 \times 10^{-3}$ *M*

$[HC_8H_7O_2] = 0.085 - 2.09 \times 10^{-3} = 0.0829 = 0.083$ *M*

$K_a = \frac{(2.09 \times 10^{-3})^2}{0.0829} = 5.3 \times 10^{-5}$

16.46 $[H^+] = 0.110 \times [CH_2ClCOOH]_{initial} = 0.0110$ *M*

	$CH_2ClCOOH(aq)$	$\rightleftharpoons$	$H^+(aq)$	+	$CH_2ClCOO^-(aq)$
initial	0.100 *M*		0		0
equil.	0.089*M*		0.0110 *M*		0.0110 *M*

$K_a = \frac{[H^+][CH_2ClCOO^-]}{[CH_2ClCOOH]} = \frac{(0.0110)^2}{0.089} = 1.4 \times 10^{-3}$

16.48 $[H^+] = 10^{-pH} = 10^{-2.70} = 1.995 \times 10^{-3} = 2.0 \times 10^{-3}$ *M*

$K_a = 6.8 \times 10^{-4} = \frac{[H^+][F^-]}{[HF]} = \frac{(1.995 \times 10^{-3})^2}{x - 1.995 \times 10^{-3}}$

$6.8 \times 10^{-4}(x - 1.995 \times 10^{-3}) = (1.995 \times 10^{-3})^2$;

$6.8 \times 10^{-4} x = 1.357 \times 10^{-6} + 3.981 \times 10^{-6} = 5.338 \times 10^{-6}$

$x = 7.85 \times 10^{-3} = 7.9 \times 10^{-3}$ *M* HF

mol = *M* × L = 7.85×10^{-3} *M* × 0.500 L = $3.925 \times 10^{-3} = 3.9 \times 10^{-3}$ mol HF

16.50

	$HClO(aq)$	$\rightleftharpoons$	$H^+(aq)$	+	$ClO^-(aq)$
initial	0.0075 *M*		0		0
equil.	(0.0075 - x) *M*		x *M*		x *M*

$$K_a = \frac{[H^+][ClO^-]}{[HClO]} = \frac{x^2}{(0.0075 - x)} \approx \frac{x^2}{0.0075} = 3.0 \times 10^{-8}$$

$x^2 = 0.0075\,(3.0 \times 10^{-8})$; $x = 1.5 \times 10^{-5}$ $M = [H^+] = [H_3O^+] = [ClO^-]$

$[HClO] = 7.5 \times 10^{-3} - 1.5 \times 10^{-5} = 7.485 \times 10^{-3} = 7.5 \times 10^{-3}$ M

Check. $\frac{4.7 \times 10^{-5}\ M\ H^+}{0.0075\ M\ HClO} \times 100 = 0.20\%$ ionization; the assumption is valid

16.52 (a)

	$HOCl(aq)$	$\rightleftharpoons$	$H^+(aq)$	+	$OCl^-(aq)$
initial	0.125 M		0		0
equil	(0.125 - x) M		x M		x M

$$K_a = \frac{[H^+][OCl^-]}{[HOCl]} = \frac{x^2}{(0.125 - x)} \approx \frac{x^2}{0.125} = 3.0 \times 10^{-8}$$

$x^2 = 0.125\,(3.0 \times 10^{-8})$; $x = [H^+] = 6.1 \times 10^{-5}$ M, pH = 4.21

Check. $\frac{6.1 \times 10^{-5}\ M\ H^+}{0.125\ M\ HOCl} \times 100 = 0.049\%$ ionization; the assumption is valid

(b)

$$K_a = \frac{[H^+][C_6H_5O^-]}{[C_6H_5OH]} = \frac{x^2}{(0.0085 - x)} \approx \frac{x^2}{0.0085} = 1.3 \times 10^{-10}$$

$x^2 = 0.0085\,(1.3 \times 10^{-10})$; $x = [H^+] = 1.1 \times 10^{-6}$ M, pH = 5.98

Check. Clearly 1.1×10^{-6} M H^+ is small compared to 8.5×10^{-3} M C_6H_5OH, and the assumption is valid.

(c)

	$HONH_2(aq)$ + $H_2O(l)$	$\rightleftharpoons$	$HONH_3^+(aq)$	+	$OH^-(aq)$
initial	0.095 M		0		0
equil	(0.095 - x) M		x M		x M

$$K_b = \frac{[HONH_3^+][OH^-]}{[HONH_2]} = \frac{x^2}{(0.095 - x)} \approx \frac{x^2}{0.095} = 1.1 \times 10^{-8}$$

$x^2 = 0.095\,(1.1 \times 10^{-8})$; $x = [OH^-] = 3.2 \times 10^{-5}$ M, pH = 9.51

Check. $\frac{3.2 \times 10^{-5}\ M\ OH^-}{0.095\ M\ HONH_2} \times 100 = 0.034\%$ ionization; the assumption is valid

16.54 Calculate the initial concentration of $HC_9H_7O_4$.

$$2 \text{ tablets} \times \frac{500 \text{ mg}}{\text{tablet}} \times \frac{1 \text{ g}}{1000 \text{ mg}} \times \frac{1 \text{ mol } HC_9H_7O_4}{180.2 \text{ g } HC_9H_7O_4} = 0.005549 = 0.00555 \text{ mol } HC_9H_7O_4$$

$$\frac{0.005549 \text{ mol } HC_9H_7O_4}{0.250 \text{ L}} = 0.002220 = 0.0222\ M\ HC_9H_7O_4$$

	$HC_9H_7O_4(aq)$ $\rightleftharpoons$	$C_9H_7O_4^-(aq)$ +	$H^+(aq)$
initial	0.0222 *M*	0 *M*	0 *M*
equil	(0.0222 - x)	x *M*	x *M*

$$K_a = 3.3 \times 10^{-4} = \frac{[H^+][C_7H_9O_4^-]}{[HC_7H_9O_4]} = \frac{x^2}{(0.00222 - x)}$$

Assuming x is small compared to 0.0222,

$x^2 = 0.00222\ (3.3 \times 10^{-4})$; $x = [H^+] = 2.7 \times 10^{-3}\ M$

$$\frac{2.7 \times 10^{-3}\ M\ H^+}{0.0222\ M\ HC_9H_7O_4} \times 100 = 12\%\ \text{ionization; the assumption is not valid}$$

Using the quadratic formula, $x^2 + 3.3 \times 10^{-4}\,x - 7.325 \times 10^{-6} = 0$

$$x = \frac{-3.3 \times 10^{-4} \pm \sqrt{(3.3 \times 10^{-4})^2 - 4(1)(-7.325 \times 10^{-6})}}{2(1)} = \frac{-3.3 \times 10^{-4} \pm \sqrt{2.941 \times 10^{-5}}}{2}$$

$x = 2.547 \times 10^{-3} = 2.5 \times 10^{-3}\ M\ H^+$; pH = -log$(2.547 \times 10^{-3})$ = 2.594 = 2.59

16.56 (a) $HCrO_4^-(aq) \rightleftharpoons H^+(aq) + CrO_4^{2-}(aq)$

$$K_a = 3.0 \times 10^{-7} = \frac{[H^+][CrO_4^{2-}]}{[HCrO_4^-]} = \frac{x^2}{0.250 - x}$$

$x^2 = 0.250\ (3.0 \times 10^{-7})$; $x = 2.74 \times 10^{-4} = 2.7 \times 10^{-4}\ M\ H^+$

$$\%\ \text{ionization} = \frac{2.74 \times 10^{-4}\ M H^+}{0.250\ M HCrO_4^-} \times 100 = 0.11\%$$

(b) $\dfrac{x^2}{0.0800} \approx 3.0 \times 10^{-7}$; $x = 1.549 \times 10^{-4} = 1.5 \times 10^{-4}\ M\ H^+$

$$\%\ \text{ionization} = \frac{1.55 \times 10^{-4}\ M H^+}{0.0800\ M HCrO_4^-} \times 100 = 0.19\%$$

(c) $\dfrac{x^2}{0.0200} \approx 3.0 \times 10^{-7}$; $x = 7.746 = 7.7 \times 10^{-5}\ M\ H^+$

$$\%\ \text{ionization} = \frac{7.75 \times 10^{-5}\ M H^+}{0.0200\ M HCrO_4^-} \times 100 = 0.39\%$$

16.58 $HX(aq) \rightleftharpoons H^+(aq) + X^-(aq)$; $K_a = \dfrac{[H^+][X^-]}{[HX]}$

$[H^+] = [X^-]$; assume the % ionization is small; $K_a = \dfrac{[H^+]^2}{[HX]}$; $[H^+] = K_a^{1/2}\,[HX]^{1/2}$

pH = $-\log K_a^{1/2}\,[HX]^{1/2} = -\log K_a^{1/2} - \log\,[HX]^{1/2}$; pH = $-1/2 \log K_a - 1/2 \log\,[HX]$

This is the equation of a straight line, where the intercept is $-1/2 \log K_a$, the slope is -1/2, and the independent variable is log [HX].

16.60 $H_2C_4H_4O_6(aq) \rightleftharpoons H^+(aq) + HC_4H_4O_6^-(aq)$ $K_{a1} = 1.0 \times 10^{-3}$

$HC_4H_4O_6^-(aq \rightleftharpoons H^+(aq) + C_4H_4O_6^{2-}(aq)$ $K_{a2} = 4.6 \times 10^{-5}$

Begin by calculating the $[H^+]$ from the first ionization. The equilibrium concentrations are $[H^+] = [HC_4H_4O_6^-] = x$, $[H_2C_4H_4O_6] = 0.25 - x$.

$$K_{a1} = \frac{[H^+][HC_4H_4O_6^-]}{[H_2C_4H_4O_6]} = \frac{x^2}{0.25 - x};\ x^2 + 1.0 \times 10^{-3}\,x - 2.5 \times 10^{-4} = 0$$

Using the quadratic formula, $x = 1.532 \times 10^{-2} = 0.015\ M\ H^+$ from the first ionization. Next calculate the H^+ contribution from the second ionization.

	$HC_4H_4O_6^-(aq)$	$\rightleftharpoons$	$H^+(aq)$	+	$C_4H_4O_6^{2-}(aq)$
initial	0.015		0.015		0
equil.	(0.015 - y)		(0.015 + y)		y

$$K_{a2} = \frac{(0.015 + y)(y)}{(0.015 - y)} = 4.6 \times 10^{-5}$$; assuming y is small compared to 0.015,

$y = 4.6 \times 10^{-5}\ M\ HC_4H_4O_6^{2-}(aq)$

This assumption is reasonable, since 4.6×10^{-5} is only 0.3% of 0.015. $[H^+] = 0.015\ M$ (first ionization) + 4.6×10^{-5} (second ionization). Since 4.6×10^{-5} is 0.3% of 0.015 *M*, it can be safely ignored when calculating total $[H^+]$. Thus, pH = -log(0.01532) = 1.18148 = 1.181.

Assumptions:

1) The ionization can be treated as a series of steps (valid by Hess's Law).

2) The extent of ionization in the second step (y) is small relative to that from the first step (valid for this acid and initial concentration). This assumption was used twice, to calculate the value of y from K_{a2} and to calculate total $[H^+]$ and pH.

Weak Bases

16.62 Organic amines (neutral molecules with nonbonded pairs on N atoms) and anions that are the conjugate bases of weak acids function as weak bases.

16.64 (a) $C_3H_7NH_2(aq) + H_2O(l) \rightleftharpoons C_3H_7NH_3^+(aq) + OH^-(aq)$; $K_b = \frac{[C_3H_7NH_3^+][OH^-]}{[C_3H_7NH_2]}$

(b) $HPO_4^{2-}(aq) + H_2O(l) \rightleftharpoons H_2PO_4^-(aq) + OH^-(aq)$; $K_b = \frac{[H_2PO_4^-][OH^-]}{[HPO_4^{2-}]}$

(c) $C_6H_5CO_2^-(aq) + H_2O(l) \rightleftharpoons C_6H_5CO_2H(aq) + OH^-(aq)$; $K_b = \frac{[C_6H_5CO_2H][OH^-]}{[C_6H_5CO_2^-]}$

16.66 $BrO^-(aq) + H_2O(l) \rightleftharpoons HOBr(aq) + OH^-(aq)$

initial	1.15 *M*	0	0
equil.	(1.15 - x) *M*	x *M*	x *M*

$$K_b = \frac{[HOBr][OH^-]}{[BrO^-]} = \frac{x^2}{1.15 - x} \approx \frac{x^2}{1.15} = 4.0 \times 10^{-6}$$

$x^2 = 1.15\,(4.0 \times 10^{-6})$; $x = [OH^-] = 2.14 \times 10^{-3} = 2.1 \times 10^{-3}$ *M*; pH = 11.33

Check. $\dfrac{2.1 \times 10^{-3}\ M\ OH^-}{1.15\ M\ C_3H_5O_2^-} \times 100 = 0.19\%$ hydrolysis; the assumption is valid

16.68 (a) pOH = 14.00 - 9.95 = 4.05; $[OH^-] = 10^{-4.05} = 8.91 \times 10^{-5} = 8.9 \times 10^{-5}$ *M*

$C_{18}H_{21}NO_3(aq) + H_2O(l) \rightleftharpoons C_{18}H_{21}NO_3H^+(aq) + OH^-(aq)$

initial	0.0050 *M*	0	0
equil.	$(0.0050 - 8.9 \times 10^{-5})$	8.9×10^{-5} *M*	8.9×10^{-5} *M*

$$K_b = \frac{[C_{18}H_{21}NO_3H^+][OH^-]}{[C_{18}H_{21}NO_3]} = \frac{(8.91 \times 10^{-5})^2}{(0.0050 - 8.91 \times 10^{-5})} = 1.62 \times 10^{-6} = 1.6 \times 10^{-6}$$

(b) $pK_b = -\log(K_b) = -\log(1.62 \times 10^{-6}) = 5.79$

The K_a - K_b Relationship; Acid-Base Properties of Salts

16.70 (a) We need K_a for the conjugate acid of CO_3^{2-}, K_a for HCO_3^-. K_a for HCO_3^- is K_{a2}.

(b) $K_b = K_w / K_a = 1.0 \times 10^{-14} / 5.6 \times 10^{-11} = 1.8 \times 10^{-4}$

(c) K_b for CO_3^{2-} (1.8×10^{-4}) > K_b for NH_3 (1.8×10^{-5}).
CO_3^{2-} is a stronger base than NH_3.

16.72 (a) Ammonia is the stronger base because it has the larger K_b value.

(b) Hydroxylammonium is the stronger acid because the weaker base, hydroxylamine, has the stronger conjugate acid.

(c) K_a for $NH_4^+ = K_w/K_b$ for $NH_3 = 1.0 \times 10^{-14}/1.8 \times 10^{-5} = 5.6 \times 10^{-10}$

K_a for $HONH_3^+ = K_w/K_b$ for $HONH_2 = 1.0 \times 10^{-14}/1.1 \times 10^{-8} = 9.1 \times 10^{-7}$

Note that K_a for $HONH_3^+$ is larger than K_a for NH_4^+.

16.74 (a) Proceeding as in Solution 16.73(a):

$$F^-(aq) + H_2O(l) \rightleftharpoons HF(aq) + OH^-(aq)$$

initial	0.036 *M*	0 *M*	0 *M*
equil	(0.036 - x) *M*	x *M*	x *M*

$$K_b \text{ for } F^- = \frac{[HF][OH^-]}{[F^-]} = \frac{K_w}{K_a \text{ for HF}} = \frac{1.0 \times 10^{-14}}{6.8 \times 10^{-4}} = 1.47 \times 10^{-11} = 1.5 \times 10^{-11}$$

$1.5 \times 10^{-11} = \frac{(x)(x)}{(0.036 - x)}$; assume the amount of F^- that hydrolyzes is small

$x^2 = 0.036\ (1.47 \times 10^{-11})$; $x = [OH^-] = 7.276 \times 10^{-7} = 7.3 \times 10^{-7}\ M$

pOH = 6.14; pH = 14 - 6.14 = 7.86

(b) $Na_2S(aq) \rightarrow S^{2-}(aq) + 2Na^+(aq)$

$S^{2-}(aq) + H_2O(l) \rightleftharpoons HS^-(aq) + OH^-(aq)$

As in part (a) above, $[OH^-] = [HS^-] = x$; $[S^{2-}] = 0.127\ M$

$$K_b = \frac{[HS^-][OH^-]}{[S^{2-}]} = \frac{K_w}{K_a \text{ for } HS^-} = \frac{1.0 \times 10^{-14}}{1 \times 10^{-19}} = 1 \times 10^5$$

Since $K_b >> 1$, the equilibrium above lies far to the right and $[OH^-] = [S^{2-}] = 0.127\ M$. K_b for $HS^- = 1.05 \times 10^{-7}$; $[OH^-]$ produced by further hydrolysis of HS^- amounts to $1.2 \times 10^{-4}\ M$. The second hydrolysis step does not make a significant contribution to the total $[OH^-]$ and pH.

$[OH^-] = 0.127\ M$; pOH = 0.896, pH = 13.104

(c) As in Solution 16.73(c), calculate total $[C_2H_3O_2^-]$.

$[C_2H_3O_2^-]_t = [C_2H_3O_2^-]$ from $NaC_2H_3O_2$ + $[C_2H_3O_2^-]$ from $Ba(C_2H_3O_2)_2$

$[C_2H_3O_2^-]_t = 0.035\ M + 2(0.055\ M) = 0.145\ M$

The hydrolysis equilibrium is $C_2H_3O_2^-(aq) + H_2O(l) \rightleftharpoons HC_2H_3O_2(aq) + OH^-(aq)$

$$K_b = \frac{[HC_2H_3O_2][OH^-]}{[C_2H_3O_2^-]} = \frac{K_w}{K_a \text{ for } HC_2H_3O_2} = \frac{1.0 \times 10^{-14}}{1.8 \times 10^{-5}} = 5.56 \times 10^{-10} = 5.6 \times 10^{-10}$$

$[OH^-] = [HC_2H_3O_2] = x$, $[C_2H_3O_2^-] = 0.145 - x$

$K_b = 5.56 \times 10^{-10} = \frac{x^2}{(0.145 - x)}$; assume x is small compared to 0.145 *M*

$x^2 = 0.145\ (5.56 \times 10^{-10})$; $x = [OH^-] = 8.975 \times 10^{-6} = 9.0 \times 10^{-6}$

$pH = 14 + \log(8.975 \times 10^{-6}) = 8.95$

16.76 (a) neutral; both Cs^+ and Br^- are negligible.

(b) acidic; Al^{3+} is a highly charged metal cation and a Lewis acid; NO_3^- is negligible.

(c) basic; CN^- is the conjugate base of HCN; K^+ is negligible.

(d) acidic; $CH_3NH_3^+$ is the conjugate acid of CH_3NH_2; Cl^- is negligible.

(e) acidic; HSO_4^- is a negligible base, but a fairly strong acid ($K_a = 1.2 \times 10^{-2}$).

16.78 *Plan.* Estimate pH of salt solution by evaluating the ions in the salts. Calculate to confirm if necessary. *Solve:*

KBr: salt of strong acid and strong base, neutral solution. The unknown is probably KBr. Check the others to be sure.

NH4Cl: salt of a weak base and a strong acid, acidic solution

KCN: salt of a strong base and a weak acid, basic solution

K_2CO_3: salt of a strong base and a weak acid (HCO_3^-), basic solution

Only KBr fits the acid-base properties of the unknown.

16.80 The solution is basic because of the hydrolysis of PO_4^{3-}. The molarity of PO_4^{3-} is

$$\frac{50.0\text{ g } Na_3PO_4}{1.00\text{ L soln}} \times \frac{1\text{ mol } Na_3PO_4}{163.9\text{ g } Na_3PO_4} = 0.3051 = 0.305\ M\ PO_4^{3-}$$

$$PO_4^{3-}(aq) + H_2O(l) \rightleftharpoons HPO_4^{2-}(aq) + OH^-(aq)$$

$$K_b = \frac{[HPO_4^{2-}][OH^-]}{[PO_4^{3-}]} = \frac{K_w}{K_a \text{ for } HPO_4^{2-}} = \frac{1.0 \times 10^{-14}}{4.2 \times 10^{-13}} = 0.0238 = 2.4 \times 10^{-2}$$

Ignoring the further hydrolysis of HPO_4^{2-}.

$[OH^-] = [HPO_4^{2-}] = x$, $[PO_4^{3-}] = 0.305 - x$

$$2.4 \times 10^{-2} = \frac{x^2}{(0.305 - x)};\quad x^2 + 2.4 \times 10^{-2}\,x - 0.0073 = 0$$

Since K_b is relatively large, we will not assume x is small compared to 0.305.

$$x = \frac{-0.024 \pm \sqrt{(0.024)^2 - 4(1)(-0.0073)}}{2(1)} = \frac{-0.024 \pm \sqrt{0.0299}}{2(1)}$$

$x = 0.074\ M\ OH^-$; pH = 14 + log (0.074) = 12.87

Acid-Base Character and Chemical Structure

16.82 (a) Acid strength increases as the polarity of the X–H bond increases and decreases as the strength of the X–H bond increases.

(b) Assuming the element, X, is more electronegative than H, as the electronegativity of X increases, the X–H bond becomes more polar and the strength of the acid increases. This trend holds true as electronegativiy increases across a row of the periodic chart. However, as electronegativity decreases going down a family, acid strength increases because the strength of the H–X bond decreases, even though the H–X bond becomes less polar.

16.84 (a) For binary hydrides, acid strength increases going across a row, so HCl is a stronger acid than H_2S.

(b) For oxyacids, the more electronegative the central atom, the stronger the acid, so H_3PO_4 is a stronger acid than H_3AsO_4.

(c) $HBrO_3$ has one more nonprotonated oxygen and a higher oxidation number on Br, so it is a stronger acid than $HBrO_2$.

(d) The first dissociation of a polyprotic acid is always stronger because H^+ is more tightly held by an anion, so $H_2C_2O_4$ is a stronger acid than $HC_2O_4^-$.

(e) The conjugate base of benzoic acid, $C_7H_5O_2^-$, is stabilized by resonance, while the conjugate base of phenol, $C_6H_5O^-$, is not. $HC_7H_5O_2$ has greater tendency to form its conjugate base and is the stronger acid.

16.86 (a) NO_2^- (HNO_3 is the stronger acid because it has more nonprotonated O atoms, so NO_2^- is the stronger base.)

(b) PO_4^{3-} (K_a for $HAsO_4^{2-}$ is greater than K_a for HPO_4^{2-}, so K_b for PO_4^{3-} is greater and PO_4^{3-} is the stronger base. Note that P is more electronegative than As and H_3PO_4 is a stronger acid than H_3AsO_4, which could lead to the conclusion that AsO_4^{3-} is the stronger base. As in all cases, the measurement of base strength, K_b, supercedes the prediction. Chemistry is an experimental science.

(c) CO_3^{2-} (The more negative the anion, the stronger the attraction for H^+.)

16.88 (a) True.

(b) False. For oxyacids with the same structure but different central atom, the acid strength **increases** as the electronegativity of the central atom increases.

(c) False. HF is a weak acid, weaker than the other hydrogen halides, primarily because the H–F bond energy is exceptionally high.

Lewis Acids and Bases

16.90. No. If a substance is a Lewis acid, it is not necessarily a Brønsted or an Arrhenius acid. The Lewis definition of an acid, an electron pair acceptor, is most general. A Lewis acid does not necessarily fit the more narrow description of a Brønsted or Arrhenius acid. An electron pair acceptor isn't necessarily an H^+ donor, nor must it produce H^+ in aqueous solution. An example is Al^{3+}, which is a Lewis acid, but has no ionizable hydrogen.

16.92

	Lewis Acid	Lewis Base
(a)	HNO_2 (or H^+)	OH^-
(b)	$FeBr_3$ (Fe^{3+})	Br^-

		Lewis Acid	Lewis Base
	(c)	Zn^{2+}	NH_3
	(d)	SO_2	H_2O

16.94 (a) $ZnBr_2$, smaller cation radius, same charge

(b) $Cu(NO_3)_2$, higher cation charge

(c) $NiBr_2$, smaller cation radius, same charge

Additional Exercises

19.96 (a) Correct.

(b) Incorrect. A Brønsted acid has ionizable hydrogen while Lewis bases have unshared electron pairs.

(c) Incorrect. The weaker the acid, the stronger its conjugate base.

(d) Correct.

(e) Incorrect. The lower the concentration of a weak base (or weak acid), the greater its percent ionization.

16.97 (a) A high O_2 concentration displaces protons from Hb, and thus produces a more acidic solution, with lower pH.

(b) $[H^+]$ = antilog (-7.4) = 4.0×10^{-8} *M*. At body temperature, 37°C, $K_w = 2.4 \times 10^{-14}$ (see Solution 16.29). At this temperature, a 'neutral' solution has $[H^+] = 1.5 \times 10^{-7}$ and pH 6.81. Even though the frame of reference is a bit different at this temperature, blood at pH 7.4 is slightly basic.

(c) The equilibrium indicates that a high $[H^+]$ shifts the equilibrium toward the proton-bound form HbH^+, which means a **lower** concentration of HbO_2 in the blood. Thus the ability of hemoglobin to transport oxygen is impeded.

16.100 (a) $K_a = \dfrac{[H^+][C_8H_5O_4^{2-}]}{[HC_8H_5O_4^-]}$; $[H^+] = [C_8H_5O_4^{2-}] = 10^{-pH} = 10^{-4.24} = 5.754 \times 10^{-5} = 5.8 \times 10^{-5}$ *M*

$$[HC_8H_5O_4^-] = 525 \text{ mg } HC_8H_5O_4^- \times \frac{1 \text{ g}}{1000 \text{ mg}} \times \frac{1 \text{ mol } HC_8H_5O_4^-}{166.13 \text{ g } HC_8H_5O_4^-} \times \frac{1}{0.250 \text{ L}}$$

$$= 0.0126\ M$$

$$K_a = \frac{[H^+][C_8H_5O_4^{2-}]}{[HC_8H_5O_4^-]} = \frac{(5.754 \times 10^{-5})^2}{(0.0126 - 5.754 \times 10^{-5})} = 2.64 \times 10^{-7} = 2.6 \times 10^{-7}$$

(b) $$\% \text{ ionization} = \frac{[H^+]}{[HA]_{initial}} \times 100 = \frac{5.8 \times 10^{-5}}{0.0126} \times 100 = 0.46\%$$

16.102 *Analyze/Plan.* Evaluate the acid-base properties of the cation and anion to determine whether a solution of the salt will be acidic, basic or neutral. *Solve:*

(i) NH_4Cl: NH_4^+, weak conjugate acid of NH_3; Cl^-, negligible conjugate base of HCl; acidic solution

(ii) $NaNO_3$: Na^+, negligible conjugate acid of NaOH; NO_3^-, negligible conjugate base of HNO_3; neutral solution.

(iii) $NH_4C_2H_3O_2$: NH_4^+, weak conjugate acid of NH_3, $K_a = K_w/1.8 \times 10^{-5} = 5.6 \times 10^{-10}$; $C_2H_3O_2^-$, weak conjugate base of $HC_2H_3O_2$, $K_b = K_w/1.8 \times 10^{-5} = 5.6 \times 10^{-10}$; neutral solution ($K_a$ for the cation and K_b for the anion are accidentally equal, producing a neutral solution.

(iv) NaF: Na^+, negligible conjugate acid of NaOH; F^-, weak conjugate base of HF, $K_b = K_w/6.8 \times 10^{-4} = 1.5 \times 10^{-11}$; basic solution.

(v) $NaC_2H_3O_2$: Na^+, negligible; $C_2H_3O_2^-$, weak base, $K_b = 5.6 \times 10^{-10}$, basic solution.

In order of increasing acidity and decreasing pH: 0.1 M $NaC_2H_3O_2$ > 0.1 M NaF > 0.1 M $NH_4C_2H_3O_2$ ≈0.1 M $NaNO_3$ > 0.1 M NH_4Cl; (v) > (iv) > (iii) ~ (ii) > (i)

(iv) and (v) are both bases, and (v) has the greater K_b value and higher pH. (ii) and (iii) are both neutral and (i) is acidic.

16.103 Considering the stepwise dissociation of H_3PO_4:

	$H_3PO_4(aq)$	$\rightleftharpoons$	$H^+(aq)$ +	$H_2PO_4^-(aq)$
initial	0.025		0	0
equil.	(0.025 - x) *M*		x	x

$$K_{a1} = \frac{[H^+][H_2PO_4^-]}{[H_3PO_4]} = \frac{x^2}{(0.025 - x)} = 7.5 \times 10^{-3}; \quad x^2 + 7.5 \times 10^{-3}\,x - 1.875 \times 10^{-4} = 0$$

$$x = \frac{-7.5 \times 10^{-3} \pm \sqrt{(7.5 \times 10^{-3})^2 - 4(1)(-1.875 \times 10^{-4})}}{2(1)} = \frac{-7.5 \times 10^{-3} \pm \sqrt{8.06 \times 10^{-4}}}{2}$$

x = 0.01045 = 0.010 *M* H^+, 0.010 *M* $H_2PO_4^-$ available for further ionization

	$H_2PO_4^-(aq)$	$\rightleftharpoons$	$H^+(aq)$	+	$HPO_4^{2-}(aq)$
initial	0.010 *M*		0.010 *M*		0 *M*
equil.	(0.010 - y) *M*		(0.010 + y) *M*		y *M*

$$K_{a2} = \frac{[H^+][HPO_4^{2-}]}{[H_2PO_4^-]} = \frac{(y)(0.010 + y)}{(0.010 - y)} = 6.2 \times 10^{-8}$$

Since K_{a2} is very small, assume y is small compared to 0.010 *M*.

$6.2 \times 10^{-8} = \frac{0.010\,y}{0.010}$; $y = [HPO_4^{2-}] = 6.2 \times 10^{-8}\ M$

$[H_2PO_4^-] = (0.010\ M + 6.2 \times 10^{-8}\ M) \approx 0.010\ M$

$[H^+] = (0.010\ M - 6.2 \times 10^{-8}\ M) \approx 0.010\ M$

$[HPO_4^{2-}]$ available for further ionization = $6.2 \times 10^{-8}\ M$

	HPO_4^{2-}	$\rightleftharpoons$	$H^+(aq)$	+	$PO_4^{3-}(aq)$
initial	$6.2 \times 10^{-8}\ M$		$0.010\ M$		$0\ M$
equil.	$(6.2 \times 10^{-8} - z)\ M$		$(0.010 + z)\ M$		$z\ M$

$$K_{a3} = \frac{[H^+][PO_4^{3-}]}{[HPO_4^{2-}]} = \frac{(0.010 + z)(z)}{(6.2 \times 10^{-8} - z)} = 4.2 \times 10^{-13}$$

Assuming z is small compared to 6.2×10^{-8} (and 0.010),

$$\frac{(0.010)(z)}{(6.2 \times 10^{-8})} = 4.2 \times 10^{-13};\ z = 2.6 \times 10^{-18}\ M\ PO_4^{3-}$$

The contribution of z to $[HPO_4^{2-}]$ and $[H^+]$ is negligible. In summary, after all dissociation steps have reached equilibrium:

$[H^+] = 0.010\ M$, $[H_2PO_4^-] = 0.010\ M$, $[HPO_4^{2-}] = 6.2 \times 10^{-8}\ M$,

$[PO_4^{3-}] = 2.6 \times 10^{-18}\ M$

Note that the first ionization step is the major source of H^+ and the others are important as sources of HPO_4^{2-} and PO_4^{3-}. The $[PO_4^{3-}]$ is **very** small at equilibrium.

16.105 (a) Consider the formation of the zwitterion as a series of steps (Hess's Law).

$$NH_2–CH_2–COOH + H_2O \rightleftharpoons NH_2–CH_2–COO^- + H_3O^+ \quad K_a$$

$$NH_2–CH_2–COOH + H_2O \rightleftharpoons {}^+NH_3–CH_2–COOH + OH^- \quad K_b$$

$$H_3O^+ + OH^- \rightleftharpoons 2H_2O \quad 1/K_w$$

$$NH_2–CH_2–COOH \rightleftharpoons {}^+NH_3–CH_2–COO^- \quad \frac{K_a \times K_b}{K_w}$$

$$K = \frac{K_a \times K_b}{K_w} = \frac{(4.3 \times 10^{-3})(6.0 \times 10^{-5})}{1.0 \times 10^{-14}} = 2.6 \times 10^7$$

The large value of K indicates that formation of the zwitterion is favorable. The assumption is that the same $NH_2–CH_2–COOH$ molecule is acting like an acid ($–COOH \rightarrow H^+ + –COO^-$) and a base ($–NH_2 + H^+ \rightarrow NH_3^+$), simultaneously. Glycine is both a stronger acid and a stronger base than water, so the H^+ transfer should be intramolecular, as long as there are no other acids or bases in the solution.

(b) Since glycine exists as the zwitterion in aqueous solution, the pH is determined by the equilibrium below.

$$^{+}NH_3\text{–}CH_2\text{–}COO^- + H_2O \rightleftharpoons NH_2\text{–}CH_2\text{–}COO^- + H_3O^+$$

$$K_a = \frac{[NH_2\text{–}CH_2\text{–}COO^-][H_3O^+]}{[^{+}NH_3\text{–}CH_2\text{–}COO^-]} = \frac{K_w}{K_b} = \frac{1.0 \times 10^{-14}}{6.0 \times 10^{-5}} = 1.67 \times 10^{-10} = 1.7 \times 10^{-10}$$

$$x = [H_3O^+] = [NH_2\text{–}CH_2\text{–}COO^-];\ K_a = 1.67 \times 10^{-10} = \frac{(x)(x)}{(0.050 - x)} \approx \frac{x^2}{0.050}$$

$$x = [H_3O^+] = 2.89 \times 10^{-6} = 2.9 \times 10^{-6}\ M,\quad pH = 5.54$$

(c) In a strongly acidic solution the $-CO_2^-$ function would be protonated, so glycine would exist as $^{+}H_3NCH_2COOH$. In strongly basic solution the $-NH_3^+$ group would be deprotonated, so glycine would be in the form $H_2NCH_2CO_2^-$.

16.106 The general Lewis structure for these acids is

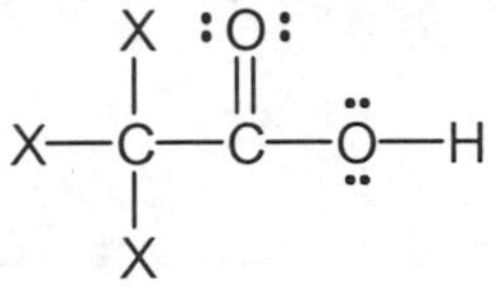

where X = H or Cl

Replacement of H by the more electronegative chlorine atoms causes the central carbon to become more positively charged, thus withdrawing more electrons from the attached COOH group, in turn causing the O–H bond to be more polar, so that H^+ is more readily ionized.

To calculate pH proceed as usual, except that the full quadratic formula must be used for all but acetic acid.

Acid	pH
acetic	3.37
chloroacetic	2.51
dichloroacetic	2.09
trichloroacetic	2.0

Integrative Exercises

16.108 $[H^+] = 10^{-pH} = 10^{-2} = 1 \times 10^{-2}\ M\ H^+$; $1 \times 10^{-2}\ M \times 0.400\ L = 4.0 \times 10^{-3} = 4 \times 10^{-3}$ mol H^+

$HCl(aq) + HCO_3^-(aq) \rightarrow Cl^-(aq) + H_2O(l) + CO_2(g)$

$$4 \times 10^{-3}\ \text{mol}\ H^+ = 4 \times 10^{-3}\ \text{mol}\ HCO_3^- \times \frac{84.01\ \text{g}\ NaHCO_3}{1\ \text{mol}\ HCO_3^-} = 0.336 = 0.3\ \text{g}\ NaHCO_3$$

16.110 (a) 24 valence e^-, 12 e^- pairs

The formal charges on all atoms are zero. Structures with multiple bonds lead to nonzero formal charges. There are 3 electron domains about Al. The electron-domain geometry and molecular structure are trigonal planar.

(b) The Al atom in $AlCl_3$ has an incomplete octet and is electron deficient. It "needs" to accept another electron pair, to act like a Lewis acid.

(c)

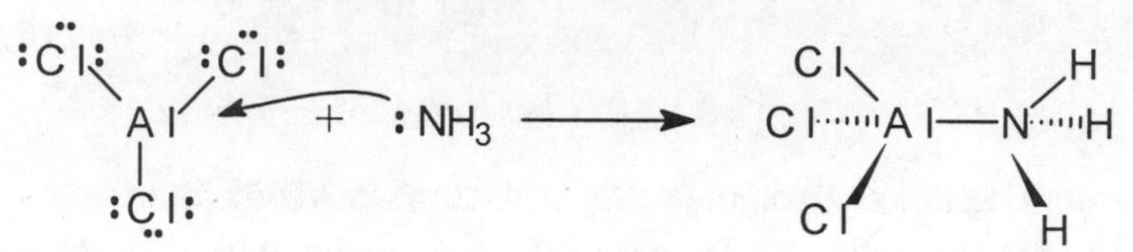

Both the Al and N atoms in the product have tetrahedral geometry.

(d) The Lewis theory is most appropriate. H^+ and $AlCl_3$ are both electron pair acceptors, Lewis acids.

16.111 *Plan.* Use acid ionization equilibrium to calculate the total moles of particles in solution. Use density to calculate kg solvent. From the molality (*m*) of the solution, calculate ΔT_b and T_b.
Solve:

	$HSO_4^-(aq)$ $\rightleftharpoons$	$H^+(aq)$ +	$SO_4^{2-}(aq)$
initial	0.10 *M*	0	0
equil.	0.10 - x *M*	x *M*	x *M*
	0.071 *M*	0.029 *M*	0.029 *M*

$$K_a = 1.2 \times 10^{-2} = \frac{[H^+][SO_4^{2-}]}{[HSO_4^-]} = \frac{x^2}{0.10 - x};$$ K_a is relatively large, so use the quadratic.

$$x^2 + 0.012\,x - 0.0012 = 0;\quad x = \frac{-0.012 \pm \sqrt{(0.012)^2 - 4(1)(-0.0012)}}{2};\quad x = 0.029\ M\ H^+,\ SO_4^{2-}$$

Total ion concentration = 0.10 *M* Na^+ + 0.071 *M* HSO_4^- + 0.029 *M* H^+ + 0.029 *M* SO_4^{2-}
= 0.229 = 0.23 *M*.

Assume 100.0 mL of solution. 1.002 g/mL × 100.0 mL = 100.2 g solution.

$$0.10\ M\ NaHSO_4 \times 0.1000\ L = 0.010\ mol\ NaHSO_4 \times \frac{120.1\ g\ NaHSO_4}{mol\ NaHSO_4}$$
$$= 1.201 = 12\ g\ NaHSO_4$$

100.2 g soln - 1.201 g $NaHSO_4$ = 99.0 g = 0.099 kg H_2O

$$m = \frac{mol\ ions}{kg\ H_2O} = \frac{0.229\ M \times 0.1000\ L}{0.0990\ kg} = 0.231 = 0.23\ m\ \text{ions}$$

$\Delta T_b = K_b(m) = 0.52°C/m \times (0.23\ m) = +0.12°C$; $T_b = 100.0 + 0.12 = 100.1°C$

16.113 (a) rate = $k[IO_3^-][SO_3^{2-}][H^+]$

(b) $\Delta pH = pH_2 - pH_1 = 3.50 - 5.00 = -1.50$

$\Delta pH = -\log [H^+]_2 - (-\log [H^+]_1)$; $-\Delta pH = \log [H^+]_2 - \log [H^+]_1$

$-\Delta pH = \log [H^+]_2 / [H^+]_1$; $[H^+]_2 / [H^+]_1 = 10^{-\Delta pH}$

$[H^+]_2/[H^+]_1 = 10^{1.50} = 31.6 = 32$. The rate will increase by a factor of 32 if $[H^+]$ increases by a factor of 32. The reaction goes faster at lower pH.

(c) Since H^+ does not appear in the overall reaction, it is either a catalyst or an intermediate. An intermediate is produced and then consumed during a reaction, so its contribution to the rate law can usually be written in terms of concentrations of other reactants (Sample Exercise 14.14). A catalyst is present at the beginning and end of a reaction and can appear in the rate law if it participates in the rate-determining step (Solution 14.66). This reaction is pH dependent because H^+ is a homogeneous catalyst that participates in the rate-determining step.

16.115 (a) The structures of the two acids are similar, but lactic acid has an –OH group on the C atom adjacent to the –COOH group. This electronegative substituent withdraws electron density from the –COOH group, increasing the strength of lactic acid relative to propionic acid. The stronger the acid, the larger the K_a value and the smaller the pK_a.

(b) pKa = 3.85, $K_a = 10^{-3.85} = 1.4 \times 10^{-4}$; $[H^+] = [C_3H_5O_3^-] = x$; $[HC_3H_5O_3] = 0.050 - x$

$$K_a = 1.4 \times 10^{-4} = \frac{[H^+]1[C_3H_5O_3^-]}{[HC_3H_5O_3]} = \frac{x^2}{0.050 - x} \approx \frac{x^2}{0.050}$$

$x^2 = 0.050(1.4 \times 10^{-4}) = 2.646 \times 10^{-3} = 2.6 \times 10^{-3}$ M $C_3H_5O_3^-$

(This represents 5.3% dissociation; solution by the quadratic yields essentially the same result.)

(c) Strategy: Assume a 100 g sample. Calculate mol Cu in sample. Use mole ratios from formula to calculate mass of O and H not due to H_2O. Subtract masses of Cu, C, H and O from 100 g to get mass of H_2O. Calculate mol H_2O and X.

Assume a 100 g sample, 22.9 g Cu.

$$22.9 \text{ g Cu} \times \frac{1 \text{ mol Cu}}{63.55 \text{ g Cu}} = 0.3603 = 0.360 \text{ mol Cu}$$

mole ratios of Cu, O and H (not due to H_2O): 1 Cu:6 O:10 H

$$\text{g O} = 0.3603 \text{ mol Cu} \times \frac{6 \text{ mol O}}{1 \text{ mol Cu}} \times \frac{16.00 \text{ g O}}{1 \text{ mol O}} = 34.59 = 34.6 \text{ g O}$$

$$\text{g H} = 0.3603 \text{ mol Cu} \times \frac{10 \text{ mol H}}{1 \text{ mol Cu}} \times \frac{1.008 \text{ g H}}{1 \text{ mol H}} = 3.632 = 3.63 \text{ g H}$$

$g\ H_2O = 100\ g\ sample - [22.9\ g\ Cu + 26.0\ g\ C + 34.6\ g\ O + 3.63\ g\ H]$

$= 12.87 = 12.9\ g\ H_2O$

$$12.87\ g\ H_2O \times \frac{1\ mol\ H_2O}{18.02\ g\ H_2O} = 0.7142\ mol\ H_2O/0.3604 = 1.98 \approx 2$$

X = 2 mol H_2O in the hydrate.

(d) Compare K_a for $Cu^{2+}(aq)$ and K_b for $C_3H_5O_3^-(aq)$.

The ion with the larger K value will undergo hydrolysis to the greater extent and will determine the pH of the solution.

pK_b for $C_3H_5O_3^- = 14 - pK_a$ for $HC_3H_5O_3 = 14.00 - 3.85 = 10.15$

$K_b = 10^{-10.15} = 7.1 \times 10^{-11}$.

Since K_a for Cu^{2+} (1.0×10^{-8}) is greater than K_b for $C_3H_5O_3^-$ (7.1×10^{-11}) the solution will be slightly acidic.

17 Additional Aspects of Aqueous Equilibria

Common-Ion Effect

17.2 (a) For a generic weak base B, $K_b = \frac{[BH^+][OH^-]}{[B]}$. If an external source of BH^+ such as BH^+Cl^- is added to a solution of B(aq), $[BH^+]$ increases, decreasing $[OH^-]$ and increasing [B], effectively suppressing the ionization (hydrolysis) of B.

(b) NH_4Cl

17.4 In general, when an acid is added to a solution pH decreases; when a base is added to a solution, pH increases.

(a) pH increases; $C_7H_5O_2^-$ decreases ionization of $HC_7H_5O_2$ and decreases $[H^+]$.

(b) pH decreases; $C_5H_5NH^+$ decreases ionization (hydrolysis) of C_5H_5N and decreases $[OH^-]$.

(c) pH increases; NH_3 reacts with HCl, decreasing $[H^+]$.

(d) pH increases; HCO_3^- decreases ionization of H_2CO_3 and decreases $[H^+]$.

(e) no change; ClO_4^- is a negligible base and Na^+ is a negligible acid.

17.6

	$(CH_3)_3N(aq) + H_2O(l)$	$\rightleftharpoons$ $(CH_3)_3NH^+(aq)$	+ $OH^-(aq)$
i	0.075 *M*	0.10 *M*	
c	-x	+x	+x
e	(0.075 - x) *M*	(0.10 + x) *M*	+x *M*

$$K_b = 6.4 \times 10^{-5} = \frac{[OH^-][(CH_3)_3NH^+]}{[(CH_3)_3N]} = \frac{(x)(0.10 + x)}{(0.075 - x)} \approx \frac{0.10\,x}{0.075}$$

$x = 4.8 \times 10^{-5} = [OH^-]$, pOH = 4.32, pH = 14.00 - 4.32 = 9.68

$[(CH_3)_3NH^+] = 0.10 + 4.8 \times 10^{-5} = 0.10005 = 0.10\ M$

17.8 (a) mol = *M* × L; mol $HC_2H_3O_2$ = 0.15 M × 0.0500 L = 7.5×10^{-3} mol

mol $C_2H_3O_2^-$ = 0.20 *M* × 0.0500 L = 0.010 mol

	$HC_2H_3O_2(aq)$	$\rightleftharpoons$ $H^+(aq)$	+ $C_2H_3O_2^-(aq)$
i	7.5×10^{-3}	0	0.010 mol
c	-x	+x	+x
e	$(7.5 \times 10^{-3}$ -x) mol	x mol	(0.010 + x) mol

$[HC_2H_3O_2] = (7.5 \times 10^{-3} - x)$ mol/0.1000 L; $[C_2H_3O_2^-] = (0.010 + x)$ mol/0.1000 L

$$K_a = 1.8 \times 10^{-5} = \frac{[H+][C_2H_3O_2^-]}{[HC_2H_3O_2]} = \frac{(x)(0.010 + x)/0.1000\text{ L}}{(0.0075 - x)/0.1000\text{ L}} \approx \frac{x(0.010)}{0.0075}$$

$x = 1.35 \times 10^{-5}\ M = 1.4 \times 10^{-5}\ M\ H^+$; pH = 4.87

(b) mol = $M \times$ L; mol HF = 0.050 $M \times$ 0.125 L = $6.25 \times 10^{-3} = 6.3 \times 10^{-3}$ mol

mol F^- = 0.10 $M \times$ 0.0500 L = 0.0050 mol

	$HF(aq)$	$\rightleftharpoons$ $H^+(aq)$	+ $F^-(aq)$
i	6.25×10^{-3} mol	0	0.0050 mol
c	-x	+x	+x
e	$(6.25 \times 10^{-3}$ - x) mol	x	(0.0050 + x) mol

$[HF] = (6.25 \times 10^{-3} + x)/0.175$ L; $[F^-] = (0.0050 + x)$ 0.175 L

Note that the volumes will cancel when substituted into the K_a expression.

$$K_a = 6.8 \times 10^{-4} = \frac{[H^+][F^-]}{[HF]} = \frac{x(0.0050 + x)/0.175}{(6.25 \times - x)/0.175} \approx \frac{x(0.0050)}{0.00625}$$

$x = 8.50 \times 10^{-4} = 8.5 \times 10^{-4}\ M\ H^+$; pH = 3.07

17.10

	$HLac(aq)$	$\rightleftharpoons$ $H^+(aq)$ +	$Lac^-(aq)$
equil (a)	0.085 - x M	x M	x M
equil (b)	0.085 - x M	x M	0.050 + x M

$$K_a = \frac{[H^+][Lac^-]}{[HLac]} = 1.4 \times 10^{-4}$$

(a) $$K_a = 1.4 \times 10^{-4} = \frac{x^2}{0.085 - x} \approx \frac{x^2}{0.085}$$; $x = [H^+] = 3.45 \times 10^{-3}\ M = 3.5 \times 10^{-3}\ M\ H^+$

$$\%\text{ ionization} = \frac{3.5 \times 10^{-3}\ M\ H^+}{0.085\ M\ Lac} \times 100 = 4.1\%\text{ ionization}$$

(b) $$K_a = 1.4 \times 10^{-4} = \frac{(x)(0.050 + x)}{0.085 - x} \approx \frac{0.050\,x}{0.085}$$; $x = 2.4 \times 10^{-4}\ M\ H^+$

$$\%\text{ ionization} = \frac{2.4 \times 10^{-4}\ M\ H^+}{0.085\ M\ Lac} \times 100 = 0.28\%\text{ ionization}$$

17 Additional Aspects of Aqueous Equilibria

Solutions to Black Exercises

Buffers

17.12 HCl is a strong acid and will react with NaF to form HF.

$$HCl(aq) + NaF(aq) \rightarrow HF(aq) + NaCl(aq)$$

As long as NaF is present in excess, the resulting solution will contain both the conjugate acid HF(aq) and the conjugate base F^-(aq), the requirement of a buffer. When HF and NaCl are combined, HF(aq) + NaCl(aq) $\rightleftharpoons$ NaF(aq) + HCl(aq), the equilibrium favors reactants, because HCl is a stronger acid than HF. Very little NaF(aq) will be present, so the conjugate base F^-(aq) is present in too small an amount to produce a buffer.

17.14 Assume that % ionization is small in these buffers (Solutions 17.9 and 17.10).

(a) The conjugate acid in this buffer is HCO_3^-, so use K_{a2} for H_2CO_3, 5.6×10^{-11}

$$K_a = \frac{[H^+][CO_3^{2-}]}{[HCO_3^-]};\ [H^+] = \frac{K_a[HCO_3^-]}{[CO_3^{2-}]} = \frac{5.6 \times 10^{-11}(0.10)}{(0.125)}$$

$[H^+] = 4.48 \times 10^{-11} = 4.5 \times 10^{-11}$ *M*; pH = 10.35

(b) mol = *M* × L; total volume = 120 mL = 0.120 L

$$[H^+] = \frac{K_a\,(0.20\ M \times 0.055\ L)/0.120\ L}{(0.15\ M \times 0.065\ L)/0.120\ L} = \frac{5.6 \times 10^{-11}(0.20 \times 0.055)}{(0.15 \times 0.065)}$$

$[H^+] = 6.32 \times 10^{-11} = 6.3 \times 10^{-11}$ *M*; pH = 10.20

17.16 NH_4^+/NH_3 is a basic buffer. Either the hydrolysis of NH_3 or the dissociation of NH_4^+ can be used to determine the pH of the buffer. Using the dissociation of NH_4^+ leads directly to $[H^+]$ and facilitates use of the Henderson-Hasselbach relationship.

(a) $NH_4^+(aq) \rightleftharpoons H^+(aq) + NH_3(aq)$

$$K_a = \frac{K_w}{K_b} = \frac{1.0 \times 10^{-14}}{1.8 \times 10^{-5}} = 5.56 \times 10^{-10} = 5.6 \times 10^{-10}$$

$$[NH_3] = \frac{5.0\ g\ NH_3}{2.50\ L\ soln} \times \frac{1\ mol\ NH_3}{17.0\ g\ NH_3} = 0.118 = 0.12\ M\ NH_3$$

$$[NH_4^+] = \frac{20.0\ g\ NH_4Cl}{2.50\ L} \times \frac{1\ mol\ NH_4Cl}{53.50\ g\ NH_4Cl} = 0.1495 = 0.50\ M\ NH_4^+$$

$$K_a = \frac{[H^+][NH_3]}{[NH_4^+]};\ [H^+] = \frac{K_a[NH_4^+]}{[NH_3]} = \frac{5.56 \times 10^{-10}(0.1495 - x)}{(0.118 + x)} \approx \frac{5.56 \times 10^{-10}(0.1495)}{(0.118)}$$

$[H^+] = 7.044 \times 10^{-10} = 7.0 \times 10^{-10}$ *M*, pH = 9.15

(b) $NH_3(aq) + H^+(aq) + NO_3^-(aq) \rightarrow NH_4^+(aq) + NO_3^-(aq)$

(c) $NH_4^+(aq) + Cl^-(aq) + K^+(aq) + OH^-(aq) \rightarrow NH_3(aq) + H_2O(l) + Cl^-(aq) + K^+(aq)$

17.18 $HC_3H_5O_3(aq) \rightleftharpoons H^+(aq) + C_3H_5O_3^-(aq)$

$[H^+] = \dfrac{K_a[HC_3H_5O_3]}{[C_3H_5O_3^-]}$; $[H^+] = 10^{-2.90} = 1.259 \times 10^{-3} = 1.3 \times 10^{-3}$ *M*

$[HC_3H_5O_3] = 0.150$ *M*; calculate $[C_3H_5O_3^-]$

$$[C_3H_5O_3^-] = \frac{K_a[HC_3H_5O_3]}{[H^+]} = \frac{1.4 \times 10^{-4}(0.150)}{1.259 \times 10^{-3}} = 0.01668 = 0.017\ M$$

$$\frac{0.01668 \text{ mol } NaC_3H_5O_3}{1.00 \text{ L}} \times \frac{112.1 \text{ g } NaC_3H_5O_3}{1 \text{ mol } NaC_3H_5O_3} = 1.9 \text{ g } NaC_3H_5O_3$$

17.20 (a) $K_a = \dfrac{[H^+][C_3H_5O_2^-]}{[HC_3H_5O_2]}$; $[H^+] = \dfrac{K_a[HC_3H_5O_2]}{[C_3H_5O_2^-]}$

Since this expression contains a ratio of concentrations, we can ignore total volume and work directly with moles.

$$[H^+] = \frac{1.3 \times 10^{-5}(0.12 - x)}{(0.10 + x)} \approx \frac{1.3 \times 10^{-5}(0.12)}{0.10} = 1.56 \times 10^{-5}$$
$$= 1.6 \times 10^{-5}\ M,\ pH = 4.81$$

(b) $HC_3H_5O_2(aq) + OH^-(aq) \rightarrow C_2H_3O_2^-(aq) + H_2O(l)$

0.12 mol	0.01 mol	0.10 mol
-0.01 mol	-0.01 mol	+0.01 mol
0.11 mol	0 mol	0.11 mol

$$[H^+] \approx \frac{1.3 \times 10^{-5}(0.11)}{(0.11)} = 1.3 \times 10^{-5}\ M;\ pH = 4.89$$

(c) $C_3H_5O_2^-(aq) + HI(aq) \rightarrow HC_3H_5O_2(aq) + I^-(aq)$

0.10 mol	0.01 mol	0.12 mol
-0.01 mol	-0.01 mol	+0.01 mol
0.09 mol	0 mol	0.13 mol

$$[H^+] \approx \frac{1.3 \times 10^{-5}(0.13)}{(0.09)} = 1.88 \times 10^{-3} = 2 \times 10^{-3}\ M;\ pH = 4.73 = 4.7$$

17.22 $\dfrac{6.5 \text{ g } Na_2HPO_4}{0.355 \text{ L soln}} \times \dfrac{1 \text{ mol } NaH_2PO_4}{120 \text{ g } NaH_2PO_4} = 0.153 = 0.15\ M$

$$\frac{8.0 \text{ g } Na_2HPO_4}{0.355 \text{ L soln}} \times \frac{1 \text{ mol } Na_2HPO_4}{142 \text{ g } Na_2HPO_4} = 0.159 = 0.16\ M$$

Using Equation [17.8] to find the pH of the buffer:

$$pH = -\log(6.2 \times 10^{-8}) + \log\frac{0.159}{0.153} = 7.2076 + 0.0167 = 7.22$$

Acid-Base Titrations

17.24 (a) The quantity of base required to reach the equivalence point is the same in the two titrations.

(b) The pH is higher initially in the titration of a weak acid.

(c) The pH is higher at the equivalence point in the titration of a weak acid.

(d) The pH in excess base is essentially the same for the two cases.

(e) In titrating a weak acid, one needs an indicator that changes at a higher pH than for the strong acid titration. The choice is more critical because the **change** in pH close to the equivalence point is smaller for the weak acid titration.

17.26 (a) At the equivalence point, moles HX added = moles B initially present = 0.1 M × 0.03 L = 0.003 moles HX added.

(b) BH^+

(c) Both K_a for BH^+ and concentration BH^+ determine pH at the equivalence point.

(d) Because the pH at the equivalence point will be less than 7, methyl red would be more appropriate.

17.28 (a) $$55.0 \text{ mL NaOH} \times \frac{0.0950 \text{ mol NaOH}}{1000 \text{ mL soln}} \times \frac{1 \text{ mol HCl}}{1 \text{ mol NaOH}} \times \frac{1000 \text{ mL soln}}{0.105 \text{ mol HCl}}$$

$$= 49.8 \text{ mL HCl soln}$$

(b) $$23.5 \text{ mL KOH} \times \frac{0.117 \text{ mol KOH}}{1000 \text{ mL soln}} \times \frac{1 \text{ mol HCl}}{1 \text{ mol KOH}} \times \frac{1000 \text{ mL soln}}{0.105 \text{ mol HCl}}$$

$$= 26.2 \text{ mL HCl soln}$$

(c) $$125.0 \text{ mL} \times \frac{1.35 \text{ g NaOH}}{1000 \text{ mL}} \times \frac{1 \text{ mol NaOH}}{40.00 \text{ g NaOH}} \times \frac{1 \text{ mol HCl}}{1 \text{ mol NaOH}} \times \frac{1000 \text{ mL soln}}{0.105 \text{ mol HCl}}$$

$$= 40.2 \text{ mL HCl soln}$$

17.30 moles OH^- = $M_{KOH} \times L_{KOH}$ = 0.200 M × 0.0300 L = 6.00×10^{-3} mol

moles H^+ = $M_{HClO_4} \times L_{HClO_4}$ = 0.150 M × L_{HClO_4}

	mL_{NaOH}	mL_{HClO_4}	Total Volume	Moles OH^-	Moles H^+	Molarity Excess Ion	pH
(a)	30.0	30.0	60.0	6.00×10^{-3}	4.50×10^{-3}	$0.0250(OH^-)$	12.398
(b)	30.0	39.5	69.5	6.00×10^{-3}	5.93×10^{-3}	$1 \times 10^{-3}(OH^-)$	11.0
(c)	30.0	39.9	69.9	6.00×10^{-3}	5.99×10^{-3}	$1 \times 10^{-4}(OH^-)$	10.2
(d)	30.0	40.0	70.0	6.00×10^{-3}	6.00×10^{-3}	$1 \times 10^{-7}(H^+)$	7.0
(e)	30.0	40.1	70.1	6.00×10^{-3}	6.02×10^{-3}	$3 \times 10^{-4}(H^+)$	3.5

$$\text{molarity of excess ion} = \frac{\text{moles ion}}{\text{total vol in L}}$$

(a) $$\frac{6.00 \times 10^{-3} \text{ mol OH}^- - 4.50 \times 10^{-3} \text{ mol H}^+}{0.0600 \text{ L}} = 0.0250\ M\ OH^-$$

(b) $$\frac{6.00 \times 10^{-3} \text{ mol OH}^- - 5.93 \times 10^{-3} \text{ mol H}^+}{0.0695 \text{ L}} = 1.01 \times 10^{-3} = 1 \times 10^{-3}\ M\ OH^-$$

(c) $$\frac{6.00 \times 10^{-3} \text{ mol OH}^- - 5.99 \times 10^{-3} \text{ mol H}^+}{0.0699 \text{ L}} = 1.43 \times 10^{-4} = 1 \times 10^{-4}\ M\ OH^-$$

(d) equivalence point, mol OH^- = mol H^+

$KClO_4$ does not hydrolyze, so $[H^+] = [OH^-] = 1 \times 10^{-7}\ M$

(e) $$\frac{6.00 \times 10^{-3} \text{ mol OH}^- - 6.02 \times 10^{-3} \text{ mol H}^+}{0.0701 \text{ L}} = 2.85 \times 10^{-4} = 3 \times 10^{-4}\ M\ H^+$$

17.32 (a) Weak base problem: $K_b = 1.8 \times 10^{-5} = \dfrac{[NH_4^+][OH^-]}{[NH_3]}$

At equilibrium, $[OH^-] = x$, $[NH_3] = (0.030 - x)$; $[NH_4^+] = x$

$$1.8 \times 10^{-5} = \frac{x^2}{(0.030 - x)} \approx \frac{x^2}{0.030};\ x = [OH^-] = 7.348 \times 10^{-4} = 7.3 \times 10^{-4}\ M$$

pH = 14.00 - 3.13 = 10.87

(b-f) Calculate mol NH_3 and mol NH_4^+ after the acid-base reaction takes place.
$0.030\ M\ NH_3 \times 0.0300\ L = 9.0 \times 10^{-4}$ mol NH_3 present initially.

		$NH_3(aq)$	+	$HCl(aq)$	→	$NH_4^+(aq)$ + $Cl^-(aq)$
				$(0.025\ M \times 0.0100\ L) =$		
(b)	before rx	9.0×10^{-4} mol		2.5×10^{-4} mol		0 mol
	after rx	**6.5×10^{-4} mol**		**0 mol**		**2.5×10^{-4} mol**

			(0.025 M × 0.0200 L) =	
(c)	before rx	9.0×10^{-4} mol	5.0×10^{-4} mol	0 mol
	after rx	**4.0×10^{-4} mol**	**0 mol**	**5.0×10^{-4} mol**
			(0.025 M × 0.0350 L) =	
(d)	before rx	9.0×10^{-4} mol	8.75×10^{-4} mol	0 mol
	after rx	**0.25×10^{-4} mol**	**0 mol**	**8.75×10^{-4} mol**
			(0.025 M × 0.0360 L) =	
(e)	before rx	9.0×10^{-4} mol	9.0×10^{-4} mol	0 mol
	after rx	**0 mol**	**0 mol**	**9.0×10^{-4} mol**
			(0.025 M × 0.0370 L) =	
(f)	before rx	9.0×10^{-4} mol	9.25×10^{-4} mol	0 mol
	after rx	**0 mol**	**0.25×10^{-4} mol**	**9.0×10^{-4} mol**

(b) Using the acid dissociation equilibrium for NH_4^+ (so that we calculate $[H^+]$ directly), $NH_4^+(aq) \rightleftharpoons H^+(aq) + NH_3(aq)$

$$K_a = \frac{[H^+][NH_3]}{[NH_4^+]} = \frac{K_w}{K_b \text{ for } NH_3} = \frac{1.0 \times 10^{-14}}{1.8 \times 10^{-5}} = 5.56 \times 10^{-10} = 5.6 \times 10^{-10}$$

$$[NH_3] = \frac{6.5 \times 10^{-4}\text{ mol}}{0.0400\text{ L}} = 0.01625\ M;\ [NH_4^+] = \frac{2.50 \times 10^{-4}\text{ mol}}{0.0400\text{ L}} = 6.25 \times 10^{-3}\ M$$

$$[H^+] = \frac{5.56 \times 10^{-10}[NH_4^+]}{[NH_3]} \approx \frac{5.56 \times 10^{-10}(6.25 \times 10^{-3})}{(0.01625)} = 2.14 \times 10^{-10};\ pH = 9.67$$

(We will assume $[H^+]$ is small compared to $[NH_3]$ and $[NH_4^+]$.)

(c) $$[NH_3] = \frac{4.0 \times 10^{-4}\text{ mol}}{0.0500\text{ L}} = 0.0080\ M;\ [NH_4^+] = \frac{5.0 \times 10^{-4}\text{ mol}}{0.0500\text{ L}} = 0.010 M$$

$$[H^+] = \frac{5.56 \times 10^{-10}(0.010)}{(0.0080)} = 6.94 \times 10^{-10} = 6.9 \times 10^{-10}\ M;\ pH = 9.16$$

(d) $$[NH_3] = \frac{0.25 \times 10^{-4}\text{ mol}}{0.0650\text{ L}} = 3.846 \times 10^{-4} = 4 \times 10^{-4}\ M;\ [NH_4^+] = \frac{8.75 \times 10^{-4}\text{ mol}}{0.0650\text{ L}}$$

$$= 0.01346 = 0.013\ M$$

$$[H^+] = \frac{5.56 \times 10^{-10}(0.01346)}{3.846 \times 10^{-4}} = 1.946 \times 10^{-8} = 2 \times 10^{-8}\ M;\ pH = 7.7$$

(e) At the equivalence point, $[H^+] = [NH_3] = x$

$$[NH_4^+] = \frac{9.0 \times 10^{-4}\ M}{0.0660\ L} = 0.01364 = 0.014\ M$$

$$5.56 \times 10^{-10} = \frac{x^2}{0.01364};\ x = [H^+] = 2.754 \times 10^{-6} = 2.8 \times 10^{-6};\ pH = 5.56$$

(f) Past the equivalence point, $[H^+]$ from the excess HCl determines the pH.

$$[H^+] = \frac{0.25 \times 10^{-4}\ mol}{0.0670\ L} = 3.731 \times 10^{-4} = 4 \times 10^{-4}\ M;\ pH = 3.4$$

17.34 The volume of NaOH solution required in all cases is

$$V_{base} = \frac{V_{acid} \times M_{acid}}{M_{base}} = \frac{(0.100)V_{acid}}{(0.080)} = 1.25\ V_{acid}$$

The total volume at the equivalence point is $V_{base} + V_{acid} = 2.25\ V_{acid}$.

The concentration of the salt at the equivalence point is $\frac{M_{acid} V_{acid}}{2.25 V_{acid}} = \frac{0.100}{2.25} = 0.0444\ M$

(a) $0.0444\ M$ NaBr, pH = 7.00

(b) $0.0444\ M\ Na^+C_3H_5O_3^-$; $C_3H_5O_3^-(aq) + H_2O(l) \rightleftharpoons HC_3H_5O_3(aq) + OH^-(aq)$

$$K_b = \frac{[HC_3H_5O_3][OH^-]}{[C_3H_5O_3^-]} = \frac{K_w}{K_a} = \frac{1.0 \times 10^{-14}}{1.4 \times 10^{-4}} = 7.14 \times 10^{-11} = 7.1 \times 10^{-11}$$

$[HC_3H_5O_3] = [OH^-]$; $[C_3H_5O_3^-] \approx 0.0444$

$[OH^-]^2 \approx 0.0444(7.14 \times 10^{-11})$; $[OH^-] = 1.78 \times 10^{-6} = 1.8 \times 10^{-6}\ M$,

pOH = 5.75; pH = 8.25

(c) $CrO_4^{2-}(aq) + H_2O(l) \rightleftharpoons HCrO_4^-(aq) + OH^-(aq)$

$$K_b = \frac{[HCrO_4^-][OH^-]}{[CrO_4^{2-}]} = \frac{K_w}{K_a} = 3.33 \times 10^{-8} = 3.3 \times 10^{-8}$$

$[OH^-]^2 \approx 0.0444(3.33 \times 10^{-8})$; $[OH^-] = 3.845 \times 10^{-5} = 3.8 \times 10^{-5}$, pH = 9.58

Solubility Equilibria and Factors Affecting Solubility

17.36 (a) *Solubility* is the amount (grams, moles) of solute that will dissolve in a certain volume of solution. *Solubility-product constant* is an equilibrium constant, the product of the molar concentrations of all the dissolved ions in solution.

(b) $K_{sp} = [Mn^{2+}][CO_3^{2-}]$; $K_{sp} = [Hg^{2+}][OH^-]^2$; $K_{sp} = [Cu^{2+}]^3[PO_4^{3-}]^2$

17.38 (a) $PbBr_2(s) \rightleftharpoons Pb^{2+}(aq) + 2Br^-(aq)$

$K_{sp} = [Pb^{2+}][Br^-]^2$; $[Pb^{2+}] = 1.0 \times 10^{-2}\ M$, $[Br^-] = 2.0 \times 10^{-2}\ M$

$K_{sp} = (1.0 \times 10^{-2}\ M)(2.0 \times 10^{-2}\ M)^2 = 4.0 \times 10^{-6}$

(b) $AgIO_3(s) \rightleftharpoons Ag^+(aq) + IO_3^-(aq)$; $K_{sp} = [Ag^+][IO_3^-]$

$$[Ag^+] = [IO_3^-] = \frac{0.0490\ g\ AgIO_3}{1.00\ L\ soln} \times \frac{1\ mol\ AgIO_3}{282.8\ g\ AgIO_3} = 1.733 \times 10^{-4} = 1.73 \times 10^{-4}\ M$$

$K_{sp} = (1.733 \times 10^{-4}\ M)(1.733 \times 10^{-4}\ M) = 3.00 \times 10^{-8}$

(c) $Cu(OH)_2(s) \rightleftharpoons Cu^{2+}(aq) + 2OH^-(aq)$; $K_{sp} = [Cu^{2+}][OH^-]^2$

$[Cu^{2+}] = x$, $[OH^-] = 2x$; $K_{sp} = 4.8 \times 10^{-20} = (x)(2x)^2$

$4.8 \times 10^{-20} = 4x^3$; $x = [Cu^{2+}] = 2.290 \times 10^{-7} = 2.3 \times 10^{-7}\ M$

$$\frac{2.290 \times 10^{-7}\ mol\ Cu(OH)_2}{1\ L} \times \frac{97.56\ g\ Cu(OH)_2}{1\ mol\ Cu(OH)_2} = 2.2 \times 10^{-5}\ g\ Cu(OH)_2$$

However, $[OH^-]$ from $Cu(OH)_2 = 4.58 \times 10^{-7}$ M; this is similar to $[OH^-]$ from the autoionization of water.

$K_w = [H^+][OH^-]$; $[H^+] = y$, $[OH^-] = (4.58 \times 10^{-7} + y)$

$1.0 \times 10^{-14} = y(4.58 \times 10^{-7} + y)$; $y^2 + 4.58 \times 10^{-7}\ y - 1.0 \times 10^{-14}$

$$y = \frac{-4.58 \times 10^{-7} \pm \sqrt{(4.58 \times 10^{-7})^2 - 4(1)(-1.0 \times 10^{-14})}}{2};\ y = 2.09 \times 10^{-8}$$

$[OH^-]_{total} = 4.58 \times 10^{-7}\ M + 0.209 \times 10^{-7}\ M = 4.79 \times 10^{-7}\ M$

Recalculating $[Cu^{2+}]$ and thus molar solubility of $Cu(OH)_2(s)$:

$4.8 \times 10^{-20} = x(4.79 \times 10^{-7})^2$; $x = 2.09 \times 10^{-7}\ M\ Cu^{2+}$

$$\frac{2.09 \times 10^{-7}\ mol\ Cu(OH)_2(s)}{1\ L} \times \frac{97.56\ g\ Cu(OH)_2}{1\ mol\ Cu(OH)_2} = 2.0 \times 10^{-5}\ g\ Cu(OH)_2$$

Note that the presence of OH^- as a common ion decreases the water solubility of $Cu(OH)_2$.

17.40 $PbI_2(s) \rightleftharpoons Pb^{2+}(aq) + 2I^-(aq)$; $K_{sp} = [Pb^{2+}][I^-]^2$

$$[Pb^{2+}] = \frac{0.54\ g\ PbI_2}{1.00\ L\ soln} \times \frac{1\ mol\ PbI_2}{461.0\ g\ PbI_2} = 1.17 \times 10^{-3} = 1.2 \times 10^{-3}\ M$$

$[I^-] = 2[Pb^{2+}]$; $K_{sp} = [Pb^{2+}](2[Pb^{2+}])^2 = 4[Pb^{2+}]^3 = 4(1.17 \times 10^{-3})^3 = 6.4 \times 10^{-9}$

17.42 $LaF_3(s) \rightleftharpoons La^{3+}(aq) + 3F^-(aq)$; $Ksp = [La^{3+}][F^-]^3$

(a) molar solubility = x = $[La^{3+}]$; $[F^-]$ = 3x

$K_{sp} = 2 \times 10^{-19}$ (x)(3x)3; $2 \times 10^{-19} = 27\ x^4$; $x = (7.41 \times 10^{-21})^{1/4}$, $x = 9.28 \times 10^{-6}$

$= 9 \times 10^{-6}$ M La^{3+}

$$\frac{9.28 \times 10^{-6} \text{ mol } LaF_3}{1 \text{ L}} \times \frac{195.9 \text{ g } LaF_3}{1 \text{ mol}} = 1.82 \times 10^{-3} = 2 \text{ g } LaF_3/L$$

(b) molar solubility = x = $[La^{3+}]$

There are two sources of F^- : KF(0.025 *M*) and LaF_3 (3 x *M*)

$K_{sp} = (x)(0.25 + 3x)^3$; assume x is small compared to 0.025 M.

$2 \times 10^{-19} = (0.025)^3$ x; $x = 2 \times 10^{-19}/1.563 \times 10^{-5} = 1.28 \times 10^{-14}$ M La^{3+}

$$\frac{1.28 \times 10^{14} \text{ mol } LaF_3}{1 \text{ L}} \times \frac{195.9 \text{ g } LaF_3}{1 \text{ mol}} = 2.51 \times 10^{-12} = 3 \times 10^{-12} \text{ g } LaF_3/L$$

= 3 pg LaF_3/L

(c) molar solubllity = x, $[F^-]$ = 3x, $[La^{3+}]$ = 0.150 *M* + x

$K_{sp} = (0.150 + x)(3x)^3$; assume x is small compared to 0.150 *M*.

$2 \times 10^{-19} = (0.150)(27\ x^3) = 4.05\ x^3$; $x = (4.94 \times 10^{-20})^{1/3} = 3.67 \times 10^{-7} = 4 \times 10^{-7}$ *M*

$$\frac{3.67 \times 10^{-7} \text{ mol } LaF_3}{1 \text{ L}} \times \frac{195.9 \text{ g } LaF_3}{1 \text{ mol}} = 7.19 \times 10^{-5} = 7 \times 10^{-5} \text{ g } LaF_3/L$$

$= 70 \times 10^{-6}$ = 70 μg/L = 70 ppb LaF_3

17.44 $Fe(OH)_2(s) \rightleftharpoons Fe^{2+}(aq) + 2OH^-(aq)$; $K_{sp} = 8.0 \times 10^{-16}$

Since the $[OH^-]$ is set by the pH of the solution, the solubility of $Fe(OH)_2$ is just $[Fe^{2+}]$.

(a) pH = 7.0, pOH = 14 - pH = 7.0, $[OH^-] = 10^{-pOH} = 1.0 \times 10^{-7}$ *M*

$$K_{sp} = 7.9 \times 10^{-16} = [Fe^{2+}](1.0 \times 10^{-7})^2;\ [Fe^{2+}] = \frac{7.9 \times 10^{-16}}{1.0 \times 10^{-14}} = 7.9 \times 10^{-2}\ M$$

Check: In pure water, $[OH^-]$ from $Fe(OH)_2$ is similar to (OH^-) from the autoionization of water, resulting in a cubic equation for $[Fe^{2+}]$. The solubility of $Fe(OH)_2$ at a buffered pH = 7.0 is actually greater than the solubility in pure water.

(b) pH = 10.0, pOH = 4.0, $[OH^-] = 1.0 \times 10^{-4}$

$$K_{sp} = 7.9 \times 10^{-16} = [Fe^{2+}][1.0 \times 10^{-4}]^2;\ [Fe^{2+}] = \frac{7.9 \times 10^{-16}}{1.0 \times 8^{-10}} = 7.9 \times 10^{-8}\ M$$

(c) pH = 12.0, pOH = 2.0, $[OH^-] = 1.0 \times 10^{-2}$

$$K_{sp} = 7.9 \times 10^{-16} = [Fe^{2+}][1.0 \times 10^{-2}]^2;\ [Fe^{2+}] = \frac{7.9 \times 10^{-16}}{1.0 \times 10^{-4}} = 7.9 \times 10^{-12}\ M$$

17.46 If the anion in the slightly soluble salt is the conjugate base of a strong acid, there will be no reaction.

(a) $MnS(s) + 2H^+(aq) \rightarrow H_2S(aq) + Mn^{2+}(aq)$

(b) $PbF_2(s) + 2H^+(aq) \rightarrow 2HF(aq) + Pb^{2+}(aq)$

(c) $AuCl_3(s) + H^+(aq) \rightarrow$ no reaction

(d) $Hg_2C_2O_4(s) + 2H^+(aq) \rightarrow H_2C_2O_4(aq) + Hg_2^{2+}(aq)$

(e) $CuBr(s) + H^+(aq) \rightarrow$ no reaction

17.48 $NiC_2O_4(s) \rightleftharpoons Ni^{2+}(aq) + C_2O_4^{2-}(aq)$; $K_{sp} = [Ni^{2+}][C_2O_4^{2-}] = 4 \times 10^{-10}$

When the salt has just dissolved, $[C_2O_4^{2-}]$ will be 0.020 *M*. Thus $[Ni^{2+}]$ must be less than $4 \times 10^{-10} / 0.020 = 2 \times 10^{-8}$ *M*. To achieve this low $[Ni^{2+}]$ we must complex the Ni^{2+} ion with NH_3: $Ni^{2+}(aq) + 6NH_3(aq) \rightleftharpoons Ni(NH_3)_6^{2+}(aq)$. Essentially all Ni(II) is in the form of the complex, so $[Ni(NH_3)_6^{2+}] = 0.020$. Find K_f for $Ni(NH_3)_6^{2+}$ in Table 17.1.

$$K_f = \frac{[Ni(NH_3)_6^{2+}]}{[Ni^{2+}][NH_3]^6} = \frac{(0.020)}{(2 \times 10^{-8})[NH_3]^6} = 5.5 \times 10^8;\ [NH_3]^6 = 1.82 \times 10^{-3};$$

$$[NH_3] = 0.349 = 0.3\ M$$

17.50

$Ag_2S(s) \rightleftharpoons 2Ag^+(aq) + S^{2-}(aq)$		K_{sp}
$S^{2-}(aq) + 2H^+(aq) \rightleftharpoons H_2S(aq)$		$1/(K_{a1} \times K_{a2})$
$2[Ag^+(aq) + 2Cl^-(aq) \rightleftharpoons AgCl_2^-(aq)]$		K_f^2

Add: $Ag_2S(s) + 2H^+(aq) + 4Cl^-(aq) \rightarrow 2AgCl_2^-(aq) + H_2S(aq)$

$$K = \frac{K_{sp} \times K_f^2}{K_{a1} \times K_{a2}} = \frac{(6 \times 10^{-51})(1.1 \times 10^5)^2}{(9.5 \times 10^{-8})(1 \times 10^{-19})} = 7.64 \times 10^{-15} = 8 \times 10^{-15}$$

Precipitation; Qualitative Analysis

17.52 (a) $Co(OH)_2(s) \rightleftharpoons Co^{2+}(aq) + 2OH^-(aq)$; $K_{sp} = [Co^{2+}][OH^-]^2 = 1.3 \times 10^{-15}$

pH = 8.5; pOH = 14 - 8.5 = 5.5; $[OH^-] = 10^{-5.5} = 3.16 \times 10^{-6} = 3 \times 10^{-6}$ *M*

$(Q = (0.020)(3.16 \times 10^{-6})^2 = 2 \times 10^{-13}$; $Q > K_{sp}$, $Co(OH)_2$ will precipitate

(b) $AgIO_3(s) \rightleftharpoons Ag^+(aq) + IO_3^-(aq)$; $K_{sp} = [Ag^+][IO_3^-] = 3.1 \times 10^{-8}$

$$[Ag^+] = \frac{0.010\ M\ Ag^+ \times 0.100\ L}{0.110\ L} = 9.09 \times 10^{-3} = 9.1 \times 10^{-3}\ M$$

$$[IO_3^-] = \frac{0.015\ M\ IO_3^- \times 0.010\ L}{0.110\ L} = 1.36 \times 10^{-3} = 1.4 \times 10^{-3}\ M$$

$Q = (9.09 \times 10^{-3})(1.36 \times 10^{-3}) = 1.2 \times 10^{-5}$; $Q > K_{sp}$, $AgIO_3$ will precipitate

17.54 $AgCl(s) \rightleftharpoons Ag^+(aq) + Cl^-(aq)$; $K_{sp} = [Ag^+][Cl^-] = 1.8 \times 10^{-10}$

$$[Ag^+] = \frac{0.10\ M \times 0.2\ mL}{20\ mL} = 1 \times 10^{-3}\ M; \quad [Cl^-] = \frac{1.8 \times 10^{-10}}{1 \times 10^{-3}\ M} = 1.8 \times 10^{-7} = 2 \times 10^{-7}\ M$$

$$\frac{1.8 \times 10^{-7}\ mol\ Cl^-}{1\ L} \times \frac{35.45\ g\ Cl^-}{1\ mol\ Cl^-} \times 0.020\ L = 1.28 \times 10^{-7}\ g\ Cl^- = 1 \times 10^{-7}\ g\ Cl^-$$

17.56 (a) Precipitation will begin when $Q = K_{sp}$.

$BaSO_4$: $K_{sp} = [Ba^{2+}][SO_4^{2-}] = 1.1 \times 10^{-10}$

$1.1 \times 10^{-10} = (0.015)[SO_4^{2-}]$; $[SO_4^{2-}] = 7.3 \times 10^{-9}\ M$

$SrSO_4$: $K_{sp} = [Sr^{2+}][SO_4^{2-}] = 3.2 \times 10^{-7}$

$3.2 \times 10^{-7} = (0.015)[SO_4^{2-}]$; $[SO_4^{2-}] = 2.1 \times 10^{-5}\ M$

The $[SO_4^{2-}]$ necessary to begin precipitation is the smaller of the two values, $7.3 \times 10^{-9}\ M\ SO_4^{2-}$.

(b) Ba^{2+} precipitates first, because it requires the smaller $[SO_4^{2-}]$.

(c) Sr^{2+} will begin to precipitate when $[SO_4^{2-}]$ in solution (not bound in $BaSO_4$) reaches $2.1 \times 10^{-5}\ M$.

17.58 Initial solubility in water rules out CdS and HgO. Formation of a precipitate on addition of HCl indicates the presence of $Pb(NO_3)_2$ (formation of $PbCl_2$). Formation of a precipitate on addition of H_2S at pH 1 probably indicates $Cd(NO_3)_2$ (formation of CdS). (This test can be misleading because enough Pb^{2+} can remain in solution after filtering $PbCl_2$ to lead to visible precipitation of PbS.) Absence of a precipitate on addition of H_2S at pH 8 indicates that $ZnSO_4$ is not present. The yellow flame test indicates presence of Na^+. In summary, $Pb(NO_3)_2$ and Na_2SO_4 are definitely present, $Cd(NO_3)_2$ is probably present, and CdS, HgO and $ZnSO_4$ are definitely absent.

17.60 (a) Make the solution slightly basic and saturate with H_2S; CdS will precipitate, Na^+ remains in solution.

(b) Make the solution acidic, saturate with H_2S; CuS will precipitate, Mg^{2+} remains in solution.

(c) Add HCl, $PbCl_2$ precipitates. (It is best to carry out the reaction in an ice-water bath to reduce the solubility of $PbCl_2$.)

(d) Add dilute HCl; AgCl precipitates, Hg^{2+} remains in solution.

17.62 The addition of $(NH_4)_2HPO_4$ could result in precipitation of salts from metal ions of the other groups. The $(NH_4)_2HPO_4$ will render the solution basic, so metal hydroxides could form as well as insoluble phosphates. It is essential to separate the metal ions of a group from other metal ions before carrying out the specific tests for that group.

17 Additional Aspects of Aqueous Equilibria

Solutions to Black Exercises

Additional Exercises

17.64 From Equation [17.9] we see that when the acid and base forms are present in equal concentrations the pH = pK_a. Thus pK_a = 7.80.

17.66 (a) $HA(aq) + B(aq) \rightleftharpoons HB^+(aq) + A^-(aq)$ $\quad K_{eq} = \dfrac{[HB^+][A^-]}{[HA][B]}$

(b) Note that the solution is slightly basic because B is a stronger base than HA is an acid. (Or, equivalently, that A^- is a stronger base than HB^+ is an acid.) Thus, a little of the A^- is used up in reaction: $A^-(aq) + H_2O(l) \rightleftharpoons HA(aq) + OH^-(aq)$. Since pH is not very far from neutral, it is reasonable to assume that the reaction in part (a) has gone far to the right, and that $[A^-] \approx [HB^+]$ and $[HA] \approx [B]$. Then

$$K_a = \frac{[A^-][H^+]}{[HA]} = 8.0 \times 10^{-5}; \text{ when pH} = 9.2, [H^+] = 6.31 \times 10^{-10} = 6 \times 10^{-10}\ M$$

$$\frac{[A^-]}{[HA]} = 8.0 \times 10^{-5} / 6.31 \times 10^{-10} = 1.268 \times 10^5 = 1 \times 10^5$$

From the assumptions above, $\dfrac{[A^-]}{[HA]} = \dfrac{[HB^+]}{[B]}$, so $K_{eq} \approx \dfrac{[A^-]^2}{[HA]^2} = 1.608 \times 10^{10}$
$= 2 \times 10^{10}$

(c) K_b for the reaction $B(aq) + H_2O(l) \rightleftharpoons BH^+(aq) + OH^-(aq)$ can be calculated by noting that the equilibrium constant for the reaction in part (a) can be written as $K_{eq} = K_a\,(HA) \times K_b\,(B) / K_w$. (You should prove this to yourself.) Then,

$$K_b\,(B) = \frac{K_{eq} \times K_w}{K_a\,(HA)} = \frac{(1.608 \times 10^{10})(1.0 \times 10^{-14})}{8.0 \times 10^{-5}} = 2.010 = 2$$

K_b (B) is larger than K_a (HA), as it must be if the solution is basic.

17.67 (a) $K_a = \dfrac{[H^+][CHO_2^-]}{[HCHO_2]}$; $[H^+] = \dfrac{K_a[HCHO_2]}{[CHO_2^-]}$

Buffer A: $[HCHO_2] = [CHO_2^-] = \dfrac{1.00 \text{ mol}}{1.00 \text{ L}} = 1.00\ M$

$$[H^+] = \frac{1.8 \times 10^{-4}\,(1.00\ M)}{(1.00\ M)} = 1.8 \times 10^{-4}\ M, \text{ pH} = 3.74$$

Buffer B: $[HCHO_2] = [CHO_2^-] = \dfrac{0.010 \text{ mol}}{1.00 \text{ L}} = 0.010\ M$

$$[H^+] = \frac{1.8 \times 10^{-4}\,(0.010\ M)}{(0.010\ M)} = 1.8 \times 10^{-4}\ M, \text{ pH} = 3.74$$

The pH of a buffer is determined by the identity of the conjugate acid/conjugate base pair (that is, the relevant K_a value) and the **ratio of concentrations** of the conjugate acid and conjugate base. The absolute concentrations of the components is not relevant. The pH values of the two buffers are equal because they both contain $HCHO_2$ and $NaCHO_2$ and the $[HCHO_2] / [CHO_2^-]$ **ratio** is the same in both solutions.

(b) Buffer capacity is determined by the absolute amount of conjugate acid and conjugate base available to absorb strong acid (H^+) or strong base (OH^-) that is added to the buffer. Buffer A has the greater capacity because it contains the greater absolute concentrations of $HCHO_2$ and CHO_2^-.

(c) Buffer A:

CHO_2^-	+ HCl	→ $HCHO_2$ + Cl^-
1.00 mol	0.001 mol	1.00 mol
0.999 mol	0	1.001 mol

$$[H^+] = \frac{1.8 \times 10^{-4}\,(1.001)}{(0.999)} = 1.8 \times 10^{-4}\,M, \text{ pH} = 3.74$$

(In a buffer calculation, volumes cancel and we can substitute moles directly into the K_a expression.)

Buffer B:

CHO_2^-	+ HCl	→ $HCHO_2$ + Cl^-
0.010 mol	0.001 mol	0.010 mol
0.009 mol	0	0.011 mol

$$[H^+] = \frac{1.8 \times 10^{-4}\,(0.011)}{(0.009)} = 2.2 \times 10^{-4}\,M, \text{ pH} = 3.66$$

(d) Buffer A: 1.00 M HCl × 0.010 L = 0.010 mol H^+ added

mol $HCHO_2$ = 1.00 + 0.010 = 1.01 mol

mol CHO_2^- = 1.00 - 0.010 = 0.99 mol

$$[H^+] = \frac{1.8 \times 10^{-4}\,(1.01)}{(0.99)} = 1.8 \times 10^{-4}\,M, \text{ pH} = 3.74$$

Buffer B: mol $HCHO_2$ = 0.010 + 0.010 = 0.020 mol = 0.020 M

mol CHO_2^- = 0.010 - 0.010 = 0.000 mol

The solution is no longer a buffer; the only source of CHO_2^- is the dissociation of $HCHO_2$.

$$K_a = \frac{[H^+][CHO_2^-]}{[HCHO_2]} = \frac{x^2}{(0.020 - x)\,M}$$

The extent of ionization is greater than 5%; from the quadratic formula, $x = [H^+] = 1.8 \times 10^{-3}$, pH = 2.74.

(e) Adding 10 mL of 1.00 M HCl to buffer B exceeded its capacity, while the pH of buffer A was unaffected. This is quantitative confirmation that buffer A has a significantly greater capacity than buffer B. In fact, 1.0 L of 1.0 M HCl would be required to exceed the capacity of buffer A. Buffer A, with 100 times more $HCHO_2$ and CHO_2^- has 100 times the capacity of buffer B.

17.69 $\frac{0.20 \text{ mol } HC_2H_3O_2}{1 \text{ L soln}} \times 0.750 \text{ L} = 0.150 = 0.15 \text{ mol } HC_2H_3O_2$

$$0.15 \text{ mol } HC_2H_3O_2 \times \frac{60.05 \text{ g } HC_2H_3O_2}{1 \text{ mol } HC_2H_3O_2} \times \frac{1 \text{ g gl acetic acid}}{0.99 \text{ g } HC_2H_3O_2} \times \frac{1.00 \text{ mL gl acetic acid}}{1.05 \text{ g gl acetic acid}}$$

$= 8.7$ mL glacial acetic acid

At pH 4.50, $[H^+] = 10^{-4.50} = 3.16 \times 10^{-5} = 3.2 \times 10^{-5}$ *M*; this is small compared to 0.20 *M* $HC_2H_3O_2$.

$$K_a = \frac{(3.16 \times 10^{-5})[C_2H_3O_2^-]}{0.20} = 1.8 \times 10^{-5};\ [C_2H_3O_2^-] = 0.114 = 0.11\ M$$

$$\frac{0.114 \text{ mol } NaC_2H_3O_2}{1 \text{ L soln}} \times 0.750 \text{ L} \times \frac{82.03 \text{ g } NaC_2H_3O_2}{1 \text{ mol } NaC_2H_3O_2} = 7.004 = 7.0 \text{ g } NaC_2H_3O_2$$

17.71 At the equivalence point of a titration, moles strong base added equals moles weak acid initially present. $M_B \times V_B$ = mol base added = mol acid initial

At the half-way point, the volume of base is one-half of the volume required to reach the equivalence point, and the moles base delivered equals one-half of the mol acid initially present. This means that one-half of the weak acid HA is converted to the conjugate base A^-. If exactly half of the acid reacts, mol HA = mol A^- and $[HA] = [A^-]$ at the half-way point.

From Equation 17.9, $pH = pK_a + \log \frac{[\text{conj. base}]}{[\text{conj. acid}]} = pK_a + \log \frac{[A^-]}{[HA^-]}$.

If $[A^-]/[HA] = 1$, $\log(1) = 0$ and pH = pK_a of the weak acid being titrated.

17.73 (a) Initially, the solution is 0.100 *M* in CO_3^{2-}.

$$CO_3^{2-}(aq) + H_2O(l) \rightleftharpoons HCO_3^-(aq) + OH^-(aq)$$

$$K_b = \frac{[HCO_3^-][OH^-]}{[CO_3^{2-}]} = \frac{K_w}{K_a[HCO_3^-]} = 1.79 \times 10^{-4} = 1.8 \times 10^{-4}$$

Proceeding in the usual way for a weak base, calculate $[OH^-] = 4.23 \times 10^{-3}$ $= 4.2 \times 10^{-3}$ *M*, pH = 11.63.

(b) It will require 40.00 mL of 0.100 *M* HCl to reach the first equivalence point, at which point HCO_3^- is the predominant species.

(c) An additional 40.00 mL are required to react with HCO_3^- to form H_2CO_3, the predominant species at the second equivalence point.

(d) At the second equivalence point there is a 0.0333 *M* solution of H_2CO_3. By the usual procedure for a weak acid:

$$H_2CO_3(aq) \rightleftharpoons H^+(aq) + HCO_3^-(aq)$$

$$K_a = \frac{[H^+][HCO_3^-]}{[H_2CO_3]} = 4.3 \times 10^{-7}; \quad \frac{(x)^2}{(0.0333 - x)} \approx \frac{x^2}{0.0333} \approx 4.3 \times 10^{-7}$$

$x = 1.20 \times 10^{-4} = 1.2 \times 10^{-4}$ M H^+; pH = 3.92

17.74 The reaction involved is $HA(aq) + OH^-(aq) \rightleftharpoons A^-(aq) + H_2O(l)$. We thus have 0.080 mol A^- and 0.12 mol HA in a total volume of 1.0 L, so the "initial" molarities of A^- and HA are 0.080 *M* and 0.12 *M*, respectively. The weak acid equilibrium of interest is

$$HA(aq) \rightleftharpoons H^+(aq) + A^-(aq)$$

(a) $K_a = \frac{[H^+][A^-]}{[HA]}$; $[H^+] = 10^{-4.80} = 1.58 \times 10^{-5} = 1.6 \times 10^{-5}$ M

Assuming $[H^+]$ is small compared to [HA] and $[A^-]$,

$$K_a \approx \frac{(1.58 \times 10^{-5})(0.080)}{(0.12)} = 1.06 \times 10^{-5} = 1.1 \times 10^{-5}, \ pK_a = 4.98$$

(b) At pH = 5.00, $[H^+] = 1.0 \times 10^{-5}$ M. Let b = extra moles NaOH.

[HA] = 0.12 - b, $[A^-]$ = 0.080 + b

$$1.06 \times 10^{-5} \approx \frac{(1.0 \times 10^{-5})(0.080 + b)}{(0.12 - b)}; \ 2.06 \times 10^{-5}\ b = 4.72 \times 10^{-7};$$

b = 0.023 mol NaOH

17.76 The simplest way to obtain the desired buffer mixture would be to titrate the H_3PO_4 solution with NaOH, using a pH meter, until the pH had risen to 7.20. From the values of K_a for phosphoric acid, we can guess that the equilibrium of importance will be the second acid dissociation.

$$H_2PO_4^-(aq) \rightleftharpoons HPO_4^{2-}(aq) + H^+(aq); \ K_a = 6.2 \times 10^{-8}, \ pK_a = 7.21$$

Using Equation [17.9]

$$7.20 = 7.21 + \log \frac{[HPO_4^{2-}]}{[H_2PO_4^-]}; \ \frac{[HPO_4^{2-}]}{[H_2PO_4^-]} = 0.98$$

That is, at pH 7.20 we have added enough 1.0 *M* NaOH to the solution to have produced approximately equal concentrations of the two anions $H_2PO_4^-$ and HPO_4^{2-}. If we had begun with 100 mL of the 1.0 *M* H_3PO_4 solution we would have added about 150 mL of 1.0 *M* NaOH, so the total volume of solution would be 250 mL. The total moles phosphate present = 1.0 *M* × 0.100 L = 0.10 mol, so mol $H_2PO_4^-$ = mol HPO_4^{2-} = 0.050 mol. The concentration of each component is 0.050 mol/0.25 L = 0.20 *M*.

17.77 The pH of a buffer system is centered around pK_a for the conjugate acid component. For a diprotic acid, two conjugate acid/conjugate base pairs are possible.

$H_2X(aq) \rightleftharpoons H^+(aq) + HX^-(aq)$; $K_{a1} = 2 \times 10^{-2}$; $pK_{a1} = 1.70$

$HX^-(aq) \rightleftharpoons H^+(aq) + X^{2-}(aq)$; $K_{a2} = 5.0 \times 10^{-7}$; $pK_{a2} = 6.30$

Clearly HX^- / X^{2-} is the more appropriate combination for preparing a buffer with pH = 6.50. The $[H^+]$ in this buffer = $10^{-6.50} = 3.16 \times 10^{-7} = 3.2 \times 10^{-7}$ *M*. Using the K_{a2} expression to calculate the $[X^{2-}] / [HX^-]$ ratio:

$$K_{a2} = \frac{[H^+][X^{2-}]}{[HX^-]};\ \frac{K_{a2}}{[H^+]} = \frac{[X^{2-}]}{[HX^-]} = \frac{5.0 \times 10^{-7}}{3.16 \times 10^{-7}} = 1.58 = 1.6$$

Since X^{2-} and HX^- are present in the same solution, the ratio of concentrations is also a ratio of moles.

$$\frac{[X^{2-}]}{[HX^-]} = \left(\frac{\text{mol } X^{2-}/\text{L soln}}{\text{mol } HX^-/\text{L soln}}\right) = \frac{\text{mol } X^{2-}}{\text{mol } HX^-} = 1.58;\ \text{mol } X^{2-} = (1.58) \text{ mol } HX^-$$

In the 1.0 L of 1.0 *M* H_2X, there is 1.0 mol of X^{2-} containing material.

Thus, mol HX^- + 1.58 (mol HX^-) = 1.0 mol. 2.58 (mol HX^-) = 1.0;
mol HX^- = 1.0 / 2.58 = 0.39 mol HX^-; mol X^{2-} = 1.0 - 0.39 = 0.61 mol X^{2-}.

Thus enough 1.0 *M* NaOH must be added to produce 0.39 mol HX^- and 0.61 mol X^{2-}.

Considering the neutralization in a step-wise fashion (see discussion of titrations of polyprotic acids in Section 17.3).

	$H_2X(aq)$	+	$NaOH(aq)$	→	$HX^-(aq)$	+	$H_2O(l)$
before	1.0 mol		1 mol		0		
after	0		0		1.0 mol		

	$HX^-(aq)$	+	$NaOH(aq)$	→	$X^{2-}(aq)$	+	$H_2O(l)$
before	1.0				0.61		
change	-0.61		-0.61		+0.61		
after	0.39		0		0.61		

Starting with 1.0 mol of H_2X, 1.0 mol of NaOH is added to completely convert it to 1.0 mol of HX^-. Of that 1.0 mol of HX^-, 0.61 mol must be converted to 0.61 mol X^{2-}. The total moles of NaOH added is (1.00 + 0.61) = 1.61 mol NaOH.

$$\text{L NaOH} = \frac{\text{mol NaOH}}{M\ \text{NaOH}} = \frac{1.61 \text{ mol}}{1.0\ M} = 1.6 \text{ L of } 1.0\ M \text{ NaOH}$$

17.79 (a) CdS: 8.0×10^{-28}; CuS: 6×10^{-37} CdS has greater molar solubility.

(b) $PbCO_3$: 7.4×10^{-14}; $BaCrO_4$: 2.1×10^{-10} $BaCrO_4$ has greater molar solubility.

(c) Since the stoichiometry of the two complexes is not the same, K_{sp} values can't be compared directly; molar solubilities must be calculated from K_{sp} values.

$Ni(OH)_2$: $K_{sp} = 6.0 \times 10^{-16} = [Ni^{2+}][OH^-]^2$; $[Ni^{2+}] = x$, $[OH^-] = 2x$

$6.0 \times 10^{-16} = (x)(2x)^2 = 4x^3$; $x = 5.3 \times 10^{-6}$ *M* Ni^{2+}

Note that $[OH^-]$ from the autoionization of water is less than 1% of $[OH^-]$ from $Ni(OH)_2$ and can be neglected.

$NiCO_3$: $K_{sp} = 1.3 \times 10^{-7} = [Ni^{2+}][CO_3^{2-}]$; $[Ni^{2+}] = [CO_3^{2-}] = x$

$1.3 \times 10^{-7} = x^2$; $x = 3.6 \times 10^{-4}$ *M* Ni^{2+}

$NiCO_3$ has greater molar solubility than $Ni(OH)_2$, but the values are much closer than expected from inspection of K_{sp} values alone.

(d) Again, molar solubilities must be calculated for comparison.

Ag_2SO_4: $K_{sp} = 1.5 \times 10^{-5} = [Ag^+]^2[SO_4^{2-}]$; $[SO_4^{2-}] = x$, $[Ag^+] = 2x$

$1.5 \times 10^{-5} = (2x)^2(x) = 4x^3$; $x = 1.6 \times 10^{-2}$ *M* SO_4^{2-}

AgI: $K_{sp} = 8.3 \times 10^{-17} = [Ag^+][I^-]$; $[Ag^+] = [I^-] = x$

$8.3 \times 10^{-17} = x^2$; $x = 9.1 \times 10^{-9}$ *M* Ag^+

Ag_2SO_4 has greater molar solubility than AgI.

17.80 pH = 10.38; pOH = 14.00 - 10.38 = 3.62; $[OH^-] = 10^{-3.62}$

$[OH^-] = 2.40 \times 10^{-4} = 2.4 \times 10^{-4}$ *M*; $[Mg^{2+}] = 0.5[OH^-] = 1.20 \times 10^{-4} = 1.2 \times 10^{-4}$ *M*

$K_{sp} = [Mg^{2+}][OH^-]^2 \approx (1.20 \times 10^{-4})(2.40 \times 10^{-4})^2 \approx 6.9 \times 10^{-12}$

17.82 $K_{sp} = [Ba^{2+}][MnO_4^-]^2 = 2.5 \times 10^{-10}$

$[MnO_4^-]^2 = 2.5 \times 10^{-10} / 2.0 \times 10^{-8} = 0.0125$; $[MnO_4^-] = \sqrt{0.0125} = 0.11$ *M*

17.83 $[Ca^{2+}][CO_3^{2-}] = 4.5 \times 10^{-9}$; $[Fe^{2+}][CO_3^{2-}] = 2.1 \times 10^{-11}$

Since $[CO_3^{2-}]$ is the same for both equilibria:

$[CO_3^{2-}] = \dfrac{4.5 \times 10^{-9}}{[Ca^{2+}]} = \dfrac{2.1 \times 10^{-11}}{[Fe^{2+}]}$; rearranging $\dfrac{[Ca^{2+}]}{[Fe^{2+}]} = \dfrac{4.5 \times 10^{-9}}{2.1 \times 10^{-11}} = 214 = 2.1 \times 10^2$

17.85 $MgC_2O_4(s) \rightleftharpoons Mg^{2+}(aq) + C_2O_4^{2-}(aq)$

$K_{sp} = [Mg^{2+}][C_2O_4^{2-}] = 8.6 \times 10^{-5}$

If $[Mg^{2+}]$ is to be 3.0×10^{-2} *M*, $[C_2O_4^{2-}] = 8.6 \times 10^{-5} / 3.0 \times 10^{-2} = 2.87 \times 10^{-3} = 2.9 \times 10^{-3}$ *M*

The oxalate ion undergoes hydrolysis:

$C_2O_4^{2-}(aq) + H_2O(l) \rightleftharpoons HC_2O_4^-(aq) + OH^-(aq)$

$$K_b = \frac{[HC_2O_4^-][OH^-]}{[C_2O_4^{2-}]} = 1.0 \times 10^{-14} / 6.4 \times 10^{-5} = 1.56 \times 10^{-10} = 1.6 \times 10^{-10}$$

$[Mg^{2+}] = 3.0 \times 10^{-2}\ M$, $[C_2O_4^{2-}] = 2.87 \times 10^{-3} = 2.9 \times 10^{-3}\ M$

$[HC_2O_4^-] = (3.0 \times 10^{-2} - 2.87 \times 10^{-3})\ M = 2.71 \times 10^{-2} = 2.7 \times 10^{-2}\ M$

$$[OH^-] = 1.56 \times 10^{-10} \times \frac{[C_2O_4^{2-}]}{[HC_2O_4^-]} = 1.56 \times 10^{-10} \times \frac{(2.87 \times 10^{-3})}{(2.71 \times 10^{-2})} = 1.652 \times 10^{-11}$$

$[OH^-] = 1.7 \times 10^{-11}$; pOH = 10.78, pH = 3.22

17.86 The student failed to account for the hydrolysis of the AsO_4^{3-} ion. If there were no hydrolysis, $[Mg^{2+}]$ would indeed be 1.5 times that of $[AsO_4^{3-}]$. However, as the reaction $AsO_4^{3-}(aq) + H_2O(l) \rightleftharpoons HAsO_4^{2-}(aq) + OH^-(aq)$ proceeds, the ion product $[Mg^{2+}]^3[AsO_4^{3-}]^2$ falls below the value for K_{sp}. More $Mg_3(AsO_4)_2$ dissolves, more hydrolysis occurs, and so on, until an equilibrium is reached. At this point $[Mg^{2+}]$ in solution is much greater than 1.5 times free $[AsO_4^{3-}]$. However, it is exactly 1.5 times the **total** concentration of all arsenic-containing species. That is, $[Mg^{2+}] = 1.5\ ([AsO_4^{3-}] + [HAsO_4^{2-}] + [H_2AsO_4^-] + [H_3AsO_4])$

Integrative Exercises

17.89 (a) For a monoprotic acid (one H^+ per mole of acid), at the equivalence point

moles OH^- added = moles H^+ originally present

$$M_B \times V_B = \text{g acid/molar mass}$$

$$\mathcal{M} = \frac{\text{g acid}}{M_B \times V_B} = \frac{0.1044\ \text{g}}{0.0500\ M \times 0.0220\ \text{L}} = 94.48 = 94.5\ \text{g/mol}$$

(b) 11.05 mL is exactly half-way to the equivalence point (22.10 mL). When half of the unknown acid is neutralized, $[HA] = [A^-]$, $[H^+] = K_a$ and pH = pK_a.

$K_a = 10^{-4.89} = 1.3 \times 10^{-5}$

(c) From Appendix D, Table D.1, acids with K_a values close to 1.3×10^{-5} are

name	**K_a**	**formula**	**molar mass**
propionic	1.3×10^{-5}	$HC_3H_5O_2$	74.1
butanoic	1.5×10^{-5}	$HC_4H_7O_2$	88.1
acetic	1.8×10^{-5}	$HC_2H_3O_2$	60.1
hydroazoic	1.9×10^{-5}	HN_3	43.0

Of these, butanoic has the closest match for K_a and molar mass, but the agreement is not good.

17.91 Calculate the initial M of aspirin in the stomach and solve the equilibrium problem to find equilibrium concentrations of $C_8H_7O_2COOH$ and $C_8H_7O_2COO^-$. At pH = 2, $[H^+] = 1 \times 10^{-2}$.

$$\frac{325 \text{ mg}}{\text{tablet}} \times 2 \text{ tablets} \times \frac{1 \text{ g}}{1000 \text{ mg}} \times \frac{1 \text{ mol } C_8H_7O_2COOH}{180.2 \text{ g } C_8H_7O_2COOH} \times \frac{1}{1 \text{ L}} = 3.61 \times 10^{-3} = 4 \times 10^{-3}\ M$$

	$C_8H_7O_2COOH(aq)$	$\rightleftharpoons$	$C_8H_7O_2COO^-(aq)$	+	$H^+(aq)$
initial	$3.61 \times 10^{-3}\ M$		0		$1 \times 10^{-2}\ M$
equil	$(3.61 \times 10^{-3} - x)\ M$		$x\ M$		$(1 \times 10^{-2} + x)\ M$

$$K_a = 3 \times 10^{-5} = \frac{[H^+][C_8H_7O_2COO^-]}{[C_8H_7O_2COOH]} = \frac{(0.01 + x)(x)}{(3.61 \times 10^{-3} - x)} \approx \frac{0.01x}{3.61 \times 10^{-3}}$$

$x = [C_8H_7O_2COO^-] = 1.08 \times 10^{-5} = 1 \times 10^{-5}\ M$

$$\% \text{ ionization} = \frac{1.08 \times 10^{-5}\ M\ C_8H_7O_2COO^-}{3.61 \times 10^{-3}\ M\ C_8H_7O_2COOH} \times 100 = 0.3\%$$

(% ionization is small, so the assumption was valid.)

% aspirin molecules = 100.0% - 0.3% = 99.7% molecules

17.92 According to Equation 13.4, $S_g = kP_g$

$$S_{CO_2} = 3.1 \times 10^{-2} \frac{\text{mol}}{\text{L} \bullet \text{atm}} \times 1.10 \text{ atm} = 0.0341 = \frac{0.034 \text{ mol}}{\text{L}} = 0.034\ M\ CO_2$$

$CO_2(g) + H_2O(l) \rightarrow H_2CO_3(aq)$; $0.0341\ M\ CO_2 = 0.0341\ M\ H_2CO_3$

Consider the stepwise dissociation of $H_2CO_3(aq)$.

	$H_2CO_3(aq)$	$\rightleftharpoons$	$H^+(aq)$	+	$HCO_3^-(aq)$
initial	$0.0341\ M$		0		0
equil.	$(0.0341-x)\ M$		x		x

$$K_{a1} = \frac{[H^+][HCO_3^-]}{[H_2CO_3]} = \frac{x^2}{(0.0341 - x)} \approx \frac{x^2}{0.0341} \approx 4.3 \times 10^{-7}$$

$x^2 = 1.47 \times 10^{-8}$; $x = 1.2 \times 10^{-4}\ M\ H^+$; pH = 3.92

$K_{a2} = 5.6 \times 10^{-11}$; assume the second ionization does not contribute significantly to $[H^+]$.

17.94 For very dilute aqueous solutions, assume the solution density is 1 g/mL.

$$\text{ppb} = \frac{\text{g solute}}{10^9 \text{ g solution}} = \frac{1 \times 10^{-6} \text{ g solute}}{1 \times 10^3 \text{ g solution}} = \frac{\mu\text{g solute}}{\text{L solution}}$$

(a) $K_{sp} = [Ag^+][Cl^-] = 1.8 \times 10^{-10}$; $[Ag^+] = (1.8 \times 10^{-10})^{1/2} = 1.34 \times 10^{-5} = 1.3 \times 10^{-5}$ *M*

$$\frac{1.34 \times 10^{-5} \text{ mol } Ag^+}{L} \times \frac{107.9 \text{ g } Ag^+}{1 \text{ mol } Ag^+} \times \frac{1 \mu g}{1 \times 10^{-6} \text{ g}} = \frac{1.4 \times 10^3 \mu g\, Ag^+}{L}$$

$= 1.4 \times 10^3$ ppb = 1.4 ppm

(b) $K_{sp} = [Ag^+][Br^-] = 5.0 \times 10^{-13}$; $[Ag^+] = (5.0 \times 10^{-13})^{1/2} = 7.07 \times 10^{-7} = 7.1 \times 10^{-7}$ *M*

$$\frac{7.07 \times 10^{-7} \text{ mol } Ag^+}{L} \times \frac{107.9 \text{ g } Ag^+}{1 \text{ mol } Ag^+} \times \frac{1 \mu g}{1 \times 10^{-6} \text{ g}} = 76 \text{ ppb}$$

(c) $K_{sp} = [Ag^+][I^-] = 8.3 \times 10^{-17}$; $[Ag^+] = (8.3 \times 10^{-17})^{1/2} = 9.11 \times 10^{-9} = 9.1 \times 10^{-9}$ *M*

$$\frac{9.11 \times 10^{-9} \text{ mol } Ag^+}{L} \times \frac{107.9 \text{ g } Ag^+}{1 \text{ mol } Ag^+} \times \frac{1 \mu g}{1 \times 10^{-6} \text{ g}} = 0.98 \text{ ppb}$$

AgBr(s) would maintain $[Ag^+]$ in the correct range.

17.95 To determine precipitation conditions, we must know K_{sp} for $CaF_2(s)$ and calculate Q under the specified conditions. $K_{sp} = 3.9 \times 10^{-11} = [Ca^{2+}][F^-]^2$

$[Ca^{2+}]$ and $[F^-]$: The term 1 ppb means 1 part per billion or 1 g solute per billion g solution. Assuming that the density of this very dilute solution is the density of water:

$$1 \text{ ppb} = \frac{1 \text{ g solute}}{1 \times 10^9 \text{ g solution}} \times \frac{1 \text{ g solution}}{1 \text{ mL solution}} \times \frac{1 \times 10^3 \text{ mL}}{1 \text{ L}} = \frac{1 \times 10^{-6} \text{ g solute}}{1 \text{ L solution}}$$

$$\frac{1 \times 10^{-6} \text{ g solute}}{1 \text{ L solution}} \times \frac{1 \mu g}{1 \times 10^{-6} \text{ g}} = 1 \mu g / 1 \text{ L}$$

$$8 \text{ ppb } Ca^{2+} \times \frac{1 \mu g}{1 \text{ L}} = \frac{8 \mu g\, Ca^{2+}}{1 \text{ L}} = \frac{8 \times 10^{-6} \text{ g } Ca^{2+}}{1 \text{ L}} \times \frac{1 \text{ mol } Ca^{2+}}{40 \text{ g}} = 2 \times 10^{-7}\, M\, Ca^{2+}$$

$$1 \text{ ppb } F^- \times \frac{1 \mu g}{1 \text{ L}} = \frac{1 \mu g\, F^-}{1 \text{ L}} = \frac{1 \times 10^{-6} \text{ g } F^-}{1 \text{ L}} \times \frac{1 \text{ mol } F^-}{19.0 \text{ g}} = 5 \times 10^{-8}\, M\, F^-$$

$Q = [Ca^{2+}][F^-]^2 = (2 \times 10^{-7})(5 \times 10^{-8})^2 = 5 \times 10^{-22}$

$5 \times 10^{-22} < 3.9 \times 10^{-11}$, $Q < K_{sp}$, no CaF_2 will precipitate

18 Chemistry of the Environment

Earth's Atmosphere

18.2 (a) The tropopause is the boundary between the troposphere and the stratosphere, the first minimum in the temperature profile of the atmosphere.

(b) Boundaries between regions of the atmosphere are at maxima and minima (peaks and valleys) in the atmospheric temperature profile. For example, in the troposphere, temperature decreases with altitude, while in the stratosphere, it increases with altitude. The temperature minimum is the tropopause boundary.

(c) Atmospheric pressure in the troposphere ranges from 1.0 atm to 0.4 atm, while pressure in the stratosphere ranges from 0.4 atm to 0.001 atm. Gas density (g/L) is directly proportional to pressure. The much lower density of the stratosphere means it has the smaller mass, despite having a larger volume than the troposphere.

18.4 $P_{Ar} = \chi_{Ar} \cdot P_{atm}$; $P_{Ar} = 0.00934\ (98.6\ \text{kPa}) = 0.921\ \text{kPa}$; $0.921\ \text{kPa} \times \dfrac{760\ \text{torr}}{101.325\ \text{kPa}} = 6.91\ \text{torr}$

$P_{CO_2} = \chi_{CO_2} \cdot P_{atm}$; $P_{CO_2} = 0.000355\ (98.6\ \text{kPa}) = 0.0350\ \text{kPa}$; $0.0350\ \text{kPa} \times \dfrac{760\ \text{torr}}{101.325\ \text{kPa}}$

$= 0.263\ \text{torr}$

18.6 (a) ppm Ne = mol Ne/1 × 10^6 mol air; $\chi_{Ne} = 1.818 \times 10^{-5}$ mol Ne/mol air

$$\frac{1.818 \times 10^{-5}\ \text{mol Ne}}{1\ \text{mol air}} = \frac{x\ \text{mol Ne}}{1 \times 10^{6}\ \text{mol air}};\ x = 18.18\ \text{ppm Ne}$$

(b) $P_{Ne} = \chi_{Ne} \cdot P_{atm} = 1.818 \times 10^{-5} \times 743\ \text{torr} \times \dfrac{1\ \text{atm}}{760\ \text{torr}} = 1.7773 \times 10^{-5}$

$= 1.78 \times 10^{-5}\ \text{atm}$

T = 295°C + 273 = 568 K

$$\frac{n_{Ne}}{V} = \frac{P_{Ne}V}{RT} = \frac{1.7773 \times 10^{-5}\ \text{atm} \times 1.0\ \text{L}}{568\ \text{K}} \times \frac{\text{K} \cdot \text{mol}}{0.08206\ \text{L} \cdot \text{atm}} = 3.8132 \times 10^{-7}$$

$= 3.813 \times 10^{-7}\ \text{mol/L}$

$$\frac{3.8132 \times 10^{-7}\ \text{mol Ne}}{\text{L}} \times \frac{6.022 \times 10^{23}\ \text{atoms}}{\text{mol}} = 2.296 \times 10^{17} = 2.30 \times 10^{17}\ \text{Ne atoms/L}$$

The Upper Atmosphere; Ozone

18.8 $$\frac{339 \times 10^3 \text{ J}}{1 \text{ mol}} \times \frac{1 \text{ mol}}{6.022 \times 10^{23} \text{ molecules}} = 5.6294 \times 10^{-19} = 5.63 \times 10^{-19} \text{ J/molecule}$$

$$\lambda = \frac{hc}{E} = \frac{(6.626 \times 10^{-34} \text{ J}\bullet\text{sec})(3.00 \times 10^8 \text{ m/sec})}{5.6294 \times 10^{-19} \text{ J}} = 3.53 \times 10^{-7} \text{ m} = 353 \text{ nm}$$

$$\frac{293 \times 10^3 \text{ J}}{1 \text{ mol}} \times \frac{1 \text{ mol}}{6.022 \times 10^{23} \text{ molecules}} = 4.8655 \times 10^{-19} = 4.87 \times 10^{-19} \text{ J/molecule}$$

$$\lambda = \frac{(6.626 \times 10^{-34} \text{ J}\bullet\text{sec})(3.00 \times 10^8 \text{ m/sec})}{4.8655 \times 10^{-19} \text{ J}} = 4.09 \times 10^{-7} \text{ m} = 409 \text{ nm}$$

Photons of wavelengths longer than 409 nm cannot cause rupture of the C--Cl bond in either CF_3Cl or CCl_4. Photons with wavelengths between 409 and 353 nm can cause C–Cl bond rupture in CCl_4, but not in CF_3Cl.

18.10 The bond dissociation energy of N_2, 941 kJ/mol, is much higher than that of O_2, 495 kJ/mol. Photons with a wavelength short enough to photodissociate N_2 are not as abundant as the ultraviolet photons which lead to photodissociation of O_2. Also, N_2 does not absorb these photons as readily as O_2 so even if a short-wavelength photon is available, it may not be absorbed by an N_2 molecule.

18.12 (a) At 120 km and beyond, oxygen atoms are primarily generated by photodissociation of O_2 molecules: $O_2(g) + h\nu \rightarrow 2O(g)$

(b) Oxygen atoms exist longer at 120 km because there are fewer particles (atoms and molecules) at this altitude and thus fewer collisions and subsequent reactions that consume O atoms.

(c) Ozone is the primary absorber of high energy ultraviolet radiation in the 200-310 nm range. If this radiation were not absorbed in the stratosphere, plants and animals at the earth's surface would be seriously and adversely affected.

18.14 32 e^-, 16 e^- pr

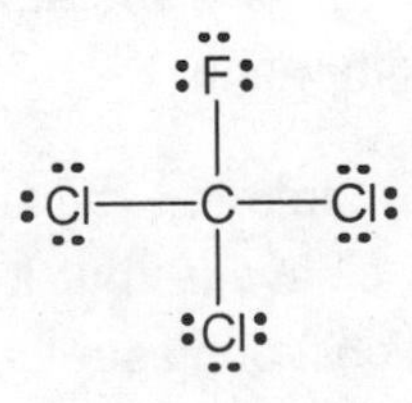

It contains C–Cl bonds that can be cleaved by UV light in the stratosphere to produce Cl atoms. It is chlorine in atomic form that catalyzes the destruction of stratospheric ozone.

CFC–11, $CFCl_3$, is chemically inert and resists decomposition in the troposphere, so that it eventually reaches the stratosphere in molecular form.

18.16 Yes. Assuming $CFBr_3$ reaches the stratosphere intact, it contains C–Br bonds that are even more susceptible to cleavage by UV light than C–Cl bonds. According to Table 8.4, the average C–Br bond dissociation energy is 273 kJ/mol, compared to 328 kJ/mol for C–Cl bonds. Once in atomic form, Br atoms catalyze the destruction of ozone by a mechanism similar to that of Cl atoms.

Chemistry of the Troposphere

18.18 CO in unpolluted air is typically 0.05 ppm, whereas in urban air CO is about 10 ppm. A major source is automobile exhaust. SO_2 is less than 0.01 ppm in unpolluted air and on the order of 0.08 ppm in urban air. A major source is coal and oil-burning power plants, but there is also some SO_2 in auto exhaust. NO is about 0.01 ppm in unpolluted air and about 0.05 ppm in urban air. It comes mainly from auto exhaust.

18.20 All oxides of nonmetals produce acid solutions when dissolved in water. Sulfur oxides are produced naturally during volcanic eruptions and carbon oxides are products of combustion and metabolism. These dissolved gases cause rainwater to be naturally acidic.

18.22 (a) $Fe(s) + H_2SO_4(aq) \rightarrow Fe^{2+}(aq) + SO_4^{2-}(aq) + H_2(g)$

(b) No. Silver is a 'noble' metal. It is relatively resistant to oxidation, and much more resistant than iron. In Table 4.5, The Activity Series of Metals in Aqueous Solution, Ag is much, much lower than Fe and it is below hydrogen, while Fe is above hydrogen. This means that Fe is susceptible to oxidation by acid, while Ag is not.

18.24 (a) Visible (Figure 6.4)

(b)
$$E_{photon} = hc/\lambda = \frac{6.626 \times 10^{-34}\ J\bullet s \times 3.00 \times 10^{8}\ m/s}{420 \times 10^{-9}\ m} = 4.733 \times 10^{-19}$$
$$= 4.73 \times 10^{-19}\ J/photon$$

$$\frac{4.733 \times 10^{-19}\ J}{1\ photon} \times \frac{6.022 \times 10^{23}\ photons}{1\ mol} \times \frac{1\ kJ}{1000\ J} = 285\ kJ/mol$$

18.26 (a) A *greenhouse gas* absorbs energy in the 10,000 - 30,000 nm or infrared region. It absorbs wavelengths of radiation emitted by earth and returns it as heat. A non-greenhouse gas is transparent to radiation in this wavelength range.

(b) Ar(g) is monatomic, while $CH_4(g)$ contains 4 C–H bonds. Infrared radiation has insufficient energy to cause electron transitions or bond cleavage, but it has an appropriate amount of energy to cause molecular deformations, bond stretching and angle bending. Monatomic gases such as Ar cannot "use" infrared radiation and are transparent to it.

The World Ocean

18.28 If the phosphorous is present as phosphate, there is a 1:1 ratio between the molarity of phosphorus and molarity of phosphate. Thus, we can calculate the molarity based on the given mass of P.

$$\frac{0.07\text{ g P}}{1\times10^6\text{ g H}_2\text{O}} \times \frac{1\text{ mol P}}{31\text{ g P}} \times \frac{1\text{ mol PO}_4^{3-}}{1\text{ mol P}} \times \frac{1\times10^3\text{ g H}_2\text{O}}{1\text{ L H}_2\text{O}} = 2.26\times10^{-6}$$

$$= 2.3\times10^{-6}\ M\ \text{PO}_4^{3-}$$

18.30 $1\times10^{11}\text{ g Br} \times \dfrac{1\times10^3\text{ g H}_2\text{O}}{0.067\text{ g Br}} \times \dfrac{1\text{ L H}_2\text{O}}{1\times10^3\text{ g H}_2\text{O}} = 1.5\times10^{12}\text{ L H}_2\text{O}$

Because the process is only 10% efficient, ten times this much, or 1.5×10^{13} L H_2O, must be processed.

18.32 Calculate the total ion concentration of sea water by summing the molarities given in Table 18.6. Then use $\pi = \Delta MRT$ to calculate pressure.

$$M_{total} = 0.55 + 0.47 + 0.028 + 0.054 + 0.010 + 0.010 + 2.3\times10^{-3} + 8.3\times10^{-4}$$
$$+ 4.3\times10^{-4} + 9.1\times10^{-5} + 7.0\times10^{-5} = 1.1257 = 1.13\ M$$

$$\pi = \frac{(1.1257 - 0.02)\text{ mol}}{\text{L}} \times \frac{0.08206\text{ L}\times\text{atm}}{\text{mol}\bullet\text{K}} \times 305\text{ K} = 27.674 = 27.7\text{ atm}$$

Check. The largest numbers in the molarity sum have 2 decimal places, so M_{total} has 2 decimal places and 3 sig figs. ΔM also has 2 decimal places and 3 sig figs so the calculated pressure has 3 sig figs. Units are correct.

Freshwater

18.34 (a) Decomposition of organic matter by aerobic bacteria depletes dissolved O_2. A low dissolved oxygen concentration indicates the presence of organic pollutants.

(b) According to Section 13.3, the solubility of $O_2(g)$ (or any gas) in water decreases with increasing temperature.

18.36 $85{,}000\text{ persons} \times \dfrac{59\text{ g O}_2}{1\text{ person}} \times \dfrac{1\times10^6\text{ g H}_2\text{O}}{9\text{ g O}_2} \times \dfrac{1\text{ L H}_2\text{O}}{1\times10^3\text{ g H}_2\text{O}} = 5.6\times10^8\text{ L H}_2\text{O}$

18.38 (a) Ca^{2+}, Mg^{2+}, Fe^{2+}

(b) Divalent cations (ions with +2 changes) contribute to water hardness. These ions react with soap to form scum on surfaces or leave undesirable deposits on surfaces, particularly inside pipes, upon heating.

18.40 $Ca(OH)_2$ is added to remove Ca^{2+} as $CaCO_3(s)$, and Na_2CO_3 removes the remaining Ca^{2+}. $Ca^{2+}(aq) + 2HCO_3^-(aq) + [Ca^{2+}(aq) + 2OH^-(aq)] \rightarrow 2CaCO_3(s) + 2H_2O(l)$. One mole $Ca(OH)_2$ is needed for each 2 moles of $HCO_3^-(aq)$ present.

$$5.0 \times 10^7 \text{ L } H_2O \times \frac{1.7 \times 10^{-3} \text{ mol } HCO_3^-}{1 \text{ L } H_2O} \times \frac{1 \text{ mol } Ca(OH)_2}{2 \text{ mol } HCO_3^-} \times \frac{74 \text{ g } Ca(OH)_2}{1 \text{ mol } Ca(OH)_2}$$

$$= 3.1 \times 10^6 \text{ g } Ca(OH)_2$$

Half of the native HCO_3^- precipitates the added Ca^{2+} so this operation reduces the Ca^{2+} concentration from 5.7×10^{-3} *M* to $(5.7 \times 10^{-3} - 8.5 \times 10^{-4})$ *M* = 4.85×10^{-3} *M*. Next we must add sufficient Na_2CO_3 to further reduce $[Ca^{2+}]$ to 1.1×10^{-3} *M*. We thus need to reduce $[Ca^{2+}]$ by $(4.85 \times 10^{-3} - 1.1 \times 10^{-3})$ *M* = 3.75×10^{-3} *M*. $Ca^{2+}(aq) + CO_3^{-2}(aq) \rightarrow CaCO_3(s)$.

$$5.0 \times 10^7 \text{ L } H_2O \times \frac{3.75 \times 10^{-3} \text{ mol } Ca^{2+}}{1 \text{ L } H_2O} \times \frac{1 \text{ mol } Na_2CO_3}{1 \text{ mol } Ca^{2+}} \times \frac{106 \text{ g } Na_2CO_3}{1 \text{ mol } Na_2CO_3}$$

$$= 2.0 \times 10^7 \text{ g } Na_2CO_3$$

18.42 $4FeSO_4(aq) + O_2(aq) + 2H_2O(l) \rightarrow 4Fe^{3+}(aq) + 4OH^-(aq) + 4SO_4^{2-}(aq)$

SO_4^{2-} is a spectator, so the net ionic equation is $4Fe^{2+}(aq) + 2H_2O(l) \rightarrow 4Fe^{3+}(aq) + 4OH^-(aq)$.

$Fe^{3+}(aq) + 3HCO_3^-(aq) \rightarrow Fe(OH)_3(s) + 3CO_2(g)$

In this reaction, Fe^{3+} acts as a Lewis acid, and HCO_3^- acts as a Lewis base.

Green Chemistry

18.44 Catalysts increase the rate of a reaction by lowering activation energy, E_a. For an uncatalyzed reaction that requires extreme temperatures and pressures to generate product at a viable rate, finding a suitable catalyst reduces the required temperature and/or pressure, which reduces the amount of energy used to run the process. A catalyst can also increase rate of production, which would reduce the net time and thus energy required to generate a certain amount of product.

18.46 (a)

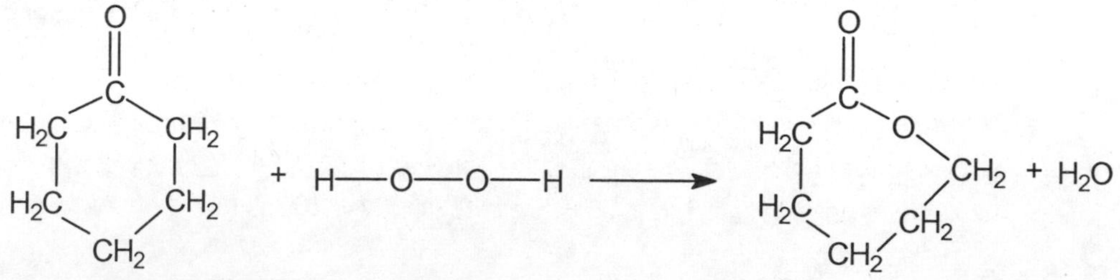

(b)

- It is better to prevent waste than to treat it. The alternative process eliminates production of 3-chlorobenzoic acid by-product, chlorine-containing waste that must be treated.
- Produce as little, nontoxic waste as possible. The by-product of the alternative process is nontoxic water. The low molar mass of water means that a small amount of 'waste' is generated.

- Chemical processes should be efficient. The alternative process is catalyzed, which could mean that the process will be more energy efficient than the Baeyer-Villiger reaction (see Solution 18.44).
- Raw materials should be renewable. The catalyst can be recovered from the reaction mixture and reused. We don't have information about solvents or other auxiliary substances.

Additional Exercises

18.47 (a) *Acid rain* is rain with a larger $[H^+]$ and thus a lower pH than expected. The additional H^+ is produced by the dissolution of sulfur and nitrogen oxides such as $SO_3(g)$ and $NO_2(g)$ in rain droplets to form sulfuric and nitric acid, $H_2SO_4(aq)$ and $HNO_3(aq)$.

(b) The *greenhouse effect* is warming of the atmosphere caused by heat trapping gases such as $CO_2(g)$ and $H_2O(g)$. That is, these gases absorb infrared or "heat" radiation emitted from the earth's surface and serve to maintain a relatively constant temperature on the surface. A significant increase in the amount of atmospheric CO_2 (from burning fossil fuels and other sources) could cause a corresponding increase in the average surface temperature and drastically change the global climate.

(c) *Photochemical smog* is an unpleasant collection of atmospheric pollutants initiated by photochemical dissociation of NO_2 to form NO and O atoms. The major components are NO(g), $NO_2(g)$, CO(g) and unburned hydrocarbons, all produced by automobile engines, and $O_3(g)$, ozone.

(d) The *ozone hole* is a region of depleted O_3 in the stratosphere over Antarctica. It is caused by reactions between O_3 and Cl atoms originating from chlorofluorocarbons (CFC's), CF_xCl_{4-x}. Depletion of the ozone layer would allow damaging ultraviolet radiation disruptive to the plant and animal life in our ecosystem to reach earth.

18.49 Stratospheric ozone is formed and destroyed in a cycle of chemical reactions. The decomposition of O_3 to O_2 and O produces oxygen atoms, an essential ingredient for the production of ozone. While single O_3 molecules exist for only a few seconds, new O_3 molecules are constantly reformed. This cyclic process ensures a finite concentration of O_3 in the stratosphere available to absorb ultraviolet radiation. (This explanation assumes that the cycle is not disrupted by outside agents such as CFCs.)

18.51 (a) The production of Cl atoms in the stratosphere is the result of the photodissociation of a C–Cl bond in the chlorofluorocarbon molecule.

$$CF_2Cl_2(g) \xrightarrow{h\nu} CF_2Cl(g) + Cl(g)$$

According to Table 8.4, the bond dissociation energy of a C–Br bond is 276 kJ/mol, while the value for a C–Cl bond is 328 kJ/mol. Photodissociation of $CBrF_3$ to form Br atoms requires less energy than the production of Cl atoms and should occur readily in the stratosphere.

(b) $CBrF_3(g) \xrightarrow{h\nu} CF_3(g) + Br(g)$

Also, under certain conditions

$BrO(g) + BrO(g) \longrightarrow Br_2O_2(g)$

$Br(g) + O_3(g) \longrightarrow BrO(g) + O_2(g)$

$Br_2O_2(g) + h\nu \longrightarrow O_2(g) + 2Br(g)$

18.52 (a) HNO_3 is a major component in acid rain.

(b) While it removes CO, the reaction produces NO_2. The photodissociation of NO_2 to form O atoms is the first step in the formation of tropospheric ozone and photochemical smog.

(c) Again, NO_2 is the initiator of photochemical smog. Also, methoxyl radical, OCH_3, is a reactive species capable of initiating other undesirable reactions.

18.54 Oxygen is present in the atmosphere to the extent of 209,000 parts per million. If CO binds 210 times more effectively than O_2, then the **effective** concentration of CO is 210 × 112 ppm = 23,520 = 23,500 ppm. The fraction of carboxyhemoglobin in the blood leaving the lungs is thus $\dfrac{23{,}520}{23{,}520 + 209{,}000} = 0.101$. Thus, 10.1 percent of the blood is in the form of carboxyhemoglobin, 89.9 percent as the O_2-bound oxyhemoglobin.

18.55 (a) $CH_4(g) + 2O_2(g) \rightarrow CO_2(g) + 2H_2O(g)$

(b) $2CH_4(g) + 3O_2(g) \rightarrow 2CO(g) + 4H_2O(g)$

(c) vol $CH_4 \rightarrow$ vol $O_2 \rightarrow$ volume air ($\chi_{O_2} = 0.20948$)

Equal volumes of gases at the same temperature and pressure contain equal numbers of moles (Avogadro's law). If 2 moles of O_2 are required for 1 mole of CH_4, 2.0 L of pure O_2 are needed to burn 1.0 L of CH_4.

$$\text{vol } O_2 = \chi_{O_2} \times \text{vol}_{air} = \frac{\text{vol } O_2}{\chi_{O_2}} = \frac{2.0\text{ L}}{0.20948} = 9.5\text{ L air}$$

(d) $2NO_2(g) + 2CH_4(g) \xrightarrow{\text{catalyst}} N_2(g) + 2C(s) + 4H_2O(l)$

$2NO(g) + CH_4(g) \xrightarrow{\text{catalyst}} N_2(g) + C(s) + 2H_2O(l)$

NO_x contains N in an oxidized form and CH_4 contains C in a reduced form, so the reaction is likely to generate a reduced form of N, N_2, and a more oxidized form of C. The carbon-containing products could also be CO(g) or $CO_2(g)$, depending on the relative amounts of NO_x.

18.57 Most of the 390 watts/m^2 radiated from Earth's surface is in the infrared region of the spectrum. Tropospheric gases, particularly $H_2O(g)$ and $CO_2(g)$, absorb much of this radiation and prevent it from escaping into space (Figure 18.10). The energy absorbed by these so-called "greenhouse gases" warms the atmosphere close to Earth's surface and makes the planet liveable.

18.58 (a) $NO(g) + h\nu \rightarrow N(g) + O(g)$

(b) $NO(g) + h\nu \rightarrow NO^+(g) + e^-$

(c) $NO(g) + O_3(g) \rightarrow NO_2(g) + O_2(g)$

(d) $3NO_2(g) + H_2O(l) \rightarrow 2HNO_3(aq) + NO(g)$

18.60 Chlorine is more convenient, because it can be shipped to the treatment sight as condensed gas and introduced in a measured way. It requires no new capital expense, because the chlorination equipment is in place. However, Cl_2 is expensive to produce and ship because it is corrosive and toxic. It is a safety hazard for workers. Its use in water treatment produces trihalomethanes, THM's, which pose a small cancer risk when dissolved in water. Perhaps more importantly, THM's are greenhouse gases and contribute to the destruction of stratospheric ozone.

18.61
- Use of chlorine as an oxidizing agent generates toxic chlorine-containing waste that must be treated.
- Cl_2 is not a renewable feed stock.
- Cl_2 is produced by electrolysis of molten NaCl. This is an energy-intensive process that reduces the net energy-efficiency of pulp bleaching.
- Cl_2 is an auxiliary substance and is certainly not innocuous.

18.62 Because NO has an odd electron, like Cl(g), it could act as a catalyst for decomposition of ozone in the stratosphere. The increased destruction of ozone by NO would result in less absorption of short wavelength UV radiation now being screened out primarily by the ozone. Radiation in this wavelength range is known to be harmful to humans; it causes skin cancer. There is evidence that many plants don't tolerate it very well either, though more research is needed to test this idea.

In Chapter 22 the oxidation of NO to NO_2 by oxygen is described. On dissolving in water, NO_2 disproportionates into NO_3^- (aq) and NO(g). Thus, over time the NO in the troposphere will be converted into NO_3^- which is in turn incorporated into soils.

Integrative Exercises

18.64 (a)

$$8{,}376{,}726 \text{ tons coal} \times \frac{83 \text{ ton C}}{100 \text{ ton coal}} \times \frac{44.01 \text{ ton } CO_2}{12.01 \text{ ton C}} = 2.5 \times 10^7 \text{ ton } CO_2$$

$$8{,}376{,}726 \text{ tons coal} \times \frac{2.5 \text{ ton S}}{100 \text{ ton coal}} \times \frac{64.07 \text{ ton } SO_2}{32.07 \text{ ton S}} = 4.18 \times 10^5$$

(b) $CaO(s) + SO_2(g) \rightarrow CaSO_3(s)$

$$4.18 \times 10^5 \text{ ton } SO_2 \times \frac{55 \text{ ton } SO_2 \text{ removed}}{100 \text{ ton } SO_2 \text{ produced}} \times \frac{120.15 \text{ ton } CaSO_3}{64.07 \text{ ton } SO_2}$$

$$= 4.3 \times 10^5 \text{ ton } CaSO_3$$

18.65 *Course sand* is removed by course sand filtration. *Finely divided particles* and some *bacteria* are removed by precipitation with aluminum hydroxide. Remaining *harmful bacteria* are removed by ozonation. *Trihalomethanes* are removed by either aeration or activated carbon filtration; use of activated carbon might be preferred because it does not involve release of TCMs into the atmosphere. *Dissolved organic substances* are oxidized (and rendered less harmful, but not removed) by both aeration and ozonation. Dissolved *nitrates* and *phosphates* are not removed by any of these processes, but are rendered less harmful by adequate aeration.

18.67 (i) $ClO(g) + O_3(g) \rightarrow ClO_2(g) + O_2(g)$

$$\Delta H_i = \Delta H_f^\circ\ ClO_2(g) + \Delta H_f^\circ\ O_2(g) - \Delta H_f^\circ\ ClO(g) - \Delta H_f^\circ\ O_3(g)$$

$$\Delta H_i = 102 + 0 - 101 - (142.3) = -141\ kJ$$

(ii) $ClO_2(g) + O(g) \rightarrow ClO(g) + O_2(g)$

$$\Delta H_{ii} = \Delta H_f^\circ\ ClO(g) + \Delta H_f^\circ\ O_2(g) - \Delta H_f^\circ\ ClO_2(g) + \Delta H_f^\circ\ O(g)$$

$$\Delta H_{ii} = 101 + 0 - 102 - (247.5) = -249\ kJ$$

(overall) $ClO(g) + O_3(g) + ClO_2(g) + O(g) \rightarrow ClO_2(g) + O_2(g) + ClO(g) + O_2(g)$

$$O_3(g) + O(g) \rightarrow 2O_2(g)$$

$$\Delta H = \Delta H_i + \Delta H_{ii} = -141\ kJ + (-249)\ kJ = -390\ kJ$$

Because the enthalpies of both (i) and (ii) are distinctly exothermic, it is possible that the ClO - ClO_2 pair could be a catalyst for the destruction of ozone.

18.68 (a) Assume the density of water at 20°C is the same as at 25°C.

$$1.00\ gal \times \frac{4\ qt}{1\ gal} \times \frac{1\ L}{1.057\ qt} \times \frac{1000\ mL}{1\ L} \times \frac{0.99707\ g\ H_2O}{1\ mL} = 3773$$

$$= 3.77 \times 10^3\ g\ H_2O$$

The $H_2O(l)$ must be heated from 20°C to 100°C and then vaporized at 100°C.

$$3.773 \times 10^3\ g\ H_2O \times \frac{4.184\ J}{g\ °C} \times 80\ °C \times \frac{1\ kJ}{1000\ J} = 1263 = 1.3 \times 10^3\ kJ$$

$$3.773 \times 10^3\ g\ H_2O \times \frac{1\ mol\ H_2O}{18.02\ g\ H_2O} \times \frac{40.67\ kJ}{mol\ H_2O} = 8516 = 8.52 \times 10^3\ kJ$$

$$energy = 1263\ kJ + 8516\ kJ = 9779 = 9.8 \times 10^3\ kJ/gal\ H_2O$$

(b) According to Solution 5.6, 1 kwh = 3.6×10^6 J.

$$\frac{9779\ kJ}{gal\ H_2O} \times \frac{1000\ J}{kJ} \times \frac{1\ kwh}{3.6 \times 10^6\ J} \times \frac{\$0.085}{kwh} = \$0.23/gal$$

(c) $\frac{\$0.23}{\$1.26} \times 100 = 18\%$ of the total cost is energy

18.69 (a) A rate constant of $M^{-1}s^{-1}$ is indicative of a reaction that is second order overall. For the reaction given, the rate law is probably rate = $k[O][O_3]$. (Although rate = $k[O]^2$ or

$k[O_3]^2$ are possibilities, it is difficult to envision a mechanism consistent with either one that would result in two molecules of O_2 being produced.)

(b) Yes. Most atmospheric processes are initiated by collision. One could imagine an activated complex of four O atoms collapsing to form two O_2 molecules. Also, the rate constant is large, which is less likely for a multistep process. The reaction is analogous to the destruction of O_3 by Cl atoms (Equation 18.7), which is also second order with a large rate constant.

(c) According to the Arrhenius equation, $k = Ae^{-E_a/RT}$. Thus, the larger the value of k, the smaller the activation energy, E_a. The value of the rate constant for this reaction is large, so the activation energy is small.

(d) $\Delta H_f^\circ = 2\Delta H_f^\circ\ O_2(g) - \Delta H_f^\circ\ O(g) - \Delta H_f^\circ\ O_3(g)$

$\Delta H_f^\circ = 0 - 247.5\ kJ - 142.3\ kJ = -389.8\ kJ$

The reaction is exothermic, so energy is released; the reaction would raise the temperature of the stratosphere.

18.71 (a) 17 e^-, 8.5 e^- pairs

Owing to its lower electronegativity, N is more likely to be electron deficient and to accommodate the odd electron.

(b) The fact that NO_2 is an electron deficient molecule indicates that it will be highly reactive. Dimerization results in formation of a N–N single bond which completes the octet of both N atoms. NO_2 and N_2O_4 exist in equilibrium in a closed system. The reaction is exothermic, Equation [22.65]. In an urban environment, NO_2 is produced from hot automobile combustion. At these temperatures, equilibrium favors the monomer because the reaction is exothermic.

(c) $2NO_2(g) + 4CO(g) \rightarrow N_2(g) + 4CO_2(g)$

$NO_2(g) + CO(g) \rightarrow NO(g) + CO_2(g)$

NO_2 is an oxidizing agent and CO is a reducing agent, so we expect products to contain N in a more reduced form, NO or N_2, and C in a more oxidized form, CO_2.

(d) No. Because it is an odd-electron molecule, NO_2 is very reactive. We expect it to undergo chemical reactions or photodissociate before it can migrate to the stratosphere. The expected half-life of an NO_2 molecule is short.

18.72 Calculate $[H_2SO_4]$ required to produce a solution with pH = 2.5. From the volume of rainfall, calculate the amount of H_2SO_4 present.

$[H^+] = 10^{-2.5} = 3.16 \times 10^{-3} = 3 \times 10^{-3}\ M$

$$H_2SO_4(aq) \rightarrow H^+(aq) + HSO_4^-(aq)$$
equil $\quad x\,M \quad x\,M$

$$HSO_4^- \rightleftharpoons H^+(aq) + SO_4^{2-} \qquad K_{a2} = 1.2 \times 10^{-2}$$
equil $\quad (x - y)\,M \quad (x + y)\,M \quad y\,M$

The first ionization of H_2SO_4 is complete; the second is not.

$[H^+] = x + y = 3.16 \times 10^{-3}\ M;\quad x = 3.16 \times 10^{-3} - y$

$$K_a = \frac{[H^+][SO_4^{2-}]}{[HSO_4^-]};\ 0.012 = \frac{(3.16 \times 10^{-3})(y)}{(3.16 \times 10^{-3} - y)}$$

$3.795 \times 10^{-5} - 0.012\,y = 3.16 \times 10^{-3}\,y;\ 3.795 \times 10^{-5} = 0.0152\,y;\ y = 2.5 \times 10^{-3}\ M$

$x = [H_2SO_4] = 3.16 \times 10^{-3}\ M - 2.5 \times 10^{-3}\ M = 6.60 \times 10^{-4}\ M = 7 \times 10^{-4}\ M\ H_2SO_4$

$$V = 1.0\text{ in} \times 150\text{ mi}^2 \times \frac{5280^2\text{ ft}^2}{\text{mi}^2} \times \frac{12^2\text{ in}^2}{\text{ft}^2} \times \frac{2.54^3\text{ cm}^3}{\text{in}^3} \times \frac{1\text{ L}}{1000\text{ cm}^3} = 9.868 \times 10^9 = 9.9 \times 10^9\text{ L}$$

$$\frac{6.60 \times 10^{-4}\text{ mol } H_2SO_4}{1\text{ L rainfall}} \times 9.868 \times 10^9\text{ L} \times \frac{98.1\text{ g } H_2SO_4}{1\text{ mol } H_2SO_4} \times \frac{1\text{ kg}}{1000\text{ g}} = 6.39 \times 10^5 = 6 \times 10^5\text{ kg } H_2SO_4$$

18.74 (a) $Al(OH)_3(s) \rightleftharpoons Al^{3+}(aq) + 3OH^-(aq) \qquad K_{sp} = 1.3 \times 10^{-33} = [Al^{3+}][OH^-]^3$

This is a precipitation conditions problem. At what $[OH^-]$ (we can get pH from $[OH^-]$) will $Q = 1.3 \times 10^{-33}$, the requirement for the onset of precipitation?

$Q = 1.3 \times 10^{-33} = [Al^{3+}][OH^-]^3$. Find the molar concentration of $Al_2(SO_4)_3$ and thus $[Al^{3+}]$.

$$\frac{2.0\text{ lb } Al_2(SO_4)_3}{1000\text{ gal } H_2O} \times \frac{453.6\text{ g}}{1\text{ lb}} \times \frac{1\text{ mol } Al_2(SO_4)_3}{342.2\text{ g } Al_2(SO_4)_3} \times \frac{1\text{ gal}}{4\text{ qt}} \times \frac{1\text{ qt}}{0.946\text{ L}}$$
$$= 7.01 \times 10^{-4}\ M\ Al_2(SO_4)_3 = 1.40 \times 10^{-3}\ M\ Al^{3+}$$

$Q = 1.3 \times 10^{-33} = (1.4 \times 10^{-3})[OH^-]^3;\quad [OH^-]^3 = 9.28 \times 10^{-31}$

$[OH^-] = 9.753 \times 10^{-11} = 9.8 \times 10^{-11}\ M;\quad pOH = 10.01;\ pH = 14 - 10.01 = 3.99$

(b) $CaO(s) + H_2O(l) \rightarrow Ca^{2+}(aq) + 2OH^-(aq);\ [OH^-] = 9.753 \times 10^{-11}$ mol/L

$$\text{mol } OH^- = \frac{9.753 \times 10^{-11}\text{ mol}}{1\text{ L}} \times 1000\text{ gal} \times \frac{4\text{ qt}}{1\text{ gal}} \times \frac{0.946\text{ L}}{1\text{ qt}} = 3.69 \times 10^{-7} = 3.7 \times 10^{-7}\text{ mol } OH^-$$

$$3.69 \times 10^{-7}\text{ mol } OH^- \times \frac{1\text{ mol CaO}}{2\text{ mol } OH^-} \times \frac{56.1\text{ g CaO}}{1\text{ mol CaO}} \times \frac{1\text{ lb}}{453.6\text{ g}} = 2.3 \times 10^{-8}\text{ lb CaO}$$

This is a **very** small amount of CaO, about 10 mg.

19 Chemical Thermodynamics

Spontaneous Processes

19.2 (a) Spontaneous; a gas, in this case perfume vapor, expands to fill its container, the room.

(b) Nonspontaneous; a mixture cannot be separated without outside intervention.

(c) Nonspontaneous; an inflated balloon doesn't burst without external stress, such as a pin pric, a squeeze or adding more gas.

(d) Spontaneous; see Figure 8.2.

(e) Spontaneous; the very polar HCl molecules readily dissolve in water to form concentrated HCl(aq).

19.4 Berthelot's suggestion is incorrect. Some examples of nonexothermic spontaneous processes are expansion of certain pressurized gases, dissolving of one liquid in another, and dissolving of many salts in water.

19.6 (a) Exothermic. If melting requires heat and is endothermic, freezing must be exothermic.

(b) At 1 atm (indicated by the term 'normal' freezing point), the freezing of 1-propanol is spontaneous at temperatures below -127°C.

(c) At 1 atm, the freezing of 1-propanol is nonspontaneous at temperatures above -127°C.

(d) At 1 atm and -127°C, the normal freezing point of 1-propanol, the solid and liquid phases are in equilibrium. That is, at the freezing point, 1-propanol molecules escape to the liquid phase at the same rate as liquid 1-propanol solidifies, assuming no heat is exchanged between 1-propanol and the surroundings.

19.8 (a) A process is *irreversible* if the system cannot be returned to its original state by the same path that the forward process took place. No work is done by the system on the surroundings during an irreversible process.

(b) Since the system returned to its initial state via a different path (different q_r and w_r than q_f and w_f), there is a net change in the surroundings.

(c) The condensation of a liquid will be irreversible if it occurs at any temperature other than the boiling point of the liquid, at a specified pressure.

19.10 (a) $\Delta E\ (1 \rightarrow 2) = -\Delta E\ (2 \rightarrow 1)$

(b) We can say nothing about the values of q and w because we have no information about the paths.

(c) If the changes of state are reversible, the two paths are the same and $w\ (1 \rightarrow 2) = -w\ (2 \rightarrow 1)$. This is the maximum realizable work from this system.

19.12 (a) The detonation of an explosive is definitely spontaneous, once it is initiated.

(b) At constant atmospheric pressure, $\Delta H = q$. The detonation reaction is highly exothermic, so the value of q is large and negative.

(c) The sign (and magnitude) of w depend on the path of the process, the exact details of how the detonation is carried out. It seems clear, however, that work will be done by the system on the surroundings in almost all circumstances (buildings collapse, earth and air are moved), so the sign of w is probably negative.

(d) $\Delta E = q + w$. If q and w are both negative, then the sign of ΔE is negative, regardless of the magnitudes of q and w.

Entropy and the Second Law of Thermodynamics

19.14 In the general case, heat gained or lost by a system is path dependent; the value of q depends on how the change occurred, as well as the initial and final states. For a reversible process, the path is specified; it is the reversible path. There is only one reversible pathway for a process. Therefore, q_{rev} depends only on the initial and final states of the system, which is the definition of a state function.

19.16 (a) The two arrangements are equally probable. This is because the identity of the molecules is specified.

(b) The answer in part (a) is consistent with the idea that gas molecules will arrange themselves equally between the two flasks. There are many more **equivalent** arrangements of equally distributed molecules [like arrangement (a)] that there are asymmetric 7:1 arrangements like (b). This means that equal distribution is more likely, but any two specific arrangements are equally probable.

19.18 (a) When a liquid freezes, the entropy of the system decreases.

(b) ΔS is negative.

(c) Entropy being a state function means that ΔS is independent of the path of the process.

19.20 (a) Solids are much more ordered than gases, so ΔS is negative.

(b) ΔS is positive for Exercise 19.1 (a), (b) and (e). (At room temperature and 1 atm pressure, H_2O is a liquid, so there are more moles of gas in the products in part (e) and $\Delta S > 0$.)

19.22 More disorder is associated with forming a gas because of the large volume expansion and increased motional freedom associated with a gas.

19.24 (a) Cs(l) → Cs(s), ΔS is negative

(b) $$\Delta H = 15.0 \text{ g Cs} \times \frac{1 \text{ mol Cs}}{132.9 \text{ g Cs}} \times \frac{2.09 \text{ kJ}}{\text{mol Cs}} = 0.2359 = 0.236$$

$$\Delta S = \frac{\Delta H}{T} = 7.2359 \text{ kJ} \times \frac{1000 \text{ J}}{1 \text{ kJ}} \times \frac{1}{(273.15 + 28.4)\text{K}} = 0.782 \text{ J/K}$$

19.26 (a) For a spontaneous process, $\Delta S_{universe} > 0$. For a reversible process, $\Delta S_{universe} = 0$.

(b) $\Delta S_{surroundings}$ is positive and greater than the magnitude of the decrease in ΔS_{system}.

(c) $\Delta S_{system} = 78$ J/K.

Molecular Interpretation of Entropy

19.28 (a) A value of zero for entropy requires that the substance is a perfectly crystalline (not disordered or amorphous, see Chapter 11) solid at a temperature of 0 K.

(b) Since CO_2 has more than one atom, the thermal energy can be distributed as translational, vibrational or rotational motion.

(c)

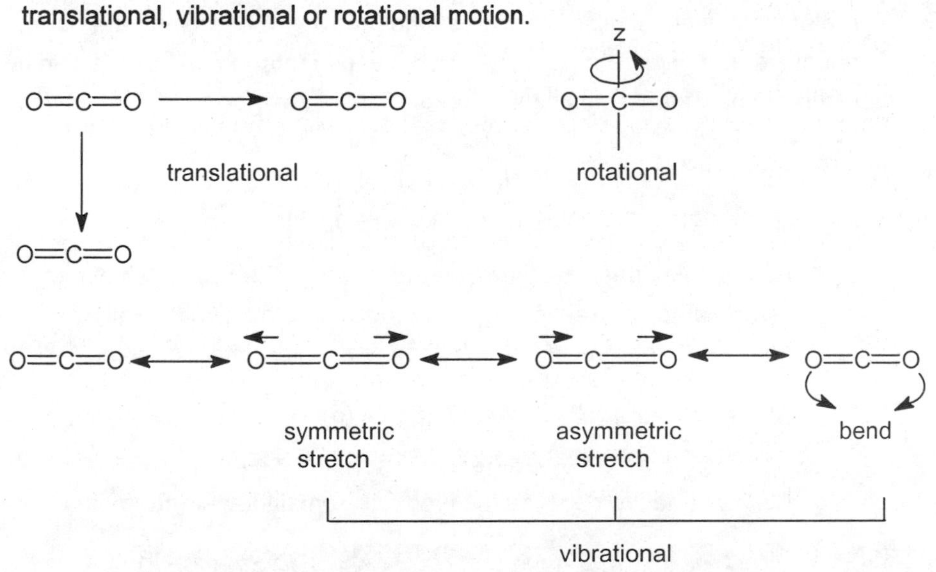

19.30 (a) 1 mol of As_4(g) at 300°C, 0.01 atm (As_4 has more massive atoms in a comparable system at the same temperature.)

(b) 1 mol H_2O(g) at 100°C, 1 atm (larger volume occupied by H_2O(g))

(c) 0.5 mol CH_4(g) at 298 K, 20-L volume (more complex molecule, more rotational and vibrational degrees of freedom)

(d) 100 g of Na_2SO_4(aq) at 30°C (more motional freedom in aqueous solution)

19.32 (a) $Fe(l) \rightarrow Fe(s)$; ΔS is negative (less motional freedom)

(b) $2Li(s) + Cl_2(g) \rightarrow 2LiCl$; ΔS is negative (moles of gas decrease)

(c) $Zn(s) + 2HCl(aq) \rightarrow ZnCl_2(aq) + H_2(g)$; ΔS is positive (moles of gas increase)

(d) $AgNO_3(aq) + KBr(aq) \rightarrow AgBr(s) + KNO_3(aq)$; ΔS is negative (less motional freedom)

19.34 (a) CuO(s), 42.59 J/mol•K ; Cu_2O(s), 92.36 J/mol•K. Molecules in the solid state have only vibrational motion available to them. The more complex Cu_2O molecule has more vibrational degrees of freedom and a larger standard entropy.

(b) 1 mol N_2O_4(g), 304.3 J/K; 2 mol NO_2(g), 2(240.45) = 480.90 J/K. More particles have a greater number of arrangements.

(c) CH_3OH(g), 237.6 J/mol•K; CH_3OH(l), 126.8 J/mol•K. Molecules in the gas phase occupy a larger volume and have more motional freedom than molecules in the liquid state.

(d) 1 mol $PbCO_3$(s), 131.0 J/K; 1 mol PbO(s) + 1 mol CO_2(g), (68.70 + 213.6) = 282.3 J/K. The second member of the pair has more total particles and half of them are in the gas phase for greater total motional freedom. Note that 1 mol of $PbCO_3$(s) has greater entropy than 1 mol of PbO(s), because of the additional ways to store energy in the more complex CO_3^{2-} anion.

19.36 For elements with similar structures, the heavier the atoms, the lower the vibrational frequencies at a given temperature. This means that more vibrations can be accessed at a particular temperature resulting in a greater absolute entropy for the heavier elements.

19.38 (a) $\Delta S° = 2S°\ NH_3(g) - S°\ N_2H_4(g) - S°\ H_2(g)$

$= 2(192.5) - 238.5 - 130.58 = +15.92$ J/K

ΔS° is small because there are the same number of moles of gas in the products as in reactants. The slight increase is due to the relatively small S° value of H_2(g), which has fewer degrees of freedom than molecules with more than two atoms.

(b) $\Delta S° = 2S°\ AlCl_3(s) - S°\ Al(s) - 3S°\ Cl_2(g)$

$= 2(109.3) - 28.32 - 3(222.96) = -478.6$ J/K

ΔS° is negative because the products contain fewer (no) moles of gas.

(c) $\Delta S° = S°\ MgCl_2(s) + 2S°H_2O(l) - S°\ Mg(OH)_2(s) - 2S°\ HCl(g)$

$= 89.6 + 2(69.91) - 63.24 - 2(186.69) = -207.20$ J/K

ΔS° is negative because the products contain fewer (no) moles of gas.

(d) $\Delta S° = S°\ C_2H_6(g) + S°\ H_2(g) - 2S°\ CH_4(g)$

$= 229.5 + 130.58 - 2(186.3) = -12.5$ J/K

ΔS° is very small because there are the same number of moles of gas in the products and reactants. The slight decrease is related to the relatively small S° value for H_2(g), which has fewer degrees of freedom than molecules with more than two atoms.

Gibbs Free Energy

19.40 (a) The *standard* free energy change, $\Delta G°$, represents the free energy change for the process when all reactants and products are in their standard states. When any or all reactants or products are not in their standard states, the free energy is represented simply as ΔG. The value for ΔG thus depends on the specific states of all reactants and products.

(b) When $\Delta G = 0$, the system is at equilibrium.

(c) The sign and magnitude of ΔG give no information about rate; we cannot predict whether the reaction will occur rapidly.

19.42 (a) $\Delta H°$ is negative; the reaction is exothermic.

(b) $\Delta S°$ is positive; the reaction leads to an increase in disorder.

(c) $\Delta G° = \Delta H° - T\Delta S° = -19.5$ kJ - 298 K (0.0427 kJ/K) = -32.225 = -32.2 kJ

(d) At 298 K, $\Delta G°$ is negative. If all reactants and products are present in their standard states, the reaction is spontaneous at this temperature.

19.44 (a) $\Delta H° = -305.3 - [0 + 0] = -305.3$ kJ

$\Delta S° = 97.65 - [29.9 + 222.96] = -155.21 = -155.2$ J/K

$\Delta G° = -259.0 - [0 + 0] = -259.0$ kJ

$\Delta G° = -305.3$ kJ $- 298(-0.15521)$ kJ $= -259.047 = -259.0$ kJ

(b) $\Delta H° = -635.5 + (-393.5) - (-1207.1) = 178.1$ kJ

$\Delta S° = 39.75 + 213.6 - (92.88) = 160.47 = 160.5$ J/K

$\Delta G° = -604.17 + (-394.4) - (-1128.76) = 130.19 = 130.2$ kJ

$\Delta G° = 178.1$ kJ $- 298(0.16047)$ kJ $= 130.28 = 130.3$ kJ

(c) $\Delta H° = 4(-1288.3) - [-2940.1 + 6(-285.83)] = -498.12 = -498.1$ kJ

$\Delta S° = 4(158.2) - [228.9 + 6(69.91)] = -15.56 = -15.6$ J/K

$\Delta G° = 4(-1142.6) - [-2675.2 + 6(-237.13)] = -472.42 = -472.4$ kJ

$\Delta G° = -498.12$ kJ $- 298(-0.01556)$ kJ $= -493.48 = -493.5$ kJ

(The discrepancy in $\Delta G°$ values is due to experimental uncertainties in the tabulated thermodynamic data.)

(d) $\Delta H° = 2(-393.5) + 4(-285.83) - [2(-238.6) + 3(0)] = -1453.1$ kJ

$\Delta S° = 2(213.6) + 4(69.91) - [2(126.8) + 3(205.0)] = -161.76 = -161.8$ J/K

$\Delta G° = 2(-394.4) + 4(-237.13) - [2(-166.23) + 3(0)] = -1404.86 = -1404.9$ kJ

$\Delta G° = -1453.2$ kJ $- 298(-0.16176)$ kJ $= -1404.996 = -1405.0$ kJ

19.46 (a) $\Delta G° = 2\Delta G°\ HCl(g) - [\Delta G°\ H_2(g) + \Delta G°\ Cl_2(g)]$

$= 2(-95.27\ kJ) - 0 - 0 = -190.5\ kJ$, spontaneous

(b) $\Delta G° = \Delta G°\ MgO(s) + 2\Delta G°\ HCl(g) - [\Delta G°\ MgCl_2(s) + \Delta G°\ H_2O(l)]$

$= -569.6 + 2(-95.27) - [-592.1 + (-237.13)] = +69.1\ kJ$, nonspontaneous

(c) $\Delta G° = \Delta G°\ N_2H_4(g) + \Delta G°\ H_2(g) - 2\Delta G°\ NH_3(g)$

$= 159.4 + 0 - 2(-16.66) = +192.7\ kJ$, nonspontaneous

(d) $\Delta G° = 2\Delta G°\ NO(g) + \Delta G°\ Cl_2(g) - 2\Delta G°\ NOCl(g)$

$= 2(86.71) + 0 - 2(66.3) = +40.8\ kJ$, nonspontaneous

19.48 (a) $\Delta G°$ should be less negative than $\Delta H°$. Products contain fewer moles of gas, so $\Delta S°$ is negative. $\Delta G° = \Delta H° - T\Delta S°$; $-T\Delta S°$ is positive so $\Delta G°$ is less negative than $\Delta H°$.

(b) We can estimate $\Delta S°$ using a similar reaction and then use $\Delta G° = \Delta H° - T\Delta S°$(estimate) to get a ballpark figure. There are no sulfite salts listed in Appendix C, so use a reaction such as $CO_2(g) + CaO(s) \rightarrow CaCO_3(s)$ or $CO_2(g) + BaO(s) \rightarrow BaCO_3(s)$. Or calculate both $\Delta S°$ values and use the average as your estimate.

19.50 $\Delta G° = \Delta H° - T\Delta S°$

(a) $\Delta G° = -844\ kJ - 298\ K(-0.165\ kJ/K) = -795\ kJ$, spontaneous

(b) $\Delta G° = +572\ kJ - 298\ K(0.179\ kJ/K) = +519\ kJ$, nonspontaneous

To be spontaneous, ΔG must be negative ($\Delta G < 0$).

Thus, $\Delta H° - T\Delta S° < 0$; $\Delta H° < T\Delta S°$; $T > \Delta H°/\Delta S°$; $T > \dfrac{572\ kJ}{0.179\ kJ/K} = 3{,}200\ K$

19.52 At $-25°C$ or 248 K, $\Delta G > 0$. $\Delta G = \Delta H - T\Delta S > 0$

$\Delta H - 248\ K\ (95\ J/K) > 0$; $\Delta H > +2.4 \times 10^4\ J$; $\Delta H > +24\ kJ$

19.54 ΔG is negative when $T\Delta S > \Delta H$ or $T > \Delta H/\Delta S$.

$\Delta H° = \Delta H°\ CH_4(g) + \Delta H°\ CO_2(g) - \Delta H°\ CH_3COOH(l)$

$= -74.8 + (-393.5) - (-487.0) = +18.7\ kJ$

$\Delta S° = S°\ CH_4(g) + S°\ CO_2(g) - S°\ CH_3COOH(l) = +186.3 + 213.6 - 159.8 = +240.1\ J/K$

$$T > \frac{18.7\ kJ}{0.2401\ kJ/K} = 77.9\ K$$

The reaction is spontaneous above 77.9 K (-195°C).

19.56 (a) $\Delta H° = \Delta H^{\circ}_f\ CH_3OH(g) - \Delta H^{\circ}_f\ CH_4(g) - 1/2\ \Delta H^{\circ}_f\ O_2(g)$

$= -201.2 - (-74.8) - 0 = -126.4\ kJ$

$\Delta S° = S°CH_3OH(g) - S°CH_4(g) - 1/2\ S°O_2(g)$

$= 237.6 - 186.3 - 1/2(205.0) = -51.2\ J/K = -0.0512\ kJ/K$

(b) $\Delta G° = \Delta H° - T\Delta S°$. $-T\Delta S°$ is positive, so $\Delta G°$ becomes more positive as temperature increases.

(c) $\Delta G° = \Delta H° - T\Delta S° = -126.4\ kJ - 298\ K(-0.0512\ kJ/K) = -111.1\ kJ$

The reaction is spontaneous at 298 K because $\Delta G°$ is negative at this temperature. In this case, $\Delta G°$ could have been calculated from ΔG_f° values in Appendix C, since these values are tabulated at 298 K.

(d) The reaction is at equilibrium when $\Delta G° = 0$.

$\Delta G° = \Delta H° - T\Delta S° = 0$. $\Delta H° = T\Delta S°$, $T = \Delta H°/\Delta S°$

$T = -126.4\ kJ/-0.0512\ kJ/K = 2469 = 2470\ K$.

This temperature is so high that the reactants and products are likely to decompose. At standard conditions, equilibrium is functionally unattainable for this reaction.

19.58 (a) As in Sample Exercise 19.11, $T_{sub} = \Delta H^\circ_{sub} / \Delta S^\circ_{sub}$

Use Data from Appendix C to calculate ΔH°_{sub} and ΔS°_{sub} for $I_2(s)$.

$I_2(s) \rightarrow I_2(l)$ melting

$I_2(l) \rightarrow I_2(g)$ boiling

$I_2(s) \rightarrow I_2(g)$ sublimation

$\Delta H^\circ_{sub} = \Delta H_f^\circ\ I_2(g) - \Delta H_f^\circ\ I_2(s) = 62.25 - 0 = 62.25\ kJ$

$\Delta S^\circ_{sub} = S°\ I_2(g) - S°\ I_2(s) = 260.57 - 116.73 = 143.84\ J/K = 0.14384\ kJ/K$

$$T_{sub} = \frac{\Delta H°_{sub}}{\Delta S°_{sub}} = \frac{62.25\ kJ}{0.14384\ kJ/K} = 432.8\ K = 159.6°C$$

(b) T_m for $I_2(s) = 386.85\ K = 113.7°C$; $T_b = 457.4\ K = 184.3°C$ (from Webelements, 2002)

(c) The boiling point of I_2 is closer to the sublimation temperature. Both boiling and sublimation begin with molecules in a condensed phase (little space between molecules) and end in the gas phase (large intermolecular distances). Separation of the molecules is the main phenomenon that determines both ΔH and ΔS, so it is not surprising that the ratio of $\Delta H/\Delta S$ is similar for sublimation and boiling.

19.60 (a) $C_2H_4(g) + 3O_2(g) \rightarrow 2CO_2(g) + 2H_2O(l)$

$\Delta H° = 2\Delta H_f^\circ\ CO_2(g) + 2\Delta H_f^\circ\ H_2O(l) - \Delta H_f^\circ\ C_2H_4(g) - 3\Delta H_f^\circ\ O_2(g)$

$= 2(-393.5) + 2(-285.83) - 52.30 - 3(0) = -1410.96 = -1411.0$ kJ/mol C_2H_4 burned

(b) $w_{max} = \Delta G° = 2\Delta G_f^\circ\ CO_2(g) + 2\Delta H_f^\circ\ H_2O(l) - \Delta G_f^\circ\ C_2H_4(g) - 3\Delta G_f^\circ\ O_2(g)$

$= 2(-394.4) + 2(-237.13) - 68.11 - 3(0) = -1331.2\ kJ$

The system can accomplish at most 1331.2 kJ of work per mole of C_2H_4 on the surroundings.

Free Energy and Equilibrium

19.62 Consider the relationship $\Delta G = \Delta G° + RT \ln Q$ where Q is the reaction quotient.

(a) $H_2(g)$ appears in the denominator of Q for this reaction. An increase in pressure of H_2 decreases Q and ΔG becomes smaller or more negative. Increasing the concentration of a reactant increases the tendency for a reaction to occur.

(b) $H_2(g)$ appears in the numerator of Q for this reaction. Increasing the pressure of H_2 increases Q and ΔG becomes more positive. Increasing the concentration of a product decreases the tendency for the reaction to occur.

(c) $H_2(g)$ appears in the denominator of Q for this reaction. An increase in pressure of H_2 decreases Q and ΔG becomes smaller or more negative.

19.64 (a) $\Delta G° = 2\Delta G°\ HF(g) - [\Delta G°\ H_2(g) + \Delta G°\ F_2(g)] = 2(-270.70) - [0 + 0] = -541.40$ kJ

(b) $\Delta G = \Delta G° + RT \ln P^2_{HF} / P_{H_2} \times P_{F_2}$

$$= -541.40 + \frac{8.314 \times 10^{-3}\ \text{kJ}}{\text{K} \bullet \text{mol}} \times 298\ \text{K} \ln[(0.36)^2/8.0 \times 4.5] = -555.3\ \text{kJ}$$

19.66 $\Delta G° = -RT \ln K_{eq}$; $\ln K_{eq} = -\Delta G° / RT$; at 298 K, RT = 2.4776 = 2.478 kJ

(a) $\Delta G° = \Delta G°\ NaOH(s) + \Delta G°\ CO_2(g) - \Delta G°\ NaHCO_3(s)$

$= -379.5 + (-394.4) - (-851.8) = +77.9$ kJ

$$\ln K_{eq} = \frac{-\Delta G°}{RT} = \frac{-77.9\ \text{kJ}}{2.478\ \text{kJ}} = -31.442 = -31.4;\quad K_{eq} = 2 \times 10^{-14}$$

$K_{eq} = P_{CO_2} = 2 \times 10^{-14}$

(b) $\Delta G° = 2\Delta G°\ HCl(g) + \Delta G°\ Br_2(g) - 2\Delta G°\ HBr(g) - \Delta G°\ Cl_2(g)$

$= 2(-95.27) + 3.14 - 2(-53.22) - 0 = -80.96$ kJ

$$\ln K_{eq} = \frac{-(-80.96)}{2.4776} = +32.68;\quad K_{eq} = 1.6 \times 10^{14}$$

$$K_{eq} = \frac{P^2_{HCl} \times P_{Br_2}}{P^2_{HBr} \times P_{Cl_2}} = 1.6 \times 10^{14}$$

(c) From Exercise 19.45(a), $\Delta G°$ at 298 K = -140.0 kJ.

$$\ln K_{eq} = \frac{-\Delta G°}{RT} = \frac{-(-140.0)}{2.4776} = 56.51;\quad K_{eq} = 3.5 \times 10^{24}$$

$$K_{eq} = \frac{P^2_{SO_3}}{P^2_{SO_2} \times P_{O_2}} = 3.5 \times 10^{24}$$

19.68 $K_{eq} = P_{CO_2}$. Calculate $\Delta G°$ at the two temperatures using $\Delta G° = \Delta H° - T\Delta S°$ and then calculate K_{eq} and P_{CO_2}.

$\Delta H° = \Delta H°\ PbO(s) + \Delta H°\ CO_2(g) - \Delta H°\ PbCO_3(s)$

$= -217.3 - 393.5 + 699.1 = 88.3$ kJ

$\Delta S° = S°\ PbO(s) + S°\ CO_2(g) - S°\ PbCO_3(s)$

$= 68.70 + 213.6 - 131.0 = 151.3$ J/K or 0.1513 kJ/K

(a) $\Delta G° = \Delta H° - T\Delta S°$. At 393 K, $\Delta G° = 88.3\text{ kJ} - 393\text{ K}(0.1513\text{ kJ/K}) = 28.84$

$= 28.8$ kJ

$$\ln K_{eq} = \frac{-\Delta G°}{RT} = \frac{-28.84 \times 10^3\text{ J}}{8.314\text{ J/K} \times 418\text{ K}} = -8.29842 = -8.83$$

$K_{eq} = P_{CO_2} = 2.5 \times 10^{-4}$ atm

(b) $\Delta G° = \Delta H° - T\Delta S°$. At 753 K, $\Delta G° = 88.3\text{ kJ} - 753\text{ K}\ (0.1513\text{ kJ}) = -25.629$

$= -25.6$ kJ

$$\ln K_{eq} = \frac{-(-25.629 \times 10^3\text{ J})}{8.314\text{ J/K} \times 753\text{ K}} = 4.0938 = 4.09;\ K_{eq} = P_{CO_2} = 60\text{ atm}$$

19.70 (a) $CH_3NH_2(aq) + H_2O(l) \rightleftharpoons CH_3NH_3^+(aq) + OH^-(aq)$

(b) $\Delta G° = -RT \ln K_b = -(8.314 \times 10^{-3})(298) \ln (4.4 \times 10^{-4}) = 19.148 = 19.1$ kJ

(c) $\Delta G = 0$ at equilibrium

(d) $\Delta G = \Delta G° + RT \ln Q$; $[OH^-] = 1 \times 10^{-14}/1.5 \times 10^{-8} = 6.7 \times 10^{-7}$

$$= 19.148 + (8.314 \times 10^{-3})(298) \ln \frac{(5.5 \times 10^{-4})(6.67 \times 10^{-7})}{0.120} = -29.4\text{ kJ}$$

Additional Exercises

19.71 (a) False. The essential question is whether the reaction proceeds far to the right before arriving at equilibrium. The position of equilibrium, which is the essential aspect, is not only dependent on ΔH but on the entropy change as well.

(b) True.

(c) True.

(d) False. **Non**spontaneous processes in general require that work be done to force them to proceed. Spontaneous processes occur without application of work.

(e) False. Such a process **might** be spontaneous, but would not necessarily be so. Spontaneous processes are those that are exothermic and/or that lead to increased disorder in the system.

19.72 The situation described is the isothermal compression of a gas.

(a) Since $nR\Delta T$ is zero, ΔE is zero. (ΔE is zero for all isothermal expansions or compressions.)

(b) $\Delta S = nR\ln(V_2/V_1)$. Since $V_2 < V_1$, $\ln(V_2/V_1)$ is negative and ΔS is negative. Qualitatively, a smaller volume means less motional freedom for the gas particles and a lower entropy.

19.74 There is no inconsistency. The second law states that in any spontaneous process there is an increase in the entropy of the universe. While there may be a decrease in entropy of the system, as in the present case, this decrease is more than offset by an increase in entropy of the surroundings.

19.75 (a) An *isolated* system is a system that does not exchange matter or energy with its surroundings.

(b) $\Delta E = 0$, $q = 0$, $w = 0$

(c) The second law is: $\Delta S_{sys} + \Delta S_{surr} \geq 0$. But for an isolated system $\Delta S_{surr} = 0$, so $\Delta S_{sys} = 0$ for a reversible process; $\Delta S_{sys} > 0$ for an irreversible process.

19.76 Melting = -126.5°C; boiling = 97.4°C.

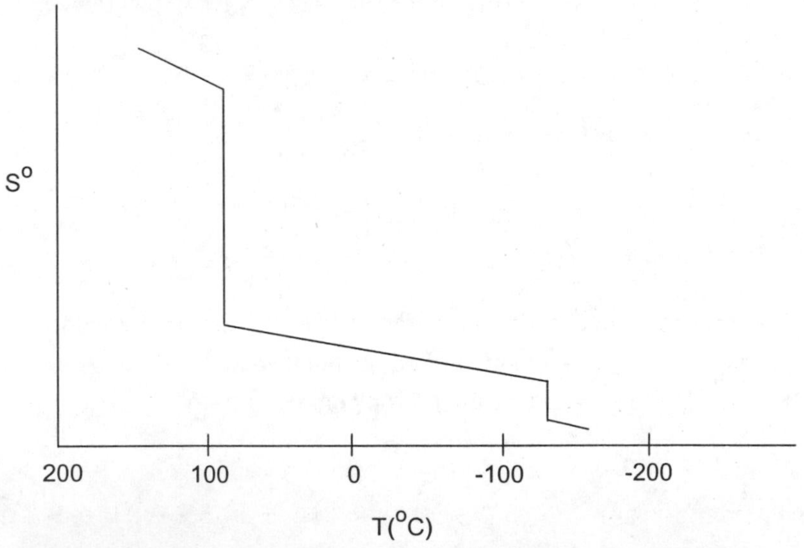

19.78 (a) C(diamond), S° = 2.43 J/mol•K; C(graphite), S° = 5.69 J/mol•K. Diamond is a network covalent solid with each C atom tetrahedrally bound to four other C atoms. Graphite consists of sheets of fused planar 6-membered rings with each C atom bound in a trigonal planar arrangement to three other C atoms. The internal entropy in graphite is greater because there is translational freedom among the planar sheets of C atoms while there is very little translational or vibrational freedom within the covalent-network diamond lattice.

(b) S° for buckminsterfullerene will be ≥ 10 J/mol•K. S° for graphite is twice S° for diamond, and S° for the fullerene should be higher than that of graphite. The 60-atom "bucky" balls have more flexibility than graphite sheets. Also, the balls have translational freedom in three dimensions, while graphite sheets have it in only two directions. Because of the ball structure, there is more empty space in the fullerene lattice than in graphite or diamond; essentially, 60 C-atoms in fullerene occupy a larger volume than 60 C-atoms in graphite or diamond. Thus, the fullerene has additional "molecular" complexity, more degrees of translational freedom, and occupies a larger volume, all features that point to a higher absolute entropy.

19.79 (a) Formation reactions are the synthesis of 1 mole of compound from elements in their standard states.

$1/2\ N_2(g) + 3/2\ H_2(g) \rightarrow NH_3(g)$

$C(s) + 2Cl_2(g) \rightarrow CCl_4(l)$

$K(s) + 1/2\ N_2(g) + 3/2\ O_2(g) \rightarrow KNO_3(s)$

In each of these formation reactions, there are fewer moles of gas in the products than the reactants, so we expect ΔS° to be negative. If $\Delta G_f^\circ = \Delta H_f^\circ - T\Delta S_f^\circ$ and ΔS_f° is negative, $-T\Delta S_f^\circ$ is positive and ΔG_f° is more positive than ΔH_f°.

(b) $C(s) + 1/2\ O_2(g) \rightarrow CO(g)$

In this reaction, there are more moles of gas in products, ΔS_f° is positive, $-T\Delta S_f^\circ$ is negative and ΔG_f° is more negative than ΔH_f°.

19.80 (a) (i) $2RbCl(s) + 3O_2(g) \rightarrow 2RbClO_3(s)$

$\Delta H^\circ = 2\Delta H^\circ\ RbClO_3(s) - 3\Delta H^\circ\ O_2(g) - 2\Delta H^\circ\ RbCl(s)$

$= 2(-392.4) - 3(0) - 2(-430.5) = +76.2$ kJ

$\Delta S^\circ = 2(152) - 3(205.0) - 2(92) = -495$ J/K $= -0.495$ kJ/K

$\Delta G^\circ = 2(-292.0) - 3(0) - 2(-412.0) = +240.0$ kJ

(ii) $C_2H_2(g) + 4Cl_2(g) \rightarrow 2CCl_4(l) + H_2(g)$

$\Delta H^\circ = 2\Delta H^\circ\ CCl_4(l) + \Delta H^\circ\ H_2(g) - \Delta H^\circ\ C_2H_2(g) - 4\Delta H^\circ\ Cl_2(g)$

$= 2(-139.3) + 0 - (226.7) - 4(0) = -505.3$ kJ

$\Delta S^\circ = 2(214.4) + 130.58 - (200.8) - 4(222.96) = -533.3$ J/K $= -0.5333$ kJ/K

$\Delta G^\circ = 2(-68.6) + 0 - (209.2) - 4(0) = -346.4$ kJ

(iii) $TiCl_4(l) + 2H_2O(l) \rightarrow TiO_2(s) + 4HCl(aq)$

$\Delta H^\circ = \Delta H^\circ\ TiO_2(s) + 4\Delta H^\circ\ HCl(aq) - \Delta H^\circ\ TiCl_4(l) - 2\Delta H^\circ\ H_2O(l)$

$= -944.7 + 4(-167.2) - (-804.2) - 2(-285.83) = -237.6$ kJ

$\Delta S^\circ = 50.29 + 4(56.5) - 221.9 - 2(69.91) = -85.43$ J/K $= -0.0854$ kJ/K

$\Delta G^\circ = -889.4 + 4(-131.2) - (-728.1) - 2(-237.13) = -211.8$ kJ

(b) (i) $\Delta G°$ is (+), nonspontaneous

(ii) $\Delta G°$ is (-), spontaneous

(iii) $\Delta G°$ is (-), spontaneous

(c) In each case the manner in which free energy change varies with temperature depends mainly on ΔS: $\Delta G = \Delta H - T\Delta S$. When ΔS is substantially positive, ΔG becomes more negative as temperature increases. When ΔS is substantially negative, ΔG becomes more positive as temperature increases.

(i) $\Delta S°$ is negative, $\Delta G°$ becomes more positive with increasing temperature.

(ii) $\Delta S°$ is negative, $\Delta G°$ becomes more positive with increasing temperature. (The reaction will become nonspontaneous at some temperature.)

(iii) $\Delta S°$ is negative, $\Delta G°$ becomes more positive with increasing temperature. (The reaction will become nonspontaneous at some temperature.)

19.82

Reaction	(a) Sign of $\Delta H°$	(a) Sign of $\Delta S°$	(b) $K_{eq} > 1$?	(c) Variation in K_{eq} as Temp. Increases
(i)	-	-	yes	decrease
(ii)	+	+	no	increase
(iii)	+	+	no	increase
(iv)	+	+	no	increase

(a) Note that at a particular temperature, positive $\Delta H°$ leads to a smaller value of K, while positive $\Delta S°$ increases the value of K.

19.84 (a) First calculate $\Delta G°$ for each reaction:

For $C_6H_{12}O_6(s) + 6O_2(g) \leftrightharpoons 6CO_2(g) + 6H_2O(l)$ (A)

$\Delta G° = 6(-237.13) + 6(-394.4) - (-910.4) + 6(0) = -2878.8$ kJ

For $C_6H_{12}O_6(s) \leftrightharpoons 2C_2H_5OH(l) + 2CO_2(g)$ (B)

$\Delta G° = 2(-394.4) + 2(-174.8) - (-910.4) = -228.0$ kJ

For (A), $\ln K_{eq} = 2879 \times 10^3/(8.314)(298) = 1162$; $K_{eq} = 5 \times 10^{504}$

For (B), $\ln K_{eq} = 228 \times 10^3/(8.314)(298) = 92.026 = 92.0$; $K_{eq} = 9 \times 10^{39}$

(b) Both these values for K_{eq} are unimaginably large. However, K_{eq} for reaction (A) is larger, because $\Delta G°$ is more negative. The magnitude of the work that can be accomplished by coupling a reaction to its surroundings is measured by ΔG. According to the calculations above, considerably more work can in principle be obtained from reaction (A), because $\Delta G°$ is more negative.

19.85 (a) $\Delta G° = -RT \ln K_{eq}$ (Equation 19.22); $\ln K_{eq} = -\Delta G°/RT$

Use $\Delta G° = \Delta H° - T\Delta S°$ to get $\Delta G°$ at the two temperatures. Calculate $\Delta H°$ and $\Delta S°$ using data in Appendix C.

$2CH_4(g) \rightarrow C_2H_6(g) + H_2(g)$

$\Delta H° = \Delta H°\ C_2H_6(g) + \Delta H°\ H_2(g) - 2\Delta H°\ CH_4(g) = -84.68 + 0 - 2(-74.8) = 64.92$
$= 64.9$ kJ

$\Delta S° = S°\ C_2H_6(g) + S°\ H_2(g) - 2S°\ CH_4(g) = 229.5 + 130.58 - 2(186.3) = -12.52$
$= -12.5$ J/K

at 298 K, $\Delta G = 64.92$ kJ - 298 K$(-12.52 \times 10^{-3}$ kJ/K$) = 68.65 = 68.7$ kJ

$$\ln K_{eq} = \frac{-68.65\ \text{kJ}}{(8.314 \times 10^{-3}\ \text{kJ/K})(298\ \text{K})} = -27.709 = -27.7,\ K_{eq} = 9.25 \times 10^{-13} = 9 \times 10^{-13}$$

at 773 K, $\Delta G = 64.9$ kJ - 773 K$(-12.52 \times 10^{-3}$ J/K$) = 74.598 = 74.6$ kJ

$$\ln K_{eq} = \frac{-74.598\ \text{kJ}}{(8.314 \times 10^{-3}\ \text{kJ/K})(773\ \text{K})} = -11.607 = -11.6,\ K_{eq} = 9.1 \times 10^{-6} = 9 \times 10^{-6}$$

Because the reaction is endothermic, the value of K_{eq} increases with an increase in temperature.

$2CH_4(g) + 1/2\ O_2(g) \rightarrow C_2H_6(g) + H_2O(g)$

$\Delta H° = \Delta H°\ C_2H_6(g) + \Delta H°\ H_2O(g) - 2\Delta H°\ CH_4(g) - 1/2\ \Delta H°\ O_2(g)$

$= -84.68 + (-241.82) - 2(-74.8) - 1/2\ (0) = -176.9$ kJ

$\Delta S° = S°\ C_2H_6(g) + S°\ H_2O(g) - 2S°\ CH_4(g) - 1/2\ S°\ O_2(g)$

$= 229.5 + 188.83 - 2(186.3) - 1/2\ (205.0) = -56.77 = -56.8$ J/K

at 298 K, $\Delta G = -176.9$ kJ - 298 K$(-56.77 \times 10^{-3}$ kJ/K$) = -159.98 = -160.0$ kJ

$$\ln K_{eq} = \frac{-(-159.98\ \text{kJ})}{(8.314 \times 10^{-3}\ \text{kJ/K})(298\ \text{K})} = 64.571 = 64.6;\ K_{eq} = 1 \times 10^{28}$$

at 773 K, $\Delta G = -176.9$ kJ - 773 K $(-56.77 \times 10^{-3}$ kJ/K$) = -133.02 = -133.0$ kJ

$$\ln K_{eq} = \frac{-(-133.02\ \text{kJ})}{(8.314 \times 10^{-3}\ \text{kJ/K})(773\ \text{K})} = 20.698 = 20.7;\ K_{eq} = 1 \times 10^{9}$$

Because this reaction is exothermic, the value of K_{eq} decreases with increasing temperature.

(b) The difference in $\Delta G°$ for the two reactions is primarily enthalpic; the first reaction is endothermic and the second exothermic. Both reactions have $-\Delta S°$, which inhibits spontaneity.

(c) This is an example of coupling a useful but nonspontaneous reaction with a spontaneous one to spontaneously produce a desired product.

$2CH_4(g) \rightarrow C_2H_6(g) + H_2(g)$ ΔG°_{298} = +68.7 kJ, nonspontaneous

$H_2(g) + 1/2\ O_2(g) \rightarrow H_2O(g)$ ΔG°_{298} = -228.57 kJ, spontaneous

$2CH_4(g) + 1/2\ O_2(g) \rightarrow C_2H_6(g) + H_2O(g)$ ΔG°_{298} = -159.9 kJ, spontaneous

(d) $CH_4(g) + 2O_2(g) \rightarrow CO_2(g) + 2H_2O(g)$

19.87 (a) The equilibrium of interest here can be written as:

$K^+\ (\text{plasma}) \rightleftharpoons K^+\ (\text{muscle})$

Since an aqueous solution is involved in both cases, assume that the equilibrium constant for the above process is exactly 1, that is, ΔG° = 0. However, ΔG is not zero because the concentrations are not the same on both sides of the membrane. Use Equation [19.21] to calculate ΔG:

$$\Delta G = \Delta G^\circ + RT \ln \frac{[K^+(\text{muscle})]}{[K^+(\text{plasma})]}$$

$$= 0 + (8.314)(310) \ln \frac{(0.15)}{(5.0 \times 10^{-3})} = 8.77 \text{ kJ}$$

(b) Note that ΔG is positive. This means that work must be done on the system (blood plasma plus muscle cells) to move the K^+ ions "uphill," as it were. The minimum amount of work possible is given by the value for ΔG. This value represents the minimum amount of work required to transfer one mole of K^+ ions from the blood plasma at 5×10^{-3} *M* to muscle cell fluids at 0.15 *M*, assuming constancy of concentrations. In practice, a larger than minimum amount of work is required.

19.88 (a) To obtain ΔH° from the equilibrium constant data, graph ln K_{eq} at various temperatures vs 1/T, being sure to employ absolute temperature. The slope of the linear relationship that should result is -ΔH°/R; thus, ΔH° is easily calculated.

(b) Use ΔG° = ΔH° - TΔS° and ΔG° = -RT ln K_{eq}. Substituting the second expression into the first, we obtain

$$-RT \ln K = \Delta H^\circ - T\Delta S^\circ; \quad \ln K = \frac{-\Delta H^\circ}{RT} - \frac{-\Delta S^\circ}{R} = \frac{-\Delta H^\circ}{RT} + \frac{\Delta S^\circ}{R}$$

Thus, the constant in the equation given in the exercise is ΔS°/R.

19.90 S = k ln W (Equation 19.8), k = R/N, $W \propto V^m$

$\Delta S = S_2 - S_1$; $S_1 = k \ln W_1$, $S_2 = k \ln W_2$

$\Delta S = k \ln W_2 - k \ln W_1$; $W_2 = cV_2^{\,m}$; $W_1 = cV_1^{\,m}$

(The number of particles, m, is the same in both states.)

$\Delta S = k \ln cV_2^{\,m} - k \ln cV_1^{\,m}$; $\ln a^b = b \ln a$

$\Delta S = k\,m \ln cV_2 - k\,m \ln cV_1$; $\ln a - \ln b = \ln (a/b)$

$$\Delta S = k\,m\ln\left(\frac{cV_2}{cV_1}\right) = k\,m\ln\left(\frac{V_2}{V_1}\right) = \frac{R}{N}m\ln\left(\frac{V_2}{V_1}\right)$$

$$\frac{m}{N} = \frac{\text{particles}}{6.022\times10^{23}} = n(\text{mol});\ \Delta S = nR\ln\left(\frac{V_2}{V_1}\right)$$

19.91 Absolute entropy is a fundamental property of matter at a specified set of conditions, that is, a state. In order to lower the entropy of the fuel, either the structure of the molecules or the conditions (temperature, pressure, amount) must be changed. Any of these changes would require energy, which would reduce the amount of energy available to drive the car, not increase it.

Integrative Exercises

19.92 (a) At the boiling point, vaporization is a reversible process, so $\Delta S^\circ_{vap} = \Delta H^\circ_{vap}/T$.

acetone: $\Delta S^\circ_{vap} = \Delta H^\circ_{vap}/T$ = (29.1 kJ/mol) / 329.25 K = 88.4 J/mol•K

dimethyl ether: ΔS°_{vap} =(21.5 kJ/mol) / 248.35 K = 86.6 J/mol•K

ethanol: ΔS°_{vap} = (38.6 kJ/mol) / 351.6 K = 110 J/mol•K

octane: ΔS°_{vap} = (34.4 kJ/mol) / 398.75 K = 86.3 J/mol•K

pyridine: ΔS°_{vap} = (35.1kJ/mol) / 388.45 K = 90.4 J/mol•K

(b) Ethanol is the only liquid listed that doesn't follow *Trouton's rule* and it is also the only substance that exhibits hydrogen bonding in the pure liquid. Hydrogen bonding leads to more ordering in the liquid state and a greater than usual increase in entropy upon vaporization. The rule appears to hold for liquids with London dispersion forces (octane) and ordinary dipole-dipole forces (acetone, dimethyl ether, pyridine), but not for those with hydrogen bonding.

(c) Owing to strong hydrogen bonding interactions, water probably does not obey Trouton's rule.

From Appendix B, ΔH°_{vap} at 100°C = 40.67 kJ/mol.

ΔS°_{vap} = (40.67 kJ/mol) / 373.15 K = 109.0 J/mol•K

(d) Use ΔS°_{vap} = 88 J/mol•K, the middle of the range for Trouton's rule, to estimate ΔH°_{vap} for chlorobenzene.

$\Delta H^\circ_{vap} = \Delta S^\circ_{vap} \times T$ = 88 J/mol•K × 404.95 K = 36 kJ/mol

19.94 The activated complex in Figure 14.13 is a single "particle" or entity that contains 4 atoms. It is formed from an atom A and a triatomic molecule, ABC, that must collide with exactly the correct energy and orientation to form the single entity. There are many fewer degrees of freedom for the activated complex than the separate reactant particules, so the *entropy of activation* is negative.

19.95 (a) $O_2(g) \xrightarrow{h\nu} 2O(g)$; ΔS increases because there are more moles of gas in the products.

(b) $O_2(g) + O(g) \rightarrow O_3(g)$, ΔS decreases because there are fewer moles of gas in the products.

(c) ΔS increases as the gas molecules diffuse into the larger volume of the stratosphere; there are more possible positions and therefore more motional freedom.

(d) $NaCl(aq) \rightarrow NaCl(s) + H_2O(l)$; ΔS decreases as the mixture (seawater, greater disorder) is separated into pure substances (fewer possible arrangements, more order).

19.97 (a) $Ag(s) + 1/2\ N_2(g) + 3/2\ O_2(g) \rightarrow AgNO_3(s)$; ΔS decreases because there are fewer moles of gas in the product.

(b) $\Delta G^\circ_f = \Delta H^\circ_f - T\Delta S^\circ_f$; $\Delta S^\circ_f = (\Delta G^\circ_f - \Delta H^\circ_f) / (-T) = (\Delta H^\circ_f - \Delta G^\circ_f) / T$

ΔS°_f = -124.4 kJ - (-33.4 kJ) / 298 K = -0.305 kJ/K = -305 J/K

ΔS°_f is relatively large and negative, as anticipated from part (a).

(c) Dissolving of $AgNO_3$ can be expressed as

$AgNO_3(s) \rightarrow AgNO_3$ (aq, 1 m)

ΔH° = ΔH° $AgNO_3$(aq) - ΔH° $AgNO_3$(s) = -101.7 - (-124.4) = +22.7 kJ

ΔH° = ΔH° $MgSO_4$(aq) - ΔH° $MgSO_4$(s) = -1374.8 - (-1283.7) = -91.1 kJ

Dissolving $AgNO_3$(s) is endothermic (+ΔH°), but dissolving $MgSO_4$(s) is exothermic (-ΔH°).

(d) $AgNO_3$: ΔG° = ΔG°_f $AgNO_3$(aq) - ΔG°_f $AgNO_3$(s) = -34.2 - (-33.4) = -0.8 kJ

ΔS° = (ΔH° - ΔG°) / T = [22.7 kJ - (-0.8 kJ)] / 298 K = 0.0789 kJ/K = 78.9 J/K

$MgSO_4$: ΔG° = ΔG°_f $MgSO_4$(aq) - ΔG°_f $MgSO_4$(s) = -1198.4 - (-1169.6) = -28.8 kJ

ΔS° = (ΔH° - ΔG°) / T = [-91.1 kJ - (-28.8 kJ)] / 298 K = -0.209 kJ/K = -209 J/K

(e) In general, we expect dissolving a crystalline solid to be accompanied by an increase in positional disorder and an increase in entropy; this is the case for $AgNO_3$ (ΔS°= + 78.9 J/K). However, for dissolving $MgSO_4$(s), there is a substantial decrease in entropy (ΔS = -209 J/K). According to Section 13.5, ion-pairing is a significant phenomenon in electrolyte solutions, particularly in concentrated solutions where the charges of the ions are greater than 1. According to Table 13.5, a 0.1 m $MgSO_4$ solution has a van't Hoff factor of 1.21. That is, for each mole of $MgSO_4$ that dissolves, there are only 1.21 moles of "particles" in solution instead of 2 moles of particles. For a 1 m solution, the factor is even smaller. Also, the exothermic enthalpy of mixing indicates substantial interactions between solute and solvent. Substantial ion-pairing coupled with ion-dipole interactions with H_2O molecules lead to a decrease in entropy for $MgSO_4$(aq) relative to $MgSO_4$(s).

19.98 (a) $K_{eq} = P^2_{NO_2} / P_{N_2O_4}$

Assume equal amounts means equal number of moles. For gases, P = n(RT/V). In an equilibrium mixture, RT/V is a constant, so moles of gas is directly proportional to partial pressure. Gases with equal partial pressures will have equal moles of gas present. The condition $P_{NO_2} = P_{N_2O_4}$ leads to the expression $K_{eq} = P_{NO_2}$. The value of K_{eq} then depends on P_T for the mixture. For any particular value of P_T, the condition of equal moles of the two gases can be achieved at some temperature. For example, $P_{NO_2} = P_{N_2O_4} = 1.0$ atm, $P_T = 2.0$ atm.

$$K_{eq} = \frac{(1.0)^2}{1.0} = 1.0;\ \ln K_{eq} = 0;\ \Delta G° = 0 = \Delta H° - T\Delta S°;\ T = \Delta H°/\Delta S°$$

$$\Delta H° = 2\Delta H°\ NO_2(g) - \Delta H°\ N_2O_4(g) = 2(33.84) - 9.66 = +58.02 \text{ kJ}$$

$$\Delta S° = 2S°\ NO_2(g) - S°\ N_2O_4(g) = 2(240.45) - 304.3 = 0.1766 \text{ kJ/K}$$

$$T = \frac{58.02 \text{ kJ}}{0.1766 \text{ kJ/K}} = 328.5 \text{ K or } 55.5°\text{C}$$

(b) $P_T = 1.00$ atm; $P_{N_2O_4} = x$, $P_{NO_2} = 2x$; $x + 2x = 1.00$ atm

$x = P_{N_2O_4} = 0.3333 = 0.333$ atm; $P_{NO_2} = 0.6667 = 0.667$ atm

$$K_{eq} = \frac{(0.6667)^2}{0.3333} = 1.334 = 1.33;\ \Delta G° = -RT \ln K_{eq} = \Delta H° - T\Delta S°$$

$$-(8.314 \times 10^{-3} \text{ kJ/K})(\ln 1.334)\ T = 58.02 \text{ kJ} - (0.1766 \text{ kJ/K})\ T$$

$$(-0.00239 \text{ kJ/K})\ T + (0.1766 \text{ kJ/K})\ T = 58.02 \text{ kJ}$$

$$(0.1742 \text{ kJ/K})\ T = 58.02 \text{ kJ};\ T = 333.0 \text{ K}$$

(c) $P_T = 10.00$ atm; $x + 2x = 10.00$ atm

$x = P_{N_2O_4} = 3.3333 = 3.333$ atm; $P_{NO_2} = 6.6667 = 6.667$ atm

$$K_{eq} = \frac{(6.6667)^2}{3.3333} = 13.334 = 13.33;\ -RT \ln K_{eq} = \Delta H° - T\Delta S°$$

$$-(8.314 \times 10^{-3} \text{ kJ/K})(\ln 13.334)\ T = 58.02 \text{ kJ} - (0.1766 \text{ kJ/K})\ T$$

$$(-0.02154 \text{ kJ/K})\ T + (0.1766 \text{ kJ/K})\quad T = 58.02 \text{ kJ}$$

$$(0.15506 \text{ kJ/K})\ T = 58.02 \text{ kJ};\ T = 374.2 \text{ K}$$

(d) The reaction is endothermic, so an increase in the value of K_{eq} as calculated in parts (b) and (c) should be accompanied by an increase in T.

19.100 (a) When the rubber band is stretched, the molecules become more ordered, so the entropy of the system decreases, ΔS_{sys} is negative.

(b) $\Delta S_{sys} = q_{rev}/T$. Since ΔS_{sys} is negative, q_{rev} is negative and heat is evolved by the system.

20 Electrochemistry

Oxidation-Reduction Reactions

20.2 (a) *Reduction* is the gain of electrons.

(b) The electrons appear on the reactants side (left side) of a reduction half-reaction.

(c) The *reductant* is the reactant that is oxidized; it provides the electrons that are gained by the substance being reduced.

20.4 (a) No oxidation-reduction

(b) I is oxidized from -1 to +5; Cl is reduced from +1 to -1.

(c) S is oxidized from +4 to +6; N is reduced from +5 to +2.

(d) S is reduced from +6 to +4; Br is oxidized from -1 to 0.

20.6 (a) $2N_2H_4(g) + N_2O_4(g) \rightarrow 3N_2(g) + 4H_2O(g)$

(b) N_2O_4 serves as the oxidizing agent; it is itself reduced. N_2H_4 serves as the reducing agent; it is itself oxidized.

20.8 (a) $Mo^{3+}(aq) + 3e^- \rightarrow Mo(s)$, reduction

(b) $H_2SO_3(aq) + H_2O(l) \rightarrow SO_4^{2-}(aq) + 4H^+(aq) + 2e^-$, oxidation

(c) $NO_3^-(aq) + 4H^+(aq) + 3e^- \rightarrow NO(g) + 2H_2O(l)$, reduction

(d) $Mn^{2+}(aq) + 4OH^-(aq) \rightarrow MnO_2(s) + 2H_2O(l) + 2e^-$, oxidation

(e) $Cr(OH)_3(s) + 5OH^-(aq) \rightarrow CrO_4^{2-}(aq) + 4H_2O(l) + 3e^-$, oxidation

20.10 (a)

$$3[NO_2^-(aq) + H_2O(l) \rightarrow NO_3^-(aq) + 2H^+(aq) + 2e^-]$$

$$Cr_2O_7^{2-}(aq) + 14H^+(aq) + 6e^- \rightarrow 2Cr^{3+}(aq) + 7H_2O(l)$$

Net: $3NO_2^-(aq) + Cr_2O_7^{2-}(aq) + 8H^+(aq) \rightarrow 3NO_3^-(aq) + 2Cr^{3+}(aq) + 4H_2O(l)$

oxidizing agent, $Cr_2O_7^{2-}$; reducing agent, NO_2^-

(b)

$$4[As(s) + 3H_2O(l) \rightarrow H_3AsO_3(aq) + 3H^+(aq) + 3e^-]$$

$$3[ClO_3^-(aq) + 5H^+(aq) + 4e^- \rightarrow HClO(aq) + 2H_2O(l)]$$

$$4As(s) + 3ClO_3^-(aq) + 6H_2O(l) + 3H^+(aq) \rightarrow 4H_3AsO_3(aq) + 3HClO(aq)$$

oxidizing agent, ClO_3^-; reducing agent, As

(c) $2[Cr_2O_7^{2-}(aq) + 14H^+(aq) + 6e^- \rightarrow 2Cr^{3+}(aq) + 7H_2O(l)]$

$3[CH_3OH(aq) + H_2O(l) \rightarrow HCO_2H(aq) + 4H^+(aq) + 4e^-]$

Net: $2Cr_2O_7^{2-}(aq) + 3CH_3OH(aq) + 16H^+(aq) \rightarrow 4Cr^{3+}(aq) + 3HCO_2H(aq) + 11H_2O(l)$

oxidizing agent, $Cr_2O_7^{2-}$; reducing agent, CH_3OH

(d) $2[MnO_4^-(aq) + 8H^+(aq) + 5e^- \rightarrow Mn^{2+}(aq) + 4H_2O(l)]$

$5[2Cl^-(aq) \rightarrow Cl_2(aq) + 2e^-]$

Net: $2MnO_4^-(aq) + 10Cl^-(aq) + 16H^+(aq) \rightarrow 2Mn^{2+}(aq) + 5Cl_2(g) + 8H_2O(l)$

oxidizing agent, MnO_4^-; reducing agent, Cl^-

(e) $H_2O_2(aq) + 2e^- \rightarrow O_2(g) + 2H^+(aq)$

Since the reaction is in base, the H^+ can be "neutralized" by adding $2OH^-$ to each side of the equation to give $H_2O_2(aq) + 2OH^-(aq) \rightarrow O_2(g) + 2H_2O(l) + 2e^-$
The other half reaction is $2[ClO_2(aq) + e^- \rightarrow ClO_2^-(aq)]$.

Net: $H_2O_2(aq) + 2ClO_2(aq) + 2OH^-(aq) \rightarrow O_2(g) + 2ClO_2^-(aq) + 2H_2O(l)$

oxidizing agent, ClO_2; reducing agent, H_2O_2

(f) $4[H_2O_2(aq) + 2OH^-(aq) \rightarrow O_2(g) + 2H_2O(l) + 2e^-]$

$Cl_2O_7(aq) + 3H_2O(l) + 8e^- \rightarrow 2ClO_2^-(aq) + 6OH^-(aq)$

Net: $Cl_2O_7(aq) + 4H_2O_2(aq) + 2OH^-(aq) \rightarrow 2ClO_2^-(aq) + 4O_2(g) + 5H_2O(l)$

oxidizing agent, Cl_2O_7; reducing agent, H_2O_2

Voltaic Cells; Cell Potential

20.12 (a) The porous glass dish in Figure 20.4 provides a mechanism by which ions not directly involved in the redox reaction can migrate into the anode and cathode compartments to maintain charge neutrality of the solutions. Ionic conduction within the cell, through the glass disk, completes the cell circuit.

(b) In the anode compartment of Figure 20.5, Zn atoms are oxidized to Zn^{2+} cations, increasing the number of positively charged particles in the compartment. NO_3^- anions migrate into the compartment to maintain charge balance as Zn^{2+} ions are produced.

20.14 (a) $Al(s) \rightarrow Al^{3+}(aq) + 3e^-$; $Ni^{2+}(aq) + 2e^- \rightarrow Ni(s)$

(b) Al(s) is the anode; Ni(s) is the cathode.

(c) Al(s) is negative (-); Ni(s) is positive (+).

(d) Electrons flow from the Al(-) electrode toward the Ni(+) electrode.

(e) Cations migrate toward the Ni(s) cathode; anions migrate toward the Al(s) anode.

20.16 (a) The Zn electrode, the anode, on the right of figure 20.4 has the higher potential energy for electrons.

(b) The units of electrical potential are volts. A potential of one volt imparts one joule of energy to one coulomb of charge.

(c) A *standard* cell potential describes the potential of an electrochemical cell where all components are present at standard conditions: elements in their standard states, gases at 1 atm pressure and 1 *M* aqueous solutions.

20.18 (a) $H_2(g) \rightarrow 2H^+(aq) + 2e^-$

(b) The platinum electrode serves as a reaction surface; the greater the surface area, the more H_2 or H^+ that can be adsorbed onto the surface to facilitate the flow of electrons.

(c)

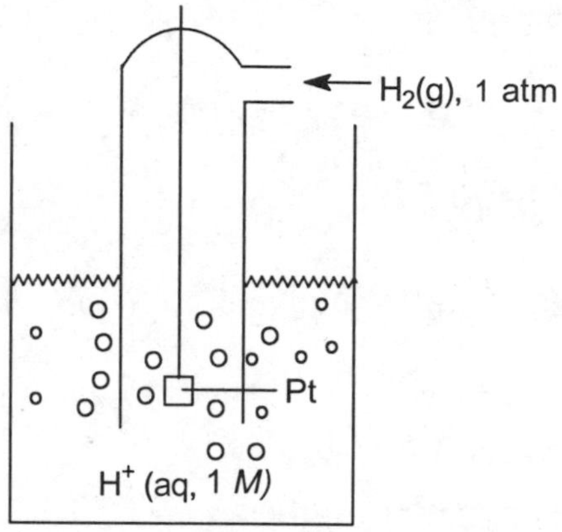

20.20 (a) It is not possible to measure the standard reduction potential of a single half-reaction because each voltaic cell consists of two half-reactions and only the potential of a complete cell can be measured.

(b) The standard reduction potential of a half-reaction is determined by combining it with a reference half-reaction of known potential and measuring the cell potential. Assuming the half-reaction of interest is the reduction half-reaction:

$E^\circ_{cell} = E^\circ_{red}(\text{cathode}) - E^\circ_{red}(\text{anode}) = E^\circ_{red}(\text{unknown}) - E^\circ_{red}(\text{reference})$;

$E^\circ_{red}(\text{unknown}) = E^\circ_{cell} + E^\circ_{red}(\text{reference})$.

(c) $Cd^{2+}(aq) + 2e^- \rightarrow Cd(s)$ $E° = -0.403$ V

$Ca^{2+}(aq) + 2e^- \rightarrow Ca(s)$ $E° = -2.87$ V

The reduction of $Ca^{2+}(aq)$ to Ca(s) is the more energetically unfavorable reduction because it has a more negative E° value.

20.22 (a) $PdCl_4^{2-}(aq) + 2e^- \rightarrow Pd(s) + 4Cl^-$ cathode $E^\circ_{red} = ?$

$Cd(s) \rightarrow Cd^{2+}(aq) + 2e^-$ anode $E^\circ_{red} = -0.403$ V

(b) $E^\circ_{cell} = E^\circ_{red}(\text{cathode}) - E^\circ_{red}(\text{anode})$; $1.03 \text{ V} = E^\circ_{red} - (-0.403 \text{ V})$;

$E^\circ_{red} = 1.03 \text{ V} - 0.403 = 0.63 \text{ V}$

(c)

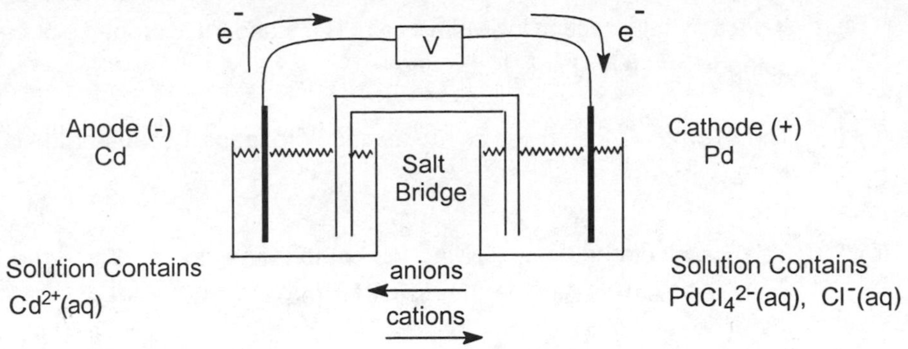

20.24 (a) $F_2(g) + 2e^- \rightarrow 2F^-(aq)$ $E^\circ_{red} = 2.87$ V

$H_2(g) \rightarrow 2H^+(aq) + 2e^-$ $E^\circ_{red} = 0.00$ V

$E^\circ = 2.87 \text{ V} - 0.00 \text{ V} = 2.87 \text{ V}$

(b) $Cu(s) \rightarrow Cu^{2+}(aq) + 2e^-$ $E^\circ_{red} = 0.337$ V

$Ba^{2+}(aq) + 2e^- \rightarrow Ba(s)$ $E^\circ_{red} = -2.90$ V

$E^\circ = -2.90 \text{ V} - (0.337 \text{ V}) = -3.24 \text{ V}$

(c) $Fe^{2+}(aq) + 2e^- \rightarrow Fe(s)$ $E^\circ_{red} = -0.440$ V

$2[Fe^{2+}(aq) \rightarrow Fe^{3+}(aq) + 1e^-]$ $E^\circ_{red} = 0.771$ V

$E^\circ = -0.440 \text{ V} - 0.771 \text{ V} = -1.211 \text{ V}$

(d) $Hg_2^{2+}(aq) + 2e^- \rightarrow 2Hg(l)$ $E^\circ_{red} = 0.789$ V

$2[Cu^+(aq) \rightarrow Cu^{2+}(aq) + 1e^-]$ $E^\circ_{red} = 0.153$ V

$E^\circ = 0.789 \text{ V} - 0.153 \text{ V} = 0.636 \text{ V}$

20.26 (a) $2[Au(s) + 4Br^-(aq) \rightarrow AuBr_4^-(aq) + 3e^-]$ $E^\circ_{red} = -0.858$ V

$3[2e^- + IO^-(aq) + H_2O(l) \rightarrow I^-(aq) + 2OH^-(aq)]$ $E^\circ_{red} = 0.49$ V

$2Au(s) + 8Br^-(aq) + 3IO^-(aq) + 3H_2O(l) \rightarrow 2AuBr_4^-(aq) + 3I^-(aq) + 6OH^-(aq)$

$E^\circ = 0.49 - (-0.858) = 1.35$ V

(b) $2[Eu^{2+}(aq) \rightarrow Eu^{3+}(aq) + 1e^-]$ $E^\circ_{red} = -0.43$ V

$Sn^{2+}(aq) + 2e^- \rightarrow Sn(s)$ $E^\circ_{red} = -0.14$ V

$2Eu^{2+}(aq) + Sn^{2+}(aq) \rightarrow 2Eu^{3+}(aq) + Sn(s)$ $E^\circ = -0.14 - (-0.43) = 0.29$ V

20.28 (a) The half-reactions are:

$2H^+(aq) + 2e^- \rightarrow H_2(g)$ $E^\circ_{red} = 0.00$ V

$Al(s) \rightarrow Al^{3+}(aq) + 3e^-$ $E^\circ_{red} = -1.66$ V

Because it has the larger E°_{red} (0.00 V vs -1.66 V), the first half-reaction is the reduction half-reaction in a voltaic cell. The standard hydrogen electrode (SHE) is the cathode and the Al strip is the anode.

(b) The Al strip will lose mass as the reaction proceeds, because Al(s) is transformed to Al^{3+}(aq).

(c) Balance electrons by multiplying the cathode reaction by 3 and the anode reaction by 2. $6H^+(aq) + 2Al(s) \rightarrow 3H_2(g) + 2Al^{3+}(aq)$

(d) $E^{\circ} = 0.00\ V - (-1.66\ V) = 1.66\ V$

20.30 (a) The two half-reactions are:

$Pb^{2+}(aq) + 2e^- \rightarrow Pb(s)$ $E^{\circ} = -0.126\ V$

$Cl_2(g) + 2e^- \rightarrow 2Cl^-(aq)$ $E^{\circ} = 1.359\ V$

Because E° for the reduction of Cl_2 is higher, the reduction of Cl_2 occurs at the Pt cathode. The Pb electrode is the anode.

(b) The Pb anode loses mass as Pb^{2+}(aq) is produced.

(c) $Cl_2(g) + Pb(s) \rightarrow Pb^{2+}(aq) + 2Cl^-(aq)$

(d) $E^{\circ} = 1.359\ V - (-0.126\ V) = 1.485\ V$

Oxidizing and Reducing Agents; Spontaneity

20.32 (a) Top. The reduction half-reactions near the top of Table 20.1 are most likely to occur; a strong oxidant is most likely to be reduced.

(b) Left. An oxidant is reduced, so it is a reactant in a reduction half-reaction.

20.34 The more readily a substance is oxidized, the stronger it is as a reducing agent. In each case choose the half-reaction with the more negative reduction potential and the given substance on the right.

(a) Mg(s) (-2.37 V vs. -0.44 V) (b) Ca(s) (-2.87 V vs. -1.66 V)

(c) H_2(g, acidic) (0.000 V vs. 0.141 V) (d) $H_2C_2O_4$(aq) (-0.49 V vs. 0.17 V)

20.36 If the substance is on the left of a reduction half-reaction, it will be an oxidant; if it is on the right, it will be a reductant. The sign and magnitude of the E°_{red} determines whether it is strong or weak.

(a) Na(s): strong reductant (on the right, E°_{red} = -2.71 V)

(b) O_3(g): strong oxidant (on the left, E°_{red} = 2.07 V)

(c) Ce^{3+}(aq): very weak reductant (on the right, E°_{red} = 1.61 V)

(d) Sn^{2+}(aq): reductant (on the right, E°_{red} = 0.154 V) **or** weak oxidant (on the left, -0.136 V)

20.38 (a) The strongest oxidizing agent is the species most readily reduced, as evidenced by a large, positive reduction potential. That species is H_2O_2. The weakest oxidizing agent is the species that least readily accepts an electron. We expect that it will be very difficult to reduce Zn(s); indeed, Zn(s) acts as a comparatively strong **reducing** agent. No potential is listed for reduction of Zn(s), but we can safely assume that it is less readily reduced than any of the other species present.

(b) The strongest reducing agent is the species most easily oxidized (the largest negative reduction potential). Zn, E°_{red} = -0.76 V, is the strongest reducing agent and F^-, E°_{red} = 2.87 V, is the weakest.

20.40 Any oxidized species from Table 20.1 or Appendix E with a reduction potential greater than 0.59 V will oxidize RuO_4^{2-} to RuO_4^-. From the list of possible oxidants in the Exercise, $Cr_2O_7^{2-}$(aq) and ClO^-(aq) will oxidize RuO_4^{2-} to RuO_4^-.

20.42 (a) $\Delta G = -nFE$. The more positive the emf of a reaction, the more negative the value of ΔG.

(b) Reactions (a) and (d) in Exercise 20.24 have positive E° values and are spontaneous.

(c) $\Delta G° = -nFE°$; F = 96,500 J/V•mol e^- = 96.5 kJ/V•mol e^-

20.24 (a) $\Delta G° = -2 \text{ mol } e^- \times \dfrac{96.5 \text{ kJ}}{\text{V} \bullet \text{mol } e^-} \times 2.87 \text{ V} = -553.91 = -554 \text{ kJ}$

20.24 (b) $\Delta G°$ = -2(96.5)(-3.24) = 625.32 = 625 kJ

20.24 (c) $\Delta G°$ = -2(96.5)(-1.21) = 233.53 = 234 kJ

20.24 (d) $\Delta G°$ = -2(96.5)(0.636) = -122.75 = -123 kJ

20.44 (a)

$$2I^-(aq) \rightarrow I_2(s) + 2e^- \qquad E^\circ_{red} = 0.536 \text{ V}$$

$$Hg_2^{2+}(aq) + 2e^- \rightarrow 2Hg(l) \qquad E^\circ_{red} = 0.789 \text{ V}$$

$$2I^-(aq) + Hg_2^{2+}(aq) \rightarrow I_2(s) + 2Hg(l) \qquad E° = 0.789 - 0.536 = 0.253 \text{ V}$$

$$\Delta G° = -nFE° = -2 \text{ mol } e^- \times \frac{96.5 \text{ kJ}}{\text{V} \bullet \text{mol } e^-} \times 0.253 \text{ V} = -48.8 \text{ kJ}$$

(b)

$$3[Cu^+(aq) \rightarrow Cu^{2+}(aq) + 1e^-] \qquad E^\circ_{red} = 0.153 \text{ V}$$

$$NO_3^-(aq) + 4H^+(aq) + 3e^- \rightarrow NO(g) + H_2O(l) \qquad E^\circ_{red} = 0.96 \text{ V}$$

$$3Cu^+(aq) + NO_3^-(aq) + 4H^+(aq) \rightarrow 3Cu^{2+}(aq) + NO(g) + 2H_2O(l)$$

E° = 0.96 - 0.153 = 0.81 V; $\Delta G°$ = -3(96.5)(0.81) = -2.3×10^2 kJ

(c)

$$\begin{array}{ll} 2[Cr(OH)_3(s) + 5OH^-(aq) \rightarrow CrO_4^{2-}(aq) + 4H_2O(l) + 3e^-] & E^\circ_{red} = -0.13\text{ V} \\ 3[ClO^-(aq) + H_2O(l) + 2e^- \rightarrow Cl^-(aq) + 2OH^-(aq)] & E^\circ_{red} = 0.89\text{ V} \\ \hline 2Cr(OH)_3(s) + 3ClO^-(aq) + 4OH^-(aq) \rightarrow 2CrO_4^{2-}(aq) + 3Cl^-(aq) + 5H_2O(l) & \end{array}$$

$E^\circ = 0.89 - (-0.13) = 1.02$ V; $\Delta G^\circ = -6(96.5)(1.02) = -591$ kJ

EMF and Concentration

20.46 (a) No. As the spontaneous chemical reaction of the voltaic cell proceeds, the concentrations of products increase and the concentrations of reactants decrease, so standard conditions are not maintained.

(b) $$0.0592 = 2.303\ \frac{RT}{F} = 2.303 \times \frac{8.314\text{ J}}{\text{mol}\bullet\text{K}} \times 298\text{ K} \times \frac{\text{V}\bullet\text{mol}}{96{,}500\text{ J}}$$

The "2.303" is a factor to change natural logs into base-10 logs. The "0.0592 V" assumes the cell operates at 298 K and that base-10 logs are used.

(c) If concentration of products increases, Q increases, and E decreases.

20.48 $Al(s) + 3Ag^+(aq) \rightarrow Al^{3+}(aq) + 3Ag(s)$; $E = E^\circ - \dfrac{0.0592}{n}\log Q$; $Q = \dfrac{[Al^{3+}]}{[Ag^+]^3}$

Any change that causes the reaction to be less spontaneous (that causes Q to increase and ultimately shifts the equilibrium to the left) will result in a less positive value for E°.

(a) Increases E by decreasing $[Al^{3+}]$ on the right side of the equation.

(b) No effect; the "concentrations" of pure solids and liquids do not influence the value of K_{eq} for a heterogeneous equilibrium.

(c) No effect; the concentration of Ag^+ and the value of Q are unchanged.

(d) Decreases E; forming AgCl(s) decreases the concentration of Ag^+, which increases Q.

20.50 (a)

$$\begin{array}{ll} 3[Ce^{4+}(aq) + 1e^- \rightarrow Ce^{3+}(aq)] & E^\circ_{red} = 1.61\text{ V} \\ Cr(s) \rightarrow Cr^{3+}(aq) + 3e^- & E^\circ_{red} = -0.74\text{ V} \\ \hline 3Ce^{4+}(aq) + Cr(s) \rightarrow 3Ce^{3+}(aq) + Cr^{3+}(aq) & E^\circ = 1.61 - (-0.74) = 2.35\text{ V} \end{array}$$

(b) $$E = E^\circ - \frac{0.0592}{n}\log\frac{[Ce^{3+}]^3[Cr^{3+}]}{[Ce^{4+}]^3};\ n = 3$$

$$E = 2.35 - \frac{0.0592}{3}\log\frac{(0.010)^3(0.010)}{(2.0)^3} = 2.35 - \frac{0.0592}{3}\log(1.250 \times 10^{-9})$$

$$E = 2.35 - \frac{0.0592(-8.903)}{3} = 2.35 + 0.176 = 2.53\text{ V}$$

(c) $$E = 2.35 - \frac{0.0592}{3}\log\frac{(0.85)^3(1.2)}{(0.35)^3} = 2.35 - 0.0244 = 2.33\text{ V}$$

20.52 (a)

$$\begin{array}{ll} 2[Fe^{3+}(aq) + 1\,e^- \rightarrow Fe^{2+}(aq)] & E^\circ_{red} = 0.771\ V \\ H_2(g) \rightarrow 2H^+(aq) + 2e^- & E^\circ_{red} = 0.000\ V \\ \hline 2Fe^{3+}(aq) + H_2(g) \rightarrow 2Fe^{2+}(aq) + 2H^+(aq) & E^\circ = 0.771 - 0.000 = 0.771\ V \end{array}$$

(b) $E = E^\circ - \frac{0.0592}{n} \log \frac{[Fe^{2+}]^2 [H^+]^2}{[Fe^{3+}]^2 P_{H_2}}$; $[H^+] = 10^{-pH} = 1.0 \times 10^{-5}$, n = 2

$$E = 0.771 - \frac{0.0592}{2} \log \frac{(0.0010)^2 (1.0 \times 10^{-5})^2}{(1.50)^2 (0.50)} = 0.771 - \frac{0.0592}{2} \log (8.9 \times 10^{-17})$$

$$E = 0.771 - \frac{0.0592\,(-16.05)}{2} = 0.771 + 0.475 = 1.246\ V$$

20.54 (a) The compartment with 0.0150 *M* Cl^-(aq) is the cathode.

(b) $E^\circ = 0$ V

(c) $E = E^\circ - \frac{0.0592}{n} \log Q$; Q = [$Cl^-$, dilute] / [$Cl^-$, conc.]

$$E = 0 - \frac{0.0592}{1} \log \frac{(0.0150)}{(2.55)} = 0.132\ V$$

(d) In the anode compartment, [Cl^-] will decrease from 2.55 *M*. In the cathode, [Cl^-] will increase from 0.0150 *M*.

20.56 (a) $E^\circ = -0.136\ V - (-0.126\ V) = -0.010\ V$; n = 2

$$0.22 = -0.010 - \frac{0.0592}{2} \log \frac{[Pb^{2+}]}{[Sn^{2+}]} = -0.010 - \frac{0.0592}{2} \log \frac{[Pb^{2+}]}{1.00}$$

$\log [Pb^{2+}] = \frac{-0.23\,(2)}{0.0592} = -7.770 = -7.8$; $[Pb^{2+}] = 1.7 \times 10^{-8} = 2 \times 10^{-8}$ *M*

(b) For $PbSO_4(s)$, $K_{sp} = [Pb^{2+}][SO_4^{2-}] = (1.0)(1.7 \times 10^{-8}) = 1.7 \times 10^{-8}$

20.58 $E^\circ = \frac{0.0592\ V}{n} \log K_{eq}$; $\log K_{eq} = \frac{nE^\circ}{0.0592\ V}$

(a) $E^\circ = 1.00\ V - (-0.799\ V) = 0.201 = 0.20\ V$; n = 2 ($Ni^{+2} + 2e^- \rightarrow Ni$)

$\log K_{eq} = \frac{2(0.201\ V)}{0.0592\ V} = 6.7905 = 6.8$; $K_{eq} = 6.17 \times 10^6 = 6 \times 10^6$

(b) $E^\circ = 1.61\ V - 0.32\ V = 1.29\ V$; n = 3 ($3Ce^{4+} + 3e^- \rightarrow 3Ce^{3+}$)

$\log K_{eq} = \frac{3(1.29)}{0.0592} = 65.372 = 65.4$; $K_{eq} = 2.35 \times 10^{65} = 2 \times 10^{65}$

(c) $E^\circ = 0.36\ V - (-0.23\ V) = 0.59\ V$; n = 4 ($4Fe(CN)_6^{3-} + 4e^- \rightarrow 4Fe(CN)_6^{4-}$)

$\log K_{eq} = \frac{4(0.59)}{0.0592} = 39.865 = 40$; $K_{eq} = 7 \times 10^{39} = 10^{40}$

20.60 $E° = \frac{0.0592\ V}{n} \log K_{eq}$; $n = \frac{0.0592\ V}{E°} \log K_{eq}$

$$n = \frac{0.0592\ V}{0.17\ V} \log 5.5 \times 10^5;\ n = 2$$

Batteries; Corrosion

20.62 (a) The emf of a battery decreases as it is used. This happens because the concentrations of products increase and the concentrations of reactants decrease. According to the Nernst equation, these changes increase Q and decrease E_{cell}.

(b) The major difference between AA- and D-size batteries is the amount of reactants present. The additional reactants in a D-size battery enable it to provide power for a longer time.

20.64 The overall cell reaction is:

$$2MnO_2(s) + Zn(s) + 2H_2O(l) \rightarrow 2MnO(OH)(s) + Zn(OH)_2(s)$$

$$12.9\ g\ Zn \times \frac{1\ mol\ Zn}{65.39\ g\ Zn} \times \frac{2\ mol\ MnO_2}{1\ mol\ Zn} \times \frac{86.94\ g\ MnO_2}{1\ mol\ MnO_2} = 34.3\ g\ MnO_2 \text{ reduced}$$

20.66 (a) $HgO(s) + Zn(s) \rightarrow Hg(l) + ZnO(s)$

(b) $E^\circ_{cell} = E^\circ_{red}$ (cathode) - E°_{red} (anode); E°_{red} (anode) = $E^\circ_{red} - E^\circ_{cell}$ = 0.098 - 1.35 = -1.25 V

(c) E°_{red} is different from $Zn^{2+}(aq) + 2e^- \rightarrow Zn(s)$ (-0.76 V) because in the battery the process happens in the presence of base and Zn^{2+} is stabilized as ZnO(s). Stabilization of the product of a reaction increases the driving force for the reaction, so E° is more positive.

20.68 (a) The alkali metal Li has much greater metallic character than Zn, Cd, Pb or Ni. The reduction potential for Li is thus more negative, leading to greater overall cell emf for the battery. Also, Li is less dense than the other metals, so greater total energy for a battery can be achieved for a given total mass of material. One disadvantage is that Li is very reactive and the cell reactions are difficult to control.

(b) Li has a much smaller molar mass (6.94 g/mol) than Ni (58.69 g/mol). A Li-ion battery can have many more charge-carrying particles than a Ni-based battery with the same mass. That is, Li-ion batteries have a greater *energy density* than Ni-based batteries.

20.70 (a) Calculate E°_{cell} for the given reactants at standard conditions.

$$O_2(g) + 4H^+(aq) + 4\,e^- \rightarrow 2H_2O(l) \qquad E^\circ_{red} = 1.23\ V$$
$$2[Cu(s) \rightarrow Cu^{2+}(aq) + 2e^-] \qquad E^\circ_{red} = 0.337\ V$$

$$2Cu(s) + O_2(g) + 4H^+(aq) \rightarrow 2Cu^{2+}(aq) + 2H_2O(l) \quad E^\circ = 1.23 - 0.337 = 0.89\ V$$

At standard conditions with $O_2(g)$ and $H^+(aq)$ present, the oxidation of Cu(s) has a positive E° value and is spontaneous. Cu(s) will oxidize (corrode) in air in the presence of acid.

(b) Fe^{2+} has a more negative reduction potential (-0.440 V) than Cu^{2+} (+0.337 V), so Fe(s) is more readily oxidized than Cu(s). If the two metals are in contact, Fe(s) would act as a sacrificial anode and oxidize (corrode) in preference to Cu(s); this would weaken the iron support skeleton of the statue. The teflon spacers prevent contact between the two metals and insure that the iron skeleton doesn't corrode when the Cu(s) skin comes in contact with atmospheric $O_2(g)$ and $H^+(aq)$.

20.72 (a) A *sacrificial anode* is a metal that is oxidized in preference to another when the two metals are coupled in an electrochemical cell; the sacrificial anode has a more negative E°_{red} than the other metal. In this case, E°_{red} for Mg^{2+} is -2.37 V, more negative than most metals present in pipes, including Fe (E°_{red} = -0.44 V) and Zn (E°_{red} = -0.763 V).

(b) No. To afford cathodic protection, a metal must be more difficult to reduce (have a more negative reduction potential) than Fe^{2+}. E°_{red} Co^{2+} = -0.28 V, E°_{red} Fe^{2+} = -0.44 V.

Electrolysis; Electrical Work

20.74 (a) An electrolytic cell is the vessel in which electrolysis occurs. It consists of a power source and two electrodes in a molten salt or aqueous solution.

(b) It is the cathode. In an electrolysis cell, as in a voltaic cell, electrons are consumed (via reduction) at the cathode. Electrons flow from the negative terminal of the voltage source and then to the cathode.

(c) A small amount of $H_2SO_4(aq)$ present during the electrolysis of water acts as a change carrier, or supporting electrolyte. This facilitates transfer of electrons through the solution and at the electrodes, speeding up the reaction. (Considering $H^+(aq)$ as the substance reduced at the cathode changes the details of the half-reactions, but not the overall E° for the electrolysis. $SO_4^{2-}(aq)$ cannot be oxidized.)

20.76 (a) anode: $2Br^-(l) \rightarrow Br_2(l) + 2e^-$

cathode: $Al^{3+}(l) \rightarrow Al(l) + 3e^-$ (Al(s) melts at a lower temperature than AlBr(s).)

(b) anode: $2Br^-(l) \rightarrow Br_2(l) + 2e^-$

cathode: $2H_2O(l) + 2e^- \rightarrow H_2(g) + 2OH^-(aq)$

The reduction potential for water is less negative than that for $Al^{3+}(aq)$, so water is reduced in preference to Al^{3+}.

(c) The minimum emf values for the two possibilities in aqueous solution are:

Al^{3+} is reduced: -1.66 V - 1.065 V = -2.73 V

H_2O is reduced: -0.83 V - 1.065 V = -1.90 V

The minus signs indicate that voltage must be applied.

20.78

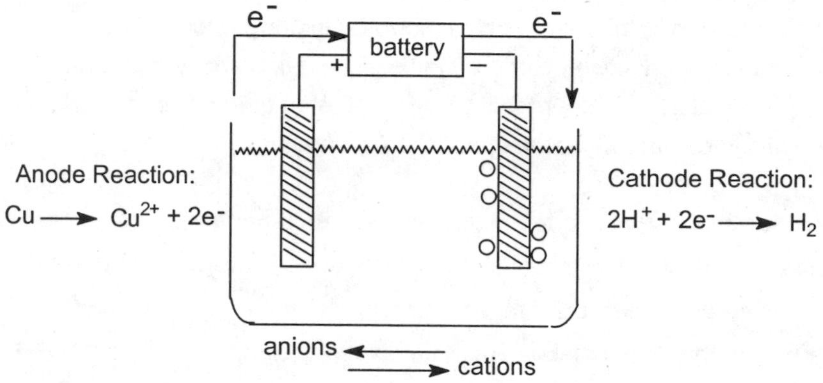

Overall cell reaction: $Cu(s) + 2H^+(aq) \rightarrow Cu^{2+}(aq) + H_2(g)$ $E° = -0.34$ V

Cu(s) is oxidized in preference to Br^- because of the smaller E°_{red} for Cu(s).

E_{min}, the **minimum** voltage required to produce the cell reaction under standard conditions, is 0.34 V. Note, however, that this value is at standard conditions $[H^+] = 1$ *M*, and $[Cu^{2+}] = 1$ *M*. This value does not include any additional voltage required to overcome kinetic effects.

20.80 Coulombs = amps•s; since this is a $2e^-$ reduction, each mole of Mg(s) requires 2 Faradays.

(a) $$5.25 \text{ A} \times 2.50 \text{ d} \times \frac{24 \text{ hr}}{1 \text{ d}} \times \frac{60 \text{ min}}{1 \text{ hr}} \times \frac{60 \text{ s}}{1 \text{ min}} \times \frac{1 \text{ C}}{1 \text{ amp} \bullet \text{s}} \times \frac{1 \text{ F}}{96{,}500 \text{ C}}$$

$$\times \frac{1 \text{ mol Mg}}{2 \text{ F}} \times \frac{24.31 \text{ g Mg}}{1 \text{ mol Mg}} = 143 \text{ g Mg}$$

(b) $$10.00 \text{ g Mg} \times \frac{1 \text{ mol Mg}}{24.31 \text{ g Mg}} \times \frac{2 \text{ F}}{1 \text{ mol Mg}} \times \frac{96{,}500 \text{ C}}{\text{F}} \times \frac{1 \text{ amp} \bullet \text{s}}{\text{C}} \times \frac{1 \text{ min}}{60 \text{ s}} \times \frac{1}{3.50 \text{ A}}$$

$$= 378 \text{ min}$$

20.82 (a) *Plan.* Use the ideal gas equation to calculate moles $H_2(g)$. Follow the progression in Figure 20.31, starting at moles of substance and moving to the left. *Solve*:

$$n = \frac{PV}{RT} = 725 \text{ torr} \times \frac{1 \text{ atm}}{760 \text{ torr}} \times \frac{5.0 \text{ L}}{296 \text{ K}} \times \frac{\text{K} \cdot \text{mol}}{0.08206 \text{ L} \cdot \text{atm}} = 0.19637 = 0.20 \text{ mol } H_2$$

$$0.19637 \text{ mol } H_2 \times \frac{2 \text{ F}}{1 \text{ mol } H_2} \times \frac{96{,}500 \text{ C}}{\text{F}} \times \frac{1 \text{ amp} \cdot \text{s}}{\text{C}} \times \frac{1}{1.5 \text{ A}} = 2.527 \times 10^4$$

$$= 2.5 \times 10^4 \text{ s (7.0 hr)}$$

(b) $2H_2O(l) \rightarrow 2H_2(g) + O_2(g)$

$$0.19637 \text{ mol } H_2 \times \frac{1 \text{ mol } O_2}{2 \text{ mol } H_2} \times \frac{32.00 \text{ g } O_2}{\text{mol } O_2} = 3.142 = 3.1 \text{ g } O_2$$

20.84 For this cell at standard conditions, E° = 1.10 V.

$w_{max} = \Delta G° = -nFE° = -2(96.5)(1.10) = -212.3 = -212$ kJ/mol Cu

$$50.0 \text{ g Cu} \times \frac{1 \text{ mol Cu}}{63.55 \text{ g Cu}} \times \frac{-212.3 \text{ kJ}}{\text{mol Cu}} = -167 \text{ kJ}$$

20.86 (a)

$$6.5 \times 10^3 \text{ A} \times 48 \text{ hr} \times \frac{3600 \text{ s}}{1 \text{ hr}} \times \frac{1 \text{ C}}{1 \text{ amp} \cdot \text{s}} \times \frac{1 \text{ F}}{96{,}500 \text{ C}} \times \frac{1 \text{ mol Ca}}{2 \text{ F}}$$

$$\times \frac{40.08 \text{ g Ca}}{1 \text{ mol Ca}} \times 0.68 = 1.586 \times 10^5 = 1.6 \times 10^5 \text{ g Ca}$$

(b) If the cell is 68% efficient, $\frac{96{,}500 \text{ C}}{\text{F}} \times \frac{2 \text{ F}}{0.68 \text{ mol Ca}} = 2.838 \times 10^5$

$= 2.8 \times 10^5$ C/mol Ca required

$$\text{Energy} = 5.00 \text{ V} \times \frac{2.838 \times 10^5 \text{ C}}{\text{mol Ca}} \times \frac{1 \text{ J}}{\text{C} \cdot \text{V}} \times \frac{1 \text{ kWh}}{3.6 \times 10^6 \text{ J}} = 0.3942 = 0.39 \text{ kWh}$$

Additional Exercises

20.88 (a)

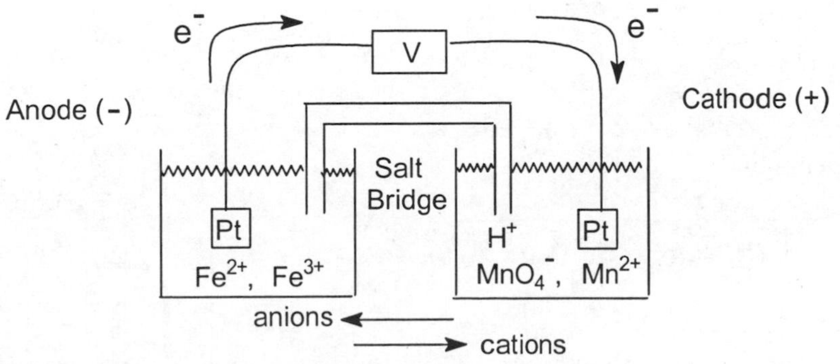

(b)

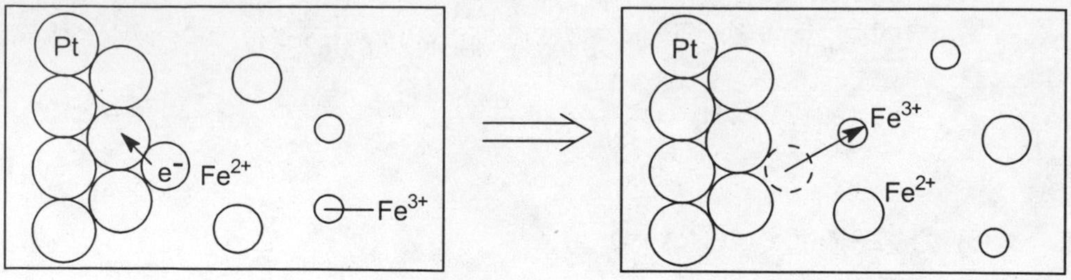

(c) $MnO_4^-(aq) + 8H^+(aq) + 5e^- \rightarrow Mn^{2+}(aq) + 4H_2O(l)$ $E^\circ_{red} = 1.51$ V

$5[Fe^{2+}(aq) \rightarrow Fe^{3+}(aq) + 1e^-]$ $E^\circ_{red} = 0.771$ V

$E° = 1.51 \text{ V} - 0.771 \text{ V} = 0.74 \text{ V}$

(d) $E = E° - \frac{0.0592}{5} \log \frac{[Fe^{3+}]^5[Mn^{2+}]}{[Fe^{2+}]^5[MnO_4^-][H^+]^8}$; pH = 0.0, $[H^+] = 1.0$

$E = 0.74 \text{ V} - \frac{0.0592}{5} \log \frac{(2.5 \times 10^{-4})^5(0.010)}{(0.10)^5(1.50)(1.0)^8}$; $Q = 6.510 \times 10^{-16} = 6.5 \times 10^{-16}$

$E = 0.74 \text{ V} - \frac{0.0592(-15.1864)}{5} = 0.74 \text{ V} + 0.18 \text{ V} = 0.92 \text{ V}$

20.89 (a)

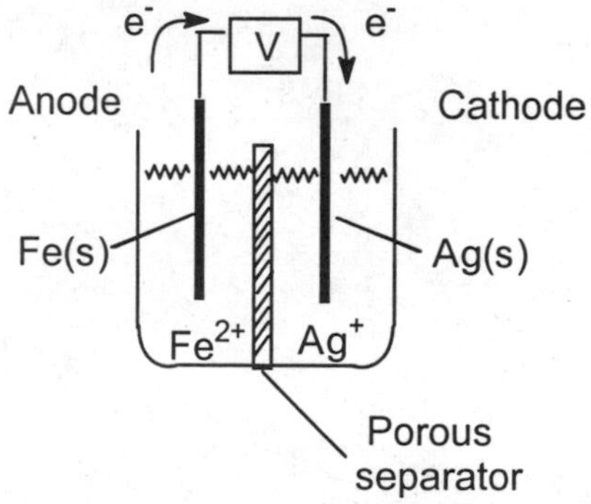

$Fe(s) \rightarrow Fe^{2+}(aq) + 2e^-$

$2Ag^+(aq) + 2e^- \rightarrow 2Ag(s)$

$Fe(s) + 2Ag^+(aq) \rightarrow Fe^{2+}(aq) + 2Ag(s)$

(b) $Zn(s) \rightarrow Zn^{2+}(s) + 2e^-$

$2H^+(aq) + 2e^- \rightarrow H_2(g)$

$Zn(s) + 2H^+(aq) \rightarrow Zn^{2+}(aq) + H_2(g)$

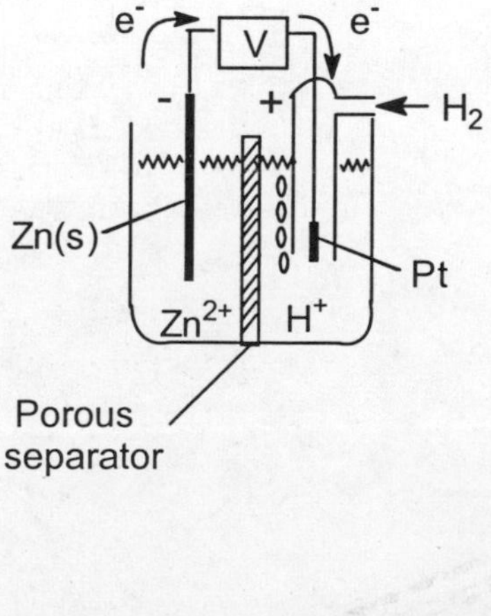

(c) $Cu|Cu^{2+}||ClO_3^-, Cl^-|Pt$ Here, both the oxidized and reduced forms of the cathode solution are in the same phase, so we separate them by a comma, and then indicate an inert electrode.

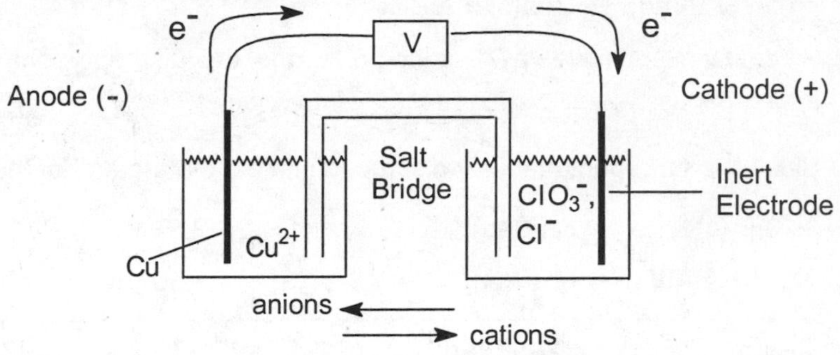

20.91 We need in each case to determine whether E° is positive (spontaneous) or negative (nonspontaneous).

(a) $I_2(s) + 2e^- \rightarrow 2I^-(aq)$ $E^\circ_{red} = 0.536$ V

$Sn(s) \rightarrow Sn^{2+}(aq) + 2e^-$ $E^\circ_{red} = -0.136$

$Sn(s) + I_2(s) \rightarrow Sn^{2+}(aq) + 2I^-(aq)$ E° = 0.536 - (-0.136) = 0.672 V, spontaneous

(b) $Ni^{2+}(aq) + 2e^- \rightarrow Ni(s)$ $E^\circ_{red} = -0.28$ V

$2I^-(aq) \rightarrow I_2(s) + 2e^-$ $E^\circ_{red} = 0.536$ V

$Ni^{2+}(aq) + 2I^-(aq) \rightarrow Ni(s) + I_2(s)$ E° = -0.28 - 0.536 = -0.82 V, nonspontaneous

(c) $2[Ce^{4+}(aq) + 1e^- \rightarrow Ce^{3+}(aq)]$ $E^\circ_{red} = 1.61$ V

$H_2O_2(aq) \rightarrow O_2(g) + 2H^+(aq) + 2e^-$ $E^\circ_{red} = 0.68$ V

$2Ce^{4+}(aq) + H_2O_2(aq) \rightarrow 2Ce^{3+}(aq) + O_2(g) + 2H^+(aq)$ E° = 1.61 - 0.68 = 0.93 V, spontaneous

(d) $Cu^{2+}(aq) + 2e^- \rightarrow Cu(s)$ $E^\circ_{red} = 0.337$ V

$Sn^{2+}(aq) \rightarrow Sn^{4+}(aq) + 2e^-$ $E^\circ_{red} = 0.154$ V

$Cu^{2+}(aq) + Sn^{2+}(aq) \rightarrow Cu(s) + Sn^{4+}(aq)$ E° = 0.337 - 1.54 = 0.183 V, spontaneous

20.92 (a) The reduction potential for $O_2(g)$ in the presence of acid is 1.23 V. $O_2(g)$ cannot oxidize Au(s) to $Au^+(aq)$ or $Au^{3+}(aq)$, even in the presence of acid.

(b) The substances need a reduction potential greater than 1.50 V. These include $Co^{3+}(aq)$, $F_2(g)$, $H_2O(aq)$ and $O_3(g)$. Marginal oxidizing agents (those with reduction potential near 1.50 V) from Appendix E are $BrO_3^-(aq)$, $Ce^{4+}(aq)$, HClO(aq), $MnO_4^-(aq)$ and $PbO_2(s)$.

(c) $3[Au^+(aq) + 1e^- \rightarrow Au(s)]$ $E^\circ_{red} = 1.69$ V

$Au(s) \rightarrow Au^{3+}(aq) + 3e^-$ $E^\circ_{red} = 1.50$ V

$3Au^+(aq) \rightarrow 2Au(s) + Au^{3+}(aq)$ $E° = 1.69 - 1.50 = +0.19$ V

Since E° is positive, ΔG° is negative and the disproportionation of $Au^+(aq)$ is spontaneous.

(d) Since the Au^+ spontaneously disproportionates, the product of the reaction is AuF_3.

$3[F_2(g) + 2e^- \rightarrow 2F^-(aq)]$ $E^\circ_{red} = 2.87$ V

$2[Au(s) \rightarrow Au^{3+}(aq) + 3e^-]$ $E^\circ_{red} = 1.50$ V

$2Au(s) + 3F_2(g) \rightarrow 2AuF_3(aq)$ $E° = 2.87 - 1.50 = 1.37$ V

20.94 (a) $I_2(s) + 2e^- \rightarrow 2I^-(aq)$ $E^\circ_{red} = 0.536$ V

$2[Cu(s) \rightarrow Cu^+(aq) + 1\ e^-]$ $E^\circ_{red} = 0.521$ V

$I_2(s) + 2Cu(s) \rightarrow 2Cu^+(aq) + 2\ I^-(aq)$ $E° = 0.536 - 0.521 = 0.015$ V

$$E = E° - \frac{0.0592}{n} \log Q = 0.015 - \frac{0.0592}{2} \log [Cu^+]^2 [I^-]^2$$

$$E = +0.015 - \frac{0.0592}{2} \log (2.5)^2(3.5)^2 = +0.015 - 0.056 = -0.041V$$

(b) Since the cell potential is negative at these concentration conditions, the cell would be spontaneous in the opposite direction and the inert electrode in the I_2/I^- compartment would be the anode; Cu(s) would be the cathode.

(c) No. At standard conditions the cell reaction is as written in part (a) and Cu(s) is the anode.

(d) $E = 0, +0.015 = \frac{0.0592}{2} \log (1.4)^2 [I^-]^2$; $\frac{2(0.015)}{0.0592} = \log (1.4)^2 + 2 \log [I^-]$;

$\log[I^-] = 0.107 = 0.11$; $[I^-] = 10^{0.107} = 1.28 = 1.3\ M\ I^-$

20.96 In order for the same electrode reactions that "normally" produce 1.5 V to produce 9 V, six of the 1.5-V cells must be connected in series; inside the 9-V battery there are six individual Zn, OH^- / MnO_2 cells connected in series. Since the 9-V battery is rectangular and the D-size battery is a cylinder, the shape of the cells and arrangement of the electrodes in the two batteries is probably different.

20.98 (a) To act as a sacrificial anode, a metal must have a more negative reduction potential (be easier to oxidize) than Fe^{2+}. E°_{red} $Sn^{2+} = -0.14$ V, E°_{red} $Fe^{2+} = -0.44$ V. Tin does not give cathodic protection to iron.

(b) Tin gives protection to iron by providing a protective coating to keep out air and water. If this coating is broken, not only does corrosion occur, it occurs more readily because tin acts as the cathode in the electrochemical cell.

20.99 The ship's hull should be made negative. By keeping an excess of electrons in the metal of the ship, the tendency for iron to undergo oxidation, with release of electrons, is diminished. The ship, as a negatively charged "electrode," becomes the site of reduction, rather than oxidation, in an electrolytic process.

20.101 A battery is a voltaic cell, so the cathode compartment contains the positive terminal of the battery. In the alkaline, Ni–Cd and NiMH batteries, $OH^-(aq)$ is produced at the cathode. The wire that turns the indicator pink is in contact with $OH^-(aq)$, so the rightmost wire is connected to the positive terminal of the battery. [The battery could not be a lead-acid battery because $OH^-(aq)$ is not present in either compartment, so neither wire would turn the indicator pink.]

20.102 (a) Total volume of Cr = 2.5×10^{-4} m × 0.32 m^2 = 8.0×10^{-5} m^3

$$\text{mol Cr} = 8.0 \times 10^{-5}\ \text{m}^3\ \text{Cr} \times \frac{100^3\ \text{cm}^3}{1\ \text{m}^3} \times \frac{7.20\ \text{g Cr}}{1\ \text{cm}^3} \times \frac{1\ \text{mol Cr}}{52.0\ \text{g Cr}} = 11.077 = 11\ \text{mol Cr}$$

The electrode reaction is:

$$CrO_4^{2-}(aq) + 4H_2O(l) + 6e^- \rightarrow Cr(s) + 8OH^-(aq)$$

$$\text{Coulombs required} = 11.077\ \text{mol Cr} \times \frac{6\ \text{F}}{1\ \text{mol Cr}} \times \frac{96{,}500\ \text{C}}{1\ \text{F}} = 6.41 \times 10^6 = 6.4 \times 10^6\ \text{C}$$

(b)
$$6.41 \times 10^6\ \text{C} \times \frac{1\ \text{amp}\cdot\text{s}}{1\ \text{C}} \times \frac{1}{10.0\ \text{s}} = 6.4 \times 10^5\ \text{amp}$$

(c) If the cell is 60% efficient, $(6.41 \times 10^6 / 0.65) = 9.867 \times 10^6 = 9.9 \times 10^6$ C are required to plate the bumper.

$$6.0\ \text{V} \times 9.867 \times 10^6\ \text{C} \times \frac{1\ \text{J}}{1\ \text{C}\cdot\text{V}} \times \frac{1\ \text{kWh}}{3.6 \times 10^6\ \text{J}} = 16.445 = 16\ \text{kWh}$$

20.104 (a) The work obtainable is given by the product of the voltage, which has units of J/C, times the number of Coulombs of electricity produced:

$$w_{max} = 300\ \text{amp}\cdot\text{hr} \times \frac{3600\ \text{s}}{1\ \text{hr}} \times \frac{1\ \text{C}}{1\ \text{amp}\cdot\text{s}} \times \frac{6\ \text{J}}{1\ \text{C}} \times \frac{1\ \text{kWh}}{3.6 \times 10^6\ \text{J}} = 1.8\ \text{kWh} \approx 2\ \text{kWh}$$

(b) This maximum amount of work is never realized because some of the electrical energy is dissipated in overcoming the internal resistance of the battery; because the cell voltage does not remain constant as the reaction proceeds; because the systems to which the electrical energy is delivered are not capable of completely converting electrical energy into work.

20.105 (a)
$$7 \times 10^8\ \text{mol}\ H_2 \times \frac{2\ \text{F}}{1\ \text{mol}\ H_2} \times \frac{96{,}500\ \text{C}}{1\ \text{F}} = 1.35 \times 10^{14} = 1 \times 10^{14}\ \text{C}$$

(b)
$$2H_2O(l) \rightarrow O_2(g) + 4H^+(aq) + 4e^- \quad E^\circ_{red} = 1.23\ \text{V}$$
$$2[H^+(aq) + 2e^- \rightarrow H_2(g)] \quad E^\circ_{red} = 0\ \text{V}$$

$$2H_2O(l) \rightarrow O_2(g) + 2H_2(g) \quad E^\circ = 0.00 - 1.23 = -1.23\ \text{V}$$

$$E = E° - \frac{0.0592}{4} \log (P_{O_2} \times P_{H_2}^2) = -1.23 \text{ V} - \frac{0.0592}{4} \log (300)^3$$

$$E = -1.23 \text{ V} - 0.11 \text{ V} = -1.34 \text{ V}; \; E_{min} = 1.34 \text{ V}$$

(c) $\text{Energy} = nFE = 2(7 \times 10^8 \text{ mol}) (1.34 \text{ V}) \frac{96{,}500 \text{ J}}{\text{V} \cdot \text{mol}} = 1.81 \times 10^{14} = 2 \times 10^{14} \text{ J}$

(d) $1.81 \times 10^{14} \text{ J} \times \frac{1 \text{ kWh}}{3.6 \times 10^6 \text{ J}} \times \frac{\$0.23}{\text{kWh}} = \$1.16 \times 10^7 = \$1 \times 10^7$

It will cost more than ten million dollars for the electricity alone.

Integrative Exercises

20.106 $2[NO_3^-(aq) + 4H^+(aq) + 3e^- \rightarrow NO(g) + 2H_2O(l)]$ $E°_{red} = 0.96$ V

$3[Cu(s) \rightarrow Cu^{2+}(aq) + 2e^-]$ $E°_{red} = 0.34$ V

$3Cu(s) + 2NO_3^-(aq) + 8H^+(aq) \rightarrow 3Cu^{2+}(aq) + 2NO(g) + 4H_2O(l)$ $E° = 0.96 - 0.34 = 0.62$ V

$2H^+(aq) + 2e^- \rightarrow H_2(g)$ $E°_{red} = 0$ V

$Cu(s) \rightarrow Cu^{2+}(aq) + 2e^-$ $E°_{red} = 0.34$ V

$Cu(s) + 2H^+(aq) \rightarrow Cu^{2+}(aq) + H_2(g)$ $E° = 0 - 0.34 = -0.34$ V

The overall cell potential for the oxidation of Cu(s) by HNO_3 is positive and the reaction is spontaneous. The cell potential for the oxidation of Cu(s) by HCl is negative and the reaction is nonspontaneous. Note that in the reaction with HNO_3, it is NO_3^- that is reduced, not H^+.

20.108 (a) The oxidation potential of A is equal in magnitude but opposite in sign to the reduction potential of A^+.

(b) Li(s) has the highest oxidation potential, Au(s) the lowest.

(c) The relationship is reasonable because both oxidation potential and ionization energy describe removing electrons from a substance. Ionization energy is a property of gas phase atoms or ions, while oxidation potential is a property of the bulk material.

20.109 (a) $NO_3^-(aq) + 4H^+(aq) + 3e^- \rightarrow NO(g) + 2H_2O(l)$ $E°_{red} = 0.96$ V

$Au(s) \rightarrow Au^{3+}(aq) + 3e^-$ $E°_{red} = 1.498$ V

$Au(s) + NO_3^-(aq) + 4H^+(aq) \rightarrow Au^{3+}(aq) + NO(g) + 2H_2O(l)$

E° = 0.96 - 1.498 = -0.54 V; E° is negative, the reaction is not spontaneous.

(b) $3[2H^+(aq) + 2e^- \rightarrow H_2(g)]$ $E^\circ_{red} = 0.000$ V

$2[Au(s) + 4Cl^-(aq) \rightarrow AuCl_4^-(aq) + 3e^-]$ $E^\circ_{red} = 1.002$ V

$2Au(s) + 6H^+(aq) + 8Cl^-(aq) \rightarrow 2AuCl_4^-(aq) + 3H_2(g)$

E° = 0.000 - 1.002 = -1.002 V; E° is negative, the reaction is not spontaneous.

(c) $NO_3^-(aq) + 4H^+(aq) + 3e^- \rightarrow NO(g) + 2H_2O(l)$ $E^\circ_{red} = 0.96$ V

$Au(s) + 4Cl^-(aq) \rightarrow AuCl_4^-(aq) + 3e^-$ $E^\circ_{red} = 1.002$ V

$Au(s) + NO_3^-(aq) + 4Cl^-(aq) + 4H^+(aq) \rightarrow AuCl_4^-(aq) + NO(g) + 2H_2O(l)$

E° = 0.96 - 1.002 = -0.04; E° is small but negative, the process is not spontaneous.

(d) $$E = E^\circ - \frac{0.0592}{3} \log \frac{[AuCl_4^-]\, P_{NO}}{[NO_3^-][Cl^-]^4[H^+]^4}$$

If $[H^+]$, $[Cl^-]$ and $[NO_3^-]$ are much greater than 1.0 *M*, the log term is negative and the correction to E° is positive. If the correction term is greater than 0.042 V, the value of E is positive and the reaction at nonstandard conditions is spontaneous.

20.111 (a) $\Delta H^\circ = 2\Delta H^\circ\ H_2O(l) - 2\Delta H^\circ\ H_2(g) - \Delta H^\circ\ O_2(g) = 2(-285.83) - 2(0) - 0 = -571.66$ kJ

$\Delta S^\circ = 2S^\circ\ H_2O(l) - 2S^\circ\ H_2(g) - \Delta S^\circ\ O_2(g)$

$= 2(69.91) - 2(130.58) - (205.0) = -326.34$ J

(b) Since ΔS° is negative, -TΔS is positive and the value of ΔG will become more positive as T increases. The reaction will become nonspontaneous at a fairly low temperature, because the magnitude of ΔS° is large.

(c) $\Delta G = w_{max}$. The larger the negative value of ΔG, the more work the system is capable of doing on the surroundings. As the magnitude of ΔG decreases with increasing temperature, the usefulness of H_2 as a fuel decreases.

(d) The combustion method increases the temperature of the system, which quickly decreases the magnitude of the work that can be done by the system. Even if the effect of temperature on this reaction could be controlled, only about 40% of the energy from any combustion can be converted to electrical energy, so combustion is intrinsically less efficient than direct production of electrical energy via a fuel cell.

20.112 First balance the equation:

$4CyFe^{2+}(aq) + O_2(g) + 4H^+(aq) \rightarrow 4CyFe^{3+}(aq) + 2H_2O(l)$; E = +0.60 V; n = 4

(a) From Equation [20.11] we can calculate ΔG for the process under the conditions specified for the measured potential E:

$$\Delta G = -nFE = -(4 \text{ mol } e^-) \times \frac{96.5 \text{ kJ}}{1 \text{ V} \cdot \text{mol } e^-}(0.60 \text{ V}) = -231.6 = -232 \text{ kJ}$$

(b) The moles of ATP synthesized per mole of O_2 is given by:

$$\frac{231.6\text{ kJ}}{O_2\text{ molecule}} \times \frac{1\text{ mol ATP formed}}{37.7\text{ kJ}} = \text{approximately 6 mol ATP/mol } O_2$$

20.114 The reaction can be written as a sum of the steps:

$Pb^{2+}(aq) + 2e^- \rightarrow Pb(s)$ $\quad E^\circ_{red} = -0.126$ V

$PbS(s) \rightarrow Pb^{2+}(aq) + S^{2-}(aq)$ $\quad$ "E°" = ?

$PbS(s) + 2e^- \rightarrow Pb(s) + S^{2-}(aq)$ $\quad E^\circ_{red} = ?$

"E°" for the second step can be calculated from K_{sp}.

$$E^\circ = \frac{0.0592}{n}\log K_{sp} = \frac{0.0592}{2}\log(8.0 \times 10^{-28}) = \frac{0.0592}{2}(-27.10) = -0.802\text{ V}$$

E° for the half-reaction = -0.126 V + (-0.802 V) = -0.928 V

Calculating an imaginary E° for a nonredox process like step 2 may be a disturbing idea. Alternatively, one could calculate K_{eq} for step 1 (5.4×10^{-5}), K_{eq} for the reaction in question ($K_{eq} = K_1 \times K_{sp} = 4.4 \times 10^{-32}$) and then E° for the half-reaction. The result is the same.

20.115 (a)

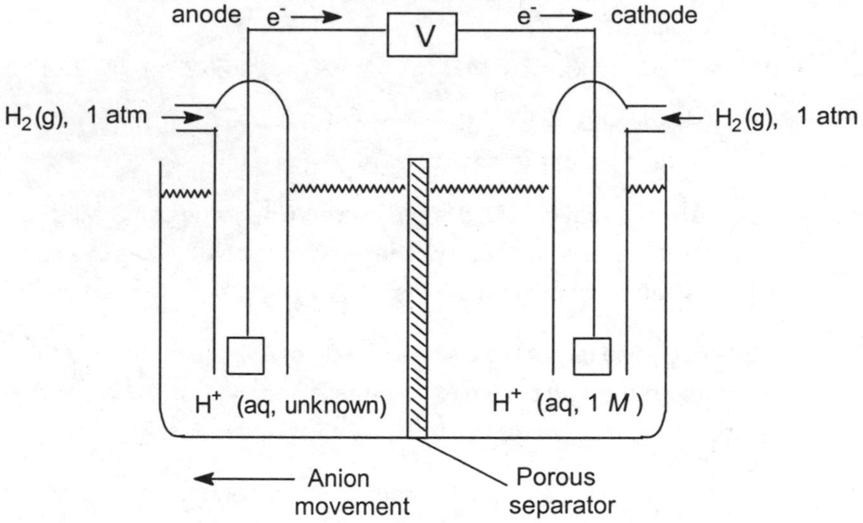

(b) $2H^+(aq, 1\ M) + 2e^- \rightarrow H_2(g)$ $\quad E^\circ_{red} = 0$

$H_2(g) \rightarrow 2H^+(aq, 1\ M) + 2e^-$ $\quad E^\circ_{red} = 0$

$2H^+(aq, 1\ M) + H_2(g) \rightarrow 2H^+(aq, 1\ M) + H_2(g)$ $\quad E^\circ = 0$

(c) At standard conditions, $[H^+] = 1\ M$, pH = 0

(d) $$E = E^\circ - \frac{0.0592}{2}\log\frac{[H^+(\text{unknown})]^2 P_{H_2}}{[H^+(1\ M)]^2 P_{H_2}}$$

$$E = 0 - \frac{0.0592}{2}\log[H^+]^2 = \frac{0.0592}{2} \times 2(-\log[H^+]) = 0.0592(\text{pH}) = 0.0592(5.0)$$

$$= 0.30\text{ V}$$

(e) E_{cell} changes 0.0592(0.01) = 0.000592 = 0.0006 V for each 0.01 pH unit. The voltmeter would have to be precise to at least 0.001 V to detect a charge of 0.01 pH units.

20.117 The two half-reactions in the electrolysis of $H_2O(l)$ are:

$$2[2H_2O(l) + 2e^- \rightarrow H_2(g) + 2OH^-]$$

$$2H_2O(l) \rightarrow O_2(g) + 4H^+ + 4e^-$$

$$2H_2O(l) \rightarrow 2H_2(g) + O_2(g)$$

4 mol e^-/2 mol $H_2(g)$ or 2 mol e^-/mol $H_2(g)$

Using partial pressures and the ideal-gas law, calculate the mol $H_2(g)$ produced, and the current required to do so.

$P_T = P_{H_2} + P_{H_2O}$. From Appendix B, P_{H_2O} at 25.5°C is approximately 24.5 torr.

P_{H_2} = 768 torr - 24.5 torr = 743.5 = 744 torr

$$n = PV/RT = \frac{(743.5/760)\text{ atm} \times 0.0123\text{ L}}{298.5\text{ K} \times 0.08206\text{ L}\bullet\text{atm/mol}\bullet\text{K}} = 4.912 \times 10^{-4} = 4.91 \times 10^{-4}\text{ mol } H_2$$

$$4.912 \times 10^{-4}\text{ mol } H_2 \times \frac{2\text{ mol e}^-}{\text{mol } H_2} \times \frac{96{,}500\text{ C}}{1\text{ mol e}^-} \times \frac{1\text{ amp}\bullet\text{s}}{1\text{ C}} \times \frac{1\text{ min}}{60\text{ s}} \times \frac{1}{2.00\text{ min}}$$

$$= 0.790\text{ amp}$$

21 Nuclear Chemistry

Radioactivity

21.2 p = protons, n = neutrons, e = electrons; number of protons = atomic number; number of neutrons = mass number - atomic number

(a) $^{126}_{55}Cs$: 55p, 71n (b) ^{119}Sn: 50p, 69n (c) ^{141}Ba: 56p, 85n

21.4 (a) $^{1}_{0}n$ (b) $^{0}_{-1}e$ or $^{0}_{-1}\beta$ (c) $^{4}_{2}He$ or $^{4}_{2}\alpha$

21.6 (a) $^{141}_{60}Nd + ^{0}_{-1}e$ (orbital electron) $\rightarrow ^{141}_{59}Pr$ (b) $^{201}_{79}Au \rightarrow ^{201}_{80}Hg + ^{0}_{-1}\beta$

(c) $^{81}_{34}Se \rightarrow ^{81}_{35}Br + ^{0}_{-1}\beta$ (d) $^{83}_{38}Sr \rightarrow ^{83}_{37}Rb + ^{0}_{1}e$

21.8 (a) $^{24}_{11}Na \rightarrow ^{24}_{12}Mg + ^{0}_{-1}e$; a β particle is produced

(b) $^{188}_{80}Hg \rightarrow ^{188}_{79}Au + ^{0}_{1}e$; a positron is produced

(c) $^{122}_{53}I \rightarrow ^{122}_{54}Xe + ^{0}_{-1}e$; a β particle is produced

(d) $^{242}_{94}Pu \rightarrow ^{238}_{92}U + ^{4}_{2}He$; an α particle is produced

21.10 This decay series represents a change of (232-208 =) 24 mass units. Since only alpha emissions change the nuclear mass, and each changes the mass by four, there must be a total of 6 α emissions. Each alpha emission causes a decrease of two in atomic number. Therefore, the 6 alpha emissions, by themselves, would cause a decrease in atomic number of 12. The series as a whole involves a decrease of 8 in atomic number. Thus, there must be a total of 4 β emissions, each of which increases atomic number by one. Overall, there are 6 α emissions and 4 β emissions.

Nuclear Stability

21.12 (a) $^{66}_{32}Ge$ - low neutron/proton ratio, positron emission

(b) $^{105}_{45}Rh$ - high neutron/proton ratio, beta emission

(c) $^{137}_{53}I$ - high neutron/proton ratio, beta emission

(d) $^{133}_{58}Ce$ - low neutron/proton ratio, positron emission

21.14 (a) Yes - within the belt of stability

(b) Close - With 51 neutrons and 43 protons, this nuclide is close to the lower edge of the stability belt. The neutron/proton ratio is somewhat low; if decay occurs, it would be positron emission or orbital electron capture.

(c) Close - slightly low neutron/proton ratio; if decay occurs, it would be positron emission or orbital electron capture.

(d) Yes - within the belt of stability

21.16 Use criteria listed in Table 21.3.

(a) $^{112}_{48}Cd$ even, even more abundant

(b) $^{27}_{13}Al$ odd proton, even neutron more abundant

(c) $^{106}_{46}Pd$ even, even more abundant

(d) $^{128}_{54}Xe$ even proton, even neutron much more abundant than odd proton; odd neutron

21.18 $^{112}_{50}Sn$ has a magic number of protons and even numbers of protons and neutrons, good indications of nuclear stability. $^{112}_{49}In$ has no magic numbers and odd numbers of protons and neutrons, indicators of nuclear instability or radioactivity.

21.20 The criterion employed in judging whether the nucleus is likely to be radioactive is the position of the nucleus on the plot shown in Figure 21.2. If the neutron/proton ratio is too high or low, or if the atomic number exceeds 83, the nucleus will be radioactive. Radioactive: (b) low neutron/proton ratio; (e) high atomic number; stable: (a), (c) and (d).

Nuclear Transmutations

21.22 A major difference is that the charge on the nitrogen nucleus, +7, is much smaller than on the gold nucleus, +79. Thus, the alpha particle could more easily penetrate the coulomb barrier (that is, the repulsive energy barrier due to like charges) to make contact with the nitrogen nucleus than the gold nucleus. Rutherford used alpha particles that were being emitted from some radioactive source. He did not have access to machines that can accelerate particles to very high energy. It would be necessary to do just that to observe reaction of an alpha particle with a gold nucleus.

21.24 (a) $^{252}_{98}Cf + ^{10}_{5}B \rightarrow 3\,^{1}_{0}n + ^{259}_{103}Lr$ (b) $^{2}_{1}H + ^{3}_{2}He \rightarrow ^{4}_{2}He + ^{1}_{1}H$

(c) $^{1}_{1}H + ^{11}_{5}B \rightarrow 3\,^{4}_{2}He$ (d) $^{122}_{53}I \rightarrow ^{122}_{54}Xe + ^{0}_{-1}e$

(e) $^{59}_{26}Fe \rightarrow ^{0}_{-1}e + ^{59}_{27}Co$

21.26 (a) $^{238}_{92}U + ^{4}_{2}H \rightarrow ^{241}_{94}Pu + ^{1}_{0}n$ (b) $^{14}_{7}N + ^{4}_{2}He \rightarrow ^{17}_{8}O + ^{1}_{1}H$

(c) $^{59}_{26}Fe + ^{4}_{2}He \rightarrow ^{63}_{29}Cu + ^{0}_{-1}e$

Rates of Radioactive Decay

21.28 The suggestion is not reasonable. The energies of nuclear states are very large relative to ordinary temperatures. Thus, merely changing the temperature by less than 100 K would not be expected to significantly affect the behavior of nuclei with regard to nuclear decay rates.

21.30 Calculate the decay constant, k, and then $t_{1/2}$.

$$k = \frac{-1}{t}\ln\frac{N_t}{N_o} = \frac{-1}{5.2\text{ min}}\ln\frac{0.250\text{ g}}{1.000\text{ g}} = 0.2666 = 0.27\text{ min}^{-1}$$

Using Equation 21.20, $t_{1/2} = 0.693/k = 0.693/0.0.2666\text{ min}^{-1} = 2.599 = 2.6\text{ min}$

21.32 Using Equation 21.19, $k = \frac{-1}{t}\ln\frac{N_t}{N_o} = \frac{-1}{120\text{ hr}} \times \ln\frac{457}{2310} = 0.01350 = 0.0135\text{ hr}^{-1}$

Using Equation 21.20, $t_{1/2} = 0.693/k = 0.693/(0.01350\text{ hr}^{-1}) = 51.3\text{ hr}$

21.34 $k = 0.693 / t_{1/2} = 0.693/5.26\text{ yr} = 0.1317 = 0.132\text{ yr}^{-1}$; $N_t/N_o = 0.75$

$$t = \frac{-1}{k}\ln\frac{N_t}{N_o} = -(1/0.1317\text{ yr}^{-1})\ln(0.75) = 2.18\text{ yr}$$

2.18 yr = 26.2 mo = 797 d. The source will have to be replaced sometime in the fall of 2002, probably in October.

21.36 (a) Proceeding as in Solution 21.35, calculate k in s^{-1}.

$$5.26\text{ yr} \times \frac{365\text{ d}}{1\text{ yr}} \times \frac{24\text{ hr}}{1\text{ d}} \times \frac{3600\text{ sec}}{1\text{ hr}} = 1.659 \times 10^8 = 1.66 \times 10^8\text{ s}$$

$$k = \frac{0.693}{t_{1/2}} = \frac{0.693}{1.659 \times 10^8} = 4.178 \times 10^{-9} = 4.18 \times 10^{-9}\text{ s}^{-1}$$

$$\ln\frac{N_t}{N_o} = -kt = -(4.178 \times 10^{-9}\text{ s}^{-1})(45.5\text{ s}) = -1.901 \times 10^{-7} = -1.90 \times 10^{-7}$$

$$\frac{N_t}{N_o} = e^{-1.90 \times 10^{-7}} = (1.000 - 1.90 \times 10^{-7});\ N_t = 2.44 \times 10^{-3}\text{ g}\,(1.000 - 1.90 \times 10^{-7})$$

The amount that decays is $N_o - N_t$:

$$2.44 \times 10^{-3}\text{ g} - [2.44 \times 10^{-3}\text{ g}\ (1.000 - 1.90 \times 10^{-7})] = 2.44 \times 10^{-3}\text{ g}\ (1.90 \times 10^{-7})$$

$$= 4.638 \times 10^{-10} = 4.64 \times 10^{-10}\text{ g Co}$$

$$N_o - N_t = 4.638 \times 10^{-10}\text{ g Co} \times \frac{1\text{ mol Co}}{60\text{ g Co}} \times \frac{6.022 \times 10^{23}\text{ Co atoms}}{1\text{ mol Co}} \times \frac{1\ \beta}{1\text{ Co atom}}$$

$$= 4.655 \times 10^{12} = 4.66 \times 10^{12}\ \beta \text{ particles emitted in 45.5 seconds}$$

(b) $$\frac{4.655 \times 10^{12}\text{ dis}}{45.5\text{ s}} \times \frac{1\text{ Bq}}{1\text{ dis/s}} = 1.02 \times 10^{11}\text{ Bq}$$

21.38 Calculate k in yr^{-1} and solve Equation 21.19 for t. $N_o = 15.2/\text{min/g}$, $N_t = 8.9/\text{min/g}$

$k = 0.693/t_{1/2} = 0.693/5715\text{ yr} = 1.213 \times 10^{-4} = 1.21 \times 10^{-4}\text{ yr}^{-1}$

$$t = \frac{-1}{k}\ln\frac{N_t}{N_o} = \frac{-1}{1.213 \times 10^{-4}\text{ yr}^{-1}}\ln\frac{8.9}{15.2} = 4.414 \times 10^3 = 4.4 \times 10^3\text{ yr}$$

21.40 $k = 0.693/1.27 \times 10^9\text{ yr} = 5.457 \times 10^{-10} = 5.46 \times 10^{-10}\text{ yr}^{-1}$

If the mass of ^{40}Ar is 3.6 times that of ^{40}K, then the original mass of ^{40}K must have been 3.6 + 1 = 4.6 times that now present.

$$t = \frac{-1}{5.457 \times 10^{-10}\text{ yr}^{-1}} \times \ln\frac{1}{(4.6)} = 2.8 \times 10^9\text{ yr}$$

Energy Changes

21.42 $$\Delta E = c^2\Delta m = (3.0 \times 10^8\text{ m/s})^2 \times 0.1\text{ mg} \times \frac{1\text{ g}}{1000\text{ mg}} \times \frac{1\text{ kg}}{1000\text{ g}} \times \frac{1\text{ kJ}}{1000\text{ J}} = 9 \times 10^6\text{ kJ}$$

21.44 Δm = mass of individual protons and neutrons - mass of nucleus

$$\Delta m = 10(1.0072765\text{ amu}) + 11(1.0086649\text{ amu}) - 20.98846\text{ amu} = 0.1796189$$

$$= 0.17962\text{ amu}$$

$$\Delta E = (2.9979246 \times 10^8\text{ m/s})^2 \times 0.1796189\text{ amu} \times \frac{1\text{ g}}{6.0221421 \times 10^{23}\text{ amu}} \times \frac{1\text{ kg}}{1000\text{ g}}$$

$$= 2.680664 \times 10^{-11} = 2.6807 \times 10^{-11}\text{ J / }^{31}\text{P nucleus required}$$

$$2.680664 \times 10^{-11}\frac{\text{J}}{\text{nucleus}} \times \frac{6.0221421 \times 10^{23}\text{ nuclei}}{\text{mol}}$$

$$= 1.6143 \times 10^{13}\text{ J/mol }^{31}\text{P binding energy}$$

21.46 In each case, calculate the mass defect, total nuclear binding energy and then binding energy per nucleon.

(a) $\Delta m = 7(1.0072765) + 7(1.0086649) - 13.999234 = 0.1123558 = 0.112356$ amu

$$\Delta E = 0.1123558 \text{ amu} \times \frac{1 \text{ g}}{6.0221421 \times 10^{23} \text{ amu}} \times \frac{1 \text{ kg}}{1000 \text{ g}} \times \frac{8.987551 \times 10^{16} \text{ m}^2}{\text{s}^2}$$

$= 1.676817 \times 10^{-11} = 1.67682 \times 10^{-11}$ J

binding energy/nucleon = 1.676817×10^{-11} J / 14 = 1.19773×10^{-12} J/nucleon

(b) $\Delta m = 22(1.0072765) + 26(1.0086649) - 47.935878 = 0.4494924 = 0.449492$ amu

$$\Delta E = 0.4494924 \text{ amu} \times \frac{1 \text{ g}}{6.0221421 \times 10^{23} \text{ amu}} \times \frac{1 \text{ kg}}{1000 \text{ g}} \times \frac{8.987551 \times 10^{16} \text{ m}^2}{\text{s}^2}$$

$= 6.708304 \times 10^{-11} = 6.70830 \times 10^{-11}$ J

binding energy/nucleon = 6.708304×10^{-11} J / 48 = 1.39756×10^{-12} J/nucleon

(c) Calculate the nuclear mass by subtracting the electron mass from the atomic mass.

$200.970277 - 80(5.485799 \times 10^{-4} \text{ amu}) = 200.926391$ amu

$\Delta m = 80(1.0072765) + 121(1.0086649) - 200.926391 = 1.7041819 = 1.704182$ amu

$$\Delta E = 1.7041819 \text{ amu} \times \frac{1 \text{ g}}{6.0221421 \times 10^{23} \text{ amu}} \times \frac{1 \text{ kg}}{1000 \text{ g}} \times \frac{8.987551 \times 10^{16} \text{ m}^2}{\text{s}^2}$$

$= 2.543351 \times 10^{-10}$ J

binding energy/nucleon = 2.543351×10^{-10} J / 201 = 1.265348×10^{-12} J/nucleon

21.48 (a) $\Delta m = 4.00260 + 1.0086649 - 3.01605 - 2.01410 = -0.0188851 = -0.01889$ amu

$$\Delta E = 0.0188851 \text{ amu} \times \frac{1 \text{ g}}{1 \text{ amu}} \times \frac{1 \text{ kg}}{10^3 \text{ g}} \times (2.99792458 \times 10^8 \text{ m/sec})^2$$

$= 1.697 \times 10^{12}$ J/mol

(b) $\Delta m = 3.01603 + 1.0086649 - 2(2.01410) = -3.5051 \times 10^{-3} = -3.51 \times 10^{-3}$ amu

$\Delta E = 3.15 \times 10^{11}$ J/mol

(c) $\Delta m = 4.00260 + 1.00782 - 3.01603 - 2.01410 = -1.971 \times 10^{-2}$ amu

$\Delta E = 1.771 \times 10^{12}$ J/mol

21.50 In a fission reactor absorption of neutrons causes a single heavy nucleus to undergo fission, producing two medium mass nuclei. These are seen in Figure 21.13 to have a larger total mass defect than the starting single heavier nucleus, so energy is released.

Effects and Uses of Radioisotopes

21.52 (a) Add ^{36}Cl to water as a chloride salt. Then dissolve ordinary CCl_3COOH. After a time, distill the volatile materials away from the salt; CCl_3COOH is volatile, and will distill with water. Count radioactivity in the volatile material. If chlorine exchange has occurred, there will be radioactivity.

(b) Prepare a saturated solution of $BaCl_2$ containing a small amount of solid $BaCl_2$. Add to this solution solid $BaCl_2$ containing ^{36}Cl. If the solid-solution equilibrium is dynamic, some of the ^{36}Cl in the solid will find itself in solution as chloride ion. After allowing some time for equilibrium to become established, filter the solution, measure radioactivity in the solution that is separated from the solid. If there were no dynamic equilibrium, the $^{36}Cl^-$ would remain in the added solid, since the solution is already saturated before the addition of more solid.

(c) Utilize ^{36}Cl in soils of various pH values; grow plants for a given period of time. Remove plants, and directly measure radioactivity in samples from stems, leaves and so forth, or reduce the volume of plant sample by some form of digestion and evaporation of solution to give a dry residue that can be counted.

21.54 (a) In a *chain reaction*, one neutron initiates a nuclear transformation that produces more than one neutron. The product neutrons initiate more transformations, so that the reaction is self-sustaining.

(b) *Critical mass* is the mass of fissionable material required to sustain a chain reaction so that only one product neutron is effective at initiating a new transformation.

21.56 (a) ${}^{2}_{1}H + {}^{2}_{1}H \rightarrow {}^{3}_{2}He + {}^{1}_{0}n$ (b) ${}^{233}_{92}U + {}^{1}_{0}n \rightarrow {}^{133}_{51}Sb + {}^{98}_{41}Nb + 3\,{}^{1}_{0}n$

21.58 (a) If the spent fuel rods are more radioactive than the original rods, the products of fission must lie outside the belt of stability and be radioactive themselves.

(b) The heavy ($Z > 83$) nucleus has a high neutron/proton ratio. The lighter radioactive fission products, (e.g., barium-142 and krypton-91) also have high neutron/proton ratios, since only 2 or 3 free neutrons are produced during fission. The preferred decay mode to reduce the neutron/proton ratio is β decay, which has the effect of converting a neutron into a proton. Both barium-142 (86 n, 56 p) and krypton-91 (55 n, 36 p) undergo β decay.

21.60

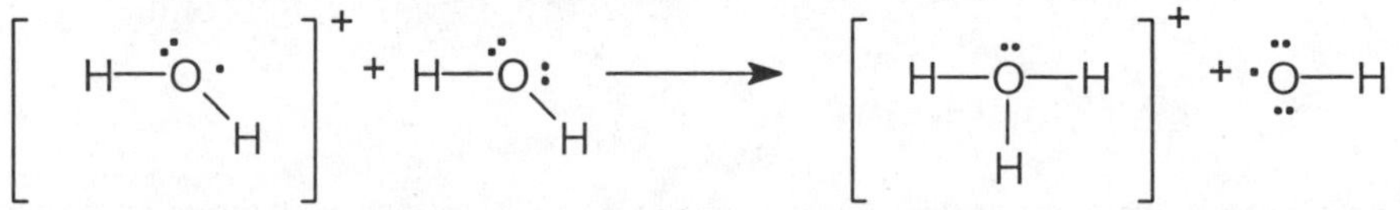

H_2O^+ is a free radical because it contains seven valence electrons. Around the central O atom there are two bonding and one nonbonding electron pairs and a single unpaired electron (3(2) + 1 = 7 valence electrons).

21.62 (a) $1\ \text{Ci} = 3.7 \times 10^{10}$ dis/s; $1\ \text{Bq} = 1$ dis/s

$$21\ \text{mCi} \times \frac{1\ \text{Ci}}{1000\ \text{mCi}} \times 3.7 \times 10^{10}\ \text{dis/s} = 7.77 \times 10^{8} = 7.8 \times 10^{8}\ \text{dis/s} = 7.8 \times 10^{8}\ \text{Bq}$$

(b) $1\ \text{Gy} = 1\ \text{J/kg}$; $1\ \text{Gy} = 100\ \text{rad}$

$$7.77 \times 10^{8}\ \text{dis/s} \times 116\ \text{s} \times 0.065 \times \frac{8.75 \times 10^{-14}\ \text{J}}{\text{dis}} \times \frac{1}{65\ \text{kg}} = 7.887 \times 10^{-6}$$

$$= 7.9 \times 10^{-6}\ \text{J/kg}$$

$$7.9 \times 10^{-6}\ \text{J/kg} \times \frac{1\ \text{Gy}}{1\ \text{J/kg}} = 7.9 \times 10^{-6}\ \text{Gy};\ 7.9 \times 10^{-6}\ \text{Gy} \times \frac{100\ \text{rad}}{1\ \text{Gy}} = 7.9 \times 10^{-4}\ \text{rad}$$

(c) rem = rad (RBE); Sv = Gy (RBE)

$$7.9 \times 10^{-4}\ \text{rad}\ (1.0) = 7.9 \times 10^{-4}\ \text{rem} \times \frac{1000\ \text{mrem}}{1\ \text{rem}} = 0.79\ \text{mrem}$$

$$7.9 \times 10^{-6}\ \text{Gy}\ (1.0) = 7.9 \times 10^{-6}\ \text{Sv}$$

(d) From Figure 21.23, the average annual background radiation is 360 mrem, or about 1 mrem/day. This 0.79 mrem exposure is less than the average background radiation for a day.

Additional Exercises

21.64 (a) $^{1}_{0}\text{n} \rightarrow {}^{1}_{1}\text{p} + {}^{0}_{-1}\text{e}$ (or $^{0}_{-1}\beta$)

The other product of neutron decay is a β particle (with the mass and charge of an electron).

(b) Neutrons in atomic nuclei do not decay at this rate because they are stabilized by the strong forces among subatomic particles in a nucleus. Evidence for strong forces in the nucleus includes nuclear binding energies and the coexistence of like-charged protons in the very small volume of the nucleus.

21.66 (a) $^{36}_{17}\text{Cl} \rightarrow {}^{36}_{18}\text{Ar} + {}^{0}_{-1}\text{e}$

(b) According to Table 21.3, nuclei with even numbers of both protons and neutrons, or an even number of one kind of nucleon, are more stable. ^{35}Cl and ^{37}Cl both have an odd number of protons **but** an even number of neutrons. ^{36}Cl has an odd number of protons and neutrons (17 p, 19 n), so it is less stable than the other two isotopes. Also, ^{37}Cl has 20 neutrons, a nuclear closed shell.

21.67 (a) $^{6}_{3}\text{Li} + {}^{56}_{28}\text{Ni} \rightarrow {}^{62}_{31}\text{Ga}$

(b) $^{40}_{20}\text{Ca} + {}^{248}_{96}\text{Cm} \rightarrow {}^{288}_{116}\text{X}$

(c) $^{88}_{38}\text{Sr} + {}^{84}_{36}\text{Kr} \rightarrow {}^{116}_{46}\text{Pd} + {}^{56}_{28}\text{Ni}$

(d) $^{40}_{20}Ca + ^{238}_{92}U \rightarrow ^{70}_{30}Zn + 4\ ^{1}_{0}n + 2\ ^{102}_{41}Nb$

21.69

Time (hr)	N_t (dis/min)	ln N_t
0	180	5.193
2.5	130	4.868
5.0	104	4.644
7.5	77	4.34
10.0	59	4.08
12.5	46	3.83
17.5	24	3.18

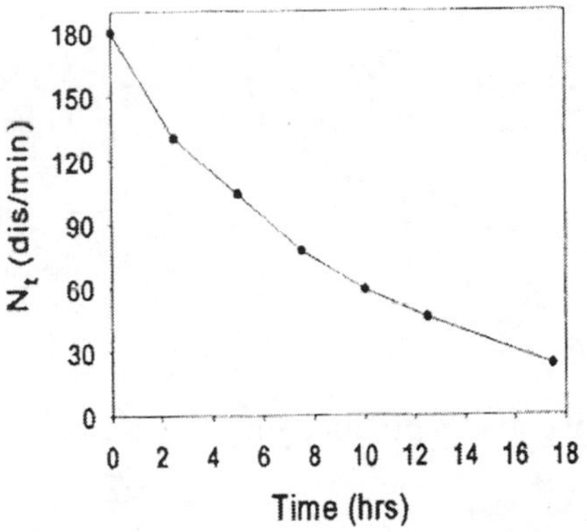

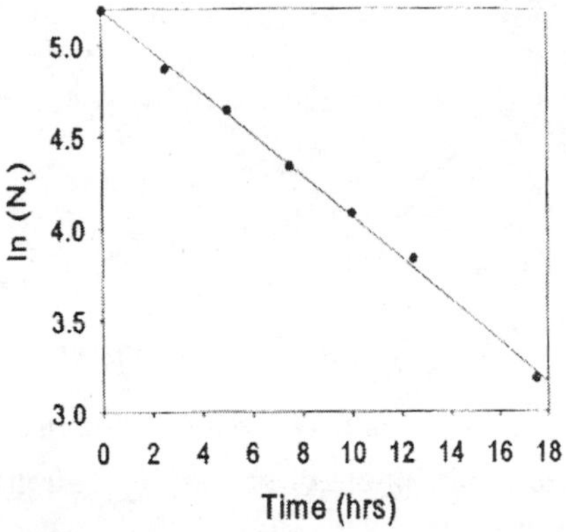

The plot on the left is a graph of activity (disintegrations per minute) vs. time. Choose $t_{1/2}$ at the time where $N_t = 1/2\ N_o = 90$ dis/min. $t_{1/2} \approx 6.0$ hr.

Rearrange Equation 21.19 to obtain the linear relationship shown on the right.

$\ln(N_t\ /\ N_o) = -kt$; $\ln N_t - \ln N_o = -kt$; $\ln N_t = -kt + \ln N_o$

The slope of this line = $-k = -0.11$; $t_{1/2} = 0.693/0.11 = 6.3$ hr.

21.71 First calculate k in s^{-1}

$$k = \frac{0.693}{2.4 \times 10^4\ yr} \times \frac{1\ yr}{365 \times 24 \times 3600\ s} = 9.16 \times 10^{-13} = 9.2 \times 10^{-13}\ s^{-1}$$

Now calculate N:

$$N = 0.500\ g\ Pu \times \frac{1\ mol\ Pu}{239\ g\ Pu} \times \frac{6.022 \times 10^{23}\ Pu\ atoms}{1\ mol\ Pu} = 1.26 \times 10^{21} = 1.3 \times 10^{21}\ Pu\ atoms$$

rate = $(9.16 \times 10^{-13}\ s^{-1})(1.26 \times 10^{21}$ Pu atoms$) = 1.15 \times 10^9 = 1.2 \times 10^9$ dis/s

21.72 The C–OH bond of the acid and the O–H bond of the alcohol break in this reaction. Initially, ^{18}O is present in the C–^{18}OH group of the alcohol. In order for ^{18}O to end up in the ester, the ^{18}O–H bond of the alcohol must break. This requires that the C–OH bond in the acid also breaks. The unlabeled O from the acid ends up in the H_2O product.

21.74 First, calculate k in s^{-1}

$$k = \frac{0.693}{12.3\text{ yr}} \times \frac{1\text{ yr}}{365\text{ d}} \times \frac{1\text{ d}}{24\text{ hr}} \times \frac{1\text{ hr}}{3600\text{ sec}} = 1.7866 \times 10^{-9} = 1.787 \times 10^{-9}\ s^{-1}$$

From Equation 21.18, $1.50 \times 10^3\ s^{-1} = (1.7866 \times 10^{-9}\ s^{-1})(N)$;

$N = 8.396 \times 10^{11} = 8.40 \times 10^{11}$ In 26.0 g of water, there are

$$26.0\text{ g } H_2O \times \frac{1\text{ mol } H_2O}{18.02\text{ g } H_2O} \times \frac{6.022 \times 10^{23}\ H_2O}{1\text{ mol } H_2O} \times \frac{2\text{ H}}{1\ H_2O} = 1.738 \times 10^{24}$$

$$= 1.74 \times 10^{24}\text{ H atoms}$$

The mole fraction of ^3_1H atoms in the sample is thus

$8.396 \times 10^{11}/1.738 \times 10^{24} = 4.831 \times 10^{-13} = 4.83 \times 10^{-13}$

21.76 (a) $\Delta m = \Delta E/c^2$; $\Delta m = \frac{3.9 \times 10^{26}\text{ J/s}}{(3.00 \times 10^8\text{ m/s})^2} \times \frac{1\text{ kg}\bullet\text{m}^2/\text{s}^2}{1\text{ J}} = 4.3 \times 10^9\text{ kg /s}$

The rate of mass loss is 4.3×10^9 kg/s.

(b) The mass loss arises from fusion reactions that produce more stable nuclei from less stable ones, e.g. Equations 21.26-21.29.

21.78 $2 \times 10^{-12}\text{ curies} \times \frac{3.7 \times 10^{10}\text{ dis/s}}{1\text{ curie}} = 7.4 \times 10^{-2} = 7 \times 10^{-2}$ dis/s

$$\frac{7.4 \times 10^{-2}\text{ dis/s}}{75\text{ kg}} \times \frac{8 \times 10^{-13}\text{ J}}{\text{dis}} \times \frac{1\text{ rad}}{1 \times 10^{-2}\text{ J/g}} \times \frac{3600\text{ s}}{\text{hr}} \times \frac{24\text{ hr}}{1\text{ d}}$$

$$\times \frac{365\text{ d}}{1\text{ yr}} = 2.49 \times 10^{-6} = 2 \times 10^{-6}\text{ rad/yr}$$

Recall that there are 10 rem/rad for alpha particles.

$$\frac{2.49 \times 10^{-6}\text{ rad}}{1\text{ yr}} \times \frac{10\text{ rem}}{1\text{ rad}} = 2.49 \times 10^{-5} = 2 \times 10^{-5}\text{ rem/yr}$$

Integrative Exercises

21.80 Calculate the amount of energy produced by the nuclear fusion reaction, the enthalpy of combustion, ΔH° , of C_3H_8, and then the mass of C_3H_8 required.

Δm for the reaction $4\ ^1_1H \rightarrow\ ^4_2He + 2\ ^0_1e$ is 4(1.00782) - 4.00260 amu - 2(5.4858×10^{-4} amu)

= 0.027583 = 0.02758 amu

$$\Delta E = \Delta mc^2 = 0.027583 \text{ amu} \times \frac{1 \text{ g}}{6.02214 \times 10^{23} \text{ amu}} \times \frac{1 \text{ kg}}{1000 \text{ g}} \times (2.9979246 \times 10^8 \text{ m/s})^2$$

$$= 4.11654 \times 10^{-12} = 4.117 \times 10^{-12} \text{ J / 4 } ^1\text{H nuclei}$$

$$1.0 \text{ g } ^1\text{H} \times \frac{1\ ^1\text{H nucleus}}{1.00782 \text{ amu}} \times \frac{6.02214 \times 10^{23} \text{ amu}}{\text{g}} \times \frac{4.11654 \times 10^{-12} \text{ J}}{4\ ^1\text{H nuclei}}$$

$= 6.1495 \times 10^{11}$ J $= 6.1 \times 10^8$ kJ produced by the fusion of 1.0 g ^{1}H.

$C_3H_8(g) + 5O_2(g) \rightarrow 3CO_2(g) + 4H_2O(g)$

$\Delta H° = 3(-393.5 \text{ kJ}) + 4(-241.82 \text{ kJ}) - (-103.85) - (0) = -2043.9 \text{ kJ}$

$$6.1495 \times 10^8 \text{ kJ} \times \frac{1 \text{ mol } C_3H_8(g)}{2043.9 \text{ kJ}} \times \frac{44.094 \text{ g } C_3H_8}{\text{mol } C_3H_8} = 1.327 \times 10^7 \text{ g} = 1.3 \times 10^4 \text{ kg } C_3H_8$$

13,000 kg $C_3H_8(g)$ would have to be burned to produce the same amount of energy as fusion of 1.0 g ^{1}H.

21.82 Calculate N_t in dis/min/g C from 1.5×10^{-2} dis/0.788 g $CaCO_3$. N_o = 15.3 dis/min/g C. Calculate k from $t_{1/2}$, calculate t from $\ln (N_t / N_o) = -kt$.

$C(s) + O_2(g) \rightarrow CO_2(g) + Ca(OH_2)(aq) \rightarrow CaCO_3(s) + H_2O(l)$

1 C atom $\rightarrow$ 1 $CaCO_3$ molecule

$$\frac{1.5 \times 10^{-2} \text{ Bq}}{0.788 \text{ g } CaCO_3} \times \frac{1 \text{ dis/s}}{1 \text{ Bq}} \times \frac{60 \text{ s}}{1 \text{ min}} \times \frac{100.1 \text{ g } CaCO_3}{12.01 \text{ g C}} = 9.52 = 9.5 \text{ dis/min/g C}$$

$k = 0.693/t_{1/2} = 0.693/5.715 \times 10^3 \text{ yr} = 1.213 \times 10^{-4} = 1.21 \times 10^{-4} \text{ yr}^{-1}$

$$t = -\frac{1}{k} \ln \frac{N_t}{N_o} = \frac{-1}{1.213 \times 10^{-4} \text{ yr}^{-1}} \ln \frac{9.52 \text{ dis/min/g C}}{15.3 \text{ dis/min/g C}} = 3.91 \times 10^3 \text{ yr}$$

21.83 Calculate the energy required to ionize one H_2O molecule, and then the wavelength associated with this energy.

$$\frac{1216 \text{ kJ}}{\text{mol } H_2O} \times \frac{1000 \text{ J}}{1 \text{ kJ}} \times \frac{1 \text{ mol } H_2O}{6.02214 \times 10^{23} \text{ molecules}} = 2.0192 \times 10^{-18}$$

$$= 2.019 \times 10^{-18} \text{ J/molecule}$$

$$\lambda = hc/E = \frac{6.626 \times 10^{-34} \text{ J} \cdot \text{s} \times 2.998 \times 10^8 \text{ m/s}}{2.0192 \times 10^{-18} \text{ J}} = 9.838 \times 10^{-8} \text{ m} = 98.38 \text{ nm}$$

21.84 Determine the wavelengths of the photons by first calculating the energy equivalent of the mass of an electron or positron. (Since **two** photons are formed by annihilation of **two** particles of equal mass, we need to calculate the energy equivalent of just one particle.) The mass of an electron is 9.109×10^{-31} kg.

$\Delta E = (9.109 \times 10^{-31}\ kg) \times (2.998 \times 10^8\ m/s)^2 = 8.187 \times 10^{-14}\ J$

Also, $\Delta E = h\nu$; $\Delta E = hc/\lambda$; $\lambda = hc/\Delta E$

$$\lambda = \frac{(6.626 \times 10^{-34}\ J \cdot s)(2.998 \times 10^8\ m/s)}{8.187 \times 10^{-14}\ J} = 2.426 \times 10^{-12}\ m = 2.426 \times 10^{-3}\ nm$$

This is a very short wavelength indeed; it lies at the short wavelength end of the range of observed gamma ray wavelengths (see Figure 6.4).

21.85 (a) $Ba(NO_3)_2(aq) + Na_2SO_4(aq) \rightarrow BaSO_4(s) + 2NaNO_3(aq)$

(b) 1.25 mmol Ba^{2+} + 1.25 mmol SO_4^{2-} → 1.25 mmol $BaSO_4$

Neither reactant is in excess, so the activity of the filtrate is due entirely to $[SO_4^{2-}]$ from dissociation of $BaSO_4(s)$. Calculate $[SO_4^{2-}]$ in the filtrate by comparing the activity of the filtrate to the activity of the reactant.

$$\frac{0.050\ M\ SO_4^{2-}}{1.22 \times 10^6\ Bq/mL} = \frac{x\ M\ \text{filtrate}}{250\ Bq/mL}$$

$[SO_4^{2-}]$ in the filtrate $= 1.0246 \times 10^{-5} = 1.0 \times 10^{-5}\ M$

$K_{sp} = [Ba^{2+}][SO_4^{2-}]$; $[SO_4^{2-}] = [Ba^{2+}]$

$K_{sp} = (1.0246 \times 10^{-5})^2 = 1.0498 \times 10^{-10} = 1.0 \times 10^{-10}$

22 Chemistry of the Nonmetals

Periodic Trends and Chemical Reactions

22.2 Metals: (a) Re, (d) Zr, (f) Ga nonmetals: (c) Ar metalloid: (b) As, (e) Te

22.4 (a) O (b) Br (c) Ba (d) O (e) Co

22.6 (a) Nitrogen is a highly electronegative element. In HNO_3 it is in its highest oxidation state, +5, and thus is more readily reduced than phosphorus, which forms stable P-O bonds.

(b) The difference between the third row element and the second lies in the smaller size of C as compared with Si, and the fact that Si has 3d orbitals available to form an sp^3d^2 hybrid set that can accommodate more than an octet of electrons.

(c) Two of the carbon compounds, C_2H_4 and C_2H_2, contain C-C π bonds. Si does not readily form π bonds (to itself or other atoms), so Si_2H_4 and Si_2H_2 are not known as stable compounds.

22.8 (a) $NaOCH_3(s) + H_2O(l) \rightarrow NaOH(aq) + CH_3OH(aq)$

(b) $CuO(s) + 2HNO_3(aq) \rightarrow Cu(NO_3)_2(aq) + H_2O(l)$

(c) $WO_3(s) + 3H_2(g) \rightarrow W(s) + 3H_2O(g)$

(d) $4NH_2OH(l) + O_2(g) \rightarrow 6H_2O(l) + 2N_2(g)$

(e) $Al_4C_3(s) + 12H_2O(l) \rightarrow 4Al(OH)_3(s) + 3CH_4(g)$

Hydrogen, the Noble Gases, and the Halogens

22.10 Tritium is radioactive. ${}^3_1H \rightarrow {}^3_2He + {}^{0}_{-1}e$

22.12 Hydrogen does not have a strictly comparable electronic arrangement. There are no closed shells of electrons underlying the valence shell. When hydrogen completes its valence shell it has only two electrons therein, a characteristic it shares only with He.

22.14 (a) Electrolysis of brine; reaction of carbon with steam; reaction of methane with steam; byproduct in petroleum refining

(b) Synthesis of ammonia; synthesis of methanol; reducing agent; hydrogenation of unsaturated vegetable oils

22.16 (a) $2Al(s) + 6H^+(aq) \rightarrow 2Al^{3+}(aq) + 3H_2(g)$

(b) $Mg(s) + H_2O(g) \rightarrow MgO(s) + H_2(g)$

(c) $MnO_2(s) + H_2(g) \rightarrow MnO(s) + H_2O(g)$

(d) $CaH_2(s) + 2H_2O(l) \rightarrow Ca(OH)_2(aq) + 2H_2(g)$

22.18 (a) Ionic (metal hydride) (b) molecular (nonmetal hydride)

(c) metallic (nonstoichiometric transition metal hydride)

22.20 The noble gases are colorless, odorless, diamagnetic, inert gases. They make up a very small fraction of the atmosphere and do not exist in naturally occurring compounds. Because they are rare and unreactive, they were difficult to detect.

22.22 (a) CaO**Br**, +1 (b) H**Br**O_3, + 5 (c) **Xe**O_3; Xe, +6

(d) **Cl**O_4^-, +7 (e) H**I**O_2, +3 (f) **I**F_5; I, +5; F, -1

22.24 (a) iron(III) chlorate (b) chlorous acid (c) xenon hexafluoride

(d) bromine pentafluoride (e) xenon oxide tetrafluoride (f) iodic acid

22.26 (a) The more electronegative the central atom, the greater the extent to which it withdraws charge from oxygen, in turn making the O-H bond more polar, and enhancing ionization of H^+.

(b) HF reacts with the silica which is a major component of glass:

$6HF(aq) + SiO_2(s) \rightarrow SiF_6^{2-}(aq) + 2H_2O(l) + 2H^+(aq)$

(c) Iodide is oxidized by sulfuric acid, as shown in Figure 22.12.

(d) The major factor is size; there is not room about Br for the three chlorides plus the two unshared electron pairs that would occupy the bromine valence shell orbitals.

22.28 (a) $3CaBr_2(s) + 2H_3PO_4(l) \rightarrow Ca_3(PO_4)_2(s) + 6HBr(g)$

(b) $2HF(aq) + CaCO_3(s) \rightarrow CaF_2(s) + H_2O(l) + CO_2(g)$

22.30

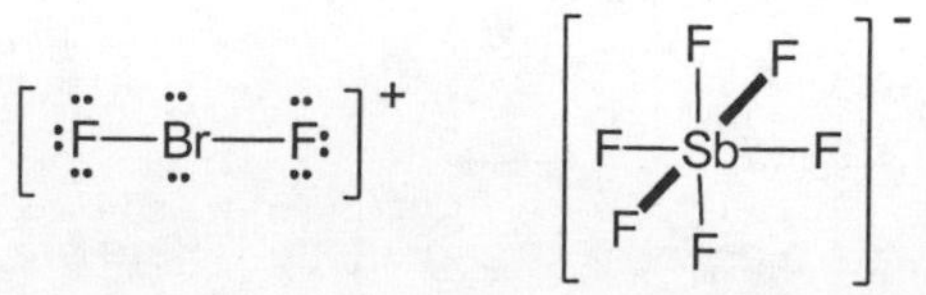

(For clarity, the three unshared electron pairs on each F in the anion are omitted.) The VSEPR model predicts a bent structure for the cation, and an octahedral geometry about Sb for the anion.

Oxygen and the Group 6A Elements

22.32 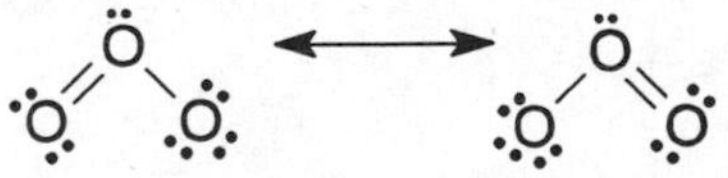

Ozone has two resonance forms (Section 8.7); the molecular structure is bent, with an O–O–O bond angle of approximately 120°. The π bond in ozone is delocalized over the entire molecule; neither individual O–O bond is a full double bond, so the observed O–O distance of 1.28 Å is greater than the 1.21 Å distance in O_2, which has a full O–O double bond.

22.34 (a) $2HgO(s) \xrightarrow{\Delta} 2Hg(l) + O_2(g)$

(b) $2Cu(NO_3)_2(s) \xrightarrow{\Delta} 2CuO(s) + 4NO_2(g) + O_2(g)$

(c) $PbS(s) + 4O_3(g) \rightarrow PbSO_4(s) + 4O_2(g)$

(d) $2ZnS(s) + 3O_2(g) \rightarrow 2ZnO(s) + 2SO_2(g)$

(e) $2K_2O_2(s) + 2CO_2(g) \rightarrow 2K_2CO_3(s) + O_2(g)$

22.36 (a) Mn_2O_7 (higher oxidation state of Mn)

(b) SnO_2 (higher oxidation state of Sn)

(c) SO_3 (higher oxidation state of S)

(d) SO_2 (more nonmetallic character of S)

(e) Ga_2O_3 (more nonmetallic character of Ga)

(f) SO_2 (more nonmetallic character of S)

22.38 (a) $H_2\mathbf{Se}O_3$, +4 (b) $KH\mathbf{S}O_3$, +4 (c) $H_2\mathbf{Te}$, -2 (d) $C\mathbf{S}_2$, -2 (e) $Ca\mathbf{S}O_4$, +6

22.40 (a)

$$2[MnO_4^-(aq) + 8H^+(aq) + 5e^- \rightarrow Mn^{2+}(aq) + 4H_2O(l)]$$
$$5[H_2SO_3(aq) + H_2O(l) \rightarrow SO_4^{2-}(aq) + 4H^+(aq) + 2e^-]$$

$$2MnO_4^-(aq) + 5H_2SO_3(aq) \rightarrow 2MnSO_4(s) + 3SO_4^{2-}(aq) + 3H_2O(l) + 4H^+(aq)$$

(b)

$$Cr_2O_7^{2-}(aq) + 14H^+(aq) + 6e^- \rightarrow 2Cr^{3+}(aq) + 7H_2O(l)$$
$$[H_2SO_3(aq) + H_2O(l) \rightarrow SO_4^{2-}(aq) + 4H^+(aq) + 2e^-]$$

$$Cr_2O_7^{2-}(aq) + 3H_2SO_3(aq) + 2H^+(aq) \rightarrow 2Cr^{3+}(aq) + 3SO_4^{2-}(aq) + 4H_2O(l)$$

(c)

$$Hg_2^{2+}(aq) + 2e^- \rightarrow 2Hg(l)$$
$$H_2SO_3(aq) + H_2O(l) \rightarrow SO_4^{2-}(aq) + 4H^+(aq) + 2e^-$$

$$Hg_2^{2+}(aq) + H_2SO_3(aq) + H_2O(l) \rightarrow 2Hg(l) + SO_4^{2-}(aq) + 4H^+(aq)$$

22.42 SF_4, 34 e^-

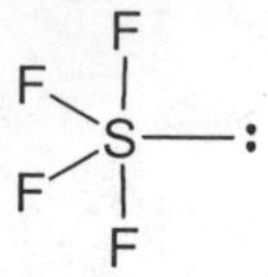

(lone pairs on F atoms omitted for clarity)

trigonal bipyramidal electron pair geometry

see saw molecular geometry

SF_5^-, 42 e^-

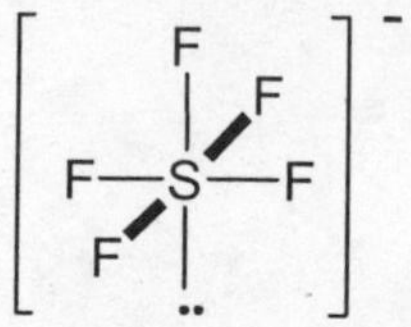

octahedral electron pair geometry

square pyramidal molecular geometry

22.44 (a) $Al_2Se_3(s) + 6H^+(aq) \rightarrow 2Al^{3+}(aq) + 3H_2Se(g)$

(b) $Cl_2(aq) + S_2O_3^{2-}(aq) + H_2O(l) \rightarrow 2Cl^-(aq) + S(s) + SO_4^{2-}(aq) + 2H^+(aq)$

Nitrogen and the Group 5A Elements

22.46 (a) HNO_2, +3 (b) N_2H_4, -2 (c) KCN, -3 (d) $NaNO_3$, +5

(e) NH_4Cl, -3 (f) Li_3N, -3

22.48 (a)

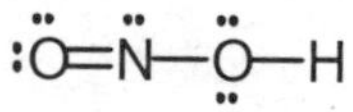

The molecule is bent around the central oxygen and nitrogen atoms; the four atoms need not lie in a plane.

(b)

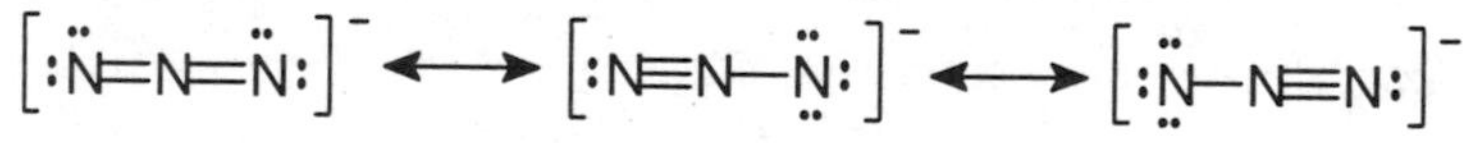

The molecule is linear.

(c)

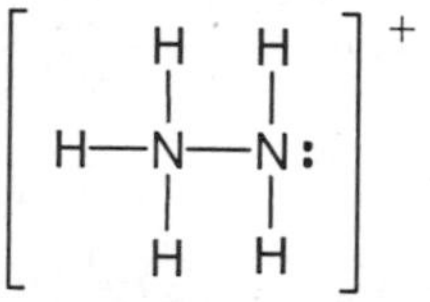

The geometry is tetrahedral around the left nitrogen, trigonal pyramidal around the right.

(d)

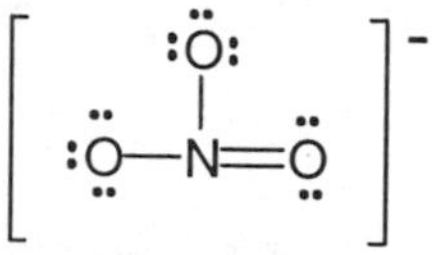

(three equivalent resonance forms)
The ion is trigonal planar.

22.50 (a) $4Zn(s) + 2NO_3^-(aq) + 10H^+(aq) \rightarrow 4Zn^{2+}(aq) + N_2O(g) + 5H_2O(l)$

(b) $4NO_3^-(aq) + S(s) + 4H^+(aq) \rightarrow 4NO_2(g) + SO_2(g) + 2H_2O(l)$

(or $6NO_3^-(aq) + S(s) + 4H^+(aq) \rightarrow 6NO_2(g) + SO_4^{2-}(aq) + 2H_2O(l)$

(c) $2NO_3^-(aq) + 3SO_2(g) + 2H_2O(l) \rightarrow 2NO(g) + 3SO_4^{2-}(aq) + 4H^+(aq)$

(d) $N_2H_4(g) + 5F_2(g) \rightarrow 2NF_3(g) + 4HF(g)$

(e) $4CrO_4^{2-}(aq) + 3N_2H_4(aq) + 4H_2O(l) \rightarrow 4Cr(OH)_4^-(aq) + 4OH^-(aq) + 3N_2(g)$

22.52 (a) $NO_3^-(aq) + 4H^+(aq) + 3e^- \rightarrow NO(g) + 2H_2O(l)$ $E^\circ_{red} = +0.96$ V

(b) $HNO_2(aq) \rightarrow NO_2(g) + H^+(aq) + 1e^-$ $E^\circ_{red} = 1.12$ V

22.54 (a) H_3PO_3, +3 (b) $H_4\mathbf{P}_2O_7$, + 5 (c) $\mathbf{Sb}Cl_3$, +3 (d) $Mg_3\mathbf{As}_2$, +5 (e) $\mathbf{P}_2O_5$, +5

22.56 (a) Only two of the hydrogens in H_3PO_3 are bound to oxygen. The third is attached directly to phosphorus, and not readily ionized, because the H–P bond is not very polar.

(b) The smaller, more electronegative nitrogen withdraws more electron density from the O–H bond, making it more polar and more likely to ionize.

(c) Phosphate rock consists of $Ca_3(PO_4)_2$, which is only slightly soluble in water. The phosphorus is unavailable for plant use.

(d) N_2 can form stable π bonds to complete the octet of both N atoms. Because phosphorus atoms are larger than nitrogen atoms, they do not form stable π bonds with themselves and must form σ bonds with several other phosphorus atoms (producing P_4 tetrahedral or sheet structures) to complete their octets.

(e) In solution Na_3PO_4 is completely dissociated into Na^+ and PO_4^{3-}. PO_4^{3-}, the conjugate base of the very weak acid HPO_4^{2-}, has a K_b of 2.4×10^{-2} and produces a considerable amount of OH^- by hydrolysis of H_2O.

22.58 (a) $PCl_5(l) + 4H_2O(l) \rightarrow H_3PO_4(aq) + 5HCl(aq)$

(b) $2H_3PO_4(aq) \xrightarrow{\Delta} H_4PO_7(aq) + H_2O(l)$

(c) $P_4O_{10}(s) + 6H_2O(l) \rightarrow 4H_3PO_4(aq)$

Carbon, the Other Group 4A Elements, and Boron

22.60 (a) H_2CO_3 (b) NaCN (c) $KHCO_3$ (d) C_2H_2

22.62 (a) The CH_3 carbon is tetrahedral; it employs an sp^3 hybrid orbital set. The other two carbons have a linear geometry about them; they employ an sp hybrid orbital set.

(b) The carbon in CN^- uses an sp hybrid orbital set. The Lewis structure of CN^- is $[:C\equiv N:]^-$. The lone pair and the C-N σ bond electrons occupy the sp hybrid orbitals. The other two p orbitals are employed in π bonding to N.

(c) The carbon in CS_2 has an sp hybrid orbital set, consistent with the linear geometry.

(d) In C_2H_6 each carbon is in a tetrahedral environment of one C–C and three C–H bonds. The C cations employ sp^3 hybrid orbitals.

22.64 (a) $CO_2(g) + OH^-(aq) \rightarrow HCO_3^-(aq)$

(b) $NaHCO_3(s) + H^+(aq) \rightarrow Na^+(aq) + H_2O(l) + CO_2(g)$

(c) $2CaO(s) + 5C(s) \xrightarrow{\Delta} 2CaC_2(s) + CO_2(g)$

(d) $C(s) + H_2O(g) \xrightarrow{\Delta} H_2(g) + CO(g)$

(e) $CuO(s) + CO(g) \rightarrow Cu(s) + CO_2(g)$

22.66 (a) $2Mg(s) + CO_2(g) \rightarrow 2MgO(s) + C(s)$

(b) $6CO_2(g) + 6H_2O(l) \xrightarrow{h\nu} C_6H_{12}O_6(aq) + 6O_2(g)$

(c) $CO_3^{2-}(aq) + H_2O(l) \rightarrow HCO_3^-(aq) + OH^-(aq)$

22.68 (a) **SiO_2**, +4 (b) **$GeCl_4$**, +4 (c) **$NaBH_4$**, +3 (d) **$SnCl_2$**, +2 (e) **B_2H_6**, +3

22.70 (a) Carbon (b) lead (c) germanium

22.72 (a)

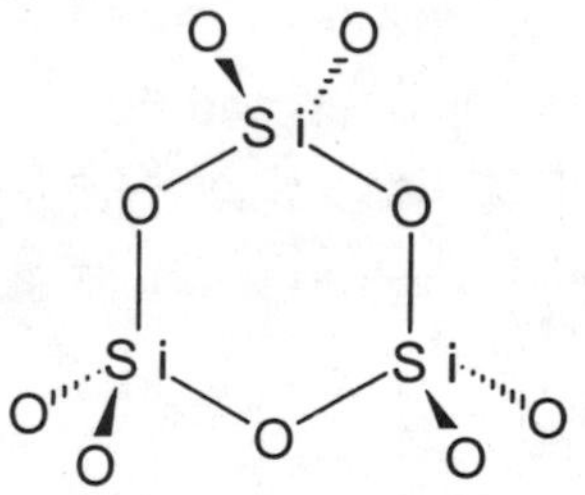

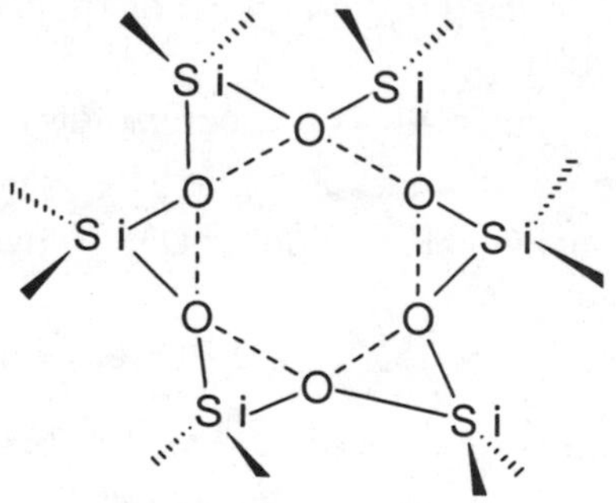

(b) $Si_3O_9^{6-}$ $Si_6O_{18}^{12-}$

22.74 (a) $B_2H_6(g) + 6H_2O(l) \rightarrow 2H_3BO_3(aq) + 6H_2(g)$

(b) $4H_3BO_3(s) \xrightarrow{\Delta} H_2B_4O_7(s) + 5H_2O(g)$

(c) $B_2O_3(s) + 3H_2O(l) \rightarrow 2H_3BO_3(aq)$

Additional Exercises

22.75 (a) *Isotopes* are atoms of the same element with different masses; their nuclei have the same number of protons but different numbers of neutrons.

(b) *Allotropes* are different structural forms of the same element. They are composed of atoms of a single element bound into different structures. For example, graphite, diamond and buckey balls are all allotropes of carbon.

(c) *Disproportionation* is an oxidation-reduction process where the same element is both oxidized and reduced.

(d) *Interhalogen* is a compound formed from atoms of two or more halogens.

(e) *Frasch* process is a mining technique for extracting deposits of elemental sulfur. Superheated water is forced into the deposit and melts the sulfur. Compressed air forces the molten sulfur to the surface, where it solidifies.

(f) *Ostwald* process is a commercial process for converting ammonia to nitric acid. It begins with the catalytic oxidation of NH_3 to NO, followed by oxidation of NO to NO_2 and hydration of NO_2 to form HNO_3.

(g) A *condensation reaction* is the combination of two molecules to form a large molecule and a small one such as H_2O or HCl.

22.77 (a) React an ionic nitride with D_2O, e.g.,

$Mg_3N_2(s) + 6D_2O(l) \rightarrow 2ND_3(aq) + 3Mg(OD)_2(s)$

(b) React SO_3 with D_2O: $SO_3(g) + D_2O(l) \rightleftharpoons D_2SO_4(aq)$

(c) React Na_2O with D_2O: $Na_2O(s) + D_2O(l) \rightarrow 2NaOD(aq)$

(d) Dissolve $N_2O_5(g)$ in D_2O: $N_2O_5(g) + D_2O(l) \rightarrow 2DNO_3(aq)$

(e) React CaC_2 with D_2O: $CaC_2(s) + 2D_2O(l) \rightarrow Ca^{2+}(aq) + 2OD^-(aq) + C_2D_2(g)$

(f) Add NaCN to the D_2SO_4 solution prepared in (b):

$$NaCN(s) + D^+(aq) \xrightarrow{\Delta} DCN(aq) + Na^+(aq)$$

The DCN can be removed as gas from the reaction.

22.78 $BrO_3^-(aq) + XeF_2(aq) + H_2O(l) \rightarrow Xe(g) + 2HF(aq) + BrO_4^-(aq)$

22.80 (a) $SO_2(g) + H_2O(l) \rightleftharpoons H_2SO_3(aq)$

(b) $Cl_2O(g) + H_2O(l) \rightleftharpoons 2HClO(aq)$

(c) $Na_2O(s) + H_2O(l) \rightarrow 2Na^{2+}(aq) + 2OH^-(aq)$

(d) $BaC_2(s) + 2H_2O(l) \rightarrow Ba^{2+}(aq) + 2OH^-(aq) + C_2H_2(g)$

(e) $2RbO_2(s) + 2H_2O(l) \rightarrow 2Rb^+(aq) + 2OH^-(aq) + O_2(g) + H_2O_2(aq)$

(f) $Mg_3N_2(s) + 6H_2O(l) \rightarrow 3Mg(OH)_2(s) + 2NH_3(g)$

(g) $Na_2O_2(s) + 2H_2O \rightarrow H_2O_2(aq) + 2NaOH(aq)$

(h) $NaH(s) + H_2O \rightarrow NaOH(aq) + H_2(g)$

22.82 $8Fe(s) + S_8(s) \rightarrow 8FeS(s)$

$S_8(s) + 16F_2(g) \rightarrow 8SF_4(g)$ or $S_8(s) + 24F_2(g) \rightarrow 8SF_6(g)$

$S_8(s) + 8O_2(g) \rightarrow 8SO_2(g)$

$S_8(s) + 8H_2(g) \rightarrow 8H_2S(g)$

Sulfur acts as an oxidizing agent in reactions with Fe or H_2 and as a reducing agent in reactions with O_2 or F_2. Incidentally, these reactions are often written using the symbol S rather than S_8 for sulfur.

22.83

$S(g) + O_2(g) \rightarrow SO_2(g)$	$\Delta H = -296.9$ kJ	(1)
$SO_2(g) + 1/2\ O_2(g) \rightarrow SO_3(g)$	$\Delta H = -98.3$ kJ	(2)
$SO_3(g) + H_2O(l) \rightarrow H_2SO_4(aq)$	$\Delta H = -130$ kJ	(3)
$S(g) + 3/2\ O_2(g) + H_2O(l) \rightarrow H_2SO_4(aq)$	$\Delta H = -525$ kJ	

$$1 \text{ ton } H_2SO_4 \times \frac{2000 \text{ lb}}{\text{ton}} \times \frac{453.6 \text{ g}}{1 \text{ lb}} \times \frac{1 \text{ mol } H_2SO_4}{98.09 \text{ g}} \times \frac{-525 \text{ kJ}}{\text{mol } H_2SO_4}$$

$$= -4.86 \times 10^6 \text{ kJ of heat/ton } H_2SO_4$$

22.85 (a) P_4, P_4O_6 and P_4O_{10} all contain a tetrahedron of phosphorus atoms with P–P–P angles of approximately 60°. In the acids containing phosphorus in the +5 oxidation state, H_3PO_4, $H_4P_2O_7$, and $(HPO_3)_n$, P is bound to four O atoms with tetrahedral geometry and approximate 109° bond angles around phosphorus.

(b)

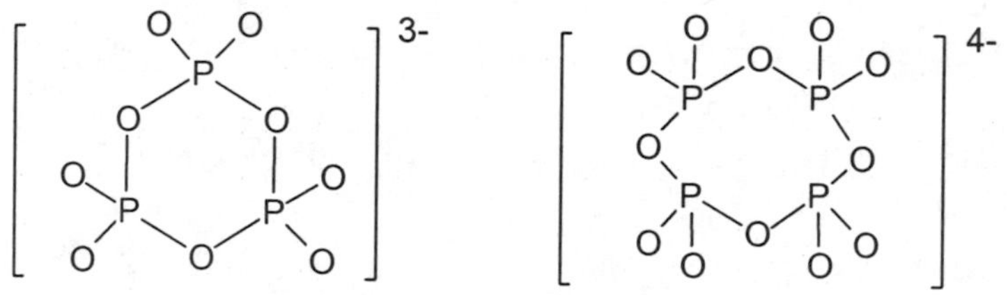

In both structures there are unshared pairs on all oxygens to give octets and the geometry around each P is approximately tetrahedral.

22.86 (a) Use the formula that relates the length of a side of a triangle to the lengths of the other two sides and the opposite angle: $a^2 = b^2 + c^2 - 2bc \cos A$. In this case, a = b = the P–O distance, and A is the P–O–P angle:

For P_4O_6, $a^2 = 2b^2(1 - \cos A) = 2(1.65)^2(1 - \cos 127.5°)$ $a = 2.96$ Å

For P_4O_{10}, $a^2 = 2b^2(1 - \cos A) = 2(1.60)^2(1 - \cos 124.5°)$ $a = 2.83$ Å

(b) The shorter P–P distance in P_4O_{10} is due both to the sharper angle and to the shorter P–O distance. The shorter P–O distance may be due to the higher oxidation state and concomitant higher effective charge of P in P_4O_{10}.

22.88 (a)

$$2[5e^- + MnO_4^-(aq) + 8H^+(aq) \rightarrow Mn^{2+}(aq) + 4H_2O(l)]$$
$$5[H_2O_2(aq) \rightarrow O_2(g) + 2H^+(aq) + 2e^-]$$

$$2MnO_4^-(aq) + 5H_2O_2(aq) + 6H^+(aq) \rightarrow 2Mn^{2+}(aq) + 5O_2(g) + 8H_2O(l)$$

(b)

$$2[Fe^{2+}(aq) \rightarrow Fe^{3+}(aq) + e^-]$$
$$H_2O_2(aq) + 2H^+(aq) + 2e^- \rightarrow 2H_2O(l)$$

$$2Fe^{2+}(aq) + H_2O_2(aq) + 2H^+(aq) \rightarrow 2Fe^{3+}(aq) + 2H_2O(l)$$

(c)

$$2I^-(aq) \rightarrow I_2(s) + 2e^-$$
$$H_2O_2(aq) + 2H^+(aq) + 2e^- \rightarrow 2H_2O(l)$$

$$2\,I^-(aq) + H_2O_2(aq) + 2H^+(aq) \rightarrow I_2(s) + 2H_2O(l)$$

(d)

$$MnO_2(s) + 4H^+(aq) + 2e^- \rightarrow Mn^{2+}(aq) + 2H_2O(l)$$
$$H_2O_2(aq) \rightarrow O_2(g) + 2H^+(aq) + 2e^-$$

$$MnO_2(s) + 2H^+(aq) + H_2O_2(aq) \rightarrow Mn^{2+}(aq) + 2H_2O(l) + O_2(g)$$

(e)

$$2I^-(aq) \rightarrow I_2(s) + 2e^-$$
$$O_3(g) + H_2O(l) + 2e^- \rightarrow O_2(g) + 2OH^-(aq)$$

$$2I^-(aq) + O_3(g) + H_2O(l) \rightarrow O_2(g) + I_2(s) + 2OH^-(aq)$$

22.89 Assume that the reactions occur in basic solution. The half-reaction for reduction of H_2O_2 is in all cases $H_2O_2(aq) + 2e^- \rightarrow 2OH^-(aq)$.

(a) $H_2O_2(aq) + S^{2-}(aq) \rightarrow 2OH^-(aq) + S(s)$

(b) $SO_2(g) + 2OH^-(aq) + H_2O_2(aq) \rightarrow SO_4^{2-}(aq) + 2H_2O(l)$

(c) $NO_2^-(aq) + H_2O_2(aq) \rightarrow NO_3^-(aq) + H_2O(l)$

(d) $As_2O_3(s) + 2H_2O_2(aq) + 6OH^-(aq) \rightarrow 2AsO_4^{3-}(aq) + 5H_2O(l)$

(e) This reaction must be occurring in acidic solution, since $Fe(OH)_3$ would form if the solution were basic. The half-reactions are:

$$2H^+(aq) + H_2O_2(aq) + 2e^- \rightarrow 2H_2O(l)$$
$$2[Fe^{2+}(aq) \rightarrow Fe^{3+}(aq) + e^-$$

$$2Fe^{2+}(aq) + H_2O_2(aq) + 2H^+(aq) \rightarrow 2Fe^{3+}(aq) + 2H_2O(l)$$

22.90 (a) $Li_3N(s) + 3H_2O(l) \rightarrow 3Li^+(aq) + 3OH^-(aq) + NH_3(aq)$

(b) $NH_3(aq) + H_2O(l) \rightleftharpoons NH_4^+(aq) + OH^-(aq)$

(c) $3NO_2(g) + H_2O(l) \rightarrow NO(g) + 2H^+(aq) + 2NO_3^-(aq)$

(d) $2NO_2(g) \rightleftharpoons N_2O_4(g)$

(e) $4NH_3(g) + 5O_2(g) \xrightarrow{\text{catalyst}} 4NO(g) + 6H_2O(g)$

(f) $2CO(g) + O_2(g) \rightarrow 2CO_2(g)$

(g) $H_2CO_3(aq) \xrightarrow{\Delta} H_2O(g) + CO_2(g)$

(h) $Ni(s) + CO(g) \rightarrow NiO(s) + C(s)$

(i) $CS_2(g) + O_2(g) \rightarrow CO_2(g) + S_2(g)$

(j) $CaO(s) + SO_2(g) \rightarrow CaSO_3(s)$

(k) $2Na(s) + 2H_2O(l) \rightarrow 2NaOH(aq) + H_2(g)$

(l) $CH_4(g) + H_2O(g) \xrightarrow{\Delta} CO(g) + 3H_2(g)$

(m) $LiH(s) + H_2O(l) \rightarrow LiOH(aq) + H_2(g)$

(n) $Fe_2O_3(s) + 3H_2(g) \rightarrow 2Fe(s) + 3H_2O(g)$

Integrative Exercises

22.92 From Appendix C, we need only ΔH_f° for F(g), so that we can estimate ΔH for the process:

$F_2(g) \rightarrow F(g) + F(g)$; $\Delta H^\circ = +160$ kJ.

$XeF_2(g) \rightarrow Xe(g) + F_2(g)$ $-\Delta H_f^\circ = +109$ kJ

$XeF_2(g) \rightarrow Xe(g) + 2F(g)$ $\Delta H^\circ = +269$ kJ

The average Xe-F bond enthalpy is thus 269/2 = 134 kJ. Similarly,

$XeF_4(g) \rightarrow Xe(g) + 2F_2(g)$ $-\Delta H_f^\circ = +218$ kJ

$2F_2(g) \rightarrow 4F(g)$ $\Delta H^\circ = 320$ kJ

$XeF_4(g) \rightarrow Xe(g) + 4F(g)$ $\Delta H^\circ = 538$ kJ

Average Xe-F bond energy = 538/4 = 134 kJ

$XeF_6(g) \rightarrow Xe(g) + 3F_2(g)$ $-\Delta H_f^\circ = 298$ kJ

$3F_2(g) \rightarrow 6F(g)$ $\Delta H^\circ = 480$ kJ

$XeF_6(g) \rightarrow Xe(g) + 6F(g)$ $\Delta H^\circ = 778$ kJ

Average Xe-F bond energy = 778/6 = 130 kJ

The average bond enthalpies are: XeF_2: 134 kJ, XeF_4: 134 kJ, XeF_6: 130 kJ. They are remarkably constant in the series.

22.94 First calculate the molar solubility of Cl_2 in water.

$$n = \frac{1\text{ atm }(0.310\text{ L})}{\frac{0.08206\text{ L}\cdot\text{atm}}{1\text{ mol}\cdot\text{K}} \times 273\text{ K}} = 0.01384 = 0.0138\text{ mol }Cl_2;\quad M = \frac{0.01384\text{ mol}}{0.100\text{ L}} = 0.1384$$

$$= 0.138\ M$$

$$K_{eq} = \frac{[Cl^-][HOCl][H^+]}{[Cl_2]} = 4.7 \times 10^{-4}$$

$[Cl^-] = [HOCl] = [H^+]$ Let this quantity = x. Then, $\frac{x^3}{(0.1384 - x)} = 4.7 \times 10^{-4}$

Assuming that x is small compared with 0.1384:

$x^3 = (0.1384)(4.7 \times 10^{-4}) = 6.504 \times 10^{-5}$; $x = 0.0402 = 0.040\ M$

We can correct the denominator using this value, to get a better estimate of x:

$$\frac{x^3}{0.1384 - 0.0402} = 4.7 \times 10^{-4};\ x = 0.0359 = 0.036\ M$$

One more round of approximation gives x = 0.0364 = 0.036 *M*. This is the equilibrium concentration of HClO.

22.95 (a) $N_2H_4(g) + O_2(g) \rightarrow N_2(g) + 2H_2O(l)$

(b) $\Delta H° = \Delta H_f^\circ\ N_2(g) + 2\Delta H_f^\circ\ H_2O(l) - \Delta H_f^\circ\ N_2H_4(aq) - \Delta H_f^\circ\ O_2(g)$

$$= 0 + 2(-285.83) - 95.40 - 0 = -667.06\text{ kJ}$$

(c) $$\frac{9.1\text{ g }O_2}{1 \times 10^6\text{ g }H_2O} \times \frac{1.0\text{ g }H_2O}{1\text{ mL }H_2O} \times \frac{1000\text{ mL}}{1\text{ L}} \times 3.0 \times 10^4\text{ L} = 273 = 2.7 \times 10^2\text{ g }O_2$$

$$2.73 \times 10^2\text{ g }O_2 \times \frac{1\text{ mol }O_2}{32.00\text{ g }O_2} \times \frac{1\text{ mol }N_2H_4}{1\text{ mol }O_2} \times \frac{32.05\text{ g }N_2H_4}{1\text{ mol }N_2H_4} = 2.7 \times 10^2\text{ g }N_2H_4$$

22.97 *Plan.* vol air → kg air → g H_2S → g FeS. Use the ideal-gas equation to change volume of air to mass of air, (assuming 1.00 atm, 298 K and an average molar mass ($\mathcal{M}$) for air of 29.0 g/mol. Use 20 mg H_2S/kg air to find the mass of H_2S in the given mass of air. *Solve:*

$$V_{air} = 2.7\text{ m} \times 4.3\text{ m} \times 4.3\text{ m} \times \frac{(100)^3\text{ cm}^3}{1\text{ m}^3} \times \frac{1\text{ L}}{1000\text{ cm}^3} = 4.9923 \times 10^4 = 5.0 \times 10^4\text{ L}$$

$$g_{air} = \frac{PV\mathcal{M}}{RT};\ \text{assume } P = 1.00\text{ atm, } T = 298\text{ K, } \mathcal{M}_{air} = 29.0\text{ g/mol}$$

$$g_{air} = \frac{1.00\text{ atm} \times 4.9923 \times 10^4\text{ L} \times 29.0\text{ g/mol}}{298\text{ K}} \times \frac{\text{K} \bullet \text{mol}}{0.08206\text{ L} \bullet \text{atm}} = 59{,}204 = 5.9 \times 10^4\text{ g air}$$

$$5.9203 \times 10^4\text{ g air} \times \frac{1\text{ kg}}{1000\text{ g}} \times \frac{20\text{ mg }H_2S}{1\text{ kg air}} \times \frac{1\text{ g}}{1000\text{ mg}} = 1.184 = 1.2\text{ g }H_2S$$

$FeS(s) + 2HCl(aq) \rightarrow FeCl_2(aq) + H_2S(g)$

$$1.184\text{ g }H_2 \times \frac{1\text{ mol }H_2}{34.08\text{ g }H_2S} \times \frac{1\text{ mol FeS}}{1\text{ mol }H_2S} \times \frac{87.91\text{ g FeS}}{1\text{ mol FeS}} = 3.054 = 3.1\text{ g FeS}$$

22.99 *Plan.* Calculate the required [H^+] from the given pH. Then determine the concentration and amount of H_2SO_4 needed to achieve this [H^+]. The first dissociation step of H_2SO_4 is complete, but the second is not, so we must solve an equilibrium problem. Let x equal the initial concentration of H_2SO_4. *Solve:*

$[H^+] = 10^{-pH} = 10^{-3.5} = 3.16 \times 10^{-4} = 3 \times 10^{-4}\ M\ H^+$

$H_2SO_4(aq) \rightarrow H^+(aq) + HSO_4^-(aq)$

$HSO_4^-(aq) \rightleftharpoons H^+(aq) + SO_4^{2-}(aq)$ $K_a = 1.2 \times 10^{-2}$

	HSO_4^-	H^+	SO_4^{2-}
initial	x	x	0
change	- y	+ y	+ y
equil.	x - y	x + y	y

$$K_a = \frac{[H^+][SO_4^{2-}]}{[HSO_4^-]} = \frac{(x+y)(y)}{(x-y)}; [H^+] = x + y = 3.16 \times 10^{-4}\ M;\ y = 3.16 \times 10^{-4} - x$$

$$1.2 \times 10^{-2} = \frac{(3.16 \times 10^{-4})(3.16 \times 10^{-4} - x)}{[x - (3.16 \times 10^{-4} - x)]} = \frac{1.00 \times 10^{-7} - 3.16 \times 10^{-4} x}{2x - 3.16 \times 10^{-4}}$$

$1.2 \times 10^{-2}(2x - 3.16 \times 10^{-4}) = 1.00 \times 10^{-7} - 3.16 \times 10^{-4}x;$

$2.4 \times 10^{-2}x - 3.79 \times 10^{-6} = 1.00 \times 10^{-7} - 3.16 \times 10^{-4}x$

$2.43 \times 10^{-2}x = 3.89 \times 10^{-6};\ x = 1.60 \times 10^{-4}\ M = 2 \times 10^{-4}\ M\ [H^+]$

$$\frac{1.60 \times 10^{-4} \text{ mol } H_2SO_4}{1 \text{ L } H_2SO_4} \times 1.00 \times 10^3 \text{ L seawater} \times \frac{98.09 \text{ g } H_2SO_4}{\text{mol}} = 15.7 \text{ g} = 2 \times 10^1 \text{ g } H_2SO_4$$

Check. The calculated concentration should be slightly greater than one-half the desired $[H^+]$, since the second dissociation of H_2SO_4 is not quite complete.

$1.60 \times 10^{-4}\ M > (3.16 \times 10^{-4})/2 = 1.58 \times 10^{-2}\ M$. Substituting into the K_a expression:

$$\frac{(3.16 \times 10^{-4})(1.56 \times 10^{-4})}{(1.60 \times 10^{-4} - 1.56 \times 10^{-4})} = 1.2 \times 10^{-2}$$

Also note that the pH indicates 1 sig fig for the result, but this level of precisionis not very useful during calculations.

Calculate the mass of Br^- present. L seawater $\xrightarrow{\text{density}}$ g seawater $\xrightarrow[Br^-]{\text{ppm}}$ mass Br^-.

Write the balanced equation for the reaction of Cl_2 with Br^- to form Br_2 and Cl^-. Solve the stoichiometry problem to get mass Cl_2 needed. Add 15%.

$$1.00 \times 10^3 \text{ L seawater} \times \frac{1.03 \text{ g}}{\text{mL}} \times \frac{1000 \text{ mL}}{1 \text{ L}} = 1.03 \times 10^6 \text{ g seawater}$$

$$67 \text{ ppm } Br^- = \frac{67 \text{ g } Br^-}{1 \times 10^6 \text{ g seawater}};\ \frac{67 \text{ g } Br^-}{1 \times 10^6 \text{ g seawater}} \times 1.03 \times 10^6 \text{ g seawater}$$

$= 69.01 = 69$ g Br^- total

$2Br^-(aq) + Cl_2(aq) \rightarrow Br_2(aq) + 2Cl^-(aq)$

$$69.01 \text{ g } Br^- \times \frac{1 \text{ mol } Br^-}{79.904 \text{ g } Br^-} \times \frac{1 \text{ mol } Cl_2}{2 \text{ mol } Br^-} \times \frac{70.906 \text{ g } Cl_2}{\text{mol } Cl_2} = 30.619 = 31 \text{ g } Cl_2$$

Accounting for the 15% excess: $0.15(30.619 \text{ g } Cl_2) = 4.593 \text{ g } Cl_2$ excess;

total g $Cl_2 = 30.619 + 4.593 = 35.212 = 35$ g Cl_2

22.100 $N_2H_5^+(aq) \rightarrow N_2(g) + 5H^+(aq) + 4e^-$ $\quad E^\circ_{red} = -0.23$ V

Reduction of the metal should occur when E°_{red} of the metal ion is more positive than about -0.15 V. This is the case for (b) Sn^{2+} (marginal), (c) Cu^{2+} and (d) Ag^+.

22.102 First write the balanced equation to give the number of moles of gaseous products per mole of hydrazine.

(A) $(CH_3)_2NNH_2 + 2N_2O_4 \rightarrow 3N_2(g) + 4H_2O(g) + 2CO_2(g)$

(B) $(CH_3)HNNH_2 + 5/4\ N_2O_4 \rightarrow 9/4\ N_2(g) + 3H_2O(g) + CO_2(g)$

In case (A) there are nine moles gas per one mole $(CH_3)_2NNH_2$ plus two moles N_2O_4. The total mass of reactants is 60 + 2(92) = 244 g. Thus, there are

$$\frac{9 \text{ mol gas}}{244 \text{ g reactants}} = \frac{0.0369 \text{ mol gas}}{1 \text{ g reactants}}$$

In case (B) there are 6.25 moles of gaseous product per one mole $(CH_3)HNNH_2$ plus 1.25 moles N_2O_4. The total mass of this amount of reactants is 46.0 + 1.25(92.0) = 161 g.

$$\frac{6.25 \text{ mol gas}}{161 \text{ g reactants}} = \frac{0.0388 \text{ mol gas}}{1 \text{ g reactants}}$$

Thus the methylhydrazine (B) has marginally greater thrust.

22.103 (a) $HOOC{-}CH_2{-}COOH \xrightarrow{P_2O_5} C_3O_2 + 2H_2O$

(b) 24 valence e^-, 12 e^- pair 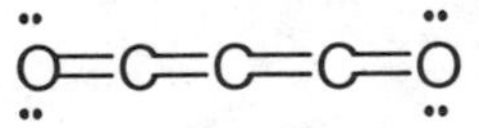

(c) C=O, about 1.23 Å; C=C, 1.34 Å or less. Since consecutive C=C bonds require sp hybrid orbitals on C (as in allene, C_3H_4), we might expect the orbital overlap requirements of this bonding arrangement to require smaller than usual C=C distances.

(d) The product has the formula $C_3H_4O_2$.

28 valence e^-, 14 e^- pr

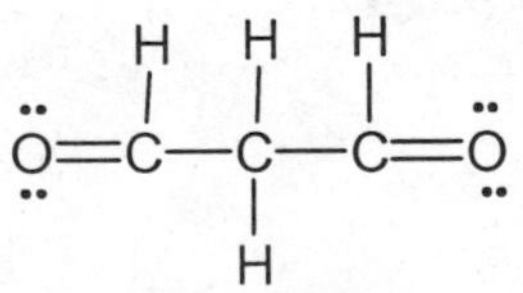

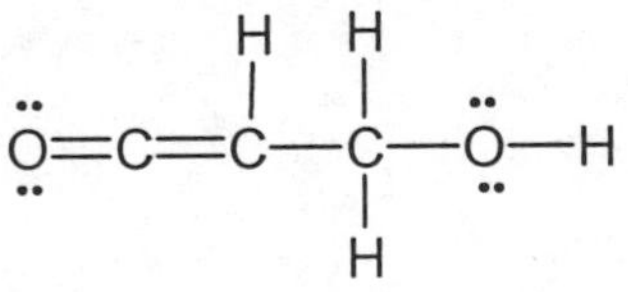

Two possibilities are shown above. The O=C=C group in the structure on the right is uncommon and less likely than the symmetrical structure on the left.

22.104 BN has the same number of valence electrons per formula unit as carbon. (Three from B, five from N, for an average of four per atom.) To the extent that we can neglect the difference in nuclear charges between B and N, we can think of BN as carbon-like. Indeed, BN takes on the same structural forms as carbon. However, because the B–N bonds are somewhat polar, BN is in fact even harder than diamond.

23 Metals and Metallurgy

Metallurgy

23.2 (a) +4

(b) $MnO_2(s) + 4H^+(aq) + 2e^- \rightarrow Mn^{2+}(aq) + 2H_2O(l) \quad E^\circ_{red} = 1.23\ V$

$Mn^{2+}(aq) + 2e^- \rightarrow Mn(s) \quad E^\circ_{red} = -1.18\ V$

Standard reduction potentials indicate that a very strong reducing agent is required to reduce the ore to Mn(s), at least if $Mn^{2+}(aq)$ is an intermediate product. According to Appendix E, only Group I and Group II metals (Li, Na, Mg, etc.) are strong enough to reduce Mn^{2+} to Mn. In practice, $MnO_2(s)$ is reduced by coke in blast furnaces, into which MnO_2 is added to incorporate Mn into steel.

23.4 (a) *Calcination* is heating an ore to decompose the mineral of interest into a simple solid and volatile compound. Calcination usually produces a metal oxide and a gas that is a nonmetal oxide.

(b) *Leaching* is dissolving the mineral of interest to remove it from an ore. The solvent is usually water or an aqueous solution of acid, base or salt.

(c) *Smelting* is heating an ore, often in a reducing atmosphere, to a very high temperature so that two immiscible liquid layers form. The layers are usually the molten metal or metals of interest and slag.

(d) *Slag* is the unwanted layer of the smelting process. It contains molten silicate, aluminate, phosphate or fluoride compounds.

23.6 (a) $2CdS(s) + 3O_2(g) \xrightarrow{\Delta} 2CdO(s) + 2SO_2(g)$

(b) $CoCO_3(s) \xrightarrow{\Delta} CoO(s) + CO_2(g)$

(c) $Cr_2O_3(s) + 6Na(l) \rightarrow 2Cr(s) + 3Na_2O(s)$

(d) $VCl_3(g) + 3K(l) \rightarrow V(s) + 3KCl(s)$

(e) $3BaO(s) + P_2O_5(l) \rightarrow Ba_3(PO_4)_2(l)$

23.8 (a) $CoO(s) + CO_2(g)$ (b) $CO(g)$

(c) $CoCO_3(s) \xrightarrow{\Delta} CoO(s) + CO_2(g)$; $CoO(s) + CO(g) \rightarrow Co(s) + CO_2(g)$

23.10 The major reducing agent is CO, formed by partial oxidation of the coke (C) with which the furnace is charged.

$Fe_2O_3(s) + 3CO(g) \rightarrow 2Fe(l) + 3CO_2(g)$

$Fe_3O_4(s) + 4CO(g) \rightarrow 3Fe(l) + 4CO_2(g)$

23.12 (a) In the *converter*, oxidation of C, Si and metals by O_2 are exothermic reactions that raise the temperature.

(b) $2C(s) + O_2(g) \rightarrow 2CO(g)$; $S(s) + O_2(g) \rightarrow SO_2(g)$; $Si(s) + O_2(g) \rightarrow SiO_2(l)$

23.14 Gold appears in elemental form in ores. The $O_2(g)$ in air oxidizes Au(s) to $Au^+(aq)$ and the $CN^-(aq)$ stabilizes the Au^+ in the form of the soluble complex ion $Au(CN)_2^-(aq)$. This enables the unwanted solids (gangue) to be filtered away from the gold-containing solution.

23.16 $SnO_2(s) + C(s) \xrightarrow{\Delta} Sn(l) + CO_2(g)$

$Sn(s) \rightarrow Sn^{2+}(aq) + 2e^-$ (anode)

$Sn^{2+}(aq) + 2e^- \rightarrow Sn(s)$ (cathode)

Metals and Alloys

23.18 Since Si has the same crystal structure as diamond, it is a covalent-network solid with its bonding electrons localized between Si atoms. Since there is no significant delocalization in Si, it is not likely to have the metallic properties of malleability, ductility and high electrical and thermal conductivity. It is likely to be hard and high-melting like other covalent-network solids.

23.20 (a) Cr: $[Ar]4s^13d^5$, Z = 24; Se: $[Ar]4s^23d^{10}4p^4$, Z = 34

Both elements have the [Ar] core configuration and both have six valence electrons. The orbital locations of the six valence electrons is different in the two elements, because Se has more electrons.

(b) Different Z and Z_{eff} for the two elements, and the different orbital locations of the valence electrons are the main factors that lead to the differences in properties. In Cr, the 4s and 3d electrons are the valence electrons. Its Z and Z_{eff} are smaller than those of Se and it is not likely to gain enough electrons to achieve a noble-gas configuration. Thus, Cr loses electrons when it forms ions, acting like a metal. Se is in the same row of the periodic table as Cr, but its 3d subshell is filled, so its valence electrons are in 4s and 4p. Because Se has a larger Z and Z_{eff}, it is more likely to hold its own valence electrons and gain other electrons when it forms ions. That Se needs only two additional electrons to achieve the noble-gas configuration of Kr is also a driving force for it gaining electrons when it forms ions, acting like a nonmetal.

23.22 The ΔH_{atom} is an indication of the strength of metallic bonding in the metals. According to the molecular orbital or band theory of metallic bonding, the strength of metallic bonding increases with the number of electrons in bonding molecular orbitals, up to a maximum of six valence electrons. As the number of valence electrons in the series increases from two for Ca to five for V, the ΔH_{atom} and the strength of metallic bonding increases.

23.24 Germanium doped with arsenic (Ge/As) is a better conductor than germanium. Ge, a semiconductor, has a filled valence band but an energetically accessible conduction band. In Ge/As, the additional valence electrons of the doped As atoms cannot fit into the filled valence band and occupy the conduction band. These electrons have access to the vacant orbitals within the conduction band and serve as carriers of electrical current. Ge/As is an *n-type* semiconductor.

23.26 According to the MO model of metallic bonding, electrical and thermal conductivity are high when electrons can be delocalized throughout the substance. In graphite, the layers are sheets of interconnected benzene rings, with extensive delocalization of π electrons. This facilitates conductivity within the layers, but not in the direction perpendicular to them.

23.28 Substitutional and interstitial alloys are both solution alloys. In a *substitutional* alloy, the atoms of the "solute" take positions normally occupied by the "solvent." Substitutional alloys tend to form when solute and solvent atoms are of comparable size and have similar bonding characteristics. In an *interstitial* alloy, the atoms of the "solute" occupy the holes or interstitial positions between "solvent" atoms. Solute atoms are necessarily much smaller than solvent atoms.

Transition Metals

23.30 (b) NiCo alloy and (c) W will have metallic properties. The lattices of these substances are composed of neutral metal atoms. Delocalization of valence electrons via the MO model of metallic bonding produces metallic properties.

(d) Ge is a metalloid, not a metal. (a) $TiCl_4$ is an ionic compound and (e) Hg_2^{2+} is a metal ion. In ions and ionic compounds, electrons are localized on the individual ions, precluding metallic properties.

23.32 Zr: $[Kr]5s^24d^2$, Z = 40; Hf: $[Kr]6s^24f^{14}5d^2$, Z = 72

Moving down a family of the periodic chart, atomic size increases because the valence electrons are in a higher principle quantum level (and thus further from the nucleus) and are more effectively shielded from the nuclear charge by a larger core electron cloud. However, the build-up in Z that accompanies the filling of the 4f orbitals causes the valence electrons in Hf to experience a much greater relative nuclear charge than those in La, its neighbor to the left. This increase in Z offsets the usual effect of the increase in *n* value of the valence electrons and the radii of Zr and Hf atoms are similar.

23.34 (a) CdO (b) WO_3 (c) Nb_2O_5

23.36 V: $[Ar]4s^2 3d^3$, (V^{2+}: $[Ar]3d^3$); Sc: $[Ar]4s^2 3d^1$; (Sc^{2+}: $[Ar]3d^1$)

V has a slightly larger Z (23) and Z_{eff} than Sc (Z > 21), so the 3d electrons in V are more tightly held than those in Sc. Also, losing the lone 3d electron in Sc^{2+} leads to the stable noble-gas configuration of [Ar] for Sc^{3+}.

23.38 (a) Ti^{3+}: $[Ar]3d^2$ (b) Co^{3+}: $[Ar]3d^6$ (c) Pd^{2+}: $[Kr]4d^8$

(d) Mo^{3+}: $[Kr]4d^3$ (e) Ru^{3+}: $[Kr]4d^5$ (f) Ni^{4+}: $[Ar]3d^6$

23.40 The stronger reducing agent is more easily oxidized; Cr^{2+} is more easily oxidized (see Solution 23.39), so it is the stronger reducing agent.

23.42 Chromate ion, CrO_4^{2-}, is bright yellow. Dichromate, $Cr_2O_7^{2-}$, is orange and more stable in acid solution than CrO_4^{2-} because of the equilibrium $2CrO_4^{2-}(aq) + 2H^+(aq) \rightleftharpoons Cr_2O_7^{2-}(aq) + H_2O(l)$.

23.44 (a) $MnO_2(s) + 4HCl(aq) \rightarrow MnCl_2(aq) + Cl_2(g) + 2H_2O(l)$

(b) Yes. MnO_2 is the oxidizing agent; HCl is the reducing agent.

23.46 (a) *Ferromagnetic* materials can form "permanent" magnets, whereas *paramagnetic* materials cannot.

(b) In order for a substance to be ferromagnetic, the magnetic moments on sites throughout the lattice must interact with one another. That is, the sites must be physically close and the overlap of orbitals must enable the individual magnetic sites to couple forming a much larger magnetic moment throughout the solid. Because of these interactions, the sustained existence of the magnetic moment does not require application of an external magnetic field.

(c) No. Other metals (Co and Ni, for example), alloys and some oxides (CrO_2) are also ferromagnetic.

Additional Exercises

23.48 Al^{3+}, Mg^{2+} and Na^+ all have large negative reduction potentials (Al, Mg and Na are very active metals). A substance with a more negative reduction potential would have to be used to chemically reduce them. All such substances are more expensive and difficult to obtain than Al, Mg and Na. Electrolysis is thus the most cost efficient way to reduce Al^{3+}, Mg^{2+} and Na^+ to their metallic states.

23.50 (a) $2VCl_3(s) + O_2(g) \rightarrow 2VOCl_3(s)$

(b) $Nb_2O_5(s) + 5H_2(g) \rightarrow 2Nb(s) + 5H_2O(l)$

(c) $2Fe^{3+}(aq) + Zn(s) \rightarrow 2Fe^{2+}(aq) + Zn^{2+}(aq)$

(d) $NbCl_5(s) + 3H_2O(l) \rightarrow HNbO_3(s) + 5HCl(aq)$

23.51 (a) $NiO(s) + 2H^+(aq) \rightarrow Ni^{2+}(aq) + H_2O(l)$

(b) The simple answer is that the solid is subjected to acid hydrolysis:
$CuCo_2S_4(s) + 8H^+(aq) \rightarrow Cu^{2+}(aq) + 2Co^{3+}(aq) + 4H_2S(g)$
However, in the absence of a strong complexing ligand, Co^{3+} is not stable in water. It oxidizes water according to the following reaction:
$4Co^{3+}(aq) + 2H_2O(l) \rightarrow 4Co^{2+}(aq) + O_2(g) + 4H^+(aq)$

(c) $TiO_2(s) + C(s) + 2Cl_2(g) \rightarrow TiCl_4(g) + CO_2(g)$

(d) In this reaction O_2 is reduced and sulfide is oxidized. Writing the sulfur product as S_8, the balanced equation is:
$8ZnS(s) + 4O_2(g) + 16H^+(aq) \rightarrow 8Zn^{2+}(aq) + S_8(s) + 8H_2O(l)$

23.53 All transition metals have the generic electron configuration $ns^2(n\text{-}1)d^x$. Regardless of the number of d electrons, each transition metal has 2 *ns* valence electrons that are the first electrons lost when metal ions are formed. Thus, almost every transition metal has a stable +2 oxidation state.

After the 2 *ns* electrons are lost, a varying number of (*n*-1)d electrons can be lost, depending on the identity of the transition metal. The availability of different numbers of d electrons leads to a wide variety of accessible oxidation states for the transition metals.

23.54 Assuming that SO_2 and N_2 are the nonmetallic products, two half-reactions can be written:

$$5[MoS_2(s) + 7H_2O(l) \rightarrow MoO_3(s) + 2SO_2(g) + 14H^+(aq) + 14e^-]$$

$$7[12H^+(aq) + 2NO_3^-(aq) + 10e^- \rightarrow N_2(g) + 6H_2O(l)]$$

$$5MoS_2(s) + 14H^+(aq) + 14NO_3^-(aq) \rightarrow 5MoO_3(s) + 10SO_2(g) + 7N_2(g) + 7H_2O(l)$$

$$MoO_3(s) + 2NH_3(aq) + H_2O(l) \rightarrow (NH_4)_2MoO_4(s)$$

$$(NH_4)_2MoO_4(s) \xrightarrow{\Delta} 2NH_3(g) + H_2O(g) + MoO_3(s)$$

$$MoO_3(s) + 3H_2(g) \xrightarrow{\Delta} Mo(s) + 3H_2O(g)$$

23.56 Silicon has the diamond structure. As with carbon, the four valence electrons of silicon are completely involved in the four localized bonds to its neighbors. There are thus no electrons free to migrate throughout the solid. Titanium exists as a close-packed lattice; each Ti atom has twelve equivalent nearest neighbors. The valence shell electrons cannot be localized between pairs of atoms; rather they are delocalized and mobile throughout the structure. In terms of the band model described in Figure 23.15, Ti has an incompletely occupied allowed energy band. The origin of the different behaviors with regard to structure has to do with the extent of the orbitals in space. Electrons in Si feel a greater attraction to the nucleus than electrons in Ti, so they are more localized.

23.58 In a paramagnetic substance, the unpaired electrons on one atom are not affected by (coupled to) the unpaired electrons on adjacent atoms. The unpaired electrons are in random orientations. The external magnetic field causes rough alignment and therefore weak attraction to the magnetic field. In a ferromagnetic substance, unpaired electrons on adjacent atoms are coupled and aligned in the same direction. This permanent magnetic moment causes the ferromagnetic substance to be strongly attracted into the magnetic field.

23.59 (a) Nb^{5+}: [Ar]; diamagnetic, no unpaired electrons

(b) Cr^{2+}: $[Ar]3d^4$ paramagnetic, unpaired electrons

(c) Cu^+: $[Ar]3d^{10}$; diamagnetic, no unpaired electrons

(d) Ru^{8+}: [Ar]; diamagnetic, no unpaired electrons

(e) Ni^{2+}: $[Ar]3d^8$; paramagnetic, unpaired electrons

23.61 (a) $Mn(s) + 2HNO_3(aq) \rightarrow Mn(NO_3)_2(aq) + H_2(g)$

(b) $Mn(NO_3)_2(s) \xrightarrow{\Delta} MnO_2(s) + 2NO_2(g)$

(c) $3MnO_2(s) \xrightarrow{\Delta} Mn_3O_4(s) + O_2(g)$

(d) $2MnCl_2(s) + 9F_2(g) \rightarrow 2MnF_3(s) + 4ClF_3(g)$

23.62 (a) Nothing. As noted in Section 20.8, a basic environment (OH^-) inhibits oxidation of Fe^{2+} to Fe^{3+}, even in the presence of $O_2(g)$.

(b) $Cu(NO_3)_2(aq) + 2KOH(aq) \rightarrow Cu(OH)_2(s) + 2KNO_3(aq)$

$Cu(OH)_2(s)$ precipitates. Cu^{2+} forms a soluble complex ion with $NH_3(aq)$, but not $OH^-(aq)$.

(c) The color of the solution changes from orange ($Cr_2O_7^{2-}$) to yellow (CrO_4^{2-}). The equilibrium is

$Cr_2O_7^{2-}(aq) + H_2O(l) \rightleftharpoons 2CrO_4^{2-}(aq) + 2H^+(aq)$

As $OH^-(aq)$ is added, it reacts with and removes $H^+(aq)$ from solution, shifting the equilibrium to the right in favor of the yellow CrO_4^{2-}.

23.64 (a) insulator (b) p-type semiconductor (c) metallic conductor

(d) metallic conductor (e) insulator (f) metallic conductor

Integrative Exercises

23.66 (a) Calculate mass Cu_2S and FeS, then mass SO_2 from each.

3.3×10^6 kg sample $\times 0.27 = 8.91 \times 10^5 = 8.9 \times 10^5$ kg $= 8.9 \times 10^8$ g Cu_2S

3.3×10^6 kg sample $\times 0.13 = 4.29 \times 10^5 = 4.3 \times 10^5$ kg $= 4.3 \times 10^8$ g FeS

$$8.91 \times 10^8 \text{ g } Cu_2S \times \frac{1 \text{ mol } Cu_2S}{159.1 \text{ g } Cu_2S} \times \frac{1 \text{ mol } SO_2}{1 \text{ mol } Cu_2S} \times \frac{64.07 \text{ g } SO_2}{1 \text{ mol } SO_2} = 3.588 \times 10^8$$

$$= 3.6 \times 10^8 \text{ g } SO_2$$

$$4.29 \times 10^8 \text{ g FeS} \times \frac{1 \text{ mol FeS}}{87.9 \text{ g FeS}} \times \frac{1 \text{ mol } SO_2}{1 \text{ mol FeS}} \times \frac{64.07 \text{ g } SO_2}{1 \text{ mol } SO_2} = 3.127 \times 10^8 \text{ g}$$

$$= 3.1 \times 10^8 \text{ g } SO_2$$

$g\ SO_2 = 3.588 \times 10^8 + 3.127 \times 10^8 = 6.715 \times 10^8 = 6.7 \times 10^8$ g SO_2

(b) Calculate mol Cu, mol Fe and mole ratio Cu: Fe.

$$8.91 \times 10^8 \text{ g } Cu_2S \times \frac{1 \text{ mol } Cu_2S}{159.1 \text{ g } Cu_2S} \times \frac{2 \text{ mol Cu}}{1 \text{ mol } Cu_2S} = 1.12 \times 10^7 = 1.1 \times 10^7 \text{ mol Cu}$$

$$4.29 \times 10^8 \text{ g FeS} \times \times \frac{1 \text{ mol FeS}}{87.9 \text{ g FeS}} \times \frac{1 \text{ mol Fe}}{1 \text{ mol FeS}} = 4.88 \times 10^6 = 4.9 \times 10^6 \text{ mol Fe}$$

1.12×10^7 mol Cu/4.88×10^6 mol Fe = 2.3 mol Cu/mol Fe

(c) The oxidizing environment of the converter is likely to produce CuO and Fe_2O_3.

(d) $Cu_2S(s) + 2O_2(g) \rightarrow 2CuO(s) + SO_2(g)$

$4FeS(s) + 7O_2(g) \rightarrow 2Fe_2O_3(s) + 4SO_2(g)$

23.67 Recall from the discussion in Chapter 13 that like substances tend to be soluble in one another, whereas unlike substances do not. Molten metal consists of atoms that continue to be bound to one another by metallic bonding, even though the substance is liquid. In a slag, on the other hand, the attractive forces are those between ions. The slag phase is a highly polar, ionic medium, whereas the metallic phase is nonpolar, and the attractive interactions are due to metallic bond formation. There is little driving force for materials with such different characteristics to dissolve in one another.

23.69 (a) $\Delta G° = \Delta H° - T\Delta S°$ (assume $\Delta H°$ and $S°$ are constant with changes in temperature)

$Si(s) + 2MnO(s) \rightarrow SiO_2(s) + 2Mn(s)$

$\Delta H° = \Delta H_f^\circ\ SiO_2(s) + 2\Delta H_f^\circ\ Mn(s) - 2\Delta H_f^\circ\ MnO(s) - \Delta H_f^\circ\ Si(s)$

$\Delta H° = -910.9 + 2(0) - 2(-385.2) + 0 = -140.5$ kJ

$\Delta S° = S°\ SiO_2(s) + 2S°\ Mn(s) - 2S°\ MnO(s) - S°\ Si(s)$

$= 41.84 + 2(32.0) - 2(59.7) - 18.7 = -32.26 = -32.3$ J/K

$\Delta G° = -140.5$ kJ $- 1473$ K$(-0.03226$ kJ/K$) = -93.0$ kJ

(b) At 1473 K, the reactants and products are all solids, so they are in their standard states. Since $\Delta G°$ is negative at this temperature, the reaction should be spontaneous and thus feasible.

23.71 $2[Cu^+(aq) + 1e^- \rightarrow Cu(s)]$ $E^\circ_{red} = 0.521$ V

$Cu(s) \rightarrow Cu^{2+}(aq) + 2e^-$ $E^\circ_{red} = 0.337$ V

$2Cu^+(aq) \rightarrow Cu^{2+}(aq) + Cu(s)$ $E^\circ = (0.521\text{ V} - 0.337\text{ V}) = 0.184$ V

According to Equation 20.18, $\log K_{eq} = \dfrac{nE^\circ}{0.0592}$; n = 2

$$\log K_{eq} = \frac{2(0.184)}{0.0592} = 6.2162 = 6.22;\ K_{eq} = 1.6 \times 10^6$$

23.72 $\Delta G^\circ = -RT \ln K$; $\Delta G^\circ = \Delta H^\circ - T\Delta S^\circ$

Calculate ΔH° and ΔS° using data from Appendix C, assuming ΔH° and ΔS° remain constant with changing temperature. Then calculate ΔG° and K at the two temperatures.

$\Delta H^\circ = 2\Delta H_f CO(g) - \Delta H^\circ_f\ C(s) - \Delta H^\circ_f\ CO_2(g)$

$\Delta H^\circ = 2(-110.5) - 0 - (-393.5) = +172.5$ kJ

$\Delta S^\circ = 2S^\circ\ CO(g) - S^\circ\ C(s) - S^\circ\ CO_2(g)$

$= 2(197.9) - 5.69 - 213.6 = +176.5$ J/K $= 0.1765$ kJ/K

$\Delta G^\circ_{298} = 172.5$ kJ $- 298$ K$(0.1765$ kJ/K$) = +119.9$ kJ

$$\ln K_{eq} = \frac{\Delta G^\circ}{-RT} = \frac{119.9\text{ kJ}}{-(8.314 \times 10^{-3}\text{ kJ/K})(298\text{ K})} = -48.3942 = -48.39;\ K_{eq} = 9.6 \times 10^{-22}$$

$\Delta G^\circ_{2000} = 172.5$ kJ $- 2000$ K $(0.1765$ kJ/K$) = -180.5$ kJ

$$\ln K_{eq} = \frac{-180.5}{-(8.314 \times 10^{-3}\text{ kJ/K})(2000\text{ K})} = 10.8552 = 10.86;\ K_{eq} = 5.2 \times 10^4$$

23.74 (a) The very low melting and boiling points for VF_5 indicate that it is molecular rather than ionic, and that the intermolecular forces are probably weak London-dispersion forces. In order for the molecule to experience only London-dispersion forces, it must be nonpolar covalent, which requires the symmetrical trigonal bipyramidal structure shown below. PF_5 also has this structure.

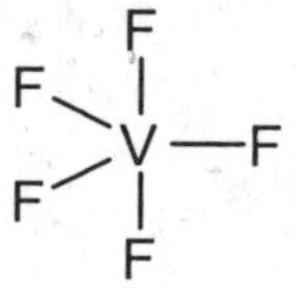

(b) $VCl_3(s) + 3HF(g) \xrightarrow{\Delta} VF_3(s) + 3HCl(g)$

(c) V(V) has a relatively small covalent radius. F is the smallest and most electronegative halogen. The steric repulsions associated with placing five larger halogens around the small V(V) central atom would be substantial. Also, the extreme electron attracting nature of F might be required to coax V into the +5 oxidation state.

23.75 Calculate the mass of Zn(s) that will be deposited.

$$2.0 \text{ m} \times 80 \text{ m} \times \frac{(100)^2 \text{ cm}^2}{1 \text{ m}^2} \times 0.49 \text{ mm} \times \frac{1 \text{ cm}}{10 \text{ mm}} \times \frac{7.1 \text{ g}}{\text{cm}^3} \times 2 \text{ sides}$$

$$= 1.113 \times 10^6 = 1.1 \times 10^6 \text{ g Zn}$$

$$1.113 \times 10^6 \text{ g Zn} \times \frac{1 \text{ mol Zn}}{65.39 \text{ g Zn}} \times \frac{2 \text{ F}}{0.90 \text{ mol Zn}} \times \frac{96{,}500 \text{ C}}{\text{F}} = 3.651 \times 10^9 = 3.7 \times 10^9 \text{ C}$$

(2 F/0.90 mol Zn takes the 90% efficiency into account.)

$$3.651 \times 10^9 \text{ C} \times 3.5 \text{ V} \times \frac{1 \text{ J}}{\text{C}\bullet\text{V}} \times \frac{1 \text{ kWh}}{3.6 \times 10^6 \text{ J}} = 3{,}550 = 3.6 \times 10^3 \text{ kWh}$$

$$3.550 \times 10^3 \text{ kWh} \times \frac{\$0.082}{1 \text{ kWh}} = \$291.06 \rightarrow \$291$$

23.77 (a) M(s) → M(g). The process of atomization is essentially breaking the "metallic bonds" in the solid metal and separating the particles into isolated gas-phase atoms. This requires relocalizing electrons from the solid lattice onto the individual metal atoms.

(b) ΔH_{atom} is the difference between the energy of a mole of gaseous metal atoms, isolated from one another, and a mole of the metal, with all its metal-metal bonding. The difference will be smaller if: 1) the gaseous atoms have some special stability relative to other metallic elements or 2) the metal-metal bonding in the solid is weaker.

The data indicate that Cr and Mn, in the middle of the first transition series, and Cu at the end, have smaller ΔH_{atom} than their neighbors. The electron configurations for these elements are: Cr, [Ar]$4s^1 3d^5$ (exception); Mn, [Ar]$4s^2 3d^5$; Cu, [Ar]$4s^1 3d^{10}$. The gaseous atoms of each of these elements have special stability due to either full or half-full subshells. Assuming relatively constant metal-metal bond strength, the special stability of the gaseous atoms reduces ΔH_{atom} for these elements, relative to their neighbors.

The lower values of ΔH_{atom} for Fe, Co and Ni relative to the elements around V (after taking account of the variations in stability of the gaseous atoms) is likely due to decreasing metal-metal bond strength. Moving to the right across the transition series from the middle onward, effective nuclear charge increases, the radial extension of the d-orbitals decreases and the strength of metallic bonding decreases. This is somewhat of a trend.

24 Chemistry of Coordination Compounds

Introduction to Metal Complexes

24.2 (a) In Werner's theory, *primary valence* is the charge of the metal cation at the center of the complex. *Secondary valence* is the number of atoms bound or coordinated to the central metal ion. The modern terms for these concepts are oxidation state and coordination number, respectively. (Note that 'oxidation state' is a broader term than ionic charge, but Werner's complexes contain metal ions where cation charge and oxidation state are equal.)

(b) Ligands are the Lewis base in metal-ligand interactions (see Solution 24.1(b)). As such, they must possess at least one unshared electron pair. NH_3 has an unshared electron pair but BH_3, with less than 8 electrons about B, has no unshared electron pair and cannot act as a ligand. In fact, BH_3 acts as a Lewis acid, an electron pair acceptor, because it is electron-deficient.

24.4 (a) Yes. There are 6 possible ligands, 3 H_2O molecules and 3 Cl^- ions. Any Cl^- ions that are not coordinated to the metal will form AgCl(s) precipitate when the complex is treated with $AgNO_3$(aq). Absence of AgCl(s) would mean all Cl^- ions were ligands and a coordination number of 6. One mole of AgCl(s) per mole of complex would mean one uncoordinated ligand, and so on. This assumes that all 3 H_2O molecules act as ligands. In fact, they could serve as water of hydration (Section 13.1, A Closer Look: Hydrates). Reaction with $AgNO_3$ gives no information about the nature of H_2O molecules.

(b) Yes. Conductivity is directly related to the number of ions in a solution. The lower the conductivity, the more Cl^- ions that act as ligands. Conductivity measurements on a set of standard solutions with various moles of ions per mole of complex would provide a comparative method for quantitative determination of the number of free and bound Cl^- ions.

24.6 (a) Coordination number = 6, oxidation number = +3

(b) 6, +2 (c) 6, +4 (d) 6, +2 (e) 6, +3 (f) 6, +3
octahedral

24.8 (a) 6 C (see Solution 24.7(d)) (b) 5 O, 1 Br^- (c) 3 N, 3 Br^- (d) 2 O, 4 N
(e) 2 O, 2 S (f) 4 N, 2 F

Polydendate ligands; Nomenclature

24.10 (a) 2 coordination sites, 2 N donor atoms

(b) 2 coordination sites, 2 N donor atoms

(c) 2 coordination sites, 2 O donor atoms (Although there are four potential O donor atoms in $C_2O_4^{2-}$, it is geometrically impossible for more than two of these to be bound to a single metal ion.

(d) 4 coordination sites, 4 N donor atoms

(e) 6 coordination sites, 2 N and 4 O donor atoms

24.12 (a) 4 (b) 4 (c) 6 (d) 6

24.14 (a) Monodentate; py has only one N donor atom.

(b) K_{eq} for this reaction will be less than one. Two free pyridine molecules are replaced by one free bipy molecule. There are more moles of particles in the reactants than products, so ΔS is predicted to be negative. Processes with a net decrease in entropy are usually nonspontaneous, have positive ΔG, and values of K_{eq} less than one. This equilibrium is likely to be spontaneous in the reverse direction.

24.16 (a) $[Mn(H_2O)_5Br]SO_4$ (b) $[Ru(bipy)_3](NO_3)_2$ (c) $[Fe(o\text{-phen})_2Cl_2]ClO_4$
(d) $Na[Co(en)Br_4]$ (e) $[Ni(NH_3)_6]_3[Cr(ox)_3]_2$

24.18 (a) trichloroethylenediamineniobium(V) sulfate

(b) tricarbonyltripyridinemolybdenum(0)

(c) ammonium tetrachloroaurate(III)

(d) tetraamminediaquairidium(III) nitrate

Isomerism

24.20 (a)

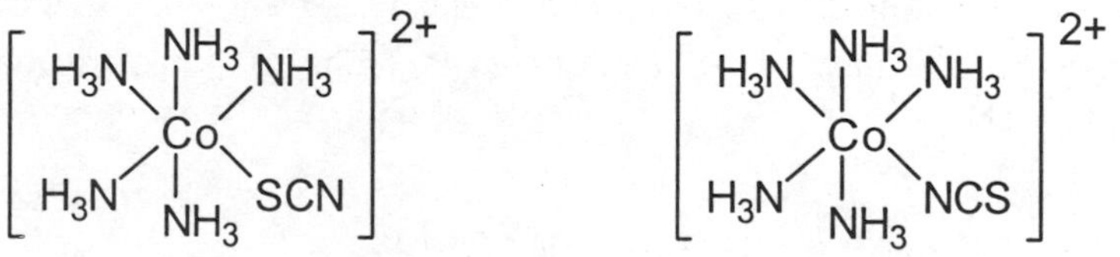

coordination sphere isomerism

24.20 (continued)

(b) 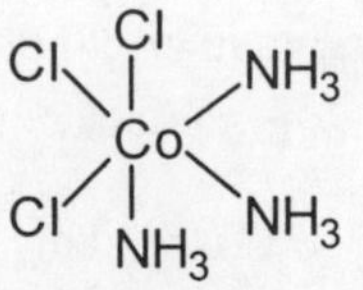 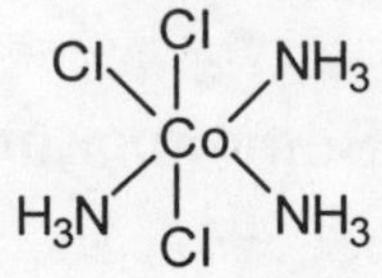

(c) 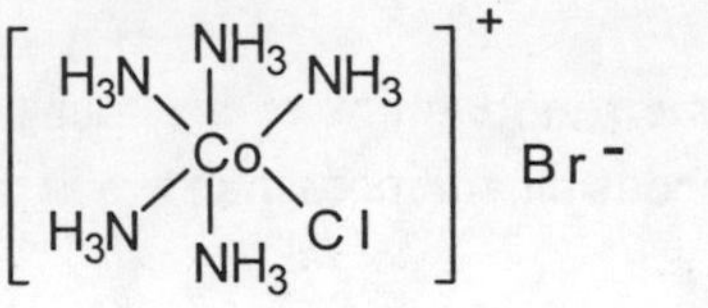 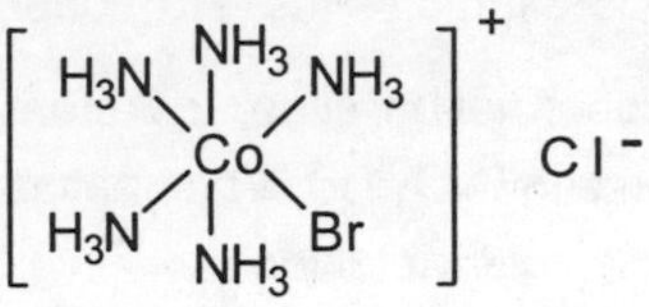

coordination sphere isomerism

24.22 Two geometric isomers are possible for an octahedral MA_3B_3 complex (see below). All other arrangements, including mirror images, can be rotated into these two structures. Neither isomer is optically active.

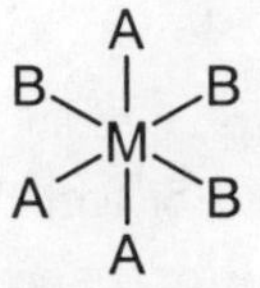

(i)

(ii)

24.24 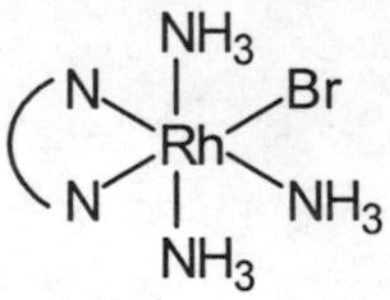 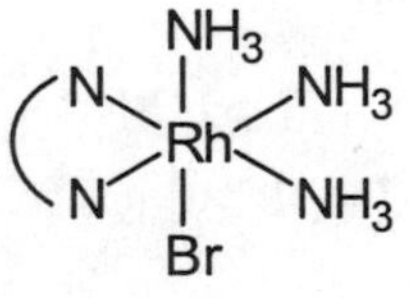

The symbol N N represents the bidentate ligand (bipy).
There are no optical isomers. The mirror image of each structural isomer can be superimposed on the structure above by a 180° rotation.

24.26 (a) 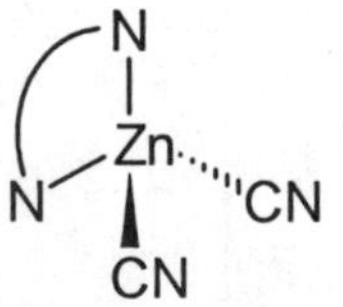

(b) 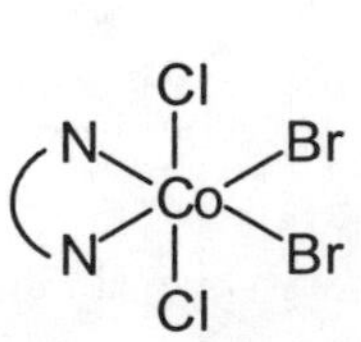 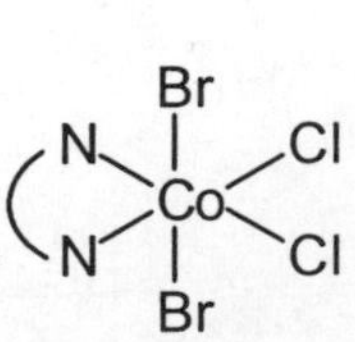

(c) 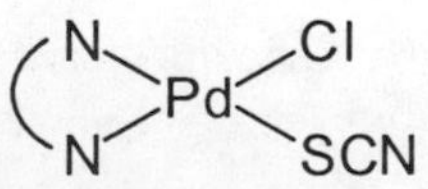

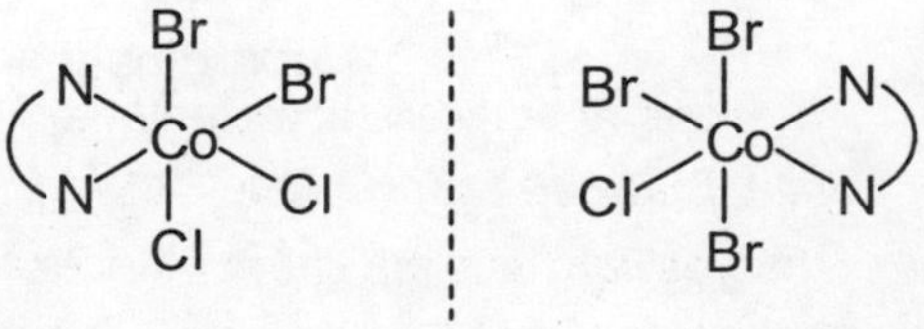

Color, Magnetism; Crystal-Field Theory

24.28 (a) Yes. A complex that absorbs visible light of one wavelength or color will appear as the complementary color. This complex absorbs green light and will appear red.

(b) No. A solution can appear green by transmitting or reflecting only green light (the situation stated in the exercise) **or** by absorbing red light, the complementary color of green.

(c) A visible absorption spectrum shows the amount of light absorbed at a given wavelength. It is a plot of absorbance (dependent variable, y-axis) vs. wavelength (independent variable, x-axis).

24.30

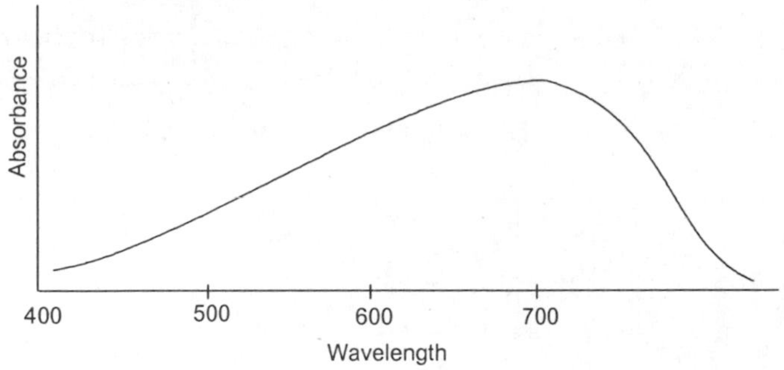

24.32 Six ligands in an octahedral arrangement are oriented along the x, y and z axes of the metal. These negatively charged ligands (or the negative end of ligand dipoles) have greater electrostatic repulsion with valence electrons in metal orbitals that also lie along these axes, the d_{z^2}, and $d_{x^2-y^2}$. The d_{xy}, d_{xz} and d_{yz} metal orbitals point between the x, y, and z axes, and electrons in these orbitals experience less repulsion with ligand electrons. Thus, in the presence of an octahedral ligand field, the d_{xy}, d_{xz} and d_{xy} metal orbitals are lower in energy than the $d_{x^2-y^2}$ and d_{z^2}.

24.34 (a) $$\Delta E = hc/\lambda = \frac{6.626 \times 10^{-34}\ J \bullet s \times 2.998 \times 10^{8}\ m/s}{500 \times 10^{-9}\ m} = 3.973 \times 10^{-19}$$

$$= 3.97 \times 10^{-19}\ J/photon$$

$$\Delta = 3.973 \times 10^{-19}\ J/photon \times \frac{6.022 \times 10^{23}\ photons}{1\ mol} \times \frac{1\ kJ}{1000\ J} = 239.25 = 239\ kJ/mol$$

(b) If H_2O is replaced by NH_3, the magnitude of Δ would increase because NH_3 is higher in the spectrochemical series and creates a stronger ligand field.

24.36 The ions absorb the complement of the color they appear. Green $[Ni(H_2O)_6]^{2+}$ absorbs red light, 650-800 nm. Purple $[Ni(NH_3)_6]^{2+}$ absorbs yellow light, 560-580 nm. Thus, $[Ni(NH_3)_6]^{2+}$ absorbs light with the shorter wavelength. This agrees with the spectrochemical series, which indicates that H_2O will produce a smaller d orbital splitting (Δ) than NH_3. Thus, $[Ni(H_2O)_6]^{2+}$ should absorb light with a smaller energy and longer wavelength.

24.38 (a) Fe^{3+}, d^5 (b) Mn^{2+}, d^5 (c) Co^{2+}, d^7 (d) Ag^+, d^{10} (e) Sr^{2+}, d^0

24.40 (a) Ru: $[Kr]5s^14d^7$ (b) Mo: $[Kr]5s^14d^5$ (c) Co: $[Ar]4s^23d^7$

Ru^{2+}: $[Kr]4d^6$ Mo^{2+}: $[Kr]3d^4$ Co^{2+}: $[Ar]3d^7$

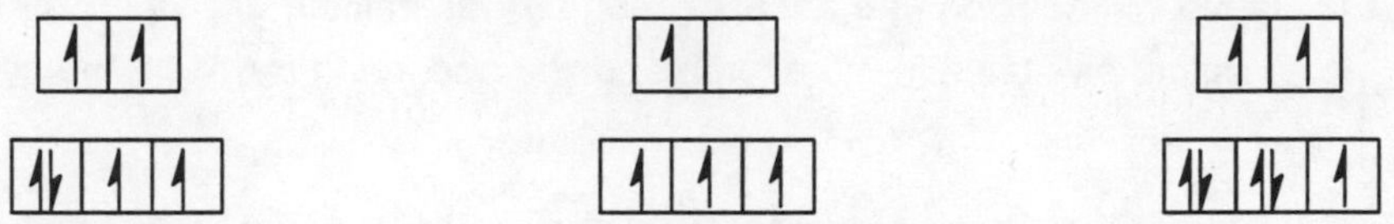

4 unpaired electrons 4 unpaired electrons 3 unpaired electrons

24.42

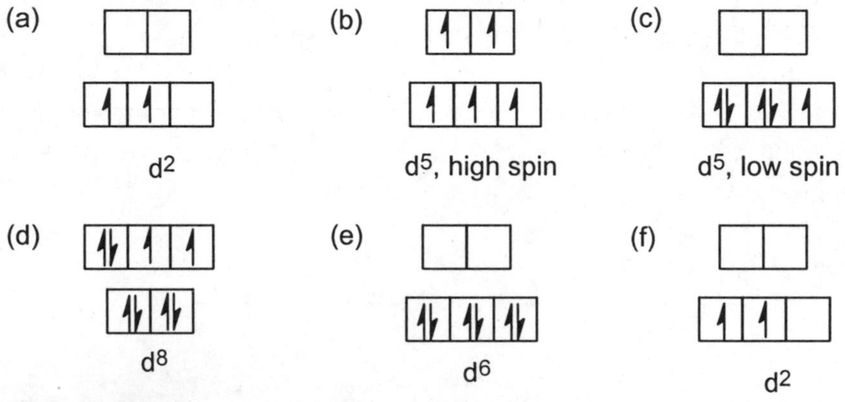

24.44

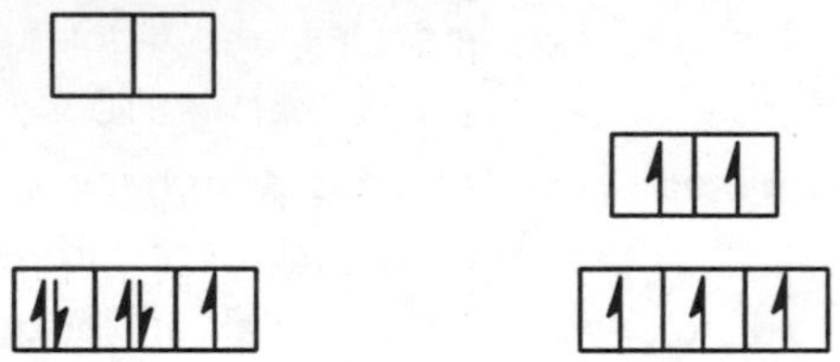

$[Fe(CN)_6]^{3-}$ low spin $[Fe(NCS)_6]^{3-}$ high spin

Both complexes contain Fe^{3+}, a d^5 ion. CN^-, a strong field ligand, produces such a large Δ that the splitting energy is greater than the pairing energy, and the complex is low spin. NCS^- produces a smaller Δ, so it is energetically favorable for d electrons to be unpaired in the higher energy d orbitals. NCS^- is a much weaker-field ligand than CN^-. It is probably weaker than NH_3 and near H_2O in the spectrochemical series.

Additional Exercises

24.46 $[Pt(NH_3)_6]Cl_4$; $[Pt(NH_3)_4Cl_2]Cl_2$; $[Pt(NH_3)_3Cl_3]Cl$; $[Pt(NH_3)_2Cl_4]$; $K[Pt(NH_3)Cl_5]$

24.47 (a) 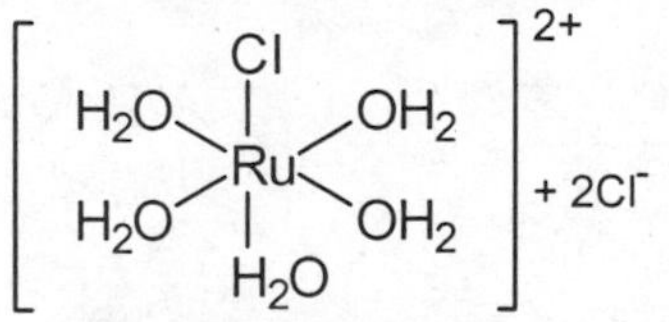

(b) 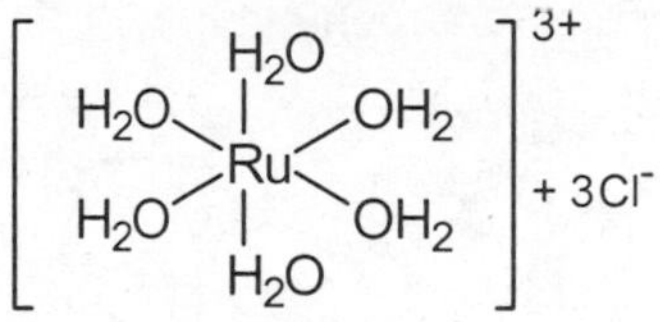

$[Ru(H_2O)_5Cl]Cl_2$ ⟶ $[Ru(H_2O)_6]Cl_3$

24.49 (a) [24.48(a)] *cis*-tetraamminediaquacobalt(II) nitrate

[24.48(b)] sodium aquapentachlororuthenate(III)

[24.48(c)] ammonium *trans*-diaquabisoxalatocobaltate(III)

[24.48(d)] *cis*-dichlorobisethylenediamineruthenium(II)

(b) Only the complex in 24.48(d) is optically active. The mirror images of (a)-(c) can be superimposed on the original structure. The chelating ligands in (d) prevent its mirror images (enantiomers) from being superimposable.

24.50 (a) Valence electrons: 2P + 6C + 16H = 10 + 24 + 16 = 50 e^-, 25 e^- pr

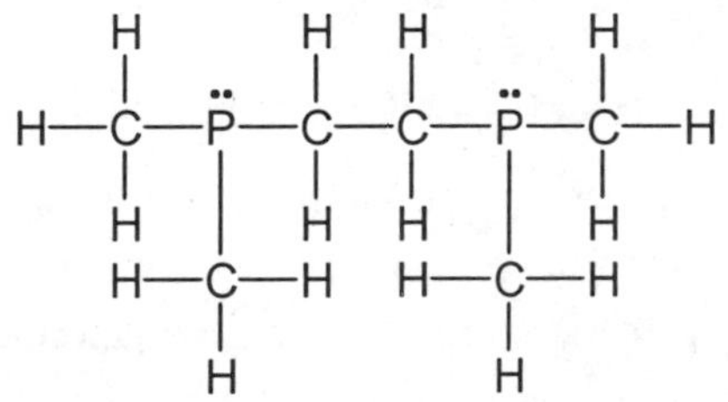

(b) Both CO and dmpe are neutral molecules, so the oxidation state of Mo must be zero.

(c) 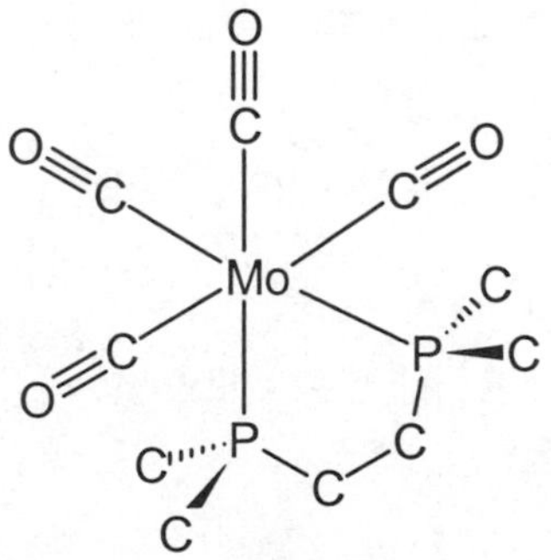

(H atoms omitted for clarity)

C≡O coordinates through C, because it is less electronegative than O, and a better electron pair donor. The molecule has only a single isomer. The dmpe ligand cannot span *trans* positions, so there are no geometric isomers. The mirror image of the structure above is easily superimposable, so there are no optical isomers.

24.52 We will represent the end of the bidentate ligand containing the CF_3 group by a shaded oval, the other end by an open oval:

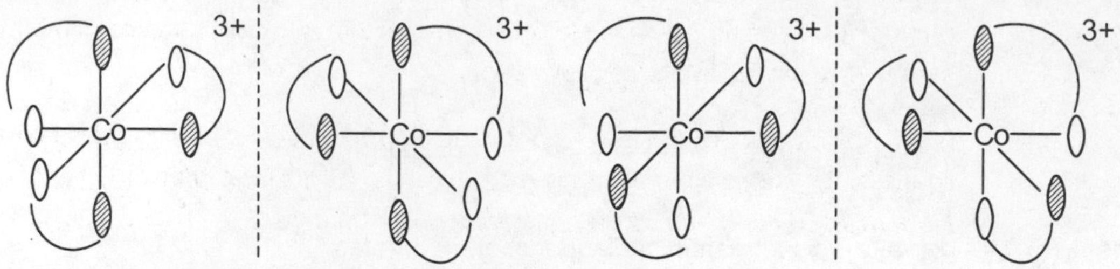

24.53 (a) *Hemoglobin* is the iron-containing protein that transports O_2 in human blood.

(b) *Chlorophylls* are magnesium-containing porphyrins in plants. They are the key components in the conversion of solar energy into chemical energy that can be used by living organisms.

(c) *Siderophores* are iron-binding compounds or ligands produced by a microorganism. They compete on a molecular level for iron in the medium outside the organism and carry needed iron into the cells of the organism.

24.55 (a) pentacarbonyliron(0)

(b) Since CO is a neutral molecule, the oxidation state of iron must be zero.

(c) $[Fe(CO)_4CN]^-$ has two geometric isomers. In a trigonal bipyramid, the axial and equatorial positions are not equivalent and not superimposable. One isomer has CN in an axial position and the other has it in an equatorial position.

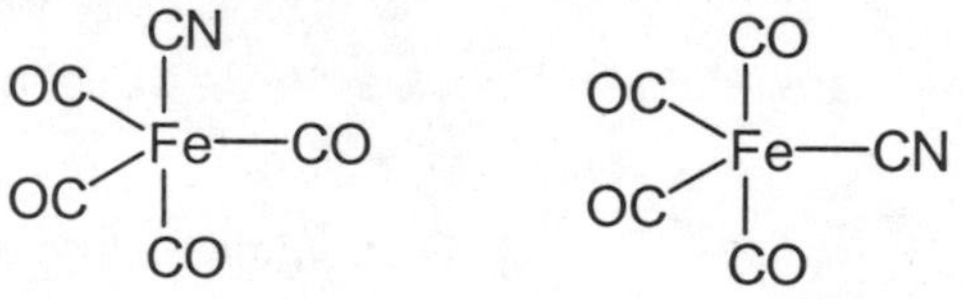

24.56 The ligands that possess the greatest ability to interact with the central metal atom cause the largest splitting. The properties of ligands that are important are **charge** (usually the more negatively charged ligands produce larger splittings) and **polarizability**, which measures the ability of the ligand to distort its charge distribution as it interacts with the positively charged metal ion.

24.58 (a)

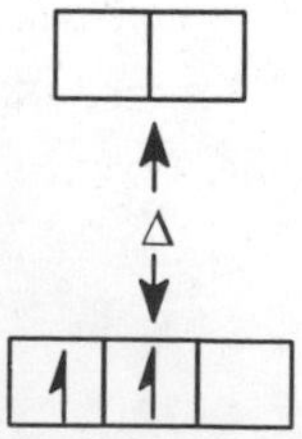

d^2

(b) These complexes are colored because the crystal-field splitting energy, Δ, is in the visible portion of the electromagnetic spectrum. Visible light with $\lambda = hc/\Delta$ is absorbed, promoting one of the d electrons into a higher energy d orbital. The remaining wavelengths of visible light are reflected or transmitted; the combination of these wavelengths is the color we see.

(c) $[VF_6]^{3-}$ will absorb light with a longer wavelength and lower energy. As a weak-field ligand in the spectrochemical series, F^- causes a smaller Δ than H_2O. Since Δ and λ are inversely related, smaller Δ corresponds to longer λ.

24.59 (a) Formally, the two Ru centers have different oxidation states; one is +2 and the other is +3.

(b) Ru^{2+}, d^6 Ru^{3+}, d^5

(c) There is extensive bonding-electron delocalization in the isolated pyrazine molecule. When pyrazine acts as a bridging ligand, its delocalized molecular orbitals provide a pathway for delocalization of the "odd" d electron in the Creutz-Taube ion. The two metal ions appear equivalent because the odd d electron is delocalized across the pyrazine bridge.

24.61 oxyhemoglobin Fe^{2+} : d^6 deoxyhemoglobin Fe^{2+} : d^6

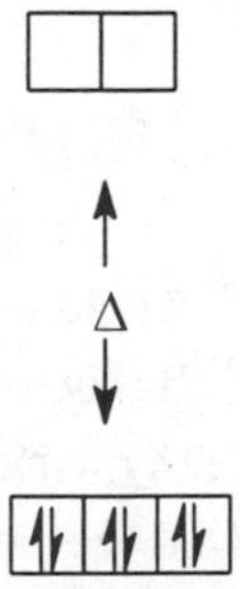

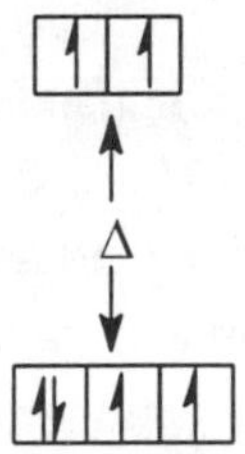

low spin, no unpaired electrons high spin, 4 unpaired electrons

In general, the crystal field splitting, Δ, is greater in low spin than high spin complexes. The energy, Δ, corresponds to the wavelength of light absorbed by the complex and determines its color. Since oxyhemoglobin absorbs higher energy, shorter wavelength light, longer wavelengths remain and the sample appears red. Deoxyhemoglobin absorbs lower energy (orange-red) light, and the sample appears blue.

24.62

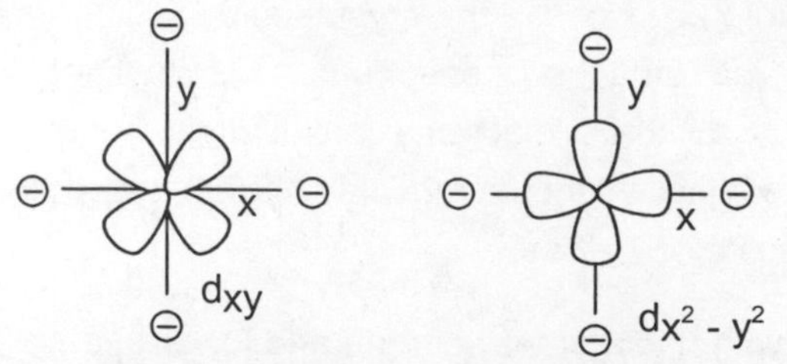

The lobes of the d_{xy} orbital point between the *x* and *y* axes, while the lobes of the $d_{x^2-y^2}$ orbital point along the axes. In a square-planar crystal field with ligands along the axes, an electron in a $d_{x^2-y^2}$ orbital is closer to the electron cloud of the ligands. Electron-electron repulsion with ligand electrons is greater for an electron in the $d_{x^2-y^2}$ orbital of the metal, so the $d_{x^2-y^2}$ orbital has a higher energy than the d_{xy} orbital.

24.64 (a) The term *isoelectronic* means that the three ions have the same number of valence electrons and the same electron configuration.

(b) In each ion, the metal is in its maximum oxidation state and has a d^0 electron configuration. That is, the metal ions have no *d*-electrons, so there should be no *d-d* transitions.

(c) A ligand-metal charge transfer transition occurs when an electron in a filled ligand orbital is excited to an empty d-orbital of the metal.

(d) Absorption of 565 nm yellow light by MnO_4^- causes the compound to appear violet, the complementary color. CrO_4^{2-} appears yellow, so it is absorbing violet light of approximately 420 nm. The wavelength of the LMCT transition for chromate, 420 nm, is shorter than the wavelength of LCMT transition in permanganate, 565 nm. This means that there is a larger energy difference between filled ligand and empty metal orbitals in chromate than in permanganate.

(e) Yes. A white compound indicates that no visible light is absorbed. Going left on the periodic chart from Mn to Cr, the absorbed wavelength got shorter and the energy difference between ligand and metal orbitals increased. The 420 nm absorption by CrO_4^- is at the short wavelength edge of the visible spectrum. It is not surprising that the ion containing V, further left on the chart, absorbs at a still shorter wavelength in the ultraviolet region and that VO_4^{3-} appears white.

24.65 Application of pressure would result in shorter metal ion-oxide distances. This would have the effect of increasing the ligand-electron repulsions, and would result in a larger splitting in the d orbital energies. Thus, application of pressure should result in a shift in the absorption to a higher energy and shorter wavelength.

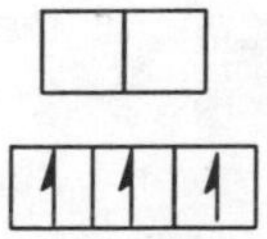

24.67

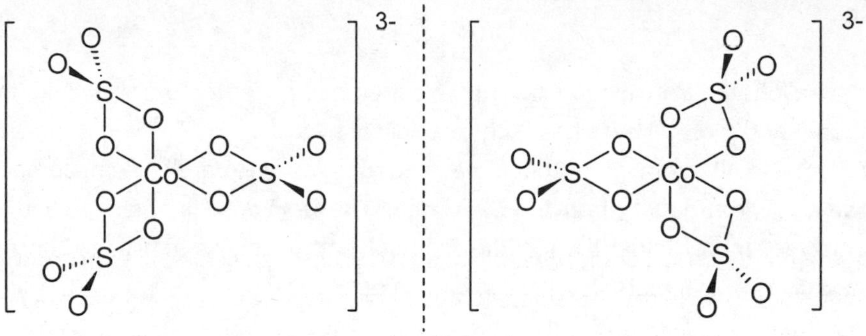

24.68 (a) Only one

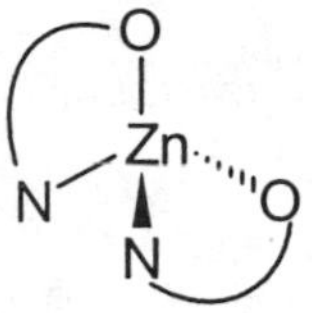

(b) Two

trans *cis*

(c) Four; two are geometric, the other two are stereoisomers of each of these.

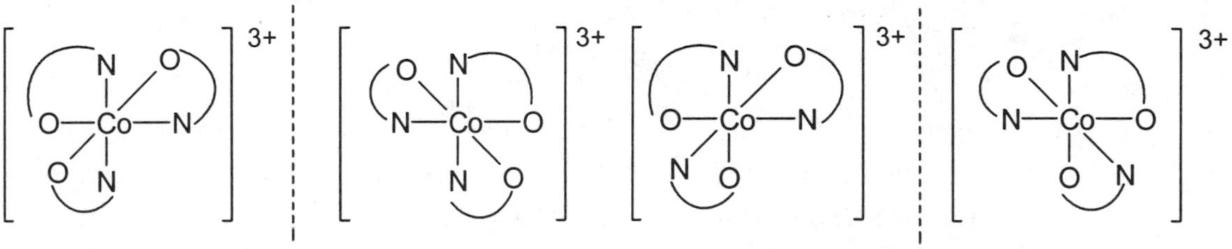

24.69

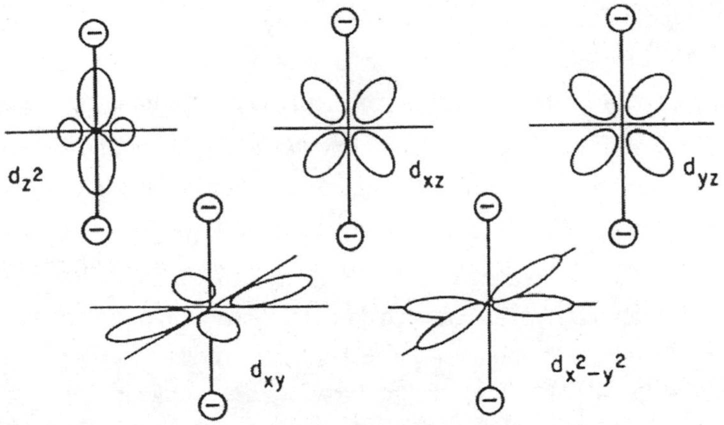

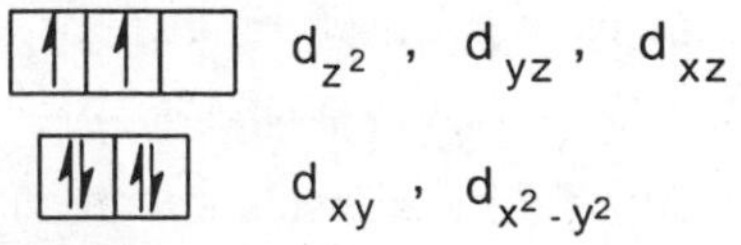

For a d^6 metal ion in a strong ligand field, there would be two unpaired electrons.

Integrative Exercises

24.70 In a complex ion, the transition metal is an electron pair acceptor, a Lewis acid; the ligand is an electron pair donor, a Lewis base. In carbonic anhydrase, the Zn^{2+} ion withdraws electron density from the O atom of water. The electronegative oxygen atom compensates by withdrawing electron-density from the O–H bond. The O–H bond is polarized and H becomes more ionizable, more acidic than in the bulk solvent. This is similar to the effect of an electronegative central atom in an oxyacid such as H_2SO_4.

24.72 (a)

$$[Cd(CH_3NH_2)_4]^{2+} \rightleftharpoons Cd^{2+}(aq) + 4CH_3NH_2(aq) \qquad \Delta G° = 37.2 \text{ kJ}$$
$$Cd^{2+}(aq) + 2en(aq) \rightleftharpoons [Cd(en)_2]^{2+}(aq) \qquad \Delta G° = -60.7 \text{ kJ}$$

$$Cd(CH_3NH_2)_4]^{2+} + 2en(aq) \rightleftharpoons [Cd(en)_2]^{2+}(aq) + 4CH_3NH_2(aq) \qquad \Delta G° = -23.5 \text{ kJ}$$

$\Delta G° = -RT\ln K_{eq}$; $-23.5 \text{ kJ} = -2.35 \times 10^4 \text{ J}$

$$-2.35 \times 10^4 \text{ J} = \frac{-8.314 \text{ J}}{\text{K}\bullet\text{mol}} \times 298 \text{ K} \times \ln K_{eq}; \ \ln K_{eq} = 9.485, \ K_{eq} = 1.32 \times 10^4$$

(b) The magnitude of K_{eq} is large, so the reaction favors products. The bidentate chelating ligand en will spontaneously replace the monodentate ligand CH_3NH_2. This is an illustration of the chelate effect.

(c) Using the stepwise construction from part (a),

$\Delta H° = 57.3 \text{ kJ} - 56.5 \text{ kJ} = 0.8 \text{ kJ}$

$\Delta S° = 67.3 \text{ J/K} + 14.1 \text{ J/K} = 81.4 \text{ J/K}$

$-T\Delta S = -298 \text{ K} \times 81.4 \text{ J/K} = -2.43 \times 10^4 \text{ J} = -24.3 \text{ kJ}$

The chelate effect is mainly the result of entropy. The reaction is spontaneous due to the increase in the number of free particles and corresponding increase in entropy going from reactants to products. The enthalpic contribution is essentially zero because the bonding interactions of the two ligands are very similar and the reaction is not 'downhill' in enthalpy.

(d) $\Delta H°$ will be very small and negative. When NH_3 replaces H_2O in a complex (Closer Look Box), the tighter bonding of the NH_3 ligand causes a substantial negative $\Delta H°$ for the substitution reaction. When a bidentate amine ligand replaces a monodentate amine ligand of similar bond strength, $\Delta H°$ is very small and either positive (part (c)) or negative (Closer Look Box). In the case of NH_3 replacing CH_3NH_2, the bonding characteristics are very similar. The presence of CH_3 groups in CH_3NH_2 produces some steric hinderance in $[Cd(CH_3NH_2)_4]^{2+}$. This complex is at a slightly higher energy than $[Cd(NH_3)_4]^{2+}$, which experiences no steric hinderance, so $\Delta H°$ will have a negative sign but a very small magnitude. Relief of steric hindrance leads to a very small negative $\Delta H°$ for the substitution reaction.

24.73 First determine the empirical formula, assuming that the remaining mass of complex is Pd.

$$37.6 \text{ g Br} \times \frac{1 \text{ mol Br}}{79.904 \text{ g Br}} = 0.4706 \text{ mol Br; } 0.4706/0.2361 = 2$$

$$28.3 \text{ g C} \times \frac{1 \text{ mol C}}{12.01 \text{ g C}} = 2.356 \text{ mol C; } 2.356/0.2361 = 10$$

$$6.60 \text{ g N} \times \frac{1 \text{ mol N}}{14.01 \text{ g N}} = 0.4711 \text{ mol N; } 0.4711/0.2361 = 2$$

$$2.37 \text{ g H} \times \frac{1 \text{ mol H}}{1.008 \text{ g H}} = 2.351 \text{ mol H; } 2.351/0.2361 = 10$$

$$25.13 \text{ g Pd} \times \frac{1 \text{ mol Pd}}{106.42 \text{ g Pd}} = 0.2361 \text{ mol Pd; } 0.2361/0.2361 = 1$$

The chemical formula is $[Pd(NC_5H_5)_2Br_2]$. This should be a neutral square-planar complex of Pd(II), a nonelectrolyte. Because the dipole moment is zero, we can infer that it must be the *trans*-isomer.

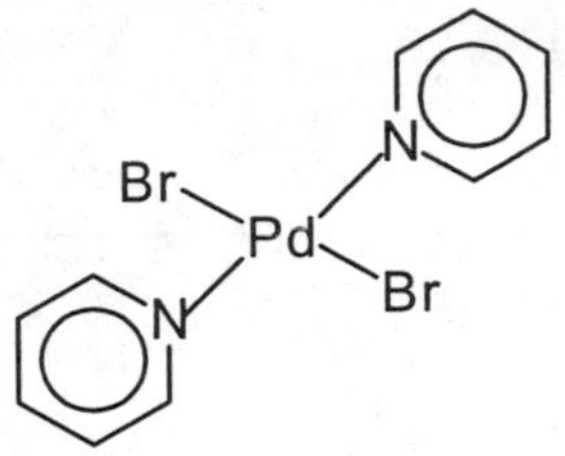

24.75 (a) The reaction that occurs increases the conductivity of the solution by producing a greater number of charged particles, particles with higher charges, or both. It is likely that H_2O from the bulk solvent exchanges with a coordinated Br^- according to the reaction below. This reaction would convert the 1:1 electrolyte, $[Co(NH_3)_4Br_2]Br$, to a 1:2 electrolyte, $[Co(NH_3)_3(H_2O)Br]Br_2$.

(b) $[Co(NH_3)_4Br_2]^+(aq) + H_2O(l) \rightarrow [Co(NH_3)_4(H_2O)Br]^{2+}(aq) + Br^-(aq)$

(c) Before the exchange reaction, there is one mole of free Br^- per mole of complex. mol Br^- = mol Ag^+

M = mol/L; L $AgNO_3$ = mol $AgNO_3$/M $AgNO_3$

$$\frac{3.87 \text{ g complex}}{0.500 \text{ L soln}} \times \frac{1 \text{ mol complex}}{366.77 \text{ g complex}} \times 0.02500 \text{ L soln used} = 5.276 \times 10^{-4} = 5.28 \times 10^{-4} \text{ mol complex}$$

$$5.276 \times 10^{-4} \text{ mol complex} \times \frac{1 \text{ mol Br}^-}{1 \text{ mol complex}} \times \frac{1 \text{ mol Ag}^+}{1 \text{ mol Br}^-} \times \frac{1 \text{ L Ag}^+(aq)}{0.0100 \text{ mol Ag}^+(aq)}$$

$$= 0.05276 \text{ L} = 52.8 \text{ mL } AgNO_3(aq)$$

(d) After the exchange reaction, there are 2 mol free Br^- per mol of complex. Since M $AgNO_3$(aq) and volume of complex solution are the same for the second experiment, the titration after conductivity changes will require twice the volume calculated in part (c), 105.52 = 106 mL of 0.0100 M $AgNO_3$(aq).

24.77 $\frac{182 \times 10^3 \text{ J}}{1 \text{ mol}} \times \frac{1 \text{ mol}}{6.022 \times 10^{23} \text{ molecules}} = 3.022 \times 10^{-19} = 3.02 \times 10^{-19}$ J/photon

$\Delta E = h\nu = 3.02 \times 10^{-19}$ J; $\nu = \Delta E/h$

$\nu = 3.022 \times 10^{-19} \text{ J}/6.626 \times 10^{-34} \text{ J}\cdot\text{s} = 4.561 \times 10^{14} = 4.56 \times 10^{14} \text{ s}^{-1}$

$\lambda = \frac{2.998 \times 10^8 \text{ m/s}}{4.561 \times 10^{14} \text{ s}^{-1}} = 6.57 \times 10^{-7} \text{ m} = 657 \text{ nm}$

We expect that this complex will absorb in the visible, at around 660 nm. It will thus exhibit a blue-green color (Figure 24.25).

24.78 The process can be written:

$H_2(g) + 2e \rightarrow 2H^+(aq)$ $E^\circ_{red} = 0.0$ V

$Cu(s) \rightarrow Cu^{2+} + 2e^-$ $E^\circ_{red} = 0.337$ V

$Cu^{2+}(aq) + 4NH_3(aq) \rightarrow [Cu(NH_3)_4]^{2+}(aq)$ "E°_f" = ?

$H_2(g) + Cu(s) + 4NH_3(aq) \rightarrow 2H^+(aq) + [Cu(NH_3)_4]^{2+}(aq)$ E = 0.08 V

$E = E^\circ - RT \ln K_{eq}$; $K_{eq} = \frac{[H^+]^2[Cu(NH_3)_4^{2+}]}{P_{H_2}[NH_3]^4}$

$P_{H_2} = 1$ atm, $[H^+] = 1$ *M*, $[NH_3] = 1$ *M*, $[Cu(NH_3)_4]^{2+} = 1$ *M*, K = 1

$E = E^\circ - RT \ln(1)$; $E = E^\circ - RT(0)$; $E = E^\circ = 0.08$ V

Since we know E° values for two steps and the overall reaction, we can calculate "E°" for the formation reaction and then K_f, using $E^\circ = \frac{0.0592}{n} \log K_f$ for the step.

$E_{cell} = 0.08 \text{ V} = 0.0 \text{ V} - 0.337 \text{ V} +$ "E°_f" "E°_f" $= -0.08 \text{ V} + 0.337 \text{ V} = 0.417 \text{ V} = 0.42$ V

"E°_f" $= \frac{0.0592}{n} \log K_f$; $\log K_f = \frac{n(E^\circ_f)}{0.0592} = \frac{2(0.417)}{0.0592} = 14.0878 = 14.09$

$K_f = 10^{14.0878} = 1.2 \times 10^{14}$

24.79 (a) The units of the rate constant and the rate dependence on the identity of the second ligand show that the reaction is second order. Therefore, the rate-determining step cannot be a dissociation of water, since that would be independent of the concentration and identity of the incoming ligand. The alternative mechanism, a bimolecular association of the incoming ligand with the complex, is indicated.

(b) The relative values of rate constant are a reflection of the kinetic basicities of the three ligands: Pyridine > SCN^- > CH_3CN.

(c) Ru(III) is a d^5 ion. In a low-spin d^5 octahedral complex, there is one unpaired electron.

25 The Chemistry of Life Organic and Biological Chemistry

Introduction to Organic Compounds; Hydrocarbons

25.2 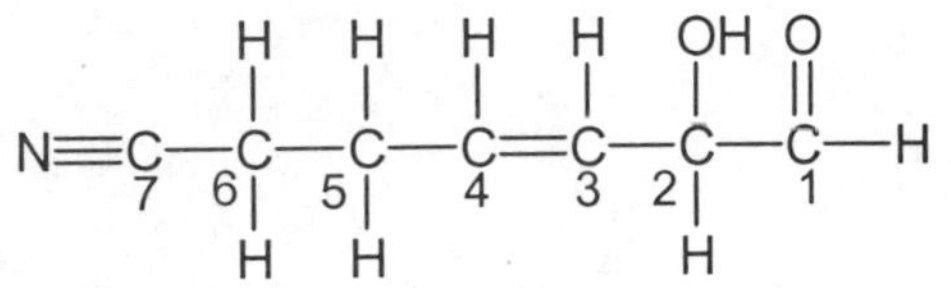

(a) C2, C5 and C6 have sp^3 hybridization (4 e^- domains around C)

(b) C7 has sp hybridization (2 e^- domains around C)

(c) C1, C3 and C4 have sp^2 hybridization (3 e^- domains around C)

25.4 In an organic molecule, bonds with unequal charge distribution are reactive, because they attract reactants that are either electron deficient (electrophilic) or electron rich (nucleophilic). These bonds are either polar bonds with permanent dipole moments, or polarizable bonds with electron clouds that are easily disturbed, or polarized. Of the bonds listed, C–O and C–Cl are reactive. C–O is polar; C–Cl is slightly polar, and polarizable due to the diffuse electron cloud about Cl.

25.6 All the classifications listed are hydrocarbons; they contain only the elements hydrogen and carbon.

(a) *Alkanes* are hydrocarbons that contain only single bonds.

(b) *Cycloalkanes* contain at least one ring of three or more carbon atoms joined by single bonds. Because it is a type of alkane, all bonds in a cycloalkane are single bonds.

(c) *Alkenes* contain at least one C=C double bond.

(d) *Alkynes* contain at least one C≡C triple bond.

(e) A *saturated hydrocarbon* contains only single bonds. Alkanes and cycloalkanes fit this definition.

(f) An *aromatic hydrocarbon* contains one or more planar, six-membered rings of carbon atoms with delocalized π-bonding throughout the ring.

25.8 cycloalkane, 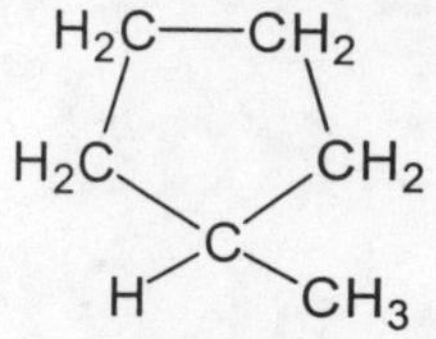 , C_6H_{12}, saturated

cycloalkene, 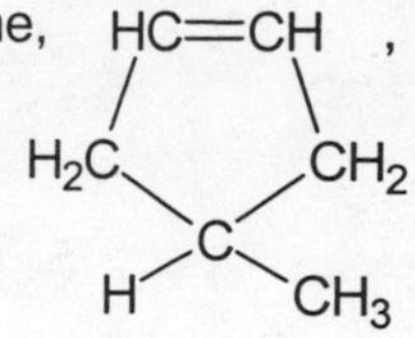 , C_6H_{10}, unsaturated

alkyne, $CH_3—CH_2—C\equiv C—CH_2—CH_3$, C_6H_{10}, unsaturated

aromatic hydrocarbon, 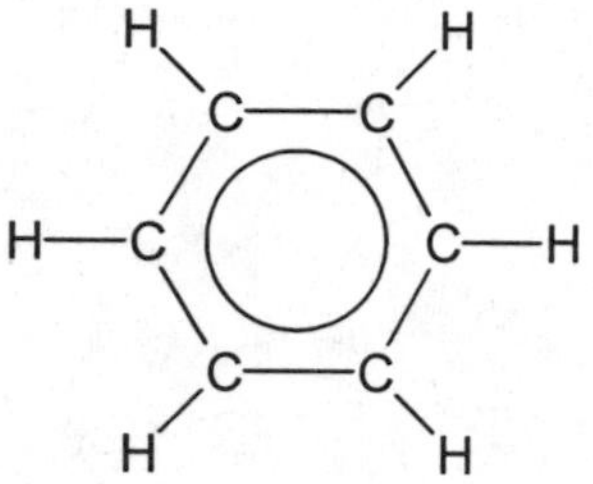 , C_6H_6, unsaturated

25.10 C_nH_{2n-2}

25.12

$CH_3CH_2CH_2CH_2C\equiv CH$

$CH_3CH_2CH_2C\equiv CCH_3$

$CH_3CH_2C\equiv CCH_2CH_3$

CH_3
$CH_3CHCH_2C\equiv CH$

CH_3
$CH_3CH_2CHC\equiv CH$

CH_3
$CH_3CHC\equiv CCH_3$

$CH_3CH_2CH=CHCH=CH_2$

$CH_3CH=CHCH_2CH=CH_2$

$CH_2=CHCH_2CH_2CH=CH_2$

$CH_3CH=CHCH=CHCH_3$

CH_3
$CH_2=CHCHCH=CH_2$

CH_3
$CH_2—CCH_2CH=CH_2$

CH_3
$CH_2=CCH=CHCH_3$

CH_3
$CH_2=CHC=CHCH_3$

CH_3
$CH_2=CHCH=CCH_3$

CH_2CH_3
$CH_2=CHC=CH_2$

CH_3 CH_3
$CH_2=C—C=CH_2$

CH_2CH_3
$CH_2=CHCH=CH_2$

25.12 (continued)

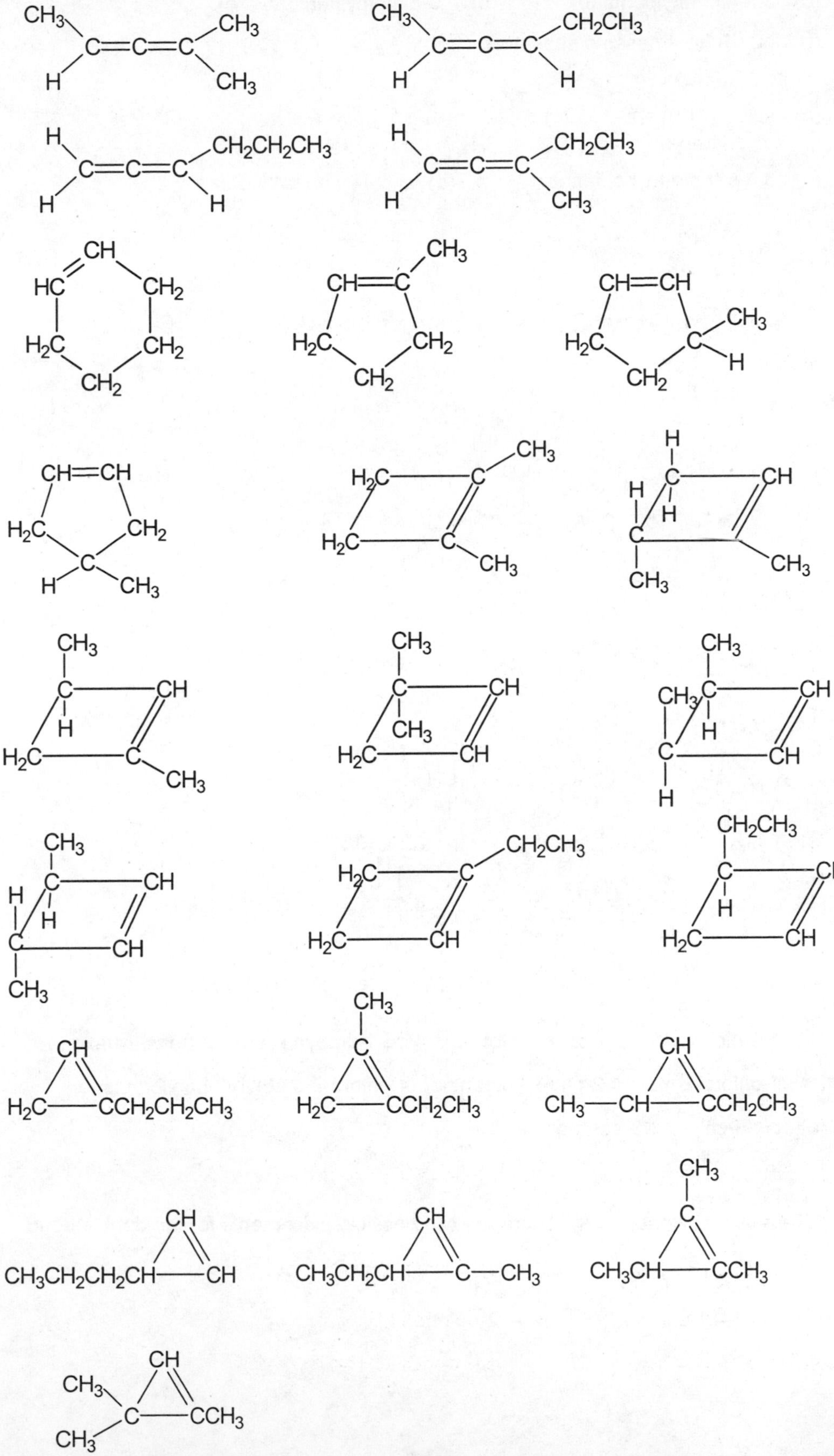

25.14 (a) 3-ethylpentane (b) 2,3-dimethylpentane

(c) 3,3-dimethylpentane (d) 2,3-dimethylpentane

(b) and (d) are the same substance

25.16 (a) sp^3 (b) sp^2 (c) sp^2 (d) sp

25.18 (a) 3,3,5-trimethylheptane (b) 3,4,4-trimethylheptane

(c) 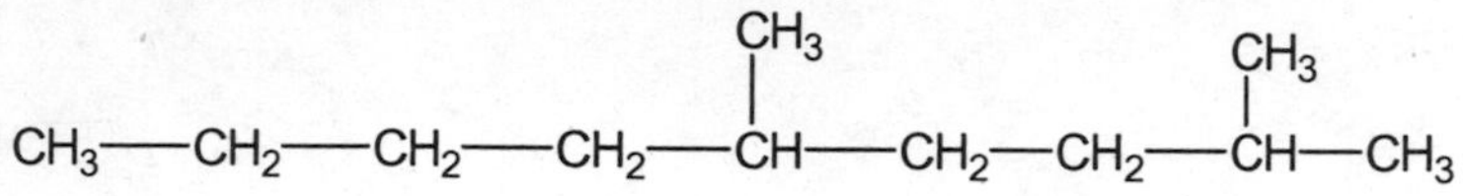

(d) 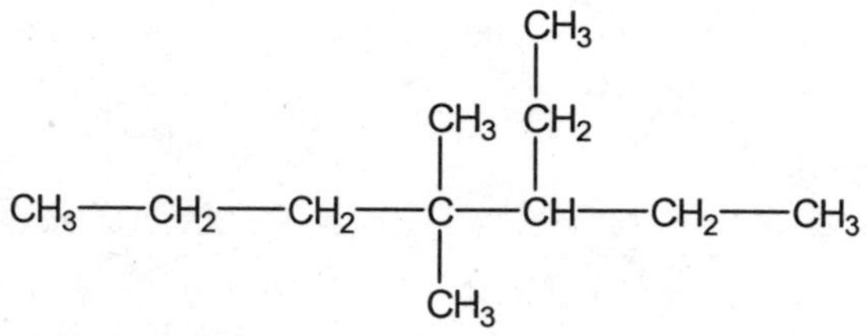

(e) 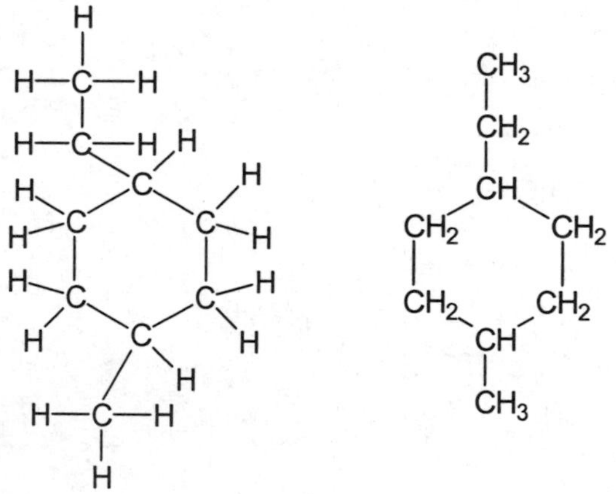

25.20 (a) 1,4-dichlorocyclohexane (b) 3-chloro-1-propyne (c) *trans*-2-hexene

(d) 1-chloro-2-methyl-2-phenyl-butane or (1-chloro-2-methyl)-2-butylbenzene

(e) *cis*-5-chloro-1,3-pentadiene

25.22 Butene is an alkene, C_4H_8. There are two possible placements for the double bond:

$CH_2{=}CHCH_2CH_3$ or $CH_3CH{=}CHCH_3$

1-butene 2-butene

These two compounds are structural isomers. For 2-butene, there are two different, noninterchangeable ways to construct the carbon skeleton (owing to the absence of free rotation around the double bond). These two compounds are geometric isomers.

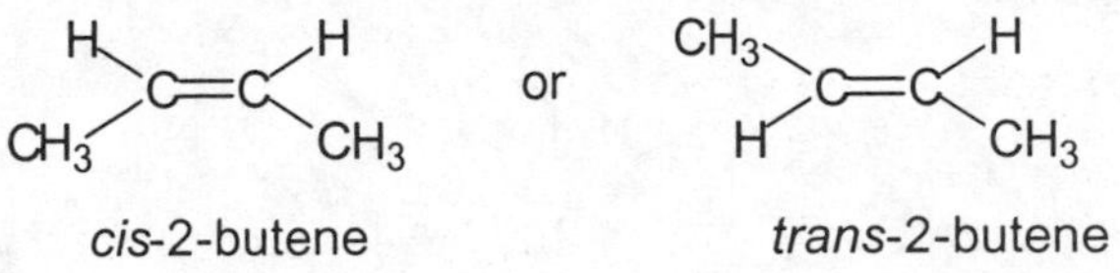

25.24

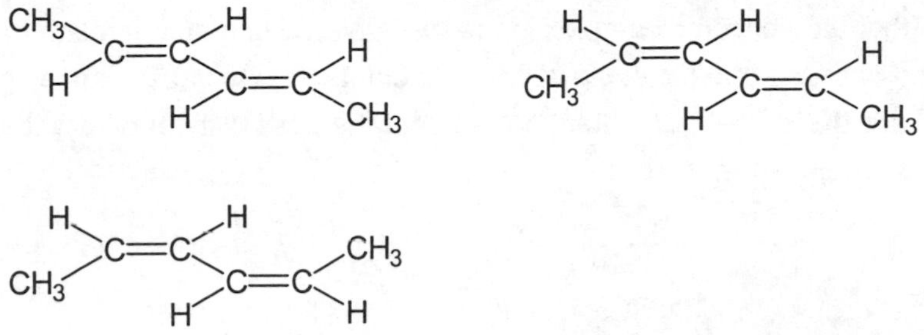

25.26 Octane number can be increased by increasing the fraction of branched-chain alkanes or aromatics, since these have high octane numbers. This can be done by cracking. The octane number also can be increased by adding an anti-knock agent such as tetraethyl lead, $Pb(C_2H_5)_4$ (no longer legal), methyl t-butyl ether, MTBE, or an alcohol, methanol or ethanol.

Reactions of Hydrocarbons

25.28 (a)

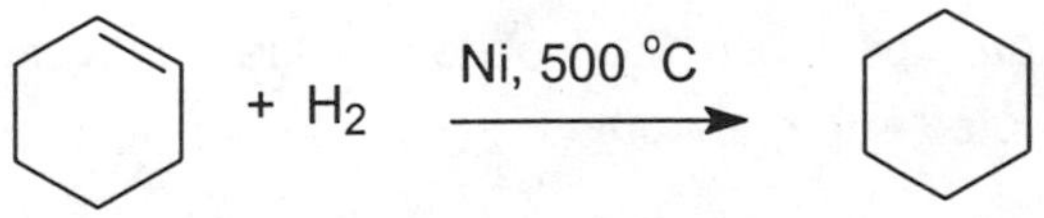

(b)

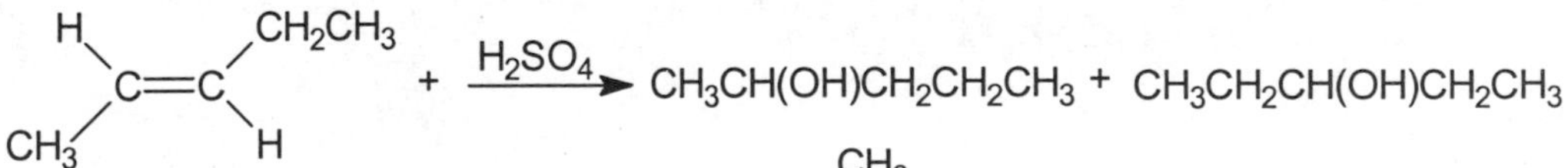

(c)

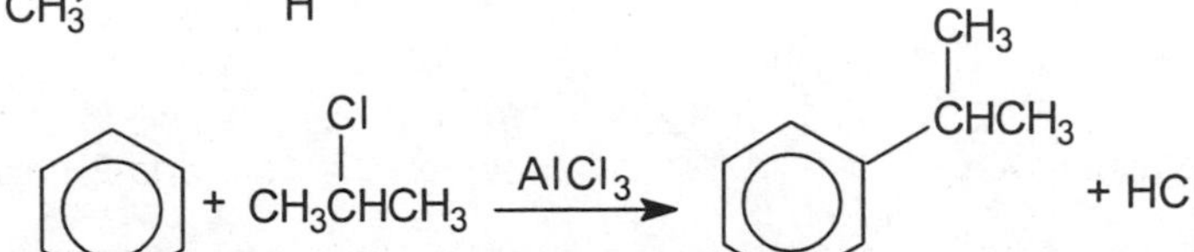

25.30 (a) The reaction of Br_2 with an alkene to form a colorless halogenated alkane is an addition reaction. Aromatic hydrocarbons do not readily undergo addition reactions, because their π-electrons are stabilized by delocalization.

(b) *Plan.* Both the *ortho* and *para* isomers are formed; they must be separated by distillation or some other technique. *Solve*:

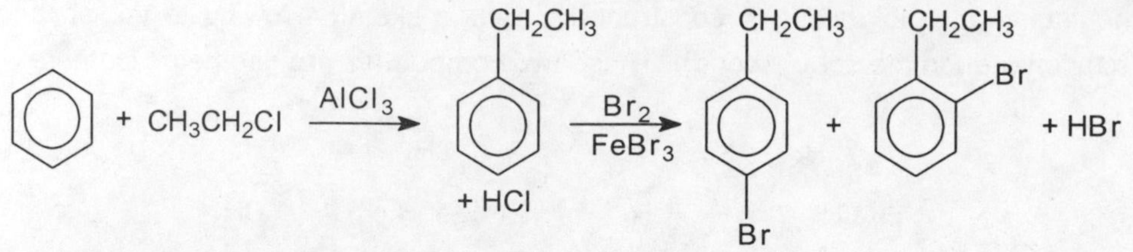

25.32 Not necessarily. That the rate laws are both first order in both reactants and second order overall indicates that the activated complex in the rate-determining step in each mechanism is bimolecular and contains one molecule of each reactant. This is usually an indication that the mechanisms are the same, but it does not rule out the possibility of different fast steps, or a different order of elementary steps.

25.34

	ΔH
$C_{10}H_8(l) + 12O_2(g) \rightarrow 10CO_2(g) + 4H_2O(l)$	-5157 kJ
$-[C_{10}H_{18}(l) + 29/2\ O_2(g) \rightarrow 10CO_2(g) + 9H_2O(l)]$	-(-6286) kJ
$C_{10}H_8(l) + 5H_2O(l) \rightarrow C_{10}H_{18}(l) + 5/2\ O_2(g)$	+1129 kJ
$5/2\ O_2(g) + 5H_2(g) \rightarrow 5H_2O(l)$	5(-285.8) kJ
$C_{10}H_8(l) + 5H_2(g) \rightarrow C_{10}H_{18}(l)$	-300 kJ

Compare this with the heat of hydrogenation of ethylene:

$C_2H_4(g) + H_2(g) \rightarrow C_2H_6(g)$; $\Delta H = -84.7 - (52.3) = -137$ kJ. This value applies to just one double bond. For five double bonds, we would expect about -685 kJ. The fact that hydrogenation of napthalene yields only -300 kJ indicates that the overall energy of the napthalene molecule is lower than expected for five isolated double bonds and that there must be some special stability associated with the aromatic system in this molecule.

Functional Groups and Chirality

25.36 (a) —C≡C—, alkyne; 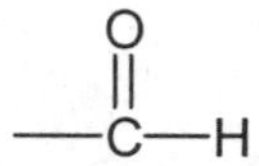 , aldehyde

(b) 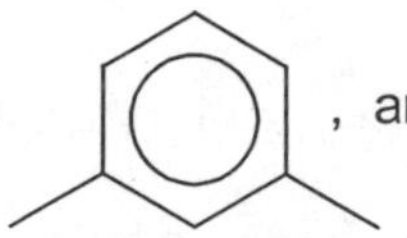 , aromatic hydrocarbon (phenyl group); —Cl, halogen;

—C=C—, alkene; —COOH, carboxylic acid

(c) 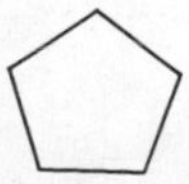 , cycloalkane; —Cl, halogen; 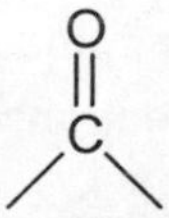 , ketone

(d) 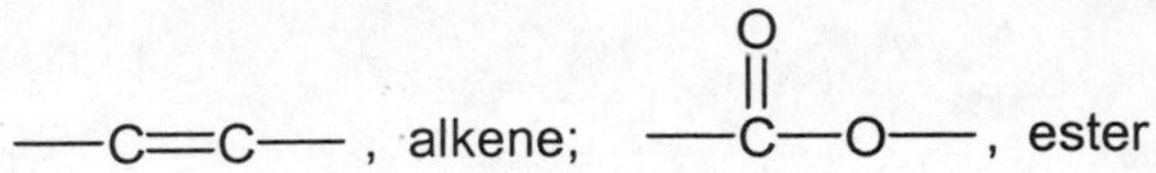

(e) 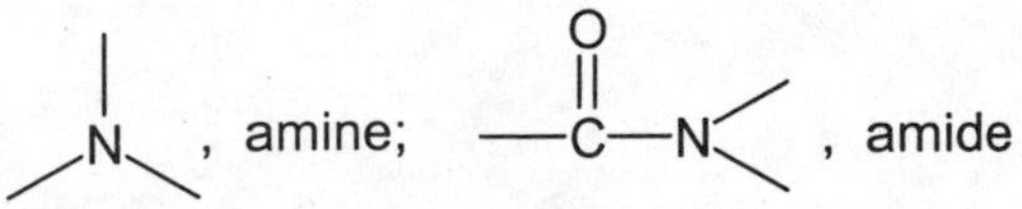

25.38 (a) C_4H_8O, (b)
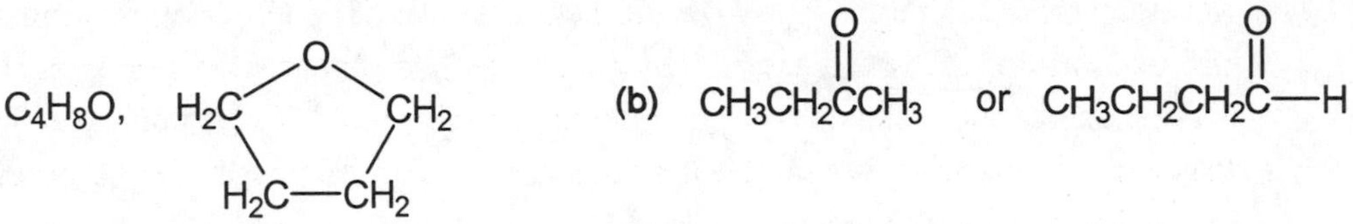

25.40 (a) (b) (c) (d)
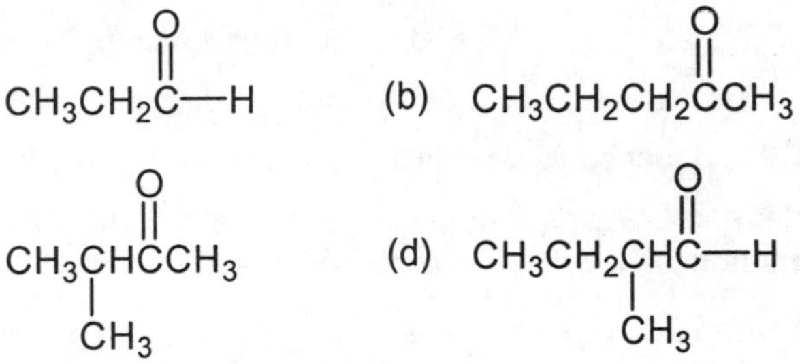

25.42 (a) (b) (c)
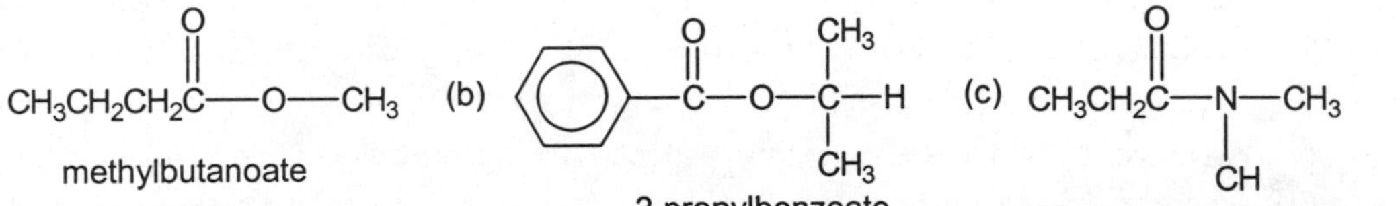

25.44 (a)
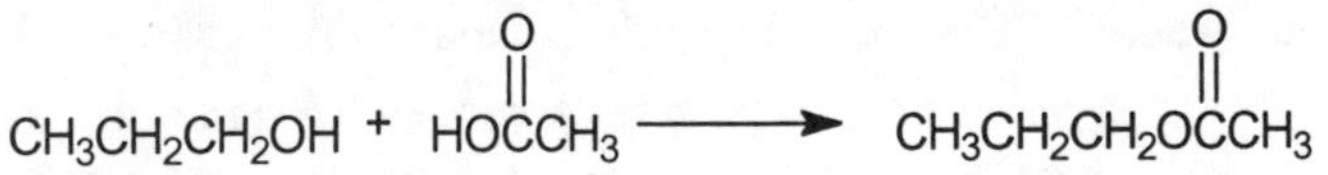

(b)
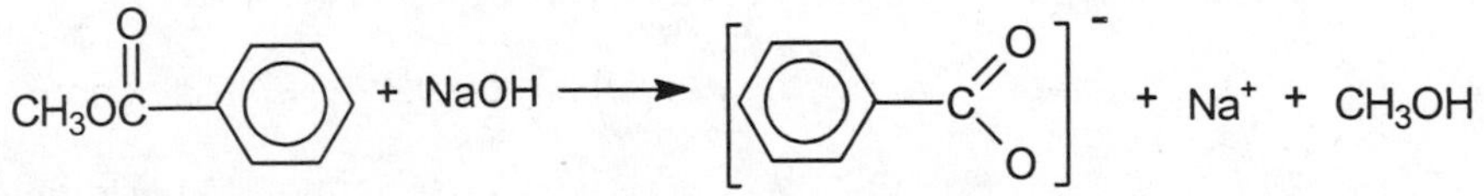

25.46 (a)

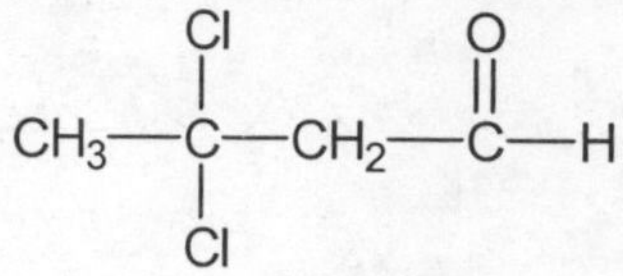

(b)

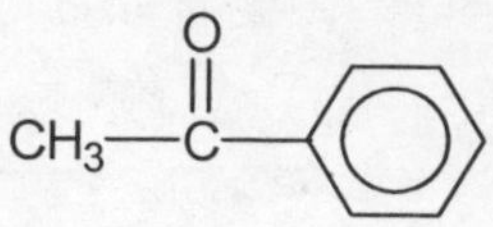

(c)

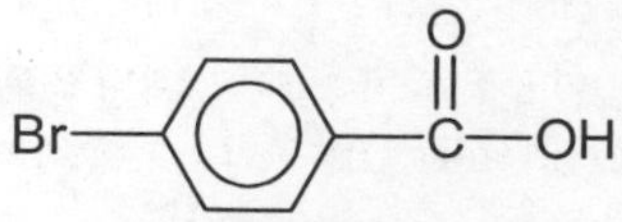

(d)

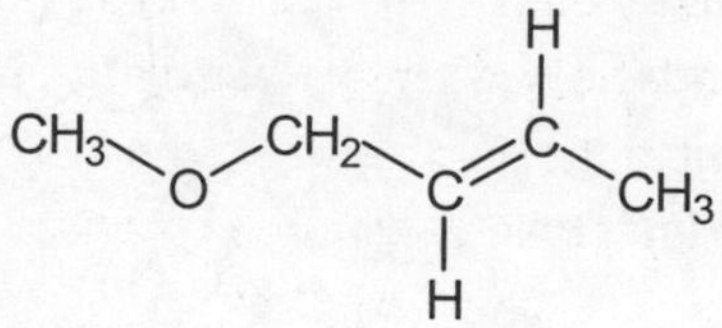

(e)

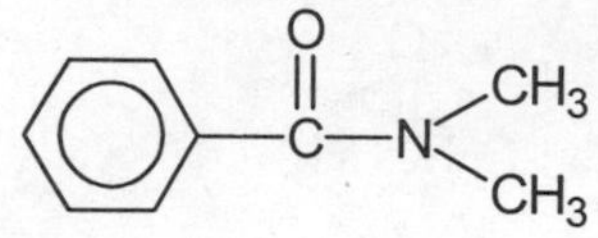

25.48 (a) Compounds in 25.18:

25.18(a) Yes, C5 is attached to H, methyl, ethyl and a complex group.

25.18(b) Yes, C3 is attached to H, methyl, ethyl and a complex group.

25.18(c) Yes, C5 is attached to H, methyl and two different complex groups.

25.18(d) No, C3 is attached to two ethyl groups, C4 to two methyl groups.

25.18(e) No, the ring C atoms with substituents are not chiral because the ring is symmetrical in both directions from these C atoms.

(b) Compounds in 25.20: Only molecule (d) has a C atom with four different groups attached; it is chiral. In molecule (a), the C atom bound to Cl and H is connected to two alkyl groups that are identical because the ring is symmetrical; molecule (a) is not chiral.

Proteins

25.50 The side chains possess three characteristics that may be of importance. They may be bulky (e.g., the phenyl group in phenylalanine) and thus impose restraints on where and how the amino acid can undergo reaction. Secondly, the side chain may possess a polar group (e.g., the -OH group in serine), that will in part determine solubility. Finally, the side chain may contain an acidic (e.g., the -COOH group in glutamic acid) or basic (e.g., the $-NH_2$ group in lysine) functional group that will partially determine solubility in acidic or basic media, and that may become involved in hydrogen-bonding with other amino acids.

25.52

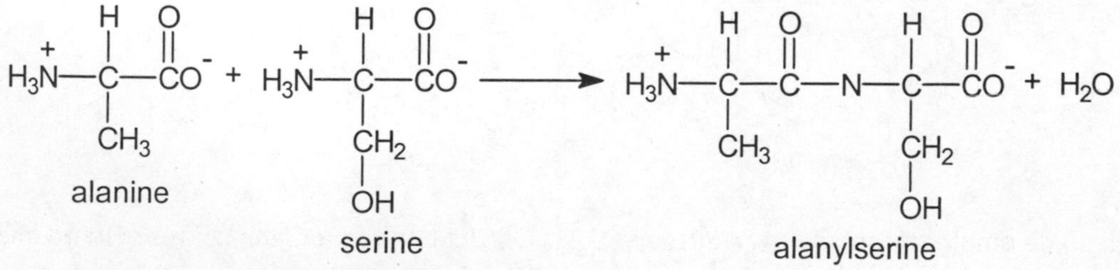

25.54 (a) Valine, serine, glutamic acid

(b) Six: Gly-Ser-Glu; Gly-Glu-Ser; Ser-Gly-Glu; Ser-Glu-Gly; Glu-Ser-Gly; Glu-Gly-Ser

25.56 It is quite evident from Figure 25.24 that the hydrogen bonds between an NH group along the chain and the unshared electron pairs of a carbonyl group further along are responsible for maintaining the helix. Indeed, the pitch and general shape of the helix are determined by what specific interactions produce a good hydrogen-bonding arrangement.

Carbohydrates

25.58 Glucose exists in solution as a cyclic structure in which the aldehyde function on carbon 1 reacts with the OH group of carbon 5 to form what is called a hemiacetal, Figure 25.27. Carbon atom 1 carries an OH group in the hemiacetal form; in α-glucose this OH group is on the opposite side of the ring as the CH_2OH group on carbon atom 5. In the β (beta) form the OH group on carbon 1 is on the same side of the ring as the CH_2OH group on carbon 5.

The condensation product of two glucose units looks like this:

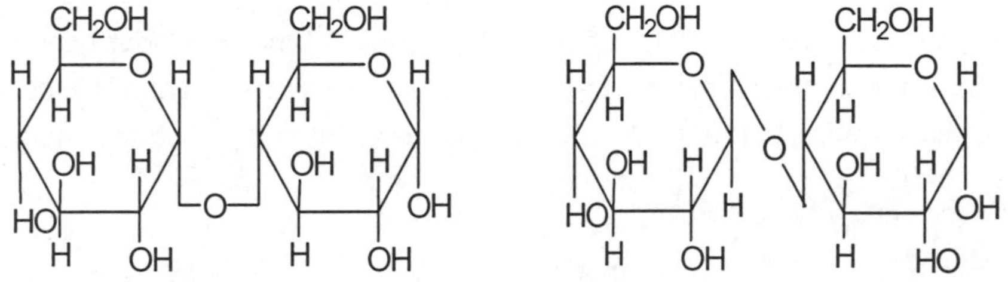

α-linkage β-linkage

25.60 (a) In the linear form of mannose, the aldehydic carbon is C1. Carbon atoms 2, 3, 4 and 5 are chiral because they each carry four different groups. Carbon 6 is not chiral because it contains two H atoms.

(b) Both the α (left) and β (right) forms are possible.

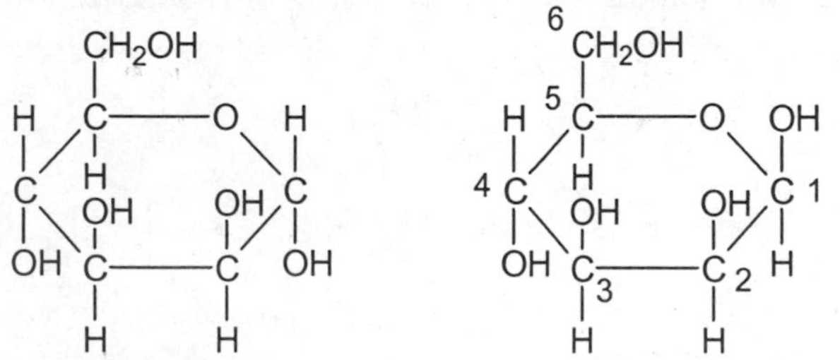

25.62 The empirical formula of cellulose is $C_6H_{10}O_5$. As in glycogen, the six-membered ring form of glucose forms the monomer unit that is the basis of the polymer cellulose. In cellulose, glucose monomer units are joined by β linkages.

Nucleic Acids

25.64

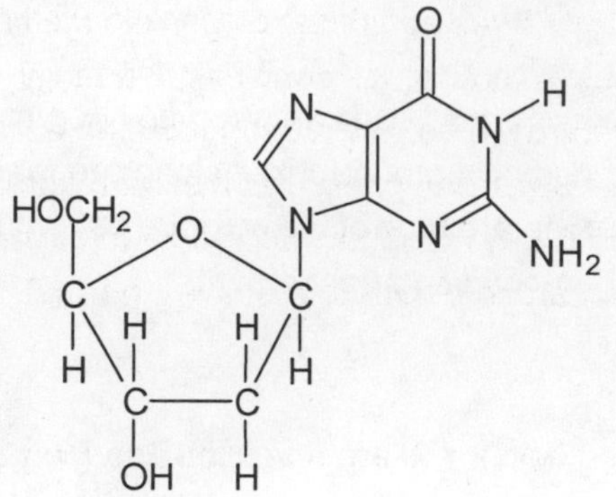

25.66

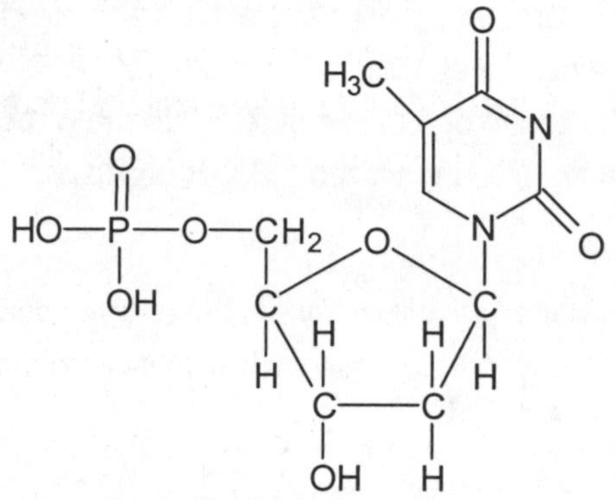

25.68

—A—C—T—C—G—A—

—T—G—A—G—C—T— ← complementary strand

Additional Exercises

25.70 *Analyze/Plan*. We are asked the number of structural isomers for two specified carbon chain lengths and a certain number of double bonds. Structural isomers have different connectivity. Since the chain length is specified, we can ignore structural isomers created by branching. We are not asked about geometrical isomers, so we ignore those as well. The resulting question is: How many ways are there to place the specified number of double bonds along the specified C chain? *Solve*:

5 C chain with one double bond: 2 structural isomers

C=C–C–C–C C–C=C–C–C

6 C chain with two double bonds: 6 structural isomers

C=C–C=C–C–C C=C–C–C=C–C C=C–C–C–C=C

C–C=C–C=C–C C=C=C–C–C–C C–C=C=C–C–C

25.71 Because of the strain in bond angles about the ring, cyclic alkynes with less than eight carbons are not stable. Alkyne carbon atoms preferentially have 180° bond angles; this requires a linear four-carbon group in the ring. Three additional carbons in the ring does not provide enough flexibility to make this possible without gross bond length or angle distortions. It is possible that a ring with eight or more carbons could accommodate an alkyne linkage. To test this with models, construct a linear four-carbon group and then add tetrahedral C-atoms until you can complete the ring and it stays together without intervention. This is a good indication of the minimum number of carbon atoms in a stable ring that contains an alkyne linkage.

25.73 The structural features that produce *cis-trans* isomerism are restricted rotation about a bond and two different groups attached to the two atoms that form the rigid bond. Alkanes have only C–C single bonds, and there is free rotation of attached groups about the single bond. Alkanes fail the criterion of restricted rotation. Alkynes have restricted rotation about the triple bond, but only one group is attached to the C atoms that form the bond. There is only one relative orientation (linear) for the two attached groups, so *cis* and *trans* isomers are not possible.

25.74 The C-Cl bonds in the *trans* compound are pointing in exactly opposite directions. Thus, the C-Cl bond dipoles cancel (Section 9.3). This is not the case in the *cis* compound, as can be seen by drawing the structure:

cis

25.76 One. One molecule of HBr would add to the C=C according to the reaction

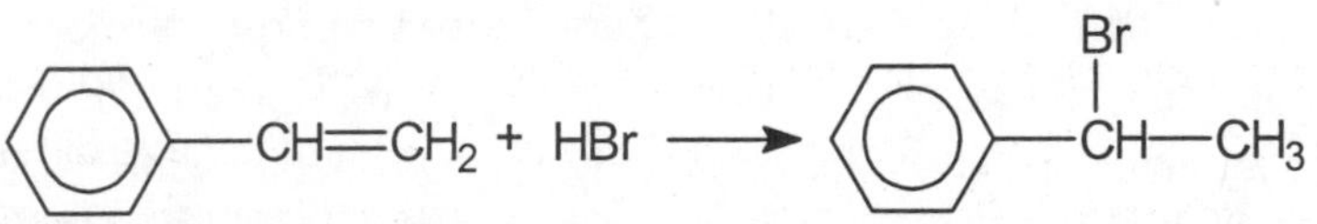

Because the π electrons in the phenyl ring are delocalized, the group is particularly stable and resistant to addition reactions. The phenyl group could undergo substitution with HBr, but only with a catalyst or special conditions.

25.77 Two plausible decomposition reactions are:

(i) $CH_2Cl_2(l) \rightarrow C(s) + H_2(g) + Cl_2(g)$

(ii) $CH_2(NO_2)_2(l) \rightarrow N_2(g) + CO_2(g) + H_2O(g) + 1/2O_2(g)$

Use bond dissociation energies (Table 8.4) to evaluate approximate ΔH values for each reaction.

(i) $\Delta H = 2D(C\text{-}H) + 2D(C\text{-}Cl) - D(H\text{-}H) - D(Cl\text{-}Cl)$

$= 2(413) + 2(328) - 436 - 242 = +804$ kJ

(ii) $\Delta H = 2D(C\text{-}H) + 2D(C\text{-}N) + 2D(N{=}O) + 2D(N\text{-}O) - D(N{\equiv}N) - 2D(C{=}O) - 2D(O\text{-}H) - 1/2D(O{=}O)$

$= 2(413) + 2(293) + 2(607) + 2(201) - 941 - 2(799) - 2(463) - 1/2(495)$

$\Delta H = -685$ kJ

Clearly, the decomposition of $CH_2(NO_2)_2$ is thermodynamically favorable, while the decomposition of CH_2Cl_2 is not. In particular, this is because of the stability of N_2 and CO_2 relative to $CH_2(NO_2)_2$. For CH_2Cl_2, no oxygen atoms are available to form stable products such as CO_2 and H_2O.

25.79 (a) 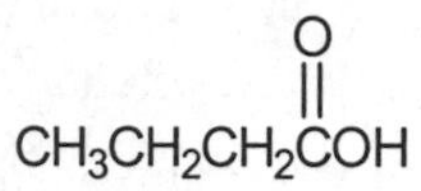 (b) 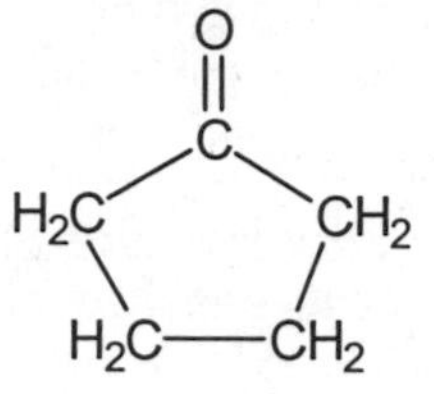 (c) 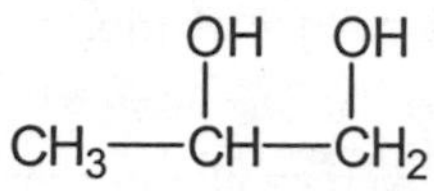

(d) 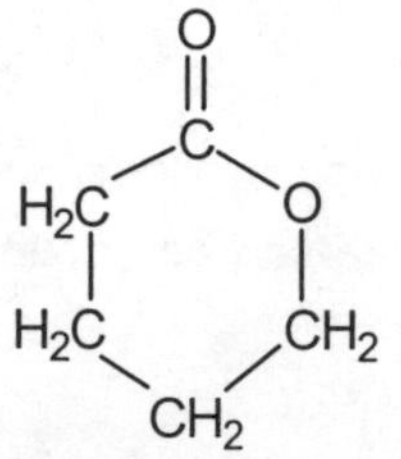

25.81 (a) 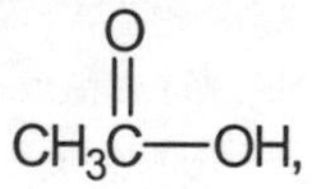 C_6H_5OH (b) 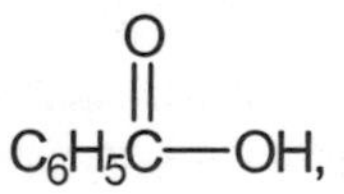 CH_3OH

25.82 In order for indole to be planar, the N atom must be sp^2 hybridized. The nonbonded electron pair on N is in a pure p orbital perpendicular to the plane of the molecule. The electrons that form the π bonds in the molecule are also in pure p orbitals perpendicular to the plane of the molecule. Thus, each of these p orbitals is in the correct orientation for π overlap; the delocalized π system extends over the entire molecule and includes the "nonbonded" electron pair on N. The reason that indole is such a weak base (H^+ acceptor), is that the nonbonded electron pair is delocalized and a H^+ ion does not feel the attraction of a full localized electron pair.

25.84 (a)

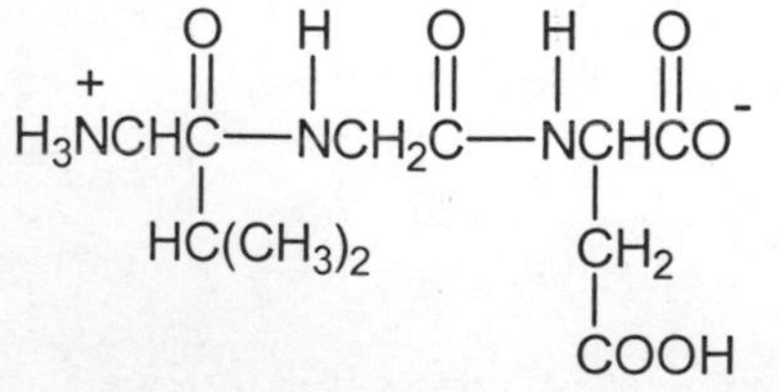

(b)

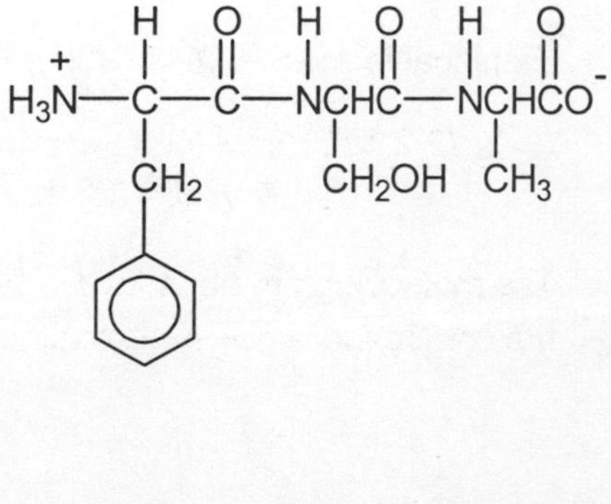

25.86 Starch, glycogen and cellulose are all biopolymers built by linking glucose monomers. Starch and glycogen have alpha (α) glucose linkages, where the bridging O atom is on the same side of the ring as the CH_2OH group. The smallest repeating unit in starch and glycogen is a single glucose unit.

Cellulose has beta (β) glucose linkages, where the bridging O atom is on the same side of one of the rings as the CH_2OH group and on the opposite side of the CH_2OH group on the second ring. The geometry of the β linkage requires that the two linked glucose units have different orientations and that the smallest repeating unit in cellulose is two glucose units with a β linkage.

The molecular weight of a polymer is an indication of the number of monomer units present. Starch, glycogen and cellulose all have a range of molecular weights. Glycogen has the widest range of molecular weights, 5,000-5,000,000 amu, and is potentially the largest polymer. Cellulose is intermediate in size with an average molar mass of 500,000 amu. Starch and cellulose are produced in plants, while glycogen is produced in animals and serves as an energy storage mechanism.

25.88

```
—G—G—T—A—C—T—
 :  :  :  :  :  :
—C—C—A—T—G—A— ←— complementary strand
```

Integrative Exercises

25.90 The compound is clearly an alcohol. Its slight solubility in water is consistent with the properties expected of a secondary alcohol with a five-carbon chain. The fact that oxidation results in a ketone rather than an aldehyde and subsequently a carboxylic acid tells us that it is a secondary alcohol:

```
CH3CHCH2CH2CH3      CH3CHCHCH2CH3       CH3CHCH(CH3)2
   |                      |                 |
   OH                     OH                OH
```

25.92 Determine the empirical formula, molar mass and thus molecular formula of the compound. Confirm with physical data.

$$85.7 \text{ g C} \times \frac{1 \text{ mol C}}{12.01 \text{ g C}} = 7.136 \text{ mol C; } 7.136 / 7.136 = 1$$

$$14.3 \text{ g H} \times \frac{1 \text{ mol H}}{1.008 \text{ g H}} = 14.19 \text{ mol H; } 14.19 / 7.136 \approx 2$$

Empirical formula is CH_2. Using Equation 10.11 ($\mathcal{M}$ = molar mass):

$$\mathcal{M} = \frac{(2.21 \text{ g/L})(0.08206 \text{ L}\bullet\text{atm/mol}\bullet\text{K})(373 \text{ K})}{(735/760) \text{ atm}} = 69.9 \text{ g/mol}$$

The molecular formula is thus C_5H_{10}. The absence of reaction with aqueous Br_2 indicates that the compound is not an alkene, so the compound is probably the cycloalkane, cyclopentane.

According to the *Handbook of Chemistry and Physics*, the boiling point of cyclopentane is 49°C at 760 torr. This confirms the identity of the unknown.

25.94 (a) A = adenosine = $C_{10}H_{10}O_3N_5$

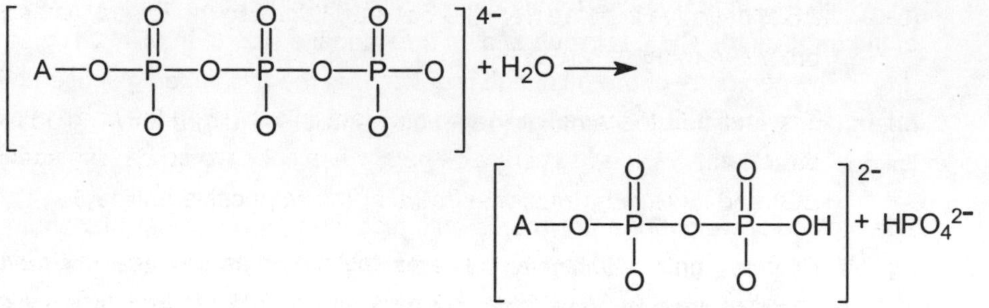

$$[A—P_3O_{10}]^{4-} + H_2O \longrightarrow [A—P_2O_6(OH)]^{2-} + HPO_4^{2-}$$

(b) If the hydrolysis reaction is spontaneous, the sign of ΔG must be negative.

(c) Adenosine monophosphate (AMP) + inorganic phosphate

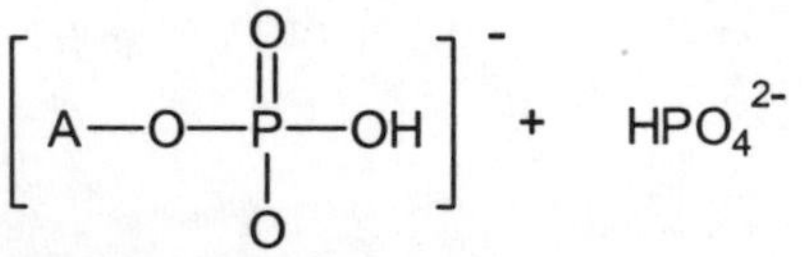

(The placement of the H^+ in these reactions is somewhat arbitrary; H^+ is attracted to the strongest base, but the equilibria are complex.)

25.95 (a) At low pH, the amine and carboxyl groups are protonated.

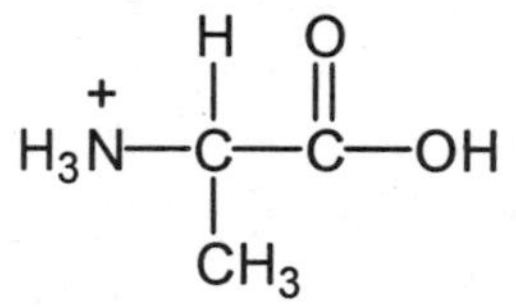

At high pH, the amine and carboxyl groups are deprotonated.

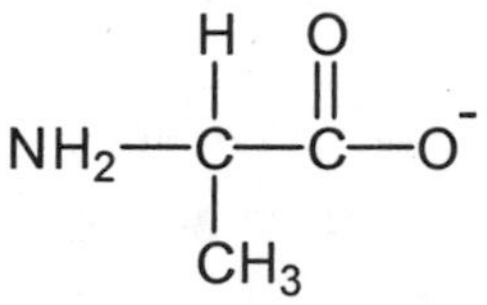

(b) $CH_3C(=O)—OH(aq) \longrightarrow CH_3C(=O)—O^-(aq) + H^+(aq)$

$K_a = 1.8 \times 10^{-5}$, $pK_a = -\log(1.8 \times 10^{-5}) = 4.74$

The conjugate acid of NH_3 is NH_4^+.

$NH_4^+(aq) \rightarrow NH_3(aq) + H^+(aq)$

$K_a = K_w / K_b = 1 \times 10^{-14} / 1.8 \times 10^{-5} = 5.55 \times 10^{-10} = 5.6 \times 10^{-10}$

$pK_a = -\log(5.55 \times 10^{-10}) = 9.26$

In general, a –COOH group is a stronger acid than a $-NH_3]^+$ group. The lower pK_a value for amino acids is for the ionization (deprotonation) of the –COOH group and the higher pK_a is for the deprotonation of the $[NH_3]^+$ group.

25.96 (a) The native form has a lower, more negative free energy than the denatured form.

(b) ΔS is negative in going from the denatured form to the folded (native) form; the native protein is more ordered.

(c) The four S-S linkages are strong covalent links holding the chain in place in the folded structure. A folded structure without these links would be less stable (more positive ΔG) and have more motional freedom (more positive entropy).

(d) At first glance, the answer seems the same as part (c). However, the eight S–H linkages are capable of forming hydrogen-bond-like interactions, which would decrease ΔG and S. Although these interactions are not as strong as S–S covalent bonds, there are more of them, so this reduction might not have much effect on ΔG and S.